Quantitative Economic
Policy and Planning

Quantitative Economic Policy and Planning
Theory and Models of Economic Control

Nicolas Spulber
Indiana University

Ira Horowitz
University of Florida

 W·W·NORTON & COMPANY·INC·

New York

Library of Congress Cataloging in Publication Data

Spulber, Nicolas.
  Quantitative economic policy and planning.

  Includes bibliographical references and index.
  1. Economic policy. 2. Economic policy—Mathe-
matical models. I. Horowitz, Ira, joint author.
II. Title.
HD82.S72 1976   338.9   75-38741
ISBN 0-393-09181-3

For Pauline and Nancy

CONTENTS

Preface   xi

I. Elements of Quantitative Economic Control   1

Chapter 1. *Policy Analysis in a Systems Control Context*   5

    1.1 Models of the Firm and Policy Models   5
    1.2 Considerations in Economic Policy Model Building   8
    1.3 Models and Systems   15
    1.4 Illustrations of Control and Coordination   30
    1.5 Cybernetics and Systemic Change   34

Chapter 2. *Information and Control*   36

    2.1 The Main Issue   36
    2.2 Information Network: Elements of a Communication
         System   37
    2.3 Measurements and Efficiency   43
    2.4 The Decision Process   53
    2.5 Concluding Comments   57

Chapter 3. *Models of Rational Policy Choice*   59

    3.1 Policy Decision Analysis   59
    3.2 The Tinbergen Model   62
    3.3 Related Models   68
    3.4 A Summary View   80
         Appendices   82

Chapter 4. *Performance Indicators: Preference Functions*   84

    4.1 On "Social" Preference Functions   84
    4.2 Individual versus Social Preference Functions   87
    4.3 Formalized Preference Functions   90
    4.4 Preferences in an Operational Context   104
    4.5 Conclusion   105

Chapter 5. *Instruments and Measures*   107

    5.1 Nature of Instruments   107
    5.2 The Array of Instruments   108

5.3 Instrument Choice 116
5.4 The Selection of Measures in the General Policy
Problem 119
5.5 Conclusion 130

Chapter 6. *Characteristics of the Processor: Structural Frameworks* 131

6.1 Generalities on Structures 131
6.2 Technical and Accounting Relationships 133
6.3 Behavioral and Causal Relationships 146
6.4 Institutional Relationships 149
6.5 Conclusion 151

II. Systems, Subsystems, and Plans 153

Chapter 7. *Planning Models* 157

7.1 The Theoretical Background 157
7.2 Planning: Introductory Remarks 159
7.3 The Hard Core of the Plan: Models 163
7.4 The Marxian Model 174
7.5 Concluding Comments 175

Chapter 8. *Planning Techniques and Procedures* 176

8.1 Types of Planning 176
8.2 Planning Techniques 178
8.3 Welding Plans: Iteration; Horizons; Stages 185
8.4 Conclusions 189
Appendices 191

Chapter 9. *Planning for Technological Change* 194

9.1 Endogenous and Exogenous Changes 194
9.2 Available Paths for Technological Transformation 195
9.3 From "Technology on the Shelf" to New
Technologies 198
9.4 TF: Techniques and Models 200
9.5 Growth, Change, and Public Policy 207

Chapter 10. *Problems of Investment Planning* 211

10.1 Introduction 211
10.2 Consistency, Optimization, and Horizons 214
10.3 Investment Decision Rules 222
10.4 From Project Choice to a Consolidated Plan 230
10.5 On the Improvement of Investment Planning 234

Chapter 11. *Planning Foreign Trade* 236

11.1 Basic Problems of Foreign Trade Planning 236
11.2 Import and Export Projections and World Trade
Matrices 240

11.3 Trade, Aid, and Planning Alternatives   247
11.4 Project Selection, Exports and the "Make or Import"
       Issue   251
11.5 Concluding Comments   252

Chapter 12. *Manpower and Employment Planning*   255

12.1 Problems of Manpower Planning   255
12.2 Demographic Dynamics and Labor Availability   258
12.3 Projections of Labor "Requirements"   264
12.4 Planning the "Educational" Component   267
12.5 Concluding Comments   271

Chapter 13. *Planning of Industrial Activities*   273

13.1 Problems of Industrial Planning   273
13.2 Linkage, Priorities, and Rates   276
13.3 Projects and Interdependencies   284
13.4 Some Special Issues: Quality and "Size"   287
13.5 Concluding Comments: On the "Yardstick" of
       Performance   288

Chapter 14. *Planning Agricultural Production*   289

14.1 Problems of Agricultural Planning   289
14.2 Interrelations of the Agricultural and Industrial
       "Complexes"   290
14.3 Planning Models in Different Environments   294
14.4 Feedback and Program Sequences   300
14.5 Demand and Production Possibilities   302
14.6 Concluding Comments   305

Chapter 15. *Locational and Regional Planning*   307

15.1 Growth and Change in the Spatial Context   307
15.2 Classification of Regions and Activities   309
15.3 Frameworks for Regional Analysis   312
15.4 Nodal Centers and the Spatial Movement of Goods   322
15.5 Concluding Comments   328

III.   Economic Control: Scope and Issues   331

Chapter 16. *State's "Agenda" under Capitalism*   333

16.1 Economic Theory and the State   333
16.2 From Haphazard Measures to Coordinated
       Management   339
16.3 Efficiency Criteria for the "Agenda"   343
16.4 Growth of the Public Sector and Perspective
       Planning   345

Chapter 17. *State's "Agenda" under Socialism*   347

17.1 The Marxian Theory of the State   347
17.2 Centralization, Decentralization, Optimization Models   351
17.3 Efficiency and Interaction-Coordination Modes   358
17.4 The State as a Perpetual Prime Mover   363

Chapter 18. *Convergence Theories and Optimal Systems*   367

18.1 The Problem Posed   367
18.2 Convergence Tendencies and Paradigms   371
18.3 The Issues   374
18.4 Other Paradigms   381
18.5 The Issues Reconsidered   384
18.6 Concluding Comments   390

Index   393

PREFACE

Quantitative economic policy, "the infant discipline of mathematical politics" as Paul A. Samuelson once called it, has thus far failed to provide a single, comprehensive quantitative treatment to the formulation of policy decisions, the exercise of government intervention in the economy in the pursuit of its aims (that is, economic management), and the integration of policies and instrument use into consistent national, sectoral, or regional programs or plans. Actually, economic policy, economic management, and economic planning, no matter how much varying in scope and overlapping in practice, are substantively one and the same thing: acts of economic control. It is with this unifying aspect that we shall be concerned. The problem of plan implementation in the administrative sense is an extremely serious one, but one that by its very nature relates to specific issues generating unique problems that fall somewhat outside of the purview of the present project and, happily, beyond our present ambitions. To the extent that implementation *qua* administration takes a back seat in the discussion, this is a reflection of a purposeful neglect on our part, and neither an oversight, nor a negative judgment as to its import.

Obvious pitfalls confront a project aiming at a comprehensive treatment of complex problems that are a concern of philosophically disparate societies, and that occur at various levels of economic significance—national, sectoral, and regional. This apparent diversity notwithstanding, we believe that a unified framework for the study of economic control is now furnished by what Oskar Lange called economic cybernetics by analogy with Norbert Wiener's path-breaking theory of "Cybernetics: the Control and Communication in the Animal and the Machine." The reference here is to the theory of systems autoregulation or programmed control, and the analysis of the informational networks of decisions and actions within such systems. As we hope to show, modern economic systems are interesting subjects for joint study because of certain identical relations between controls and the underlying economic process. We shall notably show that interactions of the "software"—that is, *policies* (or descriptive structures by which a programmer controls the computer), and of the "hardware"—that is, the *physical structures* of the economy, can be studied independently of the specific arrangements of a given economic system.

The present study has greatly benefited from, and indeed has been made possible by, the considerable progress that has taken place of late in the general theory of control, and more specifically in the theories of multi-level systems, information, and planning. Progress has notably been made in exploring the interrelations between (a) the regulation, stability, reliability, and adaptability of multi-level systems; (b) the role of information as a specific input in decision making; (c) the formulation of policy goals; (d) the choice of policy instruments for consideration as potential measures to effect these goals; (e) the specification of the constraints that limit the government's freedom and ability to intervene in the ordinary operations of the economy; and (f) the utilization of mathematical optimization techniques. These advances have proceeded in two main directions: (1) as logical extensions of the engineering theories of control, and, (2) as extensions of, or by analogy to, the theory of the firm and the theory of consumer behavior.

Progress has further been made in the versatile utilization of input-output economics, activity analysis, and large-scale linear models. Input-output economics, originally devised by Professor Wassily Leontief for the study of economic structures, has been increasingly put to use in the study of variations in structures for the purposes of planning. Additionally, advances in constrained optimization techniques, and developments in econometrics and statistical decision theory, have made it feasible to attack policy and management problems through complex models that were hitherto either mathematically intractable, or statistically unapproachable.

It is interesting to observe at the outset that although "planning" has been taking place in the Soviet Union for almost half a century, the most decisive progress in the formulation and the development of the theory of policy, management, and planning—developments that have clarified the nature and limits of planning as such—has occurred in the West. In fact, the Soviet economy is a centrally administered, as opposed to a centrally planned, economy. That is, the focus of Soviet planning is on the translation of policy decisions (more or less arbitrarily taken) into binding instructions for the enterprises and in checking the results, rather than on determining optimal policies and plans for achieving prespecified goals. Even in the Soviet Union, however, which is a special rather than a general case, binding instructions are often thwarted, and plans often go awry. In contrast, in a centrally planned economy policy makers would focus on reaching internally consistent, or feasible policies that, when judged in accordance with prespecified criteria, can also be said to be optimal. The Soviet experience, in effect, offers only a method of planning, as opposed to a theory of planning.

Our approach in this book is to analyze how in practice, (a) the government's decision-making apparatus can be made more effective, (b) plans can be formulated and the optimal plan chosen from among a feasible set, and (c) transitions can be made from general to sectoral and decentralized plans. The present approach contrasts with that taken in the vast and expanding literature on "mathematical politics" and management on the one hand, and on planning (macro and micro, Western and Soviet) on the other hand, insofar as we shall attempt to (a) provide a unified treatment of all the subjects involved and (b) show their deeper interconnections. We are encouraged to do this because of our conviction that policy models, management theory, and planning of all kinds are all reducible to a small core of models and their variables.

We have also made a decision, a resolute and conscious decision, but one that we recognize to be arguable, to bypass, in the main, some very important issues—in particular, some of the more complex questions raised by the social and political structures—that impact upon policy and planning decisions. In neglecting these issues we do not mean to imply that we judge them to be unimportant, or even, indeed, of lesser importance than the technical questions and models to which we address ourselves. Rather, in the classical tradition, we prefer to include them in our *ceteris paribus* assumptions, in order that we may stress and focus exclusively upon the models and techniques that are proving to be of the greatest use to planners in the West and in the East, without adding further and controversial distractions. It is our observation that it is this narrower *comprehensive technical* guide that is missing from the literature, rather than the broader social and political discussion. We wish to stress, however, that the approach presented in this book can be easily adapted to the analysis of issues now in vogue, such as the question of the preservation of the environment, and the question of whether growth is or is not desirable.

By its very nature, quantitative analysis of policy and planning necessarily demands some familiarity with and tolerance for relatively advanced mathematics and statistics, and upon occasion the demands can be high indeed. In order to be able to address the work to as wide an audience as possible, mathematical and statistical materials that seem to us of undue difficulty but of more than passing interest have been provided in appendices to various chapters. The book is indeed intended for a wide and diversified audience. As an outgrowth of graduate courses on policy and planning which one of the authors has offered at Indiana University for the past several years, the work should serve, first of all, graduate students of economics and political science interested in policy formulation and implementation. It should, furthermore, be of value to the ever-increasing population of planners and policy makers who have become aware of the need to *quantify* the governmental decision-making process, thereby endowing it with the mathematical and statistical precision that "better" decision making demands. Finally, it should be of interest to students and practitioners of economic development, for the quantitative analysis of economic policy and planning theory are also indispensable parts of development theory. The latter, we believe, tends to be too oriented toward the study of general "drawbacks" to development, and insufficiently oriented toward (a) the ways in which the economic variables that affect development might be manipulated, and (b) the existing limits to such manipulations.

The book is divided into three parts, each of which contains a brief introductory discussion of purpose and rationale. These introductions are intended to set the stage for what follows. Part I is concerned with the *Elements of Quantitative Economic Control*. Here we (a) introduce the policy problem as a problem of economic management which can be analyzed using the theory of control and information, in particular, (b) define the jargon common to the world of economic policy, (c) develop some of the classic policy models based on the theory of rational policy choice, and (d) discuss the major empirical issues that arise in their application.

Part II is concerned with *Systems, Subsystems, and Plans.* Here we (a) discuss the planning models and techniques that have commanded the greatest attention among planners and within the literature, in order to describe the steps involved in *overall* planning, and point out the problems involved in *decentralized* planning; (b) explore goal formulation and integration within each economic sector, and the problems of coordination of their interacting activities.

Finally, in Part III we deal with *Economic Control: Scope and Issues,* drawing the logical inferences of our earlier analyses. In particular, we shall suggest (a) that the economist's conception of the role of the government as coordinator and controller of the nation's economic affairs has undergone significant change, and that these roles are gaining ever-increasing acceptance and recognition, (b) that certain government controls in the East and West which, to begin with, were highly dissimilar, may tend to become less so, and (c) that notwithstanding paraeconomic factors precluding East's and West's systematic convergence, policy making, management, and planning in dissimilar systems can and must be analyzed with the same set of tools.

ACKNOWLEDGMENTS

The book has evolved from a graduate course taught over a number of years at Indiana University. We wish to express our gratitude, first of all to our students, for their probing questions, stimulating criticisms, and valuable suggestions. We are particularly grateful to a number of our former students who showed continuous interest over the years in the progress of the preparation of the manuscript for publication, and who helped with various comments and suggestions: we are especially indebted to E. Mark Kloc, Jr., and to Dr. Ulrich Ernst who read parts of the manuscript in various stages and who made invaluable suggestions and comments.

A number of our colleagues read parts of, or whole drafts of various chapters. Among them, Professor George M. von Furstenberg, Scott H. Gordon, Michael J. P. Magill, Clarence C. Morrison, Richard L. Pfister, Claude Schochet, Robert N. Taaffe, and George J. Stolnitz of Indiana University (Bloomington campus), J. Ronnie Davis, Antal Majthay and Jerome W. Milliman of the University of Florida deserve our special thanks for their help. We are also greatly indebted to Distinguished Professor Gerhard Tintner of the University of Southern California, Los Angeles, who read drafts of the first six chapters, and to Professor Prohena Betancort of the University of Maryland, who did a close reading of the entire manuscript.

As usual, none of the persons mentioned necessarily agrees with our exposition or with our arguments, nor shares any responsibility for the book's failings and shortcomings.

PART ONE
Elements of Quantitative Economic Control

In formulating the goals it proposes to accomplish—that is, in establishing "policies"—a government takes the initial steps toward assuming a conscious role in regulating the nation's economic affairs. This role is analogous to that of top management in the modern corporation, wherein managerial judgments as to what is in the best interests of the corporation as an entity, as well as in the best interests of its stockholders, its employees, and the public at large, determine the actions taken by the corporation. It is in this sense that the government, making judgments as to what is in the best interests of the nation as an entity, as well as in the best interests of the citizenry and the world at large, is behaving as the top *economic manager* confronted by *managerial problems* that are not dissimilar to those of corporate top management. The scope of the public manager's role, that is, the *extent* to which the government will intervene in the economy and whether or not there is a deliberate, overall policy of government intervention, will, however, differ between various economic and political systems and philosophies, whereas the scope of the private manager's role, which is defined for each individual manager by the *established* lines of authority and responsibility, is limitless and "intervention" is mandatory.

Government's managerial or economic problems of "steering" and choice are examined herein within the framework of *the theory of regulation and adaptive control* associated with the contributions of the Nobel laureate Kenneth Arrow, Oskar Lange, and a number of distinguished mathematical economists. In addition, consideration of certain *operational aspects* of policy formulation and of instrument's use necessitates the resort to what might be called *the theory of rational policy choice* developed by analogy to the theory of rational consumer choice by another Nobel laureate, Jan Tinbergen. As we shall see below, Tinbergen's theory is conceptually related to the former, but it tackles the problem from different angles, and yields, because of this, different useful insights.

The term *control theory* as used in this book refers to *multi-level multi-goal* hierarchical systems—that is, *layered* systems of interrelated functional elements that transform inputs into outputs and that display a *supreme* coordinator or regulator (governor). The lower-level units' purposive actions (that is, their goal-seeking activities) are not necessarily fully controlled by the higher-level units, nor are these goals identical or similar to the goals of the higher-level units. As typically referred to in the economic literature, control theory deals with systems with a direct controller-processor relationship, and with *single-goal* decision problems. Game theory and the theory of teams deal with associated systems with direct controller-processor relationships, and with *multiple goals*. In this book, a regulated system may be a simple or complex process with *single* or *multiple* controllers, with or without layered subsystems acting independently or interdependently through a hierarchical arrangement.

A regulated system is usually conceived as a *simple* or a *complex* process—investment, consumption, national product, for instance—tending to a desired value or norm, while the regulator (the government or some other agency) is viewed as a specific device that influences the process. The desired norm of the state of output toward which the controlled system tends may be a constant or a variable quantity. If it is a constant, the regulator attempts to determine its every value, and seeks to maintain the system's course along the desired path. The former case is that of *stabilization;* the latter case is that of *controlled regulation.* In any event, either the constant or the variable norm may be determined as a function of a single or a multi-parameter argument. The parameters may be time, some preceding state of output, an extremum, and so on, and the regulator's problem becomes one of programmed, adaptive control to "steer" the economy in the desired direction. An economic system must, however, be approached also as a hierarchical setup of interacting goal-seeking subsystems (for example, manpower, foreign trade, regions, and so on) each with its own goals, which the supreme unit (the government) attempts to coordinate in some optimally defined way.

In the classic policy models of rational policy choice devised by Jan Tinbergen, the decision-making authority first expresses and orders its preferences for various combinations of variables consisting of both (a) economic quantities, such as disposable income, income distribution, and total output, and (b) economic structures, such as the technical, behavioral, and institutional organization of the society, via its so-called preference function. The latter serves as the objective function in a constrained optimization problem wherein the task of the decision-making authority is to determine *the optimal feasible program*—that is, the most preferred mutually compatible and achievable rates of the economic quantities and structures. For this purpose, it will have to select from the array of fiscal, monetary, and institutional-reform instruments at its disposition, the rates for the decision variable(s) (instrument or instruments) which will ensure the preferred result. While such models are based on the highly simplified assumptions of a *direct* relationship between the supremal controller and the economic process, and of a single-goal decision problem, they clarify numerous operational aspects of policy choice in which we are interested.

The two approaches—the cybernetic approach and the modeling à la Tinbergen—apply the same end-means analysis. The "economic processor" of the first is comparable to the "economic structure" of the second; the performance criterion of the first is the equivalent of the preference function of the second; and, finally, the regulator, or the system's managing agent, plays the role of decision maker choosing the appropriate instrument rate. The crucial differences lie in the fact that the two approaches yield *different insights* into the problem of economic management. The first yields insights into the complex interrelations between control and information, the role of "feedback," the question of centralization and decentralization, and the problem of coordination of interacting goal-seeking subsystems. The second yields insights into the scope of specific goals-instruments combinations and variations.

The basic definitions and concepts of the cybernetic or control and communication approach are presented in the first two chapters of this section. The first chapter emphasizes how the government as such, or any of its agencies, as the system's supremal and infimal *controllers,* may either (a) regulate monetary, physical, and informational inputs into the system in order to help effect the outputs that it wishes to generate, or (b) alter the existing network of arrangements between the elements that comprise the system and subsystems, as well as alter the operations of the elements themselves, in order to carry out a given policy, or make the system a more effective vehicle for generating the desired outputs. Here the economy is described as a *purposeful* system whose rationale is to satisfy various social concerns as specified in a societal preference function, effectively and efficiently.

The second chapter is concerned with (a) developing the concept of information, and with (b) introducing the more general problem of communication. Information is a major input and output in any system, and its generation, transmission, and processing raises some very critical issues. Organization, coordination, and control involve issuing, interpreting, and evaluating data, and modifying as needed either previous messages, or the parameters under which the various component units operate, in order to attain the overall system objectives. The cybernetic approach seeks to determine the most efficient means of transmitting and processing these informational flows—that is, to determine the most efficient communications network—and this goal in turn suggests the need for a *measure* of information. This subject, too, is taken up in the second chapter.

The third chapter presents, in its most general form, the classic policy problem confronting the policy maker. This is seen to be a nonlinear programming problem in which the rates of a set of prespecified policy instruments are the decision variables. These rates are to be chosen so as to maximize the objective function that summarizes the policy makers' preferences. This is to be done, subject to a set of constraints and boundary conditions describing (a) the structure of the system, (b) the definitions that bind together the system's variables, and (c) any uncompromisable demands that the policy makers seek to impose upon any policy. Some special cases of the general model, in particular Tinbergen's linear programming model and Theil's quadratic programming variation on Tinbergen's now classic theme, are also considered and appraised here.

It is seen in Chapter 3 that the elements required by the theory of rational policy choice for the solution of a policy problem are (a) the preference function that is to be optimized, (b) the instruments that the policy makers have at their disposal, and (c) the constraints and boundary conditions that define the set of feasible policies. The theoretical issues that are raised, and the empirical problems that arise, with respect to each of these, are taken up in turn in Chapters 4, 5, and 6.

Chapter 4 discusses (a) some suggestions offered in the literature for specifying the preference function, as well as (b) some of the difficulties that are necessarily encountered in putting these suggestions into practice. Chapter 5 (a) considers the sorts of policy instruments that are generally available, (b) describes the most frequently employed policy instruments of the East and the West, and (c) indicates the circumstances that commonly underlie the use of these instruments. Finally, Chapter 6 presents some of the more useful formats for describing (a) the technical, (b) the behavioral, and (c) the institutional constraints or characteristics that define the processor of a system, or its structure. Here, particular attention is given to Leontief's input-output model, the Marxian model, and the relationship between the two.

CHAPTER 1

Policy Analysis in a Systems Control Context

1.1 MODELS OF THE FIRM AND POLICY MODELS

Economists have long been involved in model-building. The neoclassical model of the firm in which a single decision maker, a profit-maximizing entrepreneur-manager, makes all the firm's decisions, accepts responsibility for these choices, and enjoys or suffers their consequences, is probably the most familiar illustration of these efforts.

The entrepreneur makes decisions *as if* all elements incorporated into the decision-making process are known with certainty. The "as if" suggests that elements such as product demand and factor supply may be uncertain. Still, the entrepreneur is willing to conjure up and act on the basis of a summary body of data, or a *certainty-equivalent,* describing all that one knows about such ordinarily stochastic variables as product demand. The fact that a certainty-equivalent value will not necessarily hold in any given instance does not inhibit the entrepreneur. The latter is *assumed* to behave *as if* it will.[1]

Even the multi-product, multi-process neoclassical firm selling in several markets is an exceedingly well-run organization. Its plans simply do not go awry. Thus, an entire set of decisions is automatically implied by any one of several subsets. For example, from the decision to employ specific quantities of the various factors of production—given the production function and the demand curve—one can infer the quantities to be produced and the prices to be charged for *all* products of the profit-maximizing firm. Further, it is presumed

---

[1] For a discussion of the "as if" assumption in economic theory see I. Horowitz, *Decision Making and the Theory of the Firm* (New York: Holt, Rinehart and Winston, 1970), particularly pp. 91–92, 323–327, and 336–337.

that the factors will produce these exact quantities, and that the anticipated profits will be realized for their sale.

The economist assumes a well-defined measure of the firm's performance, based on well-defined entrepreneurial objectives, to be maximized subject to a set of well-defined constraints. In the simplest model of the firm, for example, profit is the sole measure of performance, maximizing profit is the entrepreneur's single objective, and the production function, product demand, and factor supply curves represent the firm's constraints. In an advanced model, sales may replace profits as the performance measure, sales maximization may become the objective, and a lower bound to profits may be introduced as an additional constraint. There remains, nonetheless, readily available and easily processed perfect information about these. Thus, an optimal solution is always achieved and all aims are always realized. There are no surprises.

The real-world firm differs from that of the neoclassical model in many respects. This firm may have many decision makers, and the complexity of its operations may *demand* the delegation of decision-making authority throughout a managerial hierarchy. The separation of ownership and management in the modern corporation means that the persons responsible for making decisions are not necessarily going to be the ones to enjoy or suffer the full consequences of these acts; and the objectives, the performance measures, and the constraints of owners and managers, as well as among the members of each group, will not necessarily coincide or be unique. They are, therefore, unlikely to be as readily specified as the theory assumes them to be.

Uncertainty abounds in the real world. The firm's decision makers are ordinarily not satisfied with a gratuitous recognition of its existence, because uncertainty implies that they will bear the risk of being unable to perfectly forecast the consequences of a prospective act. Thus, uncertainty will be incorporated into a manager's decision-making calculus with varying degrees of analytical sophistication. Further, because attitude toward risk, and willingness to undertake it or determination to avoid it, is a *personal* characteristic that differs between individuals, it is an aspect of decision making that can lead different persons confronted with the same problem and information to rationally arrive at different decisions. Thus, the uncertainty itself is a vital element that can influence decisions.

In the modern corporation one decision does not necessarily imply all others, and decision making is not as compartmentalized as in its neoclassical counterpart. Management does not make a single output decision for a given production period in isolation from all other problems and aspects of the firm's operations, and its past and future history. Rather, decision making in the modern corporation ordinarily entails a planned *sequence* of decisions—that is, a *strategy*—that establishes a production, pricing, and inventory *policy*. This strategy will be followed over a *series* of time periods, and from it will evolve *tactics* for dealing with any individual *contingencies* that might arise in the future.

Modern management must also live with imperfect information. In con-

trast to the neoclassical situation, the information required for real-world decision making is not thrust upon the modern manager. Instead, the appropriate information must be specified, gathered, and processed. In contrast to the
neoclassical model, in the real world this is a time-consuming process, and
often a very costly one. Yet, the information upon which decisions will be
based, may well be erroneous. In particular, the input data may be unreliable
and the basic assumptions invalid. When this occurs, except by chance either
the right solution is reached to the wrong problem, or the wrong solution to the
right problem. In either event, the manager quickly realizes the importance of a
steady flow of accurate information. But, information is not necessarily, nor ordinarily cost free.

The result of data imperfections and real-world complexities, then, is
that aims are not always achieved, and small though they may be, there are
usually some surprises. The observed outcomes of past decisions, as well as the
passage of time, provide management with new information that can be incorporated into the decision-making process. Thus, operations in the real-world
firm are frequently sufficiently flexible to permit (1) a revision of initial input
data to take account of new information, (2) a control mechanism to process
data and compare forecasts and facts, and (3) an automatic adjustment of an
initial decision in light of the revised data and/or the controlled comparison.

The primary considerations in constructing a model of the firm are not
unique to microeconomic theory. Rather, they are germane to economic models
in general, and to economic policy models in particular. Microeconomic models are concerned with managing the *firm's* economic affairs; economic policy
models are concerned with managing the *nation's* economic affairs. Both types
of models are therefore concerned with *economic management*. But, whereas
the firm's survival is dependent upon and *demands* conscious entrepreneurial
guidance, an economic policy is a governmental action that is *imposed* upon a
nation so as to influence its economic affairs. Thus, entrepreneurial decision
making is *required* in a model of the firm, but governmental policy making is a
form of *voluntary intervention* that only enters into a model of the economy by
intent. Assuredly, there is no *realistic* alternative to such intervention, and the
only relevant question is the *extent* of the intervention. It is in the answer to this
question that we find the major distinction between the controlled economies of
the East and the free market, or, more appropriately, the mixed economies of
the West.

Economic policy models therefore differ from the neoclassical model of
the firm in two major respects. The first concerns management's role in the
decision-making process, and the extent to which economic mangement is
employed to deal with macroeconomic problems. The second concerns the
model's size and complexity, and the sophistication of the analytical tools that
are required because of these. Since modern society is so much larger and more
complex than the neoclassical firm, larger and more complex models are
required to represent it, and more sophisticated techniques are needed to analyze and deal with its economic problems. This is, however, also true of the

modern corporation, vis-à-vis the necolassical firm. Indeed, the problems confronting corporate management are not dissimilar to those confronting "the" government, especially insofar as the corporations are multi-national giants, and the societies are those of the smaller, perhaps emerging nations. This suggests that the analytical tools used by the former in the decision-making process may well be of assistance to the latter in the policy-making process. It is this observation that provides our starting point in the development of quantitative economic policy and planning models.

1.2 CONSIDERATIONS IN ECONOMIC POLICY MODEL-BUILDING

a. Social settings and policy models

An economic policy model is a simplified representation of both the *structural* characteristics and inner relationships of any economic region (such as a city, state, or nation) and of the possible ways of manipulating its parameters. As such, policy models are essentially normative, while their foundations are sets of behavioral, technological, and institutional components.

A behavioral model *describes* behavioral characteristics of the system being modeled. Consider a particularly abstract behavioral model of gross domestic investment in which current annual investment is described as being dependent upon the previous year's rate of economic activity, and the trend in economic activity over the two-year period. Translating this verbal description into a mathematical description, we may write $I_t = i_t(Y_{t-1}, Y_{t-1} - Y_{t-2})$; or, investment I_t in year t is a function i_t of the previous year's gross national product, Y_{t-1}, and the previous annual change in gross national product, $Y_{t-1} - Y_{t-2}$. This mathematical translation has a threefold justification: (1) the language of mathematics is more compact and manipulable than are verbal languages; (2) its use demands greater precision and less obfuscation; and (3) the "grammar" or rules of mathematics frequently permit one to draw from the model inferences that would otherwise remain obscured. Building models and translating them into mathematics—mathematical model-building—is therefore a prominent activity in this book.

By making the form of the function explicit, say by specifying a linear relationship between the variables, we can write

$$I_t = i_t(Y_{t-1}, Y_{t-1} - Y_{t-2}) = \alpha_0 + \alpha_1 Y_{t-1} + \alpha_2(Y_{t-1} - Y_{t-2}) \tag{1.1}$$

The α_i's are *parameters* that describe the particular linear relationship. These might be assigned in various ways, but the most widely employed methods in policy models are those of econometrics.

The econometric approach to parameter estimation recognizes both that the relationship between the dependent variable, in this case investment, and the independent variables, in this case gross national product and its most recent trend, ordinarily offers only a partial explanation for the behavior of the dependent variable, and that the influence of certain other factors affecting the dependent variable cannot be captured systematically. Rather, these factors influence investment in a random manner through some prespecified stochastic process. Thus, the econometric version of the original verbal model contains both a deterministic and a stochastic component. In particular, it specifies current annual investment as the sum of a *systematic linear term*, $\alpha_0 + \alpha_1 Y_{t-1} + \alpha_2(Y_{t-1} - Y_{t-2})$, that is invariant, and a *random disturbance term*, ϵ_t, that behaves in accordance with some stochastic process; or,

$$I_t = \alpha_0 + \alpha_1 Y_{t-1} + \alpha_2(Y_{t-1} - Y_{t-2}) + \epsilon_t \qquad (1.1a)$$

Techniques such as least-squares or maximum-likelihood estimation can then be applied to a set of historical data in order to assign values a_i to the α_i ($i = 0$, 1, 2); that is, to *precisely describe the systematic component of behavior* in the economy's investment sector. The ϵ_t's which are never observed, can then be estimated by the *residuals,* $e_t = I_t - a_0 - a_1 Y_{t-1} - a_2(Y_{t-1} - Y_{t-2})$. The latter are simply the differences between the actual values of the dependent variables and the values that would be predicted on the basis of the estimated systematic relationship.

In contrast to behavioral models, *normative* models *prescribe* behavior in a system for which one has formulated a set of goals. Thus, a normative model in which investment is a dependent variable might indicate the level at which the prime interest rate would have to be pegged *if* the current rate of investment is to be maximized. Normative models will ordinarily have behavioral features. Thus, pegging the interest rate may result in the rate of investment *prescribed* by a normative model, only because of the predictability of investment behavior as *described* by the model's behavioral components.

A policy model is therefore normative insofar as it is used to suggest policies that will help to achieve a set of objectives. It will, however, be built on a behavioral foundation that includes a set of assumptions with respect to the prevailing economic *order*—that is, the political, legal, and institutional framework within which any policy must be developed. Thus, policy models generally have normative goals, and the extent to which these goals can be realized will be constrained from several directions, one of the most important of which is the established economic order. At one extreme the government relies on the *market mechanism* to achieve such aims as the maximization of a social welfare function; at the other extreme, that of *statism,* policy makers attempt to regulate *all* economic variables, including prices, quantities, and the allocation of market shares among producers, in order to achieve a preestablished state goal. In modern societies, however, neither of these extremes is seen as a viable alternative.

On the one hand, recognition that the economic order cannot survive if the social and economic inequities that the market mechanism tends to perpetuate and that the vicissitudes of economic life tend to exaggerate are not relieved, has in turn led to the realization that *some* governmental intervention in economic affairs is both necessary and desirable. On the other hand, the size and complexity of modern society makes it equally apparent that *all* aspects of economic life cannot be effectively regulated, and that while the relief of *all* inequities may be a desirable goal, it is not a very practical one. Thus, some form of *economic management* is imposed on all modern societies. The only real issue is the *extent* to which the economy is managed, and the *forms* of intervention that are employed.

In general, then, policy models built to deal with the problems of one society differ from those built to deal with the problems of another only with respect to: (1) the *specific rules* of economic order that all solutions must respect—that is, the existing political, legal, and institutional framework that must house any policy; (2) the *particular variables* that policy makers are permitted to control, and the extent to which they are permitted to exercise such control; (3) the *normative goals* that policies seek to achieve; and (4) the *behavioral* and *technological* basis upon which the society has been constructed. More general differences can also arise concerning the nature of the input data employed and the complexity of the decision-making process. Specifically, whether the model is deterministic or stochastic, and whether the model is single-stage or multi-stage.

Deterministic models assume that *all* elements of the system are known with *certainty,* whereas *stochastic* models recognize that virtually all aspects of the real world are subject to various degrees of *uncertainty.* Although stochastic models tend to be more realistic, and as a result are frequently more rewarding than deterministic models, they also tend to be less tractable. The model-builder must decide on the level of abstraction compatible with the model's purposes and the technical limitations of the people that will be working with the model. Complexity in model-building is not necessarily a virtue, nor is simplification necessarily a vice. On the one hand, then, a deterministic investment model that implies the *direction* in which investment will change if the prime interest rate increases by a quarter of a point, will *suffice* for some purposes. On the other hand, a stochastic model of investment that implies the *extent* to which the change in investment will be affected by increased risk aversion on the part of entrepreneurs, will be *mandatory* for other purposes.

A second important dimension of model complexity relates to whether a *single decision,* or a series of *independent decisions,* is extracted from the model, or whether a *sequence of decisions,* or a set of *interdependent decisions,* is to be derived. The former case is that of a *single-stage* model; the latter case describes a *multi-stage* model. Once again the appropriate level of abstraction depends on the purposes to which the model is to be put. Thus, limited goals and a lack of the requisite mathematical techniques frequently lead to the development of essentially *static* economic models that either imply a unique decision in a given situation, or else permit one to study the effects of change on a given situation—the method of comparative statics. Alternatively, the fact that the results of a current decision may well influence or determine the inputs of future decisions may lead one to build *dynamic* economic models that imply a planned sequence of decisions, and require a higher level of modeling sophistication.

Each of these characteristics is a consideration in the various models discussed and developed in this book. One type of model is not necessarily "better" than another. The important issue is to determine the most appropriate type of model for the specific problem; that is, to determine the optimal level of abstraction, given the particular problem, and the modeling, mathematical, and statistical tools that one is prepared to bring to bear on it.

b. Some specific issues

Policy models seek optimal solutions for given sets of *objectives* and *restrictions*. Some of the restrictions are *definitional* and *behavioral conditions inherent* within the structure of the system being modeled; others are *normative demands imposed* on the solution by the decision-making body. Thus, the behavioral, technological, and institutional constraints that *describe* the structure of the system appear as a set of *endogenous* restrictions initially defining what is for *it* a set of *feasible* solutions. The policy goals that *prescribe* objectives for this system can enter the model through a set of *exogenous* restrictions, as well as through an *objective function*. Objectives appearing as constraints represent inviolable goals whose accomplishment is required of *any* solution. For an optimal policy to exist, these goals must be mutually compatible. An important contribution that a model can make is to show these goals to be incompatible. This could then force the policy makers to *establish priorities* with respect to the goals that are to be satisfied, and those that must be sacrificed. In effect, the exogenous restrictions impose upon any policy a set of minimally acceptable standards and trade-offs. This further reduces the set of feasible solutions to those meeting these standards.

The policy-making problem is to determine the *optimal* feasible solution, and the concept of optimality implies the acceptance of a *performance criterion*. In economics, performance criteria associate numbers to outcomes so as to reflect *ordinal* preferences. Thus, the criterion is a *function* of those attributes of an outcome that are of concern for decision-making purposes. It is *ordinal* as opposed to cardinal, in the sense that a *ranking* of the outcomes based on the performance criterion *signals* the policy maker's *preferences,* although not necessarily the strength of these preferences. The criterion is said to be an *objective* function, because it is a function that provides policy makers with an unequivocal objective: determination of the preferred decision.

Assuredly, there have been occasional and short-lived efforts to attach a cardinal interpretation to the preference function. Their lack of staying power has three main sources. First, on philosophical grounds it stretches credibility to ascribe to an individual, no less than to a group, the ability or willingness to issue statements to the effect that one "basket of desiderata" is, in any meaningful sense, twice as desirable, say, as is another; and, still further, that the numbers assigned to the relation are meaningful measures of the strength of the preference for the "basket." Second, cardinality also lends itself open to the possibility of interpersonal comparisons, which again are anathema to utility theorists. Finally, and perhaps the most compelling argument against cardinality, is the fact that the assumption of an ordinal preference measure is in and of itself sufficient to deduce the major principles of both consumer behavior and welfare theory. Under these circumstances, it makes little sense to demand of the preference function a property that is both questionable and unnecessary.

The policy makers' preferences, and consequently the objective function, will depend on the specific attributes of an outcome, and their attitudes with respect to these attributes—that is, the goals. Thus, *ceteris paribus,* the outcome promising the lowest rate of unemployment or the highest rate of real per capita income, will ordinarily be preferred. The trade-offs that policy makers are willing to accept among the attributes subsequently determine the complete ordering among *all* outcomes.

The attributes are in turn dependent upon a set of variables. Included among these are the *decision variables* or policy *instruments.* These are the variables over which policy makers exercise control. Since the performance criterion is a function of the attributes, it is in turn a function of the decision variables. The general policy problem is therefore to select rates for the decision variables so as to optimize the objective function, while assuring that the constraints are respected. A solution to this problem is called a *program.* The preferred solution, or optimal program, can include variables such as tax rates and government expenditures—*economic quantities*—as well as variables such as the political organization of society—*economic structures.* When a particular economic quantity or structure is used for policy purposes, this use is referred to as a policy *measure.*

There is, however, a considerable difference between (1) developing the general framework for a policy model, and (2) filling in the details of a specific model and obtaining and applying a solution for a particular problem. To accomplish the latter, it is necessary to (1) identify the actual policy makers, (2) specify both the objective function and the constraints, (3) determine, gather, and process the information upon which a solution will be based, (4) perform the required mathematical manipulations and arithmetic computations, and (5) implement the solution. Each of these requisites offers potential complications.

It is important to identify *policy makers, planners,* and *controllers* at all levels. It is the responsibility of the policy makers to define the goals, order preferences, and specify the objective function of the system as a whole. It is the responsibility of the planners to redefine these goals in an operational way and to compare them with the performances of, and the projections for the system and its subsystem's activities, as defined by lower-level controllers and managers. The policy makers' goals are, presumably, the goals, preferences, and objectives of the larger society on whose behalf decisions are being taken. There will not necessarily be a single policy maker, nor will there necessarily be unanimity within a decision-making body with respect to these vital issues. On the one hand, then, we can attempt to reach a consensus permitting the derivation of a compromise solution, but one that may well be unsatisfactory to all. On the other hand, we can attempt to initially eliminate from the set of feasible solutions those that *all* decision makers agree are less preferable than others. This requires sufficient model flexibility to permit one to extract the subset of potential candidates for a final *negotiated* program. In effect, the problem of *converting* input information into an output solution in an economic and mathematical setting becomes the first stage in a process requiring the *reduction* of one set of inputs to a second set of inputs to be employed in a political setting.

Additionally, policy is not necessarily made in a single decision center. Rather, the policy-making process may be decentralized, either by the successive delegation of decision-making authority throughout layers of bureaucracy, or by the spatial decentralization of the policy makers. In this case, clearly, one decision may work at cross-purposes with another. Successful application of policy models therefore requires a decision-making *network* through which decisions can be coordinated and controlled.

Specifying the objective function and the constraints—that is, defining the problem—is a particularly complex issue for policy models, because they deal with the problems of complex societies in an uncertain environment. As a result, the problems tend to be intricate, and require a few large models capable of dealing with sets of interrelated decisions under uncertainty. This is as opposed to many small models, each of which deals with a single deterministic decision considered in isolation from the others. In defining the problem, then, the interrelationships among the various decisions and their consequences must be clearly delineated. Moreover, in anticipating the possibility of a decision judged in retrospect to have been nonoptimal, the availability of an evaluation and control mechanism must be explored. One must be especially concerned with implementing the solution. The implementation process may offer the opportunity to develop a procedure for exploiting observed results elsewhere in the economic system, and making automatic corrective adjustments in the solution as new data are received, as the vagaries of chance lead to nonoptimal outcomes, and as errors are detected and their causes diagnosed.

The interdependency among decisions arises in two basic ways. On the one hand, in a *sequential* decision process the output of one decision provides the input for a subsequent decision. On the other hand, in *parallel* decision processes two or more decisions are made independently of one another in the sense that, while they may employ common inputs, they can be considered to have been made simultaneously and to have led to outputs that will be required, albeit perhaps after further processing, as inputs into another decision in a common sequence. Thus, *parallel sequences* can also occur in which intermediate decisions ultimately link up in providing the inputs for a final program.

The availability of a control mechanism implies that the results of a decision are to be evaluated and interpreted, and in the event they are found to be nonoptimal, the decision can be altered. Specifically, the model contains a *feedback* mechanism producing information about the extent to which a decision has had a nonoptimal result. This information is then fed back as input and a new decision is made. The feedback process can be carried out repeatedly. Indeed, a sequential decision process can be a feedback process wherein the output of a decision made at a given point in time, irrespective of its predictability, is recycled as an input into this very same decision made at a later point in time.

Determining, gathering, and processing the necessary input data is always a potential problem for the model-builder. Relevant data do not just appear; they must be specified and collected. These data take two distinct forms, "hard" and "soft." Hard data consist of historical information and facts. These are objective in the sense that knowledgeable persons would accept these data, independent of personal beliefs, as answering given questions or fulfilling given definitions or conditions. This does not imply, however, that there will necessarily be agreement with respect to either the data's interpretation, or the validity of the use to which they are being put. It does imply that the data are reliable, and that there is general agreement that a particular situation is correctly represented by the data.

Soft data consist of individual judgments. These are subjective in the sense that they represent personal beliefs, and not all knowledgeable persons would concur in these beliefs. Unlike hard data which can be judged to be either correct or incorrect, there are no correct or incorrect soft data. Some soft data, however, stand up better under the test of time than do others.

In economic analysis the distinction between hard and soft data is often somewhat blurred because of the need to rely upon surrogates to measure the variables of interest. Thus, when the most appropriate data to measure a variable are not available or cannot be obtained, less appropriate data must be used for this purpose. For example, per capita income, gross national product, and real national income have all been employed as surrogates for economic welfare. The figures themselves may be hard data, although they very quickly become somewhat soft when interpreted as reflecting economic welfare. In building complex models, one is unlikely to be employing data in a manner closed to criticism. The model-builder's problem is to seek out the "best" data for the purpose, and to recognize that not all knowledgeable persons will judge it to be so.

Processing the data involves determining the appropriate statistical techniques, as well as the format for introducing the data into the model. Thus, in lieu of introducing into the model an entire series of data for a particular variable, one might want to incorporate only the arithmetic mean of the series, or the mean and the standard deviation; or, one might assume that the series behaves *as if* it was generated by a particular probabilistic process. In any event, a large-scale computer will almost surely play an integral role, both as a medium for storing input as well as output data, and as a computational device for converting a set of basic information into either final output, or into output to be employed as input in a subsequent stage.

Finally, the model must be solved. Even with comparatively small models this will not necessarily be either pleasant or possible. In particular, the mathematical requirements may be beyond the existing state of mathematical knowledge; and, while it is often possible to make a model more tractable, and ultimately solvable, via further simplifying assumptions, or while it is frequently possible to obtain reasonable approximations to a solution, these options will not necessarily be either practical or feasible.

Assuredly, a model's mathematical complexity and the likelihood of failing to solve it, tend to mount as the model itself expands and becomes more complex. Because of their complexity, then, policy models are often not amenable to solution by mathematical and analytical techniques. Fortunately, the large-scale computer's ability to rapidly process vast amounts of data has led to the development of computational techniques for solving complex models. These techniques take advantage of the computer as a research tool. Thus, although the computer is singularly lacking in wit, it nonetheless possesses rather remarkable powers of memory, and it is extraordinarily obedient. It does what one tells it to do; but it only does so with the information with which it has been provided. It can therefore be used as an accounting and data-processing device, as well as a problem-solving tool. It is the computer's willingness and capacity to serve in both of these respects that has facilitated the analyses of complex policy problems in a systems control context.

1.3 MODELS AND SYSTEMS

a. Systems

The public manager is the decision maker, or the *controller* of the economic *system*. There are two extremely important and easily overlooked observations in this otherwise noncontroversial statement. First, it is *natural* to view an economy as a system. Moreover, since we know a good deal about systems in general—that is, their characteristics, their rationale, and how to go about analyzing them and improving their design and performance—the application of this knowledge to *economic systems* could prove to be extremely important in understanding how *they* operate, how *their* performance can be improved, and how the goals that have been established for *them* can be better achieved. Second, the public manager plays quite a specific role in this system; namely, that of the controller. Thus once we understand the functions of the controller in systems in general, we can have an improved perspective of the functions of the public manager—their scope and limitations.

The systems approach to viewing organizations, public and private, as well as the managerial *process* within these organizations, has proved to be very fruitful. It is the success in these areas that encourages us to approach the larger managerial problems confronting the public manager of the macroeconomic system from the same systems point of view. But this approach requires an initial investment of time in the acquisition of some vocabulary, as well as in establishing an acquaintance with some of the more important systems concepts.

In its broadest sense, a *system* is an arrangement of a set of interrelated *elements* whose function is to *transform* inputs into outputs. The transformation might be the *conversion* of a set of factor inputs into a set of product outputs,

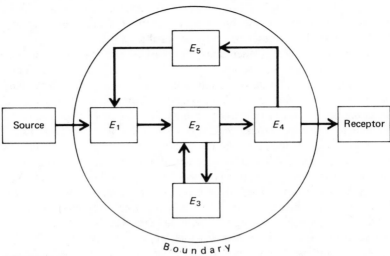

FIGURE 1-1

the *exchange* of personal income for consumption goods, or the *translation* of one set of information into a second set. The interrelationship between any two elements involves the output of one being employed as an input by the other, in which case the elements are said to be *coupled*. Figure 1.1 presents a *flow diagram* of a five-element system. The direction of the arrowhead indicates an input (entering) or an output (leaving). Thus, the output of E_1 is an input to E_2, both E_3 and E_4 receive the output of E_2, and E_2 and E_3 employ each other's output as input.

    The size of a system depends on the number of its elements, which may be few or extremely large (for example, in the central nervous system). Our concern here, however, will not be with systems' *sizes,* but rather with systems *functions*. Specifically, we shall confine our attention to *purposive* systems whose elements have an underlying unity that binds them to a common purpose. We shall refer to the elements so bound as *endogenous* to the system. Thus, when two endogenous elements are coupled, as with E_2 and E_4, the output of one becomes an *endogenous input* to the other. The rationale for these couplings, that is, the rationale for the existence of the particular system is that it permits the common purpose—the system's objective—to be achieved effectively and efficiently.

    The interrelationships and communality of interest suggest that the problems faced by individual elements must ultimately become problems for the entire system, and that the solutions applied to these problems will ultimately have wider implications for the other elements and the system as a whole. Under these circumstances, a solution that is optimal from the narrow perspective of any one element, or system component, will not necessarily be optimal from the wider perspective of the entire system. Indeed, such a solution may be at variance with those being proposed to deal with the problems facing other components. By the same token, the interactions of these components, if the system is well designed, will produce a *synergistic* effect; that is, a result whereby the whole is greater than the sum of the parts. Thus, working *in concert* these elements can together accomplish more in total than would be achieved through their individual, uncoordinated efforts. Similarly, through *coordinated* effort as orchestrated by the system's managers, the benefits of *symbiosis* can be realized; that is, the ability of apparently dissimilar elements to work together for their mutual advantage.

To a large extent, whether an element is or is not incorporated into a system is arbitrarily decided by the model-builder as a matter of problem definition. The decision not to include the *universe* of all elements as part of the system will ordinarily result in the exclusion of elements whose behavior can either influence, or can be influenced by, the system. Such elements comprise the system's *environment* and are said to be *exogenous* to the system. Thus, although elements in the environment are not integral parts of the system itself, they may, nonetheless, provide it with *exogenous inputs*. In the flow diagram of Figure 1.1, the endogenous element E_1 receives an exogenous input from a source in the environment, and ultimately the endogenous element E_4 transmits output as an exogenous input to a receptor in the environment. The verbal or mathematical distinction between the system and the environment appears in a flow diagram as a *boundary* separating the exogenous from the endogenous elements.

An operating definition of a system would therefore describe it as an organization of interrelated elements having a functional unity and a common purpose, as well as a boundary distinguishing these elements from their environment. In somewhat tautological fashion, then, an *organization* is a set of interrelated elements constrained, by a set of decision rules, to choose acts that will further their common interests—that is, their tastes and beliefs. In the particular instance wherein *all* elements have only common interests—that is, there are no differences in preferences and judgments—the elements are said to comprise a *team*. [2]

The systems control approach to the analysis of economic policy and planning is based on *two* premises. First, economic systems, and complex organizations—though not necessarily teams—of individual related elements, differ from one another only insofar as the particular couplings, or the transformation mechanisms differ. Different systems can therefore have much in common; the study of any one may suggest solutions to the problems of any other. Second, as is true of other organizations, economic systems are susceptible to *management* and *control* as well as to *"redesigning"* (that is, they are susceptible to alterations in their basic arrangements, changes in the manner in which the individual components transform inputs into outputs, the selective introduction of exogenous inputs, and the detection and correction of errors). Closely bound together with systems' *control* is *information*. Similarities and differences in

[2] See J. Marschak and R. Radner, *Economic Theory of Teams* (New Haven, Conn.: Yale University Press, 1972), pp. 123–126.

the type and nature of communication within systems are of paramount importance for distinguishing among the forms of control.

There are various ways of defining the components of an economic system. The components might be thought of as the individual firms and consumers generating economic activity. Alternatively, boundaries might be set up so as to group these components into *subsystems,* such as industries, economic sectors, or cities and regions, each of which have their own functional unity. In any event, they share common ties encouraging them to organize, or to be organized, into a single economy or system, and thereby to achieve, for this subsystem, a synergism of its own.

Because of this communality, a policy that is implemented to relieve the problems of any one element—such as the employment of a particular instrument in the form of an exogenous input—may well create problems for other endogenous elements. Recognizing this, the cybernetic approach suggests that although policy problems can vary considerably in terms of their difficulty, all are *complex* problems because they affect *complex* systems. Moreover, to deal with complex problems one must focus on the whole, rather than on any individual part. That is, policy models must deal with the problems of the economic system, treating the problems of the individual economic unit as a subsidiary aspect of the broader issue.

b. Complexity and modeling

It is conceptually feasible to build a mathematical model of the most complex system. Indeed, many such models have been built to aid in economic policy and planning. As these models become more realistic, however, they also tend to become mathematically intractable. This occurs both because the functional forms defining the problem will not necessarily have the pleasant properties and mutual compatibility that the mathematics demands of them, and because most of our mathematical tools are not equipped to handle the interrelationships inherent in complex systems. This forces the model-builder to either introduce additional simplifying assumptions that frequently have the effect of severely limiting the model's applicability and subsequent usefulness, or else to seek nonanalytical methods of solution. It is for the latter purpose that the technique of computer *simulation* has been developed and refined.

Simulation is a means of solving problems in models that are not amenable to analytical solution. Thus, the simulation technique is not employed because it is generally the best way to solve problems. Rather, it is a technique that we often resort to, because it may be the only practical means of solving a particular problem. We *experiment* with the model and *computationally* obtain an array of variegated *experience* that will *suggest* a solution. Experimenting with a model via the computer is likely to be a less costly and more practical option than experimenting with the actual system being modeled.

It is the latter aspect of simulation that makes it a particularly powerful tool of *systems design* and *systems analysis.* Systems design is ultimately concerned with determining an optimal arrangement of the system's elements. As a practical matter it may not be possible to determine *the* optimal arrangement, nor even to recognize it as such should we happen to stumble across it. Nonetheless, it *is* practical to seek *better* systems designs; that is, alternative component arrangements that enhance the elements' ability to achieve their common purpose. Then, again, a performance measure and an objective function are required, and improvements in the system will be signaled by higher values of the objective function governing decisions.

The cybernetic approach to economic policy and planning therefore both affords an *opportunity,* and entails an *obligation,* to consider two related aspects of policy problems. On the one hand, we can seek better ways of *organizing* an economic system so as to enable the planner to more effectively achieve society's goals. On the other hand, we can seek better solutions to the problems *confronting* a particular system, not merely those confronting a particular component, so as to more effectively employ the instruments—the decision variables—that policy makers have at their disposal.

c. An analogy

The systems concept is not new. Indeed, science has always been systems oriented. In biology, for example, the mammalian circulatory system has of necessity been a source of interest for centuries. Knowledge of how this system operates helps the physician analyze problems affecting the system's components and, although there is little that one can do to alter the basic design, some components can in fact be modeled, modified, and replaced. The mammalian circulatory system, for instance, is an organization of components whose twofold purpose is to distribute nutrients and oxygen to all parts of the body, while removing the body's waste products. In this system, unoxygenated blood is admitted to the heart through the right auricle. The pumping action of the heart sends the blood to the pulmonary arteries and, after the blood is oxygenated as a result of an input of oxygen through the lungs, it is recirculated through the heart and to the brain, as well as reprocessed throughout the circulatory system. Undoubtedly it is this system that inspired the physician François Quesnay to conceptualize the circulation of expenditures and products between the actors of the economic process (the "social classes" of his time) as an integrated *Tableau Economique.* This eventually inspired Marx, Walras, and Leontief.

All systems have one common aspect: the outputs of one element are processed and transformed into the outputs of related elements. Thus, all systems deal with *flows.* Economic systems, in particular, deal with three basic kinds of flows: information, materials, and energy, including human energy. Therefore, we shall not only be concerned with the flows of physical commodities and services throughout the economic system, but, of at least equal importance, with the informational flows as well. Similarly, systems differ only in the nature of the inputs and outputs, the networks linking the elements, the mechanisms through which transformation takes place, the type and amount of information they handle, and the ways in which *coordination* and *control* is achieved in each of them.

Economic systems have a particular distinction in that human beings are intimately involved. The vagaries of human behavior, and the fallibility of man's creations, invariably means that it will be impossible to perfectly forecast the behavior of all elements in an economic system. Therefore, from the standpoint of economic policy and planning, an economic system requires (1) a representation of its underlying structures and (2) an information-gathering, processing, and organizing network to handle what normally are complex stochastic multi-stage problems to be resolved by (3) a set of policy makers whose decisions are guided by (4) an objective function that reflects the preferences of a set of citizens that will inevitably bear the consequences of these policies. The result of the decision-making process is generally a policy that is amenable to modification and control.

d. System characteristics

Principles evolving from other disciplines are often of considerable value in economic analysis. For example, knowledge of the graphic arts helped Viner's famed Chinese draftsman recognize the impossibility of obtaining the neoclassical firm's U-shaped long-run average cost curve as the locus of minima of U-shaped short-run average cost curves.[3] Similarly, knowledge of the calculus makes it clear that the marginal-revenue-equals-marginal-cost solution to the neoclassical firm's production problem will only maximize profits if the marginal cost curve has a greater slope than does the marginal revenue curve at their point of intersection. By the same token, an understanding of the general principles of systems is helpful in analyzing the particular problems of economic systems. Assuredly, an extensive discussion of systems would in itself provide subject matter sufficient for a volume of its own. Nonetheless, even a cursory description of some basic concepts will contribute to an understanding of economic systems, and thereby abet efforts to manage them.

As previously stated, system elements are mechanisms that accept inputs and transform them into outputs. In general, it will be convenient to denote an input by an $n \times 1$ column *vector* $\mathbf{x}$ with typical element x_j, whose transpose is the row vector $\mathbf{x}' = (x_1, \ldots, x_j, \ldots, x_n)$. Similarly, the output is represented by a second $m \times 1$ column vector $\mathbf{y}$ with typical element y_i, so that $\mathbf{y}' = (y_1, \ldots, y_i, \ldots, y_m)$. We adopt the convention that a "prime" indicates transpose, and unless otherwise indicated, all vectors will be column vectors. Writing the transformation mechanism as the $m \times n$ *matrix A* with typical element a_{1j}, the system of Figure 1.2 can be described mathematically as $A\mathbf{x} = \mathbf{y}$. Thus, suppose A is a $1 \times n$ matrix of consumer demands and x is a vector of product prices. In this case, then, A is a row vector whose typical element a_{1j} is the quantity demanded of the jth product, and x_j is the price of the product. The element E is a market that transforms these demands into a total

---

[3] See J. Viner, "Cost Curves and Supply Curves" *Zeitschrift für Nationalökonomie*, III, 1932.

FIGURE 1-2

consumption expenditure of $y = \Sigma a_{1j}x_j$. More generally, we might simply write $y = f(x)$, or in the present context, consumption expenditure is a function of price.

The *structure* of a system is determined by the coupling of its elements, or how they are paired off with one another. Let $z' = (z_1, \ldots, z_k, \ldots, z_r)$ denote a second vector of outputs and B be an $r \times m$ *matrix with typical element* b_{ki}. The coupling of Figure 1.3(a) can then be described in general as $z = g(y)$, where $y = f(x)$; or, in the specfic case where the transformation functions of E_1 and E_2 are matrices, $Ax = y$ and $By = z$. Continuing with the previous illustration, E_2 might represent an information center in which government expenditures are based on total private consumption, with the behavioral rule being that government expenditure z is a constant proportion B of consumption expenditure y.

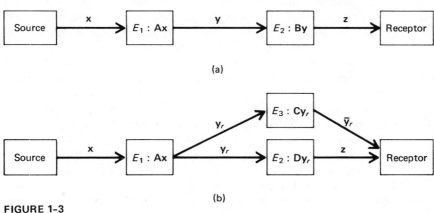

FIGURE 1-3

Assuredly, every element of y need not be employed in the second transformation process. This is the case in the flow diagram of Figure 1.3(b). Here, y_r is the $r \times 1$ vector of outputs consisting of, say, the last r elements of y, and $z = g(y_r)$. Where the transformation functions are matrices, we can partition B into submatrices C and D such that $B' = (C, D)$. If C is an $r \times r$ *identity matrix and D is an $(m - r) \times r$ matrix, the system of Figure 1.3(b) can be written:* $Ax = y$ and $B'y = (C, D)y = (\bar{y}_r, z)$, where $\bar{y}_r$ is the $(r - m) \times 1$ vector consisting of the first $r - m$ *elements of y.* In the previous economic context, we can think of the information center as determining government expenditures on the basis of, say, consumer expenditures on durable goods, the last r commodities in the vector of demands.

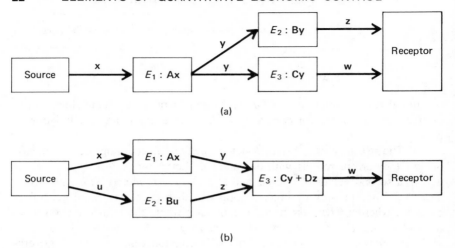

(a)

(b)

FIGURE 1-4

When an element's output becomes the input for more than one other element, this is referred to as *ramification* of output. In general, ramification of output can be described mathematically as $y = f(x)$, $z = g(y)$, and $w = h(y)$. In Figure 1.4(a), for instance, E_2 represents the government information center, while E_3 might be an industry information center relying on consumption expenditure data to determine the rate of private investment expenditure. Consumption expenditure will therefore influence both government expenditure and private investment expenditure in this system. Similarly, Figure 1.4(b) illustrates ramification of input, wherein two elements contribute inputs to a third element. This particular system might be written $y = f(x)$, $z = g(u)$, and $w = h(y, z)$. Here, y might again be consumption expenditure determined as a function of product demand, z might be private investment expenditure determined as a function of the interest rate, and w might be government expenditure, determined as a function of private consumption *and* investment.

Putting this in matrix notation, ramification of output would be written $Ax = y$, $By = z$, and $Cy = w$. One type of ramification of input would be $x = y$, $Bu = z$, and $w = Cy + Dz$. Thus, the coupling of elements provides an *explicit* description of the interrelationships within a system, and the degree of ramification of inputs and outputs determines the complexity of the system. It should be apparent, however, that in order for a system to operate the elements must be *compatible* with one another. That is, if two elements are coupled the transformation process of one must indeed be able to accept as input the output of the other. Thus, we explicitly *defined* the vectors and matrices of the earlier examples so as to assure they would be compatible and that the matrix operations could be performed. This is not necessarily the case in the previous two situations where, for example, if y is $m \times 1$ and C is $m \times n$, the operation Cy is not defined. The moral is: the coupling of elements in a single system demands the compatibility of the outputs of one with the transformation function of the other.

In the preceding examples (Figures 1.2 through 1.4) we have been concerned with so-called *open-loop* systems which are usually used when precise input or output control are not required. Indeed, in such systems we normally rely on the *absence* of nonneglectable external disturbances to give us the required output. When precise control is of the essence—in order to improve in some way the process to be controlled—a *feedback* mechanism must be provided. Such control requires identification, computation, and actuation—that is, steering correction [see Figure 1.5(a)].

The basic function of a feedback element such as E_4, referred to as a *transducer*, is to act as a *measuring* device, or *identifier*. What the identifier identifies is the extent to which the output of an element, in this case E_3, deviates from some preestablished standard or performance measure that the element is expected to maintain. Thus, an exogenous input into the system might be expected to yield a particular rate of output Q^*. To assure that it does, the actual output rate Q is employed as an information input to the identifier which performs the arithmetic operation $Q^* - Q$. This difference $\overline{Q}$ is then fed back

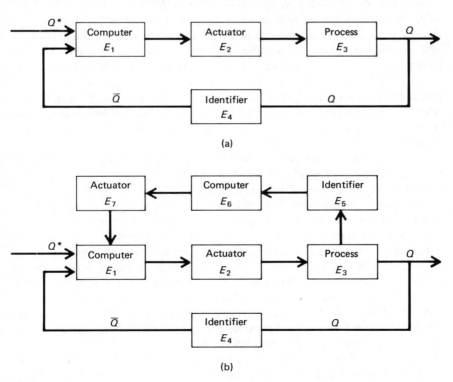

(a)

(b)

FIGURE 1-5

as an input to E_1 whose function now is to perform a transformation that will bring the final output into line with the original plan.

Since few of us lead error-free lives, it is easy to sympathize with both the failure of a real system to perform in exact accordance with our wishes, and with efforts to equip the system with a corrective network to detect and rectify any errors that occur. Nevertheless, as we shall discuss below, the "error" that a feedback loop is designed to correct is often somewhat misnamed. In general, an element such as E_1, through which exogenous inputs enter the system, or feedback output is reintroduced to it, is called the *controller*. The controller is any managing agent, perhaps an electronic computer, that determines the inputs entering the system. In effect, the controller is a decision-making body regulating the system by *selecting* exogenous inputs for processing, and by *reacting* to the results of its most recent decision.

The controller in the previous feedback system can be considered to be a combination of consumers and government. The input in Figure 1.5(a), for example, might be a given increment in government expenditures. The government exercises the initial control over the selection of exogenous inputs, *choosing* to admit, say, the input ΔG into the system. Thus, the initial output of the controller is an *instruction* to the element E_2 that ΔG is to be spent. This element, the *actuator*, then sends an input *signal* to the *process mechanism E_3* to add ΔG to total economic activity and hence to gross national product. The process mechanism performs its function and, via the feedback element E_4, feeds back the *information* to the controller that consumers have additional spending power of ΔG. Consumers now have control over how much of this ΔG will be permitted to reenter the system, and they make the decision to spend $c\Delta G$, where c is the marginal propensity to consume. They do this by sending an instruction to the actuator, the process is actuated anew, and the sequence is repeated.

There are three *unique* features of any single closed-loop system that are important from the standpoint of economic policy. *First,* there is the notion of a *controller*. In the context of economic policy and planning, the controller is a policy-making management that selects from among exogenous inputs or *instruments* a particular set, the *measures,* in order to optimize an objective function; that is, in order to help the system best achieve its purpose. *Second,* there is the notion of *information* to be gathered, processed, and transmitted. In the context of economic policy and planning, decisions are occasionally made on the basis of inaccurate information, instructions are issued that will occasionally be interpreted incorrectly, and results are achieved and analyzed in the form of information output that is occasionally inaccurate. *Third,* there is the notion of *feedback* and *control* permitting a controller to modify previous decisions having unanticipated consequences. In the context of economic policy and planning, policy-making management is given additional information to incorporate into subsequent decisions. As we shall see later (more specifically in Chapter 10 when we discuss investment planning) the mathematical development and resolution of control problems such as these is currently being abetted by advances that are being made in the techniques of optimal control theory.

The notions of a controller, information, and feedback in turn suggest three major issues upon which a study of policy models must focus: (1) the instruments available to planners, the selection of measures, and the choice of an objective function to reflect the purpose of the system; (2) the nature, quality, and quantity of information to be transmitted through the system, the method of transmission, the system's ability to convert plans into achievements, and the extent to which information will be lost or erroneous information will be transmitted in the system; and (3) the opportunities that exist for correcting errors, dealing with unexpected contingencies, and modifying previous acts.

We shall be concerned with each of these issues in succeeding chapters, as well as how they are resolved in particular economic systems. We shall also be concerned with two additional issues that the concept of a system calls to our attention: the possibilities of adaption and learning.

If the environment in which the system operates is not sufficiently stationary—or, in more complex systems—a second, third, and so on, loops have to be added, whose functions are to adjust different parameters (see Figure 1.5b). Such systems, called *adaptive* systems, automatically react to environmental changes in a way favorable to the system's purpose. In the economic system of Figure 1.5(a), for example, suppose that the input to E_2 and E_3 is an increment ΔG in government expenditure that might encourage the industrial sector classified as part of the environment, to increase investment expenditures. Such an increase might be transmitted back to the controller vis-à-vis the government to increase taxes. Thus, inherent in the notion of adaption is a concept that is dear to the economist's heart; namely, the concept of *stability* and the economic, social, and psychological forces that both direct a system toward a predictable end, and maintain that end once it has been achieved.

Whereas adaptive systems adjust to contingencies for which they are prepared, *learning* systems adjust to *new* circumstances for which a backlog of remembered experience that automatically effects an appropriate response is unavailable. Learning is particularly important in policy models, where it implies endowing a system with sufficient flexibility to permit the elements to react to new and unpredictable events in what may have to be new and unpredictable ways. Both controller and system will learn from the experience, so that adjustments take place that will better enable the system to achieve its purpose.

A variety of characteristics can be designed into a system. The *ideal* system is one achieving the maximum performance level hoped for in its initial conception. The ideal economic system might have as its goal a set of social welfare objectives, and contain a set of functional relationships among the elements to guarantee that these objectives will be met. Dreams of Utopia notwithstanding, it will be more reasonable for us to seek optimum systems; that is, systems containing components and functions arranged so as to effect a set of consequences that *approach* the desired objectives. It is to this more realistic end that policy models must be directed if the designing of those systems being modeled is to be improved.

e. Specialization, decentralization, and coordination [4]

Complex organizations require that a variety of jobs be performed, a variety of decisions taken, and lines of authority and responsibility be established. *Efficient* complex organizations require division of labor and specialization, which implies the need for the decentralization and *delegation* of authority among a variety of decision-making units, or controllers. Thus, a major corporation might be divided into divisions and departments, each of which operates as an independent profit center, and each of which has its unique responsibilities, but each of which is ultimately accountable to a central corporate management. It is the obligation of this corporate management to *coordinate* the individual activities and decisions so as to achieve the optimal operation of the organization as a whole. Alternatively, in the Soviet Union—surely the largest, and perhaps the least efficient major corporation in the world—limited independence exists between the individual divisions and departments. Rather, the decision-making authority is centralized in a "corporate management" that issues directives to the individual units whose only obligation is to carry out what in theory, at least, are *coordinated* instructions.

It seems apparent, then, that the problem of coordination of decentralized activities in a complex organization such as an economic system is a key problem for planners to resolve. In a free-market economy this coordination is achieved through the price mechanism under which, for example, excess demand at given prices will *ordinarily* both call forth additional supply, and result in higher prices that coordinate buyers' demands with sellers' supplies. Similarly, in either planned economies or large corporations a system of shadow prices will result—whether tacitly understood or explicitly computed—and these shadow prices can be equally as effective as a set of actual prices obtaining in a market, insofar as coordinating the organization's decentralized activities toward a common purpose is concerned. Nonetheless, there is no reason to assume that equally effective nonprice coordination mechanisms could not be devised.

To help place the issue of coordination and decentralization within our systems control framework, consider the economic system of Figure 1.6. This is a variant of the Arrow and Hurwicz model.[5] In this system there are $n + 3$ components: a set of n firms, F_i ($i = 1, \ldots, n$); a consumption sector C; an

---

[4] Much of what follows in this and the next section is based on M. D. Mesarović, D. Macko, and Y. Takahara, *Theory of Hierarchical, Multilevel Systems* (New York: Academic Press, 1970), particularly Chapters 1 and 2.

[5] K. J. Arrow and L. Hurwicz, "Decentralization and Computation in Resource Allocation" in R. W. Pfouts (ed.) *Essays in Economics and Econometrics* (Chapel Hill: University of North Carolina Press, 1963).

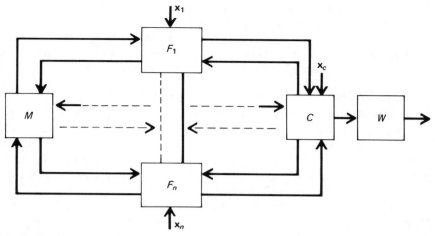

FIGURE 1-6

industrial market M; and a computer center W responsible for evaluating the system's performance.

The purpose of this system *qua* organization is to allocate its resources among firms and the consumption sector so as to maximize the welfare of the consumption sector. This welfare is some prespecified function $w(g_1, \ldots, g_m)$ of the basket of m goods $(g_1, \ldots, g_m)$ that are consumed. Each firm F_i receives an initial allocation of resources x_i. It transforms these into outputs, perhaps with the aid of goods received from other firms. The industrial market M is the medium through which industrial goods are exchanged. Consumers receive both initial resources in the amount x_c, and goods from the n firms. The latter are determined in accordance with consumer demands, the pricing system, and consumer wealth. Information about final consumption is inputted to the computer which, via the welfare function w, transforms this information into a measure of how well the initial endowment of resources has been allocated under the given state of technology; that is, given the firms' transformation functions.

In principle, the problem of selecting the $x = (x_1, \ldots, x_n, x_c)$ that maximizes $w(g_1, \ldots, g_m)$ can be solved by the controller of the planned economy. A decision-making body might, for instance, take further advantage of the computer, and simulate the results of *all* alternative allocation schemes and component decision rules, select the scheme and rules that result in the highest value of the welfare function, and then issue the resources, and finally the orders to each of the components to behave in accordance with the prescribed rules. In fact, however, some if not all of the components will have their own independent decision-making units, as is the case in either free-market or mixed economies. Under these circumstances, the controller—the government—might at best *influence* the decisions taken by the individual units which while *pursuing their own aims,* will not necessarily, and indeed are unlikely to, achieve the maximization of w. How to accomplish this "induced" maximization is the problem of coordination, as viewed through multi-level hierarchical systems theory. This creates two problems: (1) How to optimally decentralize authority when relationships between departments are not strictly on a competitive basis; and (2) how to effect optimal coordination.

f. Systems and subsystems: classifications

A multi-level system can be viewed as a *hierarchy of subsystems*. Suppose there are n such subsystems S_i ($i = 1, \ldots, n$) with S_1 being the highest level subsystem, S_2 the next highest, and so forth. The meaning of "highest," "next highest," and "lowest" is that the decision unit of S_1, the *supremal* unit, makes the most important decisions—that is, the decisions that can influence the acts taken by the lower-level *infimal* subsystems—the decisions reached in S_2 can influence the decisions of S_3 through S_n, and so forth. There can also be feedback between the subsystems. Thus, the effects of a decision reached by the supremal unit upon the decisions and outputs of the infimal units might be relayed to the highest level, and result in the subsequent alteration of an upper-level decision. But, it is the objective function of the supremal unit that dictates the final decision sequence, taking precedence over the preferences of the infimal units. In effect, any alteration of a decision at the S_3 level, say as a result of feedback received from S_4, is *voluntary* on the part of the S_3 decision-making body; but, the latter decision-making body can *impose its will* upon the S_4 decision-making body, should it choose to do so. When, in such a multi-level system, the entire series of subsystem decisions is essentially *simultaneously* determined in the sense that there is a flow of information between the subsystems, and the decisions reached at *any* one level might be altered as a result of information received with respect to the decisions reached at *any* other level, this is said to represent an *on-line* system. When, however, decisions are reached *sequentially,* so that each subsystem reaches a decision only *after* receiving information with respect to the decisions reached at the next highest level, this is said to represent an *off-line* system.

Typically, in the economies of the West as well as in the organizations that they house, the hierarchical structure, even when multi-level, allows the infimal subsystems some latitude in the decision-making process, which permits their decision-making bodies to reach decisions that are not *completely* controlled by higher-level subsystems. In general, the decision-making bodies of higher-level subsystems exercise varying degrees of *influence* over those of the lower-level subsystems. The influence can invariably be extended to complete control, or dictatorship by the supremal unit, although it is rare when such is actually the case. Rather, there are certain sets of activities for which each subsystem has a set of decision rules, or accepted and well-recognized standards for decision making, and certain activities over which higher-level decision-making bodies might seek to exercise dictatorial powers. Yet there are other activities over which each decision-making body may be permitted virtually complete freedom to exercise its best judgment.

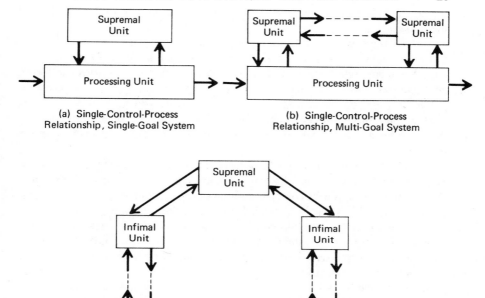

(a) Single-Control-Process
Relationship, Single-Goal System

(b) Single-Control-Process
Relationship, Multi-Goal System

(c) Multi-Level,
Multi-Goal System

FIGURE 1-7

Following Mesarović *et al.*,[6] we may distinguish between three basic hierarchical arrangments: (1) direct controller-processor relationship *single*-goal systems; (2) direct controller-processor relationship *multi*-goal systems; and (3) hierarchical *multi*-level, *multi*-goal systems. These structures appear as in Figure 1.7.

The direct controller-processor single-goal system provides the simplest format for decision making. Such an organization is comparable to the single-product, single-process, profit-maximizing firm. Even in this specialized instance, however, the *problems* confronting the organization can be quite complex, and therefore the resolution of the problems may require some quite sophisticated decision-making tools. Thus, even in this classical firm the entrepreneur must make a difficult decision when demand is stochastic, when output commitments must be made prior to the marketing period, and when unsold output can be stored at a given holding cost for *possible* sale at a subsequent point in time. Most economic systems, to be sure, are much more complex than this, although the Soviet system, for instance, is organized and run—in principle at least—as an integrated, directly guided controller-processor multi-goal

[6] *Op. cit.*, pp. 50–51.

system, with the intermediate actuators faithfully complying to the decisions of the *supremal* unit.[7]

Theoretically, the "competitive economy" is also a direct controller-processor multi-goal system; here, however, there are a *series of co-equal firms* each of which might have a different goal. Any subset of these firms can form a *coalition* and, when all share exclusively common goals and have common judgments, they comprise a *team*. Clearly, however, their goals will frequently conflict, and thus a variety of decision-making techniques, including especially those of game theory, may be employed to resolve individual decision problems.

Finally, in the multi-level, multi-goal system we see the main characteristics of Western economies: namely, the existence of a supremal unit whose goals will not necessarily coincide with those of the infimal units. In such systems there are three kinds of decision problems: those existing at the supremal level, those existing at the infimal levels, and the overall problems of the entire system. For the overall system to be effective, the supremal unit must *coordinate* and *control* the decisions of the infimal units, and, for this coordination and control to be effective, it is required: (1) that the decisions of the infimal units be compatible with each other and with those of the supremal unit; (2) that the supremal unit send instructions and otherwise influence the infimal units so that the decisions that they reach will be compatible with the goals of the supremal unit; and (3) that while no one unit has total responsibility for the overall system, the problems that confront the system be defined so as to be amenable to resolution in some overall sense. For such systems, it is apparent, complex analytical and decision-making techniques are required, perhaps utilizing what are as yet undeveloped and undiscovered tools.

1.4 ILLUSTRATIONS OF CONTROL AND COORDINATION

a. Automaticity

Feedback, adaptive, and learning systems are, in engineering terminology, *servomechanisms:* devices reacting to information about change in a manner so as to direct the system toward its desired objectives. The transformation elements are "black boxes," a blanket description used to convey the idea that a *detailed* description of *how* inputs are processed into outputs may be unnecessary for systems design and analysis. That is, the transformation operation can remain obscure and hidden within the "black box" so long as we know the elements from which the process accepts inputs, and the elements to which the

---

[7] If once a decision is taken it is implemented as an *order* to a processing unit *P*, this does not mean that in Soviet target *planning* there is no exchange of information between the lower units and the supremal unit—the center. As we shall see, preliminary plan targets are formulated by the center and transmitted (through ministries) to the plants together with proposed plant targets. The managers of the plants propose modification of these projections. These proposals are then consolidated and modified centrally. They then become orders to the actuators (ministries) and processors (enterprises).

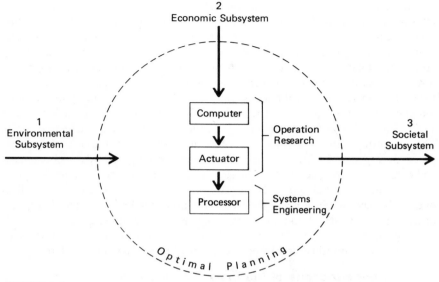

FIGURE 1-8

process sends outputs, and know that the inputs, the process, and the outputs are all mutually compatible.

To the extent that economic "cyberneticists" have a goal, it is to develop *automatic control systems* that accept and process information, react to change, and modify their own operations. This does not necessarily mean the elimination of the human element in a decision-making role. Rather it means an ever-increasing empathy between people and the machines they have created (see Figure 1.8).

Cybernetics—or the unified and expanded theories of engineering control and engineering communication—is, in effect, concerned with the very issues that plague policy makers in their efforts to direct economic systems.[8] Whether intended or not, upon occasion we shall therefore be cast into the role of cyberneticists. This will not necessarily improve our accomplishments, but it will serve to add an extra bit of lustre to what we do.

b. The Keynesian multiplier

The linear Keynesian model is an illustration of simplified "closed sequences of dependence" intensively studied in control-system engineering.[9] Consider again the closed-sequence model, represented in Figure 1.5 (a) and suppose that the input to E_2 and then to E_3 is an increment ΔG in government expenditures. The output of E_3 is the increment ΔY in gross national product. If

[8] N. Weiner, *Cybernetics* (New York: John Wiley, 1948), pp. xii ff.
[9] See A. Tustin, *The Mechanism of Economic Systems,* An Approach to the Problem of Economic Stabilization from the Point of View of Control System Engineering (Melbourne, London: Heinemann, 1953), pp. 7 ff.

c is the marginal propensity to spend and $M = 1/(1-c)$ is the multiplier, the total increment ΔY will be given by $(M)\Delta G$. In the present flow diagram, this process can be described simply by having E_3 generate as output an increment in gross national product equal to the input it receives. Without the feedback element, the total increment in gross national product would be ΔG. Suppose, however, that the feedback element receives as input the output of E_3, and performs the operation of subtracting zero from this output multiplied by the marginal propensity to spend. The difference $c\Delta G - 0$ is then fed back as input to E_1. The result is that E_3 initially generates ΔG so that E_4 generates $c\Delta G$. This, in turn, leads E_1 to supply $c\Delta G$ as input to E_2 and hence to E_3 which proceeds to generate $c\Delta G$ as output. This output is identified by E_4, processed, and $c^2\Delta G - 0$ is fed back to E_1. The process continues in this fashion, with the *total* output of E_3 being $Y = \Delta G + c\Delta G + c^2\Delta G + \cdots = (M)\Delta G$. Assuredly, one might have initially made the transformation function of E_3 the multiplier operation. The feedback loop, however, sets out the multiplier process in *detail* as a logical consequence of the economic behavior of an economic system, and not merely as a mystical and incomprehensible bit of economic folklore.

c. Imperfections of the market as a controller

A classic case of the failure of the market as controller obtains when, because of an inability of competitive producers to immediately adjust a perishable output to price, the decision to supply a total industry output of Q_{t+1} at time $t+1$ is based on the price P_t at which the total industry output of Q_t was sold at time t. This situation gives rise to the classic cobweb theorem.

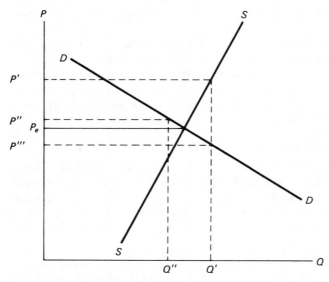

FIGURE 1-9

In the case of linear demand and supply curves seen in Figure 1.9, suppose that producers, anticipating a market price of P', produce a quantity of Q'. In order to sell their entire output of the perishable product, producers will have to reduce price to P''. This reduction in price results in the decision to produce Q'' for sale in the following period, and the reduced quantity results in buyers bidding up the price to P''', and so forth. In situations of instability, it is clear that the free market is a rather ineffective servomechanism. A governmental controller, such as would exist in a Socialist economy could simply *dictate* a price of P_e—a price that would be easily determined, given knowledge of the supply and demand curves. In situations such as these, modifying the market mechanism may well work to the benefit of the participants in the market.[10]

d. Coordination and control in two-tier decision systems

Complex systems have various levels of decision making involving priority of action. This raises problems concerning the relationship between the units of different levels, and the coordination of the goal-seeking (decision-making) subsystems so as to achieve a goal and goals identified for the entire system.

Mesarović *et al.* provide, among their other illustrations of such problems, the particularly illuminating example of a two-level electric power system with a single supremal decision unit and n infimal control units.[11] There are n electricity-generating areas. The relationships between these $2n + 1$ components are displayed in Figure 1.10. The twofold problem is to determine the amount of electricity to generate in each area, given the system objective of minimizing the total cost of electric power generation.

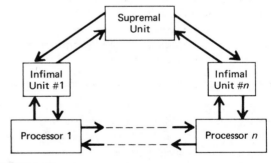

FIGURE 1-10

Denoting by u_i the *net* power exchange between area 1 and the other areas, we can immediately write $\Sigma u_i = 0$, since what one area receives must be provided by other areas, and what one area sends must be received by other

---

[10] For a discussion see O. Lange, "The Computer and the Market," in C. H. Feinstein (ed.) *Socialism, Capitalism, and Economic Growth* (Cambridge, Mass.: Cambridge University Press, 1967).
[11] *Op. cit.*, pp. 4–14.

areas. Denoting also the electricity generated in area i by q_i, the total cost of the electricity generated in this area can be written $C_i(q_i)$. The total cost of power generation in the system will be given by $C(q_1, \ldots, q_n) = C(q_1) + \cdots + C_n(q_n)$. Finally, with k_i the power-generating capacity in area i, for each of the n areas we require that $q_i + u_i \leq k_i$. Thus, the system's problem can be written as

$$\text{Minimize} \qquad C = C_1 + \cdots + C_n \tag{1.2a}$$
$$\text{subject to } u_1 + \cdots + u_n = 0 \tag{1.2b}$$
$$q_i + u_i \leq k_i \qquad i = 1, \ldots, n \tag{1.2c}$$
$$q_i \geq 0 \qquad i = 1, \ldots, n \tag{1.2d}$$

through the appropriate choice of the decision variables u_i and q_i. That is, determine the amount of electricity to be generated in each area, as well as the amount to be sent or received by each area, so as to minimize the total cost of power generation, while respecting the constraints.

Although the system's problem can be defined and, given the specification of the cost functions and the capacities, in principle be solved either by analytical (mathematical programming) techniques, or by computer (numerical) methods, the further question arises as to *where* the responsibility for solution rests; in particular, whether each infimal decision unit should be left to its own devices to minimize costs in its area, with the supremal unit simply attempting to *coordinate* the independent decisions reached in the individual areas, or whether the supremal unit should take the dictatorial initiative of solving the cost-minimization problem for the system as a whole, and simply issue instructions to the infimal units. The answer does not rest on purely philosophical issues, inasmuch as the supremal unit will not necessarily be able to solve the overall problem, say because the data to solve it may be distorted when transmitted from infimal to supremal units, the analytical or computer techniques required by the specific problem are not available, or the solution, once arrived at, is not readily implemented. The problem of coordination, even in two-level systems, is not easily solved.

1.5 CYBERNETICS AND SYSTEMIC CHANGE

Cybernetics—the unified approach to systems' control and communication—provides a conceptual framework for the analysis of the interrelationship between policies and economic processes. This framework, which enables us to analyze various types of economies as well as certain processes within them, is broad enough to encompass market-type economies as well as Soviet-type and underdeveloped economies. A convenient medium is thus available for analyzing and understanding, contrasting and comparing, not only policy solutions, but also *differences* between various couplings within systems. At the same time, this approach holds out the promise that the solutions developed for the problems of any one system might be modified to resolve the problems of another. Thus, the cybernetic approach also provides the framework for examining *systemic change;* that is, changes in individual elements, or changes in their couplings, or changes in coordination methods, that determine the system's behavior and overall performance.

This approach therefore provides opportunities for reframing the entire comparative systems' analysis and theory. The new analysis will highlight similarities and differences in patterns of generating and processing information, of identifying performance and of correcting imbalances of controls, as well as call attention to patterns of decision making and planning, of economic centralization and decentralization. At the same time, it will provide us with a common language for the interdisciplinary exchange of ideas regarding various types of systems.

CHAPTER 2
Information and Control

2.1 THE MAIN ISSUE

An important aspect of the cybernetics concept is its focus on *flows,* not the least of which are *information* flows. These are crucial, because information gleaned from the environment and generated internally, perhaps through feedback, as well as historical information, data, and accumulated knowledge, are the *inputs* upon which controllers make decisions and coordinate activities. Moreover, the controller's *output* is information in the form of instructions given to actuators, and subsequently to processors to implement these decisions. And, it is feedback information from an identifier which enables the system's managers to exercise their control function so as to ensure that the desired outputs have in fact been achieved. Additionally, information, especially technological information, can enter *directly* into the processor's transformation (production) function as a factor of production, and, indeed, can be substituted for the traditional factors of labor and capital; that is, the physical and energy flows. In light of our view of the economy as a purposeful system amenable to control, it is therefore incumbent upon us that we concern ourselves with various aspects of information—gathering, storage, coding, transmission, distortion, and measurement—as the *medium* of coordination and control, since even the most sophisticated policy and planning models, indeed, perhaps, *particularly* the most sophisticated models, make considerable *demands* on the system's *information network.*

In the broadest sense, information means communicated *knowledge, data, news, instructions.*[1] In the more technical framework of information or communication theory, the term relates to *signal processes,* and to their relations in communication and data-processing devices. It is synonymous with *un-*

[1] C. E. Shannon and W. Weaver, *The Mathematical Theory of Communication* (Champaign-Urbana: University of Illinois Press, 1949).

certainty with respect to which of a specific set of messages will be sent or received. In the context of cybernetics, information refers to messages or signals *in their connection with* a given control system.

As we already know, process control involves the measurement of the variables to be controlled (namely, the system's output), its comparison with the reference input, and, where necessary, the adjustment of the entire process so that, despite any unanticipated disturbances that throw the system off course, output will approach as closely as possible the reference input. Control, "reverse" information to the controller or actuator via feedback on how the target has been approached, and measurement and comparisons of targets and reference input, involves signals and messages. The production and transmission of messages, as well as any accompanying disturbances, can be studied and analyzed from either one of two differing points of view: (1) that of *statistical information theory,* as an essentially *abstract* mathematical and statistical process; or, (2) that of *signal structure theory,* as essentially a transmission problem wherein the *concrete* processes and the physical properties of the communication devices are also considered. The analysis of the processes of coordination and control within systems requires a firm understanding of the basic concepts of information from *both* viewpoints, and we shall therefore introduce these below.

Control involves not only a communication process, but also a decision process: the decision makers—coordinators, controllers, and even actuators—must *select* certain data for analysis, storage, or transmission. Due to the greater importance of external effects in modern production processes, the greater time lags in production, the increasing rate of technological progress, and the development and spread of the large-scale computer, information now is more varied and ample than ever before, and also plays a more decisive role than ever before. Systems differ as to the kinds of information they generate, the extent to which they facilitate or hamper voluntary or involuntary information distortion, and the effectiveness with which they handle information. The questions of information selection, the nature and type of information flows within systems, and of the value and cost of information have been examined from a variety of angles in both information and decision theory, which we briefly set forth in this chapter.

2.2 INFORMATION NETWORK: ELEMENTS OF A COMMUNICATION SYSTEM

The purpose of a *communication system* is the exchange of information; its so-called "fundamental problem" is the successful reproduction of messages sent from an information source to a known destination. For many purposes the reproduction need not be exact, so long as the essential *meaning* that the source intends the message to convey is correctly interpreted at the destination. In one version of a simple feedback system, messages—information—are sent to the system from the environment. These messages, or exogenous inputs, enter the system via a *receptor* that is responsible for their correct interpretation and their subsequent translation and transmission to the controller. The latter then uses this information in the decision-making process, in turn, first serving as an information source that seeks to implement its decisions by sending instructions to an actuator, and second, in order to exercise control, serving as a destination for information recycled to it by the identifier. The controller that wants to send instructions to initiate a plan in two months, might do so through the coded message "oga nia wota onthmas." It is doubtful whether a reasonably alert actuator receiving the message "og ni wot onthmas" would ever misinterpret its meaning. Indeed, in a communication system in which, say, at least 75 percent of the symbols are correctly received and no symbols are out of sequence, the meaning of the *message* might always be correctly understood. Under these circumstances the 75 percent level of accuracy will suffice.

Messages are *sequences of symbols*. The written English language is a communication medium using the twenty-six Latin letters as its symbols. A sequence of these symbols is a word; a sequence of these words is a sentence, or a message. Assuredly, some messages are meaningless, in the sense that they are neither associated with specific ideas nor physical entities. In the context of economic systems, however, concern with communication is essentially a concern with the availability of a communication subsystem—be it the stock market or a five-year plan—that permits the reproduction of *meaningful* messages—such as instructions, knowledge, and data—between the system's components and subsystems.

A typical communication system, such as illustrated in Figure 2.1, contains five basic components: (1) an *information source* responsible for (a) *gathering* data from both the external and internal environments—that is, acting as the receptor for *exogenous* information as well as *recycled* information that is fed back into the system from the final destination—and (b) *storing* the data for both immediate transmission and eventual recall and use; (2) a *transmitter* that receives stored messages from the information source, *codes* the messages, and then sends out coded *signals;* (3) a transmitting *channel* over which the signals are sent; (4) a *receiver* that *translates* the signals into decoded messages; and (5) a *destination* that receives the decoded messages and is responsible for (a) *analyzing* them, and (b) *instructing* the processor, say, as to the intentions of the information source. There may also be a sixth element, a *noise source* in the subsystem's environment, sending signals that interfere with the transmission process; and, additionally, there might be information *feedback* whereby information is *recycled* from the processor to the information source for possible storage.

In any system there may be a number of different types of communication systems. These exist because of the intentions of one of the system components, acting as an information source, to send any one of a number of possible messages to another component of the system, acting as a destination. Thus, for example, the communication system that exists between a supremal controller—the Central Administration—and the infimal controllers—the Gov-

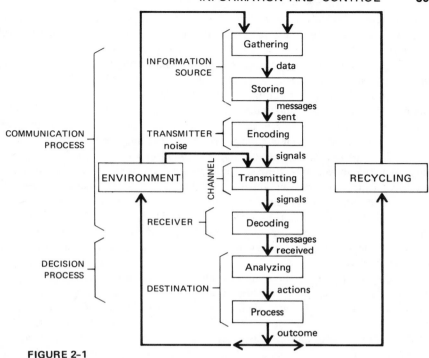

FIGURE 2-1

ernment Branch Offices—in a multi-level hierarchy is likely to be quite formal, and to consist of written instructions and memoranda, whereas the communication system that exists between the infimal controllers—that is, among the officers in a given Branch—might be quite informal, and consist of lunchhour scuttlebutt exclusively. If the information source never varies the message, a communication system serves no purpose, because the content of the message is always known with certainty at the intended destination. If the source sends either one of two messages, then the transmitter can code these messages using only two symbols, say a 1 and a 0, where a 1 indicates that the first message is being sent, and a 0 indicates the second. This same transmitter, which is only capable of emitting 1's and 0's, can also be used when four messages might be sent, by allowing it to transmit any one of four sequences: 00, 01, 10, and 11. Thus, 01 is a code that could be used to indicate to the receiver that the second message has been sent.

In the highly specialized and abstract context of statistical information theory, the *probability* that a particular message *will be* sent determines the amount of information conveyed over the communication system, when that message has in fact been sent. The *meaning* of the message is irrelevant. Similarly, the probabilities of sending particular messages determine the *expected* amount of information conveyed through the system. By the same token, the injection of additional random elements—noise or interference—reduces the information flow. Where, for example, a two-symbol process is constantly subjected to a dominant noise force that prevents the receiver from receiving the symbol sent by the information source, and instead substitutes its own unrelated sequence of 1's and 0's, no information is ever received at the destination. In effect, then, in the absence of uncertainty there is no information and no need for communication; but, in order for it to generate information, the uncertainty must come from the possible messages that might be sent by the information source, and not be the result of an inability on the part of the communication system to precisely reproduce messages.

Information flows may be single channel or multi-channel, depending upon whether they derive from a single source—the former case—or whether they reach their final destination from several sources simultaneously—the latter. Second, they may be either single-phased or multi-phased, depending on whether they relate to the same event or to a series of events. Third, they may be anterior, simultaneous, or posterior to the event(s) to which they relate. Finally, they may reflect this (other) event(s) in an accurate or a "distorted" (that is unreliable) way.

Gathering information entails both the collection of judgmental, historical, and institutional data, and the specification of desiderata and noninstitutional constraints. Judgmental data consist primarily of sets of *probability assessments* with respect to the stochastic elements and uncertain parameters that can affect the system and influence decisions. Historical data consist of factual information, time-series and cross-section data, and the assumptions that underlie decisions. These assumptions might include, for example, acceptance of specific demand and production functions as appropriate representations of actual demand and technology. The institutional data relate to the economy's structure, insofar as they describe its institutions and their functions. Clearly, then, the information source or the receptor gathers information, as it gathers lilies—where it may—both from the other system components, from the external environment, and from its own internal operations and sources.

Once gathered, information must be *stored,* and this entails the maintenance of data in the appropriate forms until required for use. Sherlock Holmes, for example, believed that the capacity of the human brain for storing information was extremely limited. Thus, he consciously selected for storage, from all the information that entered his personal galaxy, only those highly specialized little gems of information that he believed would someday be useful to recall for possible assistance in the solution of a crime. Although Holmes would probably deny it, the large-scale computer's memory and core is distinctly superior to even his rather remarkable brain in performing storage services, and thus is commonly employed in the storage function in any modern organization's decision-making unit, or primary information source. The choice of format in which the data are to be stored and presented rests largely with the user. So too does the selection process.

While the capacity of the computer often permits the average user to be somewhat less selective than was Holmes, it also frequently results in one's being literally inundated with *unwanted* and *unnecessary* data that only delays the decision-making process, or adds to its cost. The problem, then, is to adjust storage capacity to the needs of the source. In particular, different data and different capacities might be needed for administration and control and accounting, or for product research and innovation, purchasing and inventory control, scheduling, sales forecasting, long-term and short-term planning, and simulation. The appropriate data are those required by the particular decision-making procedures and models employed by the controller or information source. On the one hand, sufficient storage capacity must be available to assure that those data selected for storage for one purpose can, in fact, be stored. On the other hand, by exercising diligence and discretion in the selection process, it might be possible to reduce the total capacity below the levels required to *simultaneously* handle data for *all* possible purposes—as is apparent to any administrator that has ever changed jobs or offices and has, in the process, discovered the vast quantities of data stored in vertical files, which are easily and logically relegated to the too rarely used circular file.

The transmitter has the responsibility for *coding* messages, and the receiver has the responsibility for *decoding* the messages that are sent over the channel. Thus, there are two aspects to coding: the transformation of message inputs into signals amenable first to transmission over a communication channel, and second to translation into message outputs capable of interpretation and analysis, to be sent to a prescribed destination. The choice of a particular code from among all the known forms for conveying information represents a significant capital investment. Each code is designed to best convey a particular type of information. Introducing a particular code, while beneficial to the attainment of the primary goals of the subsystem, requires an initial human capital investment in order to acquaint decision makers with the unique features of the code employed. Such specialization may inhibit the decision maker's ability to process and interpret information in unfamiliar forms, or to adapt to changing organizational roles. As a consequence, the characteristics of the code chosen tend to define the nature of the information acquired and transmitted. This, of course, is why our world of unintelligible forms to be filled out in triplicate is actually controlled by a secretarial elite that is becoming less and less successful at concealing this increasingly obvious fact!

The communication *channel* is the medium through which the coded signals are sent from the transmitter to the receiver, and this is the point at which noise—inputs from the environment which might cause a signal other than that entering the channel as input, to be outputted from the channel to the receiver—could enter the communication system.

Analyzing information entails interpreting and evaluating the decoded signals that are sent by the receiver to their destination in the system. Thus, policy makers and their technical advisors must interpret preferred solutions and the results of any plans implemented on the basis of these solutions. Similarly, actuators must interpret and analyze the controllers' instructions, and identifiers must first interpret output information and then feed the controllers information as to, say, any forecasting errors that have occurred. A crucial problem in information analysis is the extent and nature of *deliberately* distorted information injected into the system, and the capacity of the system to evaluate and correct it. Decision makers at all levels may want to hide their true preferences, may tend to circulate irrelevant or distorted data so as to conceal their plans and performance, may "dress up" the information in order to appear in a favorable light, and so on. Such distortions can be major roadblocks to rational policy making in *any* type of system. The decisive factors in this respect are the interests and purposes attached to information distortion, for example, whether and in which ways reference inputs serve as standards of performance, the penalties and rewards attached to the distortion, the forms and extent of centralization and decentralization of the given system, and so on. Many of these problems concern, therefore, both the stimuli at work in the system, as well as the system design (and, in particular, the methods of control of managerial decision processes and performance).

Finally, *information recycling* entails the establishment of a feedback network that enables the economic managers to control the system. In particular, managers must be kept advised of a policy's results, prediction errors must be detected, and either the appropriate instructions in the form of new decision inputs intended to correct deviations from the desired results must be issued, understood, and implemented, or else the standards of performance must be reassessed.

In general, then, the transmission of information entails providing input information to, and obtaining output information from the system's components—subsystems and their elements. Where elements are coupled, the output information of one must be compatible with the transformation function of the element to which the information will flow as input. That is, each component must be capable of *correctly interpreting* the messages sent to it by the components to which it is coupled. Thus, although reliance on the black-box concept suggests that knowledge of each element's *specific* operations may be unnecessary for systems analysis or design, knowledge of the sort of information, and of the format that each element requires, and knowledge of the sort of information and its format that each element generates, *will* be necessary.

Within the economy at large, information flows are often distinguished by the various control subsystems with which they are associated; for instance, goods and services markets, monetary and credit markets, factor markets, and so forth. The subsystems are differently organized and linked within and between the mixed and the statist economies; but, irrespective of the system, different classes of information *type*—prices, outputs, qualities, demands, and supplies—are relevant within particular subsystems, as we shall see in detail further on.

The information required by the decision-making techniques employed by policy makers is of many kinds, and of different levels of complexity. A policy problem is not defined solely by the data, but rather by policy makers' desiderata and the constraints that restrict policy choice. As already noted, the desiderata consist of both the preference function that guides the choice between policies, and any side conditions that the policy makers choose to impose or to respect; the noninstitutional constraints consist of those side conditions that are imposed from within the system, representing as they do the behavioral and technological basis of the economy. Determining *what* information is required by policy makers and planners—and then *acquiring, storing,* and *updating* this information—is thus a critical problem of public management.

2.3 MEASUREMENTS AND EFFICIENCY

a. Information content

In the ordinary usage, information relates to communicated knowledge. A system's effectiveness often depends on how efficiently knowledge is communicated between its various components; that is, on the transmission of information between the coordinator, the controllers and the actuators, the actuators and the processors, the processors and the identifiers, the identifiers and the controllers. A study of systems therefore also requires a measure of information, in order that we might determine how effectively knowledge is being communicated between its various components.

The technical usage of the term information relates to such a measure. In particular, *information* is defined as a measure of one's *freedom of choice* in selecting a piece of knowledge—or, technically, a *message*—to communicate. It abstracts from the meaningfulness of the message. Thus, information reflects, and is measured by, the *likelihood* that a specific piece of knowledge *will be* transmitted, rather than some *quantification* of the knowledge that actually is transmitted.

Consider, for example, the amount of information contained in each of the last four letters of the five-letter English word, Q _ _ _ _. The second letter contains *no information*, because the English language offers no *freedom of choice* for this letter: doubtless the second letter is U. In effect, the absence of freedom of choice means that the knowledge is already possessed, no *new* knowledge is being communicated, and thus there is no information contained in the message "the second letter is U." But, there is considerable information contained in the message "the last three letters include an I, a T, and an E." Moreover, *given* this message, there is no (additional) information in the message "the third letter is I," because the third letter *must* be I. Thus, there is only one piece of information left to convey: namely, which of the last two letters is the E.

The *information content* of a message measures the amount of new knowledge contained therein. There are two perspectives from which this information content can be viewed: that of the source and that of the destination. In the former instance we are concerned with the source's freedom of choice in selecting among the messages that *might be sent;* in the latter instance we are concerned with the receiver's freedom of choice in selecting among the messages that *might be received.* The scope of our concern with information content is further widened with the recognition that the message received will not necessarily be the message sent. Thus, one can also consider the freedom of choice in selecting among messages that might be received, *given* knowledge of the message sent; or conversely, freedom of choice in selecting among messages that might have been sent, *given* knowledge of the message received. Information and probability are therefore intimately linked; if one can always guess the contents of a message—that is, the *probability equals one* that the message can be correctly anticipated—it conveys no new knowledge. Alternatively, if one "does not have the foggiest idea" as to the contents of the message—that is, the probability of correctly anticipating the message equals zero—then a considerable amount of information is being sent. In effect, the higher is the probability of correctly anticipating a message, the lower is its information content.

In essence, then, the search for a measure of information is also, and *equivalently,* a search for a measure of *uncertainty.* Specifically, it will be a measure of the uncertainty as to the message that was or will be sent or received.

Consider, for example, messages from a controller that either approves or disapproves of plans proposed by the technical staff. Suppose that past experience indicates that the controller is equally likely to approve or disapprove any given proposal. The message sent by the controller to the actuator is whether or not to initiate some positive action, in accordance with the staff's recommendations. Either instruction would be equally surprising, and either message is *defined* as containing a unit, or a *bit,* of information. The term "bit," which provides the common denominator for measuring information, is a contraction of "*b*inary dig*it*." The latter suggests itself because the binary digits 1 and 0 can provide a *code* for the instructions "initiate" and "do not initiate," respectively. When the instructions and thus the binary digits are equally likely to occur, the actuator receives a "bit" of information. If the controller always approves of staff proposals and issues instructions to initiate these plans, there is no information in the message "initiate," although there would be considerable information in the message "do not initiate." Indeed, this message comes as something of a refreshing shock, and indicates that either there has been a shake-up in the controller's office, or that there has been interference with the true message. If the probability of an "initiate" instruction is "almost" one, the message "initiate" comes as no surprise, and thus conveys virtually no new information. This contrasts with the great surprise caused by, and vast amount of information in, the message "do not initiate."

To measure the information content of a message, let p represent the probability that the message will be sent. Then its *information content* is given by

$$H = \log_2 \left(\frac{1}{p}\right) = -\log_2 p \tag{2.1}$$

To help grasp the intuitive appeal of this measure, consider the case of the controller as an information source for which $p = \frac{1}{2}$ for either message, "initiate" = 1 or "do not initiate" = 0. Each message has an information content of $H = -\log_2(\frac{1}{2}) = 1$ (bit). When $p = 1$ and the message is certain to be received, $H = -\log_2 1 = 0$ (bits). Clearly, the closer is p to unity, the lower is the information content H of the message sent and received.

In the case of the ambivalent controller, the measure behaves as we want a measure of information to behave. As we shall see, it is equally applicable in more general circumstances. In particular, it is the *only* measure that satisfies a small set of properties that one would logically *demand* of a measure of information. Since uncertainty and information are directly related in communication theory, it will be useful here to consider the properties that one would demand of a measure of *uncertainty*, for a measure of *information* should have equivalent properties, and these will be somewhat more readily understood when discussed in the more familiar contexts of uncertainty and systems.

Suppose that a controller might send any one of n different symbols $S_i (i = 1, \ldots, n)$ with probability $p(S_i)$. The measure of uncertainty about the symbol that will actually be sent is denoted $H = h(p(S_1), \ldots, p(S_i), \ldots, p(S_n))$; or, H is a function of the individual probabilities. Specifically, H depends on the uncertainty about a symbol that the controller might send, averaged over all the possible symbols. For present purposes it suffices to consider only *discrete* communication systems in which a finite number of n symbols can be sent.

The first property that we require of such a measure is that it be *continuous* in the $p(S_i)$. That is, the function must be defined for all possible combinations of the $p(S_i)$, where $0 \leq p(S_i) \leq 1$, such that small perturbations in the $p(S_i)$ induce small changes in H.

A second and related requirement is that when all $p(S_i)$ are equal, or $p(S_i) = 1/n$, the measure should be a monotonically increasing function of n. That is, when the symbols are equally likely to be sent, uncertainty about the symbol that will actually be chosen is greater, the greater is the number of available symbols. This function might appear as in Figure 2.2 where n is only permitted to take on integer values.

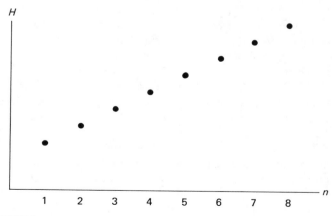

FIGURE 2–2

The third requirement is more complex and less easily understood than are the first two, but its inherent good sense is no less apparent. Suppose the symbol S_i is only the first of two symbols that the controller will send, and that the second can be any one of m symbols $T_j (j = 1, \ldots, m)$. Moreover, suppose the probability that the appearance of S_i will be followed by the appearance of T_j is given by the conditional probability $p(T_j | S_i)$.

There are nm possible two-symbol messages $S_i T_j$ that the controller might send, any one of which occurs with probability $p(S_i)p(T_j | S_i) = p(S_i; T_j)$. The uncertainty as to the two-symbol message that will be selected is given by $H = (p(S_1; T_1), \ldots, p(S_n; T_m))$. The demand we make of the measure is that this uncertainty be *decomposable* into the sum of the uncertainty with respect to the first symbol, plus the *expected* uncertainty with respect to the second symbol—that is, the second-symbol uncertainty weighted by the likelihood of facing it. Thus, the uncertainty due to the first symbol is measured by $h(p(S_1), \ldots, p(S_i), \ldots, p(S_n))$; *given* the occurrence of S_i, the uncertainty due to the second symbol is measured by $h(p(T_1 | S_i), \ldots, p(T_j | S_i), \ldots, p(T_m | S_i))$; and, the uncertainty for the two-stage process is then given by

$$H = h(p(S_1), \ldots, p(S_i), \ldots, P(S_n)) + \sum_i p(S_i) h(p(T_1 | S_i),$$
$$\ldots, p(T_j | S_i), \ldots, p(T_m | S_i)) \qquad (2.2)$$

It is easily shown [2] that the *only* measure satisfying these three properties is the logarithmic function

$$H = h(p(S_1), \ldots, p(S_i), \ldots, p(S_n)) = K \sum_i p(S_i) \log_a \left(\frac{1}{p(S_i)}\right)$$

$$= -K \sum_i p(S_i) \log_a p(S_i) \qquad (2.3)$$

where K is an arbitrary constant. By convention K is set equal to 1 and a to 2.

Consider, for example, a controller sending coded messages using 1 and 0 with equal probabilities of $p(1) = p(0) = \frac{1}{2}$. Here $H = -(\frac{1}{2})\log_2(\frac{1}{2}) - (\frac{1}{2})\log_2(\frac{1}{2}) = -\log_2(\frac{1}{2}) = 1$. That is, this situation contains a unit of uncertainty, or a *bit* of information. With four equally likely possibilities, $H = \log 4 = 2$; with eight equally likely possibilities $H = \log 8 = 3$; and, in general, doubling the number of equally likely possibilities adds one bit of information, and another unit of uncertainty.

As a further illustration, suppose that the symbols 1 and 0 are equally likely to occur at any stage in a three-symbol sequence. This situation contains three bits of information, because each of the eight sequences, 111, 110, 100, 101, 011, 010, 001, and 000 is equally likely. In this case there is a unit of uncertainty about the first symbol, a unit of uncertainty about the second symbol, and a unit of uncertainty about the third symbol. Thus, although the number of possible outcomes in the three-symbol sequence is four times that obtaining

[2] *Ibid.*, pp. 116–118.

with a single symbol, the degree of uncertainty is only three times as great. Similarly, there are two units of uncertainty about the last two symbols, given either one of the equally likely first symbols. Hence, by the decomposition property, $H = h(\frac{1}{2}, \frac{1}{2}) + (\frac{1}{2}) h(\frac{1}{4}, \ldots, \frac{1}{4}) + (\frac{1}{2}) h(\frac{1}{4}, \ldots, \frac{1}{4}) = 1 + (\frac{1}{2})(2) + (\frac{1}{2})(2) = 3$, since $h(\frac{1}{2}, \frac{1}{2}) = 1$, and $h(\frac{1}{4}, \ldots, \frac{1}{4}) = 2$.

As a weighted sum of logarithms, H is an *expectation*. It is a measure of uncertainty as to what might occur, or the *expected* information in an information-generating process. Equivalently, it measures the *entropy* or disorder of the process. The *information content* of an already observed outcome of this process is thus measured by $\log p(S_i)$. In effect, if an outcome is expected to occur with probability $p(S_i)$ and it does occur, the information contained in its occurrence is measured by $\log p(S_i)$; and, prior to actually observing the outcome, the amount of expected information is given by the weighted average of the information contents, or $H = -\Sigma p(S_i) \log p(S_i)$. To reiterate, the information content depends solely on the *probability* $p(S_i)$, and is independent of the *meaning* of the symbol S_i.

In addition to satisfying the properties initially required of an uncertainty vis-à-vis information measure, H has several additional properties and features that are no less appealing and certainly no less important,[3] and that encourage its application to a wide variety of problems. Of particular interest are its interpretations as a measure of uncertainty or a measure of dispersion. These have been the basis for much of its use in economic analysis, and its interpretation as an information measure, which is of interest from the systems' control standpoint. Interest in this connection, for example, is in the *amount* of information flowing from a controller to an actuator, or in the *amount* of information

---

[3] *Ibid.*, pp. 51–52. The key properties are:

(1) If all $p(S_i) = 0$ $(i \neq k)$ and $p(S_k) = 1$, then $H = 1(\log 1) = 0$. That is, when the outcome is known in advance there is no uncertainty, and the symbol-producing mechanism—the information source—generates no information.

(2) H is maximized for a given number of n outcomes, when all $p(S_i)$ are equal, and $p(S_i) = 1/n$. That is, uncertainty is at its greatest, and the average amount of information generated is maximized for a given number of outcomes, when the outcomes are equally likely.

(3) Any tendency toward an equalization of the $p(S_i)$ increases H. That is, the greater the uncertainty with respect to which of any two outcomes will occur, the greater is the uncertainty and expected information associated with the entire process.

(4) Where there are two processes P and P' having n and m outcomes, respectively such that $p(S_i)$ and $p(T_j)$ are the probabilities of occurrence of the ith outcome in P and the jth outcome in P', $H(P, P') \leq H(P) + H(P')$, where $H(P, P') = -\Sigma_i \Sigma_j p(S_i; T_j) \log p(S_i; T_j)$; or, the uncertainty associated with the *joint* occurrence of an outcome from P and an outcome from P' is not greater than the sum of the individual uncertainties. When the two outcomes are independent, $p(S_i; T_j) = p(S_i)p(T_j)$ and the equality $H(P, P') = H(P) + H(P')$ holds. That is, in the case of independent events the joint uncertainty is the sum of the individual uncertainties, but the joint uncertainty is less than the sum, when the outcome of one event influences the outcome of the other.

(5) $H(P' | P) \leq H(P) + H(P') - H(P) = H(P')$, or knowledge about the outcome in P always reduces the uncertainty about the outcome of P' unless the events are independent, in which case the latter uncertainty is unaffected. That is, a second information source can only reduce the expected information generated by some first source, except insofar as the two sources are independent, in which case the expected information is unaffected by the output of the second source.

contained in the instructions from, say, two controllers as opposed to one. In the first instance, the ability of the controller to better achieve its purpose may depend on the complexity of the information network that *must be* designed in order to handle all the information that *might be* transmitted. In the second instance, the efficiency of the system and the cost of operating it might be improved by determining whether or not and which information sources are generating superfluous or *redundant* information.

b. Maximal communication rate

Each of the latter two issues is closely tied to the concept of channel *capacity*, or the *maximum possible rate* at which information can be transmitted through a channel. This rate depends on the number of different symbols that *might* be transmitted, the "duration" of each symbol—for example, whether it takes longer to send one symbol versus another—and the rules or constraints on the permissible sequences of symbols—for example, whether "X" is permitted to follow "Q" in an English word.

Consider an information source that selects from among n symbols S_i ($i = 1, \ldots, n$) of equal duration, with no *prior* constraints on allowable sequences. The maximum information content of each symbol is $\log(n)$ bits, achieved when the S_i are equi-probable. Then, if the system transmits N symbols per second, its capacity is $C = N \log(n)$ bits per second.

Suppose, for example, that two symbols are transmitted per second. The maximum *expected* information content of any sequence occurs when the symbols are equally likely, and successive symbols are independent of one another. The probability of any particular sequence is $(1/n)$ $(1/n)$, and the expected information is

$$H = -\sum_i \sum_i \left(\frac{1}{n}\right)\left(\frac{1}{n}\right) \log\left(\frac{1}{n}\right)\left(\frac{1}{n}\right) = -n^2 \left(\frac{1}{n}\right)^2 \log\left(\frac{1}{n}\right)^2 = 2 \log (n) \text{ bits per}$$

second

When the rules of the communications system either do not permit certain sequences, or in some way *constrain* the allowable sequence of symbols, the channel capacity is reduced. The maximum rate of information transmission over an unconstrained channel will therefore exceed the rate for a constrained channel using the same symbols of equal duration; and, in either case, the actual average rate of transmission might fall below these maxima. In particular, when the rules *permit* sequences that *in fact* are never used, as in the case of "QX" in the English language, the average rate of transmission falls short of the capacity. The ratio of (1) the expected information transmitted over a channel to (2) its capacity is referred to as the channel's *efficiency*, or *relative entropy* $E = H/C$. Since $H \leq C$, $E \leq 1$. The extent to which E falls below unity reflects the extent to which the available capacity for transmitting information is not being used, or the *redundancy* in the system. This is measured either by $R_1 = 1 - E$ or $R_2 = C - H$. In general, effective use of a communication channel requires minimal redundancy, and transmission of the maximum amount of information consistent with the channel's capacity. Thus, if the actuators, say, always send one of eight messages to the processors in the economic system, and if there is no possibility of an actuator's signal being misunderstood by a processor, then a three-symbol sequence of ones and zeros would suffice as a "code" to transmit *all* of the actuator's instructions. A code that permits nine messages to be sent is inefficient, because the ninth message is *never* sent. From the standpoint of the economic system as a multi-level hierarchical organization of interconnected subsystems, this suggests that, *ceteris paribus,* one of the economic managers' concerns should be the development of the most efficient "code"—in verbal memos, forms, charts, and the like—for transmitting information between the system's components.

c. Conditional entropy and sample data

A principal component of statistical decision theory is *Bayes' Rule,* which provides a convenient, orderly, and technically sound basis for revising an initial set of probability assignments to allow for additional information. In particular, let $p(S_i)$ denote a prior probability assignment of the relative likelihood of outcome S_i ($i = 1, \ldots, n$) and let $p(T_j \mid S_i)$ denote the probability that a sampling experiment will lead one to observe T_j ($j = 1, \ldots, m$), given that the outcome of the actual event will indeed turn out to be S_i. Then the revised probability of S_i—revised on the basis of the additional information that T_j has been observed—is denoted $p(S_i \mid T_j)$ and is given by

$$p(S_i \mid T_j) = \frac{p(S_i)p(T_j \mid S_i)}{\sum_i P(S_i)p(T_j \mid S_i)} \tag{2.4}$$

Equation (2.4) is Bayes' Rule. It follows immediately from the identity $p(S_i)p(T_j \mid S_i) = p(T_j)p(S_i \mid T_j)$, by dividing both sides of the identity by $p(T_j) \neq 0$. When one's prior judgments are dogmatic, that is, where one assigns probabilities of either 1 or 0 to $p(S_i)$, $p(S_i \mid T_j)$ will also equal either 1 or 0. In effect, if one is certain that an outcome will or will not occur, additional data will not shake this certainty. Assuredly, there are few instances when one is truly "certain" about a future outcome or the value of an unobserved parameter, although frequently our confidence is sufficiently strong so as to lead us to behave *as if* the outcome or parameter value is a certainty. In point of fact, most persons are ordinarily willing to reconsider and alter probability assignments to take account of new information; but this willingness only serves to emphasize the fact that dogmatic judgments are generally inappropriate.

In the context of communication theory and the economic system, the prior probability $p(S_i)$ can be interpreted as the probability that the ith symbol, S_i, will be sent from a controller to an actuator. The *likelihood* $p(T_j \mid S_i)$ is the probability that the jth symbol will be received, given that the ith has been sent. The sample probability, $p(T_j) = \sum_i p(S_i)p(T_j \mid S_i)$, is the prior probability that the jth symbol will be received. Finally, $p(S_i \mid T_j)$ is the posterior probability that the ith symbol has been sent, given that the jth symbol has been received.

Under this interpretation, $H(S \mid T) = -\sum_i \sum_j p(S_i; T_j) \log p(S_i \mid T_j)$ is the conditional uncertainty, or *conditional entropy*, of the symbol that was sent, given the symbol that was actually received. It can be shown that $H(S \mid T) \leq H(S) = -\sum p(S_i) \log p(S_i)$. That is, unless there is complete independence between symbols sent and received, in which case the equality holds, on average knowledge of the received symbol reduces the uncertainty about the original symbol. It is also true that $H(T \mid S) \leq H(T) = -\sum p(T_j) \log p(T_j)$, which implies that, on average, uncertainty about the symbol to be received is reduced by knowledge of the symbol that was sent, unless these two events are independent; in the latter case the equality holds and the uncertainty is unaffected. In this context $-\log [p(S_i \mid T_j)/p(S_i)] = -\log p(S_i) + \log p(S_i \mid T_j)$ is referred to as the *information gain* from observing T_j. This information gain may be positive, zero, or negative, depending on whether the probability of S_i is raised, unaffected, or reduced by observing T_j. The *expected* information gain, $H(S) - H(S \mid T)$, is necessarily nonnegative. That is, *prior* to observing the outcome of an experiment, one can "expect" that the observation will at worst be uninformative. Again, however, these measures depend solely on *probabilities*. There are neither differing *penalties* nor *rewards* attached to the different S_i, in accordance with their *meaning*.

As an ideal, knowledge of a received symbol T_j eliminates *all* uncertainty as to the symbol S_i that was sent. That is, when $p(T_j \mid S_i) = 1$ and $p(T_k \mid S_i) = 0$ $(k \neq j)$,

$$p(S_i \mid T_j) = \frac{p(S_i)p(T_j \mid S_i)}{\sum_i p(S_i)p(T_j \mid S_i)} = \frac{p(S_i)p(T_j \mid S_i)}{p(S_i)p(T_j \mid S_i)} = 1$$

and $p(S_r \mid T_j) = 0$ $(r \neq i)$. Because it is certain that S_i was sent when T_j is received, $H(S \mid T) = -p(S_i; T_j) \log(1) = 0$, since $\log(1) = 0$ and $p(S_j; T_k) = 0$ $(k \neq j)$. Unfortunately, however, a symbol may be misinterpreted, or there could be some other form of interference or *noise* which upon occasion might cause an incorrect identification of the symbol originally transmitted. In this case, then, *two* sources act upon the channel, an information source and a noise source, and each is guided by its own statistical process.

In a noiseless process there is no uncertainty about the symbols sent given the symbols received, and the *rate of information transmission* equals the entropy of the source; or, $R = H(S)$. In a noisy channel $H(S \mid T) > 0$; due to interference there is, on average, some uncertainty with respect to the symbols that were sent, given the symbols received. In *this* connection conditional entropy $H(S \mid T)$ is referred to as the *equivocation*: it reflects the remaining uncertainty as to the message intended by the sender.

The difference between the entropy at the source and the equivocation, $H(S) - H(S \mid T)$, is the rate of information transmission over a noisy channel. Without noise, $H(S \mid T) = 0$ and $R = H(S)$. When the noise, in effect, completely obscures the message, $H(S \mid T) = H(S)$; or, the messages received and sent are independent of one another, and $R = 0$. Thus, noise introduces some ambiguity into the message, making the rate of transmission in a noisy channel $R \leq H(S)$.

Analogously, the capacity of a noisy channel is $C = \text{Max} (H(S) - H(S \mid T)) = \text{Max } R$. That is, channel capacity is the *maximum* rate at which information can be transmitted, given the symbols, the sequencing rules, and the noise. This leads to the fundamental theorem for a noisy channel: it is possible to develop a set of symbols and rules—that is, a code—such that the equivocation can be made arbitrarily small. This could be accomplished, say, by repeating the original message several times, or by the design of an appropriate code. In any event, there is no method of coding that gives an equivocation less than $C - H(S)$.

The importance of this theorem for system control is its suggestion that in the presence of a noise source that interferes with, say, the actuator's ability to correctly interpret the instructions issued by the controller, a format for transmitting these instructions could be designed to make the degree of ambiguity arbitrarily small. A necessary concern of economic planning, then, is the format used for communication, and the reduction of ambiguity in communication, in order that the actual rate of information transmission through a communication channel approach the channel's information-transmitting capacity.

As a final observation, the third demand that was made of the information measure permits us to write $H = h(p(S_1), \ldots, p(S_i), \ldots, p(S_n)) + \sum_i p(S_i) h(p(T_1 \mid S_i), \ldots, p(T_m \mid S_i))$, or to *decompose* the entropy of a source into two parts. The first of these parts, $h(p(S_1), \ldots, p(S_1), \ldots, p(S_n))$, is the *between-group* entropy: this measures the uncertainty *between* a *primary* set of groups. In the original formulation, for example, $p(S_i)$ represented the probability of the ith symbol being the first one transmitted, or the initial basis for distinguishing between sequences of symbols. The second part, $\sum_i p(S_i) h(p(T_1 \mid S_i), \ldots, p(T_j \mid S_i), \ldots, p(T_m \mid S_i))$, is the *within-group entropy:* this measures the average uncertainty *within* each of the primary groups. In the original formulation, for example, $p(T_j \mid S_i)$ represented the probability that the jth symbol will follow the ith symbol.

The decomposition property provides a generally useful analytical framework.[4] Suppose, for example, that there are n controllers and that each might send any one of m messages. Let $p(S_i)$ now denote the probability that the ith controller ($i = 1, \ldots, n$) will send a message, and let $p(T_j \mid S_i)$ denote the probability that the ith controller will send the jth message ($j = 1, \ldots, m$). In this case, the between-group entropy measures the uncertainty with respect to which controllers might send a message; the within-group entropy measures the expected uncertainty of the message that will be sent. Similarly, $h(p(T_1 \mid S_i), \ldots, p(T_j \mid S_i), \ldots, p(T_m \mid S_i))$ measures the uncertainty as to the message to be sent by the ith controller, and the sum of the between- and within-group entropies measures the uncertainty as to both the sender and the message.

[4] For example, see D. C. Murphy, "Entropy as a Measure of Decentralization," in M. W. Hopfe (ed.) *Proceedings of the Fifth Annual Meeting of AIDS,* pp. 67–69.

d. Efficiency

The rationale for the existence of any purposeful system is to accomplish certain objectives efficiently and effectively. This is no less true of a communication system. Two alternative approaches suggest themselves for determining whether, in fact, a communication system is operating efficiently. The first would involve a comparison of the data production, transmission, and processing in the system with that in a large-scale computer; the second would involve analyzing certain systemic features with the help of the information-theoretic measurements discussed above. In either event, the underlying motive would be to *improve* the system's information network.

In the former instance, there are three fundamental criteria that provide the basis for any comparison between communication systems: the *speed* with which the communication process occurs; the *idling time* during which various elements in the communication system are waiting to perform their function in the communication process; and the amount of data that the system can handle, or its *capacity*. In this connection, it may be possible to design more efficient communication systems with respect to any one, or all of these criteria, in which case it then becomes a matter of balancing off the costs of the improvements versus the benefits that they yield. The latter may not be as easily quantified as the former. Moreover, the issues of speed, idling time, and capacity relate to all aspects and adjuncts of the communication system, including data gathering, processing, transmission, analysis, and control. Increased efficiency in one area, transmission, say, will not necessarily be accomplished without impairing efficiency in another area, control, for example. Thus, paradoxically, the ability of the managers of the modern organization, including public managers, to analyze all of the available data, to coordinate and reconcile decisions, and to control the processor, may actually be impaired by the increased capacity of the large-scale computer and the speed with which it operates, because of the vast amounts of data that it imposes upon them. In effect, management may be so *swamped* with data that the control process suffers delays because of the time that is spent filtering through data that management feels obliged not to ignore. The problem, then, is to determine those data that are necessary to accomplish the system's purpose, and to develop the optimal communication network for processing *these* data. That is, the *selection* issue must first be resolved, and the network compatible with the optimal selection—given the cost considerations—must be established.

In the latter instance, the analysis involves *locating the centers generating* the most information and *determining the sources of redundancy* in the system. Here, the purpose is to determine the optimal codes so as to assure that the amount of information transmitted through the system approaches the system's capacity for transmitting information. In this connection, *some* redundancy might be desirable where, for example, noise interferes with the communication process and raises the possibility of errors in the messages received. The problem, then, is to determine the optimal redundancy, given the cost of error, and the cost of introducing redundancy—that is, using a portion of the system's transmitting capacity to, in effect, repeat messages.

2.4 THE DECISION PROCESS

a. Acquisition and information

It is always possible, often necessary, and sometimes optimal to base decisions on immediately available historical data, personal knowledge, and judgments. Frequently, however, additional information—knowledge, data, facts, and experience—that could alter an initial assumption can either be acquired, or automatically becomes available. Over time, for example, additional time-series observations that might be used to reestimate the parameters of a structural regression equation in a policy model, become available. Alternatively, an initial set of probability assignments might be made with respect to a particular parameter. Additional data relating to the parameter could then be obtained by sampling, and the original probability assignments revised in light of these new data.

The initial historical and judgmental inputs into a decision-making model are called *prior* data because of the possibility of acquiring additional information through experimentation. When additional information has been acquired and then used to revise the original inputs, the revisions are referred to as *posterior* data. Once the possibility of obtaining yet additional information arises, the posterior data becomes "prior" with respect to this prospective information. Thus, the terms prior and posterior are actually relative to particular stocks of information and experiments.

In practice, it is impossible to obtain *perfect* information with respect to all the parameters in a problem. A particular population's marginal propensity to spend, for instance, is never known. Rather, economists commonly rely upon time-series or cross-section data to supply *estimates* of such parameters. As the sample of observations upon which an estimate is based approaches the universe (or more realistically, the population), the estimate can be expected to approach the true parameter value, assuming that such exists, and that it is invariant. Extrapolating this idea to the limit, perfect information can be likened to an exhaustive sample.

Unfortunately, exhaustive samples are rarely available or worth the acquisition cost, so that perfect information is rarely sought or obtained. Instead, the common practice is to settle for *sample* information. But ordinarily such information will not convert a stochastic problem into a deterministic one. Rather, by altering some of the premises upon which a decision is to be reached, it will convert one stochastic problem into a second stochastic problem. In the process, however, sample information can be expected to help policy makers reach better decisions, by making them "better informed" with respect to the stochastic process.

From the policy-making standpoint, then, the opportunity to acquire additional information raises several important issues. First, there must be an efficient mechanism for processing this information, and a clear-cut procedure for its use in the revision of the prior data. Second, where additional information has an acquisition cost of time and money, this cost must be determined. Third, whether or not to acquire additional information is itself a problem whose resolution depends on the potential *value* of the information once it has been acquired. That is, whether the search will be worth the cost. Finally, it might be possible to acquire alternative packages or samples of information, and the questions of which packages, and how much information to acquire, must also be resolved.

These problems are, of course, not unique to the question of system control. They are, nonetheless, particularly pertinent issues here, because not only does information flow between the system's components and subsystems, but to all intents and purposes this flow is a source of new information to be added to that already contained in the black box. How this input is used to transform prior into posterior data therefore represents an important issue toward which we shall now direct our attention.

Concerned with the acquisition of additional information and the choice of decision rules, statistical decision theory attempts to analyze decision problems under uncertainty.[5] In this approach, the decision maker's preferences and attitude toward risk are summarized in an ordinal risk preference function—the von Neumann-Morgenstern "utility" function, discussed below. Also, the decision maker's beliefs about the possible outcomes of an event, the payoffs from which will depend on both the outcomes and the action taken by the decision maker, are quantified in a set of probability assignments. The "rational" decision maker—that is, the decision maker abiding by a small set of quite palatable behavioral axioms that most persons would want their own decision-making processes to obey—will choose the act that maximizes "expected utility" in the von Neumann-Morgenstern sense. Utilizing Bayes' Rule to determine how all of the various pieces of information that might be obtained from a sampling experiment would affect the initial probability assignments, the expected utility given each sample result can be computed. Weighting each of these expected utilities by the prior probability of obtaining the sample results and summing yields the expected utility of the experiment. By comparing this expected utility with the expected utility prior to sampling, one can, in principle, determine the value of sample information, or the value of the experiment, to the decision maker. The value of perfect information, or the value of an experiment that gives an infinite sample, is simply a special case.[6]

b. Value and forms of information

i. "Value" of Information A key dimension in the cost-benefit analysis of information is the possible *value* associated with each message. Such val-

---

[5] The terms risk and uncertainty will be used interchangeably here.
[6] For the full dose, see H. Raiffa and R. Schlaifer, *Applied Statistical Decision Theory* (Cambridge, Mass.: The M.I.T. Press, 1968).

uation is related, on the one hand, to the *vision* of the decision makers of the system of which they are a part, a vision dependent on the *a priori* information about that system and on their interpretation of its meaning; and, on the other hand, on the controllers' conception of the extent and nature of their control; that is, of (a) the economic validity of any given information in the *total decision-making context,* (b) the time dimension concerned, (c) the position of each decision maker in the decision hierarchy, and (d) the impact of that decision on the system's parts or on its totality.

The value of any given message or communication system can be appraised through some benefit function of the von Neumann-Morgenstern type. Comparable to the sample information of statistical decision theory, the communication system provides messages of varying information content. The value of the information contained in these messages can vary from decision maker to decision maker; but the value can, nonetheless, in principle be computed as indicated above. Thus, after determining the value of a message-generating process, and given the readily computed expected information content of the process, one could, presumably, determine the value of the expected information content. The economics of information is therefore concerned with the *economic* choice between alternative communication systems and organization structures, insofar as the latter entail both information flows whose net benefits can be assessed, and determinable or assignable costs.[7]

Various technical concepts previously discussed have some direct application in such analysis. In addition, the entropy concept has been successfully employed by economists in a variety of ways, particularly in the *analysis* of economic value-share data—most notably, in analyzing seller's competition, and in studying trends in income distribution—as well as in the *analysis* of probability functions—most notably, in evaluating forecasting procedures.[8]

For example, one can consider the expected information gain of a forecasting procedure that assigns probabilities to future outcomes. Alternatively, by interpreting an individual's share of national income, or a firm's proportion of industry sales, as a "probability," entropy can be used as a measure of disorder or inverse concentration. Thus, the larger is the entropy in, say, sales among firms in an industry, the greater is the uncertainty as to the firm that would actually have captured the custom of a buyer chosen at random, the lesser is seller's concentration in the industry, and the greater, presumably, is competition. Similarly, the greater is the income entropy among individuals, the more equal is the distribution of income shares. Moreover, the decomposition property allows one to analyze these distributions for grouped data—which is often the format of economic data. In particular, if H_{gi} is the entropy in the *i*th group, and p_i is the share that the *i*th group has of the total of some economic variable, then the entropy for this variable would be

$$H = -\sum_i p_i \log(p_i) + \sum_i p_i H_{gi} \tag{2.5}$$

[7] See J.Marshak, "Economics of Information Systems," in M. D. Intriligator (ed.) *Frontiers of Quantitative Economics* (Amsterdam: North-Holland, 1971), pp. 32–107.

[8] See H. Theil, *Economics and Information Theory* (Chicago: Rand McNally, 1967).

This breakdown thus permits one to measure the extent to which it is the relative inequality between or within groups that contributes to the overall inequality in that economic variable.

ii.   Organization and the **Forms** *of Information* In discussing the question of the role of information in systems' organization Leonid Hurwicz has suggested [9] that centralized and decentralized allocative processes may be viewed as poles of a *continuum.* Focusing on the relations among the component parts of economic systems (and neglecting the internal structures of the components) Hurwicz has noted that at one pole of the continuum, information bids of *prices and quantities* are dispersed among economic units anonymously; at the other pole, all dispersed information, *including complete descriptions of technologies, preferences, and resource holdings,* is addressed to a single, central unit. All allocative mechanisms could then be classified according to whether their requirements were similar to those of one or the other type. Hurwicz has also pointed out that "partioning" of components (namely, administrative changes at various administrative levels) would not be viewed as "decentralization" per se, while reductions in the volume of central directives and increased contractual relations among enterprises, clearly would. In the USSR and Soviet-type economies, most "economic reforms" have been of the first type rather than of the second.

In the Hurwicz scheme, the differences between the two poles of the continuum rightly involve not only a systemic *organization,* but *also the forms and the nature* of *the information* respectively required by the centralized and the decentralized poles. One should note that, in addition, a number of other factors may influence the *nature, form, content,* and volume of the information circulating in tightly centralized systems. These elements are notably: (a) the reliability of the information *generated* in such systems; (b) the question of the *language* available for communication between the various elements of the system; (c) the *volume* of the information *required;* and (d) the possible speed of the processing.

In a tightly regulated "servomechanism" in which the center plays the role of both target setter and overseer of results, that is, in situations in which the targets are both *commands* and *standards of performance,* strong tendencies to distort information are built into the system. Withholding the basic data, furnishing unimportant or trival information, and distorting the uses of communication in general, become, indeed, a protective device for counteracting commands and for reducing their significance, and the *more* information required from below, the higher the likely tendency toward its distortion.

Conversely, in this system, in order to ensure as much accuracy in execution as is feasible, the center is led to prescribe either all commodity flows or all prices. In these circumstances the "language" available for communication between the center and the producing or consuming units represents

[9] L. Hurwicz, "On the Concepts and Possibility of Informational Decentralization," *American Economic Review,* Vol. 59, No. 2, May 1969.

a formidable constraint. Such language must indeed cope with the highly complex requirement of describing perfectly all the properties of all the items produced or exchanged, if it is to prevent abuses in contracts and their interpretation. Limited decentralization may in such cases prove to be difficult to carry out in the conditions desired by the center. In market-directed, rather than administratively directed economies, contracts are used as *complements* to market exchanges; market pressures, therefore, do not need a "common language" to be effective.

The *volume* of information may thus tend to be extremely large in a directed economy both under the form of commands from above and reports of all kinds including data on fulfillment from below. Typically, as delineated earlier, these data of an *endogenous* nature would be essentially focused on *administration and control,* as well as on *accounting*—while in decentralized systems attention would be paid to *exogenous* elements, namely, sales forecasting, study of credit availabilities, and so on, along with product research, purchasing, inventory control, and related problems of supply, scheduling, planning, and simulation.

In any centralized system, bent on carrying out some overriding objective—for example, "victory" in war, rapid "industrialization" or some similar superior target—a tendency arises toward shortening the chains of command, replacing the important economic stimuli with injunctions, and increasing to the utmost vertical concentration in production. The mainsprings of this tendency are not only speed, but also the pursuit of the elusive goal of reliability of information—since both speed and reliability decrease as the number of elements coupled in a series increases. A high degree of centralization in decision making raises, however, a host of problems of its own. To start with, the central authority has a *limited capacity* for processing information into decisions, and, consequently, information is often "queueing" at the center, awaiting its processing into final decisions; the "shortening" of the chain thus increases rather than decreases delays; and, finally, weakens the overall efficiency of the information and command network.[10]

2.5 CONCLUDING COMMENTS

With increasing economic development there is an *ever increasing outpouring of information from a variety of sources and in a variety of forms:* supply and demand for information are continuously growing. Concomitantly and paradoxically, because of the increased complexity of economic decisions in any modern economic setting, and because of the increased risks which any important decision entails, uncertainty is also growing.

Although increased information complexity tends thus to characterize all modern economies, the *concrete forms of information flows* tend, as we saw, to differ appreciably in the East from those in the West. Typically, nonprice information flows are characteristic for the former, and price-type information is

[10] Oskar Lange, *Introduction to Economic Cybernetics* (London: Pergamon Press, 1970), pp. 172 ff.

characteristic for the latter. Further, the anterior (planning) time horizon is relatively longer in the former than in the latter. Finally, since the Soviet supreme controller aims at directly controlling the activities of the actuators and of the processors alike, the amount of information under the form of instructions from the top, and the reverse flows of operational reports from the bottom—tend to be *extremely detailed*. Paradoxically, then, the sheer volume of information required for controlling economic actuators and processors, and its probable redundancy and cost, may be *much higher* in centrally administered economies—that is, in the systems that otherwise like to suppress "information" in the society at large—than in primarily market-directed, decentralized systems.

CHAPTER 3

Models of Rational Policy Choice

3.1 POLICY DECISION ANALYSIS

In the preceding chapters we first presented the *schemas* of various systems: inter-connecting channels in which controlling and coordinating policy decisions must be effected. We then examined the *issues* related to the flow and processing of the information required for the purpose. We now turn to the *analysis* of such decisions; that is, to the interrelation of policy *goals, instruments,* and *constraints,* and to *optimization* procedures. All of these ingredients appear in Jan Tinbergen's initial set of policy models devised in the 1950s,[1] which provide the underlying philosophy for virtually all such efforts.[2] It is the means of dealing with these ingredients, and the treatment of *time, uncertainty,* and the rate of *foreign trade* that distinguishes the truly innovative models from those that represent only minor variations on a Tinbergian theme. In Tinbergen's analysis, the mechanics of government control are clarified with particular reference to a *single-controller, open-loop model,* rather than for multi-level coordinating-controlling feedback frameworks. The latter have not been ignored, however, as we shall see below when H. Theil's early contributions to the subject [3] are discussed.

The objectives with which policy models are concerned are presumed to be those of the society. In fact, however, they are the objectives of the policy makers who, at the extremes, either impose their own value systems on the so-

[1] J. Tinbergen, *On the Theory of Economic Policy* (Amsterdam: North-Holland, 1952).

[2] See, for example, K. A. Fox and E. Thorbeke, "Specifications of Structure and Data Requirements in Policy Models," in B. G. Hickman (ed.) *Quantitative Planning of Economic Policy* (Washington, D.C.: Brookings Institution, 1965), pp. 1–110; J. Tinbergen and H. C. Bos, *Mathematical Models of Economic Growth* (New York: McGraw-Hill, 1962); H. Theil, *Economic Forecasts and Policy* (Amsterdam: North-Holland, 1961).

[3] *Ibid.*

ciety, or attempt to interpret the wills, and achieve a satisfactory compromise among the frequently divergent goals, of a heterogeneous citizenry. However formulated, the objectives fall into three distinct categories. On the one hand, there are uncompromisable *demands* that enter as constraints to be respected by *any* policy. On the other hand, there are *wants* that are amenable to trade-off, and that enter through a social preference function purporting to order "the" preferences of the society. Superimposed on each of these are the attitudes toward risk of the policy-making body. These become relevant once we move from deterministic to stochastic models. As such, they must be *explicitly* incorporated into the model once the uncertainties prevailing in the real world are recognized, lest they be introduced implicitly, and thereby perhaps inappropriately.

In addition to describing the policy makers' demands, the constraints describe the society's technological, economic, sociological, and governmental structure. The model will therefore contain technical, behavioral, and institutional constraints that delineate the interrelationships among those variables over which policy makers exercise some control, as well as those over which they do not. The former are of particular interest, for included among them are the instruments to effect policy. These consist of both economic quantities and economic structures. Ordinarily, limitations will be imposed on the extent to which any one instrument can be either applied or ignored. These will appear in a set of boundary conditions that impose yet additional restrictions on any solution that the policy makers might reach.

Given a model's basic ingredients and structure, three additional issues must be resolved by the model-builder: namely, the treatment of uncertainty, time, and foreign trade.

In the case of uncertainty, the issue is whether to build either a *deterministic* model in which policy makers behave "as if" the world were one of certainty, or a necessarily more complex *stochastic* model in which the policy makers' risk-taking propensities and the vagaries of chance play vital roles in the decision-making process and its consequences. In the case of time, the issue is whether to build either a *static* model based on a set of predetermined input data and assumptions, and capable of handling only single-period decision problems, or a necessarily more complex *dynamic* model capable of yielding a decision-making *strategy*, a planned sequence of interdependent multi-period decisions based on a set of *initial* assumptions and data, as well as the perhaps random consequences of preceding decisions. In the case of foreign trade, the issue is whether to build either a *closed* model that treats the economy as a self-sufficient and independent entity operating in isolation from the rest of the world, or a necessarily more complex *open* model in which the economy is coupled into a global economic network wherein a set of interdependent economies, prodded by their own self-interests, engage in universally rewarding foreign trade. Still further, where an economy itself is composed of a number of interrelated sectors, an open *microeconomic* model can be built that incorporates the flow of commerce among them. This would replace the *macro-economic* model in which the various sectors are aggregated into a single unit.

Assuredly, a dynamic and stochastic microeconomic model of a multi-sector open economy would be the most sophisticated type of policy model. But, sophistication and utility are not synonymous. The latter depends on both the ease with which the model can be solved, and the applicability of the policy prescriptions that its simplest and most unrefined forms offer. These prescriptions, or *programs,* consist of a specification of the set of instruments, or *decision variables,* and their rates that will *optimize* the *preference function,* subject to the *constraints* and the *boundary conditions.*

It was toward this end that Tinbergen's efforts were directed. Tinbergen viewed the twofold purpose of a policy model as determining (1) whether economic policies are mutually consistent, and (2) facilitating the choice among feasible policies. In contrast to models that attempt to *forecast* the rates of a set of variables of interest to policy makers, Tinbergen's policy models focus on two subsets of these variables: (1) the so-called *target* variables whose rates can be influenced; and (2) the so-called *instrument* variables from among which will be chosen the so-called *measures* whose role is to influence the target variables in the direction desired by the policy-making body.

Assuredly, a model's basic structure should depend on its purpose. Economic policy is concerned with economic welfare, and this can prompt concern with (1) the current and future *rates* of economic variables such as output, (2) the *distribution* of these variables among various economic sectors, such as the distribution of output between the consumption and investment sectors, and (3) the *allocation* of these variables among individual economic units, such as the allocation of output and productive activity among individual consumers and producers. The allocation problem, while a pressing and important one, will be relegated to a subsidiary position in subsequent discussions, for this is a *detail* evoking highly personalized value-judgment issues that, while relevant when planning for a *specific* economy, would only divert us from our primary purpose of developing a general framework for economic planning.

In the context of planning, concern with the rates and distribution of economic variables ordinarily implies concern with these variables at a particular point or period in time, or over a given time horizon, concern with their growth, or concern with regulating their intertemporal movements. It is in part because of these time-related concerns that we shall employ the term *rate* as opposed to *level* when discussing economic quantities. In particular, total output, say, over the time period from T_1 to T_2 is given by $Q^T(t) = \int_{T_1}^{T_2} Q(\tau)/dt$ where $Q(t) = dQ^T(t)/dt$ is the *rate* of output at time t, and $[dQ(t)/dt]/Q(t) = [d^2Q^T(t)/dt^2]/Q(t)$ is the *rate of growth* in output at time t. Although we shall be especially concerned with policy models that relate to discrete time periods as opposed to continuous points in time, we shall also be concerned with total performance over a *series* of time periods. For purposes of consistency, we shall therefore uniformly use ''rate'' to indicate the magnitude of an economic variable—output, employment, foreign trade, and the like—either at any *point* in time or for any reference *period,* as is relevant for the particular model.

This chapter introduces models that reflect each of these basic concerns: (1) Tinbergen's static models; (2) Theil's stochastic and multi-period models; (3) the Mahalanobis growth model; and (4) Phillips' stabilization model.

3.2 THE TINBERGEN MODEL

Tinbergen's model contains a set of M variables that may initially be dichotomized into M_c *controlled,* and M_u *uncontrolled,* variables. The M_c controlled variables can be further dichotomized into I *known targets* y_i $(i = 1, \ldots, I)$ and J *unknown* instruments z_j $(j = 1, \ldots, J)$. Similarly, the uncontrolled variables can be divided into K *known* pieces of data, or fixed factors u_k $(k = 1, \ldots, K)$, and S unknown irrelevant variables, or *side-effects* x_s $(s = 1, \ldots, S)$. Thus, $I + J = M_c$ variables, y_i and z_j, represent economic quantities and structures that can be manipulated or influenced, and $K + S = M_u$ variables, u_k and x_s, represent the "givens" and extraneous consequences, respectively, of economic analysis. The side-effects are thus endogenous variables determined by the model, the instruments and data are exogenous variables determined by the controller and the environment, and the target rates can be either endogenously determined by the model, or exogenously fixed by the controller.

Prominent among the targets are such policy-oriented variables as consumption, employment, the rate of inflation—that is, the rate of growth in prices—and the balance of payments. These so-called "important" policy variables can be treated in two ways. Specifically, Tinbergen introduces the concept of a fixed, or an *absolute* target wherein policy makers *require* that the targets achieve *specific rates*. Alternatively, with a *flexible* target, policy makers may prefer one rate to another, but the target's rate is ultimately determined by the model so as to optimize the policy-making preference function, rather than being prespecified.

The instruments are decision variables under the policy makers' control. Instruments such as the income tax rate, the rate of government spending, and the money supply are particularly important *economic quantities;* the antitrust *laws,* price and wage *controls that temper* the activity of a free market, and a fundamental change in the *organization* of the banking system are important *economic structures.* The latter are policy instruments that when activated become measures involving significant changes in the institutional arrangements for carrying out economic activity.

To the extent that current rates of economic activity depend on past rates, predetermined variables such as past consumer purchases or the more recent history of net foreign trade, may exert exogenous influences on the economy. The given capital stock *level*—the result of past *rates* of investment and depreciation—and commitments to provide specific amounts of foreign aid are additional fixed factors that, along with prior data, enter the model as uncontrolled variables. Similarly, variables such as the weather, an energy crisis, the possibility of strike-provoking labor-management intransigence, and the surprise reevaluation of a foreign currency, although unpredictable with certainty, nonetheless influence the endogenous variables—the targets—and are amenable to probability judgments and forecasts. Although the rates of these variables *may* be the result of purposeful acts taken elsewhere, as far as the given economic system and *its* controllers are concerned, they are random influences, or noise, that can be incorporated into the model when accompanied by probabilistic statements, or the most refined forecasts that existing knowledge and the state of the art permit.

Finally, there is a set of side-effects. Like the targets, their rates will also be influenced by the data and instruments. Unlike the targets, however, policy makers are not concerned with these irrelevant variables or their rates. Thus, the consequences of an act may be felt in other economies or, like the government debt, may be borne by future generations; but, from the policy makers' perspective they are irrelevant to policy decisions.

The selection of variables to include in a model, and the classification of variables from the policy standpoint, provide two of the three principal elements that determine its "physique." The third element is the specification of the structural relationships—the couplings among the variables. This defines the system's structure. Each model is grounded on certain assumptions about the relationships between the different elements in the system, and each model must take into account constraints and boundary conditions on the goals and instruments available to the policy-making body. The Tinbergen model is defined by a set of N equations that describe its structural relations.

The usual form of a Tinbergen-like model presents the general programming problem:

$$\text{Maximize}_{y, z} \quad W = w(y, z) \tag{3.1}$$

$$\text{subject to} \quad g_r(u, z) = f_r(y) \qquad r = 1, \ldots, R \tag{3.2}$$

$$g_n(u, z) = f_n(x) \qquad n = R + 1, \ldots, N$$

$$y_0 \leq y \leq y_1; \qquad z_0 \leq z \leq z_1 \tag{3.2a}$$

where $u' = (u_1, \ldots, u_K)$, $x' = (x_1, \ldots, x_S)$, $y' = (y_1, \ldots, y_I)$, and $z' = (z_1, \ldots, z_J)$ are row vectors of the controlled variables (y_i and z_j) and the uncontrolled variables (u_k and x_s), respectively; the prime ($'$) indicates transpose. Thus, Equation (3.1), $W = w(y, z)$ is a preference function to be maximized by the appropiate choice of rates for the instruments and targets. This preference function, originally called a social utility function by Tinbergen, has alternatively been referred to as a target-preference function,[4] a macro-economic preference function,[5] and a social welfare function.[6] This general formulation em-

[4] B. Hansen, *Lectures in Economic Theory II* (Lund, Sweden: Studentlitteratur, 1967), p. 4.

[5] R. Frisch, *General Outlook on a Method of Advanced and Democratic Macroeconomic Planning* (Oslo: Institute of Economics, Dec. 1965), p. 17.

[6] Abram Bergson, *Essays in Normative Economics* (Cambridge, Mass.: Harvard University Press, 1966), pp. 27–49.

phasizes that both instruments and targets can be arguments in the preference function. Indeed, by its very nature as an objective, every target, whether fixed or flexible, will *necessarily* enter the preference function, although any individual instrument, such as the rediscount rate or the rate of government spending, need not.

Equations (3.2), the N constraints $g_r(u, z) = f_r(y)$ and $g_n (u, z) = f_n(x)$, describe the chain of causality between the exogenous independent variables—the instruments and the data—and the endogenous dependent variables—the targets and side-effects, respectively. Equations (3.2a), the boundary conditions $y_0 \leq y \leq y_1$ and $z_0 \leq z \leq z_1$, indicate the tolerable target rates, and impose limits on the extent to which any particular instrument may be employed or ignored.

The policy problem defined by Equations (3.1), (3.2), and (3.2a) is comparable to the somewhat more pedestrian distribution problems of the theories of consumer behavior and production. In the former, the objective function is a Marshallian utility function to be maximized subject to a single budget constraint. This is accomplished by the appropriate distribution of the consumer's income among the commodities available for purchase. In the latter, the objective function is a production function to be maximized subject to a single cost constraint and any fixed factor commitments incurred by the firm. This is accomplished among the variable factors of production available for hire. As is true of consumer behavior and production, the difficulty of solving a policy model depends on the exact form of its equations; the applicability of the solution depends on the extent to which the chosen specification captures the structure of the economic system being modeled. In order to gain the virtue of simplicity, Tinbergen assumed linear functions, continuous in all the variables. Thus, Tinbergen's policy problem is one of linear programming.

In particular, define $a' = (a_1, \ldots, a_I)$ and $b' = (b_1, \ldots, b_J)$ as known $1 \times I$ and $1 \times J$ row vectors, respectively, and $A = [a_{ri}]$, $B = [b_{rj}]$, and $C = [c_{rk}]$ as known $R \times I$, $R \times J$, and $R \times K$ matrices, respectively. For notational convenience we ignore the side-effects, since they do not affect the solution. With fixed targets $y = \bar{y}$, the general programming problem assumes the linear programming format

Maximize $W = a'\bar{y} + b'z$ (3.3)

subject to $Bz - A\bar{y} = -Cu = d_1$ (3.4)

$z_0 \leq z \leq z_1$ (3.4a)

With flexible targets, the values of the y_i are not assigned in advance, so that these too become, in effect, decision variables whose rates are to be determined in the solution to the model. In this case, the additional set of boundary conditions, $y_0 \leq y \leq y_1$, appears in Equations (3.4a), and Equations (3.4) would be written $Bz - Ay = -Cu = d_2$.

Consider, for example, the economic system of Figure 3.1. The controller can employ two instruments at rates of z_1 and z_2, and instructions to implement such a policy are sent to the actuator. The actuator implements the policy with inputs of z_1 and z_2 into the industrial subsystem, Processor A. This

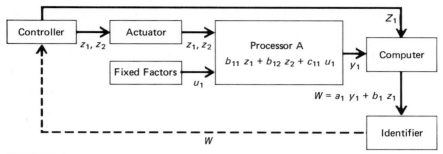

FIGURE 3-1

subsystem also receives a fixed factor input u_1. The transformation (production) function for this subsystem is $b_{11}z_1 + b_{12}z_2 + c_{11}u_1 = a_{11}y_1$; or, $y_1 = (b_{11}/a_{11})z_1 + (b_{12}/a_{11})z_2 + (c_{11}/a_{11})u_1$.

Information about the output rate and the employment of the first instrument is fed to the computer, because each of the variables enters into the policy makers' preference function W. The computer then computes the value of W. This information *might*, as indicated by the dashed line, be fed back to the controller. In such a system, then, the controller can either (1) test the impact of various policies through simulation or actual implementation, in the latter event perhaps altering the policy depending on feedback information, or (2) fix a target and determine, mathematically or through simulation and feedback, the instrument selection that will effect this target.

As a set of equalities, Equations (3.4) define a set of R simultaneous linear equations in J unknowns—the instruments. We shall assume that $a_{ii} \neq 0$ and that $a_{ri} = 0$ $(r \neq i)$, so that each equation in (3.4) specifies a unique linear relationship between the instruments, the data, and a *single* fixed target. With respect to the ith target, for example,

$$b_{i1}z_1 + b_{i2}z_2 + \cdots + b_{iJ}z_J + c_{i1}u_1 + \cdots + c_{iK}u_K = a_{ii}\bar{y}_i . \tag{3.4i}$$

indicates the manner in which the z_j and u_K effect the given target level $\bar{y}_i$. Subtracting $\Sigma_k c_{ik}u_k$ from both sides of the equation yields

$$b_{i1}z_1 + b_{i2}z_2 + \cdots + b_{iJ}z_J = a_{ii}\bar{y}_i - \Sigma_k c_{ik}u_k = d_{1i} \tag{3.4i'}$$

where d_{1i}, as the weighted sum of a series of constants—the fixed target and the data—is itself a constant. Still further, $R = I$. That is, the number of equations equals the number of absolute targets. Thus, Equations (3.4) define I simultaneous linear equations in J unknowns. Under the assumption that these equations are independent, they will have either an infinite number of solutions, a unique solution, or no solution (except, perhaps, by coincidence) depending on whether $I < J$, $I = J$, or $I > J$. In the former two cases it is additionally assumed that the equations are mutually consistent. Whereupon with $I < J$ the maximization problem is solvable by linear programming, and with $I = J$ there is a unique simultaneous solution to the constraint equations; in the third case with $I > J$, there will not necessarily be any set of values for the unknown z_j satisfying all I equations simultaneously.

Two additional observations result from the fact that Equations (3.3), (3.4), and (3.4a) define a linear programming problem: (1) the fundamental theorem of linear programming must hold; and (2) the problem has a dual, the linear programming problem

$$\text{Minimize}_{\lambda} \quad W_d = d_1' \lambda \tag{3.3'}$$

$$\text{subject to} \quad B' \lambda = b \tag{3.4'}$$

$$\lambda \geq 0 \tag{3.4a'}$$

where $\lambda' = (\lambda_1, \ldots, \lambda_R)$ is a vector of dual variables, λ_i being associated with the ith constraint. Additional dual variables $\lambda_{R+j0} \geq 0$ and $\lambda_{R+j1} \geq 0$ would be introduced for given boundary conditions, $z_j \leq \bar{z}_j$ and $z_j \geq \bar{z}_j$, respectively.

The former observation implies that the number of variables included at nonzero levels in the optimal solution cannot exceed the number of constraints. Thus, unless Equation (3.4a) *demands* the inclusion of certain instruments in the optimal solution by setting $z_0 > 0$, the number of instruments (variables) included in the optimal solution cannot exceed the number of constraints (absolute targets).

The latter observation implies that a dual variable will be associated with each constraint and boundary condition. The value of this variable in the optimal solution to the *dual* can be interpreted as a *shadow price* or opportunity cost. In the present context, it represents the welfare loss suffered *at the margin* as a result of fixing a target at the given rate as opposed to keeping it flexible or alternating its rate; or the loss suffered by restricting the permissible rate of the instrument. Moreover, the *ratio* of dual variables for any two constraints yields the *rate of substitution* between targets; that is, the compensating change in the rate of one target which is required when the rate of a second target is changed, in order to leave the value of the objective function unchanged. Thus, as with duals in general, the information yielded by the dual to the Tinbergen problem can be extremely important and useful to policy makers in that it assigns *implicit* values to targets, and *costs* to boundary conditions. In addition, the Tinbergen model as well as its successors can provide considerable *insights* into specific policy decisions, even in the absence of *specific* parameter estimates, or even without employing them as the *sine qua non* in every planning decision. In particular, through various types of *sensitivity analysis* and *simulations*—that is, putting the model on the computer and perturbing the parameters or exogenous inputs in various ways—one can study the potential impact of alternative programs under alternative, plausible *scenarios*.

Despite its considerable impact and importance there are, nonetheless, two aspects of the Tinbergen model which detract from its overall applicability. First, the linearity assumption is overly restrictive, particularly when applied to the preference function. It is difficult to accept either that the function is linear in both targets and instruments, or even that it is additively separable so that it can be written as the sum of a series of functions of the individual variables. The continuity assumption, although convenient and frequently nondistortive even when known to be invalid, is also restrictive in a very important sense; namely, it precludes the inclusion of economic *structures*—which would have to be treated as binary variables—among the instruments without framing the problem as an *integer* programming problem. Given the existing algorithms for the solution of such problems, this would severely limit the scope of an actual policy model. Thus, we could define the problem, but even with the help of an electronic computer, a multi-integer-variable, multi-equation problem might not be solvable. Further, the implication of the fundamental theorem of linear programming that the maximum number of instruments employed in the optimal solution will not exceed the number of constraints, will be invalid when one or more of the variables is required to be an integer. Thus, even linear models with both economic quantities and economic structures will not yield nice, neat generalities.

Second, it is a deterministic model to be used to determine policy in a stochastic world. There are two unfortunate aspects to the certainty assumption. First, it obscures both the need to introduce feedback and controls in order to specifically allow for and rectify the unanticipated and undesired outcomes of a policy, and the need to consider the policy makers' risk preferences. Second, such a model lacks the stochastic ingredients obtaining in the real world in general, and in econometric models and parameter estimates in particular. Thus the values of the data variables, the u_k, will often be error-prone forecasts or estimates. Similarly, the parameters in the constraints are usually estimated by linear regression techniques. Each equation thus estimates the *systematic* relationship between a set of independent instruments and data, and a dependent target. Because their influence is nonsystematic, the equation thus ignores the presence of random factors that also influence the target. As a result, a policy appearing to be optimal a priori can be disastrous ex post. Assuredly, recognizing uncertainty and explicitly allowing for it in the decision-making process, will not guarantee against its potentially adverse consequences. Nonetheless it will permit one to take these adverse consequences, as well as all other possible outcomes, into consideration before reaching a decision, which guarantees that the risk preferences of the policy-making body will be respected.

A final issue, and one confronting all models, is that parameter values may change over time. Thus, by the time parameter estimates become available they may already be outdated. This problem is particularly prevalent where time-dependent dynamic models are involved. Thus, there is always the risk that the model will offer last year's solutions to solve next year's problems.

Notwithstanding these criticisms, Tinbergen has suggested a solid framework within which to build policy models. Indeed, his basic concepts are applicable to a wide variety of policy problems of both economic stabilization and growth by appropriate selection of target and instrument variables, and accurate structural specification for a given planning horizon.

3.3 RELATED MODELS

a. The Theil approach

Theil contributed a major modification of the basic Tinbergen model, stemming from his recognition that the nondefinitional structural constraints are ordinarily developed through econometric analysis. In this event the rates of the uncontrolled dependent variables cannot be forecast with certainty, and maximizing a preference function that assumes that the values of the arguments *will* obtain with certainty is neither appropriate nor meaningful. Indeed, Theil suggested, it is unlikely that the most preferred rate for any single target, or indeed any prespecified rate, can ever be acquired through any but the most fortuitous selection of instruments. This is so, because in addition to the *systematic* relationship between the dependent target and the independent variables—the instruments—there will be a *stochastic* component influencing the target. Inasmuch as the target is subject to random shocks, it too will behave as a random variable. The econometric relationship only suggests the possibility of determining the *expected value* of the dependent variable by specifying values for the independent variables. For example, suppose

$$\beta_{10} + \beta_{11}z_1 + \beta_{12}z_2 = \hat{y}_1$$

is the true regression line for predicting the first target's rate for given values of the first two instruments, and $\hat{y}_1$ is the target rate in the absence of random shocks; $\hat{y}_1 + \epsilon_1 = y_1$ is the *actual* target rate and depends on the value of the random disturbance term, ϵ_1. Empirically, β_{1j} will be *estimated* by b_{1j}, and ϵ_1 will be estimated by the error term

$$e_1 = y_1 - b_{10} - b_{11}z_1 - b_{12}z_2.$$

Similarly, the most preferred values of the instruments will not necessarily be achieved because of the need to move away from the preferred instrument values, say in response to feedback data, in order to reach the desired targets. In any event, the preference function employed in Tinbergen's model cannot be employed in Theil's model, for the former requires a statement of ordinal preferences under certainty and a Marshallian analysis, while the latter requires a statement of ordinal preferences under uncertainty, and a von Neumann-Morgenstern analysis.

Suppose, then, that Equation (3.1) represents an ordinal preference function in the von Neumann-Morgenstern sense. Then, in accordance with the von Neumann-Morgenstern behavioral axioms, where y and z are vectors of random variables the optimal decision will maximize the expected value of W, denoted $E[w(y, z)]$, subject to any constraints. In the present instance, the values of the z_j may be selected with certainty, and hence only the rates of the targets, the y_i, are subject to stochastic variation.

Denote by y^0 and z^0 the vectors of the most preferred values of the targets and instruments. Then, $w(y^0, z^0) - w(y, z) = l(y, z) = L$ is defined as the *loss function*. In particular, for the given preference function, the loss function measures the *opportunity* loss suffered as a result of (1) a failure to set the instruments at their most preferred values, and (2) the failure of the target variables to achieve their most preferred rates. Since $w(y^0, z^0)$, the maximum value of the welfare function for the given instruments and targets, is a constant, maximizing $E[w(y, z)] = E[w(y^0, z^0)] - E[l(y, z)] = w(y^0, z^0) - E[l(y, z)]$, is equivalent to minimizing $E[l(y, z)]$, and results in the same optimal solution. To emphasize that there are, in fact, preferred values for the controlled and uncontrolled variables, we shall stress the minimum-loss approach, confident that this will also yield the maximum-welfare solution.

Theil assumes the preference function to be quadratic in each of its arguments; or

$$W = a'y + b'z + y'D_1y + z'D_2z + y'D_3z \qquad (3.5)$$

where a' and b' are row vectors as in Equation (3.3) and D_1, D_2, and D_3 are appropriately chosen matrices such that $w(y, z)$ is a strictly concave function of y and z. Thus, Equation (3.5) in Theil's model is equivalent to Equation (3.3) in Tinbergen's model. The associated equivalent quadratic loss function is

$$\begin{aligned} L = {}& a'(y^0 - y) + b'(z^0 - z) + (y^0 - y)'E_1(y^0 - y) \\ &+ (z^0 - z)'E_2(z^0 - z) + (y^0 - y)'E_3(z^0 - z) \end{aligned} \qquad (3.5a)$$

where E_1, E_2, and E_3 are appropriately chosen matrices such that L is a strictly convex function of y and z. In its simplest version, Theil's approach is to determine the vector of the controlled variables that minimizes the *expected* quadratic loss, subject to a set of linear constraints (3.4) and (3.4a), where the expectation is with respect to the random variable.

Just as Tinbergen's model defines a *linear* programming problem, Theil's model defines a *quadratic* programming problem. For a given set of constraints, the only difference in the two problems is that the former requires the maximization of a linear objective function, while the latter requires the minimization of a quadratic and strictly convex objective function. Figure 3.2 illustrates the difference for a two-instrument problem with a constraint set of the form.

$$Bz \leq A\bar{y} - Cu = Ay^0 - Cu = d_1 \qquad (3.4')$$
$$z \geq 0 \qquad (3.4a')$$

In Tinbergen's problem of Figure 3.2(a), we seek the highest of the parallel lines defined by the linear objective function, at least one point of which lies in the set of feasible solutions—the shaded area—defined by the constraints. In Theil's problem of Figure 3.2(b), we seek the smallest of the concentric ellipses centered at (y^0, z^0) defined by the quadratic objective function, at least one point of which lies in the same set of feasible solutions. In the linear programming case, the optimal solution is at a vertex—in two dimensions, a point of intersection of two or more constraints; in the quadratic programming case the optimal solution is on a boundary—in two dimensions, the locus of points defined by one or more constraints when the strict equality

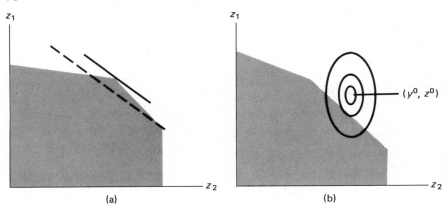

FIGURE 3-2

applies. As Figure 3.2 emphasizes, then, both models seek solutions among the same set of alternatives and within the same economic structure. Policy differences arise only because of differences that occur in the shape of the preference function stemming from a differing awareness of, and desire to allow for, forecasting errors. Unlike the linear programming model, however, the number of instruments (variables) in the optimal solution can exceed the number of targets (constraints). The interpretation of the quadratic programming dual is unchanged from that of the linear programming dual.

In a more complex format, Theil's model is made dynamic by allowing the results of a period t decision to become data, or predetermined variables, to be used in reaching decisions in future periods $t + m$ ($m > 0$). Thus, if (1) the policy makers' time horizon consists of T consecutive periods, (2) each of J instruments can be employed, and (3) each of I targets is of policy-making concern in each of these T periods, there will be a total of $(I + J)T$ variables entering into a multi-period quadratic loss function. The expectation of this function is to be minimized with respect to the J instruments, subject to a set of linear constraints. In general, there will be IT constraints, each of which describes an econometric relationship between the instruments, the data, and a given target during each of the T periods. For example, the ith constraint in the tth period will be

$$b_{i1t}z_{1t} + \cdots + b_{iJt}z_{Jt} + c_{i1t}u_{1t} + \cdots + c_{iKt}u_{Kt} = a_{iit}y_{it} \qquad (3.4\text{ii})$$

where for any particular data variable u_{kt}, we may find $u_{kt} = y_{v(t-m)}$; that is, the kth data variable in the tth period is the observed target rate in the $(t - m)$th period. In this case, then, information received in period t influences decisions reached in period $t + m$; and since this information cannot be predicted with certainty, each decision complex becomes a *strategy:* a planned sequence of decisions that allows for feedback—recognition of the consequences of prior decisions. Figure 3.3 presents a flow diagram of a simple version of such a system, which is a rather modest modification of the system of Figure 3.1.

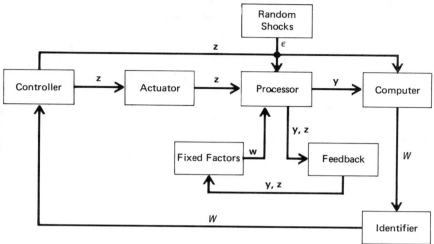

FIGURE 3-3

Theil's approach goes two important steps beyond Tinbergen's pioneering efforts. First, it recognizes and explicitly deals with the stochastic elements inherent in the estimated relationship between the controlled variables and the targets. Second, it recognizes the possibility that the policy maker will be required to plan for a multi-period time horizon with a strategy, as opposed to a unique policy. At the same time, to maintain computational simplicity and take advantage of linear regression techniques, the model retains the restrictive assumptions of continuity in all variables and linear constraints, and replaces the restrictive and implausible assumption of a linear objective function and risk-neutrality, with the equally restrictive, but somewhat more plausible assumption of the quadratic objective function that reflects risk-averse behavior.

b. The Mahalanobis model

Theil-Tinbergen policy models are essentially short run in nature. They are concerned with effecting the rates of given targets in *each* of one or more time *periods*. Alternatively, however, policy might take on a long-run outlook and be concerned with effecting some *future* target rate, or the *total* "experience" of a target over some time *interval*. A primary concern of models to aid in the formulation of a future-oriented policy will be the *rate of growth* in the economy and its subsystems. The Mahalanobis model [7] is a particular case in point.

The Mahalanobis model is a growth-oriented planning model for a "frictionless" full-employment economy in which a single instrument—investment—is employed to effect desired rates in a single target—national income.

[7] P. C. Mahalanobis, "Some Observations on the Process of Growth of National Income," *Sankhyā,* Vol. 12, 1953; and "The Approach of Operational Research to Planning in India," *Sankhyā,* Vol. 16, 1955.

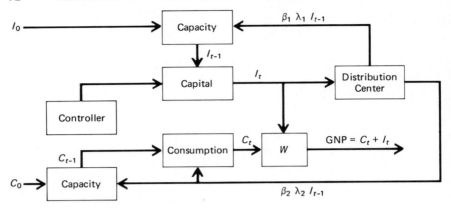

FIGURE 3-4

The model is of interest because it was originally formulated as a planning aid for a specific economy—India—and has subsequently provided the foundation for several more advanced and refined models of a similar genre.

The simplest version of the model—the system depicted in Figure 3.4—divides the economy into two subsystems or economic sectors: a capital sector and a consumption sector. The "frictionless," full employment nature of the economy is seen in the fact that the output of each sector is assumed to equal that sector's productive capacity. Thus, I_t denotes *both* the total productive *capacity* of the capital sector in period t—that is, the maximum amount of capital available to produce either additional capital capacity or consumption capacity during t—and the *actual input* of capital services during period t. Similarly, C_t denotes *both* the total productive *capacity* of the consumption sector during t—that is, the maximum amount of consumer goods that the economy is capable of producing during t—and the *actual output* of consumer goods during this period. Thus, the model completely ignores demand conditions in the sense that it implicitly assumes both a demand-and-supply equality that will also equal capacity in each sector, and a price mechanism that will automatically effect this. National income, Y_t, is given as the sum of consumption and investment:

$$Y_t = C_t + I_t \tag{3.6}$$

In each sector (1) input or output equals capacity, and (2) additional "frictions" such as obsolescence and depreciation which would effect, with time, *ceteris paribus* decreases in the productive capacities of the sectors are absent. Hence, in any period t these capacities will be increased above their period $t - 1$ levels by the amount of additional consumption and investment productive capacity generated by the capital goods sector during $t - 1$.

In particular, let λ_1 denote the proportion of productive capacity in the capital goods sector devoted to the production of additional investment capacity. This proportion is assumed fixed for all t during the relevant time horizon of T. Then $\lambda_1 I_{t-1}$ represents the total volume of investment capacity employed as input during $t-1$ in the production of *additional* capacity for the capital goods sector. Letting β_1 denote the fixed output:capital ratio for this sector, $\beta_1(\lambda_1 I_{t-1})$ determines the change in the sector's productive capacity. Hence, the total input of investment during period t equals the rate of investment during period $t-1$ plus the increment in capacity achieved during $t-1$; or,

$$I_t = I_{t-1} + \beta_1 \lambda_1 I_{t-1} = (1 + \beta_1 \lambda_1) I_{t-1} \qquad (3.7)$$

Similarly a fixed λ_2 denotes the proportion of the capital goods sector's productive capacity devoted to the production of additional capacity for the consumption goods sector. With just two sectors, $\lambda_1 + \lambda_2 = 1$. Thus it is further assumed that a clearly maintainable distinction exists between capacity used for consumption and capacity used for investment. The assumption is not easily justified.

Letting β_2 denote the fixed output:capital ratio for the consumption goods sector, $\beta_2(\lambda_2 I_{t-1})$ determines the change in productive capacity in the consumption goods sector, since $\lambda_2 I_{t-1}$ is the total volume of investment capacity employed during $t-1$ in the production of *additional* consumption goods capacity. Here, then, it is important to recognize that for either sector the output:capital ratio refers to the output of productive *capacity* generated by a unit of capital; and, in the consumption goods sector in particular, total output equals total productive capacity; or,

$$C_t = C_{t-1} + \beta_2 \lambda_2 I_{t-1} \qquad (3.8)$$

As shown in Appendix 3.1, Equations (3.6)–(3.8) can be solved to yield general solutions for I_t, C_t, and Y_t as functions of t, given initial rates of investment, consumption, and income at time $t=0$ of I_0, C_0, and Y_0, respectively. In particular, as a first-order homogeneous difference equation, (3.7) is readily solved to yield

$$I_t = (1 + \lambda_1 \beta_1)^t I_0 \qquad (3.9)$$

This solution is then substituted into Equation (3.8) which then also becomes a first-order difference equation

$$C_t = C_{t-1} + \beta_2 \lambda_2 (1 + \lambda_1 \beta_1)^{t-1} I_0 \qquad (3.10)$$

whose solution is

$$C_t = C_0 + \frac{\beta_2 \lambda_2}{\beta_1 \lambda_1} [(1 + \lambda_1 \beta_1)^t - 1] I_0 \qquad (3.11)$$

Substituting (3.9) and (3.11) into (3.6), the rate of the target, national income, is determined as

$$Y_t = Y_0 + (1 + \frac{\beta_2 \lambda_2}{\beta_1 \lambda_1})[(1 + \lambda_1 \beta_1)^t - 1] I_0 \qquad (3.12)$$

In this model of a closed economy, $\beta_i (i = 1, 2)$ describes, in effect, the technological constraints under which the planner must operate. The $\lambda_i (i = 1,$

2) are the decision variables whose values will establish both the fixed allocation, and, in effect, the rate of the instrument, investment. The target may be either flexible or fixed. In the fixed-target case, we would determine λ_1 and therefore $\lambda_2 = 1 - \lambda_1$ in order to achieve a prespecified rate of $Y_t^* = Y^*$ at some *particular future date t**. The concern in the flexible-target case is with determining values of the λ_i to maximize *total* national income over some *prespecified time horizon T*. Thus, the fixed-target problem consists of solving the equation

$$Y^* = Y_0 + (1 + \frac{\beta_2(1 - \lambda_1)}{\beta_1 \lambda_1})[(1 + \lambda_1 \beta_1)^t - 1] I_0 \tag{3.13}$$

for λ_1 in terms of predetermined values of Y^*, Y_0, I_0 β_1, and β_2. The flexible-target problem consists of solving the equation

$$\underset{\lambda_1}{\text{Max}} \sum_{t=1}^{T} Y_t = TY_0 + \sum_{t=1}^{T} (1 + \frac{\beta_2(1 - \lambda_1)}{\beta_1 \lambda_1})[(1 + \lambda_1 \beta_1)^t - 1] I_0 \tag{3.14}$$

by first computing $d(\Sigma Y_t)/d\lambda_1$, setting the latter equal to zero, and solving the resulting equation. This will not necessarily be a pleasant undertaking.

As discussed in Chapter 7, the Mahalanobis model can be expanded into a multi-sector framework. Given the restrictiveness of its assumptions, however, the model is of questionable value for actual planning purposes. Nonetheless, its framework and implications are suggestive, and the model is a potentially valuable source of interesting offspring.

c. The Phillips model

The Mahalanobis model is a dynamic model of a closed economy, and its primary focus is on growth. The Phillips model [8] is also a dynamic model of a closed economy, but its focus is on stabilization, particularly short-run stabilization.

As with the Theil and Mahalanobis models, Phillips' model acquires its dynamic character through the introduction of a lagged relationship. Unlike the former models, however, Phillips' model assumes a time continuum rather than a sequence of discrete time periods.

Phillips distinguishes between total demand and total output vis-à-vis national income. The former, denoted D, is given as the sum of the amount consumers *want* to consume plus an autonomous expenditure. For convenience we shall assume that the latter consists solely of investment I, although it may also be defined to include an autonomous consumption component. With Y denoting national income or output, desired consumption is assumed to be proportional to output, or $C = cY = (1 - s)Y$ where c is the marginal propensity to consume and $s = 1 - c$ is the marginal propensity to save. The time subscripts are deleted, reflecting the continuous nature of the model, and for con-

[8] A. W. Phillips, "Stabilization Policy in a Closed Economy," *Economic Journal*, Vol. 64, June 1954.

venience we write $Y(t) = Y$ and $C(t) = C$. Note that I is assumed constant. Thus,

$$D = C + I = (1 - s)Y + I \tag{3.15}$$

The key to the simplest Phillips model is the assumption that output reflects supply, and that *supply* will be adjusted over time in response to any discrepancies between supply and demand. Hence, with $Y - D$ the discrepancy between supply and demand at any given moment in time, the change in output will be a function of this discrepancy, or $dY/dt = f(Y - D)$. In particular, Phillips assumes a linear relationship such that

$$\frac{dY}{dt} = -\lambda(Y - D) \tag{3.16}$$

When supply exceeds demand, supply is reduced; when demand exceeds supply, supply is increased. The greater is the value of $\lambda > 0$, the greater is the adjustment in supply, and the more rapid is the response to any discrepancy. Thus, λ is a measure of the speed of response of supply to demand excesses or deficiencies.

Combining Equations (3.15) and (3.16) we obtain

$$\frac{dY}{dt} = -\lambda Y + \lambda D = -\lambda Y + \lambda(1 - s)Y + \lambda I \tag{3.17}$$

or

$$\frac{dY}{dt} + \lambda sY = \lambda I \tag{3.17a}$$

This is an easily solved differential equation whose solution is given by

$$Y = \bar{Y} + (Y_0 - \bar{Y})e^{-\lambda st} \tag{3.18}$$

where Y_0 is the national income rate at time $t = 0$. It is readily verified that this solution is obtained as the sum of a homogeneous solution of the form $Y = ae^{xt}$, and a particular solution obtained "at equilibrium" where $dY/dt = 0$. In the latter case, $\lambda s\bar{Y} = \lambda I$, whereupon $\bar{Y} = I/s$. That is, the equilibrium rate of national income equals the rate of autonomous investment divided by the marginal propensity to save.

This is the simplest version of the Phillips model, and it yields an expression that describes the time path of national income. It is, in effect, a dynamic multiplier model. The economic system that it models is depicted in Figure 3.5. Additionally, we can introduce a second dynamic feature in the form of investment that takes place in response to output *changes*. As depicted by the dashed lines in Figure 3.5, this so-called *induced investment*, denoted I_n, enters the model in two ways. First, it enters in the same manner as autonomous investment. In this case, then, Equation (3.15) is revised to read

$$D = (1 - s)Y + I + I_n \tag{3.19}$$

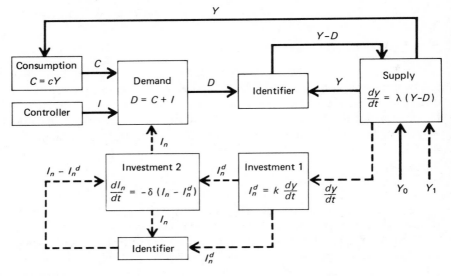

FIGURE 3-5

Second, it enters via its relationship to the change in output, dY/dt. In particular, Phillips assumes a linear *accelerator*

$$I_n^d = k[\frac{dY}{dt}]$$ (3.20)

where $k > 0$ is the investment coefficient, so that the *desired* rate of investment induced by the change in output, denoted I_n^d, is proportional to the output change. But, the *actual* rate of induced investment need not equal the desired rate. Indeed, I_n is assumed to lag behind I_n^d, with the discrepancy between them equaling

$$I_n - I_n^d = I_n - k[\frac{dY}{dt}]$$ (3.21)

Induced investment changes over time so as to remove this discrepancy;

$$\frac{dI_n}{dt} = -\delta(I_n - k[\frac{dY}{dt}])$$ (3.22)

A linear adjustment function is again assumed where, as in the case of λ, $\delta > 0$ is a measure of the speed of response of induced investment to discrepancies from its desired rate.

As shown in Appendix 3.2, this more complex dynamic multiplier-accelerator model is also reducible to a single differential equation. Now, however, it is a second-order equation that, given a *pair* of initial conditions Y_0 and Y_1, yields the time path of national income and hence of induced investment, with the equilibrium income rate of $Y = I/s$ determined as before. Although the latter model does not in itself offer policy makers a means of regulating economic activity, it is amenable to yet a further refinement that does. Specifically, government expenditure of G can be introduced into Equation (3.19), as induced investment was previously introduced into Equation (3.15). And, as with induced investment, the *planned rate* of government expenditure, G_p, will not necessarily equal actual expenditures. Rather, actual expenditures are assumed to lag behind the planned rate, which introduces yet another lag effect into the model. Now, however, planned expenditures become an instrument whose purpose is to stabilize economic activity; that is, to dampen national income fluctuations.

Phillips considers three forms of stabilization policy, each of which specifies a different functional relationship between G_p and Y: (1) planned expenditure is inversely proportional to the difference between the actual and target rates of national income; (2) planned expenditure is inversely proportional to the cumulated difference between national income and its desired rate; and (3) planned expenditure is inversely proportional to the rate of change in national income. Mathematically, these three policies can be written: (1) $G_p = -g_1(Y - Y^*)$; (2) $G_p = -g_2 (\int_0^t (Y - Y^*)dt)$; and (3) $G_p = -g_3[dY/dt]$. Assuredly, these policies may be applied either individually or in combination. Then, as before, we assume a linear corrective factor to remove the discrepancy between planned and actual expenditure, or

$$\frac{dG}{dt} = -\theta(G - G_p) \qquad\qquad (3.23)$$

where, again, $\theta > 0$ is a speed-of-response constant.

Depending on the form of stabilization policy, the resulting differential equation might be quite difficult to solve. The solution, however, will generally yield as measures an *initial* rate of government spending, *as well as* a spending time path required by the particular policy. Nonetheless the simplicity of the model's structure, the sensitivity of the model to the parameter estimates, and the complexity of its solution, combine to make it a useful analytical device *suggesting directions* that stabilization policies might follow, as opposed to suggesting the specific policies themselves.

d. Multi-equation econometric policy models

Following on the heels of Tinbergen's econometric modeling of structural relationships, a series of multi-equation econometric models designed to aid in policy formulation have been developed during the past two decades. Their scope has ranged well beyond that of Tinbergen's original conceptions, as the collection of more extensive time series of reliable data, advances in econometric methodology, and advances in computer technology which have made it feasible to estimate the parameters of large and complex systems of equations, have encouraged the more detailed description and specification of the interrelationships that determine an economic system's structure. The most prominent models in this category are the Klein-Goldberger,[9] Brookings-SSRC,[10] and Wharton [11] models.

The original Klein-Goldberger model of the U.S. economy was fitted to *annual* data for the 1929–1952 period. The model consists of twenty equations, five of which are definitional and fifteen behavioral. The twenty endogenous variables include eleven targets, such as consumer expenditures and corporate profits, and the eighteen exogenous variables include nine fiscal policy instruments, of which six are tax variables and three are spending variables, and a single monetary policy instrument, excess reserves as a percent of total reserves. This model is the prototype for the more recent models developed at the Brookings Institution, some of which have extended to over three hundred equations, incorporated more than one hundred variables, and been fitted to quarterly data for periods as long as thirteen years.

As implied by the greater number of equations and variables, the latest large-scale models are constructed at a much higher level of disaggregation and with considerably greater detail than was true of their predecessors. The basic structure of these models is *block-recursive*. This means that certain endogenous variables are functions solely of a set of the exogenous variables and the past rates of some of the endogenous variables, whereas other endogenous variables are directly influenced by exogenous variables and predetermined rates of endogenous variables, as well as by *current rates of other endogenous variables*. The recursive appellation stems from the fact that current rates determined for some of the endogenous variables can influence future rates of these and other endogenous variables. The block appellation stems from the fact that the endogenous variables themselves can logically be grouped into various "blocks." Thus, there is one block of endogenous variables whose rates are determined by the exogenous variables and the past rates of endogenous variables. There are also blocks of "price" variables and blocks of "quantity" variables, and so forth.

Recursive policy models are of particular interest because their structure reveals the chain of *causality* among the variables. This helps to distinguish the direct and indirect effects of policy measures. In particular, endogenous variables of the *first order* are those that are influenced only by exogenous variables and each other. Thus, where y_{1i} is an exogenous variable of the first order, z is a vector of exogenous variables, and y_1 is a vector of first-order endogenous variables not including the ith, $y_{1i} = f_{1i}(z, y_1)$.

[9] L. Klein and A. S. Goldberger, *An Econometric Model of the United States, 1929–1952* (Amsterdam: North-Holland, 1955).
[10] J. S. Duesenberry *et al.* (eds.) *The Brookings Quarterly Econometric Model of the United States* (Amsterdam and Chicago: North-Holland; Rand McNally, 1965).
[11] The Wharton Quarterly Econometric Forecasting model was first specified in 1965 and revised in 1968/69. See M. K. Evans and L. R. Klein, *The Wharton Quarterly Econometric Forecasting Model*, Wharton School of Finance and Commerce, University of Pennsylvania, Studies in Quantitative Economics, No. 2. Its successor is the Mark III. See, M. D. McCarthy, *The Wharton Quarterly Econometric Forecasting Model Mark III*, Wharton School of Finance and Commerce, University of Pennsylvania, Studies in Quarterly Economics, No. 6, 1972.

Similarly, endogenous variables y_{2j} of the *second order* are influenced only by each other, the exogenous variables and endogenous variables of the first order. They do not influence endogenous variables of the first order. Thus, where y_2 is a vector of second-order endogenous variables not including the jth, $y_{2j} = f_{2j}(z_{1i}, y_{1i}, y_1, y_2)$. Clearly, *each* variable need not appear in both f_{1i} and f_{2j}. And, in analogous fashion we would write

$$y_{nk} = f_{nk}(z, y_{1i}, y_1, y_{2j}, y_2, \ldots, y_{n-1,r}, y_{n-1}, y_n) \tag{3.24}$$

Thus, once a suitable exchange policy, say, has been determined, a certain wage policy may be achieved in order to determine full employment; and, once this is accomplished, other instruments may be used so that a certain balance-of-payments figure will be achieved. The extent to which a multi-order chain of causality can be developed will depend on the degree of interdependency among the endogenous variables, and whether certain "one-way" patterns can be detected and isolated.

The block-recursive system parallels the multi-level organization consisting of a hierarchy of subsystems. Here, in effect, the supremal unit—the policy makers—send exogenous inputs to the economic system. The highest-order infimal subsystems react to these and other exogenous inputs, and may interact with each other before reaching decisions and transmitting physical outputs or informational outputs to the next-highest order of infimal subsystems, and so forth. The econometric model attempts to portray and estimate the input-output process, either for physical *or* informational flows.

From the policy standpoint, one of the major advantages of a detailed econometric model is that it provides a convenient medium for *experimentation* with alternative policies. This experimentation is carried out through a series of *simulations* in which the inputs of the different instruments controlled by the policy makers are shifted in order to study *how* the various targets are affected, the *sensitivity* of the targets to changes in the instruments, as well as *why* past policies were ineffective and what the correct policies would have been. To achieve this, the instrument variables must be appropriately defined so as to make them amenable to direct control. Thus, in the larger Brookings and Wharton models, tax variables are defined in terms of tax *rates* that can be altered rather than tax receipts that might be effected; and in the Brookings model, say, the monetary sector is described by almost thirty equations with, for example, the interest rate becoming a key variable, and one whose impact can be fully explored.

Evaluation of the results of such simulation experiments implies the need for a well-defined set of targets and preferences. With a quarterly model, these will tend to be short term in nature. As a result, planning with the model will be oriented toward short-term stabilization rather than long-term growth. Thus, while the model's detail, scope, and complexity take it far beyond Tinbergen's original specification, the difference is one of degree rather than character. Nonetheless, it is sufficient to negate the possibility of an analytical solution, which accounts for the use of simulation as the means of exploring for appropriate policy decisions. Alternatively, the econometric model can be used by specifying values for the *dependent* variables—including the targets—and then solving for the *independent* variables to determine the values that they would *have to* assume in order to effect the specified values for the dependent variables. The model can therefore also be used to help determine the policies necessary to achieve given objectives.

3.4 A SUMMARY VIEW

The Tinbergen model and its successors have thus far made what is perhaps their greatest contribution in providing a basic structure for the development and analysis of policy decisions. The specific models built within this structure have all been suggestive rather than definitive. As such, they have brought out a series of defects. Some of these have been subsequently corrected, while others remain a source of current attention and concern. The resolution of all these defects will not necessarily be readily achieved, if indeed it can ever be achieved. In any event, the issue of modeling gives rise to four important theoretical possibilities that should be noted: (a) that the model has a "solution" that can be found by standard algorithms; (b) that the model has "solutions" in the sense that their existence can be proved, even if they are difficult if not impossible to locate except by happenstance; (c) that the model has no solution; and (d) that we cannot clearly decide upon the appropriate model. These possibilities must be borne in mind by the model-builder and, indeed, they may ultimately dictate the model that is built, or the degree of reliance and credibility given to the inferences drawn from the modeling exercise.

Although it is conceptually feasible to build into a model the capability to handle *qualitative* shifts in the economic structure, such as occurs with the onslaught of an unaccustomed and unanticipated prolonged period of peace, lack of experience with such dramatic shifts makes model reliability under these circumstances somewhat suspect. Thus, regression parameters estimated from time-series data during the cold war and a series of warm-to-hot wars will not necessarily be valid during a protracted peace. Further, because of the *time required to assemble and amass data,* it may be impossible to obtain parameter estimates in time to employ a model for policy purposes a priori, rather than ex post.

A perennial concern of policy models is the *classification of variables.* Yesterday's irrelevant variable, say the balance of payments, can become today's target and tomorrow's instrument. Yet, this distinction is important, because it will influence the model's structure. Moreover, what is an *appropriate structure* and *level of disaggregation* for one set of instruments and targets will not necessarily be appropriate for another.

Above all, it must be remembered that a *model is not reality:* the forecasts generated will be *estimates;* the outcomes anticipated need not be realized; and, neither the model nor the economic system itself will necessarily be adaptable to change, or able to learn from and automatically adjust for previous errors. Policy makers can benefit from formal models, but by the same token, formal models can benefit from policy makers' and technicians' judgmental and informational inputs. These inputs could, for example, be used in the *original* estimation of regression coefficients, as in the Bayesian approach to regression. Alternatively, the so-called random disturbances that impact on the dependent variables might be random as far as the formal regression is concerned, but might often be at least in part predictable by knowledgable and alert economic managers and their staffs. Such abilities should not be wasted, but rather should be used, even if only informally, *in support of* the formal models.

A model is a *tool,* and the transformation of the prescriptions it yields into a set of policies will not ordinarily be a frictionless transformation. Policy must be *implemented,* and the techniques for enforcing and carrying out a control measure may be crucial in determining its effectiveness. It is all too easy to become immersed in a model's technicalities, and to forget that because the model is not the reality it can only *suggest* policy. Even if it is a good model, the policies it suggests will not necessarily be readily implemented and controlled, nor will *all* their effects necessarily have been anticipated and considered. Models should be updated and refined. Most of all, however, they must be kept in proper perspective.

APPENDIX 3.1

To solve for the general solutions in the Mahalanobis model, observe that since Equation (3.7) is a first-order homogeneous difference equation, its solution will be of the form $I_t = ax^t$, where a and x are constants. Substituting ax^t for I_t in (3.7), it is immediately determined that $x = (1 + \lambda_1\beta_1)$. The initial condition is a given investment rate I_0 at time $t = 0$ whereupon $I_0 = ax^0 = a$, so that

$$I_t = (1 + \lambda_1\beta_1)^t I_0 \tag{3.9}$$

Substituting (3.9) into (3.8), we determine

$$C_t = C_{t-1} + \beta_2\lambda_2(1 + \lambda_1\beta_1)^{t-1} I_0 \tag{3.10}$$

The solution to this equation is somewhat more complex, consisting of the sum of a homogeneous solution of the form $C_{th} = ax^t$ and a particular solution of the form $C_{tp} = Bb^t$. These solutions are determined to yield the general solution

$$C_t = C_{th} + C_{tp} = C_0 + \frac{\beta_2\lambda_2}{\beta_1\lambda_1}[(1 + \lambda_1\beta_1)^t - 1] I_0 \tag{3.11}$$

with Equation (3.12) determined from $Y_t = C_t + I_t$.

APPENDIX 3.2

To solve for the general solutions in Phillips' dynamic multiplier-accelerator model, substitute (3.19) into (3.16), to determine

$$\frac{dY}{dt} = -\lambda Y + \lambda(1-s)Y + \lambda I + \lambda I_n \tag{3.25}$$

Solving in terms of I_n,

$$I_n = \frac{1}{\lambda}\frac{dY}{dt} + sY - I \tag{3.26}$$

Now, differentiating with respect to t,

$$\frac{dI_n}{dt} = \frac{1}{\lambda}\frac{d^2Y}{dt^2} + s\frac{dY}{dt} \tag{3.27}$$

since $dI/dt = 0$ because I is assumed fixed. Equating the latter expression for dI_n/dt to that in Equation (3.22), combining terms and substituting for I_n from Equation (3.26), we determine

$$\frac{1}{\lambda}\frac{d^2Y}{dt^2} + (s + \frac{\delta}{\lambda} - \delta k)\frac{dY}{dt} + \delta sY = \delta I \tag{3.28}$$

This equation is a second-order differential equation whose solution, like that of the first-order equation of the simpler model, is of the form $Y_t = ae^{rt}$. After computing dY/dt and d^2Y/dt^2 and substituting, this equation can be solved to yield the time path of national income, and hence of induced investment, given a *pair* of initial conditions. In particular, letting $\lambda s + \delta - \lambda\delta k = c_1$, and $\lambda\delta s = c_2$, the homogeneous part of (3.28) becomes

$$\frac{d^2Y}{dt^2} + c_1\frac{dY}{dt} + c_2Y = 0$$

Substituting $d^2Y/dt^2 = ax^2e^{rt}$ and $dY/dt = axe^{rt}$,

$$ax^2e^{rt} + c_1axe^{rt} + c_2ae^{rt} = 0,$$

or $x^2 + c_1 x + c_2 = 0$,

and $x = \dfrac{-c_1 \pm \sqrt{c_1^2 - 4c_2}}{2}$

Hence, the homogeneous solution is

$$Y_{th} = a_1 e^{\frac{-c_1 + \sqrt{c_1^2 - 4c_2}}{2} t} + a_2 e^{\frac{-c - \sqrt{c_1^2 - 4c_2}}{2} t}$$

The particular solution, found by setting $dY/dt = d^2Y/dt^2 = 0$, is $Y_{Pt} = I/s$.

The general solution is $Y_t = Y_{th} + Y_{Pt}$, and values for a_1 and a_2 are determined from the two initial conditions by solving the two simultaneous equations

$$Y_0 = a_1 + a_2 + \frac{I}{s}$$

$$Y_1 = a_1 e^{\frac{-c_1 + \sqrt{c_1^2 - 4c_2}}{2}} + a_2 e^{\frac{-c_1 - \sqrt{c_1^2 - 4c_2}}{2}} + \frac{I}{s}$$

CHAPTER 4

Performance Indicators: Preference Functions

4.1 ON "SOCIAL" PREFERENCE FUNCTIONS

In the previous chapters we have seen that an economy can be described as a hierarchical system that can be managed and controlled. At the lowest level, management can be accomplished through a set of decision makers each selecting instruments to inject as inputs into the system's economic process. Conceptually, control of each subprocess may be viewed as achieved via a feedback mechanism, or a computer that has as its transformation operation the decision maker's criterion function that translates informational inputs with respect to the variables—instruments and targets—of interest to the decision maker into a measure of overall subprocess performance. Such criterion functions are what is referred to in economic policy models as *preference functions*. Put otherwise, a preference function is the specification of the decision maker's desiderata, formulated in a meaningful and operational way, and then carried out through the manipulation of a set of controllable variables called instruments. At each successive level in the hierarchical structure, management by each decision maker constitutes an attempt on the latter's part to achieve some desiderata, as expressed in a preference function, subject to the constraining action of lower-level choice. At the upper level, then, the planner seeks to coordinate the actions of all lower-level agents, attempting to resolve or remove the conflict in preferences existing both within and among decision levels, in order to obtain a degree of system's performance compatible with some overall system's criterion function—often called society's *social preference function*. Thus in the general hierarchical policy problem the planner, as central decision maker, seeks to obtain the objectives of a policy-making body, as expressed by a well-defined social preference function to be optimized, or a set of prespecified target rates to be achieved, subject to the decisions of lower-level agents as expressed in a set of structural constraints and boundary conditions on the instruments and, perhaps, the targets. In defining the social preference function, determining the constraints, and specifying the instruments and targets, very complex issues arise. These issues do not resolve themselves, nor can they be ignored. There are, however, various approaches to dealing with them, and these draw our attention in the last three chapters of Part I.

The concern of this particular chapter is the *social preference function*. This preference function—determined by a man or woman, a small group of people, a parliament, or the whole population through a plebiscite—is, as Frisch puts it, the opposite of economic structure; it is indeed what the authority—by whomsoever represented—"would like to see realized disregarding provisionally the question whether it is feasible or not structurally." [1] The formulation of such a function may well be the most nebulous issue of all, inasmuch as it involves the personal and societal desiderata that policy makers are presumed to respect in the decision-making process. The basic questions that we must examine in this respect are: (1) How do we relate in terms of a preference function what the individuals or groups of individuals within a society want, and what the policy makers want? (2) How do we "formalize" the policy makers' desiderata? (3) How do we coordinate and systematize the preferences from a quantitative point of view? (4) How do we cut through the myriad of possible alternatives to select the most relevant ones? (5) How do we draw their bounds and test their feasibility?

To get a feel for the almost overwhelming magnitude of the problem of defining a social preference function, consider a society that divides evenly into two groups, or more precisely into two *teams*. Suppose that the teams must choose between all guns $= G$ and all butter $= B$, or else indicate indifference between these choices. Each team is asked to vote as to whether guns are preferred to butter $(G \wr B)$, butter is preferred to guns $(B \wr G)$, or whether the team is indifferent between which is chosen $(G \sim B)$. Because these are teams in the formal sense, the vote will be unanimous: by definition, the members all have common interests. Given the two equally strong bloc votes, the policy makers need some social preference function—or here, in a sense discussed below, more aptly a decision rule or *constitution*—to choose between guns and butter.

The decision rule can be written $W = w(T_1, T_2)$ where T_i is the preference of team $i = 1, 2$. With two choices yielding three possible votes, and two teams, there are $3^2 = 9$ possible vote combinations: $(G \wr B, G \wr B)$, $(G \wr B, B \wr G)$, $(G \wr B, B \sim G)$, ... , $(G \sim B, B \sim G)$. Suppose that the function assigns numbers $+1$, 0, and -1 to any combination, where $+1$ indicates that guns is "society's choice" (because that is how the function is set up), 0 indicates "indifference" (so that the policy makers can decide by, say, the flip of

[1] R. Frisch, *An Implementation System for Optimal National Economic Planning Without Detailed Quantity Fixation from a Central Authority* (Oslo: Institute of Economics, January, 1963), p. 13.

a coin), and -1 indicates that butter is "society's choice." The following possible assignments exist:

$$w(G \wr B, G \wr B) = +1; -1; 0$$
$$w(G \wr B, B \wr G) = -1, +1; 0$$
$$w(G \wr B, B \sim G) = 0; +1; -1$$
$$w(B \wr G, G \wr B) = +1; -1; 0$$
$$w(B \wr G, B \wr G) = -1; +1; 0$$
$$w(B \wr G, B \sim G) = 0; +1; -1$$
$$w(B \sim G, G \wr B) = +1; -1; 0$$
$$w(B \sim G, B \wr G) = -1; +1; 0$$
$$w(B \sim G, B \sim G) = 0; +1; -1$$

As there are three possible numerical assignments or choices for each of the nine vote combinations, there are $3^9 = 19{,}683$ possible decision rules. For example, the three columns indicate three such functions; but taking the first number in the first column ($+1$) and attaching it to the other two columns in place of the -1 and 0, respectively, yields two more functions, and so forth—for a total of an additional 19,680 functions.

Certainly, some of these 19,683 functions are frivolous. Thus, $w(G \wr B, G \wr B)$ should surely be assigned $+1$, and lead to guns, and $w(B \wr G, B \wr G)$ should surely be assigned -1, and lead to butter. Similarly, $w(G \sim B, G \wr B)$ and $w(G \wr B, G \sim B)$ should never *automatically* select butter (and, indeed, the Pareto criterion, which urges the choice of the alternative that makes somebody better off and nobody worse off, would argue for guns), and $w(B \wr G, B \sim G)$ and $w(B \sim G, B \wr G)$ should never select guns. Even then, in the absence of a dictator choosing counter to both groups, there are $(1)^3(2)^4(3)^2 = 144$ possible decision rules. And, in this instance, there are only two blocs of voters and two choices.

To specify a meaningful social preference function is, then, an exceedingly difficult problem for the policy maker. Resolution of this problem involves three distinct, yet intimately related aspects: (1) individuals' preference functions as such; (2) group preference functions as such, where the policy makers must mediate among the groups; and (3) the policy makers' preference function. These distinct aspects mean that the definition of a social preference function can be attacked from either of two different angles. On the one hand, policy makers can attempt to specify a decision rule that abstracts from their own views and provides a social preference function that translates individual or group preferences directly into system preferences. On the other hand, policy makers can attempt to specify a social preference function, giving weight to their own views, and presumably those of their constituents—either as individuals or interest groups—as they interpret the latter's views. The former situation commonly arises in writing a constitution that determines who will assume the policy makers' role, and, in many instances in which the policy makers are either reluctant or prohibited from acting on their own, determines the measures that the society's members—as a group—prefer or prevent. Indeed, in both Eastern and Western systems, the problem of defining what is meant by information is compounded by the possibility that decision makers at all levels may want to hide their true preference functions—that is, *distort* the information that is provided to, say, decision makers at other levels, technicians, and constituents. This could be a major roadblock to rational policy making in any type of system! The latter situation commonly arises in the policy makers' day-to-day job of making policy and selecting among alternative courses of action.

4.2 INDIVIDUAL VERSUS SOCIAL PREFERENCE FUNCTIONS

The neoclassical conception of a social preference function is Bergson's social welfare function.[2] Here, *social* welfare is a reflection of *individual* preference orderings in the Marshallian sense. In particular, let $U^j = u^j (q_1^j, \ldots, q_i^j, \ldots, q_m^j)$ denote the Marshallian utility function of the jth individual, where q_i^j is the amount of the ith entity ($i = 1, \ldots, m$) allocated to the jth individual ($j = 1, \ldots, n$). Then the Bergsonian social welfare function is given by

$$W = w(U^1, \ldots, U^j, \ldots, U^n) = w(q_1^1, \ldots, q_i^j, \ldots, q_m^n)$$

In practice, such a unanimously agreed upon function will not exist, because no set of observers possesses a mandate to make the ethical judgments necessary to specify the unique interrelationships between the individual functions which will allow "equitable" trade-offs between the society's members. Lacking this, most societies rely upon the market mechanism to accomplish a distribution of goods and services in accordance with the members' preferences. In fact, however, although a social welfare function capable of handling *all* problems of societal choice may never have actually been formulated, conceptually it does exist, and its conceptual existence provides certain *broad* policy guidelines to handle *some* problems of social choice. Thus, we expect the function to have the property that if some combination of the q_i^j say Q_1, is *preferred to another combination* Q_2 by at least one individual, and Q_2 is not preferred to Q_1 by any individuals, then Q_1 should be the choice of any social action involving these two alternatives alone. This rule may be applicable to a limited number of situations, and it provides a useful guideline when such situations arise; but it will not lead to a universally applauded ordering of *all* alternatives.

Even a cursory consideration of the issues involved makes apparent the pitfalls and difficulties that any entire population, a small group of policy makers, or a single individual would encounter in attempting to define a preference function to guide social policy. In point of fact, it would be difficult enough to secure agreement as to the desiderata, to say nothing of the acceptable trade-offs between their various levels. In the United States, for example, neither God, Motherhood, nor the Flag has succeeded in retaining its erstwhile position as a *universally* accepted desideratum. There are differences in the value judgments of different politicians of the same party, of the same party at different times, of different parties at different times, and the public at large and the various pressure groups within the public at large at all times. Indeed, Dorfman

[2] A. Bergson, *Essays in Normative Economics* (Cambridge, Mass.: Harvard University Press, 1966), pp. 27–49.

has suggested [3] that in fact "social preferences" do not exist. What exists are *groups* with preferences, groups that coalesce and "trade-off" certain preferences when they coalesce. These groups form coalitions that, although themselves lacking in objectives, are comprised of interest groups, say teams, that do have coinciding objectives.

To the extent that such groups and coalitions exist—and empirical observation suggests that they are universal—the resolution of problems of social choice involves elements of *game theory;* in particular, various *bargaining* principles, *voting* strategies, *arbitration* schemes, and the underlying theoretical bases for the evolution of various *coalitions.* In this instance, the individual's problem is either (1) to develop a *strategy,* including the formation of a coalition, that will best accomplish the individual's objectives in a *conflict* situation—that is, a situation in which there are conflicting preferences and differences of opinion as to the appropriate action; or (2) to develop an appropriate *compromise* solution among individuals or groups that have conflicting preferences. [4]

The policy makers' problem basically falls into the latter category. It is to accomplish for the citizenry and the interest groups that which they may not be able to accomplish on their own; that is, to act as an arbitrator, albeit an arbitrator subject to external pressures and internal biases, that effects compromises and interprets "the will of the people." To effect such compromises, it is tempting to assert that policy makers should seek to define a social preference function that reflects the various individual and group preferences "to the greatest extent possible." That is, it should be some sort of consensus that allows for a compromising of differences of opinion where such are not wholly irreconcilable. Unfortunately, however, even from the theoretical standpoint, to say nothing of the practical issues involved, this is at best a specious assertion, akin to requiring individual preference functions to reflect individual preferences. As is the case with individual preference functions, the development of a social preference function should also proceed from a set of prior axioms to which all "reasonable" persons would subscribe as a basis for social decision making. The difficulty here, however, is twofold. First, as we have already seen, even when society divides into two teams, and there are only two alternatives to choose between, a large number of decision rules can be defined for selecting between these alternatives. Second, even a finitely small set of such axioms will not necessarily be mutually compatible, and the choice of the axioms themselves will involve individual value judgments. This is the important thrust of Arrow's famous "Impossibility Theorem" and the controversy that has followed it. [5] Whereas Bergson's concern was in defining a social *preference* func-

[3] R. Dorfman, "Social Decisions Without Social Preferences," in M. Kaser and R. Portes (eds.) *Planning and Market Relations* (London: MacMillan, 1971), pp. 117–129.

[4] For an excellent overall discussion see R. D. Luce and H. Raiffa, *Games and Decisions* (New York: John Wiley, 1957).

[5] K. Arrow, *Social Choice and Individual Value* (New York: John Wiley, 1951). Also see, for example, G. Tullock, "The General Irrelevance of the General Impossibility Theorem," *Quarterly Journal of Economics,* Vol. 81, No. 2, May 1967; and J. Coleman, "The Possibility of a Social Welfare Function," *American Economic Review,* Vol. 56, No. 5, December 1966.

tion that would provide a welfare ordering for the society, Arrow's concern was with defining a social *choice* function—*a* decision rule—that would permit the *derivation* of a social ordering of alternatives *based on* knowledge of the individual or group orderings.[6] The "Impossibility Theorem" yields the conclusion that there exists no rule for social decision making—or in Arrow's terminology, there exists no *constitution*—that will always satisfy the bare minimum of requirements that "reasonable" persons would demand of such a rule.

Arrow suggests four basic conditions that might reasonably be required of a constitution: (1) Collective Rationality; (2) Pareto Principle; (3) Independence of Irrelevant Alternatives; and (4) Nondictatorship.

Collective rationality imposes upon the *social* decision-making scheme a basic property of the *individual's* Marshallian utility function; namely, the existence of a system of social choice that reflects a transitive ordering of a set of preferences. Thus, any ordering of preferences among alternatives implies a social choice function $W = w(\mathbf{Q})$ that associates higher numerical values to the more preferred choices, although the values do not themselves have cardinal significance. Here, whenever society's decision-making procedure—say a one-person, one-vote rule—would indicate that $\mathbf{Q}_j \succ \mathbf{Q}_k$, this will be reflected in the *assignment* of $W_j = w(\mathbf{Q}_j) > W_k = w(\mathbf{Q}_k)$.

The *Pareto Principle* states that when alternative $\mathbf{Q}_j$ is preferred to alternative $\mathbf{Q}_k$ by at least one individual, and all individuals that do not prefer $\mathbf{Q}_j$ to $\mathbf{Q}_k$ are indifferent between the two, then the social ordering should rank $\mathbf{Q}_j$ higher than it ranks $\mathbf{Q}_k$. In effect, the selection of $\mathbf{Q}_j$ rather than $\mathbf{Q}_k$ makes at least one individual better off without harming any other individual, and therefore the social decision-making scheme should select $\mathbf{Q}_j$ over $\mathbf{Q}_k$. That is, if for all individuals $\mathbf{Q}_j \succeq \mathbf{Q}_k$, and for at least one individual $\mathbf{Q}_j \succ \mathbf{Q}_k$, we *assign* $W_j > W_k$.

The *independence of irrelevant alternatives* requires that social decision making only be influenced by viable alternatives. Thus, suppose the constitution signals $\mathbf{Q}_j$ over $\mathbf{Q}_k$ as the preferred alternative when these are the only two possible choices. It should still signal this ordering between the same two choices even though there exists some *unavailable* alternative $\mathbf{Q}_k$ that might be preferred to both. Alternatively, when $\mathbf{Q}_j$ is ranked higher than $\mathbf{Q}_k$, the constitution should not lead to the choice of $\mathbf{Q}_k$ over $\mathbf{Q}_j$ simply because $\mathbf{Q}_r$ has now been introduced as a third possibility.

The requirement of *nondictatorship* is for for most of us the most palatable of this set of very palatable conditions. It asserts that there is no individual or interest group whose preference map automatically determines the social choice ordering for the society, except when all individual or group preferences coincide. That is, no individual can dictate the constitution irrespective of the preferences of the rest of the society; or, in effect, the individual should "count."

Despite the fact that none of these conditions is terribly controversial,

[6] K. Arrow, *op. cit.*

Arrow's *Impossiblility Theorem* asserts that there can be no universally applicable constitution simultaneously satisfying all four. A particularly appealing illustration of the theorem results from considering one of the more popular modes of social choice, majority rule, and applying it to a situation in which there are three alternatives, Q_1, Q_2, and Q_3. Suppose that for one-third of the population $Q_1 \succ Q_2$ and $Q_2 \succ Q_3$. Similarly, for one-third of the population $Q_3 \succ Q_1$ and $Q_1 \succ Q_2$; and for the final third of the population, $Q_2 \succ Q_3$ and $Q_3 \succ Q_1$. Then, from the first and second groups we discover that two-thirds of the population prefer Q_1 to Q_2, from the first and third groups we discover that two-thirds of the population prefer Q_2 to Q_3, and from the second and third groups we discover that two-thirds of the population prefer Q_3 to Q_1. In this case, then, a majority-rule constitution would not lead to a transitive ordering of alternatives, since $Q_1 \succ Q_2 \succ Q_3 \succ Q_1$—a somewhat disturbing development.

Since it is unlikely that anyone's sensibilities will be offended by any of the four conditions that have been suggested as reasonable requisites of constitutions, the Impossibility Theorem makes it clear that *any* rule for social decision making is necessarily going to offend *somebody's* sensibilities, and that there is no strictly *logical* constitution. Indeed, a further implication of the Impossibility Theorem is that there is no clear-cut way to determine which of the four conditions should be sacrificed in order to arrive at a constitution satisfying the other three—for, in fact, any set of the other three conditions can be satisfied if we are prepared to sacrifice the fourth, so long as we do not sacrifice collective rationality.

4.3 FORMALIZED PREFERENCE FUNCTIONS

Notwithstanding the difficulties involved, as a practical matter planners, as coordinators, require *some* preference function, and *some* set of value judgments to employ in the analysis of alternatives. Whether we or they like it or not, it is the policy makers' *responsibility* to define this function. Indeed, such definition is imperative for establishing priorities, evaluating performance, and assessing the impact of the measures taken by the center (supremal unit). Certainly, the planner will frequently express preferences in the form of inviolable *demands*—that is, constraints—that narrow down the set of feasible alternatives, and limit decisions; for example, *maximum* acceptable rates of inflation and/or unemployment, or *minimum* acceptable rates of economic growth and/or technological progress. Without an explicit preference function, however, preferences so expressed can only determine admissable decisions, without signaling the *optimal* decision. Certainly, too, the planner might always be able to immediately and correctly identify the preferred decision, especially if the possible alternatives are few in number; but this only indicates that there is in fact a preference function guiding selections. Formalizing and revealing this function would both assure consistent decisions that are in fact preferred, and perhaps permit the planner to take advantage of mathematical and computer-based algorithms for determining optimal solutions.

In the absence of dictatorship, the policy makers' job thus becomes one of "interpreting the will *and* the needs of the people"; therefore, the social preference function actually used to resolve problems of social choice is neither wholly a consensus or compromise of a set of individual preference functions, nor an overall welfare judgment with respect to society as a whole. Formally defined, a preference function is a *rule* that assigns to any variable or combination of variables—such as, for example, a commodity, a service, or an unemployment rate—a number such that the more preferred is a given combination, the higher is the number that is assigned to it. In particular, let $q_{ik}(i = 1, \ldots, m; k = 1, \ldots, n)$ denote the value of the ith variable in the kth combination. For example, q_{11} might be the unemployment rate obtained as a result of a particular project whose institution also effects given rates of inflation q_{21} and deficit spending q_{31}. Then, whenever combination $q_r = (q_{1r}, \ldots, q_{ir}, \ldots, q_{mr})$ is preferred to combination $q_s = (q_{1s}, \ldots, q_{is}, \ldots, q_{ms})$, the rule assigns a higher number to q_r than is assigned to q_s; when the two combinations are equally preferred, the rule assigns them the same number.

For actual policy-making purposes it is necessary to (1) formally define the *variables*, both targets and instruments to be incorporated into the function, (2) determine *whose* judgments and preferences are to be reflected in the numerical assignments, and (3) specify the *rule* for making the assignments. The product of this procedure will be a *cardinal preference function* generating numbers that *signal ordinal preferences*. Thus, whenever q_r is preferred to $q_s(q_r \succ q_s)$ the preference function $W = w(q)$ assigns $W_t = w(q_r) > W_s = w(q_s)$. Whenever q_r and q_s are equally preferred $(q_r \sim q_s)$ the function *assigns* $W_r = W_s$. Hence, the ex post *computation* $W_r > W_s$ is a *signal* of an earlier expression of the ex ante judgment $q_r \succ q_s$, and this preference may now be inferred. The *preference* relation " $\succ$ " therefore signals the ordinal relation " $>$," and " $=$ " signals " $\sim$ " because the ordinal preferences were the initial basis for making the earlier numerical assignments.

In principle, where q^t is the combination selected at time t, it is also possible to specify an *intertemporal* preference function $W^T = w_T(q^1, \ldots, q^T)$. The arguments of the function are the combinations of variables selected from the present time ($t = 1$) to some future time ($t = T$). In this preference function, as in all preference functions considered in this chapter, we assume a *finite time horizon* of T selection "points." This implies that although time is, of course, continuous, decision making takes place at discrete points on the continuum. This suffices for present purposes, inasmuch as planners and policy makers prefer to operate within finite horizons; but in later chapters, particularly Chapter 10, we shall also remark on preference functions having an infinite time horizon.

To derive a well-defined preference function demands a *systematic* exploration of the attitudes held by one or more individuals with respect to what may be an irreconcilable, if nonetheless relevant, set of desiderata and instruments, so that these attitudes might be meaningfully coordinated and quantified, and the optimal combination chosen from among the set of feasible alternatives. As *individuals* forced to allocate such scarce resources as income, time and personal energy among the myriad combinations of commodities and activities of which they might avail themselves, few consumers bother to *systematically* express their preferences, or to evaluate alternatives with the hedonistic precision implied in the theory of consumer behavior. Rather, consumers either grant themselves the luxury of the nonoptimal decisions that accompany the inability or unwillingness to apply the theory's decision-making calculus, or else they are forced to accept nonoptimal decisions because they do not know how to avoid these. Preferences are revealed in the market place by the choices made among *available* commodities. At a given set of prices, consumers elect to purchase some goods and to reject others. Frequently, however, the selections are made in at least partial ignorance of the available and feasible alternatives.

Policy makers, however, are not expected to take as cavalier an attitude toward the public policy-making process as most consumers take toward the personal decision-making process. This is so because the implications of a nonoptimal policy decision are usually much greater and far reaching than those of a nonoptimal personal decision, and because policy makers are accountable to constituents for their decisions. Policy making is a job that the citizenry ''hires'' policy makers to perform, and to perform well. As a consequence, policy makers are under pressure to provide a clear and precise definition of the preference function to be employed in the policy-making process.

In the present context, a preference function serves a twofold purpose. On the one hand, it provides (a) the objective function to be optimized in the policy-making problem, or (b) the performance criterion to evaluate how well the system is functioning and how effectively the controller has employed the available instruments, or (c) the feedback computer's informational input-output function that helps the economic managers to control the system and guide it in the desired direction. This is essential in systematic policy making. On the other hand, it provides a means of keeping the public at large informed as to the policy makers' goals, and what the policy makers consider to be acceptable trade-offs and compromises. In the former regard, it is to the policy makers' advantage to provide the technicians—the economists and their computers— with as much accurate and meaningful information as is required by their decision-making models. In the latter regard, it is also to the policy makers' advantage, or so they frequently presume it to be when donning their politicians' hats, to provide their constituents with no more accurate, meaningful, or plentiful information than is required by their efforts to placate the electorate and get its support. Thus, politicians tell the electorate that they favor more of everything that is ''good,'' such as higher employment and higher wages, and that they disdain everything that is ''bad,'' such as across-the-board price increases and personal taxes. Ordinarily, however, they fail to either acknowledge the incompatibility of many of these objectives, or to admit that despite their sincere interests in achieving *all* of these objectives, compromises will have to be made. One of the technician's problems is to determine the compromises that the policy makers are prepared to accept; that is, to formalize the preference function. As far as uncompromisable issues are concerned, these enter the policy-making calculus either through the constraints or the boundary conditions. Here, the policy makers are imposing mandatory *demands* on any policies that are selected.

One proposal for determining the preference function is a direct-interview procedure wherein an interviewer first attempts to elicit what policy makers *allege* to be acceptable trade-offs. The policy makers are then informed of the policy implications of these trade-offs. This feedback might prompt a revision of their initial statements in the light of the implied policies. Thus, for example, the policy makers might be asked to express a preference for, say, an x percent unemployment rate and a y percent rate of inflation, as opposed to an x' percent unemployment rate and a y' percent rate of inflation. The responses to a series of such questions would yield several points on the preference function. These could then be used to *approximate* the entire array of ordinal preferences.

Given the economy's structure as expressed in a series of constraints, and given the bounds imposed upon any solution, the approximating preference function would be optimized with respect to the decision variables in a hypothetical problem. The solution would then be presented to the policy-making body, and its members would then have the opportunity to analyze the solution and indicate those aspects of it that they approve, and those that they do not. The technician subsequently attempts to determine which of the initial statements—that is, which characteristics of the preference function—have led to the undesirable results. The policy makers then have the opportunity to reconsider their initial statements and alter those to which they do not have an unwavering allegiance. Alternatively, they may simply have to face up to the fact that, given the economy's structure, some of the consequences of their preferred decisions will be objectionable. In essence, they will either have to (1) correct the errors and inconsistencies that have been called to their attention, (2) alter the preference schedule that will guide policy, or else (3) accept a solution that they really do not like at all. Once the initial statements have been reconsidered and perhaps revised, the procedure is repeated. This process continues through a succession of revisions until an "acceptable" solution, perhaps a *local* maximum, is achieved. Unhappily, the *global* maximum may remain obscured.

Essentially three approaches for developing the preference function have been suggested in the literature. In the first of these—the so-called "Santa Claus" approach—the policy makers express their desiderata, and the analysts then attempt to define the function that would capture these expressions of preference. In the second approach—that involving the establishment of a "Basic Policy Chart"—the analyst provides a graphical description of the infinite variety of policies available to the policy-making body, in combination with the consequences associated with each. This enables the policy makers to directly choose the most preferred plan and its consequences, without forcing them to establish a *complete* preference ordering. The third approach—that involving the "Establishment of a Set of Priorities"—requires the policy makers to establish a priority ordering over the various desiderata. Weights attached to each of the desiderata permit the computation of an overall index for ranking any policy or project. Other schemes have been suggested, but they are basically variants of these three, which we now consider in greater detail.

a. The "Santa Claus" approach

The *Santa Claus* approach is so-named because in this approach the policy makers are first asked to suppose they are in the presence of a beneficent visitor—presumably bearded and dressed in red—who is both willing *and* able to grant any requests that they might make with respect to the economy. It is implicitly assumed, although the assumption is not necessarily valid, that under these circumstances policy makers can blank their minds of the *realistic* restrictions of which they are aware, and in the process come up with a list of outcomes that they would most prefer—the desiderata. In the second stage, the policy makers are asked to choose between any two of the desiderata, or different rates of the desiderata, when given a free choice as to which of the alternatives will be bestowed upon the society by "Santa Claus." It is supposed that a series of such paired comparisons will provide the analyst with sufficient insight into the policy makers' thoughts to permit an *approximation* of an overall preference function.

The "Santa Claus" approach puts into practice the theoretical precepts underlying problems of choice. It attempts to *force* policy makers to reveal their preferences. In the theory of consumer behavior under certainty, for example, it is assumed that individuals can order their preferences between any two entities or packages of entities. That is, when either q_s or q_r is certain to be received, the individual is capable of asserting that either (1) $q_s \succ q_r$, (2) $q_r \succ q_s$, or (3) $q_r \sim q_s$. It is further assumed that the "rational" individual that prefers q_v to q_s and q_s to q_r, also prefers q_v to q_r. This is the transitivity assumption, and it asserts that whenever $q_v \succ q_s$ and $q_s \succ q_r$, it should also be true that $q_v \succ q_r$. These "individual rationality" assumptions suffice for the derivation of a Marshallian utility function that fully describes the individual's *ordinal* preferences in a world of certainty.

Unfortunately, however, there can be a serious gap between *normative* standards of what is and what is not rational, and the *behavioral* standards of rationality under which we all live and under which policy makers reach decisions. Thus, the policy maker that asserts indifference between a GNP of 10.0 billions and a GNP of 10.00000000000000001 billions is unlikely to be accused of a loss of sanity; and a similar assertion with respect to a GNP of 10.00000000000000002 billions is also likely to be shrugged off, and so on up the line. Indeed, should this policy maker also assert indifference between GNPs of 10.9999999999999999 billions and 11.0 billions, our confidence in these judgments would remain unaltered. But, despite our appreciation of the policy maker's indifference between any single GNP rate and the rate that exceeds it by exactly .00000000000000001 billions, should the same policy maker indicate indifference between a GNP of 10.0 billions and a GNP of 11.0 billions, the citizenry might consider demanding a new election. That is, from a practical standpoint we do not necessarily insist that individual preferences be transitive, and we do not necessarily consider intransitive preferences to be "irrational." Indeed, just the reverse might be true—from a practical standpoint!

From the Marshallian utility function, one can determine the very important *rates of substitution* between any two variables. These rates are important because they reveal the change in the value of one variable that would be required to offset a change in a second variable so as to leave the individual indifferent between either of two combinations. In general, consider any combination $q = (q_1, \ldots, q_i, \ldots, q_m)$ where q_i is the value assumed by the ith variable. $U = u(q) = u(q_1, \ldots, q_i, \ldots, q_m)$ is the number assigned to the combination q. Totally differentiating, $du = (\partial u/\partial q_i)dq_i + (\partial u/\partial q_k)dq_k = 0$ when q_i and q_k are varied so as to leave the numerical assignment unaltered. Hence $dq_i/dq_k = -(\partial u/\partial q_k)/(\partial u/\partial q_i)$ is the rate of substitution that the individual is willing to accept between the two entities, while remaining indifferent between the resulting combinations.

Individual behavior under uncertainty provides a somewhat more complex situation, and requires several additional assumptions or *axioms* about "rational" decision making, beyond those of individual rationality. In this new context, it is further assumed that individuals can express indifference or preference between (a) a simple "lottery" in which some most preferred "prize" q_1 is offered with probability p and a least preferred "prize" q_m is offered with probability $(1-p)$, and (b) an alternative q_k to be received with certainty, where $q_1 \succeq q_k \succeq q_m$, and $\succeq$ is the relation "preferred or indifferent to." The individual's willingness to accept risk is indicated by the level of p at which the lottery and the certain alternative become indifferent. Denoting by $\tilde{q}_k = (p_k[q_1];$ $(1-p_k)[q_m])$ the *lottery* in which the most preferred prize q_1 is won with probability p_k and the least preferred prize is won with probability $(1-p_k)$, $\tilde{q}_k \sim q_k$ at p_k. With $\tilde{q}_k \sim q_k$, it is also assumed that the individual would accept the lottery $\tilde{q}_k$ in place of the certainty q_k, in any combination in which the latter appeared. It is further assumed that one is prepared to abide by the laws of probability, the sole concern being that, in any risky situation involving q_1 and $\tilde{q}_m$, $\tilde{q}_k \succeq \tilde{q}_j$ whenever $p_k > p_j$. That is, the individual seeks the highest probability of winning the most preferred prize, whenever the situation requires a choice between alternatives involving *only* the most and least preferred prizes. Then it is possible to establish a second *cardinal* relationship, $V = v(q)$, reflecting *ordinal* preferences *and* attitudes toward risk, such that $V_k = v(q_k) > V_j = v(q_j)$ *signals* $q_k \succeq q_j$. In the case of this relationship, there is, however, a distinctly cardinal aspect to the numerical assignments. In particular, they are linearly related to the *probabilities*—say, the p_j. Thus, in effect, the numerical assignments given to the "prizes" can be given a probabilistic interpretation; namely, they represent the probabilities of winning in a simple lottery involving only the best and worst prize, which is equivalent to the prizes in question. Thus they can be interpreted as having the same "cardinal virtues" as probabilities; notably, they reflect relative likelihoods.

The function, $V = v(q)$, is a von Neumann-Morgenstern utility or risk-preference function.[7] It provides the basis for determining optimal alternatives in risky situations. In particular, the previous axioms lead to the decision-making principle that the preferred decision is the one that maximizes *expected utility*. Assuredly, however, axioms that *seem* reasonable will not necessarily be followed in practice. Persons will not *necessarily* order preferences in a manner that is intransitive; persons will not *necessarily* choose the alternative that is consistent with their preference functions. In effect, persons will not *necessarily* make decisions in accordance with the axioms; that is, decision making in practice will not *necessarily* be a rational procedure. This does not imply, however, that persons desiring to make rational decisions and accepting the von Neumann-Morgenstern axioms would not alter their decisions should the decisions be determined to be at variance with those that maximize expected utility. As a corollary to the latter observation, persons that determine at the outset that they want to reach optimal—that is, most preferred—decisions, should immediately specify their utility functions, and should choose the decision that maximizes expected utility. Here, however, the term utility is used in the von Neumann-Morgenstern sense, and expected is used in the statistical sense. In general, then, Marshallian utility will be germane for resolving problems of individual choice under certainty, and von Neumann-Morgenstern utility will be germane for resolving problems of individual choice under uncertainty. Thus, Marshallian utility is relevant for a Tinbergen-type model, and von Neumann-Morgenstern utility is relevant for a Theil-type model.

Until recently, however, the problems of uncertainty were pushed into the background in policy analysis, and previous attempts to deal with the problems of *eliciting* preferences focused on certainty-related situations. Nonetheless, the subsequent discussions will be relevant for either situation.

As a *practical* matter, no individual ever could or ever would specify an entire preference map, either under certainty or uncertainty. Rather, an individual might be able to indicate several points on this map. The remaining points are then to be filled in by extrapolation. The "Santa Claus" approach rests on this philosophy.

The first stage in the process attempts to elicit variables such as rates of employment, gross national product, and inflation, which *should* be included in the preference function *because* they focus on issues of concern to the policy makers. The second stage attempts to determine sufficient points on the preference map to permit the analyst to make a "reasonable" approximation of the entire map through a series of extrapolations. In effect, the analyst uses interviewing expertise to help the *policy makers* concerned with *social choice* derive

[7] J. von Neumann and O. Morgenstern, *Theory of Games and Economic Behavior* (Princeton, N.J.: Princeton University Press, 1944). For a discussion of the distinction between von Neumann-Morgenstern utility and Marshallian utility see I. Horowitz, *Decision Making and the Theory of the Firm* (New York: Holt, Rinehart and Winston, 1970), pp. 340–343, 369–374.

preference functions equivalent to those that *individuals* are assumed to be capable of deriving on their own accord to resolve problems of *individual choice*. Given the policy makers' approximated preference function, the analyst can then determine the rates of substitution between any pair of the previously elicited desiderata.

As is true of individual preferences, the policy makers' preferences may change over time. Moreover, and particularly when the policy makers are indifferent, or close to being indifferent, between two alternatives, expressions of preference made at one point in time will not necessarily agree with those made at a second point, nor will they necessarily be an accurate reflection of the policy-making body's "true" feelings. It is therefore considered advisable to repeat the interviewing procedure several times, both in order to expand the amount of data gained with respect to the preference function, and to assure that accurate and up-to-date data are obtained.

Information can enter the analysis through several directions. Under uncertainty, for example, it can be employed to revise prior probability judgments so that the decision that maximizes prior expected utility will not necessarily maximize posterior expected utility. Alternatively, von Neumann-Morgenstern risk preference functions have been posited that *automatically* allow for changing preferences over time as the results of previous decisions are realized—that is, as new information is fed back to the decision maker.[8] In the present context, for example, the risk preference function $V = v(q)$ might instead be written as $V = v(q_0 + q)$, where q_0 denotes the "present stock" of the "prizes" contained in the project q. Thus, q_0 might be a vector of present GNP, employment, and balance-of-trade rates; q is the random vector of *increments* in these variables that is associated with a particular decision. Then, at a subsequent point in time a new project p will be evaluated in accordance with the function $v(p + q_0 + \bar{q})$, where $\bar{q}$ is the vector of increments in GNP, employment and balance of trade that were actually realized from the earlier decision.

In the Marshallian framework, we might simply consider preferences as changing over time as new information is received, or as the results of previous decisions are actually experienced. Thus, the package q_r that appeared to be preferable to q_s may no longer be so-judged once it has been received. In effect, the stock of information that the policy makers possess may influence their preferences. Hence, the preference function $W = w(x, y)$ might perhaps be written $W = w(x, y, H)$; that is, it is a function of the instrument and target rates, for a *given* stock of information available to the controller qua policy maker. As such, the objective function in the policy-making problem becomes a function of the policy makers' information, and the decision that is optimal for one stock of information will not necessarily be optimal for another.

Traditional attempts to elicit preferences have neglected the informational aspects, and instead have focused on determining preferences, given the

[8] In his "Risk Aversion in the Small and in the Large," *Econometrica*, Vol. 32, Nos. 1–2, January–April 1964, J. Pratt, for example, explicitly introduces the decision maker's wealth into the risk preference function.

stock of information actually possessed at the particular point in time. The principal advocate for accomplishing this via the direct-interview approach has been Ragnar Frisch.[9] Frisch has especially emphasized the importance of forcing policy makers to think in terms of broad desiderata as opposed to specific projects and the specific targets that they would affect. This separation permits the analyst to place in apposition with one another that which the policy makers prefer and the trade-offs they are *prepared* to accept, and that which policy can achieve and the trade-offs that the economic structure *forces* them to accept.

In effect, this procedure seeks to apply a very traditional model of economic decision making. On the one hand, the interviewing procedure is employed to derive a *subjective preference surface,* a two-dimensional cut of which yields the familiar indifference curve. The curves labeled W_1, W_2, and W_3 in Figure 4.1, for example, describe alternative rates of two policy objectives, I and C, which will leave the policy makers indifferent between two "packages" of I and C, and consequently describe the *ceteris paribus* trade-offs they are prepared to accept between these objectives. As with the individual's indifference curves, policy makers judge any combination of C and I on curve W_3 to be preferable to any combination on W_2; and, any point on W_2 is judged preferable to any point on W_1. But, each point on W_i ($i = 1$, 2, 3) is equally preferred.

On the other hand, the economic structure, including the state of technology, determines an *objective production-possibilities surface* or *frontier,* a two-dimensional cut of which yields the familiar production-possibilities curve. The curve labeled *PP* in Figure 4.1, for example, describes the *maximum* alternative rates of the two policy objectives, I and C, that the society is capable of achieving. The area between the curve and the axes therefore encompasses the set of *feasible* points from which the optimum will be selected. Given the strict concavity of the economy's production-possibilities curve and the strict convexity of the policy makers' indifference curve, the optimal policy is that which obtains at the point W^*. [10] This is the point of tangency of the curve *PP* and W_2, the highest indifference curve that can be reached under the structural constraints.

This policy-making framework, then, is refreshingly traditional. As will be discussed in the next chapter, the assumption that a sufficient, accurate, and descriptive production-possibilities surface can be developed for policy-making purposes does not seem too far-fetched in light of the significant advances made in econometric estimation techniques in recent years, and the constantly expanding volumes of data that are being gathered by government and industry sources worldwide. Moreover, any policy-making procedure must assume the availability of sufficient information to permit the generation of such a surface. Whether a set of policy makers can concur on a preference function, and

---

[9] R. Frisch, *General Outlook on a Method of Advanced and Democratic Macro-Economic Planning, op. cit.,* p. 18.

[10] Indeed, W^* is optimal so long as the convexity of the indifference curves is greater than that of the production-possibilities curve.

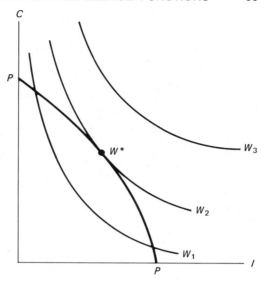

FIGURE 4-1

whether a series of interviews can be conducted that will produce sufficient information to enable an analyst to approximate this function—either for a group or even for a single individual—is, however, quite another matter.

It should nonetheless be stressed that each point on the production-possibilities frontier will be optimal for *some* set of preferences so that, in any event, we will want to choose a point on the frontier. Specifying a preference function eliminates the need for the economist to choose this point by default. Assuredly, in this world of highly diverse and differently motivated individuals, it is unlikely that the specific function employed in the analysis will correspond to the preference of all members of society, or indeed to those of all the policy makers. But it is vital that some effort be undertaken to recognize the considered judgment of those individuals to whom the regulation of the economy's affairs has been entrusted. It is in this spirit that the "Santa Claus" approach represents an ideal, although not one that is easily realized.

b. The basic policy chart

A *Basic Policy Chart* is a practical device intended to side-step the problem of establishing the policy makers' entire preference map. Instead, the chart attempts to offer policy makers a clear and comprehensive description of the *feasible* alternatives and their associated consequences, after eliminating choices that are necessarily nonoptimal because they promise, say, lower rates of a desideratum, such as employment, than that available from a feasible alternative that is the equal of those eliminated in all other respects. This description includes relevant information about the alternative rates of the desiderata that can be achieved, given the economy's structure, as well as information about

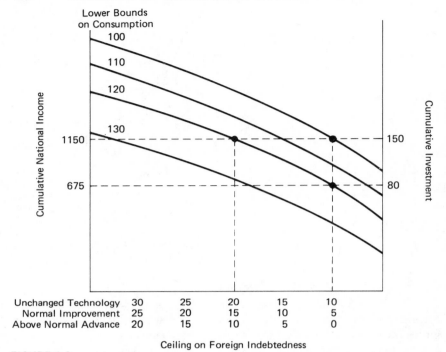

Unchanged Technology	30	25	20	15	10
Normal Improvement	25	20	15	10	5
Above Normal Advance	20	15	10	5	0

Ceiling on Foreign Indebtedness

FIGURE 4-2

the measures required to effect them. In terms of Figure 4.1, for example, each point on the production-possibilities frontier might be accompanied by a description of the measures necessary to achieve it. Points falling below *PP*, although achievable, would never be considered. Instead of initially posing to the policy makers a series of questions that would permit the derivation of the entire preference function, they would only be asked to select the preferred point on the *PP* curve.

Figure 4.2 is an illustration of a Basic Policy Chart. The term "basic" refers to the fact that the chart describes the interrelationships between the economy's *basic* components. The present chart has the same format as one developed by Frisch for the Egyptian economy.[11] Here, the imposed ceiling on foreign indebtedness is shown on the horizontal axis, the vertical axis on the left indicates the *attainable* cumulative level of national income during the planning period, and the vertical axis on the right indicates the *required* cumulative investment during the period.

Each of the curves represents the mix of three variables, income, investment, and foreign debt, for given *lower bounds* on private consumption. Implicit in the chart, then, is the assumption that specific projects have already been analyzed so as to determine for, say, a given peak rate of two in-

[11] R. Frisch, "Planning for the U.A.R.," *Economics of Planning*, Vol. 5, Nos. 1–2, 1965.

struments—foreign indebtedness and total investment during a specific planning period—the lower bounds on the target variables—annual private consumption and accumulated national income—that can be effected.

Thus, let us consider just a few of the alternatives among which, the chart suggests, policy makers can choose. With a foreign indebtedness ceiling of 20, policy makers that insist upon a lower bound on annual consumption of 120 can accomplish this with a cumulative investment of 150. The accompanying rate of accumulated national income will be 1150. This same lower bound on consumption of 120 can also be achieved with half as much foreign indebtedness; but, given the economy's structure, a total of 80 of investment is required, and accumulated national income will only reach 675. Alternatively maintaining investment at the previously noted figure of 150 and halving the foreign indebtedness to 10 reduces the lower bound on private consumption to 100, although maintaining accumulated national income at the previous level of 1150.

In a further expansion of the chart for the Egyptian case, Frisch has also provided the figures on the horizontal axis, the foreign investment ceiling, under various assumptions about technological progress. Thus, the first (upper) set of figures in the present chart might assume unchanged technology during the planning period. Additional sets of figures reflecting alternative assumptions about technological progress might also be presented. In the simplest case, for example, where there is a unique relationship between the ceiling on foreign indebtedness and technological progress, the relationship might be $D_1 = D_0 - 5$, where D_1 is the ceiling when there is a "normal" advance made in technology, and D_0 is the ceiling with unchanged technology, for $10 > D_0 \geq 5$. Similarly, we might also have $D_2 = D_0 - 10$, where D_2 is the ceiling with "above-normal" technological progress, for $D_0 \geq 10$. Thus, if there is normal technological progress, the same objectives can be accomplished with a given total of investment and reduced ceiling of foreign investment—reduced by five—as when technology is unchanged. In particular, with a ceiling of 15 on foreign investment and total investment of 150, a lower bound of 120 on consumption and an accumulated national income of 1150 can be obtained. When technological progress is above normal, the ceiling on foreign investment can be further reduced to 10, without affecting the objectives.

The present chart therefore encompasses five basic variables: foreign debt, technological progress, private consumption, accumulated national income, and cumulative investment. Technological progress can represent an instrument, a target, or a given datum. The foreign investment ceiling and total investment can be taken as policy instruments, with annual private consumption and accumulated national income as unequivocal targets. Then, with technological progress a datum determined in the environment, the policy makers' problem is to select among the alternative rates of the instruments those that, given knowledgeable judgments about technological progress, will combine with the effected rates of the targets into the most desirable package, as evaluated by a specific policy-making body.

The philosophy underlying the development of the Basic Policy Chart has considerable appeal: present policy makers with an easily comprehended picture of the alternatives and then let them choose for themselves. Unfortunately, as is true with graphical techniques in general, as soon as the number of relevant dimensions extends beyond four or five, it becomes impossible to adequately represent the alternatives in a single picture and manageable format. Thus, while the technique is of interest, its potential is severely limited, and its use is restricted to situations in which there are relatively few instruments and targets.

c. Establishing priorities

In asking policy makers to *establish priorities*,[12] the technician is implicitly requiring them to frame their preferences within a linear preference function wherein each target is assigned a weight in accordance with its priority ordering. On the one hand, the restrictiveness of the linearity assumption raises serious questions about the usefulness of the results and the validity of employing them in determining policy. On the other hand, the linearity framework forces policy makers to immediately think in terms of trade-offs between priorities, rather than trade-offs between particular target rates. In this procedure, the technician only requires the answers to a relatively small number of questions. We need not rely on any guesses or extrapolations to fill in the answers to unasked questions, because these are implied by the linearity assumption.

Suppose, for example, that there are m policy objectives; the rate of the ith objective is denoted q_i. The policy makers are then required to determine the number of units of the ith objective that they would be prepared to sacrifice for an additional unit of the jth. On the basis of the responses, and assigning the first objective, say, a weight of $w_1 = 1$, the ith objective is assigned a weight w_i. Then, with the first objective playing the role of numeraire, a preference index $W_k = \Sigma_i w_i q_{ik}$ can be associated to any particular policy, where q_{ik} is the rate of the ith objective obtained from the kth policy. The ratio w_j/w_i is the implicit rate of substitution that the policy makers assign between the jth objective and the ith. The policies can then be ranked in accordance with the values of the preference index that they generate.

The attraction of this approach is that once the weights have been assigned, alternative projects are readily ranked in order of preference, provided only that their effects can be forecast. Unfortunately, however, the linearity assumption is untenable. It is scarcely likely that policy makers will view *all* the various objectives as being substitutable for one another, and that the acceptable trade-offs will be independent of the specific rates of attainment. The approach is an obvious one, but its shortcomings are too serious to recommend its use.

In point of fact, *any* additively separable preference function $W = \Sigma w_i(q_i)$ raises similar concerns. That is, if $w_i(q_i)$ is a strictly concave func-

[12] United Nations, *Programming Techniques for Economic Development* (Bankok: United Nations, 1961).

tion the classical assumption of "diminishing marginal utility" is restored. But *all* the objectives remain noncomplementary, in the loose sense that, say, increases in the rate of one must be accompanied by increases in the rate of another in order to raise the welfare index. Thus, the rate of industrial output and the rate of exports, for example, are likely candidates for complementarity, since the relationship is symmetric, and increasing exports without increasing domestic output will ordinarily be undesirable.

d. Opportunities and commitments

Policy making is a *dynamic* process involving a series of decisions that have current impact, effect future opportunities, and entail future commitments. This occurs in two distinct ways. First, the controller makes decisions with respect to *assets* that can yield services over an extended period of time. Second, the controller may be concerned with the system's performance over some future time period, or at some future point in time, rather than "immediately."

The role that assets play in the preference function is unique, because assets are valued for the services that they are able to provide. But the exact timing and extent of these services will not necessarily be known in advance. In view of this, Koopmans has suggested incorporating as arguments in the preference function neither the assets nor the services, but rather the *opportunities* that the assets offer; that is, the future *opportunity* to draw upon the asset for services, without making a prior *commitment* to utilize these services at any particular time.[13] A hydroelectric dam, a government plane, and a military arsenal are examples of typical assets about which policy makers must make decisions.

The opportunity to use or not to use a particular service at any point in time carries with it the virtue of *flexibility* with regard to future choice. In the absence of a distinct preference for entering into commitments that remove uncertainty about the future, even though such commitments might result in decisions that will be regretted, policies that offer flexibility and deferred choices will, *ceteris paribus,* always be preferred to policies that do not, because new information, including feedback from previous choices, may become available, tastes and preferences may change, and new and unforeseen options may arise.

Firm *commitments* relating to the future can be dealt with in two basic ways. First, policy makers might be concerned with the system's performance at *each* point in time, over either some finite or infinite time horizon. Comparatively little successful research has been accomplished on this very difficult problem, about which we will have more to say in Chapter 10. The reason for this lack of success is apparent. Here, the system's measure of performance must be a *dynamic* or *intertemporal* social preference function that includes as its arguments the desiderata at each and every point in time, and thus the policy makers must not only specify acceptable trade-offs between targets at any point

[13] T. C. Koopmans, *Scientific Papers of T.C. Koopmans* (New York: Springer Verlag, 1970), pp. 243–254.

in time, but in addition they must specify acceptable trade-offs between targets, as well as for a given target, *over* time. Given this specification, the policy problem is to determine for the economic system a *continuously optimal* policy.

Alternatively, the exclusive focus of policy might be on the performance of the system at some specific future date. In this case, the variables entering the preference function relate solely to that target point, and we must deal with what is referred to as a *turnpike* preference function. [14] The fact that the rates of these variables at intermediate time points do not enter the social preference function implies that the effects on these variables at any point in time other than the target date can be ignored in determining a *terminally optimal* policy. Indeed, under these circumstances the "turnpike theorem" of balanced growth confirms that optimizing the preference function at the target date might mean that the optimum will not be most efficiently reached by the most obvious *direct* path. Rather, it will be achieved through an indirect route that, although in a sense roundabout, nonetheless permits a more rapid pace and hence an earlier arrival at the desired end. For example, to maximize consumption at some future date $t + n$, it might be best to accept consumption sacrifices during all earlier intermediate periods $t + i$ ($i < n$) in favor of additional increments in investment whose payoffs in consumption will be realized at $t + n$.

There are, however, two especially important considerations that should at least be mentioned in this connection. First, it is necessary to specify so-called terminal conditions in order to determine an optimal policy. For example, in virtually all policy problems it is necessary to specify a capital stock bequest for the generation beyond the terminal date. On the one hand, it can be argued that this future generation and such a bequest are "not our concerns." On the other hand, most of us, including policy makers, accept these as quite legitimate concerns, witness the current preoccupation with conserving resources and preserving the environment. Determining the amount of the bequest is therefore yet another "preference" that must be extracted from the policy-making body.

Second, it is not easy to impose sacrifices whose justification *is not obvious* to the electorate. Policy makers are therefore almost certain to be tempted by those objectives that have not yet been achieved when, at any intermediate time point, they are confronted with a choice between alternatives, and the one with the greatest short-term attraction will not be optimal in the long term. Insofar as they are truly operating with a turnpike preference function, however, the turnpike theorem suggests that this is a temptation that must be overcome.

4.4 PREFERENCES IN AN OPERATIONAL CONTEXT

The preceding suggestions for extracting the policy makers' preferences are not quite as practical as originally hoped by their proponents. Although the preference functions that have been posited make only the seemingly harmless as-

[14] S. Chakravarty, "Alternative Preference Functions in Problems of Investment Planning on the National Level," in E. Malinvaud *et al.* (eds.) *Activity Analysis in the Theory of Growth and Planning* (New York: Macmillan, 1967), pp. 150–166.

sumption that the transitive ordering of preferences can be accomplished by a policy-making body, or that the actual ordering can be approximated by a technician provided with partial information with respect to the complete ordering, the assumption may nonetheless be demanding too much of policy makers that are simply not prepared to compromise certain of their desiderata.

Hansen, for example, has suggested that policy makers tend to think in terms of absolute targets, such as full employment and price stability, and that even though these targets might not be mutually consistent, given the economy's structure, policy makers will be reluctant to compromise either target.[15] Indeed, this reluctance may stem from a very real *inability* on the policy makers' part to assess acceptable trade-offs between the targets. On the one hand, the policy makers' reluctance to assert a preference for, say, an x percent rate of inflation and a y percent unemployment rate, as opposed to an x' percent rate of inflation and a y' percent unemployment rate, might be interpreted as reflecting indifference between the two situations. On the other hand, the policy makers might in fact express very strong preferences for one situation or the other *if* they were aware of the full implications of each. But, policy makers that have been *conditioned* to think in terms of idealistic optima upon which we can *all* agree, might not *know* which of the two less desirable, if more feasible, alternatives they prefer, because they have not fully evaluated the potential impact of deviations from the optimum. Alternatively, where the absolute targets, say, *are* mutually consistent, these should be introduced into the problem via the constraints or the boundary conditions, and not solely through the preference function.

In essence, the operational problem is one of training—training policy makers to recognize and understand the sort of options among which they may be forced to choose, as they abandon the universally admirable desiderata to which they adhere when playing their politician's roles, and consider and evaluate the compromises with which they will be forced to live in their policy-making roles. This will not be an easy job, but the difficulty is by no means insurmountable.

4.5 CONCLUSION

Elements of Bergsonian welfare functions are present in the social preference functions specified by policy makers. In these preference functions, individual interests take a back seat to the interests of society as a whole; in these functions, policy makers must take into consideration what they judge to be individual preferences, and then make some value judgments as to the ordering of alternatives which would be best for the group, given these individual preferences. The specification of such a function is a practical necessity. In selecting the society's political leaders, its members are thus assigning their policy-making proxies to those individuals that have convinced them of their ability to make "sound" judgments about the social preference function.

Assuredly, the "selection" of the political leaders in a Western econ-

---

[15] B. Hansen, *Lectures in Economic Theory, op. cit.,* p. 130.

omy, and their responsiveness to the will of the people will not necessarily be mirrored in an Eastern economy; and, the desiderata and trade-offs that claim a place in the policy makers' preference function in a basically capitalist economy do not, as we shall see in detail in Part III, correspond with those in a Socialist economy. In this chapter we have been concerned with the *technical* issues and difficulties surrounding the specification of a preference function; but it is the political, economic, and social philosophies existent in the given society which ultimately determine its shape.

Moreover, as we have repeatedly emphasized, the economy is a hierarchical system with a number of controllers. Thus, while the supremal controller is essentially concerned with the social preference function, the infimal controllers will also be confronted with the need to establish some preference function. In a centrally administered economy—that is, in a fully controlled economy—the specification might be trivial; namely, *exactly* carry out the orders of the central authority. In a mixed economy, however, the preference function can be quite complex. Thus, management of a major corporation in a capitalist country will ordinarily gauge its performance not simply by the "business of business is business" criteria of profits, rate of return, sales, growth, and the like, but also by various criteria of *social* responsibility such as, for example, control of pollution, truth in advertising, and nondiscriminatory hiring practices. Whether the private firm *should* be "socially responsible" as an ethical-moral concern, or simply because it is "good business" to be so, is a debatable issue. In any event, however, it is an issue that the infimal controllers of these firms must resolve.

It appears, then, that the main questions surrounding the determination of the social preference function can still be best answered by relying on subjective beliefs, and its determination essentially rests with the policy makers. In the process, citizens' individual preferences, at least at the supremal level, are relegated to a secondary position, and the politicians' value judgements become of primary importance. Unlike the individual consumer's preferences which are revealed through the market, society's preferences are revealed through political channels. There also exists conflict between the policy-planner or economist, and the policy maker or politician. The former is primarily concerned with efficiency conditions and policy feasibility; the latter is preoccupied with social welfare. This is an ambiguous goal that, when not clearly defined, may apply to interest groups or political institutions, when it is actually intended to apply to the society at large.

CHAPTER 5

Instruments and Measures

5.1 NATURE OF INSTRUMENTS

The control variables that the policy makers can manipulate in seeking to achieve their objectives, or to improve the performance of the economic system, consist of three types of instruments: (1) an economic quantity such as a tax rate; (2) a legislative rule such as an antitrust regulation; and (3) a reform such as might be accomplished by a major revision in the structure of the agricultural sector, which effects a radical adjustment in the economy's institutional character.

On the one hand, then, economic quantities are quantitative instruments that affect neither the structure nor the foundation of the economic system, but rather deal solely with the magnitudes of those economic variables whose rates fall within the exclusive province of the government, as the system's controller, to determine. These instruments *could* be treated as exogenous inputs from the environment into the economic system. They are, however, more appropriately treated as inputs to the system from a governmental controller participating as one of the system's basic components. As such, particularly in a dynamic system with a feedback loop, these inputs might at one point in time evolve from the controller as an *exogenous input* to the actuator, and at a later point in time as an *endogenous output* from the controller or the actuator reacting to, say, an informational input from the feedback element and its computer. In neither event, however, is there any interference with either the couplings or the transformation operations of the system's components.

Legislative rules, on the other hand, are qualitative instruments that do not affect the foundation, that is, the basic *structure* of the economic system, but that do alter the details of social organization. These instruments, in effect, establish restrictions on the behavior of the system's individual components, but like the quantitative instruments, they do so without altering the basic couplings. Thus, the qualitative instruments either (1) restrict, or in some other manner influence, the inputs into and/or the outputs from some system component, or else they (2) influence the transformation operations that the components perform. Finally, reforms also represent qualitative instruments, but use of such instruments results in a substantial alteration in either a component's or the economy's structural organization. These changes, then, are those that are sufficiently fundamental so as to define what may eventually become a new economic system. A reform will therefore either (1) *radically* alter the transformation operation performed by a component so as, in effect, to replace an old component with a new one, or else it will (2) alter the couplings between existing components.

When an instrument is actually used in an economic policy, it becomes a *measure*. In the sense that economic policy requires some *positive action* on the government's part, the employment of a measure implies that a *change* has been made, either in some economic quantity within the existing institutional setting, or else in the setting itself; that is, in either the details or the foundations of the economy.

In this chapter we shall (1) discuss the particular instruments available to policy makers, (2) indicate how the Capitalist or Western nations, and how the Socialist or Eastern nations, have tended to differ in their employment of these instruments as measures, and (3) discuss some of the factors that have historically tended to be important considerations in dictating the choice of one instrument as opposed to another.

5.2 THE ARRAY OF INSTRUMENTS

a. The four primary classifications

In both Western and Eastern economics, policy makers have the same family of instruments at their disposal. *Quantitative* instruments include, besides direct controls and actions that affect the institutional setting, the traditional array of public finance and money and credit instruments. Often, the distinction between (a) newly imposed direct controls or the removal of existing controls, and (b) *fundamental* changes in the existing institutional framework becomes quite blurred. Thus, an instrument that some might view as a reform, might with equal conviction and logic be viewed by others as merely a legislative rule.

As part of one of the most important empirical studies of economic policy, Kirschen and his associates [1] surveyed nine Western nations in order to determine the instruments considered, and measures undertaken, by Western policy makers in the years following World War II. The results of this survey provide a useful basis for classifying, describing, and discussing the major policy instruments and measures.

The instruments of *public finance* are composed of government expendi-

[1] E. S. Kirschen *et al.*, *Economic Policy in Our Time* (Chicago: Rand McNally, 1964).

ture and revenue items. These items are the basic elements in the national budget. Thus, the use of these instruments involves a complex of budgetary and financial considerations, in addition to the policy objectives of most immediate concern.

The expenditure items consist of government spending for (1) collective goods, (2) so-called merit goods, and (3) transfer payments. Collective goods commonly make up the bulk of government spending. These range from public roads and national parks to nuclear arsenals and military forces; they are goods of which all members of the society can "take advantage." Merit goods, however, are only intended to benefit a specific segment of the population. Thus, "free milk" programs for school children and fellowship programs for scholars are grouped under merit spending. Finally, transfer payments are those for which services are not required; they are made by the government to benefit particular segments of the population. Social security payments and negative income tax payments would fall in this category. The distinction between merit goods and collective goods, or merit goods and transfers is, however, frequently a more theoretical than practical distinction, depending as it often does on the approach that one takes toward the item. A government contribution to the development of the arts, for example, would initially benefit a small group of individuals, but, theoretically at least, the ultimate effects might be enjoyed by all citizens; or, in any event, these *ultimate* benefits would be *available* to all citizens, should any be inclined to take advantage of them. Similarly, whether a "free milk" program bestows a merit good on a segment of the population, or whether it is merely a transfer payment enjoyed solely by this segment, is largely a matter of definition.

Musgrave [2] has provided a further convenient delineation of public finance items according to whether they have stabilization, distribution, or allocation purposes and effects. Although as will be indicated there is not a one-to-one correspondence between the latter classes and the previous expenditure groupings, one can, nonetheless, draw some important correspondences between them. In particular, spending for collective goods is commonly undertaken either for stabilization purposes, or in order to effect an allocation of resources that the society could not achieve on its own. As a practical matter, all citizens do not take advantage of collective goods, and hence these will ordinarily have effects on the distribution of society's resources. This, however, is a coincidental side-effect rather than a preconceived purpose. Similarly, transfer payments might be made in order to stabilize the economy, but their primary aim is to redistribute income from one segment of the population to another. Here too any effect on the allocation of resources is strictly an unanticipated by-product. Finally, insofar as merit goods have aspects of collective goods, their purpose will be to reallocate resources, and insofar as they have aspects of transfer payments, their purpose will be to affect the distribution of income. Again, however, this is not an inviolable rule.

[2] R. A. Musgrave, *The Theory of Public Finance* (New York: McGraw-Hill, 1959).

The revenue items consist of both the broad spectrum of taxes that the government might impose, and duties such as tariffs and tolls. As is true of the expenditures that these revenues are intended to finance, the method of collection can have stabilization, allocation, and distribution purposes and effects. Thus, the intent of an increase in the personal income tax rate might be to reduce the consumer's purchasing power in order to stem an inflationary tide, while an increase in the corporate tax rate might, in its most simplistic sense, be intended to help achieve a more equitable distribution of income between labor and the owners of capital. Similarly, by placing a high tax on tobacco products the government might hope to achieve a reallocation of the economy's resources into more productive pursuits that are less inimical to the health of the citizenry—both those who indulge and those who are innocent victims of the latter group's vice. Thus, while the *major* objective of, say, a liquor tax might be to raise revenues, the tax will also have allocation effects; and, while the *major* objective of a tariff on foreign goods might be to protect a domestic industry from foreign competition, this tariff will also raise revenues. Revenue-generating instruments will therefore ordinarily have two-pronged effects, and the policy makers must evaluate them in this light. In each of these cases, the policy makers' desiderata can be affected both directly and indirectly. In the former instance, for example, the allocation of resources *could* be a desideratum in the social preference function and, additionally, the revenues raised *could* in turn be used in a manner that affects other desiderata in the preference function. The *overall* impact of the tax on the economic system would then be evaluated by the "computer" which would accept informational inputs from the economic system, and transform these into a performance measure informational output via the social preference function that has been stored in it.

The difference between government expenditures and revenues—the government debt—is itself an important instrument of government policy, and not simply a by-product of the use of the expenditure and revenue instruments. In particular, the government that seeks to put upward pressure on the economy might attempt to do so by *initially* recognizing that an increase in the national debt will help to exert such pressure, and *then* formulating the expenditure and tax policies that will produce this debt. From this perspective, then, the debt becomes the instrument, and the specific expenditure and revenue items that the controller inputs into the system in order to implement the measure, become the by-products.

To the extent that the government engages in borrowing and lending and otherwise affects the national debt, Kirschen considers this to fall within the *money and credit* instrument category. Again, however, this categorization would seem to be a matter of preference and definition, and the distinction is not substantively important.

In general, the instruments of money and credit are those that reflect the interplay between the government and some Central Banking authority. Here, control is usually divided between the government and the Central Bank, and sometimes a National Credit Council. Inasmuch as a Central Bank or Credit

Council will not ordinarily exercise more than a secondary influence on the central government's decision to employ, say, deficit spending as a means of bolstering the economy, it is questionable whether all government borrowing and spending should appear as a money and credit instrument, as opposed to a public finance instrument. Operations in the *existing* debt, such as the issuance of government bonds, are, however, quite another matter, and are clearly money and credit instruments. Similarly, those variables that are under the government's control and that influence the lending and borrowing activities of other government agents, and those variables that influence credit creation in the banking system, as well as the interest rate established by the Central Bank, are money and credit instruments. As with the public finance instruments, these instruments can also affect the allocation of resources and the distribution of income, but the motivation that underlies their use is ordinarily the stabilization of economic activity, particularly in the short run.

Direct controls of prices and quantities, or market operations in general, are powerful instruments with quick effects. Such controls are grouped into the regulation of foreign trade, foreign exchange, and immigration, control of prices, the regulation of output, and other controls on the internal economy and its operations.

The use of direct controls as instruments will not necessarily take place via statutory regulation. Rather, the government will frequently employ moral suasion which, when supported by the implicit threat of legal action, can be most persuasive. Even in the international sphere moral suasion can be effective where, for example, the government engages in an extensive promotional campaign in an effort to persuade the populace to purchase domestically produced products, to curtail foreign travel in favor of domestic travel, or to take advantage of domestic carriers rather than foreign carriers for international travel. Similarly, the government can buy and sell on foreign currency markets in an attempt to influence foreign exchange rates in the absence of statutory regulation; or, depending on the sanctions and *quid pro quos* available to it, the government can attempt to persuade foreign governments to alter *their* policies in the directions dictated by domestic conditions.

The powers of persuasion are, however, somewhat less effective when applied to domestic markets, unless, as in the foreign sphere, supported by a substantial threat of subsequent government action, such as restrictive legislation.

Price controls as an instrument generally means the establishment of maxima and minima, as opposed to direct price fixing. Thus, legislation might be enacted to establish rent controls, or to prevent firms from charging prices that are either higher than some preestablished maximum, or that would result in a profit that exceeds some preestablished maximum. Similarly, minimum wage laws might be enacted to prevent firms from paying their employees wages (which after all are only prices paid for services) that fall below some preestablished minimum.

Quantity controls are generally accomplished by the adoption of some rationing scheme. Here too, however, upper and lower bounds might be imposed on output or sales. Thus, airlines might be forced to maintain some minimum level of service between two locations, and farmers might be paid to restrict their outputs of given commodities to certain preestablished maxima. Further, by setting certain standards of production, the government can exercise direct control over the method of production or the inputs employed in a production process. Thus, the government can, in effect, exercise direct control over the internal operations of the economic system, including both the couplings and the transformation operations.

Finally, the government can effect *changes in the economy's institutional framework*. This can be accomplished either by (1) an institutional change that in turn affects one of the previously mentioned instruments, by (2) a *radical* change in the existing economic system, or by (3) the creation of a new institution. In the former category we might, for example, list a change in the *system* of transfers and subsidies that results in an alteration in the way in which these public finance instruments could be employed. In the latter categories we might list changes in the antitrust laws that would alter the market structures and the systems of production that can evolve, and that might even affect the existing system of production, as well as the creation of new systems such as, for example, an international labor organization or corporate cartel in a given industry.

b. Instruments and objectives in the West and the East

The array of instruments available to policy makers therefore cuts a rather wide swath. Kirschen's analysis reveals that those in all four groups have in fact been used in the Western nations. Nonetheless, there have been differences in the degree of reliance placed upon certain groups of instruments, and differences in the situations in which certain groups have been employed. Spulber [3] provides a convenient summary of the main interconnections elicited by Kirschen between instruments and objectives, which is reproduced here as Figure 5.1.

The figure delineates three specific short-term, and three specific long-term objectives, in addition to "expansion of product" which can be placed in either category, and the convenient "other objectives" catch-all. It should be recognized, however, that the classification of objectives into short term and long term, as well as what instruments affect what objectives, is to some extent arbitrary. "Full employment," "control of demand pressures," and "improvement in the balance of payments" are the short-term objectives; improvement in "the structure of production," "working conditions," and "the distribution of income and wealth" are the long-term objectives. Thus, for example, one of the *foreign trade* instruments of *direct control* is the regulation of immigration and foreign travel; and, as indicated in the figure, the single objective of this instrument is *full employment*. In contrast, direct price and wage controls can

[3] N. Spulber, *The Soviet Economy* (New York: Norton, 1969).

have a much broader impact, affecting all the listed objectives with the single exception of the balance of payments. Even in these cases, however, although it is not their *intent,* the instruments can impact on other objectives as well. Thus, the categorizations are only intended to be suggestive of intent, rather than definitive.

A broad summary of the details underlying the figure would indicate that the public finance family of instruments, in particular, has played the key role in policy making, followed by the use of direct controls. Especially important controls have been those in the sphere of foreign trade which permit the regulation of imports and exports.

Assuredly, in the economies of the West which, notwithstanding the deviations from pure capitalism, are in fact basically unregulated, direct controls are commonly feasible only insofar as achieving short-term objectives is concerned, whereas changes in the institutional framework imply that a long-term objective is involved. Thus, the government of a Western nation might impose price controls in an effort to achieve short-term price stabilization, but it would normally eschew the use of market-manipulating media as a means of modifying major long-standing income distribution inequities. Instead, to accomplish such modifications the government might revamp the tax system. This would be an institutional change that affects a public finance instrument; it is invoked so as to achieve a long-term objective.

From an administrative standpoint, there is little justification for making systemic changes with which one will have to live in the future in order to rectify a temporary difficulty with which one prefers not to live in the present. From a political standpoint, it is unlikely that such systemic changes can win sufficient support from the populace and the politicians so as to permit their adoption and institution with the rapidity that temporary difficulties demand.

Similarly, unless one is prepared to dispense with much of the market mechanism and initiate moves toward establishing a regulated economy, direct controls will only be supportable as a means of countering short-term aberrations from long-term objectives. Thus, in the Soviet Union and in the ''socialist camp''—excluding Yugoslavia—direct controls have traditionally been viewed as the most important group of instruments for effecting long-term, as well as short-term, objectives. In such regulated economies, policy makers seeking to side-step the market mechanism have invoked and maintained in perpetuity direct controls on prices, quantities, and the methods of production and organization of industry. Whether in fact an abrogation of the free-market mechanism is the most effective means of dealing with long-term issues, or indeed is the most effective means of dealing with short-term issues, is a bone of considerable contention. Indeed, in more recent years there have been some shifts in domestic policy in the Soviet Union toward the employment of more indirect measures in order to *influence* economic activity in desired directions.

Except for changes in the institutional framework, in the West all other groups of instruments have been considered to be important in effecting short-term objectives. With respect to long-term objectives, public finance in-

FIGURE 5-1

SOURCE: Based on E. S. Kirschen et al., *Economic Policy in Our Time* (Amsterdam North Holland Publishing Co. 1964).

		INSTRUMENTS												
		Instruments of Direct Control												
		A. Enterprises						B. Branches and Sectors				C. Foreign Trade		
OBJECTIVES		Control of types, size, location	Control of Investment	Raw material allocation	Price fixing, cost and profitability controls	Wages and work conditions controls	Quality and standard controls	Control of Investment	Raw material allocation	Prices and wage controls	Output distribution controls	Import and export trading (prices and mixes)	Exchange control	Immigration and foreign travel control
Short Term	Full Employment	●	●	●	●	●		●	●	●		●	●	●
Short Term	Control of Pressures of Demand			●	●	●		●		●		●	●	
Short Term	Improvement in the Balance of Payments						●	●	●			●	●	
	Expansion of Production*	●	●	●	●	●		●	●	●		●		
	Improvement in the Structure of Production	●	●	●	●	●	●	●	●	●		●		
Long Term	Improvement in Working Conditions					●				●				
Long Term	Improvement in Income and Wealth Distribution				●	●				●				
Long Term	Other Objectives									●		●		

INSTRUMENTS

| | Instruments of Public Finance | | | | | | | | | | Instruments of Money and Credit | | | | | | | | | Changes in Institutional Framework | | | | | | |
| | A. Related to Direct Controls | | | | | | | | B. Other | | A. Related to Direct Controls | | | | | B. Other | | | | A. Affecting Instruments | | | | B. Affecting Production Framework | | |
Row	Direct and indirect taxes on, and subsidies of, enterprise	Public consumption	Financing control Investments	Payments to banks for loan financing	Budget surplus or deficit	Taxes on households	Taxes on cooperatives	Transfers to households	Foreign aid	Custom duties	Wage imposition of interest rates	Govt. guarantees of loans	Control of state enterprises borrowing	Control of cooperative borrowing	Other directives	Lending abroad	Borrowing from abroad	Devaluation	Revaluation	Changes in the system of direct controls	Changes in the system of subsidies to enterprises	Changes in the tax system	Changes in the court system	Changes in extent of public ownership	Changes in labor's role in management	Creation of new institutions
1	●	●	●	●	●	●																				
2	●	●		●	●	●	●			●	●															
3	●									●								●	●							
4	●	●	●	●							●	●	●	●	●	●	●			●	●	●	●	●	●	●
5	●	●	●	●			●				●	●	●	●	●		●			●	●	●	●	●	●	●
6																										
7					●	●	●																			
8	●								●							●								●	●	●

struments followed by changes in the institutional framework have been considered useful; money and credit instruments, like direct controls, have scarcely been used for this purpose.

The neglect of monetary instruments to achieve long-term purposes is occasioned by the fact that these instruments imply *changes* from an existing situation which are intended to *induce* other *changes* throughout the economic system. Thus, increases in the mortgage rate, for example, might be expected to result in short-term decreases in consumer borrowing for new home construction. But, (1) this will not *necessarily* be the case, and (2) even if it is, after sufficient time has passed and consumers have grown accustomed to the new rates, they are likely to borrow for mortgage purposes with all of their previous vigor. Indeed, because monetary instruments can only indirectly *induce* behavior, in contrast to the *direct* impact of the public finance instruments of taxes and spending, even from the short-term standpoint, policy makers are frequently reluctant to risk exclusive reliance upon them. Thus, because they are most readily imposed and removed, and because their effects are most directly observable and predictable, the public finance instruments tend to be favored for both short-term and long-term purposes, supported by direct controls in the short term and institutional changes in the long term, where such are politically feasible.

5.3 INSTRUMENT CHOICE

The desiderata of economic policy evolve from the value judgments and perceptions of the political decision makers. Thus, the selection of target variables is based solely on subjective assessments, although the target *rates* that policy attempts to achieve will also depend on objective considerations of feasibility. With respect to the instruments, however, it is tempting to believe that these will be chosen solely through objective considerations; that is, by determining what the "best" instrument is for effecting a given target under the existing economic structure. Despite its initial appeal, this is, nonetheless, a rather naive belief since not all equally effective instruments will necessarily be equally compatible with the basic philosophy of the economic system, nor that of its individual components. Moreover, any instrument must be evaluated in light of (1) its impact on *all* targets, not just the one upon which it exerts its primary thrust, as well as (2) the way its effects blend in with those of the other instruments to be employed. As a result, in any given situation the instruments chosen as measures will depend on various subjective, as well as objective, considerations. Indeed, because there are a variety of issues to be taken into account, generalizations with respect to the most appropriate instruments for realizing certain goals may prove impractical. It is apparent why, for example, reforms would not ordinarily be instituted in the solution of a short-run policy problem. But whether direct controls or the public finance instruments would be used, and in the latter case the specific instruments to be used, is not as apparent.

Some instruments will surely be more efficient in effecting certain targets than will others. In an intuitive sense what this means is that the same result can be accomplished through the comparatively minor employment of some instruments—the more efficient ones for the purpose; and the comparatively intensive use of others—the less efficient ones for the purpose. Similarly, some instruments will be more costly to apply than will others, both in terms of the directly calculable financial costs of implementation and administration, and the less direct, but by no means less important, (1) social costs that they may entail in the form of inequitable burdens imposed on particular groups, and (2) political costs to be borne by a government shouldering the responsibility for acts that may have serious domestic and international repercussions. Additionally, there will be both ideological and philosophical considerations influencing the choice among instruments, as the policy makers' economic, sociological, and political beliefs lead them to favor, *ceteris paribus*, some instruments as opposed to others. Finally, the selection of measures must be made in the context of the institutional framework that defines the basic economic system, or else the policy makers must be prepared to modify that framework.

Because the final selection of measures will at least in part depend on personal beliefs and institutional considerations, policy makers can logically disagree as to what constitutes an appropriate policy, even when they agree as to the desiderata toward which policy should be geared. In formal policy models, these beliefs and considerations are summarized in the relationships between a set of target variables that are the arguments in a preference function to be maximized, and perhaps in a series of behavioral restrictions that help to define a set of admissible policies. Determination of an optimum policy then reduces to solving a mathematical problem. The technical issues of efficiency and cost, and the institutional limitations constraining policy, are *initially* set out and dealt with when the structural constraints are specified. Similarly, differing personal beliefs and preferences with respect to the instruments should either be reconciled when the preference function is *initially* specified, or acknowledged via additional restrictions and boundary conditions to be incorporated directly into the problem. In effect, then, in the general policy model both the instruments and the targets are decision variables; and the considerations that go into selecting the instruments—both in terms of which to initially consider, and which to take as measures—are substantially the same as those which were previously discussed with respect to the targets. But, the perspective with which one views these two types of decision variables will differ.

In particular, the policy makers' value judgments and interpretations of the collective will enables them to specify a set of desiderata, as well as a preference function summarizing the acceptable trade-offs between these desiderata. Indeed, as in the case of some of the Tinbergen models, the policy makers may also specify rates for the desiderata—the fixed targets. In the latter event, the structure of the economic system as described in a set of constraining relationships determines whether or not the fixed targets are mutually compatible, and, if they are, the policies through which they can be achieved. In the case of variable targets, however, the structural relationships assume a role of equal importance to that of the preference function in determining the final target rates at which the policy makers aim. The preference function therefore indicates which of any two situations the policy makers do in fact prefer, and the set of structural equations and boundary conditions indicates which situations are attainable. With respect to the target variables, then, it is necessary to determine (1) what they are, (2) how they should be interrelated within the preference function, and how they are determined within the economic system, and (3) whether they are to be fixed or variable. The resultant variables might then be quantitative variables that are either continuous, such as unemployment rates, or discrete, such as the number of state universities; or alternatively the targets may be qualitative, such as the maintenance of price stability.

Similar issues must be resolved with respect to the instruments. In particular, the policy makers must determine the instruments available to them, and then specify how, if at all, the instruments should enter into the preference function. The manner in which the instruments influence the targets must also be determined and described in the constraining structural equations. From the perspective of the instruments, the preference function therefore indicates which of two alternative policies effecting the same results is preferred, and the set of structural equations and boundary conditions indicates the consequences, in terms of the target variables, of having the government undertake any particular feasible policy. With respect to the instruments, then, it is necessary to determine: (1) what they are; (2) whether or not they should enter the preference function, and, if so, how they should enter insofar as concerns the trade-offs that policy makers are willing to accept between (a) instrument and instrument and (b) instruments and targets; and (3) what their relationships are to the target variables insofar as their effects on the targets are concerned. The resultant variables might then be continuous quantitative variables such as tax rates, or discrete quantitative variables such as the *number* of roads to be constructed. Alternatively, the instruments might be qualitative variables, such as whether or not price controls are instituted, or reforms that essentially define a new set of structural relationships, such as might be effected by abandonment of, or reliance upon, the free market to regulate output and price. From a practical standpoint, ascertaining the impact of qualitative instruments is likely to present special difficulties, and introduce considerable uncertainty. This, however, is a matter of degree rather than substance.

On the one hand, then, irrespective of the underlying motivation, whenever policy makers do indeed discriminate between instruments and want the final choice of measures to reflect their preferences, the instruments can be directly incorporated as variables in the preference function along with the target variables. Each instrument will then be accompanied by such familiar accoutrements as the rates of substitution with respect to the other instruments as well as the targets. Alternatively, the intention to maintain an instrument, such as a tax rate, at a rate below some predetermined maximum, can be realized by specifying this in a boundary condition that all admissible policies must satisfy.

On the other hand, to the extent that certain instruments are more effective in realizing some targets than are others, to the extent that some instruments are more difficult and costly to apply than are others, to the extent that an instrument might influence many targets and not simply the single one for which it is the most effective instrument and, moreover, that these subsidiary influences will not necessarily be positive, and to the extent that the instruments involve institutional arrangements that are basic to the structure of the economic system itself, these factors will make themselves known within the constraining structural equations and boundary conditions that define the system.

5.4 THE SELECTION OF MEASURES IN THE GENERAL POLICY PROBLEM

a. The Tinbergen model

Much of the traditional lore concerning the actual selection of measures from among the available instruments derives from Tinbergen's original model, discussed in Chapter 3. In this model, the policy makers specify I targets y_i, and consider J instruments z_j. As was previously indicated, in the case of fixed targets whether the model can be solved for a unique set of measures will depend on whether the number of targets exceeds, equals, or is less than the number of available instruments.

Suppose, in particular, that $I > J$; that is, the number of targets exceeds the number of available instruments with which they might be achieved. Except by chance, no single combination of the instruments will effect the given targets. This is the situation illustrated in Figure 5.2(a) in which the policy maker can utilize only two instruments in order to achieve three targets. The three lines represent three equations of the form of Equation (3.4i'):

$$b_{i1}z_1 + b_{i2}z_2 = d_i \qquad i = 1, 2, 3$$

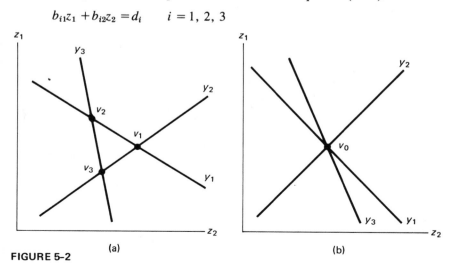

(a)   (b)

FIGURE 5-2

Although any *two* of the targets can be reached, as indicated by the three points v_1, v_2, and v_3 at which two of the lines intersect, there is no point that lies on all three lines. Figure 5.2(b) illustrates the more fortuitous case where all three lines do indeed intersect at a single point v_0, and the three targets can be achieved by the appropriate use of just two instruments. Clearly, however, this would be a rather pleasant happenstance.

With $I = J$, the number of targets equals the number of instruments through which they will be effected, and a unique solution exists. This is illustrated in Figure 5.3 for the case of two targets and two instruments. The solution is given at the point v_0 where the two lines

$$b_{i1}z_1 + b_{i2}z_2 = d_i \qquad i = 1, 2$$

intersect.

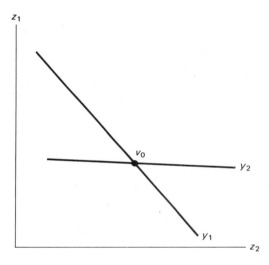

FIGURE 5-3

In each of these cases, if a solution exists it will be unique. Under these circumstances, then, the solution is independent of the preference function specified by the policy makers. Be preestablishing values for all I targets, the policy makers have, in effect, chosen to ignore the *direct* impact that the instruments can have on the objective function. Instead, the instruments have been relegated to a subsidiary role wherein their ability to effect the given targets fails to take into account their ancillary effects on the preference function.

With $I < J$, the number of instruments exceeds the number of targets, and there are an infinite number of solutions. This is illustrated in Figure 5.4 for the case of a single target and two instruments:

$$b_{11}z_1 + b_{12}z_2 = d_1$$

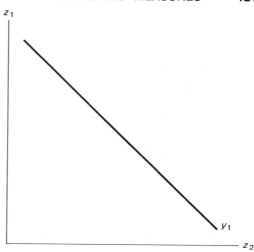

FIGURE 5-4

Here, any point on the line will satisfy the single equation. The policy makers' problem, then, is to determine the point on the line, and hence the combination of instruments, at which the preference function is maximized. In general, with $I < J$, any set of $J - I$ of the instruments can be determined arbitrarily, and the remaining I instruments are then uniquely determined by the I constraints. In this case, then, we are said to have $J - I$ *degrees of freedom* to arbitrarily establish rates for the instruments. With $I = J$ and $J - I = 0$ degrees of freedom, the rates of *all* J instruments are uniquely determined by the constraints; with $J - I < 0$, there will commonly be no solution.

Implicit in the previous discussion is the assumption that any solution that evolves will also satisfy any boundary conditions that have been imposed. Although such a possibility is by no means far-fetched, by the same token it cannot be taken for granted. Moreover, when the boundary conditions are violated, the added complication may not be easily resolved—if it can be resolved at all.

Consider, for example, Figure 5.5 illustrating the case of two targets and two instruments. Here there is a unique solution at the point v_0 which, unfortunately occurs at a rate of z_1 in excess of its upper bound of z_1^0. In this case, then, as in the case where $I > J$, a unique solution satisfying all constraints, including the boundary constraints, does not exist; and, in general, when a boundary condition is violated, except by coincidence a unique solution, or indeed *any* solution satisfying *all* constraints, will not necessarily exist.

Assuredly, the clever model-builder makes certain to incorporate a sufficient number of instruments into the model so as to achieve the degree of flexibility that almost guarantees the existence of alternative solutions satisfying the constraints. When the functions are nonlinear the previous comments no longer

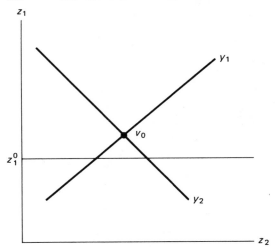

FIGURE 5-5

hold. Introducing nonlinearities may make a solution difficult to determine, but at the same time it could assure the existence of a feasible solution where one did not exist in the linear case. Figure 5.6, for example, illustrates a case in which there are two targets, two instruments, and nonlinear constraints. Here, there are two solutions satisfying both constraints, located at the points v_0 and v_1. When neither solution violates the boundary conditions, the solution that maximizes the preference function will be selected. But even if one of the solutions does violate a boundary constraint, the other will not necessarily do so,

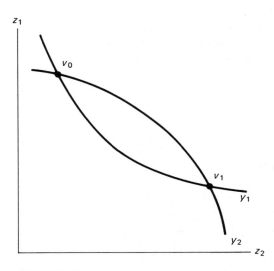

FIGURE 5-6

and can be implemented. Thus, although Tinbergen's linear specification might initially be viewed as introducing an important simplification, it might at the same time be creating unanticipated difficulties.

Although it enlarges the set of decision variables without increasing the number of constraints, a Tinbergen policy model with flexible targets will not necessarily be more or less easily solved than the same model with fixed targets. Indeed, if the format of a single target, albeit a flexible one, within each constraint is maintained, there will now be $I + J$ variables, but still only I constraints. The policy problem then assumes a linear programming format, and the fundamental theorem of linear programming tells us that no more than I of these $I + J$ variables can be positive, unless so specified in the boundary conditions. Thus, in the absence of a boundary condition specification, for every instrument that becomes a measure, one of the target variables *must* assume a zero value.

On the one hand, then, preestablishing the target rates eliminates the need to determine them, and thereby reduces the number of possible solutions and, in general, the model's algebraic complexity. It does this by replacing a variable with a constant, which is the ultimate aim of all methods of solving simultaneous equations, and limiting the policy problem to the choice of measures. On the other hand, keeping the targets flexible increases the degrees of freedom within which the policy makers operate, and hence both enhances the possibility that a solution exists, and, by increasing the number of possible solutions in terms of target rates and combinations of measures, raises the maximum value that the objective function can take on, given the set of constraints.

b. The general policy model

Relaxing the linearity assumption permits us to convert the Tinbergen model into a nonlinear model that specifies the general policy problem under certainty. Here, the policy makers are assumed to seek measures that will maximize the social preference function

$$W = w(y_1, \ldots, y_I; z_1, \ldots, z_J) \tag{5.1a}$$

subject to the constraints

$$g_m(y_1, \ldots, y_I; z_1, \ldots, z_J) \leq d_m \qquad m = 1, \ldots, M \tag{5.1b}$$

and boundary conditions

$$y_i^0 \leq y_i \leq y_i^1 \qquad i = 1, \ldots, I \tag{5.1c}$$

$$z_j^0 \leq z_j \leq z_j^1 \qquad j = 1, \ldots, J$$

where the y_i's are the (variable) targets, and the z_j's are the instruments.

For simplicity, initially suppose that all functions are twice-differentiable, and that all targets and instruments are continuous quantitative variables. Suppose, too, that policy makers exhibit a positive preference for y_i and z_j so that $\partial W/\partial y_i$, $\partial W/\partial z_j > 0$. In the process of solving the problem, then, we would define a set of "multipliers" $\lambda_m (m = 1, \ldots, M)$, where λ_m is the implicit cost of imposing the mth restriction, and cost is expressed in the same units as W—social utility. We would also define "multipliers" θ_j^0 and θ_j^1 that assign an implicit cost to imposing a lower and upper bound, respectively, on the jth instrument ($j = 1, \ldots, J$). "Multipliers" ϕ_i^0 and ϕ_i^1 with similar interpretations are attached to the boundary constraints on the ith target ($i = 1, \ldots, I$). Hence, the Lagrangian to be maximized is

$$L = W - \Sigma_m \lambda_m (g_m - d_m) - \Sigma_i \phi_i^0 (y_i - y_i^0) - \Sigma_i \phi_i^1 (y_i - y_i^1)$$
$$- \Sigma_j \theta_j^0 (z_j - z_j^0) - \Sigma_j \theta_j^1 (z_j - z_j^1) \tag{5.2}$$

With particular reference to the instruments, we note that $\partial L / \partial z_j^0 = \theta_j^0$ and $\partial L / \partial z_j^1 = \theta_j^1$. That is, at the optimum solution where $y_i = y_i^*$ and $z_j = z_j^*$, θ_j^0 gives the change in L, or the change in social utility resulting from a marginal increase in the lower bound on the jth instrument; θ_j^1 gives the change in social utility that results when the upper-bound restriction is relaxed. With $z_j^1 > z_j^0$, either $\theta_j^1 = 0$ or $\theta_j^0 = 0$; if the optimal solution $z_j = z_j^* = z_j^0$, then $\theta_j^0 \leq 0$; if $z_j^* = z_j^1$, then $\theta_j^1 \geq 0$; and, if $z_j^0 < z_j^* < z_j^1$, then $\theta_j^0 = \theta_j^1 = 0$. That is, there is no cost to increasing either boundary condition so long as neither is binding at the optimum. But, when the lower bound is effective at the optimum, then increasing it *may* reduce the maximum level of social utility that can be achieved; and, when the upper bound is effective at the optimum, then increasing it *may* increase the maximum level of social utility that can be achieved. The ϕ_i^0 and ϕ_i^0 have similar interpretations with respect to the targets, and the λ_m have similar interpretations with respect to the structural constraints.

The Kuhn-Tucker first-order necessary conditions for a maximum to this nonlinear programming problem [4] state that if in the optimal solution $z_j^0 < z_j^* < z_j^1$, that is, if the jth instrument is employed as a measure, but its use is not constrained by a boundary condition imposed upon it, then it will be employed to the point at which

$$\frac{\partial W}{\partial z_j} = \Sigma_m \lambda_m \left(\frac{\partial g_m}{\partial z_j} \right) \tag{5.3a}$$

If, however, $z_j^* = z_j^0$, then

$$\frac{\partial W}{\partial z_j} \leq \Sigma_m \lambda_m \left(\frac{\partial g_m}{\partial z_j} \right) \tag{5.3ai}$$

while if $z_j^* = z_j^1$, then

$$\frac{\partial W}{\partial z_j} \geq \Sigma_m \lambda_m \left(\frac{\partial g_m}{\partial z_j} \right) \tag{5.3aii}$$

Similarly, if in the optimal solution the ith target obtains at a point such that $y_i^0 < y_i^* < y_i^1$, then

---

[4] See, for example, G. Hadley, *Nonlinear and Dynamic Programming* (Reading, Mass.: Addison-Wesley, 1964).

$$\frac{\partial W}{\partial y_i} = \Sigma_m \lambda_m \left(\frac{\partial g_m}{\partial y_i}\right) \tag{5.3b}$$

whereas if $y_i^* = y_i^0$, or alternatively $y_i^* = y_i^1$, then

$$\frac{\partial W}{\partial y_i} \leq \Sigma_m \lambda_m \left(\frac{\partial g_m}{\partial y_i}\right) \tag{5.3bi}$$

or

$$\frac{\partial W}{\partial y_i} \geq \Sigma_m \lambda_m \left(\frac{\partial g_m}{\partial y_i}\right) \tag{5.3bii}$$

respectively.

In essence, then, Equations (5.3a), (5.3ai), and (5.3aii) imply that when an instrument is employed to the minimum (maximum) permissible extent, at that point the marginal social utility of using it is no greater (less) than the marginal social cost associated with its use; the difference between the two is given by $\theta_j^0 (\theta_j^1)$. If, however, the boundary conditions do not affect the extent to which an instrument is used, then it will be employed to the point at which its marginal social utility is equated to its marginal social cost. Moreover, as indicated by the second-order sufficiency conditions for a maximum, at lower rates of employment, the marginal social utility exceeds the marginal social cost, and hence the use of the instrument is extended; at higher rates, the marginal social cost exceeds the marginal social utility, and hence the use of the instrument is curtailed. A similar interpretation exists with respect to the targets and their rates in the optimal solution.

When policy makers are indifferent as to the rate obtaining for the jth instrument, $\partial W/\partial z_j = 0$. Then, either the instrument is used to the minimum or maximum extent permitted by the boundary conditions, or else it is used to the point at which the marginal social cost of its use is driven to zero. In the latter event, the second-order conditions imply that at lower rates of use the marginal social costs are *negative*. Thus, at rates $z_j < z_j^*$ increased use actually implies marginal social *benefits*, while at rates $z_j > z_j^*$ there are marginal social *costs*. Similarly, when policy makers prefer lesser use of the jth instrument so that there is, in effect, a *disutility* associated with its use, $\partial W/\partial z_j < 0$. Here too, then, $z_j^0 < z_j^* < z_j^1$ implies that the first-order condition (5.3a) holds, the interpretation being that the marginal *disutility* of using the jth instrument is equated to the marginal social *benefits* derived from its use. The second-order condition states that at lower (higher) rates the marginal social benefits exceed (fall short of) the marginal social disutility.

When the instrument variables are quantitative but discontinuous, the problem takes on additional mathematical complexity, because the relevant partial derivatives will not necessarily be defined. Hence, the first-order conditions may no longer be applicable. Similarly, the methods of the calculus are inapplicable when (1) the instruments are qualitative and described by, say, a binary variable z_b that may be used to indicate the presence ($z_b = 1$) or absence ($z_b = 0$) of a rule, or (2) where a reform is involved and described by one set of structural equations rather than another. Nonetheless, depending on the functional form specified for the equations, appropriate mathematical methods for solving the problem, such as integer and zero-one programming techniques, may be available. Unfortunately, however, the economist's penchant for a marginalist interpretation of the solution is not as readily satisfied when the variables are not continuous, and the functions are not differentiable.

Recognizing the existence of uncertainty and our inability to forecast perfectly adds yet further statistical and mathematical complications. First, it will be necessary to estimate the parameters of some, if not all of the structural equations, and then to use these estimates to forecast the effects of instruments upon targets. Then, in solving the model, it will be necessary to recognize that because of (1) our inability to forecast perfectly, and (2) the need to deal with parameter *estimates,* the target variables of interest will be *random* variables. Hence, it will very likely be necessary to use mathematical expectations in manipulating the model. Depending on the functional forms specified for the equations and those of the probability densities assigned to the random variables, the manipulations may not be readily accomplished.

Perhaps the major implication of introducing uncertainty, nonlinearities, and discontinuities into policy models is that under *any one* of these conditions there is no reason to expect that the number of measures taken will correspond to the number of targets at which policy is to be aimed. Indeed, only when a policy model appears in a linear programming format a la Tinbergen can we expect an instrument-per-target rule. In fact, Theil's comparatively slight modification of the objective function to a quadratic form in order to admit uncertainty immediately invalidates the rule. More recent studies suggest that an optimal policy under uncertainty may require the use of *all* quantitative instruments, *irrespective* of the number of targets.[5]

There are at least two underlying motives behind this suggestion. On the one hand, recognizing uncertainty forces recognition of the likely need to adjust the rates of the instruments when, after measures have been taken, the target variables fail to assume their desired rates. Following Brainard,[6] the effects of the instrument I on the target Y might be given by

$$Y = aI + \mu \qquad (5.4)$$

[5] See W. Brainard, "Uncertainty and the Effectiveness of Policy," *American Economic Review,* Vol. LVII, No. 2, May 1967; F. R. Shupp, "Uncertainty and Stabilization Policies for a Nonlinear Macroeconomic Model," *Quarterly Journal of Economics,* Vol. 86, No. 1, February 1972; D. W. Henderson and S. J. Turnovsky, "Optimal Macroeconomic Policy Adjustment under Conditions of Risk," *Journal of Economic Theory,* Vol. 4, No. 1, February 1972; Robert Holbrook, "Optimal Economic Policy and the Problem of Instrument Instability," *American Economic Review,* Vol. LXII, No. 1, March 1972; and G. C. Chow, "Problems of Economic Policy from the Viewpoint of Optimal Control," *American Economic Review,* Vol. LXIII, No. 5, December 1973. As M. M. Ali and S. I. Greenbaum have shown in an unpublished paper ("Stabilization Policy, Uncertainty, and Instrument Proliferation") once one introduces an instrument use cost, it does not necessarily follow that all instruments will be used. Indeed, it is intuitively obvious that if there is an infinite cost to using an instrument, it will *never* be used.

[6] *Op. cit.*

where a is a constant, whose value might itself be uncertain,[7] and μ is a random variable having an expected value of $E[\mu] = 0$ and variance of $\sigma_\mu^2 > 0$. Then, to effect $Y = Y^*$ the policy $I = Y/a$ would be implemented. Here, however, even if the value of a is known with certainty, the random fluctuations in μ will ordinarily mean that $Y \neq Y^*$, and hence subsequent adjustments in I will be called for. When Y^* can be effected through multiple instrument use, as in the case where

$$Y = a_1 I_1 + a_2 I_2 + \mu \tag{5.4a}$$

and where there are adjustment costs and these increase with the rates of the instruments, it will be desirable to employ many instruments at lower rates, rather than a few instruments at higher rates, in order to reduce the costs of adjustments. Indeed, this result will hold even under certainty when the instrument rates are going to undergo future change, and the cost of adjustment is positive. Further, such changes in the instrument use rates under certainty will not necessarily occur solely because the target rate Y^* is varied.

Suppose, for example, that

$$Y_t = a_1 I_t + a_2 I_{t-1} \tag{5.4b}$$

where the subscript t is a time index, so that the target rate at time t depends on the instrument rates at times t and $t - 1$. Attempts to achieve a constant target rate of $Y_t = Y_{t-1} = Y^*$ for all $t \geq 0$ require that

$$Y_t = a_1 I_t + a_2 I_{t-1} = a_1 I_{t-1} + a_2 I_{t-2} = Y_{t-1}$$

This results in the second-order difference equation

$$I_t + \left[\frac{(a_2 - a_1)}{a_1} \right] I_{t-1} - \left[\frac{a_2}{a_1} \right] I_{t-2} = 0$$

The solution to this equation is of the form

$$I_t = K_1 \left[\frac{(a_1 - a_2)}{2a_1} + \frac{1}{2} \sqrt{ \frac{(a_1 - a_2)^2}{a_1^2} + \frac{4a_2}{a_1} } \right]^t$$
$$+ K_2 \left[\frac{(a_1 - a_2)}{2a_1} - \frac{1}{2} \sqrt{ \frac{(a_1 - a_2)^2}{a_1^2} + \frac{4a_2}{a_1} } \right]^t$$

where K_1 and K_2 are constants. Here, then, I_t will in general vary over time, and *instrument instability* can occur even though the optimal target rates are constant and there is no uncertainty.[8]

On the other hand, a multi-measure policy is encouraged by the same principle that underlies the diversification of assets in an investment portfolio. In the present instance, however, the "assets" are the instruments that can be

[7] C. Barry and I. Horowitz, "Risk and Economic Policy Decisions," *Public Finance*, Vol. XXX, No. 2, 1975.

[8] G. C. Chow, *op. cit.*

incorporated into a policy "portfolio," and the expected "return" that this portfolio generates will be an expected social utility index, which is a function of a set of desiderata. Then, in order to reduce the risk—here measured by the variance in social utility—associated with any given level of expected social utility, a diverse set of instruments, each of which has an imperfectly predictable impact on the target variables, is selected. In effect what is being accomplished by this diversification is an increase in the probability that at least one instrument will have a favorable impact on any one target, or that not all instruments will fail. Thus, diversification lowers the probability of seriously undershooting a target. Similarly, because it is unlikely that all instruments will prove to be as effective *ex post* as they are expected to be *ex ante*, the probability of seriously overshooting a target is also reduced by instrument diversification.

The choice of instruments and determination of their rates in formal policy models will therefore depend on the confidence of policy makers in their ability to accurately forecast the effects of each individual instrument on each of the target variables, as summarized in a set of probability assignments to accompany any forecasts, the presumed relationship between the instruments and the targets, as summarized in the constraints, and the extent to which policy makers elect to recognize differing attitudes toward the instruments, as summarized within the preference function, constraints, or boundary conditions.

c. Some additional considerations

These same factors have also come into play during actual policy determination in both East and West, although ordinarily with somewhat less formality and rigor than the theorists' models would suggest. Here too, however, policy makers and their technicians have attempted to establish relationships between instruments and targets, making judgments about the effects of an instrument and the likelihood that a measure will or will not have a given impact. With varying degrees of precision, policy makers have been concerned with establishing the values for expressions such as $\partial y_i/\partial z_j$ and $\partial^2 y_i/\partial z_j^2$. That is, they have attempted to determine the effects on the ith target of a change in the jth quantitative instrument, as well as whether, at the margin, the instrument tends to become either more effective ($\partial^2 y_i/\partial z_j^2 > 0$) or less effective ($\partial^2 y_i/\partial z_j^2 < 0$) as its use increases; or, whether it is equally effective ($\partial^2 y_i/\partial z_j^2 = 0$) at all rates of use.

In terms of the mathematical model, the policy makers' technicians have attempted to estimate the parameters and establish the appropriate forms of the functions.

$$g_i'(z_1, \ldots, z_J) = y_i \qquad i = 1, \ldots, I \qquad (5.5)$$

which give the "reduced form" of the constraints (5.1b). Thus, where the equations are all linear, a typical equation might be

$$a_{0i} + a_{1i}z_1 + a_{2i}z_2 + \cdots + a_{Ji}z_J = y_i \qquad (5.6)$$

where $\partial y_i / \partial z_j = a_{ji}$ is the marginal effect on the ith target of a change in the rate of the jth instrument. In the linear case, $\partial^2 y_i / \partial z_j^2 = 0$.

What this formulation makes clear, and what should be emphasized at this point, is the fact that each instrument can have spillover effects on a number of targets beyond the *primary* target that it is intended to influence. Indeed, the situation in which an instrument impacts upon only a single target would be the exception rather than the rule.

Similarly, policy makers are concerned with the costs involved in employing any instrument. Here "cost" is broadly defined. There may, for example, be rather sizable administrative costs associated with a program of price controls, whereas increases in the tax rate can be accomplished at virtually no direct financial expense. Additionally, however, there may be social costs, perhaps intangible, associated with both policies. Thus, either policy might be viewed as a means of controlling inflation, but the former will have secondary effects on the allocation of resources, while the latter will have secondary effects on the distribution of income. In either event, there is a "cost" to society which we would do well to explicitly recognize as a decision variable—a target—in the mathematical model, but one that enters only as an additional consideration in its informal counterparts.

In addition, policy makers will have to recognize the diverse preferences of different persons and interest groups with respect to the various types of instruments. Thus, rent controls will be anathema to landlords, as will price controls to corporate executives, whereas international banking interests may or may not favor adjustments in the foreign exchange rate. Similarly, some economists favor the public finance instruments as opposed to the monetary instruments, and vice versa, purely on theoretical grounds; and, some persons oppose the public finance instruments and favor the monetary instruments, and vice versa, purely on ideological grounds. Although in practice these may be issues to be thrashed out during the policy-making process, in *theory* their resolution should precede the policy-making process itself, with such individual and group beliefs and interests reflected *directly and initially* in the preference function, constraints and boundary conditions, to the extent that they are admitted at all.

Finally, policy makers must recognize the empirical record of success— or failure—achieved by the various instruments. Not only can there be theoretical disagreement over the impact of the instruments, but in addition there can be disagreement over the empirical evidence, which does not ease the policy makers' burdens. Thus, for example, in the United States regulatory commissions are being subjected to increasing abuse, as there is a heightened tendency to question their effectiveness, and indeed to question whether they actually do more harm than good. At the same time, however, their defenders point to particular areas of accomplishment that would not have been achieved in their absence. In effect, then, one always draws *inferences* from historical data, but these inferences will not necessarily be universally drawn. Even where analysts agree on the facts, they will not necessarily agree on their interpretation. We therefore elect not to impose our own interpretative biases in indicating which instruments are more effective than others.

The difference in the way that instruments are chosen in informal versus formal models, then, is that in the latter all of the technical and personal considerations are quantified and incorporated directly into the decision-making process and used as input data. The decision reached is then the optimal decision compatible with these data. In the former, however, technical issues provide some initial suggestions as to possible alternative policies, with the final choice of measures determined as the resolution of differing attitudes, judgments, and interests.

5.5 CONCLUSION

Policy makers have available to them quantitative and qualitative instruments, as well as reforms. The choice among instruments should neither be made, nor considered to be an efficacious response to the desire to achieve a particular target. Rather, a package of measures should be chosen from among the available instruments. This package will constitute an overall policy that seeks to optimize some societal welfare function. In point of fact, there has indeed been a tendency to use certain types of instruments in certain situations and to achieve specific goals. The primary factors governing their choice have been cost and efficiency criteria, subject to philosophical and ideological considerations, as well as institutional limitations. It is the differences in the latter which, perhaps, best explain the policy differences existing between East and West.

CHAPTER 6

Characteristics of the Processor: Structural Frameworks

6.1 GENERALITIES ON STRUCTURES

It is clear by now that the policy makers' problem is to choose one of a set of feasible policies defined in part by constraints and boundary conditions that the policy makers themselves *are determined* to respect, and in part by constraints and boundary conditions that *must be* respected because of the structure of the economic system. On the one hand, then, policy must take into consideration the policy makers' preferences. On the other hand, policy must take into consideration (a) the input-output transformation operations performed by the individual components, and (b) the output-input relationships implied by their couplings.

Although policy makers ordinarily have some intuitive understanding of whether or not a particular program acceptable to them is also feasible and its measures and targets mutually compatible, it is the technician's task to describe the structure of the system with the quantitative precision that efficient policy making demands. This is necessary for two reasons. First, although the policy makers' implicit view of the system might *ordinarily* lead them to select a feasible policy, it will not necessarily do so. The failure to recognize the infeasibility of a particular policy prior to its adoption necessarily results in subsequent alterations—of either targets, or goals, or both—to assure that *all* decision variables lie within the feasible set. Thus, choosing an infeasible policy is equivalent to selecting a set of measures that generates unanticipated and unwelcome values for a set of targets. Then, when the sought-after targets are incompatible with past measures, it is the targets that make the policy infeasible; lacking the option to revise a policy to which one is committed, it is the targets that will necessarily have to be revised. Second, policy makers do not merely seek a *feasible* policy. Rather, they seek the *optimal feasible* policy.

The determination of this optimum policy cannot be assured unless the entire set of feasible policies can be delineated and explored. It is the quantitative description of the structure of the economic system that makes this *exploration* possible, and it is the means of accomplishing this that commands our attention in this chapter.

As we already noted, the structure of an economic system is defined by the operations of its components and the network of their couplings. The structural framework therefore consists, for example, of (1) given forms of production activities, (2) given cultural patterns of response to various stimuli, and (3) given (a) ownership relations, (b) forms of income distribution, and (c) forms of intervention in the economy. Thus, this framework is comprised of a series of (1) technical, (2) behavioral, and (3) institutional relationships that define the system, and it is accompanied by various assumptions and hypotheses with respect, say, to war and peace and foreign relations in general, that describe the political, social, cultural, and international environment within which the system operates. *All* systems, however, are hierarchical systems. They have the communality of a controller and a processor. Where they differ *structurally* is in the specific details—the couplings, the processes and activities, and the institutions.

The same elements coupled differently define a new system as, of course, does the addition or deletion of an element from a given network. This observation points up a potentially important difference in policy making between East and West. In particular, in the West one can normally presume the policy makers' desire to maintain continuity of structure. In the East, however, both the operations of the components and their couplings are either changing or amenable to change at the discretion of the system's controllers. This is particularly the case, for example, with respect to the forms of intervention chosen by the policy makers, and with respect to the forms of production activities permitted by the policy makers—the third and first groups, respectively.

The second group focuses on the behavioral and causal relationships that describe the patterns of influence between and among each of the economic variables of interest to the policy makers, and the other variables in the economic system. These relationships have historically been expressed through various recursive or multi-equation econometric models, including the various Keynesian-type models.

The third group focuses on the institutional relationships that specify the rules under which the system operates. These relationships are introduced through the assumptions that are made as to how the system will be *permitted* to operate, such as in the Chenery family of models wherein alternative assumptions are made about, say, the upper and lower bounds on the supply of capital.

As a preliminary introduction to the models in these various categories, and to set the stage for Part II, in the next three sections we present some of the more interesting approaches within each of these groups. In the main, the approaches currently in vogue build upon these efforts.

6.2 TECHNICAL AND ACCOUNTING RELATIONSHIPS

In both East and West the economy's structure will initially be described by a series of relationships of the form

$$g_r(u, z) = f_r(y) \qquad r = 1, \ldots, R \tag{6.1}$$

where $u = (u_1, \ldots, u_K)$ is a vector of variables exogenous to the system, $z = (z_1, \ldots, z_J)$ is a vector of instruments, and $y = (y_1, \ldots, y_I)$ is a vector of target variables. In addition, there may exist a series of boundary conditions

$$z^0 \leq z \leq z^1 \qquad \text{and} \qquad y^0 \leq y \leq y^1 \tag{6.2}$$

that the instruments and targets must *necessarily* satisfy. (The tax rate, for example, must lie between zero and one, and prices and outputs cannot be negative. The problem confronting the technician is how to develop, in their most useful and descriptive forms, the structural relationships among the variables, as well as their limits.)

Economic systems can be modeled at various levels of aggregation. In general, no single level of aggregation will clearly be revealed as optimal. Instead, some levels are more *useful* and *appropriate* than others, in light of the available data and the purposes for which the model is being built. Thus, for some purposes individual plants will be considered to be the components in the industrial subsystem of a larger economic system, and the technical relationships of special interest will be the plants' transformation or production functions. In this case, then, the structural equations to model the industrial subsystem will consist of the set of joint production functions

$$q_{ir} = f_{ir}(F_{1i}, \ldots, F_{ji}, \ldots, F_{Ji}) \qquad i = 1, \ldots, I; \qquad r = 1, \ldots, R \tag{6.3}$$

where q_{ir} is the ith plant's output of the rth product, and F_{ji} is the amount of the jth factor used as input in the ith plant. In this context, the production function is seen as the most disaggregated type of input-output relationship.

At a slightly higher level of aggregation, the individual firm might be the component in an industrial subsystem, and in the multi-plant firm the input-output relationship will be the *firm's* transformation function. Thus, suppose that firm 3, say, consists of plants $i = 7, 8,$ and 9. We can then write

$$Q_{3,r} = q_{7r} + q_{8r} + q_{9r} = \sum_{i=7}^{9} f_{ir}(F_{1i}, \ldots, F_{ji}, \ldots, F_{Ji}) \tag{6.4}$$

where $Q_{3,r}$ is the third firm's output of product r. In either event, the technician's problem is to specify the form, and estimate the parameters of the transformation functions f_{ir}.

Similarly, at a still higher level of aggregation, the system components can be considered to be the individual *industries*. In this case, the transformation function might be written

$$Q_r = \sum_{p=1}^{P} Q_{p,r} = \sum_{i=1}^{I} f_{ir}(F_{1i}, \ldots, F_{ji}, \ldots, F_{Ji}) \tag{6.5}$$

where Q_r is the total output of industry r, and $Q_{p,r}$ is the amount of this industry's product produced by firm $p(p = 1, \ldots, P)$.

Just as the product outputs can be aggregated at various levels, so too can the factor inputs. Thus, $F_1 = \sum_{i=1}^{I} = F_{1i}$ might represent, say, all lathe operators, all skilled labor, all blue collar labor, or all production and nonproduction workers. And, in a similar manner, Q_r might represent, say, lager beer, malt beverages, alcoholic beverages, or all beverages. The appropriate definition depends on the purpose of the model, the practical restrictions imposed by data limitations, one's ability to manipulate complex models, and the need to operate within time and cost constraints.

Economic policy models generally employ a fairly high level of aggregation. This is because policy models are primarily concerned with the *macroeconomic* effects of economic policy, and only secondarily with its microeconomic implications. Policy models will therefore ordinarily consider "the industry" to be the basic system component, with the precise definition of "industry" depending on the level of disaggregation required by the policy-making process and its implementation.

In particular, suppose there are $R = S$ uniquely defined industries, such that $Q_{rt}(r = 1, \ldots, R)$ is the output of industry r during time period t. Suppose too that Q_{rst} is the amount of output r used as input by industry $s(s = 1, \ldots, S)$ during time period t. For convenience, the time subscript t will be suppressed in subsequent discussion. The economic system therefore contains R industrial components. For simplicity, suppose these are coupled, so that $Q_r = \sum_{s=1}^{R} Q_{rs} + D_r$. That is, the *total* output of the rth component is distributed to each of the other $R - 1$ components in the amount $Q_{rs}(s \neq r)$, some output Q_{rr} is fed back into the component to be used as an input, and some output D_r goes to a nonindustrial component. The rate of Q_{rr} will, by convention, be set at zero; the rate of $D_r \geq 0$ represents the amount of product r that is not fully absorbed within the industrial sector. In the simplest form of analysis, then, D_r is the amount of product r that flows to private households, or *final* (consumer) *demand*. In more complex models, D_r represents the amount of product that is either consumed by private households, purchased by the government, exported to a foreign sector, or retained by industry as either inventory or investment.

The input from the private sector to industry r is denoted L_r and represents labor services. Again, in the simplest form of analysis labor services are assumed to be the only autonomous inputs into the industrial sector. In more complex models, however, L_r might be separated into, say, services that generate wages and salaries, dividends, profits, rents, and taxes. Still further, flows from inventory, the using up of previous investment in the form of depreciation, and imports from the foreign sector might also be introduced. In the simplest case, then, the production function for industry r can be written as

$$Q_r = f_r(Q_{1r}, \ldots, Q_{Rr}, L_r) \tag{6.6}$$

Once again the technician's problem is the specification of the form of this function, and the estimation of its parameters. The solution to this problem was the singular contribution of Leontief.[1]

a. The Leontief model

The Leontief input-output model is a special case of a Walrasian general equilibrium model. In the Walrasian system, the N profit-maximizing firms in a competitive economy employ K factor inputs in the production of M commodities; the J utility-maximizing consumers, some of whom may be entrepreneurs that own the firms, sell services, and purchase commodities, subject to an income constraint. Equilibrium is achieved in the system through two conditions: (1) aggregate demand equals aggregate supply for all factors and all commodities; and (2) aggregate profits equal aggregate entrepreneurial income.

The Leontief model makes the Walrasian system operational through either one of two equally applicable and equally debatable assumptions: (1) the production function for each industry—that is, the transformation operation of each system component—is of the form of fixed technological coefficients of production; or (2) the production function of each industry is of the linear homogeneous form, with fixed factor-input price ratios obtaining over time. Each of these assumptions implies that $Q_{rs} = a_{rs}Q_s$ and $L_s = b_sQ_s$ where a_{rs} and b_s are fixed constants showing, per unit output of industry s, the input from industry r, and the input from the labor sector, respectively. Expressed in value terms these relationships yield $Q_{rs}^* = p_rQ_{rs}$, $Q_r^* = p_rQ_r$, and $W_s = wL_s$ where p_r and w are the price of industry r's output and the wage rate, respectively.

The assumption of fixed input-output proportions raises two immediate issues: (1) whether it is a valid assumption for an entire economy's production system, and (2) whether, even if the assumption is in fact valid, the factors of proportionality will remain unchanged over time. As regards the former issue, it is clear that the assumption is too restrictive to be generally valid. Nonetheless, it may well be a useful assumption in that it simplifies parameter estimation, while not *substantially* distorting the true picture. As regards the latter issue, it may also be useful and nondistortive to assume the proportions unchanged over "short" periods of time, say fewer than five years. In any event, the Leontief model has commanded sufficient attention and, indeed, has enjoyed sufficient application to warrant a detailed discussion.

We shall focus on Leontief's open system which abstracts from the foreign sector. The latter is included in his closed model. Recall that $Q_r = \sum_s Q_{rs} + D_r (r = 1, \ldots, R)$ with $Q_{rr} = 0$ and $\sum_s L_s = L$, where L denotes the total labor supply. In physical terms, then,

$$Q_r = \sum_s a_{rs}Q_s + D_s \qquad r = 1, \ldots, R \tag{6.7}$$

$$L = \sum_s b_sQ_s \tag{6.8}$$

---

[1] W. Leontief, *The Structure of the American Economy, 1919–1939* (Oxford: Oxford University Press, 1941).

or in value terms,

$$Q_r^* = \sum_s \alpha_{rs} Q_s^* + D_r^* \qquad r = 1, \ldots, R \tag{6.9}$$

$$W = \sum_s \beta_s Q_s^* \tag{6.10}$$

where

$$\alpha_{rs} = \frac{Q_{rs}^*}{Q_s^*} = \left(\frac{p_r}{p_s}\right) a_{rs}$$

$$\beta_s = \frac{W_s}{Q_s^*} = \left(\frac{w}{p_s}\right) b_s$$

$$W = wL \text{ and}$$

$$D_r^* = p_r D_r$$

Leontief further assumes a purely competitive economy with free entry and exit of firms. The importance of this assumption for the model is its implication that in each industry total receipts equal total costs. For each industry this equality can be written as

$$\text{total revenue} = p_s Q_s = \sum_r p_r Q_{rs} + wL_s = \text{total cost}$$

$$p_s Q_s = (\sum_r p_r a_{rs}) Q_s + w b_s Q_s$$

$$= (\sum_r p_r a_{rs} + w b_s) Q_s$$

Hence

$$p_s = \sum_r p_r a_{rs} + w b_s \qquad s = 1, \ldots, R \tag{6.11}$$

equivalently

$$I = \sum_r \frac{p_r}{p_s} a_{rs} + \frac{w}{p_s} b_s = \sum_r \alpha_{rs} + \beta_s \tag{6.12}$$

For equilibrium to be attained in the Leontief system, as expressed in physical terms, Equations (6.7), (6.8), and (6.11) must hold. The sets (6.7) and (6.8) represent $R + 1$ equations that, together with the R equations in (6.11), give a total of $2R + 1$ *linear* equalities in $2R + 1$ unknowns. The latter comprise the R industry outputs Q_r, the total labor supplied L, and the R prices p_r. The technological coefficients a_{rs} and b_s are assumed to be known, or determinable on the basis of historical data; the final demands D_r are to be specified by the policy maker; and the wage rate w acts as a numeraire to fix the price level. The Leontief model therefore yields a unique solution.

The input-output model uses interindustry output flows to describe the structural relationships within the economic system; the final demands are controlled variables—in effect, *instruments*—used to determine the system's rate of economic activity. To generalize the system, these final demands can be specified in greater detail, indicating the sources from which they derive. In particular, suppose that $D_r = C_r + I_r + G_r + \Delta_{ar} + E_r$, where C_r denotes purchases for private consumption, I_r denotes purchases for investment, G_r denotes government purchases, Δ_{ar} denotes purchases for inventory, and E_r denotes export sales in industry r. In view of the latter two specifications, we might also define an $R + 1$ "producing" sector to represent the use of stocks from inventory Δ_d, and an $R + 2$ sector to represent imports M. Here, then, Δd, M, and the components of D_r, or any subset of these, can be viewed as exogenous to the system, or, perhaps, as autonomous inputs into it. These too, then, become variables subject to regulation by the controller.

The Leontief model is also readily extended to include the various social accounting relationships of interest to policy makers. Viewed in value terms Equations (6.9), (6.10), and (6.12) form $2R + 1$ linear equations in $2R + 1$ unknowns. Here the unknowns are the R output *values* Q_r^*, the total wage *bill* W, and the R final *demand values* D_r^*. Given the wage rate as the numeraire, the R prices can be determined from the fixed price ratios.

Now, the value of total *gross* output in the economy is given by $T_{GO} = \sum_{r=1} Q_r^*$. The value of total *net* output is given by $T_{NO} = T_{GO} - \sum_r \sum_s Q_{rs}^* = \sum_r Q_r^* - \sum_r \sum_s Q_{rs}^* = D_r^*$. That is, T_{NO} nets out the interindustry flows so as not to double-count them. In the present context, suppose that $r, s = 1, \ldots, R + 2$, in order to include inventory depletions Δ_d and imports M as "producing" sectors. With the asterisk (*) indicating a monetary value rather than a physical output, by definition the gross national product Y is given by the value of total net output, less imports and decreases in inventory; or

$$Y = T_{NO} - \Delta_d^* - M^*$$

$$= \sum_{r=1} Q_r^* - \sum_r \sum_s Q_{rs}^* - \Delta_d^* - M^*$$

$$= \sum D_r^* - \Delta_d^* - M^* \tag{6.13}$$

from (6.9). Now, however, letting $C^* = \sum C_r^*$, $I^* = \sum I_r^*$, $G^* = \sum G_r^*$, $\Delta_a^* = \sum \Delta_{ar}^*$, and $E^* = \sum E_r^*$, noting that $C^* + I^* + G^* + \Delta_a^* + E^* = \sum D_r^*$, and substituting into (6.13), we obtain the familiar expression for GNP:

$$Y = C^* + I^* + C^* + (\Delta_a^* - \Delta_d^*) + (E^* - M^*) \tag{6.13a}$$

That is, gross national product is equal to the sum of private consumption, domestic investment, government expenditures, net inventory change (accretions less depletions), and net foreign trade (exports less imports).

Similarly, with total receipts equal to total cost, we may write $T_{NO} = \sum_s Q_s^* - \sum_s \sum_r Q_{rs}^* = \sum_{s-1} wL_s + \Delta_d^* + M^* = wL + \Delta_d^* + M^*$. Thus, the total wage bill, wL, equals the value of total net output less inventory depletions and imports, $T_{NO} - \Delta_d^* - M^*$; and, in the present system, the total wage bill represents total income. Assuredly, this component too can be disaggregated into such components as wages and salaries, entrepeneurial income or profits, interest, rent, dividends, taxes, and so on. Therefore, gross national income is given by

$$wL = T_{NO} - \Delta_d^* - M^* = Y$$

or, alternatively disaggregated

$$Y = WS + \pi + i + RN + d + \tau \tag{6.13b}$$

where WS is wages and salaries, π is profit, i is interest, RN is rent, d is dividends, and τ is taxes.

Moreover, the model permits the analysis of either physical or informational flows throughout the economic system. In the former case, the physical transactions matrix describes the transformation operations on physical (raw materials, products, and energy including labor) flows of inputs and outputs; in the latter case, the value transactions matrix describes the transformation operations on what is in a sense informational (monetary) flows of inputs and outputs. In each case the fundamental advantages of the systems approach for managerial decisions are maintained; that is, its recognition of the *interrelations* among a set of *mutually dependent* components, and its consideration of the *chain of reactions* set into motion by the controller's inputs into the system. Still further, just as the transformation operations of the components in a dynamic system may systematically change over time, so too the input-output relationships that describe the system in the Leontief approach can be made to systematically change over time. In particular, each of the technological coefficients—the a_{rs}, b_s, α_{rs}, and β_s—can themselves be made functions of, say, time itself.[2] Thus, for example, we could write $a_{rst} = a_{rs} + k_{rs}t$, were t denotes time and k_{rs} is a trend factor. The technological coefficients matrix would then *automatically* be revised over time.

b. The Marxian model

The Soviets have proceeded in much the same manner as the Western nations in attempting to describe the technical, structural relationships in the Soviet economy, although they have begun from a different point of departure. Nonetheless, the Soviet analytical scheme is closely akin to the Leontief input-output model, and in fact shares its analytical tractability and social accounting bonus features.

Structural relationships in the Soviet economy, are often portrayed in Soviet economic literature with the help of the Marxian two-sector model, originally devised by Marx for studying the operation of the economy under capitalism.[3] This analytical scheme, used in the USSR mostly for the study of possi-

---

[2] R. Stone and A. Brown, "Behavioral and Technical Change in Economic Models," in E. A. G. Robinson (ed.) *Problems in Economic Development* (London: Macmillan, 1965), pp. 428–438; and W. Leontief, "The Dynamic Inverse," in A. P. Carter and A. Brody (eds.) *Contributions to Input-Output Analysis* (Amsterdam: North-Holland, 1970), Vol. I, pp. 17–43.

[3] K. Marx, *Capital, A Critical Analysis of Capitalist Production* (Moscow: Foreign Languages Publishing House, 1954 [1887 edition]), Vol. 2, pp. 392 ff.

ble changes in interrelations among macro variables, also has much in common with the previously discussed Mahalanobis model. Indeed, when the broad framework of these purportedly different models is set out in very specific, mathematical terms, it becomes more and more apparent that these various illustrations of the structural relationships in the East and West are not as different as is often supposed. Rather, they differ only in the *details,* and in the preference and institutional relationships that help guide the policy makers' choice of measures.

In the basic model, that of *simple reproduction,* the Marxian framework consists of two broadly aggregated sectors: one produces new *fixed* capital and raw materials, jointly called producers' goods; the other produces consumers' goods. In particular, let Q_1^* represent the total *value* of new producers' goods, and let Q_2^* represent the total *value* of consumption goods. For simplicity it is assumed that all production takes place in a single period, and that the means of production—fixed capital, inventories, and raw materials—are completely used up during the production process. In the Marxian framework, all "values" are in terms of labor inputs; that is, in terms of some standard wage or numeraire.

The value of the new producers' goods is distributed as: (1) funds for the replacement of the fixed capital, inventories, and raw materials that are used up in the producers' goods sector while producing those new goods, denoted c_1; (2) compensation to labor or *variable* capital, with the total wages paid being denoted by w_1; and (3) profits or surplus value to the owners of the means of production in the producers' goods sector, denoted $s_1 = Q_1^* - c_1 - w_1$. (These owners are the so-called capitalists in the West, and the socialist state in the East). Similarly, the value of the consumption goods, Q_2^*, is distributed as: (1) funds to replace the fixed capital used to produce the consumption goods, denoted c_2; (2) wages paid to variable capital, denoted w_2; and (3) surplus value or profits accruing to the owners of the production facilities (viz. the capitalists or the state) in the consumption sector, denoted s_2.

Assuming that, *in value terms,* the total demand for new producers' goods, $c_1 + c_2$, is equal to the supply, Q_1^*, we find that

$$c_1 + c_2 = Q_1^* = c_1 + w_1 + s_1 \qquad (6.14)$$

or, upon cancelling c_1 on both sides of the equation

$$c_2 = w_1 + s_1 \qquad (6.14a)$$

Assuming also that all of labor's wages $(w_1 + w_2)$ and the owners' profit $(s_1 + s_2)$ is used to purchase consumption goods (Q_2^*),

$$w_1 + w_2 + s_1 + s_2 = Q_2^* = c_2 + w_2 + s_2 \qquad (6.15)$$

which once again, immediately implies (6.14a). The system is depicted in Figure 6.1.

The implications of the balancing, or equilibrium condition (6.14a) are especially interesting if, following Marx, we define $e_i = s_i/w_i$ as the *rate of exploitation*—modestly called rate of accumulation under socialism. Under this definition, the exploitation of labor by the owners of the means of production is

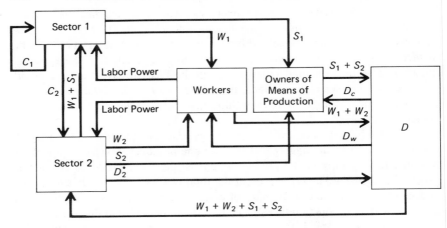

FIGURE 6-1

greater in the ith sector ($i = 1, 2$), the greater is the surplus value relative to the wages paid in that sector. Now, dividing both sides of (6.14a) by w_2 we find

$$\frac{c_2}{w_2} = \frac{w_1}{w_2} + \frac{s_1}{w_2}$$

and, assuming as Marx often did,[4] that the rate of exploitation is the same in each sector, or $e_1 = e_2$, we can write $e_1 = s_1/w_1 = e$, whereupon $s_1 = ew_1$. Hence, by substitution

$$\frac{c_2}{w_2} = \frac{w_1}{w_2} + \frac{ew_1}{w_2}$$

or

$$\frac{w_1}{w_2} = \frac{c_2/w_2}{1+e} = \frac{k_2}{1+e} \qquad (6.16)$$

where $c_i/w_i = k_i$ is the *organic composition of capital* in the ith sector ($i = 1, 2$). The latter reflects the technological productivity of labor, insofar as higher values of k_i imply greater output for a given amount of labor value. Thus, assuming that technology is fixed, k_i is also assumed fixed.

Equation (6.16) implies that for equilibrium to obtain, a unique relationship must exist between (1) the ratio of the wages paid in each sector, (2) the rate of exploitation, and (3) the organic composition of capital in the consumption sector. The latter two ratios thereby determine the distribution of labor in the economy and, given the constancy of the rate of exploitation, the owners' (capitalists' or the state's) surplus. Thus, either this relationship *will be realized* if supply equals demand and equilibrium obtains, or if this relationship *is in fact realized*, equilibrium will obtain, and supply and demand will automatically be equated.

[4] *Ibid.*, pp. 508–509.

The simple reproduction process, however, allows no room for growth. This is introduced into the Marxian model of *expanded reproduction* through the assumption that the owners of the means of production in each sector distribute a portion of their surplus value so as to *increase* the amount of goods produced, and the amount of labor that is hired. In effect, these owners *reinvest* a portion of their current profits in order to increase their future profits; but they restrict their reinvestment to the original sectors from which the funds were generated.

Let Δc_i and Δw_i ($i = 1, 2$) denote in value terms the *change* in the level of capital and the *change* in the level of labor, respectively, that the owners seek to effect. For convenience the subscript to delineate different time periods is suppressed. Thus, investment in period t is given by $I_t = \Delta c_i + \Delta w_i$. With s_{ii} denoting the surplus *retained* by the owners,

$$s_i = \Delta c_i + \Delta w_i + s_{ii} \qquad i = 1, 2 \tag{6.17}$$

Upon replacing c_i with $c_i + \Delta c_i$ ($i = 1, 2$) and s_i with $\Delta c_i + \Delta w_i + s_{11}$, Equation (6.14) now becomes

$$c_i + c_2 + \Delta c_1 + \Delta c_2 = Q_1^* = c_1 + w_1 + \Delta c_1 + \Delta w_1 + s_{11} \tag{6.14'}$$

which implies

$$c_2 + \Delta c_2 = w_1 + \Delta w_1 + s_{11} \tag{6.14a'}$$

Similarly, the sum of labor's wages $(w_1 + \Delta w_1) + (w_2 + \Delta w_2)$ and the surplus *retained* by the owners and hence available for purchasing consumption goods $(s_{11} + s_{22})$ is equated to the value of all consumption goods (Q_2^*) as in equation (6.15), to yield

$$w_1 + \Delta w_1 + w_2 + \Delta w_2 + s_{11} + s_{22} = Q_2^* = c_2 + \Delta c_2 + s_{22} \tag{6.15'}$$

which also implies (6.14a') as the equilibrium condition.

To see the implications of this new balancing condition, suppose that investment in period t is in constant proportion to the previous period's surplus, or $I_t = \alpha_i s_{i,t-1}$ where $\alpha_i (i = 1, 2)$ is the constant of proportionality. Suppose, too, that this investment is distributed between capital and labor in constant proportion such that $\Delta w_i = \lambda_i I_t$ and $\Delta c_i = (1 - \lambda_i) I_t$ ($i = 1, 2$). The growth rates for capital and the wage bill are then given by

$$g_{c_i} = \frac{\Delta c_i}{c_{i,t-1}} = \frac{(1 - \lambda_i) I_t}{c_{i,t-1}} = \frac{(1 - \lambda_i) \alpha_i s_{i,t-1}}{c_{i,t-1}}$$

$$= \frac{(1 - \lambda_i) \alpha_i s_{i,t-1}/w_{i,t-1}}{c_{i,t-1}/w_{i,t-1}} = \frac{(1 - \lambda_i) \alpha_i e_i}{k_i} \tag{6.18}$$

and

$$g_{w_i} = \frac{\Delta w_i}{w_{i,t-1}} = \frac{\lambda_i I_t}{w_{i,t-1}} = \frac{\lambda_i \alpha_i s_{i,t-1}}{w_{i,t-1}} = \lambda_i \alpha_i e_i \tag{6.18a}$$

respectively. That is, the growth rates depend on the capital owners' inclinations to invest, as well as on how they distribute their investment funds.

Now, with a constant organic composition of capital $k_i = c_i/w_i$, both c_i and w_i must grow at the same rate. Hence $g_{c_i} = g_{w_i}$, or

$$\frac{(1 - \lambda_i)\alpha_i c_i}{k_i} = \lambda_i \alpha_i e_i$$

and

$$\lambda_i = \frac{1}{(1 + k_i)} \tag{6.19}$$

which determines the proportions invested in capital and labor, as well as the growth rates, with

$$\frac{\lambda_1}{\lambda_2} = \frac{1 + k_2}{1 + k_1} \tag{6.19a}$$

Moreover, proceeding as before and suppressing the time subscript, from the balancing condition Equation (6.14a′) it follows that

$$\frac{c_2}{w_2} + \frac{\Delta c_2}{w_2} = \frac{w_1}{w_2} + \frac{\Delta w_1}{w_2} + \frac{s_{11}}{w_2}$$

But $c_2/w_2 = k_2$, $\Delta c_2 = g_{c_2}c_2$, $\Delta w_1 = g_{c_1}w_1$, and $s_{11} = s_1 - \Delta c_1 - \Delta w_1$. Hence, the previous equation becomes

$$k_2 + g_{c_2}k_2 = \frac{w_1}{w_2} + \frac{g_{c_1}w_1}{w_2} + \frac{s_1}{w_2} - \frac{\Delta c_1}{w_2} - \frac{\Delta w_1}{w_2}$$

$$= \frac{w_1}{w_2} + \frac{ew_1}{w_2} - \frac{g_{c_1}c_1}{w_2}$$

because $s_1 = ew_1$ and $g_{c_1}c_1 = \Delta c_1$. Substituting $k_1 w_1 = c_1$ and rearranging terms,

$$\frac{w_1}{w_2} = \frac{k_2(1 + g_{c_2})}{1 + e - g_{c_1}k_1} \tag{6.16'}$$

comparable to (6.16). Thus, equilibrium in the Marxian system of expanded reproduction differs from that of simple reproduction, only insofar as expanded reproduction also introduces both the organic consumption of capital in the consumption goods sector, and the growth rates in the two sectors.

Finally, since the right-hand side of (6.16′) only contains parameters, w_1/w_2 must be constant. This requires the wage bill in both sectors to grow at the same rate, or,

$$g_{w_1} = \lambda_1 \alpha_1 e_1 = g_{w_2} = \lambda_2 \alpha_2 e_2$$

which with $e_1 = e_2 = e$ implies

$$\frac{\lambda_1}{\lambda_2} = \frac{\alpha_2}{\alpha_1}$$

and, in lieu of (6.19a)

$$\frac{\alpha_2}{\alpha_1} = \frac{1 + k_2}{1 + k_1} \qquad (6.20)$$

That is, for equilibrium to obtain the ratio of rates of investment in each sector must be a constant as determined by the organic composition of capital in that sector. There is no compelling reason to expect that this will in fact be the case.

Like the Leontief model, then, the Marxian model makes some very restrictive assumptions, not the least of which relate to the absence of technological progress. This assumption, assuredly, is solely in the *formal* presentation of the model since Marx did in fact consider technological progress to be a central feature of capitalist development. Abstracting from this issue, however, the two models—that of Marx and that of Leontief—share a more common kinship than that of heroic assumptions. In particular, consider a highly aggregated, open Leontief-type model with R-2 sectors, producing a total value of Q_1^* and Q_2^* of industrial and consumer goods, respectively, such that (1) $Q_{21}^* = Q_{22}^* = O$ and $D_2^* = Q_2^*$, and (2) Q_{11}^*, $Q_{12}^* \geq O$, and $D_1^* = O$. (See Figure 6.2.) That is, all output of the consumption sector goes to final demand, but none of the output of the industrial sector is so distributed. Similarly, consider payments to labor services to be comprised of both wages and salaries, WS, and profits π, where WS_1 and WS_2, and π_1 and π_2 are the wage bill and profit earned in the industrial and consumption sectors, respectively. The value transactions matrix for this system appears as follows:

$$V = \begin{bmatrix} Q_{11}^* & Q_{12}^* & 0 \\ Q_{21}^* & Q_{22}^* & Q_2^* \\ WS_1 & WS_2 & 0 \\ \pi_1 & \pi_2 & 0 \end{bmatrix}$$

With total receipts equal to total costs, in the industrial sector,

$$Q_{11}^* + Q_{12}^* = Q_{11}^* + WS_1 + \pi_1 \qquad (6.21)$$

or

$$Q_{12}^* = WS_1 + \pi_1 \qquad (6.21a)$$

Similarly, in the consumption sector,

$$Q_2^* = D_2^* = Q_{12}^* + WS_2 + \pi_2 \qquad (6.21b)$$

But, with consumption goods purchased out of profits and wages,

$$WS_1 + \pi_1 + WS_2 + \pi_2 = D_2^* \qquad (6.22)$$

which together with Equation (6.21b) implies

$$WS_1 + \pi_1 = Q_{12}^* \qquad (6.22a)$$

Letting $Q_{12}^* = c_2$, $WS_1 = w_1$, and $\pi_1 = s_1$, (6.22a) of the Leontief model is seen to be equivalent to (6.14a) of the Marxian model—and indeed

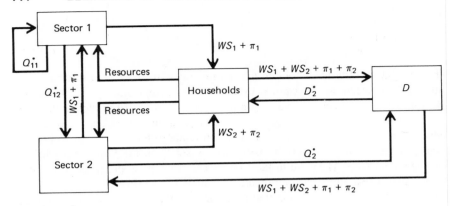

FIGURE 6-2

those variables *are* similarly defined. In the same manner, $WS_2 = w_2$, $Q_{11}^* = c_1$, and $\pi_2 = s_2$, whereupon (6.21a) and (6.21b) are seen to be equivalent to (6.14) and (6.15), respectively. In fact, then, the Marxian model of Figure 6.1 is seen to have the same basic *structural* framework as a highly aggregated Leontief model of Figure 6.2. The latter is made useful for policy purposes by its restrictive assumptions with respect to the economy's technology. The former is made useful for policy purposes by its restrictive assumptions with respect to entrepreneurial behavior and institutional arrangements.

c. The Harrod-Domar model

One of the simplest, yet important structural models is the now classic Harrod-Domar growth model.[5] It is not entirely clear whether this model deals with technical, as opposed to behavioral relationships, but this is solely a matter of interpretation. Specifically, we are concerned with interpreting the input-output relationship in the industrial sector of a two-sector economy in which the second component is a consumption sector. For mathematical convenience we shall consider a time-continuous model, instead of the discrete-time-period version.

With C denoting personal consumption, I denoting private investment, A denoting autonomous expenditures, and Y denoting gross national product, by definition we have the social accounting relationship

$$Y = C + I + A \qquad (6.23)$$

Here, then, expenditures in the amount A—either investment or consumption—are automomous to the system and may be considered to be a policy variable subject to government control. These expenditures will directly stimulate additional consumption because of the *behavioral* relationship $C = cY$, where c is the marginal propensity to consume. Specifically, personal consumption will

---

[5] R. F. Harrod, *Towards a Dynamic Economics* (London: Macmillan, 1948); E. D. Domar, "Capital Expansion, Rate of Growth, and Employment," *Econometrica*, Vol. 14, No. 2, April 1946.

increase in the amount A/s, where $s = 1 - c$ is the marginal propensity to save. But, say because of the need for additional facilities to produce the goods demanded by consumers, as well as to handle the autonomous expenditures, increased private investment will also take place. The Harrod-Domar assumption is that this so-called *induced* investment will be proportional to the change in gross national product; or

$$I = k(\frac{dY}{dt})$$
(6.24)

where the constant k is the familiar accelerator. Rewriting (6.24) in the form

$$k = \frac{I}{(dY/dt)}$$
(6.24a)

the accelerator is seen to equal the ratio of new capital investment to the change in total output. Thus, the assumption that k is constant is equivalent to assuming a constant capital:output ratio. As expressed in Equation (6.24), the relationship can therefore be viewed as a behavioral relationship reflecting an entrepreneurial response to a change in economic activity. Alternatively, it can be viewed, and we so view it here, as a manipulation of the technical relationship (6.24a) reflecting the industrial sector's *required* response to the demand for additional output as being investment in additional facilities. Moreover, this additional investment is in fixed proportion to the increment in gross national product, where the accelerator is the factor of proportionality.

By direct substitution into (6.23), we have

$$Y = cY + k(\frac{dY}{dt}) + A$$

which, after rearranging terms, yields the first-order differential equation

$$\frac{dY}{dt} - (\frac{s}{k})Y + \frac{A}{k} = 0$$
(6.25)

The general solution of Equation (6.25) depends on the value of A, and whether or not it is constant. In any event, it is easily verified that the homogeneous part of this solution will be of the form

$$Y_h = Be^{gt}$$
(6.26)

where B is a constant determined by the initial "starting" conditions, and $g = s/k$. Further, $dY_h/dt = gBe^{gt}$. Thus, $(dY_h/dt)/Y_h = g$ is the rate of growth in gross national product in the absence of autonomous expenditure (that is, with $A = 0$). In general, then, writing $Y = Y_h + Y_p$, where Y_p is the particular solution to (6.25), $(dY/dt)/Y$ will be the rate of economic growth. This growth rate will be the sum of two terms, an "inherent" component and an "autonomous" component. The former will be given by $g = s/k$, and thus will be a unique function of the marginal propensity to save and the accelerator, exclusively. Economic growth in this system will therefore partially depend on a given *tech-*

nical relationship, the fixed capital:output ratio, and a given *behavioral* relationship, the marginal propensity to save.

6.3 BEHAVIORAL AND CAUSAL RELATIONSHIPS

There are essentially two types of behavioral relationships that should be distinguished from one another. On the one hand, there are *purely behavioral* relationships, such as $C = cY$. These reflect the decision-making process of a particular component in the economic system. Like the technical relationship, the behavioral relationship is the transformation operation of a system component. In this case, however, the transformation operation or function does not depend on a given state of technology, but on a *purposeful response* to a set of what are generally, but not necessarily restricted to economic data. Thus, the transformation operation in the household sector, as one component of the system, may be a simple consumption function $C = f(Y)$. The empirical counterpart of this function might be an econometrically estimated linear function,

$$C = C_0 + cY + u \qquad (6.27)$$

where C_0 is a constant, and u is a residual term that enters because of random disturbances that, although they influence consumption, do not influence it in a systematic, and hence predictable fashion.

Broadly speaking, the consumption function describes what is, on average, the *propensity* of households to spend out of current income, with c being the marginal propensity to consume. Similarly, one can postulate, say, an investment function $I = g(Y)$ and a borrowing function $B = h(Y)$, where B denotes corporate borrowing, to reflect the *propensities* of entrepreneurs to invest and to borrow, respectively, in *purposeful response* to the rate of economic activity. In each case, the transformation operation is the mathematical statement of how, in a particular system component, an independent variable or set of variables influences some dependent variable *because of* the decision-making process within that component.

On the other hand, behavioral relationships can also be *causal,* either in the sense that we (1) explicitly *interpret* a system component's transformation operation as being a determinate *output response* to an *input stimulus,* or insofar as we can (2) trace through some series of interdependencies existing within the entire economic system or any of its subsystems, and in the process isolate certain stimulus-response relationships that can be seen to *ultimately* obtain. In either event, the advantage of this interpretation from the policy standpoint is that the policy makers may be able to manipulate some of the stimuli, and the causal behavioral relationships permit them to isolate the response to any such manipulations.

Consider, for example, a simple Tinbergen-type model. The model contains two accounting relationships:

$$Q = Y + E - M \qquad (6.28)$$

$$DB = M - E \qquad (6.29)$$

where Y, M, and E are as previously defined, Q is total expenditure, and DB is the deficit in the balance of payments. There are two behavioral relations:

$$M = mY \tag{6.30}$$

$$Q = G + cY \tag{6.31}$$

where G is the rate of public expenditure, and m and c as constants are the marginal propensities to import and consume, respectively. In this model, G is a policy instrument that the policy makers are assumed to manipulate in order to effect a full-employment rate of national income, Y_F.

The rate of exports, E, is taken as exogenous to the system. The chain of causality in the model then runs as follows. A target Y_F is established by the policy-making body. Given $Y = Y_F$, a rate of imports $M_F = mY_f$ is then determined from (6.30). With E given exogenously, the balance-of-payments deficit is now determined from (6.29) as $DB_F = M_F - E = mY_F - E$. Total expenditures can then be determined from (6.28) as $Q_F = Y_F + E - mY_F = (1 - m)Y_F - E$, and this *uniquely* determines the rate of government spending from *(6.31) as a residual*: $G_F = Q_F - cY_F = (1 - m)Y_F - E - cY_F = (1 - m - c)Y_F - E$.

Although the *causal ordering* in this model is quite straightforward, in general establishing a causal ordering means establishing a network of *precedence* relations. These relations order the variables in accordance with the number of other variables that they influence. Thus, the full employment target initially influences imports, and imports, in combination with the exogenous exports, influence both total expenditure and the balance-of-payments deficit. Total expenditure then influences the *required* rate of government spending. But, as seen through this network of precedence relations, the instrument requirement gets its basic impetus from the controller's initial establishment of a target, and an input from the environment.

As seen in Figure 6.3, this system of equations provides a formal mathematical statement of a rather simple feedback system. The demand for export

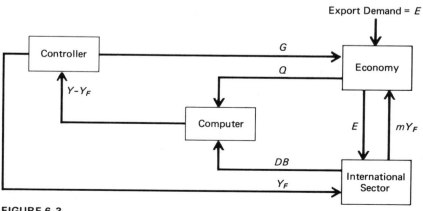

FIGURE 6-3

goods comes as an exogenous input to the system from the (international) environment. The feedback or computer component provides the controller with information with respect to the discrepancy between the actual and the targeted rate of national income. The international-sector component is assumed to have a transformation operation that provides to the economy imports in the amount of m times the target rate of national income, as well as an informational transformation operation that provides the computer with balance-of-payments information. The controller can then "experiment" with various inputs of government expenditures until such time as the computer provides the feedback information that the actual and the targeted rates of national income have been equated; or, alternatively, the controller can simply solve the set of equations as above for the full-employment income-generating rate of spending.

The preceding model is a *recursive* model in which each of the four dependent variables—imports, trade deficit, total expenditure, and government spending—can be determined in logical sequence from the two independent variables—exports and the full-employment target—and the previously determined dependent variables. Consider, however, a slightly altered version of this previous model with Equation (6.30) replaced by

$$M = m'Q \tag{6.30'}$$

That is, m' is now the marginal propensity to import relative to total *expenditures*, rather than total income. Now, with imports depending on total expenditure, from (6.30'), and with total expenditure depending on imports, from (6.28), a strictly recursive precedence relation cannot be established in this model. Rather, imports and total expenditure are determined *simultaneously*. But, once they have been so-determined, the trade deficit and the rate of government spending can also be determined.

Specifically, substituting (6.31') into (6.28), and given a $Y = Y_F$ target and a rate of exports E, we find $Q = Y_F + E - M = Y_F + E - m'Q$. Hence,

$$Q = Q_F = \frac{1}{1+m'} (Y_F + E)$$

whereupon

$$M = M_F = m'Q_F = \frac{m'}{1+m'} (Y_F + E)$$

With Q and M thus determined, from (6.29) we find

$$DB = DB_F = M_F - E = \frac{m'}{1+m'} Y_F - \frac{1}{1+m'} E$$

and

$$G = G_F = Q_F - bY_F = \frac{1-b(1+m')}{1+m} Y_F + \frac{1}{1+m'} E$$

The revised version of the original model is featured by an *interdependent* relationship between imports and total expenditure. These dependent variables are determined from the two independent variables; the remaining two dependent variables are subsequently determined on the basis of these newly obtained solutions. In a similar manner, it is often the case that *blocks* of dependent variables X_i exist such that $X_1, \ldots, X_m$ are simultaneously determined solely as functions of the independent variables. Then, $X_{m+1}, \ldots, X_n$ are simultaneously determined on the basis of the independent variables and the newly determined solutions for $X_1, \ldots, X_m$. Similarly, $X_{n+1}, \ldots, X_t$ are then simultaneously determined from the independent variables and the previously derived solutions for $X_1, \ldots, X_n$, and so forth.

In this case, there exists a series of "levels" at which the variables are determined. At the first or highest level, for example, $X_1, \ldots, X_m$ are determined solely from the independent variables. This determination is made independent of any subsequent decisions to be made with respect to the remaining $X_i (i \geq m + 1)$. At the second or next highest level, $X_{m+1}, \ldots, X_n$ are determined from the independent variables, as well as the decisions made at the first level, but independent of the decisions to subsequently be made at the lower levels with respect to $X_i (i \geq n + 1)$. Similarly, at the third level $X_{n+1}, \ldots, X_t$ are determined by the first- and second-level decisions, but independent of any lower-level decisions, $X_i (i \geq t + 1)$. This is analogous to the multilevel system with a supremal unit and several infimal decision units.

In effect, then, even with structural models that are not strictly recursive it might be possible to *partition* the variables into various subsets such that those in each subset are determined simultaneously. The set of solutions within each of the partitioned subsets will then either be independent of other solutions, or will depend on other partitioned subsets in a recursive fashion. Thus, it is often the case that in interdependent models, as well as in strictly recursive models, the variables can be thought of as being determined through a causal ordering, but with the chain of causality running through a unique sequence of blocks of dependent variables.

6.4 INSTITUTIONAL RELATIONSHIPS

The institutional relationships in an economic system reflect the *details* that are either *imposed* upon that system by actions of government, or that emerge from the philosophical beliefs of the citizenry and the existing cultural patterns of the society.

In the former instance, the relationships fall into two basic categories, each of which is easily modeled. First, there are relationships involving entities such as tax rates, reserve ratios, interest on the public debt, and the like. These may be expressed through functions of varying degrees of complexity. In the case of an ad valorem tax, for example, we can write $\tau_\Sigma = \tau P q$ where τ is the (percentage) tax rate, P is the average price at which the item has sold, q is the number of units sold, and τ_Σ is the government's tax revenue from the item. Thus, τ is an instrument whose rate will be established as part of overall government tax policy. In the case of a personal income tax, the function might be a bit more complex. In the United States, for example, it is of the form $T_\Sigma = \sum_i \sum_j (B_i + b_i I_{ij})$, where B_i is the base tax payment of an individual in the ith income class, b_i is the marginal tax rate imposed on any income earned above that base, but within that class, I_{ij} is the taxable income of the jth individual in the ith class, and T_Σ is the total tax revenue generated by the personal income tax. In all cases, if it is possible to state the relationship—as it must be—it will also be possible to set it down in equational form.

Second, there are governmentally imposed relationships that affect the feasible degree of variation in the relevant variables. These relationships can take two forms. On the one hand, they can appear as boundary conditions imposed on the decision variables, either the targets or the instruments. Thus, the government might wish to establish upper and lower bounds to, for example, the unemployment rate, the trade deficit, export growth, and so forth. Such institutional relationships will appear in a structural model in constraints of the form $X_i^0 \le X_i \le X_i^1$.

Similarly, the boundaries imposed on one variable might depend on the rates of other variables. Thus, the ratio of foreign inflow to gross national product that the government is willing to admit as feasible, might depend, say, on the savings-to-income ratio obtaining in the economy. In a simple linear model this could be introduced via constraints of the form $a_i^0 X_i \le b_i^0$ and $a_i^1 X_i \ge b_i^1$, where the X_i are the variables, and a_i^0, a_i^1, b_i^0, and b_i^1 are constants. Then, the difference between the upper bound b_i^0, and the lower bound b_i^1 might itself be a function of other variables. That is, $b_i^0 - b_i^1 = g(Y_1, \ldots, Y_K)$. In the present illustration, for example, the range between the permissible bounds of the savings ratio, for given levels of the foreign-capital:inflow ratio, might depend on the government's capacity to raise savings, expand exports, and secure foreign aid.

Just as the government can impose restrictions, so too can some restrictions be inherently imposed by the cultural milieu within which the system functions. Thus, Chenery has explicitly recognized in his models[6] that there will be bounds imposed on, for example, the supply of capital and labor, and the supply of foreign exchange. He has also recognized that the *composition* of internal and external demands might well hold to some complex relationship deriving from personal consumption patterns indigenous to the society.

One structural model of institutional relationships which is of particular interest is the so-called Oslo model developed by Frisch.[7] This model attempts to introduce, for analytical and decision-making purposes, the distribution of purchasing power among variously classified sets of households, and the distribution of demands of these households. That is, it describes both where income goes and how it is spent.

This description takes place via an *income-transformation* matrix, which is a logical extension of the input-output table. In this matrix, households are

[6] H. B. Chenery, "A Model of Development Alternatives," in R. J. Ward (ed.) *The Challenge of Development* (Chicago: Aldine, 1967), pp. 31–44, and H. B. Chenery and M. Bruno, "Economic Development in an Open Economy: The Case of Israel," *Economic Journal*, Vol. 72, May 1962.
[7] R. Frisch, *A Survey of Types of Economic Forecasting and Programming and a Brief Description of the Oslo Channel Model* (Oslo: Institute of Economics, May 1961).

divided into I classes, say in terms of income, and the primary income is divided into K classes, say in terms of the source: wages, salaries, profits, and so on. Then, the income-transformation matrix consists of elements $R_{ki}(k = 1, \ldots, K; i = 1, \ldots, I)$, such that R_{ki} is the amount of income in the kth category that flows to households in the ith class. Similarly, where there are $j = 1, \ldots, J$ producing sectors, one can develop a *demand* matrix with typical element $C_{ji}(j = , \ldots, J; i = 1, \ldots, I)$ showing the demand of the ith household for the jth commodity. These matrices can then be adjoined to the input-output matrix, in effect permitting a more detailed analysis of the impact of any autonomous decisions taken by the government. We shall discuss the Oslo model at greater length in Chapter 8.

Again, then, the institutional relationships can be modeled in a variety of ways, consistent with the format of the other structural relations, and the purposes for which the model is being built.

6.5 CONCLUSION

The set of feasible policies among which the policy makers will choose is defined by a set of constraints and boundary conditions. These are restrictions that the instruments and targets *must* satisfy either (1) because of the technology of the system, the behavioral patterns established in the society, and the institutional arrangements under which the system operates, or (2) because of requirements that the policy makers wish to directly impose upon any policy. In the latter case, we are once again concerned with the *policy makers' preferences;* in the former case, we are concerned with the *system's structure.*

The structure of an economic system can be, and has been modeled in many different ways. The modeling problem is essentially one of developing the most useful format for setting down a series of social accounting, causal and institutional relationships linking a set of prespecified instruments to a set of prespecified targets. It is within this format, and in light of the preferences that they maintain, that the policy makers will select the optimal set of measures.

PART TWO
Systems, Subsystems, and Plans

Part I was concerned with the presentation of the basic elements of Quantitative Policy Analysis—that is, with the examination of the relationships between governors of simple and/or multi-level systems, and these systems' components and couplings. Part II is concerned with the coordination of various policy decisions into national *programs* or *plans,* and with the formulation, integration, and interaction of goals within the main subsystems of the economy.

A plan has three fundamental purposes. It is a *coordinating mechanism* of policies which will commonly concern such issues as overall economic growth, technological choices, capital and labor utilization, sectoral activities, location and regional considerations. It must reconcile, for example, decisions relating to capital and manpower utilization, with decisions relating to the directions in which the research and development activities in the economy are going to proceed.

Second, it is a public *guide to action.* That is, it must detail the specific projects and processes that are necessary to effect governmental policy. Here, two different types of plans can be distinguished. On the one hand, a plan accompanied by sufficient administrative guarantees so as to assure its implementation by all the economic agents of the country is said to be a *directive* plan. On the other hand, a plan that is not supported by such guarantees, but is only suggestive of programs that the government would like to see undertaken, is said to be an *indicative* plan. In the Soviet acceptance of the term "planning," a *directive* plan supersedes the market. In the Western acceptance, an *indicative* plan *combines with the market and complements its functions.* This latter plan is a national framework of firmed-up expectations, enlightening individual behavior.

Third, a plan is a detailed *study* of both the possible and the desirable long-term consequences of short-term resource allocation decisions, and of the patterns of growth and development, whether of a nation, a sector, or an economic region. Thus, a plan not only sets out a course of action, but in addition, it details the long-term implications of this action. In contrast to growth models, or to theoretical policy models in general, plans therefore involve: (a) *detailed* empirical *estimates,* or subjective assessments of the model's parameters; (b) *complex specifications* of the development processes that will evolve from the plan; and (c) the various sectoral or branch *disaggregations* that are necessary in order to evaluate the effects that the plan will have throughout, and on all levels of the economy.

The detailed specification of disaggregated *sectoral alternatives* raises a number of problems, among which the most important are the following: the need to deal with the various *couplings* between the sectoral subsystems and the national systems of which they are a part; and the need to integrate the decision making *within* each of these subsystems. The disaggregated sectoral models are usually intended to *complement* rather than *substitute for* an aggregated national model. The results that they yield should be mutually consistent, as well as consistent with the activity of the entire economy. Sectoral and national models should be submitted to a continuous process of revision and refinement, in order to assure that their interconnections have been adequately understood and specified.

Further, planning is inherently a dynamic process rather than a static one. But, the appropriate time dimension within which to plan for one sector will not necessarily be optimal with respect to another. Thus, the technology sector might demand a long-term outlook that focuses on a continuous *path* of expenditure and effort inputs that will generate long-term technological outputs, whereas the foreign trade sector might demand a short-term focus on current exchange rates that will assure the maintenance of a favorable balance of payments. Alternatively, planning in the technology sector might imply the short-term need to translate the results of past research into products and processes that are compatible with the objectives set for the agricultural sector, whereas planning in the foreign trade sector might imply the establishment of a long-term program for raw material exports. The appropriate time dimension will depend on the particular sector under consideration, and the overall purpose of the plan.

In a general way, all plans involve the same kind of choices and the same kind of fundamental problems—namely those of consistency, efficiency, optimality. Central to most planning exercises is indeed input-output economics. As already stated, Leontief's flexible mathematical tool has found an increasingly expanding scope of application in planning of all kinds and at all levels. Its extensions by Hollis B. Chenery, Ragnar Frisch, and others, have established it in a unique position in the field. Yet, each sector is subject to its peculiar set of constraints—political, social, institutional. Thus, the agricultural sector might be privately controlled, and agricultural prices determined in the free market, whereas the industrial sector might be publicly controlled, and industrial prices determined by governmental fiat. An *optimal* plan for one sector will, therefore, not necessarily be *compatible* with the constraints imposed upon another. Moreover, in plan implementation various conflicts are bound to arise within the economy-wide controlling hierarchy. Many other econometric and mathematical programming tools are therefore required in addition to input-output economics in planning practice. In plan implementation, the center *cannot* take over all decision-making powers. It must therefore *select* a mode of coordination defining clearly its relationships with the lower levels, *modify* in various ways the lower levels' decision problems, and *establish a method* for determining and implementing an *optimal* solution with the selection of the mode of coordination. The center must, furthermore, determine the *type, quantity,* and *quality* of information that each lower-level unit will receive concerning its interaction with the rest of the system.

Disregarding here the issues connected with plan implementation, we focus in Part II on (a) the specific steps involved in overall planning, (b) the problems involved in the so-called decomposition and decentralization techniques, and (c) the specific nature of sectoral and regional plans.

In this section's first chapter, Chapter 7, we discuss (a) the steps involved in plan formulation, (b) some specific planning models, and (c) recent modeling and methodological advances—the contributions and the contributors—in the East and in the West. Particular emphasis is given to the types of models that are available to the planner, and to the types of data that are necessary in plan formulation.

In Chapter 8 the emphasis shifts to planning techniques. After discussing (a) *how* plans are constructed and, in particular, the problem of planning by "stages," we next explore (b) some of the more important *techniques* employed in economic planning; those techniques that we consider here are forecasting, activity analysis, the so-called dual methods, dynamic programming, and simulation.

Planning for *economic growth* is the particular concern of Chapters 9–15. Chapters 9–12 deal with the determination of the conditions for economic expansion; Chapters 13–15 deal with the main sectors of economic activity and with regional structuring.

The opening chapter, Chapter 9, examines the problems of choice among available technologies and of technological forecasting; the constraints under which the long-term choices of the directions of expansion must be carried out are carefully presented. Chapter 10 discusses the interplay between public and private investment decisions and between macro and micro criteria of choice for determining the *volume and pattern of capital resources and allocation.* Chapter 11 considers the role of the foreign sector as one representing a potentially important *source of product demand and capital supply,* and thereby one of the pivotal factors in economic expansion. Finally, Chapter 12 discusses the problems of deployment and development of human resources, that is, issues in estimating labor availability and manpower requirements, and issues in educational planning.

Chapters 13 and 14 turn to the main sectors of economic activity: industry and agriculture. Chapter 13 examines various aspects of *interdependence among "priority" branches,* and the differences in this respect between Soviet and Western strategies of expansion. Chapter 14 brings into relief some of the basic homogeneous characteristics and problems of agriculture which allow for common planning decisions and economic modeling, notwithstanding the complex social frameworks and traditions of this sector.

Chapter 15 concludes the section with a discussion of the problems of "evening out" economic differences among regions, and of optimally structuring the national "space." A number of the more widely used models of regional planning and regional growth models are examined in a systematic fashion.

CHAPTER 7
Planning Models

7.1 THE THEORETICAL BACKGROUND

Since the 1950s, economic planning—herein defined as the *systematic charting by government of a desired course for national sectoral or regional outputs*—has, in the West, received a powerful impetus from the need for complex economic policies, most especially under depression and war-time conditions. A major purpose of Western planning and planning models is to facilitate the policy-making process. This is accomplished both by a unified treatment of a collection of interrelated problems that one might be tempted to deal with individually, and by making planning and economic intervention respectable and accepted media that can help otherwise free-market economic systems to achieve their goals. Relying heavily on the concepts, models, applications, and combinations of income theory, social accounting theory, and growth theory developed in the past few decades, planning theory has also had to cope with a number of more specific problems: in particular, (1) the integration of multi-level, multi-stage, multi-gestation decision and production problems; (2) formulation of complex operations models; (3) concrete determination of feasibility areas; and (4) the definition of static and dynamic optimality. Thus, as in Holland, on the one hand, planning has been concerned primarily with economic behavior in the aggregate. And, as in France, on the other hand, planning has been primarily concerned with achieving sectoral adjustments, and, in a sense, only secondarily with economic behavior in the aggregate. The most notable contributions for tackling these problems have been made by Jan Tinbergen, Ragnar Frisch, Hollis B. Chenery, and Richard Bellman—to mention only a few of the more outstanding contributors to the field.[1]

[1] R. Bellman, *Adaptive Control Processes* (Princeton, N.J.: Princeton University Press, 1961); H. B. Chenery and M. Bruno, "Economic Development in an Open Economy," *Economic Journal*, Vol. LXXII, March 1962; R. Frisch, *General Outlook on a Method of Advanced and Democratic*

As previously remarked, Tinbergen's theory of rational policy choice has served as the foundation for raising and dealing with a large number of policy issues. His mathematical planning models for "hard core" planning and planning in stages, developed in conjunction with H. C. Bos,[2] have provided a concrete demonstration of how the macro-planning framework, and various subdivisions of the planning task, can be successively approached in an imaginative and fruitful fashion.

In the planning context, one of Frisch's notable efforts has been his attempt to bring into a common focus an expanded vision of interindustry transactions, including (1) certain behavioral patterns in the economy, (2) substitutability effects during a planning period, (3) the so-called carry-on impact of decisions on investment and the planning for investment startings, and (4) the interactions within a simple planning frame of input-output analysis and flow-of-funds accounts.

Chenery and his associates have exercised a great impact on current planning methods through direct empirical investigations of planning problems in less developed areas, and the resultant formulation of a family of planning models evaluating "feasibility areas" when data are crude and scarce; in particular, when it is exceedingly difficult to pinpoint the various actual or assumed resource "gaps"—that is, the simultaneous or successive constraints that exist with respect, say, to savings, foreign exchange, and skilled labor. Chenery and Clark's pioneering study, *Interindustry Economics,*[3] provides a nexus between income projections, sectoral analysis, and evaluation of individual projects, through the utilization of linear programming methods.

Bellman and his associates have presented detailed approaches to the application of dynamic programming for the solution of control theory problems, allocation of resources, price determination, and inventory and scheduling processes. This work, however, is only now starting to find increased application in complex planning analysis.

Soviet planning, the prototype for planning in the East, was inaugurated on a national scale in 1929. Some of its pioneers were liquidated physically; others were simply destroyed professionally. Remarkable pioneering attempts in input-output analysis, made in the Soviet Union in the 1920s, and in linear programming, made in the 1930s, were cut short by Stalin. He emphasized instead, central balancing of scheduled outputs and demands, product by product, and administrative orders for their execution. As a Soviet economist acknowledged it in the late 1960s, "the new ideas [concerning activity analysis] were assimilated *slowly* by our science and were also put into practice *slowly.*" [4]

Macroeconomic Planning (Oslo: Institute of Economics, December 1965); J. Tinbergen, *Development Planning* (London: World University Library, 1967).

[2] J. Tinbergen and H. C. Bos, *Mathematical Models of Economic Growth* (New York: McGraw-Hill, 1962).

[3] H. B. Chenery and P. G. Clark, *Interindustry Economics* (New York: John Wiley, 1959).

[4] V. V. Novozhilov, *Problems of Cost-Benefit Analysis in Optimal Planning* (White Plains, New York: IASP, 1970), p. 22. (Emphasis supplied).

It is erroneous to even allude to contributions to planning methodology during Stalin's era. As continues to be true throughout Eastern Europe, the purpose of Soviet planning was and remains to exert direct control over all aspects of economic activity; that is, to impose centralized control on the economic system as a whole. As we shall see in Chapter 8—implementation is in Soviet planning at least as important as the plan itself, To place the vacuum in planning methodology in the Stalin era in true perspective, one need only consider that planning techniques made rapid strides in the West precisely when they were kept frozen in the Soviet Union, so that in the end the Soviet Union fell behind in a field in which it was initially the pioneer.

Since the death of Stalin there have been various developments in planning technology in the East. Outstanding in this regard has been the work of Lange and Kalecki in Poland,[5] Kornai in Hungary,[6] and Kantorovich, Nemchinov, Novozhilov, and Dadaian in the Soviet Union.[7]

Perhaps the most notable contributions have been those of Lange, who introduced the entire Western economic apparatus into Eastern economics in the 1950s. His own unique contribution to planning modeling concerns the study of the "economic effect" of the physical composition of investment, and the employment effect of investment in various economic sectors.

Kalecki's work starts with his basic growth model, and indeed has greater relevance for growth theory than for planning models. The contributions of Kantorovich and Novozhilov primarily concern methods of "shadow price" evaluation for achieving optimal allocation of resources under planning—a singular contribution that continues to be ignored in the planning practices of the Soviet Union, as will become apparent when we explore planning techniques. Finally, we might note that other Soviet contributions primarily concern variations of the Marxian two-sector model, which is only of marginal interest in the West.

7.2 PLANNING: INTRODUCTORY REMARKS

a. What is meant by planning

A perpetual concern of management, whether of the household, the firm, or the national economy, is its necessary involvement in both short-term

[5] M. Kalecki, *Introduction to the Theory of Growth in a Socialist Economy* (Oxford: Blackwell, 1969); O. Lange, *Introduction to Econometrics* (New York: Macmillan, 2nd ed., 1963) and (with A. Banasiński) *Optimal Decisions, Principles of Programming* (Oxford: Pergamon Press, 1970).

[6] J. Kornai, *Mathematical Planning of Structural Decisions* (Amsterdam: North-Holland, 1967).

[7] L. V. Kantorovich, "Mathematical Methods of Production Planning and Organization" (1939) in V. S. Nemchinov (ed.) *The Use of Mathematics in Economics,* English edition, A. Nove (ed.) (Edinburgh and London: Oliver & Boyd, 1964), and L. V. Kantorovich, *The Best Use of Economic Resources,* English edition, G. Morton (ed.), P. F. Knightsfield (transl.) (Cambridge, Mass.: Harvard University Press, 1965); V. S. Nemchinov, *The Use of Mathematics, op. cit.,* and *Ekonomiko matematicheskie metody i modeli* (Economic Mathematical Methods and Models) (Moscow: Sotsekonlit, 1962); V. V. Novozhilov, *Problems of Cost-Benefit Analysis in Optimal Planning, op. cit.;* finally, see the important collective work *Optimal'noe planirovanie i sovershenstvovanie upravleniia narodnym khoziaistvom* (Optimal Planning and the Improvement of the Management of the National Economy) Essays for the 75th Birthday of V. S. Nemchinov (Moscow: Nauka, 1969).

and long-term *planning*. In the managerial context, planning implies the need to *specify* the projects to be undertaken, and the procedures to be followed, in order to effect the choice of policies and programs. In essence, then, planning models breathe life into policy models, first by requiring the specification of functional forms, second by utilizing accounting and statistical procedures for the estimation of relevant parameters, and finally by exploring the specific implications of alternative plans—that is, policies that might actually be adopted—for the economy and its individual sectors. The policy-making process therefore establishes the *basic framework* for achieving the short-term, medium-term, or long-term objectives set up by the controllers of the economic system, whereas the planning process provides the necessary *operating details* for the managers of the individual components within this framework. In the short term of, say, a single year, these details are commonly backed by government fiat; in the medium term of a three-to-five year period, the government will commonly commit itself to certain policies designed to assure that the plan is effective; and in the long term the government will commonly provide a framework for achieving policy objectives.

As an operative procedure, then, planning is a continuous process that may serve *any* type of policy. It is also a process that can take place at either of two levels. On the one hand, *directive planning* requires direct governmental action to assure that the policy makers' plans will in fact be implemented, and that the variables that the policy makers' want to influence will in fact be influenced in the desired direction. Thus, directive planning is generally short term in nature. On the other hand, *indicative planning* entails the use of the government's powers of persuasion and influence, and the government's credibility, to *indirectly* influence the relevant variables in the desired direction, by causing firms and individuals to voluntarily embark on the courses of action *suggested* by the policy makers' plans. Hence, indicative planning is generally longer term in nature.

In addition to understanding what is meant by planning, it is also important to recognize what is *not* meant by planning. In particular, planning models are neither forecasting models nor growth models, although the latter are in fact *related* to planning, if distinct from it. Thus, planning is related to forecasting, insofar as both seek to determine the future rates of certain variables of interest to the policy-making body. But, whereas forecasting simply seeks to ascertain these rates as policy-making informational inputs, planning seeks to influence these rates as policy-making objectives, in the desired directions—and it is predicated on the assumption that they can be so-influenced.

Similarly, long-term or *perspective* planning models are related to growth models insofar as both are *ordinarily* concerned with the *rates of change* or acceleration in the rates of certain variables of interest to policy makers. But, whereas growth models tend to be broadly defined theoretical constructs from which one can *infer* the underlying factors effecting economic growth, planning models are necessarily empirical in nature, and require a *detailed specification* of the causes and effects of economic growth. Thus, planning models require: (1) empirical estimates of both the relevant parameters, and of the short- and long-term economic consequences of implementing specific projects under consideration; (2) complex specification of development processes and policy constraints, so that projects and procedures that are incompatible with each other or with the policy makers' goals are not suggested; and (3) broad sectoral disaggregations, say in terms of regions, industrial structure, and technology, so that the feasibility and economic implications of any plan for less broadly, but logically defined subsystems of the economic system can be analyzed in detail.

Planning models, then, provide the foundation for *computational* procedures for (1) guiding policy makers in the implementation of the policy-making process, (2) studying, in detail, the long-term consequences of alternative resource allocations, and (3) theorizing about the consequences and demands of economic growth and development. The output of these procedures is a set of *figures* associated with various proposals, and this set of figures forms a plan. Since the task of coordinating and reconciling these figures is essentially a mathematical and logical process, the precise and logically consistent nature of mathematical models makes their employment in this regard especially appropriate. The task of implementing the plan means that those deviations that do occur from the anticipated results will not be tolerated, and that sufficient feedbacks and flexibility will be built into the decision-making process to permit the policy makers to take the necessary actions to correct for unforeseen disturbances and unanticipated results.

The present-day debate over planning or programming has firmly shifted from the overly vague question of its desirability to its form and its focus. Whether one favors the widest possible use of the competitive market to organize economic life or, say, the use of the state's machinery to guide economic planning raises a single crucial question: how is it to be done?—not whether it is to be done.

Experience has revealed that even in the developed countries: (1) the political defenses against cohesive minority groups are disturbingly weak; (2) the rigidity and mechanical uniformity of political controls often lead to gross inefficiencies; (3) even the best educated society may reject economic rationality because of ingrained prejudice; and (4) the forces of the market place act at times at a socially unacceptable rate in the elimination of objectionable conditions, such as poverty and the economic abuses of monopoly power. Planning is not a panacea. Rather, it is a means of better understanding how and why the economic system behaves as it does, of anticipating economic changes before they occur, and of taking positive action to move the economic system in desired directions.

b. The steps involved in planning

National planning is the logical extension of the policy-making process wherein the projects and procedures through which policy is to be implemented must be specified in detail, and the demands that these projects and procedures will make on the variously defined individual sectors or *subsystems* of the economy, the ramifications of national policy for these individual subsystems, the commitments that the central government will have to make to them consistent with national policy, and the couplings or interrelationships of these variously defined subsystems and how they relate to the overall national system, must all be spelled out with the numerical precision that effective systemic control demands. In general, then, planning consists of a fairly uniform set of steps. These are basically five in number.

The first step in planning focuses on the controller's objective function. It involves a careful inspection and determination of the major problems confronting the economy, and the essential *issues* with which the planners must be concerned, as well as the related need to define the society's *goals*. The issues might range from structural imbalances, say in output and employment patterns, and discrepancies in the GNP and population growth rates, to balance of payments problems. The choice of goals, say as expressed in the policy makers' preference functions, or as determined through popular "referendum," might include, for example, curbing unemployment over a period of T_1 years, eliminating disguised unemployment in T_2 years, and consolidating small industry, while developing heavy industry, in T_3 years. It should be noted, however, that the *true* scale of preference of the policy makers, that is, their *actual* priorities, may not be deciphered from the plan itself, but rather from *plan fulfillment patterns*. In directive planning in particular, where the supremal coordinator *sets* the goals and *oversees* the implementation, it is indeed plan fulfillment that reveals what goals the directors of the system are willing to *sacrifice first* when departures from the original plan become imperative.[8]

The second step involves defining the *data* and specifying the *constraints,* as well as formulating particular *hypotheses* concerning the future. In the former connection, such specific data will be needed as saving and import propensities, capital:output and labor:capital ratios, input-output coefficients, and, in Marxian systems, the organic compositions of capital, rates of "surplus value," and their interrelations; also constraints will have to be specified on, for example, the minimal rate of per capita consumption, the maximum level of the available labor pool, and the institutional rules and regulations that the system must respect. In the latter connection, particular hypotheses must be put forth with respect to the future of such variables as foreign aid, the composition of imports, and possible restrictions on private consumption.

The third step involves choosing and specifying a *model* that defines the key interrelations among the main variables. It is, however, a step that is especially difficult to separate from the preceding one. On the one hand, the model suggests the data requirements; on the other hand, the availability of data suggests the feasibility of selecting one model as opposed to another. The data and model specification processes therefore involve feedback from one to the other so as to assure that the demands of the latter are compatible with the ca-

[8] See J. G. Zielinski, *Economic Reforms in Polish Industry* (London: Oxford University Press for the Institute of Soviet and East European Studies, University of Glasgow, 1973), p. 35.

pabilities of the former. Steps two and three, then, are concerned with *explicitly* describing, generally in mathematical form, the transformation processes of the individual components of the system, the couplings of the components, the appropriate groupings of components into subsystems and the couplings of the latter, and any external constraints that are *imposed* upon the system, say because of the controller's demands, because of events that are taking place in the environment, or because of changes that are occurring within the system itself.

As a fourth step, it is necessary to establish both the proper projections for those variables that can either be accurately forecast, or are to be directly or indirectly controlled by the planner, and the sectoral adjustments that will have to be made or will be taking place within the chosen plan period. The former instance once again involves a data problem, insofar as it requires the specification of exogenous inputs into the economic system, as well as the determination of the outputs to be obtained, and, perhaps, reintroduced into the system through some feedback mechanism. The latter instance involves the detailed analysis of these inputs and outputs so as to explore their ramifications for the individual components and subsystems vis-à-vis components.

Finally, it is necessary to define the policies and instruments to carry out the plan implied by the projections and the required sectoral adjustments. That is, it is necessary to determine and effect the specific projects and programs— the inputs from the controller, as well as the feedback mechanism—that will make the plan viable.

The heart of the planning process is the model describing the system and thus defining the problem. Everything else—data requirements, speculations about the future, and sectoral implications—emanate from it. As remarked at the outset of the book, this is not to suggest that the *political* problems inherent in planning are minimal. Indeed, the interaction between the planners and the politicians that have to be convinced to act is critical. Given the thrust of the book, however, it is the *technical* aspects that take primacy over the *political* aspects, with models and algorithms diverting us from the subsequent issues of negotiation, bargaining, and compromise. We neglect the latter, not out of ignorance but, remembering our previous admonishments with respect to selectivity, out of *choice,* and thus it is to the planning models that we now turn.

7.3 THE HARD CORE OF THE PLAN: MODELS

We have previously discussed the·wide variety of considerations that arise in building a model for policy and/or planning purposes, and have, in fact, looked at some structural models for describing the behavioral, technological, and institutional relationships in the economy. We shall now once again consider some structural models. In the present planning context, however, our interest in doing so is to show *how* they can be handled for planning purposes, and *which* are the main planning approaches currently in use. For the first point, we shall select a few examples of aggregated macro-models and disaggregated, simplified two-sector and multi-sector micro-models; for the second point we shall examine, in particular, the basic approaches developed by, or based on, the Mahalanobis, Frisch, and Chenery models, as well as the Soviet approach. Assuredly, there are a wide variety of models that have been, and will continue to be built to suit the individual needs of planners. The intent of the present section is not to be exhaustive, but rather to indicate how some of these models are actually handled for planning purposes.

a. Overall central models

Planning, from its inception to the realization of its results, is an intertemporal process. As such, overall central planning models are primarily growth oriented and thread the interrelationships among (1) the rates of growth of such crucial economic variables as consumption, investment, and foreign trade, as well as (2) the rates of growth that the latter rates (a) imply for, say, GNP, and (b) require of, say, the labor force and agricultural productivity. These models therefore require the specification of such familiar, if elusive, coefficients as overall capital:output ratios, and the marginal propensities to save and invest.

The simplest and most familiar models in conception and execution, which can be used for judging key relationships among macrovariables and for setting up a frame within which sectoral plans may be fitted, are the Harrod-Domar models and their variants. These models determine the rates of growth in national income and its components as functions of the marginal propensity to save and the marginal capital:output ratio. In the more sophisticated variants, the possibility of leakages in the system which prevent the actual growth rates from achieving their theoretically attainable magnitudes is incorporated into the models.

An important variant on the Harrod-Domar theme, a Kalecki model,[9] has been used for preliminary studies of certain long-term planning perspectives in Poland. The model seeks to complement the traditional Soviet "priority sectors" approach to planning. The latter accepts as its fundamental precepts (1) the goal of maximum growth of national income, and (2) the constraint of a minimally acceptable standard of living. The Soviet traditional *technique* for accomplishing this (to which we have already alluded), is the method of "balances." This technique, however, is not accompanied by a model for explicitly determining this maximum rate and the temporal stream of investment that this rate requires. The Kalecki model is an attempt to rectify this neglect—an attempt that has since been expanded upon in more sophisticated versions.

Kalecki's model proceeds by *specifying* the annual change in the rate of national income. This change, ΔY, is given as the sum of three components: (1) annual gross productive expenditure, given in constant prices, denoted I, multiplied by the marginal output:capital ratio, $1/k$; (2) the base rate of national income, Y, multiplied by a capacity-reducing coefficient a_2; and (3) the base rate of national income multiplied by a capacity-increasing coefficient a_1. In the

---

[9] M. Kalecki, *Introduction to the Theory of Growth* . . . . , *op. cit.*

former case, fixed capital is worn out and depreciates; in the latter case, technological improvements, say, effect improved utilization of fixed capacity. Then,

$$\Delta Y = (\frac{1}{k})I + a_1Y - a_2Y \tag{7.1}$$

whereupon

$$\frac{\Delta Y}{Y} = \frac{1}{k}\frac{I}{Y} + a_1 - a_2 \tag{7.2}$$

yields the rate of growth in national income. It is commonly assumed that the improvements in capital utilization just balance off depreciation, so that $a_1 = a_2$, and

$$\frac{\Delta Y}{Y} = \frac{1}{k}\frac{I}{Y} \tag{7.2a}$$

akin to Equation (6.26) and the growth rate in the Harrod-Domar model.

Equation (7.2a) suggests that economic growth is limited solely by the rate of investment expenditure and the capital:output ratio. The latter is estimated on the basis of past experience and future projections; the former is constrained from three directions.

First, when productive investment increases, the immediate short-term impact is to reduce consumption and unproductive investment—that which effects short-term consumption increases without longer-term benefits. But, because of the minimum living-standard constraint, this reduction is limited, and, consequently, so is the rate of productive investment.

Foreign trade imposes a second constraint. There is a need to balance imports and exports over the long term. As the demand for imports increases, the supply and sale of exports must increase commensurately. This in turn requires diverting investment to the export-producing sector, and exerts still further pressure on the acceptable rate of investment.

A third constraint may arise from the need to raise labor productivity—that is, to obtain greater output from a given labor force—and this too may require additions to the capital stock that further pressure the investment boundary.

Finally, a number of assumptions and projections are necessary in order to apply the model. Even casual consideration of the three major constraining factors suggests, for example, the need to be concerned with demographic changes, changing consumption patterns, developments in international markets, technological change, and changes in the labor force. This assuredly is true of Harrod-Domar-type models in general. In addition to being over-simplified, they are highly sensitive to parameter values that will ordinarily be difficult to estimate and that, in any event, are likely to be changing regularly, albeit perhaps systematically, in response to technological change as well as changing consumption versus savings preferences effected by changes in the economic, political, and social conditions of the society. Moreover, because they are highly aggregated they give no clue as to, say, the specific regional and industrial sectoral allocations of investment. In the West, therefore, the models find their greatest use in the *suggestions* that they make regarding the broader implications of alternative investment policies for economic growth, or, alternatively, regarding the rates of economic growth that *appear* to be achievable. In the East, however, the model's variants have been given more direct application, with the specifics dealt with as part of the more general balance approach.

b. Two-sector models

For sectoral planning purposes the economic system can be divided into a series of interconnected subsystems, or industrial sectors. One such division, the simplified two-sector version of the Mahalanobis model, was previously discussed in Chapter 3. In the present section we shall consider a pair of two-sector models suggested by Ichimura.[10]

As in the Mahalanobis model, the initial Ichimura model divides the economy into a consumption and an investment goods sector. Unlike the former model, however, intersectoral transactions are ignored, so that the combined net output of both sectors determines national income. Thus, with C the net output in the consumption goods sector, and I the net output in the investment goods sector, $Y = C + I$.

Ichimura assumes that consumption will be proportional to national income, or $C = cY$ where c is the marginal propensity to consume, and $s = 1 - c$ is the marginal propensity to save. Hence,

$$C = (1 - s)(C + I) \tag{7.3}$$

Additionally, on the supply side it is assumed that (1) expansion in the capacity of the consumption goods industry will be required so as to keep up with the scheduled demand for consumer's goods, and therefore that (2) new investment within the investment goods sector will also be required. In particular, with ΔC and ΔI the increments in output requirements in the consumption and investment goods sectors, respectively, and with k_1 and k_2 the marginal capital:output ratios in the two respective sectors

$$I = k_1 \Delta C + k_2 \Delta I \tag{7.4}$$

or net output of investment goods equals the sum of the increased capacity requirements for consumption goods ($k_1 \Delta C$) and investment goods ($k_2 \Delta I$).

The model offers planners virtually no flexibility, in that the rates of growth in both sectors are uniquely determined by the parameter estimates, k_1, k_2, and s, and are necessarily equal to each other. This assures a fixed ratio of consumption-to-investment output over time. Specifically from Equation (7.3) it is easily seen that $sC = (1 - s)I$, so that $C = [(1 - s)/s]I$. Hence

[10] In United Nations, *Programming Techniques for Economic Development* (Bangkok: United Nations, 1961).

$$\Delta C = [\frac{(1-s)}{s}] \Delta I \tag{7.5}$$

Upon making this substitution for ΔC in (7.4) and solving, we immediately determine that

$$\frac{\Delta I}{I} = \frac{s}{k_1(1-s) + k_2 s} = \frac{s}{k} \tag{7.6}$$

It is also immediately clear that $\Delta C/C = \Delta I/I$. Thus, in typical Harrod-Domar fashion, the rate of growth in each sector, and thus in national income, equals the ratio of the marginal propensity to save to "the" capital:output ratio. In the present instance, however, the overall capital:output ratio is a weighted average of the capital:output ratios in each of the two sectors. In the case of the consumption goods sector, the weight is the marginal propensity to spend; in the case of the investment goods sector, the weight is the marginal propensity to save.

As an illustration, suppose that $c = .8$, $k_1 = 3$, and $k_2 = 6$. The overall capital:output ratio is then given by $k = (.8)(3) + (.2)(6) = 3.6$. Suppose that total income is initially at a rate of 1000. Then, given a marginal propensity to consume of .8, income will be divided between consumption of $C = 800$ and investment of $I = 200$. Further, it follows from Equation (7.6) that the rates of growth in consumption, investment, and income will all equal $.2/3.6 = 5.56$ percent. Hence, during the first plan year income can be expected to increase by a total of $1000(1.0556) = 55.56$. Eighty percent of this increment, or 44.45, will be for increased consumption; the remaining 20 percent, or 11.11, will be for increased investment goods. The latter figures represent the 5.56 percent increases in consumption and investment above their initial rates of 800 and 200, respectively.

Given an overall capital:output ratio of 3.6, a national income increment of 55.56 requires capital of $3.6(55.56) = 200$; the latter is precisely the initial rate of investment. Similarly, an increase in consumption of 44.45 requires capital in the amount of $3(44.45) = 133.34$; and, the increase in investment output of 11.11 requires capital in the amount of $6(11.11) = 66.66$. Thus, the initial investment outlay of 200 is divided in a 2:1 ratio in favor of capital for the consumption goods sector as opposed to the investment goods sector; that is, in inverse proportion to their capital:output ratios. At the end of the first plan year, then, $C = 844.45$ and $I = 211.11$. During the second plan year, the latter investment outlay will again be divided so as to allocate one-third to investment goods, or 70.37, with the remaining 140.74 allocated to the consumption goods sector. This two-to-one investment pattern, with each of the relevant variables increasing by 5.56 percent per year, will continue so long as the sectoral capital:output ratios, and the marginal propensity to consume, remain unchanged. The planners' problem is then to determine the specific investment projects to undertake, and the particular consumer goods to produce, to effect these totals.

Ichimura has also suggested a similar two-sector division between home and export markets. In the export sector, industries specializing in the production of export goods produce in the amount of $X = E(t)$. That is, due to changing conditions throughout the world, say with respect to prices and income rates, exports are a function of time, t. Production in the domestic industry sector, denoted H, plus imports M is equal to total domestic expenditures. Thus, with the domestic sector responsible for producing both consumption goods *and* capital goods, if output in the domestic sector increases by ΔH and the capital:output ratio in this sector is k_4, new capital in the amount $k_4\Delta H$ will be produced by the domestic industry. Similarly, with the capital:output ratio in the export goods industry denoted k_3, new capital in the amount $k_3\Delta X$ will be required by the latter, when export production increases by ΔX. Hence, given the marginal propensities to save (s) and to consume (c) out of total domestic production $H + X$, total domestic expenditures of $H + M$ will equal consumption of $c(H + X)$ plus new capital investment of $k_3\Delta X$ for the export goods sector, and $k_4\Delta H$ for the domestic goods sector.

The initial two equations of the second Ichimura model are, therefore,

$$X = E(t) \tag{7.7}$$

$$H + M = (1 - s)(H + X) + k_3\Delta X + k_4\Delta H \tag{7.8}$$

In addition, it is assumed that imports are a function of the rate of production in the domestic goods sector; or, where m is the marginal propensity to import relative to domestic goods production,

$$M = mH \tag{7.9}$$

Given a specific function $E(t)$, the values of H, X, and M are then uniquely determined in terms of the capital:output ratios and the marginal propensities to save and import.

Assuming the equality of imports and exports, this model is manipulated in much the same fashion as the previous model. Thus, with $M = mH$ and $X = M$, $X = mH$, and Equation (7.8) can be rewritten

$$H + mH = (1 - s)(H + mH) + k_3m\ \Delta H + k_4\ \Delta H$$

whereupon we immediately determine

$$\frac{\Delta H}{H} = \frac{s(m + 1)}{mk_3 + k_4} = \frac{s(m + 1)}{k} \tag{7.10}$$

as the *unique* rate of growth in domestic output; and, clearly $\Delta H/H = \Delta X/X$.

Comparable to the previous model, then, suppose $c = .8$, $k_4 = 3$, and $k_3 = 6$, and that the import:domestic-production ratio is set at $m = .25$. With an initial income rate of 1000, once again consumption is at the rate of 800. Hence, since exports equal imports, investment production in the domestic industry must be 200. Total production is, therefore, $H + X = 1000$; and, with $M = X = .25H$ we immediately determine $M = X = 200$ and $H = 800$. From

Equation (7.10), the rates of growth both in production in the domestic sector and in exports again equal $.2(.25 + 1)/(.25(6) + 3.0) = .25/4.5 = 5.56$ percent. In particular, then, $X = 200(1.0556)^t$ *must* be the rate of exports t years after the initial plan date—that is, exports must grow at the rate of 5.56 percent per year—if the nation's foreign exchange problems are to be avoided. The planners' problem is to develop and implement programs that will assure that this rate of growth is achieved.

A variety of two-sector models suggest themselves from the "dual" nature of economic systems as being comprised of farm and industrial sectors, rural and urban sectors, advanced and lagging sectors, and the like. Ichimura points out that an important consideration in such two-sector models is often the increase in population in the traditionally lagging agricultural or rural sector, and the estimated requirements for absorbing population into the more advanced industrial or urban sector. The crucial issue, then, is to determine the factors that limit the absorption of the population of the former sectors—most particularly, the farmers—into the latter sectors. The two-sector models are therefore especially useful vehicles for speculating as to the factors that inhibit economic growth, as well as about the problems of development.

c. Multi-sector models

The intent of the original two-sector Mahalanobis model discussed in Chapter 3 was to provide a simple operational model for the second Indian plan. In this model, the "instrument" is the allocation of investment between two commodity sectors; the objective is maximum growth. The Mahalanobis model can also be expanded into a multi-sector model in which the economic system is described in terms of a *number* of subsystems. Mahalanobis [11] accomplished this by subdividing the consumption sector into three distinct subsectors: (1) a sector housing modern technology; (2) a sector producing consumption goods in a smaller, more traditional setting, which would include agriculture; and (3) a service sector. Denoting consumption and hence productive capacity in these sectors in period t by C_{1t}, C_{2t}, and C_{3t}, respectively, total consumption is given by $C_t = C_{1t} + C_{2t} + C_{3t}$. Comparable to the earlier model λ_{2j} denotes the proportion of productive capacity in the capital goods sector devoted to the production of additional productive capacity in consumption sector $j(j = 1, 2, 3)$; in turn, λ_1 denotes the proportion of productive capacity in the capital goods sector devoted to the production of additional productive capacity in the capital goods sector, so that $\lambda_1 = \lambda_{21} + \lambda_{22} + \lambda_{23} = 1$. Similarly, $\beta_{2j} = 1/k_{2j}$ denotes the output:capital ratio in consumption sector j.. A set of three equations of the form

$$C_{tj} = C_{(t-1)j} + \beta_{2j}\lambda_{2j}I_{t-1} \qquad (j = 1, 2, 3) \tag{7.11}$$

[11] P. C. Mahalanobis, "Some Observations on the Process of Growth of National Income," *Sankhyā*, Vol. 12, 1953; and "The Approach of Operational Research to Planning in India," *Sankhyā*, Vol. 16, 1955.

then replaces Equation (3.8) and the model is solved as before for *four* decision variables: λ_1 and λ_{2j} ($j = 1, 2, 3$). The values of these variables then determine the optimal rates of the *four* instruments: additional investment in the capital goods sector, and additional investment in the three consumption subsectors.

In this form, the multi-sector Mahalanobis model is indeterminate, since there is but a single target—whether flexible or fixed—and four instruments with which it can be achieved. There are, however, only two rather than three degrees of freedom, since the decision variables must sum to unity. Because of this constraint, the "fourth" of the λ's is determined from the other three. The model can be made determinate simply by specifying values for any two of the λ's; but there is little sound theoretical basis for doing so. And, in view of the sensitivity of the results to the values of the λ's, this becomes a risky proposition indeed.

Alternatively, one can attempt to introduce additional targets into the model. In this vein, Mahalanobis introduced sectoral labor:capital ratios where, for example, in the investment sector, with E denoting the rate of employment, $E_{1t}/\lambda_1 I_t = \delta_1$. Thus, δ_1 represents the number of employees required in the capital goods sector, per *extra* unit of investment devoted to capital goods. Then, following Mahalanobis, the new employment generated by new investment, totaled over all four sectors, becomes an additional target. Even in this case, however, the number of instruments exceeds the now two targets, and a determinate solution can only be reached by specifying the value of one of the λ's. Moreover, the solution to the model assumes the independence of the output:capital and labor:capital ratios. This will not ordinarily be the case.

The simplest *multi-sector* model is the input-output model with fixed technological coefficients of production. As we already noted, the model is amenable to various levels of aggregation, and alternative sectoral specifications. Additionally, and without undue complication, the possibilities of (a) alternative production processes, and (b) time lags in the production process can also be incorporated into the basic model. These provide it with yet further flexibility.

In the former instance, the so-called "process approach," the option is held open that the various product categories may be susceptible to *several* fixed-coefficient processes. There will therefore be at least as many fixed technological coefficient processes available as there are product categories. Thus, not only can alternative mixes of the same set of inputs yield different output compositions, but alternative input compositions can, conceivably, yield the same output.

In the latter instance, the so-called "time-phasing" of production relationships, it is assumed that the factor inputs, including perhaps the capital inputs, are required a fixed time period in advance of the date when it is anticipated the outputs will become available.

The process approach permits the planners to utilize input-output relationships and mathematical programming techniques in determining the optimal production *processes* through which to carry out a plan; the time-phasing approach permits the planners to accurately time the *input requirements* of a plan, to assure that these inputs will be available when they are needed. In either event, however, the empirical problems are enormous. Estimating the fixed co-efficients and precisely determining the lags will not be a simple matter, and assuming these parameters fixed over a planning period may be heroic indeed.

Despite the enormity of the associated problems, Ragnar Frisch has attempted to broaden the basic input-output model in several significant ways in an attempt to make it more relevant for planning purposes. Frisch's approach appears as the so-called Oslo Channel Model.[12]

First, Frisch specifies an "income-transformation" matrix detailing the distribution of each of the primary sources of income, from wages to dividends, among various household categories. The precise definitions of these income sources depend on analytical needs and data limitations. Then, given a traditional input-output matrix from which one can ascertain the amount of an industry's output that will be demanded by each of the household categories, one can trace the flow from income to demand, and thereby determine the impact on final demand in each product class of changes occurring in any one of the primary income sources.

Second, through the introduction of "ring equations" Frisch instills the input-output model with greater flexibility by permitting substitution among factors to take advantage of possible factor complementarity, and to recognize the reality of factor rivalry. Within each so-called ring, Frisch groups together all primary inputs that can serve essentially the same purpose. Thus, for example, under metals one might group aluminum, copper, tin, and steel. If, then, a certain "quality" of metals, such as tensil strength, is demanded in a particular industry, this "quality" might alternatively be satisfied by x tons of aluminum, y tons of copper, z tons of steel, or some combination of these. Hence, an option is opened to the planner with respect to *which* metals to use to achieve a given end.

Third, investment is divided into "project channels" in accordance with three features: the so-called carry-on effect, the capacity effect, and the production or infra-effect. These make the model dynamic. The carry-on effect relates to the resources that will have to be committed in *future* periods as the result of an investment undertaken in the current planning period; the capacity effect relates to the capacity changes in each of the producing sectors that will be effected in future periods; and the infra-effect relates to future changes in the fixed technological coefficients which will result from a current investment project. Each channel groups together a stockpile of investment projects that, on average, produce similar intertemporal changes. As a practical matter, the channel definitions are commonly determined according to empirical convenience. The historical experience of those that have worked with the model is that 30 to 50 channels is an acceptable number, but 70 to 100 is more satisfactory.

[12] R. Frisch, *A Survey of Types of Economic Forecasting and Programming and Brief Description of the Oslo Channel Model* (Oslo: Institute of Economics, May 1961).

The model itself is, as Frisch describes it, a *selection* model rather than an implementation model. It is not until the constellation of volume figures have been analyzed in detail that one can turn to the practical difficulties of implementing its suggestions; that is, of determining whether the projects constituting a plan are compatible with the existing institutional, administrative, and financial constraints. Added to the considerable classifactory and technical problems that arise at the selection stage, the implementation problem would seem to make the widespread applicability of the Oslo model rather remote.

d. Gap models

The previously described Chenery model is related to another set of models—the so-called "gap" models, whose principal feature is the determination of various actual or assumed "gaps." Typical of these gaps are those between the tentative projections of ex ante demand and ex ante supply, or the spending required for, say, a welfare society for the next T years and the available resources over this period.

In essence, the gap technique, whether with respect to the short term or the long, or domestic versus international planning, consists of an analysis of the discrepancies between projections based on normative goals, and projections of the available resources. These discrepancies result in a gap that, barring some direct action on the government's part, is likely to persist. In particular, several models built around a so-called savings gap proceed along the following lines. First, a target rate of growth is posited for gross national product $[Y_n = Y_0(1 + r)^n]$. Second, it is necessary to determine the *capital* requirement $[I^n = f(Y_n)]$ to achieve this growth rate. A Harrod-Domar model, for example, might be a useful vehicle for accomplishing this. Third, from a typical consumption or savings function, the potential *savings* (S) generated by the posited GNP rate will also be projected $[S_n = g(Y_n)]$. Finally, the difference G_n between the capital requirements—the projected norm, and the potential savings rate—the available resource, is the savings gap $G_n = I_n - S_n = f(Y_n) - g(Y_n)$. (See Figure 7.1.) The planners' problem is to obtain additional funds to finance the required capital; and, foreign aid is a typical solution that is reached.

Models built around a foreign exchange gap proceed along similar lines. Again, a target rate of growth is posited for GNP (Y_n). Then, based on the expected GNP and specified functional relationships linking imports to the rate of GNP, an import forecast is derived $[M_n = h(Y_n)]$. These imports are to come from both developed and the lesser-developed countries. The difference (F_n) between the projected import rate—the norm—and a similarly projected export rate—the resource—$[X_n = p(Y_n)]$ is called the trade, or foreign exchange gap $[F_n = M_n - X_n = h(Y_n) - p(Y_n)]$. And, once again, the planners' problem is how to erase this gap (see Figure 7.2). A typical solution to this problem is to encourage, or induce, domestic investment in the export industries.

Finally both types of model are combined into the so-called two-gap model, raising the question of finding the "biggest," or the *dominant* of the

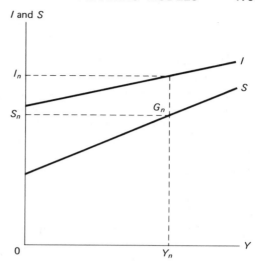

FIGURE 7-1

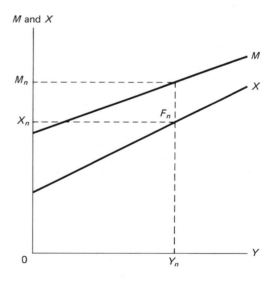

FIGURE 7-2

two gaps, and determining how it can be eliminated without further expanding the other. Having achieved this, the *secondary* gap is then attacked. It is apparent that additional, tertiary gaps and the like can also be dealt with in similar fashion. In particular, additional gaps will be introduced into the model when there are additional issues with which the planner is *specifically* concerned. Thus, if the planner is concerned with domestic regional growth patterns, or with the rates of growth in specific industrial sectors, then the latter will provide the focus for yet additional gaps.

7.4 THE MARXIAN MODEL

The discussion of structure in Chapter 6 developed the fundamental similarity of the Marxian two-sector model, and a Leontief input-output type of model, with its associated interconnections. In using the Marxian model of expanded reproduction for planning purposes, the "key" ratios are the organic composition of capital and the rate of exploitation; the "key" variables determining the rates of growth within the system are the proportions of the surplus within the producers' goods and consumers' goods sectors that will be retained by owners of the means of production (the "capitalists," or the state).

Suppose, for example, that at the beginning of the plan period $c_1 = 4000$, and $w_1 = s_1 = 1000$ in the producers' goods sector, so that $Q_1 = 4000 + 1000 + 1000 = 6000$. Similarly, suppose that $c_2 = 1500$, and $w_2 = s_2 = 750$, so that $Q_2 = 1500 + 750 + 750 = 3000$ in the consumers' goods sector. Thus, the organic composition of capital, c_i/w_i, is $k_1 = 4$ in the producers' goods sector, and $k_2 = 2$ in the consumers' goods sector; the rate of exploitation, s_i/w_i, is $e = 1$ in both sectors.

Suppose that in the producers' goods sector the owners of the means of production retain exactly half of their surplus. Then, given that $k_1 = 4$, the $(.5)1000 = 500$ that is invested in this sector so as to increase the amount of goods produced and labor hired is distributed as $\Delta c_1 = 400$ and $\Delta w_1 = 100$. Similarly, suppose that in the consumers' goods sector the owners retain 80 percent of the surplus. Then given that $k_2 = 2$, the $(.2)$ $750 = 150$ that is invested in this sector is distributed as $\Delta c_2 = 100$ and $\Delta w_2 = 50$. Therefore, in the second plan year $c_1 = 4000 + 400 = 4400$ and $w_1 = s_1 = 1000 + 100 = 1100$; here $w_1 = s_1$, because the rate of exploitation is unity. Hence, $Q_1 = 6600$. In the consumers' goods sector in the second plan year, $c_2 = 1500 + 100 = 1600$ and $w_2 = s_2 = 750 + 50$; again, $w_2 = s_2$ because the rate of exploitation is unity. Hence $Q_2 = 3200$, so that the total product $Q_1 + Q_2$ increases from 9000 to 9800.

In the illustration, and using the results of Chapter 6, $\alpha_1 = .5$ and $\alpha_2 = .2$. From Equation (6.19) we determine that $\lambda_1 = .2$ and $\lambda_2 = .33$. Hence from Equations (6.18) and (6.18a) we determine as growth rates that: $g_{c1} = (.8)(.5)(1)/4 = .1$ and $g_{c2} = (.67)(.2)(1)/2 = .067$; $g_{w1} = (.2)(.5)(1) = .1$ and $g_{w2} = (.33)(.2)(1) = .067$. It is immediately seen that these are in fact the previously determined growth rates for the two periods. With respect to wages in the producers' goods sector, for example, the rate of growth is $100/1000 = .1$. It is interesting to observe, however, that the growth of wages in the consumers' goods sector of .067 does not equal the .1 rate in the producers' goods sector. That is, the present system is not in equilibrium. The reason for this is easily seen, given the values of the organic compositions of capital and the equality of rates of exploitation in both sectors. Equilibrium requires that $(\lambda_1/\lambda_2) = .6 = (\alpha_2/\alpha_1)$. But, $\alpha_2/\alpha_1 = .4$. Thus, if the owners in the producers' goods sector continue to retain half of their surplus (that is, $\alpha_1 = .5$), equilibrium can only be achieved by having $\alpha_2 = .6\alpha_1 = .3$. That is, for equilibrium to obtain, owners in the consumers' goods sector must retain 70 percent of their surplus and reinvest 30 percent. Planners in a Marxian economy can, presumably, effect such a change!

7.5 CONCLUDING COMMENTS

Planning serves as (1) a *guide* for enlightened policy making, (2) an *integrating* framework for certain economic activities, and (3) as a frame for *consolidating expectations*, even in primarily market-guided economies. A variety of models have been built to aid in the planning process. The technical sophistication and mathematical complexity of many of these models should not be allowed to obscure the facts that in large measure planning is a political process, that the models and their solutions are dependent upon parameter values that are at the very least difficult to estimate, and at the very worst capable of constant variation in what are indiscernible, and perhaps random patterns, and that their outward complexity belies their (ordinarily) highly aggregative character that makes their solutions more suggestive of general principles than instructive of detailed actions.

The models presented in this chapter are useful insofar as they serve to indicate both the various *types* of model that are available to planners, and the various *types* of data—parameter estimates—that are required in the planning process. As we shall subsequently see, both the complexity of the models and their data requirements increase substantially once we get down to brass tacks and consider some specific models aimed at particular planning problems.

CHAPTER *8*

Planning Techniques and Procedures

8.1 TYPES OF PLANNING

Soviet economists distinguish between the *Soviet planning method,* or what they refer to as "socialist planning"—which, according to them, is the only planning possible—and *Western planning,* or what they refer to as "capitalist programming." The alleged distinction between these approaches is brought out in the writing of M. Bor who comments that, in contrast to socialist planning which "includes the entire complex of problems involved in determining plan targets for nationwide quantities like consumption, saving, national output, and national income," capitalist programming, which is primarily advisory and not ordinarily accompanied by administrative or legal guarantees, is "dependent on 'final demand' and therefore unable to go beyond the development and stimulation of general trends of sectoral production." [1] In short, Soviet planning penetrates inside the economy down to the level of the enterprise, while capitalist programming "does not transcend the framework of regulation of capitalist production, leaving economic development largely to the play of market fluctuations." [2] Thus, "the capitalist practice of programming incorporates no direct organizational-economic tie between even the most elaborate national program and the programs of individual enterprises. Therefore, even when a . . . group of entrepreneurs channel their investments in accordance with the programme, they do so because they are interested in state benefits at that particular moment . . ." [3] Soviet planning is thus seen as concerned with *both* the couplings of the components of the economic system and their trans-

[1] M. Bor, *Aims and Methods of Soviet Planning* (New York: International Publishers, 1967), p. 221.
[2] *Ibid.,* p. 220.
[3] *Ibid.,* pp. 225–226.

formation functions, whereas capitalist programming focuses primarily on the controller's choice of exogenous inputs into the system, secondarily with individual couplings, and not at all with individual transformation functions.

Bor, like most of the other Soviet economists, mistakes planning with *detailed orders* issued to enterprises and industries. Yet, there is nothing "socialist" about such orders. Indeed, in World War I, or under the Nazi regime in Germany in the late 1930s, such detailed orders concerning input and output mixes were already being issued to industries and enterprises in capitalist countries. The German war-economy methods of World War I—or the German "Kriegswirtschaft" model—organized in its essentials by Walter Rathenau, was indeed largely copied both by the Nazis and by Stalin (see Chapters 16 and 17). In fact, Lange called the Soviet economy a *sui generis Kriegswirtschaft*.[4] Still further, planning need not supersede the market; it can combine with it in innumerable ways, so that plan and market can in a sense be visualized as the ends of a continuum.

For broader purposes, a much more appropriate distinction between planning by specific and direct orders—as in a wartime, or in a totalitarian economy—and planning by other means, is that between directive and indicative planning. Directive plans are associated with administrative guarantees and legal sanctions; their aim is to obtain a prespecified output mix from a prespecified input mix. Indicative plans are programs that neither take the form of specific production assignments, nor are reinforced by juridical sanction; their aims are to provide a working framework for the government, and a "firmed-up expectations" outlook for businesses. The process of planning—that is, of operational policy making—remains the same in both cases.

Either directive or indicative planning may entail a *formalized* or a discretionary approach or procedure. A formalized procedure involves automaticity in formulation and execution. Once a core planning model is chosen, the rest of the planning process is dependent on the processing of the data needed for estimating unknown structural parameters, and determining the rates of the relevant economic variables. If the results yielded are unacceptable, either in that they do not conform with reality as it is known, or insofar as projections are patently infeasible, one can start anew by revising the assumptions, and perhaps altering the model. By contrast, in the *discretionary* approach there is no strict automaticity; intervention and change are possible at every stage of the process.

In planning, then, one is initially concerned with processing information; that is, with delineating alternative policies that might be followed, assessing the potential consequences of these policies and the likelihoods associated with these consequences, and then ranking the alternatives in accordance with the policy makers' preferences. This information processing can take place via a formal mathematical programming model wherein, for example, a prespecified objective function is maximized subject to a set of structural constraints

---

[4] O. Lange, *The Working Principles of the Soviet Economy* (New York: Research Bureau for Postwar Economics, second ed. 1944).

and boundary conditions, or through a more heuristic decision-making procedure utilizing, say, a Basic Policy Chart. Subsequently, one is concerned with executing the preferred plan. Here, too, the projects that comprise the plan might either be automatically implemented through, say, a network of controllers and actuators that have, in effect, been programmed to follow certain decision rules that cause them to behave in specific ways in reaction to given sets of data; or, alternatively, the controllers might have the freedom to improvise, bypassing a set of actions suggested by a particular plan, in favor of a course of action that, for reasons of their own, perhaps based on a heretofore unanticipated set of circumstances, they strongly favor.

Assuredly, the formal approach to planning need not be followed at both stages. In particular, a formal approach might be adopted at the initial planning stage, and a discretionary approach adopted at the subsequent execution stage. Indeed, it is not unusual with respect to formal decision-making models in general to discover that one of their most important functions is to offer *recommendations* that serve to focus the decision makers' attention upon a specific program, or within a narrowed range of feasible alternatives. The decision makers then impose their own *ad hoc* decision-making devices upon these recommendations, as they perhaps recognize that an earlier statement of preferences was either erroneous, or no longer coincides with currently held beliefs; and, in any event, this earlier statement requires up-dating as evidenced by the fact that, when forced to actually make a decision, the decision makers prefer not to accept the decision selected by the formal decision-making model. Particularly with respect to economic planning, where the planning process may be unfolding over a period of several years, and where both preferences and politicians may be changing, it is more than likely that discretionary variations will be introduced into formal themes.

Irrespective of the type of planning, the operational nature of the process requires (1) techniques for extracting from a given policy model the consequences of any proposed plan in order that all alternatives be properly evaluated, and (2) procedures for evaluating and revising the basic model as new information becomes available that enables the model-builder to refine earlier ideas. This chapter is concerned with these techniques and procedures.

8.2 PLANNING TECHNIQUES

Differences in planning techniques in the West and East reflect the fundamental philosophical difference between their respective economic systems: a predominant reliance on the market place to resolve price, output, and allocation decisions in the former case, and a predominant reliance on a bureaucratic hierarchy of actuators to carry out the price, output, and allocation decisions dictated by a centralized controller-agency in the latter case. In the West, then, planners are basically concerned with: (1) *anticipating* the consequences of alternative plans; (2) *analyzing* the economic system so as to elicit plans whose implementation they might seek to induce rather than inflict; and (3) *optimizing* the performance of the economic system—to the extent that the instruments and resources available to them can be employed as controlled inputs to the system.

In contrast, planning in the East is neither concerned with anticipating, analyzing, nor optimizing. Rather, planners vis-à-vis controllers are basically concerned with: (1) *issuing the instructions* that are seen as the means for achieving a set of prespecified targets—targets that are not necessarily either optimal or achievable; and (2) *discovering discrepancies* between the actual and the intended performance of individual components; (3) *attempts to correct* in the process of plan implementation the technical and/or analytical errors that have resulted in these discrepancies, while straining to *fulfill* the *top* priorities.

On the one hand, then, the concerns of Western planners have led to the development of forecasting, analytical, and optimization techniques. On the other hand, the concerns of Eastern planners have led to the development of "bookkeeping" devices to determine what must be done to accomplish certain ends, and to check up on the extent to which these ends have in fact been achieved. We shall briefly consider, in turn, the more important techniques that have evolved from these differing concerns.

a. Western techniques: forecasting, simulation, and mathematical programming

i. Forecasting Both short-term and long-term forecasting have become an increasingly important aspect of economic policy. The quantitative techniques involved in long-term forecasting do not differ greatly from those used for short-term forecasts. There are, however, two essential and related differences between them. First, uncertainty is markedly increased as the time horizon lengthens. Second, because of this increased uncertainty, judgment and "hunches" necessarily play a much larger role in long-term forecasting. Even disregarding unexpected wars and natural disasters, the highly volatile nature of some important variables, such as technological change, makes consistently accurate long-term forecasting a nearly impossible task, and lends to long-term forecasting the aura of art rather than science.

Nonetheless, the forecasting problem is currently attacked with considerable scientific sophistication, liberally sprinkled with hopes and prayers. This sophistication stems from the seemingly endless stream of advances that are being made in the area of econometrics. Although input-output model variants, such as the Oslo model, are occasionally used for short- and medium-term forecasting, and an increasing acceptance of the personalistic approach to probability and the Bayesian approach to decision making have made "probabilistic predictions" [5]—probability statements about the future, based on judgment, experience, and empirical evidence—a respectable and increasingly popular way to view the future, the most important vehicles for forecasting remain the single-equation and simultaneous-equation econometric models. The issue is no longer *whether* to take an econometric approach to forecasting, but rather to determine *which* econometric technique is most appropriate for estimating the

[5] H. V. Roberts, "Probabilistic Prediction," *Journal of the American Statistical Association,* Vol. 60, No. 307, March 1965, pp. 50–62.

parameters in the model at hand. Whereas prior to World War II the movements in many of the crucial economic variables might have been forecast on the basis of simple trend equations fitted to a few observations by ordinary single-equation least squares, the more important time series might now be broken down into, say, their trend and cyclical patterns via a more·complex spectral analysis.[6] Similarly, the single-equation least-squares forecasting models of the 1950s have given way to complex multi-equation models fitted by multi-stage and generalized least-squares procedures that serve to provide parameter estimates of greater validity.

It remains true, however, that different parts of the economy vary greatly in their predictability. Over the short term, individual stock price movements, for example, are virtually unpredictable, except in terms of some probabilistic process. Similarly, although it is ordinarily impossible to perfectly forecast production, most individual sectors remain easier to forecast than, say, agricultural production, which is subject to the random whims of climatic change. Over the long term the problem is still further complicated by the possibility, indeed the inevitability, of technological change. Thus, forecasters must anticipate not only when the state of an art will be advanced, but also when new developments will be translated into commercially applicable and adopted innovations.

In a systems context, forecasts are necessary in three major areas. First, planners *must* be concerned with the behavior of the noncontrolled variables, those exogenous variables whose rates are determined in the environment outside the system. Second, planners *must* be able to forecast the impact both on the system's output, as well as, perhaps, on the outputs of the individual components of an exogenous input from the controller into the system. Third, and in order to achieve the latter, the planner *must* be able to forecast the outputs of individual components in response to inputs into these components. There is little reason to suppose, however, that forecasts in one area will necessarily be more reliable than forecasts in another, either in the short term or the long.

ii. Simulation [7] As a means of experimenting with the economic system via the *comparatively* inexpensive medium of the electronic computer—inexpensive, that is, by comparison with experimenting with the real-world situation—simulation offers planners a means of (1) analyzing a wide variety of alternative plans and their consequences, as well as various decision rules, and (2) testing the sensitivity of both the system model and a plan to alternative parameter values. Thus, the computer can be used to project the time path of

[6] See G. E. P. Box and G. M. Jenkins, *Times Series Analysis: Forecasting and Control* (San Francisco: Holden-Day, 1970).

[7] For an extended discussion of simulation and its uses see T. H. Naylor, J. L. Balintfy, D. S. Burdick, and K. Chu, *Computer Simulation Techniques* (New York: John Wiley, 1966). Also, G. Fromm and P. Taubman, *Policy Simulation with an Econometric Model* (Washington, D.C.: The Brookings Institution, 1968).

results from any plan and any set of decision rules, for all economic variables of interest to the planners; and, this can be done for any set of parameter estimates. Similarly, where (1) exogenous inputs into the system, (2) parameter values, or (3) structural relationships and transformation functions are not known with certainty, given a set of probability assignments the computer can project the various time paths of results from all plans and decision rules, *together with* the probabilities of realizing these results.

Ordinarily, simulation will not provide an automatic device for determining an optimal plan—although conceptually, at least, by building into the model a component that simulates the planners' preference function, this too can be accomplished. Rather, as it is commonly applied, simulation is an information-generating technique. It is used to provide planners with the most comprehensive set of information—prospective projections—that can be obtained with respect to the economic impact of every plan under consideration. Planners will then use this information, perhaps in a formal policy-choice model, to select the optimal plan.

*iii. **Mathematical Programming*** The general *policy* problem is, as we have repeatedly mentioned, a nonlinear programming problem under uncertainty in which the policy makers' preference function is to be maximized, subject to a set of structural contraints, the policy makers' demands, and boundary conditions. For *planning* purposes, the functional relationships and restrictions must be given explicit form, the parameters must be specified, and the resulting programming model must be solvable. In view of the *practical* problems involved in estimating the parameters in nonlinear equations, and of solving even relatively small-scale nonlinear programming problems under certainty on large-scale electronic computers, planners have basically relied on linear models for national programming purposes.

Linear programming and input-output analysis are now standard planning techniques that combine into a third important technique, activity analysis, in which there are *various* fixed technological coefficient processes from among which the optimum combination must be chosen.

The mathematical framework of an activity analysis model is presented in Appendix 8.1. Basically, however, the model proceeds along the following lines. First, a series of activities or production transformation processes are defined, each of which is characterized by fixed technological coefficients. These activities can then be carried out at different levels such that, because of the fixed coefficient property, increasing the level of any activity by a factor of λ will also increase by a factor of λ the inputs required in the activity. Hence, if a_{11} is the amount of "the first" input required in "the first" activity, and a_{1s} is the amount of the first input required in the sth activity, with n unique activities and λ_s the level of the sth, $\Sigma a_{1s}\lambda_s$ is the total requirement of the first input. That is, the activities can be combined *linearly*. The extent to which the activities are undertaken, or the production processes employed, becomes a decision problem that assumes a linear programming framework where, for example, $\Sigma a_{ls}\lambda_s \leq Q_1$ represents a restriction imposed by the availability of the first input.

Activity analysis is an important planning technique because its simplified format makes feasible both the estimation of the model's parameters, and the model's solution via computer-oriented linear programming algorithms. Additionally, the duality principle of linear programming permits the assignment of shadow prices to the constraining "resources," and thereby helps planners to both evaluate the economic system's resources, and place their future options and needs, say in terms of foreign aid, in proper perspective.

A second especially significant linear programming technique for planning purposes derives from the decomposition principle,[8] which is applicable to planning situations in which (a) structure of the overall economic system can be described by, and is subjected to, a series of linear constraints, and the controller's objective is to maximize or minimize some linear objective function, and (b) the system can be logically subdivided into a set of interdependent subsystems, each of which is constrained by its own unique set of linear restrictions. In this case, as described in Appendix 8.2, the computational solution to the overall problem is often most readily achieved via an iterative procedure in which it is necessary to solve a small linear programming problem for each of the subsystems with respect to its own unique constraint set. The solutions are fed into an overall programming problem that reflects the interrelationships between the subsystems, and the solutions to this overall problem are in turn fed back to the subsystems for use in revising the parameters in the objective functions used in the subsystem problems. The procedure is repeated until the decomposition principle's systemic optimality decision rule is satisfied. The application of this technique to regional planning problems in particular is discussed in Chapter 15.

Considerable mathematical strides have also been made in recent years toward solving dynamic, multi-stage decision problems wherein a sequence of decisions—such as is ordinarily required in medium-term and long-term planning—must be made. These strides have proceeded along two separate, if related paths. On the one hand, the *dynamic programming* approach provides a disarmingly simple, but profound mathematical *philosophy* for determining the optimal sequence of decisions in a multi-stage decision problem: *if* one can determine the optimal sequence up to any stage, then one need only worry about optimizing for and beyond that stage; *how* one determines these optima depends on the problem, and simple heuristics and observation may suffice as well as advanced calculus, depending on the structure of the problem.[9]

On the other hand, the *control theory* approach, which we defer discussion of until Chapter 10, based on fundamental principles of the calculus of variations, provides a disarmingly complex mathematical *framework* for determining an optimal *path* of interdependent decisions over a given time period.

[8] G. B. Dantzig and P. Wolfe, "A Decomposition Principle for Linear Programs," *Operations Research*, Vol. 8, No. 1, January–February 1960, pp. 101–111.

[9] See R. Bellman, *Dynamic Programming* (Princeton, N.J.: Princeton University Press, 1957).

Presently, the insights provided by both approaches have been more theoretical than applied, but this is virtually certain to change in the immediate future.

d. Network theory

The *timing* of the individual components of a plan is an ever-present, and singularly important aspect of planning. Avoiding bottlenecks, such as occur when simultaneous demands on investment capital or foreign aid come from different sources, can be crucial in making it possible to carry out the plan in the most efficient manner.

The most prominent of these scheduling techniques is PERT—the Project Evaluation and Review Technique—which involves choosing an optimal time and/or expenditures pattern, or a strategy for meeting a given set of objectives.[10] Based on certain assumptions with respect to the stochastic elements in the system—for example, the likelihood that an export industry will be operating profitably and at capacity in T years as opposed to $T + i$ years—the technique considers the most optimistic, pessimistic, and most likely projections for these stochastic elements, which are the individual activities in a logical network of interrelated activities. In such a network, there is a logical sequence with which the activities can take place, with the initiation of one activity being dependent upon the successful completion of another. Thus, for example, the development of an export steel industry might depend on the prior development of both a railroad network and an open-water harbor.

In order to anticipate possible delay points, allow for interruptions, and determine, say, the shortest possible time in which the plan can be completed, it is necessary to elicit both the earliest time at which any particular activity can be completed (and therefore when subsequent activities can commence) as well as the latest time at which any particular activity can be completed without affecting the completion time of the entire plan. The difference between the latest completion time for events *terminating* at a particular activity, and the earliest starting time for events *originating* at that activity, represents *slack* in the plan. That is, this is a period during which (1) with positive slack there is one unnecessary delay that might be eliminated through a rescheduling of activities, or (2) with negative slack, some plan elements will be behind schedule.

The so-called *critical path* is the longest required time path through the network. It represents the totality of the latest completion times for one set of activities, and hence the earliest starting times for all subsequent activities. Thus, the critical path indicates the earliest possible completion time for the entire plan.

PERT, viewed as a whole, provides a procedure for coordinating activities so as to minimize both the time along the critical path, and slack. Similarly PERT can be extended to include cost factors so as to mimimize the cost of completing a plan. In either case, it is a useful managerial planning tool.

[10] For a brief, but useful discussion see F. S. Hillier and G. J. Lieberman, *Introduction to Operations Research* (San Francisco: Holden-Day, 1967), pp. 208–234.

b. Eastern techniques: the method of balances

The Soviets use the Marxian schema of simple and expanded reproduction only for the study and analysis of various changes in the economy's macro variables and in their interrelations. For constructing their plans, they use instead what they call a "balances method." This consists essentially of *resource and use balances* for *each* of the principal components in the system, including both individual commodities and the principal resources. The core of a Soviet plan is formed by the interlocking product balances of a number of *priority* commodities or group of commodities (steel, electricity, military goods, and so on); to this core are articulated all the other, overlapping, *product* balances. All these balances are then crudely aggregated into *"synthetic"* (value) balances of projected gross national product by "producers and consumers' goods sectors, industrial origin and end-use, following Marxian definitions." [11]

As noted in considering the Kalecki planning model, Soviet policy seeks to maximize national income, subject to a constraint on the minimum standard of living. This policy results, for example, in the establishment of a set of physical targets for individual commodities or commodity groups, or perhaps even for individual commodities allocated by principal users. Then, for any commodity one can construct a balance sheet indicating, on the one hand, the sources of total supply, and, on the other hand, the allocation of total demand. The planners' problem is to effect a balance between the two.

On the supply side, domestic production, imports, and inventories provide the total physical supply, Q_i, of the ith good. On the demand side, some of the good, q_{ij}, is allocated to the jth producing firm, and the remainder, q_i, is either marketed, exported, or retained as inventory. The supply-and-demand balance requires $Q_i = \Sigma_j q_{ij} + q_i$.

With respect to individual commodities, then, Soviet planning must proceed along two fronts. First, individual plant capabilities must be ascertained, and precedents established for issuing and implementing the directives that establish each plant's production quota. Simultaneously, the availability of the necessary foreign exchange for purchasing in the world market must be effected. Second, foreign and domestic prices must be fixed so as to assure the necessary demand rates and preestablished allocations. If this supply-and-demand balance is difficult to accomplish for a single commodity, it is a herculean achievement for a set of interrelated commodities consisting of both complements and rivals.

Moreover, the Soviets must also concern themselves with the physical balances of such key factors of production as plant and equipment, fuel and power, raw materials, and manpower. Indeed, because prices can generally be set low enough to guarantee sufficient aggregate demand for individual commodities, the principal limitation to economic growth generally comes from

---

[11] N. Spulber, *The Soviet Economy, Structure, Principles, Problems* (New York: Norton, rev. ed., 1969), pp. 29, and 139 ff; see also: N. P. Lebedinskii (ed.), *Metodicheskie ukazaniia k sostavleniiu gosudarstvennogo plana razvitiia narodnogo khoziaistva SSSR* (Guidelines on methods for compiling the state plan of the USSR national economy) (Moscow: Ekonomika, 1969).

supply factors, such as capital and manpower. Thus, these balances are crucial to Soviet planning, with labor resources and productivity assuming an especially important role.

With respect to labor, for example, the available labor inputs at any time are determined by first estimating population growth, and then determining the labor force as some function of the estimated population. Subsequently, labor input is given as the product of average working time and the total labor force. This labor input is then distributed among the various nonagricultural sectors in accordance with their requirements, as determined by the established production rates and sectoral labor productivity. Completing the labor balance, the agricultural labor force is determined as a residual from the available labor supply, and the requirements for nonagricultural employment. When all agricultural underemployment has been eliminated, employment in the service sector—which is also usually treated as a residual—is determined.

Similarly, the supply of capital equipment is taken as determined by the existing capacity in the domestic capital-producing sector, the technically attainable increment in this capacity, and the availability of imports. The sources to finance this capital investment are savings, depreciation, and foreign exchange, where savings are a function of national income.

Given the constrained growth-maximizing objective, Soviet "planning" thus consists in constructing and crudely integrating the product balances (and their underlying capacity expansion and utilization rates), and then in issuing the directives that are compatible with the maximum feasible rate of capital expenditure and the projected growth in, say, the labor force. These directives aim at providing an internally consistent set of output standards that will equate supply and demand for all commodities at their targeted rates of output.

The single-minded Soviet focus on the production side of the planning process, and the traditional treatment of planning as an essential arithemetic, as opposed to mathematical, process for achieving the policy makers' arbitrary goals, suffers further indignities at the hands of the duality principles of mathematical programming. These principles challenge the notion of arbitrariness in planned prices, by stressing the implicit need for a set of rational prices whose levels are intimately married to the optimal production program. Indeed, through the solution to the dual and the determination of a rational price structure, the optimal production program will *automatically* be determined. It immediately follows, then, that an arbitrary system of prices will not, except by extraordinary good fortune, be compatible with an optimal allocation of goods and resources. But such an allocation has not been the Soviet intent.

8.3 WELDING PLANS: ITERATION; HORIZONS; STAGES

a. Iteration in the formulation phase

Planning is a give-and-take process involving an exchange of ideas and information among individual agencies and agents in general, and between a central planning agency and its sectoral appendages in particular. As such, planning proceeds by a series of interations wherein an initial suggestion is transmitted, studied, and returned for reevaluation. The process repeats itself, with certain ideas solidifying and details being filled in, until such time as a mutually agreed upon proposal is ready to be approved by the appropriate legislative unit.

Although the iterative theme is common to both Eastern and Western planning, the agencies involved differ greatly.

In West European countries, planning generally starts at the governmental level with broad policy recommendations being made to a General Planning Commission (GPC). The latter determines the data necessary for formulating the plan, and instructs the appropriate statistical agencies to provide such data. When these data have been provided, a plan is formulated by the GPC and submitted to a High Planning Council (HPC) for evaluation and transmission to the government. The HPC then evaluates its options and either returns to the GPC with the request for alternative suggestions and modifications, or else it selects a plan to support, and submits its selection to the appropriate legislative body for approval.

In the East, the crucial difference is the direct involvement, within well-defined limits, of the executants in the planning process. First, preliminary *directives* are worked out by the policy makers with the help of a Central Planning Agency, with the objective of influencing projections at the sectoral and operational levels. Draft plans are then elaborated by ministerial and regional bodies, and by enterprises, all supposedly using progressive "norms." Balancing techniques and criteria of efficiency are then applied within the framework established by the "directives" from above. Subsequently, the draft plans are transmitted upward, where they are checked, amended, and integrated into a single national plan. After approval by the government, the plan becomes a "law"—that is, a compulsory set of decisions for all the system components involved.

b. Horizons

The implications of time perspective are critical in planning. Three time-period categorizations are customarily applied to plans: short term, medium term, and long term.

The short-term plan tends to correspond to the budgetary period within which the policy-making body operates, and this is generally one year; the medium-term plan corresponds to the four-to-seven year gestation period that is normally required for an investment in plant and equipment to evolve into a viable productive activity; and, the ten-to-twenty year long-term, or perspective plan corresponds to the maximum time period over which planners believe it is feasible to project in a meaningful manner. In fact, most budget expenditures are nondiscretionary.

These time periods bear an interesting relationship to the Marshallian view of the time element as it influences supply. In particular, the shortest of Marshallian short runs, the market period in which supply is virtually inelastic because firms cannot adjust output with sufficient rapidity to react to differing price offers, is analogous to the short-term planning period wherein planners must accept as given such long-term variables as the state of technology and the economy's productive capacity. In the Marshallian short run, firms can adjust production in reaction to price changes, but the *number* of firms operating in a given short-run period is fixed. This is analogous to the planners' medium-term period, wherein there is room for change in the existing economic system, but any additional production facilities will not as yet have become fully operational. Finally, in the Marshallian long run all resources are mobile, and all entrepreneurially desired adjustments to factor supply and product demand conditions are feasible. This is analogous to the long-term planning period, wherein planners can assume the economic system to be capable of accepting and adjusting in accordance with the plan's guidelines and projections.

c. Disaggregation: stages

Tinbergen [12] proposed the formulation and integration of plans by *stages*. Under this planning procedure, given the size and complexity of the task, the equations in the planning model should not be solved simultaneously, but rather by a *tâtonnement* process of successive approximations, or by trial and error. The planning process is therein cut into pieces or phases some or all of which must be repeated if the assumptions used in earlier stages are disqualified by later findings and new information. Specifically, planning begins at the macro stage, and then proceeds through the sectoral and regional stages, and ultimately to the project stage.

At the macro stage, an overall plan for the economic system is established in accordance with the policy makers' objectives and the economy's structural constraints. Thus, for example, a Harrod-Domar model, and estimates of the overall capital:output ratio and the minimally acceptable standard of living, might be used to determine the rate of investment that is required to achieve the maximum feasible rate of economic growth. Then the corresponding development of the sectors defined in the plan might be traced through an input-output model. Specific concerns here would be, for example, public consumption, exports, the allocation of investment among the various industries, and the production of intermediate goods and raw materials. This sectoral analysis is at least in part intended to reveal whether the plan developed at the macro stage is in fact compatible with the constraints that exist at the structural stage, in terms of the available human, capital, and technological resources, and the interindustry structural relationships. If it is not, then the macro plan must be modified accordingly, and the sectoral analysis repeated with the revised effort.

The regional stage is not *necessarily* the third stage in the process. Instead, it might also follow the macro stage or, indeed, might be the *final* stage in the planning process. It is at this stage that the planners must determine how, for example, the various sectoral investments will be distributed among the

---

[12] J. Tinbergen, *Development Planning, op. cit.*

various economic subsystems or regions. In this context, it is useful to distinguish between the so-called "shiftable" and "nonshiftable" projects: the former can be undertaken in several different regions, whereas the latter *must* be undertaken in a particular region, either for technical reasons, or to be consistent with its intent in the original macro plan.

The project stage details the specific investment projects and programs through which the macro plan is to be accomplished. Here, each prospective project is subjected to an economic evaluation of its estimated costs and projected benefits. It is then necessary to select from among these projects the subset whose total cost coincides with the total investment allocated to each sector, and which at the same time yields a projected stream of benefits—both direct and indirect—that are consistent with the macro plan. Once again, then, the projects necessary to accomplish the overall goals of the plan may not be available, or the available projects may not mesh with the sector and regional prerequisites, in which case additional plan modification is required, and the macro, sectoral, and regional planning processes are repeated until an internally consistent program is determined.

d. Soviet disaggregation and integration

Soviet planning, as carried out through a series of balances, works through an extensive system of equations which in some cases, as we have noted, seek to assure the precise equivalence of the available resources with the planned allocations, say of manpower, investment, and production of various major commodities, and in other cases seek to determine the residuals available for what are dealt with as subsidiary parts of the economy. There is, however, "no accepted system of consolidating the sector, branch, and product interconnections, the financial flows, and the changes in the capital stock, although the need for such a balance has been repeatedly stressed and some precise proposals have been formulated for this purpose." [13] In effect, the complexity of the Soviet balance system makes impractical a *unified* treatment of the planning process, and almost forces Soviet planners to lose sight of the forest for the trees.

Spulber has summarized as follows the Soviet problem: "The Soviet search, which is still going on, seeks to establish a balance encompassing a far broader macroeconomic field than that of either the physical balances or the income and related balances. As the Soviet economists put it, such a balance—a sort of yearly national balance sheet—should be consistent with the key indicators of the plan, should uncover all the concrete relations in the Soviet growth process, and should offer a truly dynamic view of each branch and of the economy as a whole. Actually this master balance seems to elude the researchers, first, because the physical balances as they are now drawn are fully interconnected neither conceptually nor in practice, and secondly, because the in-

[13] N. Spulber, *The Soviet Economy, op. cit.,* p. 33.

come and money flows are *inter alia* not clearly and specifically coordinated with the intersector outputs and distributions." [14]

Assuredly, there have been efforts in the Soviet Union in particular, and in the Eastern bloc in general, to provide an internally consistent and computationally manageable planning procedure. The Kornai-Liptak method,[15] for example, applied in certain countries including Hungary, proposes a type of stage planning called "two-level planning." This consists in formulating and combining two levels of interrelated linear programming exercises. In the initial stage—the higher level—a central linear programming model is solved to yield a set of input quotas and output targets for the various industries, or major productive centers comprising the economic system. At the second stage—the lower level—a series of linear programming models is solved, with each individual industry's production problems treated uniquely.

In the East, then, there has been an increasing recognition of (1) the need to be concerned with optimization in planning, and not merely with the issuance of directives to the individual productive units designed to achieve a supply-and-demand equilibrium, and (2) the responsibility of providing a mutually compatible and internally consistent set of investments, projections, and instructions.

8.4 CONCLUSIONS

The solution of planning models, and indeed often to some degree, the formulation of planning models, depends on the existence of various computational algorithms—techniques. These range from the heuristic techniques of the computer, to the more elegant, if often impractical analytical techniques of mathematical programming and control theory, each supported by various statistical and managerial techniques for forecasting and parameter estimation. Some of these techniques have been considered in this chapter; others will be introduced as we deal with planning for individual sectors and planning to handle individual issues.

In a very perceptive lecture on Development Planning included in his volume *Some Aspects of Economic Development,* Professor W. Arthur Lewis correctly remarks that "making Development Plans is the most popular activity of the governments of underdeveloped countries since the war, and is also nearly their biggest failure." [16] Addressing himself to the well-known fact that many plans are made and then put aside soon after they are made, Professor Lewis notes that some of these plans are pure political phantasy based on wild assumptions formulated primarily for propaganda purposes. A further indication of plan failure is that in planning or nonplanning countries "there has been no correlation between development planning and economic growth. That is to say, the countries which have grown most rapidly have not been the countries

---

[14] *Ibid.,* p. 34.

[15] J. Kornai, *Mathematical Planning of Structural Decisions, op. cit.,* pp. 343–384.

[16] W. A. Lewis, *Some Aspects of Economic Development* (London: Allen & Unwin, 1969), p. 37.

which have had the most elaborate plans." [17] Professor Lewis then goes on to say that growth has depended—in all these countries—on the private sector. If, however, the private sector, either alone or with the help of the plan, does not find conditions favorable for growth, the plan, however elaborate, is of no use.

Moreover, from quantitative predictions of future growth to actual stimulation of growth is a gulf that cannot be easily bridged. In Soviet planning such a gap does not exist, since industries are *ordered* to produce the planned output. The ways in which they produce it—namely the questions of quality and actual output mix—need not divert us here (particularly since these issues rarely divert Soviet plan managers). In indicative planning, the difference between plan making and plan implementation is bound to be significant, and the more significantly so in underdeveloped countries afflicted by lack of adequate personnel, adequate instruments, adequate price responsiveness, and so on. The disenchantment with planning comes from the past illusion that it would be enough to draw an internally consistent economic model of a desired future, and reality would automatically—even painlessly—conform to it. This, of course, could never come to pass.

Finally, the rigid Soviet edict system itself does not fare well, either in the Soviet Union—once a certain level of development and of military power has been achieved—or in Eastern Europe. The application of the Soviet model in the latter countries has led to innumerable crises and dislocations. How to replace orders with incentives—or how to tear off the burning Nessus shirt of Soviet-type directive planning—is a complex question that profoundly affects the socioeconomic climate in the whole "socialist world." [18]

[17] Ibid., *loc. cit.*
[18] Recall that the centaur Nessus was shot by Hercules. A shirt dropped in his blood poisoned Hercules, and caused him such agony that he killed himself.

APPENDIX 8.1

An activity is a combination of commodities—that is, a combination of products and factors. Suppose there are m commodities, and that a_{rs} is the amount of the rth commodity employed when the sth activity is carried out at its numeraire or *unit* level. Hence, the vector

$$A^s = \begin{bmatrix} a_{1s} \\ a_{2s} \\ \vdots \\ a_{ms} \end{bmatrix}$$

describes the combination of commodities that *defines* a unit level of the sth activity, where $a_{rs} > (<)0$ represents a product output (factor input).

It is assumed that (1) activities are additive, so that

$$A^s + A^t = \begin{bmatrix} a_{1s} + a_{1t} \\ a_{2s} + a_{2t} \\ \vdots \\ a_{ms} + a_{mt} \end{bmatrix}$$

and that (2) as each commodity level a_{rs} increases to some scalar multiple λa_{rs}, the activity level increases to λA^s. This implies constant returns to scale—or more particularly, fixed technological coefficients—both for individual activities and for combinations of activities.

If it is not possible to develop any activity as a positive linear combination of other activities—that is, if one cannot write $A^\mu = \sum_{s=1}^{k} \lambda_s A^s$ for $\lambda_s \geq 0$ and all $s \neq \mu$— then A^μ is called a *basic* activity. The basic activities describe the economic system's technology, as summarized in the matrix A:

$$A = [A^1, \ldots, A^n] = \begin{bmatrix} a_{11} & a_{12} \cdots a_{1n} \\ a_{21} & a_{22} \cdots a_{2n} \\ \vdots & \vdots \quad\ \vdots \\ a_{m1} & a_{m2} \cdots a_{mn} \end{bmatrix}$$

Clearly, and by definition, any other activity can be defined as a linear combination of basic activities.

Now, let $Q = (Q_1, \ldots, Q_m)'$ represent the vector of commodities produced by the system. Then, if the sth basic activity is carried out at a level of λ_s,

$$Q_k = a_{k1}\lambda_1 + a_{k2}\lambda_2 + \cdots + a_{kn}\lambda_n$$

and $Q = A\lambda$ where $\lambda = (\lambda_1, \ldots, \lambda_n)'$.

In effect, then, $A\lambda = Q(\lambda \geq 0)$ defines the structural constraints in a programming problem. Thus, if the "value" of a unit of the sth activity is given by v_s, and the total value of the economic activity in the system is obtainable by adding individual values, then this total is given by $y = \Sigma v_s \lambda_s$.

$$\text{Max} \qquad y = \Sigma v_s \lambda_s \tag{8.1a}$$

$$\text{subject to } A\lambda = Q \tag{8.1b}$$

$$\lambda \geq 0 \tag{8.1c}$$

defines a linear programming problem in which the optimal combination of basic activity levels is determined so as to maximize the value of the system's total economic activity, for given commodity levels. Thus, for example, if the commodities are labor, land, coal, iron ore, and so on, the solution to the programming problem might determine, say, how many cars—the kth activity—to produce. Indeed, the set of points $A\lambda = Q(\lambda \geq 0)$ defines the feasible technological possibilities.[19]

APPENDIX 8.2

When each of the J separate subsystems of the economic system is constrained by a set of linear restrictions

$$B_j x_j = b_j$$

and the couplings and system constraints are also described by a set of J linear restrictions

$$\sum_{j=1}^{J} A_j x_j = b_0$$

a linear programming problem

$$\text{Maximize} \qquad W = \sum_{j=1}^{J} c_j x_j \tag{8.2a}$$

$$\text{subject to } \sum_{j=1}^{J} A_j x_j = b_0 \tag{8.2b}$$

$$B_j x_j = b_j \qquad j = 1, \ldots, J \tag{8.2c}$$

$$x_j \geq 0 \qquad j = 1, \ldots, J \tag{8.2d}$$

can be defined, the solution to which may be more readily obtainable by taking advantage of the so-called *decomposition* principle.

The decomposition principle proceeds from the observation that the optimal solution to this linear programming problem will *necessarily* be some convex combination of the extreme points x_{kj}^* of the convex set of feasible solutions to $B_j x_j = b_j$; or,

$$x_j = \sum_k \rho_{kj} x_{kj}^* \tag{8.3a}$$

$$\sum_k \rho_{kj} = 1 \tag{8.3b}$$

$$\rho_{kj} \geq 0 \qquad k = 1, \ldots, K \tag{8.3c}$$

Substituting Equation (8.3a) into (8.2b) yields

$$\sum_j A_j(\sum_k \rho_{kj} x_{kj}^*) = \sum_{j,k} \rho_{kj} A_j x_{kj}^* = b_0$$

while substituting into (8.2a) yields

$$W = \sum_j c_j(\sum_k \rho_{kj} x_{kj}^*) = \sum_{j,k} \rho_{kj} c_j x_{kj}^*$$

Still further, writing $d_{kj} = A_j x_{kj}^*$ and $f_{kj} = c_j x_{kj}^*$, a linear programming problem, equivalent to the original problem,

[19] See T. C. Koopmans, *Activity Analysis of Production and Allocation* (New York: John Wiley, 1951).

Maximize $\qquad W = \sum_j \sum_k f_{kj} \rho_{kj}$ $\hfill$ (8.4a)

subject to $\sum_j \sum_k d_{kj} \rho_{kj} = b_0$ $\hfill$ (8.4b)

$\qquad\qquad \sum_k \rho_{kj} = 1 \qquad j = 1, \ldots, J$ $\hfill$ (8.4c)

$\qquad\qquad \rho_{kj} \geq 1 \qquad k = 1, \ldots, K; j = 1, \ldots, J$ $\hfill$ (8.4d)

is defined. Here, however, the problem is to determine a set of optimal weights ρ_{kj}, *given* the d_{kj} and f_{kj}. The latter require determination of the extreme points x_{kj}^*.

The computational problem is eased by the further observation that the only x_{kj}^* that are required for the optimal solution—and hence the only d_{kj} and f_{kj} required—are the optimal extreme points to the convex set $B_j x_j = b_j$. The decomposition principle takes advantage of this observation by initially solving J *small* subproblems.

Maximize $\quad w_j = \sum \alpha_j x_j$ $\hfill$ (8.5a)

subject to $B_j x_j = b_j$ $\hfill$ (8.5b)

$\qquad\qquad x_j \geq 0$ $\hfill$ (8.5c)

for a (here) unspecified set of weights α_j to determine an initial set of values for x_{kj}^* and hence for d_{kj} and f_{kj}. These values are then used in (8.4a) and (8.4b) whereupon, and without going into further detail, a new set of weights α_j' is determined. The computational procedure continues in this iterative manner until an optimal solution is signaled, and an optimal set of weights α_j^* is determined.

The computational advantage is that although *many more* linear programs are solved than would be required by solving (8.2a)–(8.2e) directly, each of these problems will be small compared to the original problem, and each will be much more easily solved. The interesting aspect from the planning point of view is that the procedure requires, in effect, a set of *sectoral* plans that must be *coordinated* at the national level, and this in turn demands a series of sectoral revisions as the supremal controller sends new objective function weights to the infimal units. As we shall see, this approach has been particularly utilized in regional planning with regional subsystems.

CHAPTER 9

Planning for Technological Change

9.1 ENDOGENOUS AND EXOGENOUS CHANGES

Planning for technological change involves the anticipation of, and the preparation for, eventual changes in both production and distribution *processes,* and *types* of products and services offered, the *diffusion* of products and services on a large scale, and, in addition, new *interdependencies* among the components of the economic system. Aware of their own limited abilities to *induce* appropriate changes in technology through borrowing and adaptation, or to *encourage* the growth of inventions and innovations, the economic managers must nonetheless try to anticipate the most decisive changes that may arise as a result of their selecting and implementing new techniques and processes from those already available, and the overall growth of knowledge and techniques at home and abroad, particularly in the MDC's, as well as the efforts of the policy makers themselves to direct, even imperfectly, the processes of economic transformation in their countries; that is, the efforts of the policy makers to "invent their own futures."

The alterations that technological change will bring about in the economy and its subsystems may affect, for example, the achievable rates of industrialization and economic growth, the future distribution of the population between urban and rural areas, and the course of the balance of payments. In so doing these changes can influence decisions with respect to *current* investment alternatives, manpower training and education programs, and government expenditure programs of all types—particularly in the area of national defense. Planning for technological change thus implies an attempt to understand and to cope with the technological transformations that can or will be brought about within a *particular* branch or sector, in order to better plan the activities of all the *other* sectors. It also implies two complementary concerns: first, developing a *long-term strategy* or perspective plan for the economic system and each of its subsystems, a strategy that both incorporates planned technological change as a policy decision variable, and also recognizes the impact of *all* technological change on the system's structure; second, developing a short-term strategy for transforming the results of past research and development (R and D) activity into new products and processes.

Although limited, an understanding of the technological transformations is *feasible* insofar as certain technological advances come about as a result of the selection and implementation of specific projects and programs already known and available, so to speak, "on the technological shelf." Moreover, it is indispensable insofar as technological change engenders concomitant changes within the economic system as a whole—in its components and in their couplings—as well as in its relations with the elements in the environments in which it operates.

On the one hand, then, it is especially important to plan for the "dynamic disequilibria" brought about by technological change in order to assure that the basic alterations that it will effect are both desired and consistent with the fundamental orientations and policies of the system's managers. The alternative—random changes in the economic system—would be akin to random mutations in the genetic structure of a biological system, and this may very well generate undesirable results. On the other hand, technological change represents what is probably the least predictable of the economic system's "period t outputs," while comprising one of the more important and least controllable "period $t + 1$ inputs;" it is, therefore, one of the most troublesome and necessary issues to consider in developing national and sectoral plans.

9.2 AVAILABLE PATHS FOR TECHNOLOGICAL TRANSFORMATION

The structure of an economic system depends in large measure upon the state or *level* of technology employed within its production and distribution subsystems. This observation can be formalized by modifying the specification of a systems model to include a technological component. Then the *implications* for the system of technological change, as well as the *potential* of technological change, can be explored and studied in the same manner as for any other variable or datum. A particularly important and interesting specification for accomplishing this is the input-output model. A variant of this model, which includes a technological factor, provides a useful portrayal of the path of technological transformation—the technologies employed in the industrial, agricultural, and service subsystems—a portrayal compatible with the planning models used in the overall system, as well as in many of the subsystems.

In particular, suppose that there are various levels of technological sophistication, or production processes p, where $p = 1, \ldots, m$. We shall first focus on the system's production relationships under the least-sophisticated technology, process $p = 1$.

Let Q_{hk}^{1t} denote the output of industrial sector h delivered at time t to a sector k that employs the initial technology, process 1. Q_k^{1t} denotes the output of sector k at time t which results from the use of process 1, and a_{hk}^1 denotes the amount of input required by sector k from sector h for the production of one unit of the kth commodity under process 1. Thus, a_{hk}^1 is the ordinary fixed technological coefficient of classical input-output analysis, whose level is determined by the given technology, process 1. In the traditional manner, then, we assume

$$Q_{hk}^{1t} = a_{hk}^1 Q_k^{1t} \tag{9.1}$$

Similarly, let H_{hk}^{1t} denote the amount of output required by sector k from sector h at time t to *increase* sector k's capacity to produce with process 1 by H_k^{1t} units at time $t+1$. In effect, then, H_k^{1t} is the *total investment* in process 1 that is taking place in industrial sector k at time t, and this investment will increase the sector's process-1 production capacity at time $t+1$. Extending the fixed-coefficients assumption to the investment sphere, it is assumed that the output required by sector k from sector h will be proportional to the former sector's total investment, where b_{hk}^1 is the factor of proportionally, or

$$H_{hk}^{1t} = b_{hk}^1 H_k^{1t} \tag{9.2}$$

Now let $\bar{Q}_k^{1t}$ denote the process-1 *capacity* of sector k at time t, and assume a single gestation period for investment. Then the total process-1 capacity of sector k at time $t+1$ will be given by

$$\bar{Q}_k^{1(t+1)} = \bar{Q}_k^{1t} + H_k^{1t}$$

or the existing capacity plus the new investment in capacity, and

$$H_k^{1t} = \bar{Q}_k^{1(t+1)} - \bar{Q}_k^{1t} \tag{9.3}$$

Hence, $I_h^t = \sum_k H_{hk}^{1t} = \sum_k b_{hk}^1 H_k^{1t}$ is the amount of sector h's output that is allocated to *investment* at time t; and, with q_h^t denoting the *final demand* at time t for sector h's output, the total *output*, Q_h^{1t}, of sector h at time t is given by

$$Q_h^{1t} = \sum_k a_{hk}^1 Q_k^{1t} + q_h^t + I_h^t \tag{9.4}$$

where total output is constrained by the available capacity; or,

$$Q_h^{1t} \le \bar{Q}_h^{1t} = \bar{Q}_h^{10} + \sum_{\tau=1}^{t-1} H_k^{1\tau} \tag{9.4a}$$

for all $h, k = 1, \ldots, n$.

Suppose, now, that in addition to the present technology, other technologies or processes $p = 2, \ldots, m$, are or become available. Still assuming a one-period gestation for investment, the previous model is readily modified for each of the alternative technologies by rewriting Equations (9.1)–(9.3) as follows:

$$Q_{hk}^{pt} = a_{hk}^p Q_k^{pt} \tag{9.1p}$$

$$H_{hk}^{pt} = b_{hk}^p H_k^{pt} \tag{9.2p}$$

where

$$H_k^{pt} = \bar{Q}^{p(t+1)}_k - \bar{Q}_k^{pt}$$ (9.3p)

for $p = 1, \ldots, m$ and $h, k = 1, \ldots, n$. The *path of technological transformation,* or the distribution of sector h outputs among the various production processes, is then defined at each time t by

$$Q_h^t = \sum_p Q_h^{pt} = \sum_p \sum_k a_{hk}^p Q_k^{pt} + q_h^t + I_h^t$$ (9.4p)

where

$$I_h^t = \sum_p \sum_k b_{hk}^p H_k^{pt}$$ (9.4ap)

under the capacity constraint

$$Q_h^{pt} \leq \bar{Q}_h^{pt} = \bar{Q}_h^{p0} + \sum_{\tau=1}^{t-1} H_h^{p\tau}$$

for $p = 1, \ldots, m$ and $h, k = 1, \ldots, n$.

The latter set of equations, although somewhat cumbersome in appearance and awesome in the data requirements, is "easily" solved once the final demands and, say, targeted capacity increments are specified. For example, consider a two-industry economy operating with two levels of technology. With the time superscript suppressed, and adopting the convention $a_{ii}^p = 0$, Equation (9.4p) becomes

$$Q_1 = a_{12}^1 Q_2^1 + a_{12}^2 Q_2^2 + q_1 + I_1$$

$$Q_2 = a_{21}^1 Q_1^1 = a_{21}^2 q_1^2 + q_2 + I_2$$

where

$$Q_1 = Q_1^1 + Q_1^2$$

$$Q_2 = Q_2^1 + Q_2^2$$

Given values for q_1, q_2, I_1, and I_2, the latter equations provide four linear equations in four unknowns: Q_1^1, Q_1^2, Q_2^1, and Q_2^2. The solutions to these equations are thus the sectoral outputs produced by each process. Similarly, in lieu of specifying the values for I_1 and I_2, these could be determined from Equation (9.4ap):

$$I_1 = b_{11}^1 H_1^1 + b_{12}^1 H_2^1 + b_{11}^2 H_1^2 + b_{12}^2 H_2^2$$

$$I_2 = b_{21}^1 H_1^1 + b_{22}^1 H_2^1 + b_{21}^2 H_1^2 + b_{22}^2 H_2^2$$

by instead specifying values for the H_h^p. As is clear, however, the addition of a third process, thereby adding variables Q_1^3 and Q_2^3 without altering the number of equations, would make the system indeterminate. Alternatively, the addition of a third industry would introduce two more equations to the initial set, but would create three more variables: Q_3, Q_3^1, and Q_3^2. Again an indeterminacy results. In effect, once we go beyond the two-industry, two-process case, it may become necessary to specify more of the variables than just the final demand and investment rates. Given such a specification, however, and respecting the capacity constraint, the path of output growth and change can be traced through a recursive process, by adding Equation (9.3p) to the system.

Policy makers seeking to pattern technological transformations in their country on the technology and processes in use in more advanced countries, could be considered to be confronted by a set of *technological transformation matrices* made up of coefficients a_{hk}^p and b_{hk}^p from which they must make a choice. In a sense, the Soviet policy makers, at the beginning of the Soviet industrialization drive in 1929, chose as their objective the adoption of the U.S. technological structure, and tried to transform the matrix of their own country into that of the United States in the shortest possible time. The Soviet leaders were not interested in maximizing consumption over the time period chosen, or in maximizing labor utilization, or some similar target.

If the policy makers of any other country would have similar powers of enforcement, they could, however, deliberately seek to avoid choosing a *rigid* model to emulate. Rather, they could, in fact, *combine* different elements from different technological matrices, and attempt to *adapt* and *adjust* these matrices to their country's own unique constraints. Unfortunately, certain techniques and processes are not flexible—each embodying a given technology that cannot be readily modified.[1] Notwithstanding its rigidities, the input-output model is especially useful insofar as it highlights some of the constraints under which technological transformation occurs; in particular, limited final demands, the distribution of final demands, capacity restrictions, the availability of existing, and perhaps technologically outmoded capacity whose abandonment cannot be justified economically, and policy makers' investment and growth targets. It is constraints such as these that limit the rate of adoption and the potential of new technological advances and industrial R and D.

9.3 FROM "TECHNOLOGY ON THE SHELF" TO NEW TECHNOLOGIES

For the *most* developed countries there are no blueprints detailing the possible speed of new inventions, the eventual stock of scientists and managers to discover and innovate, and the possible shifts in techniques, processes, products, and services. In a sense, the role of the managers of the system tends to diminish with this increased uncertainty; they no longer posses a clear map of the future, and cannot hope to secure any serious control over the speed and direction of change. Past systemic changes that have occurred in response to ear-

---

[1] The consequences of technological combinations can be assumed to be portrayed by the model, if each bundle of processes, p, is considered as consisting of a combination from various matrices. The model has, however, a severe limitation: when the initial technology is underutilized, and as a consequence certain inefficient technologies are discarded while only the more efficient ones are kept, the resulting changes as expressed by changes in the technological coefficients a_{hk}^1 and b_{hk}^1 are not portrayed.

lier technological advances provide little indication of the further alterations that might be expected to follow on the heels of the as yet unknown, indeed, perhaps unimaginable technological advances to occur in the future. To identify the issues that have never before been met, to cope with the new problems raised by the growth and diversification of the modern "invention industry" (the R & D "Industry"), and to evaluate the time element involved in the introduction and diffusion of new methods, products, and services, a special field of research has developed: *technological forecasting* (TF).

Unlike economic forecasting, which focuses on the pressures of supply and demand for substantiating short-term fiscal and monetary policies, or for ascertaining medium-term directions of the progress of the economy toward its long-term objectives, TF attempts to project future technological possibilities, make probabilistic predictions with respect to future technological advances, and project future openings of the *new* options that in turn need to be taken into account by policy makers, planners, or managers, when *planning action today* within any given time horizon. Technological forecasting has thus arisen as a result of the policy makers' and planners' need to know *what* technological changes are going to occur—*and when*—so that depending on the degree of control they have over the system they may either anticipate its changes or prepare its restructuring; that is, determine the future couplings and transformation operations of its components, as well as, perhaps, the specific components that will actually constitute the future system—in addition to influencing current R and D activity rates, and current innovations and technological changes.

In the Soviet Union of 1929, the formulation of the so-called "Soviet strategy of economic development" was prompted by the pursuit of a single, all-embracing goal within the framework of a vast and backward country— namely, the reaching and surpassing of the levels of economic development achieved in the most developed capitalist countries in the "leading" industrial-military branches. The introduction of the United States' production techniques required, then, according to the Soviet policy makers, a high rate of capital accumulation and a high degree of concentration of investment in the production of producers' goods. The need for a stepped-up overall rate of investment, and for a swift reallocation of scarce resources in favor of industry in general, of heavy industry in particular, and within heavy industry itself in favor of the "leading links"—steel, electricity, and machine tools—emerged rapidly from the prevailing policies, the prevailing possibilities and constraints, and the available "blueprints" of systematic changes in the sequences of events that precipitated them in the advanced countries.

Policy makers in the developed Western economies cannot, assuredly, formulate such clear-cut strategies, and cannot expect to impose them on their economies even when their own normative goals are well defined, and the prevailing possibilities and economic constraints are well known. Nonetheless, they need to fully *explore* future *options,* and try to determine the likely *time* when these options will actually become operational. Such an exploration is possible and fruitful inasmuch as the policy makers have, up to a point at least, the capacity to decide *what is to be anticipated*—that is, what exactly must be explored and what end-use must be picked out from an abundance of opportunities—and have up to a point the ability to determine the *interacting influences* of foreseeable forces and factors affecting identified future needs and wants.

9.4 TF: TECHNIQUES AND MODELS

In order to plan for and influence technological change, it is necessary to assess (a) the possible *directions*—both generally and specifically—in which changes might be expected, (b) the probable *magnitudes* of such changes, and (c) their eventual *implications* for the economic system, as well as (d) the probable *timing* of the changes. It is as a result of this "need to know" that technological forecasting has evolved. TF is one of the most recent additions to a family of forecasting activities—demographic, economic, social, and political—utilized by policy makers in plan formulation. TF techniques attempt to be attuned to the complex and elusive elements representing accumulated knowledge and the human capacity for imaginative thinking. They are typically partial techniques in the sense that, as Erich Jantsch has pointed out in his encyclopedic study,[2] none has thus far encompassed and integrated *all* of the various approaches to the problem—the exploratory, normative, feedback, and intuitive-thinking approaches—each of which has a unique and important contribution to make to TF, and thence to planning for technological change.

   Exploratory techniques are concerned with assessing future technological *opportunities*. This assessment can come either from an extrapolation of historical trends in technological advance within the various scientific disciplines, or from an analysis of the pattern of previous technological advances. In either case, an attempt is made to establish a historical relationship between a set of "current" independent outputs and states of the economic system, and future technological change. In contrast, *normative* techniques attempt to elicit the *needs and desires* of, say, consumers and producers, and presume that the search for technological advances will proceed with the objective of satisfying these needs and desires. *Feedback* approaches, as their name implies, work in both directions. These assume, for example, that current demands will stimulate R and D activity in given directions, that the latter activity will result in technological advance that will spread out in various directions, and that these new directions will in turn encourage new demands and ambitions, with the process perpetuating itself on into the future. Finally, *intuitive thinking* utilizes the *brainstorming activities* and considered judgments of knowledgeable and imaginative individuals whose perceptions, both individually and in concert, often tend to be more insightful than the more orderly "thoughts" generated by a systematic model. In each instance, including that of intuitive thinking, a variety of formal models exist for extracting meaningful technological forecasts. A small if representative subset is considered here.

[2] E. Jantsch, *Technological Forecasting in Perspective* (Paris: OECD, 1967).

a. Exploratory models

Exploratory TF models are generally concerned with two distinctly different aspects of planning. On the one hand, planners may be interested in obtaining some *overall impression* of the magnitude and timing of technological change that will be taking place in the economy, ceteris paribus, or the degree of technological sophistication under which the economic system will be functioning at some future time *t*. On the other hand, planners may also be interested in determining the *specific* technological advances that will take place, the sequencing of these advances, and the timing of the sequence. The former aspect requires a macro TF model; the latter requires a micro TF model.

Most of the macro-exploratory models are of the same basic genre. They are interesting, but not overwhelmingly credible. The key variables in these models typically are the level of technologies and processes available, that is, *technological information, I(t)*, and the rate of research and development activity, as reflected, say, in the *number of scientists, N(t)*, at any point in time, *t*. One might hypothesize, for example, that the rate of growth in technologies available (which may or may not remain ''on the shelf'') is proportional to the number of scientists, since the latter are presumably working to achieve technological advance. With k_1 the factor of proportionality,

$$\frac{\frac{dI}{dt}}{I(t)} = k_1 N(t) \tag{9.5}$$

Suppose, too, that the population of scientists is increasing over time in an ''S-shaped'' logistic pattern toward some upper limit of N_L; or, say

$$N(t) = \frac{N_L}{1 + k_2 e^{-k_3 t}} \tag{9.6}$$

where k_2 and k_3 are positive constants. In models such as this, it is the stock of scientists and the rate of growth in this stock which constrains the rate of R and D activity and the level of technology.

The parameters k_2 and k_3 can be, and commonly are estimated by fitting Equation (9.6) to historical data on the scientific population via ordinary least squares, for any prespecified N_L.[3] Substituting for $N(t)$ from (9.2) into (9.1), and multiplying both sides of the resulting equation by $I(t)$ yields

$$\frac{dI}{dt} = k_1 I(t) \frac{N_L}{(1 + k_2 e^{-k_3 t})} \tag{9.7}$$

or

---

[3] Write $N(t)[1 + k_2 e^{-k_3 t}] = N_L$. Then, $e^{-k_3 t} = [N_L - N(t)]/k_2$ and $-k_3 t = \ln[N_L - N(t)] - \ln k_2$, whereupon $\ln[N_L - N(t)] = \ln k_2 - k_3 t$ is immediately seen to be of the linear form $y(t) = k_2' + k_3' t$. For convenience, the residual term is deleted throughout.

$$(1 + k_2 e^{-k_3 t}) \frac{dI}{dt} = k_1 N_L I(t) \tag{9.7a}$$

Equation (9.3a) is a homogeneous first-order differential equation whose solution is

$$I(t) = I_0 e^{\dfrac{k_1 k_2 N_L (1 - e^{-k_3 t})}{(1 + k_2)(1 + k_2 e^{-k_3 t})}} \tag{9.8}$$

where I_0 is the level of technological information extant at the time $t = 0$. Thus, a precise measure of the level of available technology at any past, or more importantly any future date is not a prerequisite to analyzing changes in this level over time—given a value for k_1. In particular, let the base year level $I(0) = I_0$ act as a "numeraire," so that at time $t = 0$ the unit level of technology obtains; or, $I_0 = 1$. Further, let us assume that for all intents and purposes the productivity of the scientific community, in terms of contributions to knowledge, can be taken to exhibit constant returns to scale in the sense that, for example, a doubling of the population of scientists will double the rate of growth in technological information, or $k_1 = 1$. Then the percentage growth in technological information at time $t = T$ is immediately obtained as

$$\frac{I(T)}{I(0)} - 1 = I(T) - 1 = e^{\dfrac{k_2 N_L (1 - e^{-k_3 T})}{(1 + k_2)(1 + k_2 e^{-k_3 T})}} - 1 \tag{9.8a}$$

Hence, the level of technological techniques and processes at any time t depends on the base-period level of techniques and processes, the upper limit on the number of scientists, and the time that has passed since the base period. And, in effect then, the technological forecast takes the form of an extrapolation of past trends, albeit a complex extrapolation built on a clear, if debatable, theoretical foundation.

There are various approaches to TF at the micro level. One of the more interesting is the so-called *morphological* approach, which is basically an orderly procedure for eliciting knowledgeable judgments about technological advance. In fact it could well be used at the macro level in combination with other elements of TF. This approach attempts to catalog the various characteristics that can be built into, say, a particular product or process. With respect to airplanes, for example, the relevant characteristics might be air velocity, required landing area, passenger capacity, fuel consumption and capacity, and the like. The m_i^{th} of m characteristics could then be described in n_i different ways. Thus, the "type" of plane might be characteristic $i = 1$, and there could be $n_1 = 4$ different plane "types": supersonic = 1; jet = 2; propjet = 3; and propeller = 4. Similarly, passenger capacity, characteristic $i = 2$, might be divided into the following $n_2 = 6$ groups: 2 persons or less = 1; between 3 and 10 persons = 2; between 11 and 30 persons = 3; between 31 and 100 persons = 4; between 101 and 200 persons = 5; 200+ = 6. Then, at the $m = 2$ characteristics level *all* alternative plane designs would fit into some category $C_{m_1 m_2}$ where $m_1 = 1, \ldots, n_1 = 4$, and $m_2 = 1, \ldots, n_2 = 6$, so that, for example, a supersonic jet $(m_1 = 1)$ capable of carrying more than 200 persons $(m_2 = 6)$ would be placed in category C_{16}.

Similarly, $C_{m_1 m_2, \ldots, m_m}$ would describe any m characteristics of a project—a product or process. In the previous illustration there would be $(n_1) \times (n_2) = (4) \times (6) = 24$ different possibilities; in general, there would be $(n_1) \times (n_2) \times \ldots \times (n_m)$ alternative designs. The technological forecasting issue is then to determine *which* of the combinations contains mutually compatible characteristics, and hence to determine those combinations that, at a minimum, are real possibilities at some future date; and, subsequently, to make a determination of *when*, given the current state of the technological art, the products or processes represented by these combinations will be forthcoming.

The morphological approach is readily cast within a Bayesian framework. In particular, it provides an exhaustive listing of all possible outcomes, and it now remains the forecaster's responsibility to assign probabilities to each outcome, say for each future date. What is especially appealing in this regard is the possibility of *revising* these probabilities as new information comes in. Thus, for example, one might assign a prior probability $P(35462)$ to combination C_{35462}, as well as a conditional probability $P(.2\backslash 1)$ to reflect the likelihood of succeeding with characteristic $m_5 = 2$ given characteristic $m_5 = 1$ has been achieved. Then the probability $P(35462)$ of C_{35462} is automatically revised to $P(.2\backslash 1) = P(35462\backslash 1)$ when combination C_{35461} is achieved. Each of the technological possibilities is, therefore, *always* associated with a continually revised probabilistic statement that reflects the forecaster's best judgment as to the relative likelihood of achieving that specific possibility at some specific future date.

b. Normative models

The normative approach to technological forecasting rests on the assumption that R and D activity will in fact take place in an optimum manner coincident with social needs and objectives. The problem here, then, is to formulate a social welfare function W having as its arguments, say, a set of needs x_i $(i = 1, \ldots, n)$ at the end of the planning period, the satisfaction of which will depend on specific R and D expenditure or programs y_j $(j = 1, \ldots, m)$ taking place over the entire planning period in, say, the jth scientific discipline, or R and D category.

In particular, for illustrative purposes suppose that the y_j are R and D expenditures, and that for the planning period a total expenditure of Y *is allocated by the policy makers to R and D, or* $\Sigma y_j \leq Y$. Then, with the planners' sole focus on the *terminal* social welfare function W, the planners' problem can be written as

$$\text{Maximize} \qquad W = w(x_1, \ldots, x_i, \ldots, x_n) \qquad (9.9a)$$

$$\text{subject to } g_i(y_1, \ldots, y_m, x_i) = 0 \qquad i = 1, \ldots, n \qquad (9.9b)$$

$$\sum_{j} y_j \leq Y \qquad\qquad (9.9c)$$

$$y_j \geq 0 \qquad j = 1, \ldots, m \qquad\qquad (9.9d)$$

by manipulating the decision variables y_j. When the constraints (9.9b) are of the form

$$g_i'(y_1, \ldots, y_m) = x_i \qquad i = 1, \ldots, n \qquad\qquad (9.9b')$$

they can be directly substituted into (9.9a), and the problem reduces to

Maximize $W = w'(y_1, \ldots, y_j, \ldots, y_m)$ $\qquad\qquad$ (9.9a')

subject to $\sum_{j} y_j \leq Y$ $\qquad\qquad\qquad\qquad\qquad$ (9.9c)

$$y_j \geq 0 \qquad j = 1, \ldots, m \qquad\qquad (9.9d)$$

which is a nonlinear—or perhaps linear—programming problem with a single constraint and boundary conditions. In the latter format, the problem is readily amenable to the introduction of uncertainty and stochastic elements; in particular one can deal with it as a portfolio investment problem of the "Markowitz type," [4] in which the planners seek the optimal R and D "investment" portfolio.

In general, then, the planners that can exercise control over R and D activity will program expenditures in such a way as to maximize a societal welfare function, subject to a set of technological and, perhaps, cost constraints involving R and D activity as an exogenous input to the system, and need-satisfying products and processes as outputs, where the rate of scientific activity on any sphere cannot be negative. As a means of technological "forecasting," this approach assumes that, on an overall basis, R and D activity and technological progress will in fact occur *as if* they had been intelligently programmed in the first place. Under this approach, then, TF is actually planned technological change wherein each R and D project is treated as just another investment (see Chapter 10), and the future technology is determined as part of an overall investment program.

Equations (9.9a)–(9.9c) define a mathematical programming problem. Essentially all normative techniques can be expressed in a mathematical programming format. The only real issue to resolve here is the specific programming technique to employ, or format within which to frame the problem. This will typically hinge upon the quality of the data, and whether they permit a complex as opposed to a relatively simple model. In the technological area, and mathematical tractability aside, it is difficult to justify anything beyond the simplest type of model.

In Chapters 4 and 6 we discussed some of the difficulties that arise in specifying a social welfare function, as well as the problems that underlie the determination of the structural constraints. The latter problems are particularly

[4] H. M. Markowitz, *Portfolio Selection* (New York: John Wiley, 1959).

vexing in the present context because a sound empirical basis for establishing the parameters in each of the structural equations does not exist. Thus, historical data cannot ordinarily be employed to determine, say, a functional relationship between the various Y_j—the scientific activity in a given discipline—and a particular need-satisfying advance in the ith product or process category. Further, it makes little sense to combine a mathematically sophisticated model and very soft statistical data. Hence, relatively simplistic approaches to the programming problem are likely to be at least as appropriate as their more complex alternatives. Thus, for example, simple linear and integer programming models, and dynamic programming models, as well as models that simply rank prospective projects on the basis of such criteria as estimated rate of return or present discounted value, are often used to forecast the types of programs and projects that will actually be undertaken. Of necessity, however, because the data are so soft, and complex dynamic models are so mathematically intractable, these normative "forecasts" tend to be short and medium term by nature.

c. Feedback techniques

Scientific activity is a continuous process that involves a long-term commitment. Moreover, this commitment is one that is constantly being reviewed and updated in the light of the current state of the technological art. As such, feedback is *inherent* in the R and D process, and is part and parcel of technological change.

Technological forecasting employing a feedback framework essentially involves the description of the technological sector of the economic system as one of its subsystems, at least one component of which is a feedback mechanism. Thus, for example, an input into this subsystem from the rest of the system might take the form of $R thousand in R and D expenditures, where, say, $R = rY$ is determined as a fixed proportion r of gross national product Y.

In a more detailed analysis, the technological subsystem might receive its input from (a) consumers, (b) producers, and (c) the government, each source being treated as a separate component or subsystem, as well as from (d) the environment, which introduces the prospect of foreign developments, and (e) a feedback element that inputs into the technological system *previous* technological developments or, say, previous R and D expenditures, results, or programs. The inputs initially take the form of (a) *demands* for new developments—products, processes, and services—arising, for example, out of consumer-expressed interest, or out of producer-vexing problems, (b) *opportunities* for new developments to exploit latent demands, and (c) *new scientific knowledge,* although these might be filtered through an actuator, and ultimately translated into (d) dollars of R and D *expenditure.*

The inputs that trigger R and D are fed into the subsystem's primary components: government laboratories, industrial laboratories, and the complex of individual inventors. Within these components the inputs are transformed into (a) the tangible outputs of new products and processes, and (b) the intangible output of new scientific knowledge to be recycled and fed back into the subsystem. Thus, given a set of assumptions with respect to the exogenous inputs into the system at all future dates up to time T, the technological forecast for time T and all intervening time periods is automatically generated as either a rate of R and D activity in terms of monetary expenditure, or some measure of accumulated scientific knowledge, or both.

Assuredly, the description of this subsystem can be very simple. In particular, the linear autoregressive equation $R_t = A + aR_{t-1}$ might employ least-squares parameter estimates A and a to "predict" R_t, R and D expenditures in year t, based solely on the previous year's expenditures. The predicted R_t is then fed back into the equation and used to predict R_{t+1}, and so forth. Alternatively, a sophisticated simultaneous-equation model can be developed to fully describe, and in detail, the R and D subsystem and its relationship to the rest of the economic system. Notwithstanding the added complexity, however, the basic process is the same: R_t is predicted on the basis of previous data and exogenous inputs, and is either automatically fed back into the system of equations to yield a prediction for R_{t+1}, and so forth, or itself is treated as an exogenous input to predict R_{t+1}. In either event, it is the sophistication of the model rather than its basic operation that is different. Indeed, $R_t = A + aR_{t-1}$ is itself but a first-order difference equation that can be solved to yield as a general solution

$$R_t = \frac{A}{1-a}(1-a^t) + R_0 a^t \tag{9.10}$$

$$= A(1+a)^{t-1} + R_0 a^t \qquad t > 0 \tag{9.10a}$$

where R_0 is the rate of R and D expenditures in "year 0." Here, then, the feedback operation is automatically built into the model, and the rate of R and D expenditures in any given year or period t—which can, perhaps, be equated with the extent of technological progress—can be immediately forecast from the equation.

d. Intuitive models

The previous approaches all attack the technological forecasting problem in a *systematic* manner, either by establishing causal links between sets of exogenous and endogenous variables, or by an exhaustive quantitative or qualitative enumeration of the various alternative scenarios, and the determination of the most likely scenario, or that which will optimize some social welfare function. The technological sector is, however, particularly susceptible to the influence of important, if not vital, "random shocks" that sporadically impact on the technological scene. Thus, for example, it seems clear that scientists will ultimately discover a cure for, or preventative of malignant cancers. Such a cure will have great demographic implications that in turn will influence the demands for certain sets of goods and services. But there is no sound historical basis for predicting when such a technical breakthrough will be achieved.

Especially with respect to technological forecasting, insight dominates hindsight, and the nonquantifiable genius of imagination is more useful for predictive purposes than the logical decision processes of the methodically dull core of the computer.

Harnessing insight and imagination, and combining knowledgeable judgments for predictive purposes are the aims of the intuitive models of technological forecasting. These are, essentially, the basic managerial approaches to extracting both individual and group subjective judgments. In the former instance, one might ask the individual to write a scenario of the future; or, alternatively, one might pose a series of questions, the answers to which will provide the opinions about the future of technology of the persons queried. In the latter instance, one seeks a consensus of the group's views about technological change, through well-organized and controlled meetings in which such group decision-making techniques as the Delphi and nominal-group procedures are applied to the technological-forecasting process.

In the Delphi technique,[5] for example, a group of experts is assembled, and each member is asked to anonymously submit a set of judgments with respect, say, to the state of technology at some future date. The responses are then made public, with the anonymity of the respondents retained. The procedure is then repeated, each person having had the opportunity to revise a previously expressed opinion, in light of those held by others in the group. The procedure continues until, presumably, a consensus is reached.

In the nominal group technique,[6] the *initial* procedure is to force each individual to contribute ideas. This is done by *requiring* each person in succession to express "one idea at a time" until all thoughts have been elicited. Then, the ideas are presented to the group in structured form, say by calling attention to those upon which the group essentially agrees, and those upon which there is no apparent consensus. There then follows an open group discussion of these ideas, and, finally, there is nominal (silent) group voting for the final set of "group judgments."

In each instance, then, there is no systematic forecasting procedure that is repetitive by nature. Rather, the procedure must be started anew whenever a new forecast is desired.

9.5 GROWTH, CHANGE, AND PUBLIC POLICY

Contemporary analyses of economic growth point to the fact, not necessarily indisputable, that at least two-thirds of the increase in output per man in the United States since 1900 is attributable to technological progress rather than to

---

[5] O. Helmer, *The Uses of the Delphi Technique in Problems of Educational Innovations* (Santa Monica: RAND Corporation, December 1966). See also J. P. Martino, *Technological Forecasting for Decisionmaking* (New York: American Elsevier, 1972), pp. 18 ff.

[6] A. L. Delbecq and A. H. Van de Ven, "A Group Process Model for Problem Identification and Program Planning," *Journal of Applied Behavioral Science*, Vol. 7, No. 4, July–August 1971, pp. 466–492.

new capital formation.[7] Technological progress accounts for shifts in the relation between physical inputs and outputs so as to increase productivity, as well
as expansion in the spectrum of our choices—new processes, better products,
and new products—generating new dimensions in production possibilities.
Moreover, better planning of technological change, better management, and the
systematically up-graded labor force allow us to cope in constantly improving
fashion with the complex and evolving matters of information flows induced by
the new techniques. Latent changes in demand, as well as changes in factor
scarcities, further stimulate changes in the pace and form of technological advance. If no severe barriers hamper either the diffusion of inventions and innovations, or the play of managerial initiatives, the increasingly diversifying
activities of the "invention industry," the broadening of the "scientific box"
of scientists, engineers, and technicians, and the expansion of industry in size
and complexity, will further enhance technological advance. All these changes
necessarily have social consequences, and, as is now apparent, a crucial fact is
that many of these consequences are *undesirable, unforeseen,* and *unintended.*
In no mean measure, the question of how to foresee and cope with some of the
consequences has legitimately become part-and-parcel of TF as such.

Centralized planning of technological change is essentially defense-
oriented in the West, although governmental programs support certain aspects
of scientific engineering education and training, as well as various technical information services. R and D efforts are conducted either directly within certain
corporation departments, or within specialized firms that view TF as a necessary part of their consulting role in corporate planning (for example, in the
United States, Abt Associates, Battelle Memorial Institute, Corplan Associates
of the Illinois Institute of Technology, the Diebold Group, Arthur D. Little,
Quantum Science Corporation, Stanford Research Institute, and so on). Eventually, a network of private evaluation centers may cooperate (as in Italy) with
the government in the formulation of a national plan. In other cases (as in
France and the Soviet Union) long-range TF is devolved to specialized governmental commissions—either included in the central planning organization or
not—which notably attempt to assess the possible implications of key technological changes for current planning, and for decision making in decisive areas
with long-term economic and social implications. The various forms taken by
the organizational aspects of TF depend, to be sure, on the specific role of the
government in the economy, or its normative goals, and on the priorities that it
assigns to their implementation.

The policy makers and planners of MDC's look upon TF and the planning of technological change as a means of avoiding the pitfalls of identifica-

---

[7] See, for example, E. Dennison, *The Sources of Economic Growth in the U.S. and the Alterna-
tives Before the U.S.* (New York: Committee for Economic Development, 1962); E. Mansfield,
The Economics of Technological Change (New York: Norton, 1968); R. R. Nelson, J. J. Peck, and
E. D. Kalachek, *Technology, Economic Growth and Public Policy* (Washington: The Brookings In-
stitution, 1967); and R. Solow, "Technical Change and the Aggregate Production Function," *The
Review of Economics and Statistics,* Vol. 39, No. 3, August 1967, pp. 312–320.

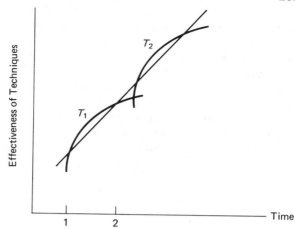

FIGURE 9-1

tion with fixed options and given technologies that might be in the process of becoming obsolete, and as an instrument for converting as much as possible of current *uncertainty* in respect to various courses of action, into probabilistically based statements about *risks*. With an appropriate forecast, the decision maker will get some idea of the odds for and against a given course of action. Systematic and continuous TF may also offer adequate *warning* and sufficient lead-time for switching over adequate resources to new technologies and areas of greater importance, when such are needed.

The problem involved can be visualized with the help of Figure 9.1 showing two successive approaches for performing some function. At year 1, TF of T_1 methods may indicate that the method is still capable of continuous progress; at year 2, a TF would indicate that T_1 is reaching its limit and that the switch over to T_2 should be prepared.

For the policy makers, not the planners, of MDC's, the greatest pitfalls of TF which will adversely affect both current options and long-term strategies are—according to Robert Ayres [8]—(a) lack of imagination and/or of "nerve" which tend to make forecasts overly pessimistic; (b) "over-compensation," or the assumption that everything is possible if only it is strongly desired—an assumption that has afflicted much of Soviet planning; (c) failure to anticipate converging developments and/or changes in competitive systems; (d) concentration on specific configurations only, and on established "expertise"; (e) incorrect calculations; and (f) intrinsic uncertainties and historical accidents.

In most countries, though, the focus in this field is not on the discovery of what the *future* may hold in terms of technological options, but in what the *present* choices imply in terms of future obligations and dependencies. Policy

[8] R. U. Ayres, *On Technological Forecasting* (Report HI-484-DP, 10 February 1965, revised version, 1966, Hudson Institute, New York) quoted in E. Jantsch, *Technological Forecasting in Perspective, op. cit.*, pp. 102–103.

makers and planners in LDC's in particular take great interest both in the specific mechanics of technological transfer, and in the investment financing that they entail, as well as in the technological and financial *dependencies* that they condition for long periods of time in the future. Hence, their primary interest is in defining norms and conditions for the "admission" of foreign technologies that necessarily involve obligations concerning terms of payment, purchase of inputs, supply of parts, and determination of the geographical areas in which the ensuing product may be distributed. They are also interested in the adaptation of the foreign technologies to suit local conditions, as well as in making the process of technological change endogenous to their economies.

CHAPTER 10

Problems of Investment Planning

10.1 INTRODUCTION

Under both capitalism and statism, and in both the more and the less developed countries, the controller influences the flow of investment through the economic system. On the one hand, planners *directly* affect the overall rate and channeling of investment through their choice of public investment budgets and projects. In some instances, such as in the construction of an inland waterway, funds to finance a profit-generating project might not be forthcoming from the private sector of a mixed economy because of the magnitudes, the risks, or the human energy commitments that are involved. In other instances, such as in the construction of a public television station, the project may not only compete with similar private ventures, but by its very intrusion into a competitive milieu it might inhibit private investment that would otherwise be effected in this area.

On the other hand, policy makers *indirectly* affect private investment through their selection of taxation and expenditure policies. The effects of such might be felt, for example, when, as a result of a sales tax on one set of goods, consumer expenditures and hence private investment are diverted toward noncomplementary alternatives. Alternatively, and in a less roundabout fashion, government expenditures on national defense might divert or encourage private investment into munitions and defense-related industries. Still further, private investment can be made less attractive through such controller-instituted policies as the adoption of a corporate income tax, or an exogenous increase in the interest rate charged by a central bank to its member banks; that is, policies that will either (a) reduce the expected future net cash flow from the investment, or (b) raise its initial financial cost.

Insofar as investment is concerned, then, policy makers actually exert a two-pronged impact upon the economic system. First, the policy makers qua controller introduce *exogenous inputs* into the system via government expenditures on goods and services, tax and interest rate adjustments, or the imposition or removal of various regulations that can affect both the transformation operations and the couplings of the individual components. Any of these can affect the attractiveness of investment to the private sector. Second, the policy makers qua investment planners manage a government investment sector that is one of the most important components of the economic system. This component may receive exogenous inputs from the controlling unit, as well as endogenous inputs from the rest of the system, depending on the components to which it is coupled. As an integral part of the system, the public investment sector would then send *endogenous inputs* to other components. Thus, for example, acting as the controller, the policy makers might issue instructions to the public investment sector through an "actuator" to institute a program of investment in atomic reactors, but the funds to support such a program might be generated endogenously as, say, a fixed proportion of corporate taxes. Similarly, some of the outputs of the public investment sector might go, for example, to the labor force and industrial sector in the form of endogenous demands for the labor and capital equipment that the particular investment requires.

As a result of the policy makers' dual role in the investment process, planning investment *demands* that consideration be given to two distinctly different issues. First, the policy makers must determine the *rates* of investment to be maintained in the economy over time. Thus, certain annual rates of investment might be compatible with the objective of maximizing economic growth, whereas other rates might be compatible with the objective of achieving a certain standard of living at some specified future date, while maintaining certain standard-of-living minima in the intervening years. To determine these rates, one set of investment planning models is needed.

Second, the policy makers must determine *which* public investment projects to undertake, or establish criteria by which the private sector may evaluate projects. This determination can be exceedingly complex, inasmuch as it means establishing certain minimum criteria that *any* prospective project must satisfy, in addition to determining the entire project *mix* to be included in an intertemporal investment program. To deal with this problem requires a second set of models. This set will include rules for evaluating individual projects, as well as techniques for selecting an investment program. In this chapter we shall consider models that fall into each of these two categories.

Although the basic issues are similar, substantial differences exist between mixed and fully centralized economies, and between more and less developed countries in dealing with the problems of (a) size and distribution of investment, and (b) rules for choice among projects. In fully centralized economies, planners *simultaneously* decide on savings *and* investment, and address *specific orders* to the *operational manager* concerning inputs and outputs flowing through the investment project. In mixed economies, savings are determined endogenously in the private sector, and once operationalized the individual public investment projects are typically permitted to function independently of the central policy-making unit. It is also typically true that the impacts of the use of the instruments of public policy are harder to ascertain in the less developed countries than in their more developed counterparts. Thus, for example, interest rates in the LDC's are usually much higher than in the MDC's, and private investors are usually less sensitive to government-inspired changes in the interest rates; perhaps more importantly, the effects on private investment of, say, changes in a corporate income tax, or the imposition of tariffs or import quotas, may be quite predictable in the MDC's, but only assessable with comparatively little confidence in the LDC's.

Numerous aspects of the problem of investment planning, with particular respect to size and distribution, have been clarified by the development of modern growth theory, particularly since the 1960s. Not *all* growth theory and its numerous developments—capital-oriented or consumption-oriented—are, however, relevant to the issues with which we are herein concerned; a judicious choice has to be made, accordingly, with specific reference to our sphere of interest. Among the main contributions to the modern theory of investment planning, a singular place is held by the early contributions of Ramsey [1] and von Neumann,[2] and by the more recent works of Frisch,[3] S. Chakravarty,[4] Lange,[5] and Arrow and Kurz.[6] The latter have contributed a particularly incisive examination of the complex aspects of investment in a mixed economy.

Similarly, numerous aspects of investment planning, particularly with respect to rules for choice, have been clarified by developments in mathematical programming, wherein the contributions of Kuhn and Tucker,[7] and Markowitz [8] are especially important, and in our understanding of "the social rate of discount," wherein the contributions of Hirschleifer,[9] Margolin,[10] Mishan,[11]

---

[1] F. Ramsey, "A Mathematical Theory of Saving," *Economic Journal,* Vol. 38, December 1928, pp. 543–559.

[2] J. von Neumann, "A Model of General Economic Equilibrium," *Review of Economic Studies,* Vol. 13, No. 1, January 1945, pp. 1–9 (G. Morgenstern, transl.).

[3] For example, R. Frisch, *A Powerful Method of Approximation in Optimum Investment Computations of the Normal Type,* and *Optimal Investments Under Limited Foreign Resources* (Oslo: Institute of Economics, June 1959 and July 1959).

[4] S. Chakravarty, *Capital and Development Planning* (Cambridge, Mass.: The MIT Press, 1969).

[5] O. Lange, "The Economic and Technological Bases of the Output and Income-Investment Ratio," in *Studies on the Theory of Reproduction and Prices* (Warsaw: Polish Scientific Publishers, 1964), pp. 5–51.

[6] K. J. Arrow and M. Kurz, "Optimal Public Investment Policy and Controllability with Fixed Private Savings Ratio," *Journal of Economic Theory,* Vol. 1, No. 1, June 1969, pp. 141–177.

[7] H. W. Kuhn and A. W. Tucker, "Nonlinear Programming," in J. Neyman (ed) *Proceedings of the Second Berkeley Symposium on Mathematical Statistics and Probability* (Berkeley, Calif.: University of California Press, 1951), pp. 481–492.

[8] H. M. Markowitz, *Portfolio Selection* (New York: John Wiley, 1959).

[9] J. Hirshleifer, "Investment Decisions Under Uncertainty: Applications of the State Preference Approach," *Quarterly Journal of Economics,* Vol. 80, No. 2, May 1966, pp. 252–277; and, "On The Theory of Optimal Investment," in E. Solomon (ed.) *The Management of Corporate Capital* (New York: The Free Press of Glencoe, 1959), pp. 205–228.

[10] S. A. Marglin, "The Social Rate of Discount and the Optimal Rate of Investment," *Quarterly Journal of Economics,* Vol. 77, No. 1, February 1963, pp. 95–112; and *Public Investment Criteria* (London: Allan and Unwin, 1967).

[11] E. J. Mishan, "Public Investment Criteria: Some Simplifying Suggestions," *Journal of Political Economy,* Vol. 75, No. 2, April 1967, pp. 139–146.

and Baumol [12] are especially notable. In this chapter we shall attempt to both set out the basic issues and approaches to these matters, and indicate where the state of the investment planning art now stands. We do this by first drawing the distinction between consistency and optimization models for determining investment and savings paths to generate targeted and optimal rates of consumption, respectively, either over time or at particular future points in time. Some of the basic issues involved are discussed here within the context, first, of one-sector models and, second, two-sector and multi-sector models. We then turn to a discussion of investment decision rules, with particular emphasis on the determination of the so-called social rate of discount. Finally, we present some particular planning models that have been suggested for the resolution of the problem of transition from individual project choice to a consolidated plan.

10.2 CONSISTENCY, OPTIMIZATION, AND HORIZONS

In a planned economy—indicative or directive—the size and structure of investment are determined as a function of the policy makers' goals. The solutions rest upon assumptions as to the achievable rates of annual investment, capital:output ratios in the various industrial sectors and geographical regions in the economy, and the probable lags between investment and output, as indicated by historical experience concerning the rate at which capital projects are planned, designed, built, and operationalized. In principle, at least, these solutions can be implemented in a Soviet-type centralized economy, since both the supply of savings and the demand for investment are government-determined: the government can vary the investment:income ratio; it can manipulate the regional allocations and basic technological choices; it can determine inputs and outputs; and, finally, it has available a variety of instruments for mobilizing or disbursing investments.

In contrast, in a mixed economy with a complex interplay of public and private decisions, the planners cannot directly determine the supply of savings and the demand for investment, but they can and do *influence* both. Arrow and Kurz point out that because of this a decision on the size and pattern of public investment should be made jointly with the choice of the instruments—such as taxes and discount rates—meant to influence private investors and consumers vis-à-vis savers.

In either case, plans can and do go awry, because the models from which they have been derived, including the data inputs, are ordinarily oversimplified, and will not necessarily be valid in our uncertainty-laden world. Nonetheless, model-building efforts are worth pursuing, because even in their oversimplification and imperfection these models can lead us in the desired direction. This is equally true of some of the more mathematically sophisticated models, such as those developed in accordance with the objective of determining and maintaining an optimal growth path.

The models in question can variously be classified as being either *con-*

---

[12] W. J. Baumol, ''On the Social Rate of Discount,'' *American Economic Review*, Vol. 58, No. 4, September 1968, pp. 788–802.

sistency or *optimization* models. In the former case, the models are concerned with determining, say, the investment and savings paths that would be *consistent* with a targeted rate of growth in consumption. In the latter case, the models are concerned with determining, say, the *optimal* investment and savings paths to achieve the maximization of an intertemporal social utility function whose arguments are the temporal rates of consumption. Whether a model serves the former or the latter purpose will, however, depend on how it is used. Thus, a mathematical programming model can be used to determine the optimal rates of a set of decision variables over which the decision maker exercises control, or it can be used to indicate the rates that these variables would assume, or the paths that they would follow over time, consistent with a set of prespecified targets, structural constraints, and boundary conditions.

Consider, for example, a mixed economy in which the state assumes a leading role in regard to the distribution of investment, or a highly centralized economy of the Soviet type. As suggested by Chakravarty [13] a first *approximation* of the size and allocation of investment could be achieved by considering the solution of the linear programming model

$$\text{Minimize} \qquad C = \sum_{j=1}^{n} c_j x_j \qquad\qquad (10.1)$$

$$\text{subject to} \ \sum_{j=1}^{n} a_{ij} x_j \geq y_i \qquad i = 1, \ldots, m$$

$$x_j \geq 0 \qquad j = 1, \ldots, n$$

where the y_i's are prespecified final commodity demands, the x_j's are the so-called activity levels, a_{ij} is a coefficient that describes the amount of commodity i that will result from undertaking activity or industrial process j at its nominal unit level, and c_j is a *capital coefficient* describing the investment that is required—say in monetary terms—by a unit level of the jth activity. Thus, if *all* activities are carried out at their unit levels, a total of $\sum_j a_{ij}$ will be produced of commodity i; if *all* activities are *to be* carried out at their unit levels, a total investment of $\sum_j c_j$ will be required.

In general, then, the linear programming problem (10.1) seeks to determine activity levels that will minimize the total investment or capital requirements, while satisfying some preestablished minimum production rates for a commodity set. Additional constraints might also be introduced into the problem. Chakravarty calls attention to two of particular interest: foreign exchange requirements and labor supply. The former might take the form $\sum_j d_j x_j \leq D$, where d_j is the amount of foreign exchange required in order to undertake activity j at the unit level, and D is the maximum available amount of foreign exchange; the latter might take the form $\sum_j l_j x_j \leq L$, where l_j is the labor input required by the unit level of activity j, and L is the total labor supply. Assuredly, the series of linearity assumptions is open to serious question, but as a first *approximation* the linear programming approach often provides valuable

[13] *Capital and Development Planning*, pp. 2 ff.

insights into an *optimal* program and yields *consistent* solutions, in the sense that, subject to the validity of the underlying assumptions, the final demands are consistent with the available capacities.

At a broader level, Chakravarty also has examined the question of optimal investment planning within a one-sector model, assuming homogeneous capital and "linear" technology, and within a two-sector model assuming shiftability and nonshiftability of capital between the two sectors, as well as within a multi-sector Leontief static and dynamic input-output model with both homogeneous and heterogeneous capital, and with "linear" technology. Chakravarty's analyses provide an excellent framework for expositing the more important of these investment planning issues.[14]

a. One-sector models

We shall first consider a one-sector model of an economy in which the policy makers' single target is to achieve a so-called "desired" rate of growth in consumption. In this connection, they will want to determine how much the economy ought to *save*, since when converted into investment, today's savings provide the foundation for tomorrow's consumption.

If $C^T(t) = \int_0^t C(\tau)d\tau$ denotes total consumption from time zero to t, then $C(t) = dC^T(t)/dt$ is the *rate* of consumption at time t, and $r(t) = [dC(t)/dt]/C(t)$—which is assumed to be constant (and, indeed, *is* approximately so)[15]—is the rate of growth in consumption at time t. If, in fact, consumption grows continuously at the desired rate of r, then in t years from the base year, time $t = 0$, the rate of consumption will be $C(t) = C_0 e^{rt}$, where $C(0) = C_0$. Given a capital stock at time t of $K(t)$, and a time-invariant capital:output ratio of k, the rate of total output, or national income $Y(t)$, will then be given by $K(t)/k$. But since the capital stock at time t is, in the assumed absence of depreciation, given by the initial capital stock, $K(0) = K_0$, plus the difference between total output $\int_0^t Y(\tau)d\tau$ and total consumption $C^T(t)$ from time zero to t, or

$$K(t) = K_0 + \int_0^t Y(\tau)d\tau - \int_0^t C(\tau)d\tau$$

then the change in the capital stock, or the rate of investment, will be given by

$$\frac{dK(t)}{dt} = Y(t) - C(t) = K(t)/k - C_0 e^{rt} \tag{10.2}$$

$$= S(t)$$

or, the rate of investment equals the rate of savings, at any time t.

---

[14] *Ibid.*, p. 111 ff.

[15] Let $C(t) = C(0)e^{rt}$. Then $C(t+1) = C(0)e^{r(t+1)}$ and $C(t+1) - C(t) = C(0)(e^{r(t+1)} - e^{rt})$ $= C(0)e^{rt}(e^r - 1) = C(0)e^{rt}(1 + r + r^2/2 + r^3/6 + \cdots - 1)$. Thus, the *rate* of increase between $t+1$ and t is $[C(t+1) - C(t)]/C(t) = (r + r^2/2 + r^3/6 + \cdots) \approx r$. That is, the rate of increase over the discrete time interval can be *approximated* by the instantaneous rate $r(t)$.

Equation (10.2) is a first-order differential equation, the solution to which is

$$K(t) = Ke^{t/k} + \frac{kC_0}{1-kr} [e^{rt} - e^{t/k}] \tag{10.3}$$

where as a necessary condition for $K(t) > 0$ for $t > 0$, we require $1/k > r$, or the output:capital ratio must exceed the desired rate of growth in consumption. The optimal savings rate in year t *consistent* with the growth rate r is then given by

$$S(t) = \frac{dK(t)}{dt} = (\frac{K}{k})^{t/k} + \frac{kC_0}{1-kr} [re^{rt} - \frac{e^{t/k}}{k}] \tag{10.4}$$

which is also a function of the base year level of the capital stock, the rate of consumption at time zero, and the capital:output ratio. Alternatively, by specifying a capital stock endowment $K(T)$ for future generations starting at time T, one can also determine from Equation (10.3) a base-year consumption rate $\hat{C}_0$ given as

$$\hat{C}_0 = \frac{1-kr}{k(e^{rt} - e^{T/k})} [K(T) - Ke^{t/k}] \tag{10.3a}$$

The way in which the model is used will depend on the policy makers' aim and "givens."

This approach ignores any intermediate depreciation in the capital stock. The implication of the $1/k > r$ assumption is that a certain amount of capital is to be bequeathed to posterity after a finite period of time. Perhaps more pertinently, the *focus* of this approach is on developing an internally *consistent set of rules* for achieving some *prespecified* objective, rather than on determining the rules for *optimizing* some objective function. The emphasis is reoriented in the latter direction through the introduction of a social welfare function.

In the context of investment *planning*, the policy makers' interest in investment does not derive from its potential multiplier impact on *current* national product, but rather from its long-term implications for *future* rates of consumption. Therefore, in determining an investment strategy to maximize some social welfare function, the arguments of the relevant function will be *all* $C(t)$, from time $t = 0$ through the investment horizon; that is, the function will be an *intertemporal social welfare function*. This immediately raises two questions: (a) what form should the function take? and (b) should the horizon be finite or infinite?

To answer the first question we should bear in mind that as a utility function, a social welfare function is merely an ordinal relation that assigns numerical values in accordance with preferences, when paired comparisons are being made between alternatives offered with certainty. Thus, in the present context, the social welfare function *might* be given by $W = w(C(T))$, or social welfare is a function solely of consumption at the horizon date T. In this particular case, the single objective would be to obtain the highest rate of consumption at time T, *irrespective* of the consumption rates suffered or enjoyed during the preceding and subsequent time periods. At the opposite extreme, for those who live only for the present the function $W = w(C(0))$ would distinguish between alternative consumption patterns solely on the basis of present consumption rates, and ignore the future entirely.

Assuredly, for nations as for individuals, the concern is generally with consumption rates over the *entire* time horizon, setting aside for the moment any discussion of what that horizon should be. And thus, recognizing that time is continuous and that a society does in fact consume continuously at all times t, from the present time zero to the horizon date T, the policy makers' most appropriate description of the society's concern is with the *time path* of consumption.

The intertemporal social welfare function over the time horizon T will be written $W = w(C(0), \ldots, C(T))$. Additionally, let $\mu(C(t), t) = \mu(C, t)$ denote the social utility function that reflects preferences, *as of time $t = 0$*, for a consumption rate of $C = C(t)$ to obtain at time t. That is, the social preference ordering depends on *both* the rate of consumption at time t, *and* the specific time t at which that rate obtains. Suppose, moreover, that this social preference ordering is independent of any considerations with respect to the rate of consumption $C(t')$ that might obtain at any *other* time $t' \neq t$. In this circumstance, as of time $t = 0$, it does not seem inappropriate for the policy makers to focus on the *total* social utility over the time horizon, in which case

$$W = w(C(0), \ldots, C(T)) = \int_0^T \mu(C, t)dt$$

In discrete time, the latter total utility would be written as the sum

$$W = \sum_{t=0}^T \mu(C, t)$$

or $W = w(C(0), \ldots, C(T))$ is assumed to be *additively separable* into the sum of a series of temporal social welfare functions. This assumption implies that "previous" consumption decisions do not impact upon the utility of "current" consumption. In point of fact, this is clearly not so, especially insofar as durable goods are concerned, or from a psychological standpoint, for example, insofar as "previous" rates of consumption effect aspiration levels that all subsequent rates are expected to maintain or surpass. Nonetheless, the assumption is convenient, and the sacrifice of reality for mathematical tractability is justified by the broad *generalizations* that can be inferred from the model.

As a further simple modification, the time factor reflecting the *preference* for $C(t)$ over $C(t')$, where $C(t) = C(t')$, so long as $t < t'$—that is, "earlier" consumption at a given rate is preferred to "later" consumption at that rate—could be introduced in the continuous case through a *discount factor* e^{-it}, where i is the rate of discount, such that $\mu(C, t) = \mu(C)e^{-it}$; in the discrete case, $\mu(C, t) = \mu(C)/(1 + i)^t$. Although a plausible case can be built for other types of relationships, for expository purposes, and given its mathematical tractability and the *authors'* time horizon, we shall restrict the discussion to the continuous case and a function of the general form $W = \int_0^T \mu(C, t)dt$.

The planners' problem is to determine $C = C(t)$ for all t ($0 \leq t \leq T$), so as to maximize W; that is, to determine a *time path* of consumption that maximizes total social welfare through the time horizon. But consumption requires output, and output, in turn, depends on investment as reflected in the capital stock. Thus, for example, the rate of total output $Y(t)$ might be assumed to be a function of the capital stock, or $Y(t) = y(K(t))$. If the capital stock depreciates at a rate of δ per unit of capital per year, then new capital formation of $dK/dt = y(K(t)) - C(t) - \delta K(t)$ will take place at time t. Hence, new capital formation at time t will depend on the capital stock $K(t)$, the time t, and the *set* of consumption decisions $\underline{C}$ that encompasses the selection of all $C(t)$. Moreover, because "future" consumption will in fact depend on the "current" capital stock, it is clear that the capital-consumption pair $(K_1(t), C(t))$ will be preferred to $(K_2(t), C(t))$ so long as $K_1(t) > K_2(t)$; or, more generally, that the capital stock should *also* be included as an argument in the social welfare function. Thus, if we now write $W = \int_0^T \mu(K, C, t)dt$, the planners' problem is to determine the time path, or consumption decision $\underline{C}$ that will

$$\text{Maximize } W = \int_0^T \mu(K, C, t)dt \tag{10.5a}$$

subject to the constraint

$$\frac{dk}{dt} = f(K, C, t) \tag{10.5b}$$

or

$$F(K, \frac{dK}{dt}, C, t) = 0 \tag{10.5b'}$$

given an initial capital stock of K_0. Determination of this set requires the simultaneous determination of the optimal investment path.

In principle, there are two ways to solve the above problem. In one, Equation (10.5b') is used to obtain a solution for, say, $C(t)$ in terms of $K(t)$, $dK(t)/dt$, and t. This solution is then substituted for $C = C(t)$ in Equation (10.5a) so that the problem reduces to

$$\text{Maximize } W = \int_0^T \mu'(K, \frac{dK}{dt}, t)dt \tag{10.5a'}$$

which is an ordinary problem in the calculus of variations, in which the optimum *function* $K(t)$ is sought. Unfortunately, however, it may not be possible to solve (10.5b') explicitly for $C(t)$.

In the other, the problem summarized in Equations (10.5a) and (10.5b), as well as many of its more complex variants, is a problem that can be solved through the calculus of variations and the principles of optimal control theory, without having to solve (10.5b'), by utilizing Pontryagin's maximum principle.[16] Assuming that a set of conventional second-order and ancillary condi-

---

[16] L. V. Pontryagin, V. G. Boltyanskii, R. V. Gamkrelidze, and E. F. Mishchenki, *The Mathematical Theory of Optimal Processes* (New York: John Wiley, 1962) (K. N. Trirogoff, transl.).

tions hold, including, for example, $\partial\mu/\partial C > 0$ and $\partial^2\mu/\partial C^2 < 0$ (that is, positive but diminishing marginal utility of consumption), and $\partial Y/\partial K > 0$ and $\partial^2 Y/\partial K^2 < 0$ (that is, positive but diminishing marginal productivity of capital), one can seek a unique time path $\underline{C}$ and set of investment requirements through the simultaneous solution of the following equations: [17]

$$\frac{dK}{dt} = f(K, C, t) \tag{10.5b}$$

$$\frac{\partial\mu}{\partial C} + \lambda\frac{\partial f}{\partial C} = 0 \tag{10.6a}$$

$$\frac{\partial\mu}{\partial K} + \lambda\frac{\partial f}{\partial K} = -\frac{d\lambda}{dt} \tag{10.6b}$$

where $\lambda = \lambda(t) = \partial(\text{Max } W)/\partial K$ is a time-dependent multiplier. As a shadow price that represents the change in the maximum attainable total utility from the optimal consumption path when the capital stock $K(t)$ changes, λ reflects the value of a unit of capital.

This is an apt stage of the discussion for considering the second of our two major issues—the time horizon. From a mathematical standpoint, an infinite horizon, $T = \infty$, is somewhat less tractable than a finite T, since as $T \to \infty$, $W = \int_0^T \mu(K, C, t) \to \infty$ unless otherwise restricted, say by introducing a satiation level of consumption C_s that limits μ to μ_s, or by a "strong enough" discounting of future preferences. The infinite horizon thus places the policy makers in the somewhat unreasonable position of choosing between alternative paths to an infinite total utility. But a finite T is also not without accompanying difficulties.

In the absence of *any* concern as to the society's welfare *after* the horizon, there is neither an intuitive nor a mathematical basis for arriving at any result other than $K(T) = 0$, because $\lambda(T) = 0$; that is, the value of capital is zero, and no capital stock is retained at T, as there is no point in "stocking up" on capital to produce for future generations whose preferences and consumptions do not concern the present population. Quite suddenly, therefore, policy makers are confronted with an additional ethical consideration: whether the present society has an obligation to bequeath a capital stock to the unborn generations, and the size of the potential bequest.

Opinion is divided on this issue, as it is on the no-less important issue of the choice of T.[18] Given the *custom* of the five-, ten-, or twenty-year plan, however, it would seem that introducing a lower-bound condition of $K(T) \geq K_T$, where $K_T \geq 0$ and, say, $T = 5$ or 10 or 20, would suffice for present purposes.

Given a set of initial and terminal conditions in terms of a capital stock

[17] For a discussion of this approach see R. Dorfman, "An Economic Interpretation of Optimal Control Theory," *American Economic Review*, Vol. 59, No. 5, December 1969, pp. 817–831.

[18] See S. Chakravarty, "Alternative Preference Functions in Problems of Investment Planning on the National Level," in E. Malinvaud, *et al.* (eds.) *Activity Analysis in the Theory of Growth and Planning* (New York: Macmillan, 1967), pp. 150–166.

endowment and bequest, in principle Equations (10.5b), (10.6a), and (10.6b) will lead to the solution of the investment planning problem. In particular, Equation (10.6a) says that at every time t, the marginal utility of additional consumption, $\partial\mu/\partial C$, should be equated to the value of investment foregone in favor of the additional consumption, $-\lambda\,(\partial f/\partial C)$; Equation (10.6b) says that the rate of change in the unit value of the new capital formation, $-d\lambda/dt$, should be equated to the sum of the new capital's contribution to utility, $\partial\mu/\partial K$, and the value of the contribution of the new capital to the capital stock, $\lambda\,(\partial f/\partial K) = \lambda\,(\partial\,(dK/dt)/\partial K)$.

b. Two- and multi-sector models

The problem of intersectoral investment planning in two- and multi-sector economies was previously discussed in Chapters 3 and 7 in terms of Mahalanobis and Fel'dman planning models. These models assume that capital investment assigned to the production of, say, additional capital goods or consumption goods, is not reassignable to another production sector at a future date. Models have also been developed, however, to deal with investment that is in fact *shiftable* between sectors. We shall discuss here what is, perhaps, the simplest of such models. For convenience, we retain the assumption of continuous time.[19]

Consider an economy that produces new capital goods and consumption goods at the rates of dK/dt and $C = C(t)$, respectively, at time t. With capital:output ratios of k_1 and k_2 in the consumption and capital goods sectors, respectively, the total capital *required* to yield a net output rate of $Y(t) - K(t) = C(t) + dK/dt$ would be $k_1 C + k_2 dK/dt$. For this output rate to be feasible, the capital requirement cannot exceed the available capital stock of $K(t) = K$; or,

$$K \geq K_1 C + k_2\frac{dK}{dt} \tag{10.7}$$

which leads to

$$C \leq \frac{1}{k_1}K - \frac{k_2}{k_1}\frac{dK}{dt} \tag{10.7a}$$

Equation (10.7a) places an upper bound on the achievable rate of consumption at time t, for a *given* level of the capital stock and the rate of new capital formation, as well as the two capital:output ratios. By assumption the marginal utility of consumption is positive, so that once the rate of new capital formation is determined, we will want to assure society of the maximum possible rate of consumption. That means that we will want Equation (10.7a) to hold as a strict equality. In this case, the utility function $\mu(C,\,t)$ can be written

$$\mu(\frac{1}{k_1}K - \frac{k_2}{k_1}\frac{dK}{dt},\,t) = \mu(K,\,\frac{dK}{dt},\,t)$$

[19] See Chakravarty, *op. cit.*

and the planners' problem becomes a calculus of variations problem in which the goal is

$$\text{Maximize } W = \int_0^T \mu(K, \frac{dK}{dt}, t)dt \qquad (10.8)$$

The solution to this problem, and the implications that the solution has for planning, depend on the boundary conditions imposed on the capital stock, $K(0)$ and $K(T)$, as well as on the specific form of the social welfare function. Clearly, however, a ceteris paribus reduction of the capital:output ratio in the capital goods sector will increase the relative rate of growth in the consumption goods sector by reducing the capital required by the former sector to achieve a given rate of new capital formation. The effects of reducing the capital:output ratio in the consumption goods sector, ceteris paribus, will depend on the specific form assumed by the social welfare function. Thus, one general implication of this model would be to stress the importance of R and D activity in the capital goods sector to effect a reduction in the capital:output ratio in this sector. A second implication would be that the optimal investment policy depends *crucially* on *both* the shape of the social welfare function and the sectoral capital:output ratios.

Although it is nice to know that there is a sound theoretical basis for these not very surprising generalizations, models such as these tend to be of little practical value for *specific* planning purposes. There are three basic reasons for this. First, even for relatively simplified models under highly restrictive assumptions, solutions that are derivable in principle will not necessarily be derivable in practice. Second, while on the one hand the functions in question might be modified so as to assure a solution, on the other hand, the construction of a really useful model might require the removal of so many restrictions, and the consequent consideration of such factors as the available labor supply, international obligations, and technological progress, that even the simplest type of model could become mathematically intractable. Third, the data requirements of these models, including at a minimum the capital:output ratios, the social welfare function, and the boundary conditions, are not unimposing.

These qualifications suggest that insofar as investment planning "in the large" is concerned, the models that have thus far been developed are unlikely to do more than yield first approximations that point planners in the right direction, providing them with a starting point from which to exercise their own unique expertise.

10.3 INVESTMENT DECISION RULES

Final acceptance of specific investment *projects* will depend on both the total investment budget and the alternatives from which the entire investment *program* will be drawn. The economic managers' initial concern is with paring down the list of prospective projects to those that will be supported in the event that the required funds are available. The basic cutoff criterion is that the present discounted value of the flow of gross returns must exceed the present discounted value of the costs. Denoting the returns in year t by R_t, the year t cost expenditure by E_t, and the fixed annual discount rate by i, the familiar criterion is

$$\text{Present Value} = PV = \sum_{t=0}^{T} \frac{R_t - E_t}{(1+i)^t} > 0$$

for a project of T years in length that involves an immediate capital investment of $K = E_0$. The discounting can be done on any other basis, such as semiannually or quarterly; in the continuous case, the criterion becomes

$$PV = \int_0^T [R(t) - E(t)] e^{-it} dt > 0 \tag{10.9}$$

The choice of present discounted value as the theoretically appropriate investment criterion is beyond dispute. In practice, however, this criterion will not necessarily be employed. Tradition has seen the frequent use and support of such rule-of-thumb ranking criteria as the internal rate of return—the discount rate that equates the present discounted value to zero, and the payback period—the number of years required to recoup the original investment. Although under *some* conditions such alternative criteria will rank projects in exactly the same way as the *PV* criterion, the results will only coincide either under very restrictive assumptions with respect to the pattern of the *net* flow of returns and the time horizons involved, or by coincidence.[20] In lieu of rehashing what are now well-known arguments, we shall take it as justifiably accepted doctrine that present discounted value is the appropriate point of departure in investment decisions. But, this only raises four major issues: (1) the measurement of the magnitudes, and the timing, of the net returns; (2) the determination of the appropriate discount factor; (3) project interdependencies; and (4) the need to deal with risk.

a. The net returns from a public investment

Neither the returns nor the costs of a public (or, for that matter, a private) investment project are easily measured. There may be tangible and intangible, as well as direct and indirect elements in each. The issues here are sufficiently well known that there is little point to belaboring them, but it would be inappropriate to ignore them entirely.

The least difficult cost to assess is the initial capital investment. In particular, the investment outlay of, say, K_t at time t might be taken as a given. Experience and observation indicate, however, that while the *initial* outlay of $K = K_0 = E_0$ tends to correspond to expectations, because immediate expenditures tend to be kept in line with budgeted allocations, such long-term capital expenditures as might be required by major plant construction rarely fall below the initial estimates, and all too frequently produce cost overruns. This suggests that the investment-data inputs should consist of probabilistic information of the

[20] See Hirshleifer, "On the Theory of Optimal Investment," *op. cit.*

following sort: an investment expenditure of K_t is anticipated at time t with probability $P_t(K_t)$, such that $\bar{K}_t = E[K_t] = \sum_{K_t} P_t(K_t)K_t \geq 0$ is the *expected* capital expenditure at time t.

Just as capital expenditures can be assessed probabilistically, so too can all other costs and returns. In the case of capital expenditures, however, these are under the economic managers' *direct control*. These expenditures relate to a specific undertaking whose underlying cost elements can be analyzed in detail and, by and large, with considerable accuracy, and they generally are to be expended in the relatively short term. In contrast, the returns and noncapital costs are unlikely to be subject to government control, elements of each may come from sources that are unamenable to accurate forecasts, and they are generally long term in nature.

A public investment project such as a dam or a road can have tangible noncapital costs of both a direct and indirect nature associated with it. Maintenance and operating costs are direct tangible costs that can be assessed probabilistically, where the assessment might be conditional upon a factor such as usage which itself could only be assessed probabilistically. One will not necessarily feel comfortable with these assessments, but such will be necessary in evaluating *any* prospective investment—public *or* private—and persons with a low tolerance of heat are well-advised to remove themselves from the kitchen. But the feeling of discomfort is positively pleasurable when contrasted with that which must accompany an assessment of the indirect costs.

The costs associated with a public investment are incurred by the *nation*. It is the nation, with the government acting as its administrative agent, that pays the direct cost of maintaining and operating the dams and highway systems. Similarly, it is the nation that bears the indirect costs associated with, say, the disappearance of a viable passenger railroad system which follows on the heels of the development of a superhighway system. These costs include the loss of tax revenues and the contribution to national product that the now defunct railways *would have made*. Thus, in order to assess the indirect costs it is necessary to both ascertain *where* indirect costs will be incurred, and then to make some determination of their *likely magnitude* at any particular time t. Assuredly, if one has available a rather large input-output table wherein the effects of a particular *type* of public investment on all other economic categories can be directly and immediately determined, and if, further, one can assume that this table and its coefficients will be valid over extended time periods, the assessment of the *net* indirect costs or returns is greatly facilitated. But, given the set of restrictive assumptions underlying the input-output approach, even in these happy circumstances the assessments are not likely to be made with great confidence. And, often investment itself is made to *change* the coefficients, and this further clouds the issue.

Assessing the *intangible* costs is just the next step up on the ladder of difficulty. There is, for example, an intangible, nonmonetary cost that is *directly* associated with the construction of a highway that necessitates the relocation of a population of families. In a very real if intangible sense, society suffers a loss when the lives of some of its members are permanently disrupted because of projects that are undertaken for the benefit of the group as a whole. In a similar vein, when the construction of a highway system leads to a deterioration in the railroad system, which in turn encourages suburban residents to commute to downtown areas by automobile, and when the result of the increased automobile usage is traffic congestion and a substantial increase in air pollution, there is an intangible, *indirect* cost being suffered by the nation at every time t. Assigning a monetary value to this cost—even with an associated probability density—is at best a tenuous proposition; but not assigning such costs is a major omission.

The very same issues arise in assessing the returns—or, more appropriately, the *benefits*—derived from a public investment. Thus, our hypothetical highway might yield tolls and tax revenues, and could, in addition, yield an indirect benefit in terms of, say, the elimination of an inefficient and unprofitable railroad service. Moreover, there could be intangible benefits in terms of, say, the facilitation of family automobile vacations and camping trips that permit the nation's citizens to enjoy its scenic beauties and, perhaps, take advantage of its outdoor bounties. But, once again, placing monetary values on these benefits, assigning probability densities to these monetary values, and doing this for all times t $(0 \le t \le T)$ is at best a herculean chore.

In effect, then, the measurement of the net benefits of any public investment, net of any costs applicable thereto, must take into account all *externalities*—the effects on the rest of the economic system—both positive and negative, which can logically be ascribed to the project, as well as the net benefits that adhere directly to the project. In practice this measurement is accomplished by a combination of analytical techniques and knowledgeable judgments.

The potential use of input-output analysis in this regard has already been noted. An alternative approach suggested by Chenery [21] is also of special interest. Investment, Chenery remarks, has several dimensions affecting various economic variables such as national income Y, the balance of payments B_a, the rate of unemployment Γ, and the distribution of income Y_d. If the social welfare function can be expressed with such variables as its arguments, so that $U = \mu(Y. B_a, \Gamma, Y_d, \ldots)$, then the increment in U resulting from a particular investment, or the *social marginal product*, SMP, can be expressed by the differential du, where

$$\text{SMP} = du = \frac{\partial U}{\partial Y}dY + \frac{\partial U}{\partial B}dB_a + \frac{\partial U}{\partial \Gamma}d\Gamma + \frac{\partial U}{\partial Y_d}dY_d + \cdots \qquad (10.10)$$

Letting $\partial U/\partial Y$ be the numeraire, and then dividing both sides by $\partial U/\partial Y = 1$, yields

$$\text{SMP} = \Delta U = \Delta Y + \frac{\partial Y}{\partial B_a}\Delta B_a + \frac{\partial Y}{\partial \Gamma}\Delta \Gamma + \frac{\partial Y}{\partial Y_d}\Delta Y_d + \cdots \qquad (10.11)$$

---

[21] H. B. Chenery, "The Interdependence of Investment Decisions," in M. Abramowitz, *et al.*, *The Allocation of Economic Resources* (Stanford: Stanford University Press, 1959).

where the difference operator Δ is used to approximate the differential operator d, and since, for example, $(\partial U/\partial B_a)/(\partial U/\partial Y) = (\partial U/\partial B_a)(\partial Y/\partial U) = \partial Y/\partial B_a$.

Concentrating only on Y and B_a, and disregarding the other impacts, the SMP can be expressed by

$$SMP = \Delta Y + \gamma \Delta B_a \tag{10.11a}$$

where $\gamma = \partial Y/\partial B_a$ is the rate of substitution between Y and B_a; that is, the increment in income that the policy makers are willing to accept in exchange for a unit improvement in the balance of payments; or alternatively, the premium attached to foreign exchange earnings or savings.

Chenery then suggests that the SMP can be empirically determined through a set of adjustments to net private profits per unit of investment, to eliminate tariffs, taxes, and subsidies, and to allow for external economies and the difference between the private and social cost of employing previously unused resources. The SMP from the marginal unit of investment employed in a given productive use can then be expressed as

$$\text{SMP}_k = \frac{V}{K} - \frac{C}{K} + \gamma \frac{\Delta B_a}{Y} \tag{10.11b}$$

where V represents domestic social value added, C is total domestic factor cost, ΔB_a denotes the impact on the balance of payments, γ is the balance premium, and K is the rate of investment. It seems clear, however, that the difficulties of measuring these few factors, which will only be compounded when such other variables as the unemployment and income-distribution effects are taken into account, make even this relatively straightforward approach hazardous indeed.

b. The social rate of discount

The classical justification for discounting future flows is as follows. If X can be invested at a maximum guaranteed annual rate of i, so that it will grow to $(1 + i)^t X = A$ at the end of t years, then one should be willing to pay X now for the *promise* of A to be received at the end of t years. This is so because the X can be invested now at the guaranteed rate to yield A at the end of t years. Hence, X is the present discounted value, or worth, of the future A, where i is the discount rate. Under continuous discounting, the $(1 + i)^t$ factor would be replaced by e^{it}. In any event, i is a *marginal* rate of return, in the sense that it represents the rate of return that would be earned with certainty on the most attractive investment alternative *remaining available* to the investor. In the context of selecting an entire investment program, however, one does not know, a priori, which projects will be included in the program and which will be excluded, and thus what the return on the marginal project *will turn out to be*. It is for this reason that Hirshleifer has argued [22] that it is not feasible to employ present discounted value, for the appropriate rate of discount cannot be known!

[22] "On the Theory of Optimal Investment," *op. cit.*

Although this argument is apt, from a *practical* standpoint it is one that must be side-stepped. As a practical matter, planners, wishing to recognize that present consumption C is preferred to future consumption C—at least by present generations—are *forced* to employ *some* rate of discount. The only really substantive issue is the determination of the rate that *will be* used. Thus, in evaluating *public* investments the government must make some *judgments* with respect to the rate of return that these funds could be expected to yield if put to their best available alternative use. A related concern is whether this rate of return is sufficiently high as to warrant investing the funds, as opposed to enjoying the *immediate* benefits that they might yield through public or private *consumption* expenditure.

The latter issue hinges on social time preference. In particular, given an intertemporal social welfare function, $U = \mu(C(0), \ldots, C(T))$, in terms of rates of consumption or benefits $C(t)$, it hinges on how much "current" consumption or benefits $C(0)$ society as a whole is willing to forego in exchange for "later" increased consumption or benefits $C(t)$. This is determinable from the differential

$$dU = \frac{\partial U}{\partial C_{(t)}} dC_{(t)} + \frac{\partial U}{\partial C_{(k+1)}} dC_{(t+1)}$$

which when equated to zero yields

$$-\frac{\partial U/\partial C_{(t)}}{\partial U/\partial C_{(t+1)}} = \frac{dC_{(t+1)}}{dC(t)} = i_s$$

as the rate of substitution between $C(t + 1)$ and $C(t)$ for all t $(0 \leq t \leq T)$. If we approximate the differential operator d by the difference operator Δ, this suggests that, for example, with a rate of substitution of $i_s = 1.1$, a $\Delta C(0) = -100$ decrease in "current" consumption can be exactly compensated for with a $\Delta C(1) = 110$ increase in "next year's" consumption. Hence, at the given rates of current and anticipated future consumption, society *demands* at least a $1.1 - 1.0 = 10$ percent annual return on any investment of current funds.

Knowledge of social time preferences would provide policy makers with important information for evaluating public investments. Thus, specification of an intertemporal social welfare function becomes of immediate concern. From an analytic standpoint it would be preferable if the rate of substitution between $C(t)$ and $C(t + 1)$ were fixed for *all t*, and independent of $C(t)$; that is, there is a single rate of substitution i_s that does not depend on the rate of consumption. Thus, at time $k \leq t$ society discounts *any* future benefit $C(t)$ by a factor of $1/(1 + i_s)^{t-k}$. Although this assumption is unrealistic, it is convenient, and is likely to yield a discount factor that will approximate the "true" rate of substitution.

Perhaps a more serious issue is the ethical one of whether there is, in fact, *any* finite rate of substitution that society would or *should* be willing to accept. It is not clear that one generation is necessarily obliged to sacrifice benefits that it might enjoy in favor of benefits to be enjoyed by subsequent generations. Notwithstanding some impressive arguments against such an obligation, policy makers seem to have little doubt that society accepts its existence. Rather than rehash this philosophical issue, we too shall simply accept the existence of an intertemporal social welfare function and an associated fixed social rate of discount i_s at which society is willing to exchange current for future benefits.

In a mixed economy with private as well as public investment, the possible redirection of private investment funds to the public investment sector, say through a corporate income tax, raises a second issue. Specifically, suppose that a 50 percent corporate income tax is imposed, so that a $100 investment yielding a $10 net profit (net of the capital investment) the following year results in a *post-tax* return of 5 percent. Suppose also, however, that the government is evaluating this *same* investment in the public sector. Then the return will not be 5 percent, but 10 percent. Should this be the marginal investment, then although 5 percent might be the discount rate that is *acceptable* in the private sector, to place public enterprises on the same footing we would require twice as large a discount factor; namely, 10 percent. If the higher rate is not required, the government would find itself engaging in inefficient investment. This is so since, by leaving resources in the hands of private investors and eliminating the tax, these resources would be expended on investments earning at least 10 percent per annum and not on those earning 5 percent per annum. That is, the private investment sector will favor investments that, ceteris paribus, "pay back" the original investment through benefits received at an earlier point in time, whereas the public investment sector will be willing to wait longer for the original investment to be paid back.

The underlying principle, which Baumol [23] originally promulgated and which has since touched off considerable debate, is that if private investors are willing to settle for, say, a 5 percent return, then this must be the private (social) rate of discount; but the rate of return that can in fact be earned on investment in the economy is, say, 10 percent. Hence, the rate of discount that the economic managers of public resources should employ when evaluating investments is ambiguous. That is, just because one is willing to *settle* for a 5 percent return does not mean that 5 percent is the appropriate discount rate when higher return options are readily available; but, by the same token, when the investment earning a pre-tax 10 percent return has been ventured in the private sector, the best remaining available options may yield something less than 10 percent. Thus, the discount factor to use on public investments would seem to lie somewhere between the pre- and post-tax rate of return.

Baumol's cautions are distressing to economists who, in the main, tend to prefer unique and clear-cut answers (a cynic might say even if wrong) to all questions. Among the interesting observations that these cautions have prompted are: (1) resources earning $s < r$ percent in the private sector should

---

[23] *Op. cit.*

not be transferred to public use unless they earn *r* percent, if such options are still available; [24] and (2) if government projects *displace* private projects, then it is the present value of the foregone private projects, discounted at the private subjective rate of time preference, that is relevant in determining whether the public investment should be undertaken, because this present value is the opportunity cost of undertaking the public project. [25]

This entire discussion provides us with an unintentionally vague answer to the question of the appropriate discount rate. This rate should be no lower than the social rate of discount, which depends on social time preferences; but it should also reflect the alternative uses to which the resources would be put if left in the private economy. There is no justification for a public investment that mirrors a rejected private investment, when the total investment in the economy remains unchanged; but *all* public investment need not be discounted at the rate that would obtain in the marginal project in a wholly private economy. What the planners must determine is the rate that resources diverted to the public sector in a mixed or statist economy would earn if left in the public's hands; that is, how the benefits foregone "today" would be compensated for by benefits to be received "tomorrow," under the existing economic system. It is at this rate that future costs and benefits should be discounted.

c. Risk

There is a long-standing presumption that a "risk factor" should be incorporated into the discount rate to reflect the uncertainties that commonly plague investment decisions in the private sector. With respect to public investments, however, and while the proposition does not have unanimous support, there is considerable sympathy for the view that because the risks of a public investment are borne by the entire population, they are negligible for any one individual. Therefore, there is little point in the economic managers' bothering to include what would be a negligible risk factor in their computations. This argument, however, is based on the implicit assumption that the project is small, and does not necessarily follow when considering an entire program.

In fact, if risk is involved, then the appropriate intertemporal social "utility" function is a von Neumann-Morgenstern function. The argument of such a function would be the present discounted value of net future benefits. Specifically $V = V(PV)$ ranks projects on the basis of present discounted value, discounted at the social rate of discount.*Then* we need only compute $E[V]$, or the *expected* utility of the public investment. The expected utility is determined by weighting the utility—in the von Neumann-Morgenstern sense—of each *possible* present discounted value, by the probability that this particular present value will indeed be received. In the special case of risk neutrality *on the part of the economic managers,* present discounted value determined on the basis of the *expected net benefits* discounted at the social rate of discount is appropriate.

[24] A. Nichols, "On the Social Rate of Discount: Comment," *American Economic Review,* Vol. 59, No. 5, December 1969, pp. 909–911.

[25] E. James, "On the Social Rate of Discount: Comment," *Ibid.,* pp. 912–916.

To the extent that the use of expected net benefits is implicit in the present value computations to which most discussions of the subject ordinarily refer, *excluding* a risk factor suggests the view that the economic *managers* are, or should be, risk neutral. This again raises a philosophical issue, and one that in all humility we do not presume ourselves capable of resolving. We can, none-theless, conveniently side-step the problem by suggesting the expected-utility-of-present-value criterion as being the appropriate means of ranking investment alternatives, irrespective of risk preferences. The next question, then, is the planners' selection among alternatives so-ranked, when they are forced to re-spect the constraint imposed by a fixed investment budget.

10.4 FROM PROJECT CHOICE TO A CONSOLIDATED PLAN

Projects chosen at various hierarchical levels in a decision-making bureaucracy may or may not be consolidated in a centrally coordinated plan. When consoli-dation is attempted, as Frisch has pointed out, the following problems must be dealt with: (a) the *timing and phasing* of investments; and (b) their *interdepen-dencies,* or their impacts on *resource demands* from each sector, on *capacities* in each delivery sector, and on *production structure* in each successive period. Chenery, Tinbergen, Steiner, and others have attempted to deal with these problems. A substantial amount of this effort has taken advantage of, and con-tributed to, advances in mathematical programming and input-output tech-niques.

Earlier in this chapter we called attention to the application of linear programming to the investment allocation problem. It should also be apparent that this same approach can be generalized in a dynamic nonlinear framework. There are, however, some *specific* formulations of particular interest.

The Markowitz model, for example, which has been formulated to de-termine an optimal allocation of *securities* investment,[26] is equally applicable to allocating public investment expenditures. In this model, the *possible* rates of return of the *j*th of *m* investments are assessed probabilistically. From these probability assessments one can then compute both an *expected return* $\bar{r}_j$ and a *variance* of returns $\sigma_{r_j r_j}$. Similarly, to reflect the extent that projects *i* and *j* are interrelated one can also assign a *covariance* of rates of return $\sigma_{r_i r_j}$. Then, if x_j is the proportion of the total budget invested in project *j,* the expected return of the entire investment *portfolio* will be given by $\bar{R} = \Sigma x_j \bar{r}_j$, and the variance of the return on the portfolio will be given by $\sigma_R^2 = \Sigma\Sigma x_i x_j \sigma_{r_i r_j}$. For a risk-averse policy maker with a *quadratic objective (utility) function,* a very simple de-scription of the investment problem is to minimize risk, as measured by the total variance, while earning *at least* $\bar{R}$ as an expected return, and exactly exhausting the investment budget. Mathematically, the problem is written

$$\text{Minimize} \quad \sigma_r^2 = \sum_{i=1}^{m} \sum_{j=1}^{m} x_i x_j \, \sigma_{r_i r_j} \qquad (10.12a)$$

[26] H. M. Markowitz, *op. cit.*

subject to $\sum_{j=1}^{m} x_j \bar{r}_j \geq \bar{R}$ (10.12b)

$$\sum_{j=1}^{m} x_j = 1$$ (10.12c)

$$x_j \geq 0 \qquad j=1, \ldots, m$$ (10.12d)

Equations (10.12a)–(10.12d) present a quadratic programming problem with the x_j's as the decision variables. By varying the required expected return $\bar{R}$, an entire *set* of optimal portfolios can be generated. To each portfolio is associated a pair $(\sigma_R^2, \bar{R})$ that indicates the minimum variance that can be achieved for a given expected rate of return. The optimal investment allocation will then depend on the policy makers' expressed preferences; that is, on the trade-offs between risk and return that the policy makers are willing to accept.

Additional constraints are readily included in the model to reflect the policy makers' insistence that *at least* $\bar{x}_k$ percent of the budget go to project k, where k might be national defense, highways, dams, and the like. The major problem, clearly, is obtaining the initial data inputs, particularly the probability assessments.

The *unidirectional* impact of public investment decisions on private investment decisions has been studied by Steiner, with the aim of optimizing net social benefits.[27]

Steiner distinguishes between projects ij that involve the use of a specific program or facility $i(i = 1, \ldots, i^*)$ for a purpose, such as providing service $j(j = 1, \ldots, j^*)$. The cost of project ij is denoted k_{ij}.

Investment choices in the public sector are divided between the set S_1, the most highly regarded projects, all of which would be selected if funds were available, but some of which may have to be eliminated, and projects in the set S_3, those that *might* be chosen should the set S_1 not exhaust the available funds. The private sector consists of projects in the set S_2, those that will be displaced if the public projects in S_1 are undertaken, and the set S_4 consisting of marginal private investment opportunities. The unidirectional aspect is that in this formulation the public authority is presumed free to choose *its* investment projects, and in so doing either *precludes* private investment for the jth purpose, or else leaves investment for the jth purpose in private hands.

If project x_{ij} in S_1 is undertaken by the government, we denote this by $x_{ij} = 1$; if not, $x_{ij} = 0$. If project j in S_2 is undertaken by the private sector, then $x_j = 1$; if not, $x_j = 0$. Hence,

$$\sum_i x_{ij} + x_j = 1 \qquad j = 1, \ldots, j^*$$ (10.13a)

for

$$x_{ij}, x_j = 0, 1 \qquad \text{all } ij, j$$ (10.13b)

[27] P. O. Steiner, "Choosing Among Alternative Public Investments in the Water Resource Field," *American Economic Review*, Vol. 49, No. 5, December 1959, pp. 893–916.

is a constraint that demands that a project serving purpose j will be undertaken in either the public ($x_{ij} = 1$) or the private ($x_j = 1$) sectors, S_1 or S_2, but not both. As further constraints, we have

$$\sum_j x_{ij} \le 1 \qquad i = 1, \ldots, i^* \tag{10.13c}$$

which states that the ith facility or project description can only be used for the jth project (or not used at all), and

$$\sum_i \sum_j x_{ij} k_{ij} \le K \tag{10.13d}$$

where K is the total budget available for financing the public investment projects in S_1 and S_3. Thus, $\sum_i \sum_j x_{ij} k_{ij}$ is the total expenditure on projects in S_1, and the funds that remain are to be spent on projects in S_3.

Finally, the planners' objective is to maximize

$$Z = \sum_i \sum_j x_{ij} y_{ij} \tag{10.13}$$

where y_{ij} is the net benefit accruing to project ij in set S_1. This net benefit is computed as (a) the gain in benefits of the ij project over alternative *public* uses of the funds k_{ij}, less (b) the gain in benefits of the jth private project over the alternative *private* uses of funds, and (c) the opportunity cost of transferring funds from the private to the public sector to finance the $x_{ij} = 1$ projects.

What Steiner has proposed, then, is a zero-one programming model for deciding whether investments should be undertaken privately or publicly. The model's unique contribution, which distinguishes it from other mathematical programming models of investment choice, is that it introduces the potential "displacement" aspects of public investment insofar as it affects the allocation of private investment. As with all such models, however, it assumes that the input data are available, and that the programming problem can be solved.

Multi-dimensional impacts of project choices consolidated in a national plan have been studied by Frisch using an input-output variant.[28] If Steiner's model has merits for studying the impact of public investment decisions in a mixed economy, Frisch's Oslo Channel model, which attempts to deal with both *timing and phasing* of investment, *and* their *interdependencies*, has a more general appeal, both in mixed and in centralized economies.

In Frisch's model, the *carry-on activity,* or the quantity of resources required in each successive period from each sector as a consequence of current investment decisions, forms the *physical* basis upon which the cost of the project to the economy can be ascertained. The *capacity effect,* or the change in productive capacity of each sector in subsequent periods, along with the *infra-effect,* or the change in the technology of production, jointly provide the generators of the stream of future benefits yielded by the investment decision.

Starting from the Leontief model,

$$Q_h^t = \sum_k (Q_{hk}^t) + C_h^t + G_h^t + J_h^t + L_h^t + E_h^t \tag{10.14}$$

[28] R. Frisch, *Oslo Decision Models* (Oslo: Institute of Economics, June, 1957); also *op. cit.*

Frisch equates the output of each sector h at time $t(Q_h^t)$ to the sum of interindustry flows $(\sum_k Q_{hk}^t)$ and final demand uses for consumption (C_h^t), government (G_h^t), investment (J_h^t), inventory changes (L_h^t), and foreign trade (E_h^t). Assuming no factor substitution, and hence no ring equations (see Chapter 7), the technological relationships of production are expressed by

$$Q_{hk}^t = a_{hk}^t Q_k^t \tag{10.15}$$

where the a_{hk}^t are the fixed technological coefficients obtaining at time t.

To incorporate the investment effects, which will be a function of both the timing and the phasing of the projects, Frisch groups all projects having similar effects into a "channel" g. That is, g is the set of all potential projects with similar average carry-on activity, capacity-effects, and infra-effects, per dollar of investment. The decision variables, H_g^d, constitute the total funds to be expended over *all* future periods in order to complete the channel g projects begun in year d of the planning period. Thus, the solution to the investment planning problem will include, for example, a value for H_2^3, the funds to be expended on channel 2 investment projects to be initiated in the third year of the planning period.

The investment coefficient b_{hg}^{td} is defined as the resources required from sector h by channel g in year t as a result of the decision to invest a dollar in channel g projects begun at time d. In the absence of substitution, the carry-on activity can then be characterized by the term $J_{hg}^{td} = b_{hg}^{td} H_g^d$. The total resources used in time t from sector h by the investment activity becomes $J_h^t = \bar{b}_h^t + \sum_d \sum_g J_{hg}^{td}$, where $\bar{b}_h^t$ is the resource use resulting from projects initiated *prior* to the current planning period.

Similarly, let c_{hg}^{td} denote the change in capacity in sector h at time t resulting from the decision to initiate a dollar of channel g projects at time d, and $\bar{c}_h^t$ denote the capacity existing in sector h at time t as a consequence of investment projects begun prior to the planning period. The total capacity of sector h at time t then becomes $Q_h^t = \bar{c}_h^t + \sum_d \sum_g c_{hg}^{td} H_g^d$.

Frisch's version of the expanded input-output model incorporating carry-on activity and capacity effects then becomes

$$Q_h^t = \sum_k a_{hk}^t Q_k^t + C_h^t + G_h^t + J_h^t + L_h^t + E_h^t \tag{10.16a}$$

$$J_h^t = \bar{b}_h^t + \sum_d \sum_g b_{hg}^{td} H_g^d \tag{10.16b}$$

$$Q_h^t = \bar{c}_h^t + \sum_d \sum_g c_{hg}^{td} H_g^d \tag{10.16c}$$

for all h and t. The infra-effect can be introduced in a similar manner by expressing the coefficients a_{hk}^t, b_{hg}^{td}, c_{hg}^{td}, and $\bar{b}_h^t$ and $\bar{c}_h^t$ as linear functions of H_g^d. As opposed to an optimization model, Frisch's approach develops a *consistency* model reflecting the ramifications of any investment decision for the economy; or, alternatively, the required investment to achieve, say, a given set of final demands.

Although all of these models are available to Eastern and Western planners alike, the differences in Eastern and Western economic philosophies, and the sensitivity of the different economic systems to the controller's actions has led to differences in *which* models are used, as well as *how* they are used.

In practice, Western planners either tend to focus on (a) the basic macro objectives of investment allocation, such as the overall growth rate, full employment, the balance of payments, and price stability, or they tend to rely on (b) isolated analyses of the impact of some key projects. The former is accomplished through the use of aggregative economic models, and the latter through the use of cost-benefit studies and their variants. No systematic integration is attempted, either between the macro and micro aspects of various public investment decisions, or between the volume and direction of public and private investment.

In the centralized economies of the Soviet type, as Lange has pointed out, the usual practice is to fix the sector allocation of investment in accordance with prespecified sector priorities, and then "to adjust the physical composition of investment in the way required to attain the sectoral composition laid down by the plan." [29] In other words, the "financial" allocation is justified by a corresponding allocation in terms of material resources. The needs for the latter are worked out on the basis of predetermined technological norms or coefficients. The cumulative accounts of, say, machinery and equipment aim at reconciling the capital investment plan with specific capital production programs.

10.5 ON THE IMPROVEMENT OF INVESTMENT PLANNING

Investment planning in either a mixed or a centralized Soviet-type economy could be substantially improved in regard to the determination of overall size and structure, and to its economic impact, if current practice would be reviewed in the light of the especially profound suggestions made by Arrow and Kurz for the former type of economy, and by Lange for the latter type.

As Arrow and Kurz note,[30] the rate of national output (Y) can be equated to either the sum of the rates of consumption (C), and government and private investment (dK_g/dt and dK_p/dt, respectively), or to the sum of the rates of consumption, taxes (T), and changes in private assets holdings (dA_m/dt), where all variables are functions of time. Now, let us define dD/dt as the rate of change in the government debt. Then, government investment will equal the sum of the change in government debt and taxes, or $dKg/dt = T + dD/dt$. It thus follows from

$$Y = C + \frac{dK_g}{dt} + \frac{dK_p}{dt} = C + T + \frac{dA_m}{dt}$$

and

---

[29] *Op. cit.*, p. 32.
[30] *Public Investment, the Rate of Return, and Optimal Fiscal Policy* (Baltimore and London: The Johns Hopkins Press for Resources for the Future, 1970), pp. 115 ff.

$$\frac{dK_g}{dt} = T + \frac{dA_m}{dt} - \frac{dK_p}{dt}$$

by direct substitution that

$$\frac{dK_p}{dt} = \frac{dA_m}{dt} - \frac{dD}{dt} \qquad\qquad (10.17)$$

which asserts that, at any point in time, the rate of private investment must be equal to the difference between the rate of change in private asset holdings and the rate of change in the public debt.

The importance of the latter observation is as follows. To put the economy on a desired feasible path, the government must simultaneously aim at *two* targets: (1) the achievement of a given total amount of savings; and (2) the achievement of a given allocation of capital between the public and the private sectors. To do this, it must not only *maintain* a certain rate of *public* investment, dK_g/dt, but it must also choose a set of instruments that will *induce* the *private* sector to choose the desired rate of dK_p/dt and hence C. Failure to control the optimal policy will result from failure to either optimally allocate capital between public and private uses, or to optimally allocate output between consumption and investment. This "controllability" depends on the workings of the private markets, as well as on the range of instruments available to the government, a dependence that is highly elusive and uncertain in less developed countries.

With respect to the centralized economies of the Soviet type, Lange notes in his paper on the economic and technological bases of investment,[31] that under given technological conditions and with a given rate of investment, there are two equivalent ways of changing the rate of increase in the national product. It can be done by "maneuvering" either the coefficients of the sectoral allocation of investment (λ_j), or the coefficients of the physical composition of investment (μ_i). The Soviet planners, as stated, start with the investment allocation and "maneuver" with the second. Lange points out, however, that these coefficients are related, and that the problem of planning consists of the proper choice of *either* kind of coefficient. When the planners choose the λ_j, the physical composition of investment, μ_i, can be calculated by solving a set of simultaneous equations. Moreover, to maximize the growth rate of the national income one must assign the highest values to those λ_j coefficients that correspond to the greatest sectoral income-investment ratios, β_j, since every shift of investment from a sector with a smaller income-investment ratio to a sector with a higher one would increase the overall rate of growth.

[31] *Op. cit.*, pp. 24 ff.

CHAPTER 11

Planning Foreign Trade

11.1 BASIC PROBLEMS OF FOREIGN TRADE PLANNING

Countries at all stages of development dread perennial problems in the balance of payments. Of special concern are balance-of-payments deficits, for these must eventuate in the need for borrowing in the foreign capital market. This can be particularly treacherous because international sources of foreign exchange may dry up abruptly, thereby throwing both the economy, and such policy objectives as full employment or industrialization, out of kilter. To "improve the balance," a whole gamut of measures or controls may be called into play. These might include (a) quantitative import or export *quotas* on various goods, or classes of goods, (b) *selective controls* of imports from, or exports to, particular currency areas, (c) the organization of *state trading agencies,* (d) multiple forms of *assistance* to import-substituting, export-promoting industries, and even, perhaps, (e) *complex controls* over foreign exchange, capital, and/or labor movements.

In an important way, foreign trade targets are *extensions* of domestic policy targets, and it is therefore open to question as to whether they should in fact be treated independently. We believe that there are two important reasons for such independent treatment. First, the international sector plays a pivotal role in the economic life of many countries; and, second, the desire for national independence, which in the post-Colonial period has become an increasingly important policy determinant, frequently plays a decisive role in shaping different *strategies* in regard to the primacy of imports or exports, import substitution or export promotion, and reliance on foreign aid.

Within the broadly *similar* framework of a perennial preoccupation with the balance of payments, and with broadly *similar* instruments at their command, the policy makers of MDC's and of LDC's tend to evaluate imports and exports in a somewhat *different* way. Specifically, *imports* play the decisive role in the growth policies of many LDC's, whereas *exports* have usually been considered as the engine of growth in most MDC's. The reason for the difference is that the concern in the LDC's is with acquiring the goods, materials, and know-how necessary for initiating the industrialization process, whereas concern in the MDC's is with securing the markets for the goods being produced in an industrialized economy.

In particular, in the LDC's on the one hand, the plans for industrialization depend on the importation of the machinery and equipment that a small and slowly developing import-substituting industry cannot provide. To pay for these imports, there is a need to generate foreign exchange earnings, particularly hard currency. Thus policy makers in the LDC's are forced to be keenly aware of the "foreign exchange gap" and of the special role that particular currency *areas* can play with respect to their own country's foreign trade. Still further, even more than in the developed countries, in the LDC's the "balance-of-payments effects" are in conflict with the "national product effect." As Frisch puts it: "If the country can obtain unlimited foreign credits or grants, and is willing to use them, it is possible to obtain an extremely rapid expansion of the national product and other desirable domestic goals. But if the policy is directed toward improving the balance of payments as much as possible, it will be necessary to acquiesce with a much slower expansion of the national product." [1]

In the MDC's, on the other hand, the export-oriented industries have been viewed as growth-propulsive. Orientation toward the opening-up of frontiers into larger common markets, toward investment abroad and toward aid to LDC's, as well as toward specialization on a broad front rather than toward "all-around development," have accordingly been prevalent, at least during the decades following World War II. As a concomitant, growth through export expansion points production at highly competitive products, forces attention to the pace of activity of the *importing* countries, and requires sophisticated maneuvering in the balance of trade and payments as between trade and services and the inflow and outflow of capital.

Neither foreign trade problems, nor the approaches to resolving them, are alien to the socialist countries. Within the framework of a policy using "all-around industrial development" in order to reach and surpass "the highest indices of industrial output" of the most advanced capitalist countries, the Soviet planners, for instance, treated imports as a crucial element of the *domestic* plan. The required volume of imports was then viewed as directly determining the volume of exports needed to secure them; or, as the Soviet writer Mishustin wrote, "the dynamics of the economic plans determine the dynamics of imports, which in their turn determines the dynamics of exports." [2]

Drawing from experiences such as that of the Soviet Union, and of sim-

---

[1] R. Frisch, *Optimal Investments Under Limited Foreign Resources* (Oslo: Institute of Economics, July 1959), p. 3.

[2] D. D. Mishustin, *Vneshniaia torgovlia SSR* (Foreign Trade of the USSR) (Moscow: Mezhdunarodnaia Kniga, 1941).

ilar policies pursued in various other countries, socialist and capitalist alike, wherein foreign trade enters into domestic planning almost as an afterthought, it has often been contended that "planning is inward looking in character," and that it can be "best applied to countries whose economy is more or less closed to foreign influences." While it is true that uncertainty with respect to forecasts and plans increases with the degree of openness of a national economy, it does not follow that planning can best be achieved in a closed economy; such a view reflects a specious interpretation of planning, and of the flexibility with which policy instruments can be used.

In fact, developments on the international scene can impact upon the economic system in two distinct ways. On the one hand, in an international, interdependent world complex, foreign nations are an integral part of the national economic system's *environment*. The inputs from this international environment to the system can take many and varied forms. First, international considerations might appear directly as arguments in the controller's objective function, or, as desiderata, be explicitly introduced by the controller in the form of constraints and/or boundary conditions. Thus, policy makers might, in the first instance, view the balance of trade as a desideratum to be incorporated in a policy-making objective function; in the second instance, the quest for a favorable balance of trade might take the form of a demand imposed on any program via a constraint. Second, the international environment can provide the controller with data, such as the available *international* capacity or supply of an important natural resource—sources of energy, metals, foods—which must be taken into account in national policy formulation. Finally, the international environment can introduce policy-influencing exogenous inputs into the system. In particular, one nation's export-import *policy* could impact upon other nations. Therefore, policy makers *must* be cognizant of policies formulated "in the environment," and then take these exogenous informational inputs into account when issuing instructions—that is, in establishing policy.

On the other hand, international ties are often sufficiently strong and stable so as to create a foreign trade *sector* that for all intents and purposes can be treated as a *subsystem* of the economic system. This subsystem can be viewed as receiving as *inputs* domestically produced goods from an industrial subsystem to which it is coupled. Thus, *exports* are treated as *inputs* into the foreign sector's transformation function wherein they provide the foreign exchange necessary to purchase imports. The *imports* purchased are the outputs of the foreign trade sector, which are in turn received as inputs by the consumer component and the industrial subsystem. To the extent that there is a foreign exchange deficit or surplus, this balance can also be looked upon as an *output* of the foreign trade subsystem. This output might be fed back into the subsystem as an input during a subsequent time period, as well as transmitted to the controller as an endogenous input affecting future policy.

There are, therefore, both endogenous and exogenous aspects to foreign trade, and it has been treated in both fashions in various planning models. Irrespective of how it is treated, however, it is vital to establish the interdependencies or *linkages* that exist between the foreign trade sector and the other sectors that make up the economic system. A still further disaggregation of the foreign sector into its national or regional subsystems or components suggests the need for establishing the linkages *among* the various national economic systems. Indeed, the establishment of these links is currently one of the more fertile fields for exploration; and the problem is particularly pressing in the developing nations, in which the potential for economic growth, as well as, perhaps, the short-term vicissitudes of economic life are generally highly dependent upon economic developments and policies in the more developed nations to which they are linked.

The orientation of these models has also differed depending upon whether they were aimed at MDC's or LDC's. In particular, studies focused on the MDC's have tended to concentrate on *projections* of imports and exports, and their interlocking, as well as on various aspects of the maneuvering in the balance of payments. Studies focused on the LDC's have, in contrast, tended to develop *procedures* for choosing among planning alternatives, once imports and the scarcity of foreign exchange have been treated as major constraints. To an extent, the emphasis on projections versus procedures hinges on whether the economy in question is mixed or controlled. In particular, in the MDC's, where the foreign trade sector is commonly viewed as part of the system's environment and therefore to a large extent outside of the controller's *direct* influence, the emphasis is on techniques for projecting the essentially uncontrollable inputs from the international environment, which in one way or another impact upon the economic system. In contrast, in the LDC's, where the overriding importance of the foreign trade sector commonly causes it to be viewed as a subsystem of the economic system—and *directly* subject to the controller's influence and inputs—the emphasis is on decision-making procedures for use by the controller in the choice among alternative inputs into each of the subsystems, including the foreign trade sector.

In this chapter we shall first discuss some of the more interesting approaches that have been employed for *projecting* imports and exports, and for constructing so-called world trade matrices. These approaches are based on international models developed, among others, by Beckerman,[3] Tinbergen,[4] Pöyhönen,[5] and Linneman.[6] We shall then turn to some of the *procedures* for choosing among investment and planning alternatives, with a view to their impact on the foreign trade sector. The most prominent of these procedures are

[3] W. Beckermann, "The World Trade Multiplier and the Stability of World Trade, 1938 to 1953," *Econometrica*, Vol. 24, 1956.

[4] J. Tinbergen, "International Economic Planning," *Daedalus*, Spring 1966.

[5] P. Pöyhönen, "A Tentative Model of the Volume of Trade Between Countries," *Weltwirtschaftliches Archiv*, Band XC, 1963.

[6] H. Linneman, *An Econometric Study of International Trade Flows* (Amsterdam: North Holland, 1966).

those suggested by Chenery,[7] Bruno,[8] and Frisch,[9] particularly with regard to small developing countries laboring under certain obvious constraints in this major sector of their economies.

11.2 IMPORT AND EXPORT PROJECTIONS AND WORLD TRADE MATRICES

Imports virtually always enter the economic system as an endogenous variable whose movements are closely attuned to those of other economic variables; in particular, variables that reflect overall economic activity, the availability of foreign exchange, and the "competitiveness" of imports relative to domestic goods. As a result of this endogenous role, import *projections* are usually based on forecasts of *other* domestic variables, some of which are within the policy makers' direct control, as well as on forecasts of various *exogenous* factors. Let M_t denote imports in year t, Y_t denote gross national product, p_t^x denote an index of domestic prices, p_t^m denote an index of prices of imported goods, and X_t denote the value of exports in year t. Then one fairly comprehensive, although not necessarily the most complete and complex model for projecting imports would be

$$M_t = f(Y_t, \frac{X_t}{Y_t}, \frac{p_t^x}{p_t^m}, t, \epsilon_t) \qquad (11.1)$$

An explicit form of Equation (11.1) might be

$$M_t = \alpha_0 Y_t^{\alpha_1} (\frac{X_t}{Y_t})^{\alpha_2} (\frac{p_t^x}{p_t^m})^{\alpha_3} e^{\alpha_4 t} \epsilon_t \qquad (11.1a)$$

where $\epsilon_t > 0$ is a random disturbance term, and the α_i's are parameters whose estimates, denoted a_i, might be obtained through ordinary log-linear regression.

One would expect to find $a_i > 0 (i = 0, \ldots, 3)$. That is, imports in year t are positively related to (1) the overall rate of economic activity (Y_t), (2) the relative availability of import purchasing power, as represented by the ratio of the foreign exchange generated by exports to overall economic activity (X_t/Y_t), and (3) the relative price advantage of imported to exported goods $(p_t^x p_t^m)$. Since all the variables are positive, a_0 must also be positive. Finally, one might also hypothesize that there will be a ceteris paribus trend in most economies toward either increasing or decreasing imports. Here we specifically hypothesize an exponential trend $(e^{\alpha_4 t})$ toward increasing $(\alpha_4 > 0)$ or decreasing $(\alpha_4 < 0)$ imports. In particular, since $\partial M_t / \partial t = \alpha_4 M_t$ and $(\partial M_t / \partial t)/M_t = \alpha_4$, the estimated import growth rate is given by a_4.

In a similar and familiar manner, define the *elasticity of imports* with re-

[7] H. B. Chenery, "A Model of Development Alternatives," in R. J. Ward (ed.) *The Challenge of Development* (Chicago: Aldine, 1967).

[8] M. Bruno, "Optimal Patterns of Trade and Development," in H. B. Chenery *et al.* (eds.) *Studies in Development Planning* (Cambridge, Mass.: Harvard University Press, 1971), pp. 173–186.

[9] *Optimal Investments* . . . , *op. cit.*

spect to the independent variable x_i by $(\partial M_t / \partial x_i)(x_i / M_t)$. Then a_1, a_2, and a_3 provide elasticity estimates. For example, the income elasticity is given by

$$\frac{\partial M_t}{\partial Y_t} \frac{Y_t}{M_t} = [(\alpha_1 - \alpha_2)(\frac{M_t}{Y_t})][\frac{Y_t}{M_t}] = \alpha_1 - \alpha_2$$

and estimated by $a_1 - a_2$. Similarly, a_2 is the estimated elasticity of imports with respect to exports, and a_3 ($-a_3$) is the estimated domestic (import) price elasticity. These elasticity formulations assume, in turn, that exports (rather than the export:GNP *ratio*), GNP and import (domestic) prices are held fixed. Alternatively, assuming that the export:GNP ratio is fixed, the estimated income elasticity of imports would simply be a_1.

In like manner, and with similar qualifications, the marginal propensity to import,

$$\frac{\partial M_t}{\partial Y_t} = (\alpha_1 - \alpha_2)\alpha_0 Y_t^{\alpha_1 - 1} (\frac{X_t}{Y_t})^{\alpha_2} (\frac{p_t^x}{p_t^m})^{\alpha_3} e^{\alpha_4 t} \epsilon_t$$

and the average propensity to import,

$$\frac{M_t}{Y_t} = \alpha_0 Y_t^{\alpha_1 - 1} (\frac{X_t}{Y_t})^{\alpha_2} (\frac{p_t^x}{p_t^m})^{\alpha_3} e^{\alpha_4 t} \epsilon_t$$

can also be estimated. In this particular formulation, however, these propensities are not fixed, and are not given solely in terms of the individual parameters. Rather, they are functions of the three economic variables—the rate of economic activity, import purchasing power, and relative prices—and changes in tastes and preferences as reflected in the trend factor.

Assuredly, there is nothing sacrosanct about the multiplicative form (11.1a), other than that it does permit direct estimates of *constant* elasticities. Suppose, however, that (11.1) is specified in linear form

$$M_t = \beta_0 + \beta_1 Y_t + \beta_2(\frac{X_t}{Y_t}) + \beta_3(\frac{p_t^x}{p_t^m}) + \beta_4 t + \omega_t \tag{11.1b}$$

where ω_t is the random disturbance term. Then the elasticities *as well as* the marginal and average propensities become very complex functions of the parameters *and* the variables. This argues in favor of the multiplicative form, at least insofar as the alternatives do not demonstrate a clear empirical or theoretical superiority, especially for analyses aimed at yielding quantitative statements with respect to the *responsiveness* of imports to the variables that directly affect them.

In addition, the parameters α_i are themselves amenable to various interpretations. Of particular interest, suppose that as a matter of policy imports are controller-regulated in accordance with economic activity. Specifically, suppose that we can write $\alpha_1 = \alpha_1^q + \alpha_1^p$. Here, the policy makers *fix* α_1^q, thereby establishing what might variously be referred to as an import policy, decision rule, or restriction that relates imports to GNP. That is, holding X_t but not (X_t / Y_t) fixed in Equation (11.1a), $\partial M_t / \partial Y_t = \alpha_1^q + \alpha_1^p - \alpha_2$, and α_1^q measures the *policy* elasticity of imports with respect to GNP. Then $\alpha_1^p - \alpha_2$ is the *unrestricted* income elasticity of imports. To estimate α_1^p requires explicit knowledge of the decision rule, or a_1^q. That is, $a_1 - \alpha_1^q$.

Clearly, these models can be varied *ad infinitum* by making the parameters themselves functions of time (so that, say, $\alpha_i = \alpha_i' + \alpha_i''t$), introducing other variables (such as employment), or introducing lagged variables (such as M_{t-1}). Interesting variations can also be obtained by segregating imports into various *categories*, such as imports for "expansion," machinery and equipment, and the like. Foreign exchange resources, which provide the import "capability" for any one class of imports, or for all imports, may then in turn be ascertained by models describing, for instance, the various interrelationships between the volume of trade turnover (imports and exports), the inflow and outflow of capital, and the relevant prices.

Specifically, now let p_t^x and p_t^m denote the average unit price of exports and imports, respectively, and Z_t^x and Z_t^m denote the *volume* of exports and imports, respectively. Then the total *value* of imports in year t, $M_t = p_t^m Z_t^m$, equals the sum of (1) the total value of exports, $X_t = p_t^x Z_t^x$, (2) the net trade balance of services, F_{1t}, (3) the net factor revenue from abroad, F_{2t}, and (4) the net inflow of long-term capital, K_{ft}; or,

$$M_t = p_t^m Z_t^m = p_t^x Z_t^x + F_{1t} + F_{2t} + K_{ft}$$

Dividing through by p_t^m, the total volume of imports, or capacity to import, will then be given by

$$Z_t^m = (\frac{p_t^x}{p_t^m})Z_t^x + \frac{F_{1t}}{p_t^m} + \frac{F_{2t}}{p_t^m} + \frac{K_{ft}}{p_t^m} \tag{11.2}$$

Given estimates of the value of exports, and the net service and factor revenue inflows, as well as the average import and export price, the import volume or capacity is immediately determined. Then, having determined the overall import capacity, Z_t^m, import *needs* for, say, goods *other than* machinery and equipment might be projected through other models, such as Equation (11.1a) specified for individual import categories i, with M_{it} replacing M_t. The remainder of foreign exchange is then earmarked for machinery and equipment, so as to yield a *total* import volume of Z_t^m.

Import needs may also be projected by sectors, with the help of input-output tables. Again letting $A = [a_{ij}]$ denote the technological coefficients matrix, and $q = [q_i]$ the column vector of final demands, in familiar fashion $q - Aq = Q$ and $q = [I - A]^{-1}Q$.

Now, let m_i be an "import coefficient" such that $m_i q_i$ is the *fixed* proportion of the output of industry i that is derived from imports. Then, with $M = [m_i]$ a column vector of import coefficients, $M'q = M'(I - A)^{-1}Q$ is the *total* projected import requirement, in volume or dollars, depending on the formulation.

In countries aiming at self-sufficiency, export projections are worked out in close relationship with the import projections. In the more developed

Western countries, however, exports are usually derived independently on the basis of policy parameters estimated for *other* countries. That is, each country's exports are projected as, say, a weighted average of the projected economic activity of the country's trading partners, or on the basis of the relation of a country's exports to projected world exports or imports. In effect, the export industries of the MDC's can be viewed as having a set of infinitely elastic supply curves—within the relevant range—so that they adjust their outputs in *response to* the demands of a fairly stable set of customers.

Export projections might also be derived through simple trend analysis. In the Ichimura model (see Section 7.3), for instance, exports are taken as a function of time, or $X_t = E(t)$. The rates of total domestic output and imports are then uniquely determined in terms of capital:output ratios and the marginal propensities to save and to import. Other models relate exports to GNP—but the GNP of the *rest of the world*—and to the ratio of domestic and foreign prices. Thus, similar to Equation (11.1) we might hypothesize

$$X_t = g(Y_{rt}, \frac{p_t^x}{p_t^m}, t) \tag{11.3}$$

where Y_{rt} is rest-of-the-world GNP.

The "rest-of-the-world" sector may be variously disaggregated into importing countries or areas. Let x_{ij} denote the flow of goods and services from country i to country j (with $x_{ii} = 0$). The flow of world trade at any time can now be specified in an import-export matrix, $X = [x_{ij}]$. The ith row of the matrix indicates the distribution of total exports of the ith country, $X_i = \sum_{j=1}^{n} x_{ij}$, among the nations of the world. The jth column, in turn, indicates how much of the jth country's total imports, $M_j = \sum_{i=1}^{n} x_{ij}$, are provided by country i. Clearly, $\Sigma X_i = \sum_i (\sum_j x_{ij}) = \Sigma M_j = \sum_j (\sum_i x_{ij}) = E = $ world trade.

Further, $m_{ij} = x_{ij}/M_j$ is the proportion, or relative share of country j's imports that is supplied by country i, where $\sum_i m_{ij} = \sum_i x_{ij}/M = 1$. The summary matrix $m = [m_{ij}]$ is the *export shares* or *market shares* matrix. Together with its source matrix—the import-export matrix—m forms the basis for the disaggregation approach to foreign trade estimation.

A Brookings model [10] of U.S. trade, for instance, distinguishes three areas: area 1—the United States; area 2—Western Europe; and area 3—the rest of the world. Trade between the industrial areas, areas 1 and 2, is assumed to depend on economic activity in the individual areas, as measured by their respective GNP's, and on the "competitiveness" of import and domestic prices in each area. U.S. imports from area 3 are assumed to depend solely on domestic GNP. Finally, the shares of areas 1 and 2 in exports to area 3 (which is assumed to spend all of its foreign receipts, R), are assumed to depend on their

[10] W. S. Salant, *The United States Balance of Payments in 1968* (Washington, D. C.: The Brookings Institution, 1963).

relative price advantages in the export market, and the availability of foreign exchange in area 3.

With the time subscript deleted, and denoting U.S. exports and imports by X_1 and M_1, respectively, with specific respect to the United States, this model can be written in functional form as

$$X_1 = x_{12}(Y_2, \frac{p^2}{p^{x_1}}) + x_{13}(\frac{p^{x_1}}{p^{x_2}}, R) \tag{11.4a}$$

$$M_1 = x_{21}(Y_1, \frac{p^1}{p^{x_2}}) + x_{31}(Y_1) \tag{11.4b}$$

Here, subscripts and superscripts refer to areas, x_{ij} denotes exports from area i to area j, and Y_i, p^i, and p^{x_i} refer to GNP, the domestic price index, and the export price index of area i. Thus, for example, the value of U.S. imports, M_1, is equal to the sum of imports from areas 2 and 3, $x_{21} + x_{31}$, where each of the latter are functions of the previously delineated variables. In principle, once these functional forms are specified, the parameters can be estimated. Then, with future rates of GNP given by assumption, given an assessment or prediction of changes in the general price level, and assuming, say, that export prices are directly related to the general price level, forecasts of X_1 and M_1 can be obtained.

Concerned with problems of broader scope than the balance of payments position of a single country, an OECD econometric analysis of international trade [11] presents an interesting attempt toward the formulation of an *integrated model* disclosing the *interaction* among the OECD member nations, and between these countries and the rest of the world as a consequence of foreign trade. Independently, for each country j, separate functions for total imports and exports, M_j and X_j, are empirically estimated. In each case, the functions would reflect the major determinants of that nation's trade activity. The import function is constructed so as to take into account domestic and foreign market factors, while the export function is constructed to reflect past market shares, competitive positions in the world market, and domestic market pressures, such as might stem from unused or fully utilized capacity.

Taken as a group, these equations form the trade flow model, whose essence can be summarized in two sets of linear functions (with all variables defined in constant prices and the time subscript deleted):

$$M_j = \alpha_{0j} + \alpha_{ij}Y_j + \alpha_{2j}PM_j + \alpha_3 PD_j \tag{11.5a}$$

where for each country j, M_j, Y_j, PM_j, and PD_j denote, respectively, total imports, GNP, the ratio of an import price index to a domestic price index, and "demand pressure" as measured by the degree of capacity utilization; and,

[11] F. G. Adams, H. Eguchi, and F. Meyer-zu-Schlochtern, *An Econometric Analysis of International Trade*, An interrelated explanation of imports and exports of OECD countries (Paris: OECD, January 1969).

$$X_j = \beta_{0j} + \beta_{1j}S_j + \beta_{2j}PX_j + \beta_{3j}PDX_j \tag{11.5b}$$

where for each country j, X_j, S_j, PX_j, and PDX_j denote, respectively, total exports, the expected rate of total exports assuming unchanged market shares, the ratio of an export price index to the export price index of competitor nations, and an index of the country's degree of capacity utilization relative to that of its competitors.

The "new" variables introduced into this model are the two capacity utilization variables, and S_j. In the former case, the suggestion is that the pressures to import (export) will be greater the greater (lesser) is the extent to which the productive capacity of domestic industries is being utilized. In the latter case, exports are presumed to follow a basic pattern, with country-by-country deviations from this pattern occurring because of price shifts and capacity problems. In particular, where $\bar{a}_{ij}$ is the base-year market share of country i in country j's total imports, S_i is defined by $S_i = \sum_{j=1}^{m} \bar{a}_{ij}M_j$. Thus, S_i introduces an interaction between imports and exports, so that the quantity of goods any nation j can export is in part determined by the willingness of all other nations to import from it.

Two major shortcomings of the OECD model stand out: (1) inconsistency between import and export forecasts, and (2) absence of feedbacks linking world trade activity to domestic income and price determination. Since the import and export functions are estimated *independently*, no guarantee exists that the sum of the national import figures will equal the sum of the national export forecast figures. Indeed, these sums will generally differ, thereby revealing a fundamental inconsistency insofar as a basic accounting identity—that world imports equal world exports—is violated. Additionally, by treating each country's GNP as an exogenous variable and limiting the linkage between national economies to the unidirectional impact of other countries' imports upon each nation's exports, the model ignores the interaction between the rates of economic activity in each nation and their international trade flows. Thus, while capable of linking the change in a particular nation's economic activity to its resulting effect upon the export activity of the rest of the world, the model fails to disclose the international transmission mechanism tracing the effects of import and export decisions on domestic economic activity.

Rhomberg[12] has singled out three basic approaches to resolving the "accounting identity" problem, which individually and in combination also admit of a number of variants.

In the *consistency* approach, imports are forecast for each nation based on a set of exogenous variables, but export forecasts for each nation are based on economic and policy variables for other nations as well. After an initial set of forecasts is obtained, these are checked for mutual consistency, and then, if

[12] R. R. Rhomberg, "Possible Approaches to a Model of World Trade and Payments," *IMF Staff Papers*, March 1970.

discrepancies exist, the initial forecasts are revised via "knowledgeable" judgments. The procedure is iterated until all accounting identities are satisfied.

In the *bilateral* approach, each nation would include in a forecasting model a forecast of imports from each *other* nation. The "other" nations would then estimate their exports from the summation of the individual import estimates.

The *structural* approach, which underlies Project LINK,[13] represents a crucial attempt to overcome the shortcomings of the previous approaches, which initially treat each country as an individual entity, by *systematically* linking the existing *individual* macroeconomic models of major industrial countries and international bodies *through their trade relations*. As Waelbroeck so aptly puts it: "Direct linkage is the procedure which best meets the basic objectives of Project LINK of using as basic building blocks real models built to solve problems of policy and forecasting in individual countries, and kept alive on a continuing basis by re-estimation and amendments inspired by everyday usage of the models. This distinguishes the project from other world models, which made good journal articles but were never tested on real problems. This philosophy makes it desirable to alter the models as little as possible, so that the models subjected to the test of LINK simulations are really the models used by country teams in their own work as forecasters and policy advisers." [14] The ultimate aim of the project is to achieve a world economic model capable of disclosing the interconnections between national economic policies, trade and payments flows, and cooperative international action.

Within the set of national-international econometric models of the participants, each of which described the economic structure of the particular country and area, the merchandise-exports functions are replaced with a market-shares matrix. In contrast to the OECD model, the LINK model replaces the import equation for each country i with an *econometric model* of that country; it replaces the export equation for each country with the equation $X_i = \sum_j a_{ij}^* M_j$ in which the *current*, rather than the base year market-shares matrix, $a^* = [a_{ij}^*]$, is used. The imports M_j are projected on the basis of the projected X_i's for some initial assumptions about world trade (and hence M_j) and a set of exogenous variables, as determined by the econometric import model. Then, given *this set* of import projections M_j', the X_i's are projected anew from the M_j''s, and these revised export projections are substituted into the econometric import model to obtain still further revised import projections, M_j''. As the process is iterated, the total import, export, and world trade figures converge toward a "plausible" value, accepted as the basis for the final individual projections. Throughout this process, the $X_i = M_i$ accounting identity necessarily holds, because each X_i is determined from the M_i and the market-shares matrix. The elements in the latter, it might be noted, can be adjusted to reflect changes in the price-relatives between the various trading partners.

[13] See R. J. Ball (ed.) *The International Linkage of National Economic Models* (Amsterdam: North-Holland, 1973) for discussions of LINK in theory and in practice.

[14] J. Waelbroeck, "The Methodology of Linkage," *Ibid.*, pp. 52–53.

Thus, instead of assuming that $m_{ij} = x_{ij}/M_j$ is a constant, one might instead assume that the market share will vary from some base, or base-year level m_{ij} as the average price of exports from country i to country j, p_{ij}^x, relative to the average price of imports between the countries, p_{ij}^m, varies. That is,

$$m_{ij} = m_{ij}^0 \left(\frac{p_{ij}^x}{p_{ij}^m}\right)^{-\eta_j}$$

where $\eta > 0$ is "the elasticity of the real market share with respect to relative export prices and is assumed to be the same for all suppliers in the jth market." [15]

The solution of a LINK model is consistent with the models for the individual countries, and also satisfies the world trade constraint. It yields a rate of world trade that permits an import rate for each country consistent with income rates and any other endogenous variables appearing in that country's import demand functions. In order to achieve this consistency between imports and exports, however, some other elements of the OECD model have been sacrificed. Of especial importance among these are the impact of competitiveness in foreign trade, and the domestic pressures for capacity utilization.

11.3 TRADE, AID, AND PLANNING ALTERNATIVES

Projections of imports and exports, by whatever methods are only part of the input necessary for determining and choosing among production and foreign trade alternatives. A crucial element in the formulation of such alternatives is, as already noted, the handling of a major bottleneck, the foreign currency shortage.

In principle, particularly in the collectivist state, planners could lay the foundation for foreign trade decisions with the help of mathematical programming models. The special significance of such models for the collectivist state derives from the controller's ability to issue instructions to effect a *variety* of individual economic decisions in specifically desired directions. One such model of particular interest has been suggested by the Hungarian economist Tardos.[16]

To describe this model, we first define the following terms: q_{jk} is the production of product j by technique k; x_{ij} is the export of product j to market i and m_{ij} is the import of product j from market i; a_{rkj} is the input of product j to a product r that is made by technique k; c_{jkl} is the input of resource l to a product j made by technique k; p_{ij}^x and p_{ij}^m are the export and import prices, respectively, of product j in market i; D_j is the domestic demand for product j, and is given external to the model; $\bar{Q}_{jk}$ is the available capacity for producing product j by technique k; $\bar{X}_{ij}$ and $\bar{M}_{ij}$ are export and import constraints, respectively, imposed on product j in market i; C_l is a constraint imposed by the

[15] B. G. Hickman, "A General Model of World Trade," *Ibid.*, p. 24.
[16] M. Tardos, "The Problem of the Central Management of Foreign Trade Turnover," in *Foreign Trade in a Planned Economy*, I. Vaida and M. Simai (eds.) (Cambridge, Mass.: Harvard University Press, 1971).

central authority—the controller—on the disposal of limited resources; and finally, b_i' and b_i'' are the minimum and maximum permitted values, respectively, of the balance of trade in market i. In general, then, i indexes market, j indexes product, k indexes technique, and l indexes resource.

Domestic demand for product j, D_j, is assumed to be *exactly* satisfied through its total domestic production, $\sum_k q_{jk}$, and net imports in the amount $\sum(m_{ij} - x_{ij})$, less the amount produced and then used for producing *other* products, or $\sum_r \sum_k a_{rkj} q_{rk}$. Thus,

$$\sum_k q_{jk} + \sum_i (m_{ij} - x_{ij}) - \sum_r \sum_k a_{rkj} q_{rk} = D_j \tag{11.6a}$$

for all j. There are five additional *definitional* constraints. These are imposed by the production maximum, the export and import maxima, the resource-disposal limitation, and the permissible bounds on the balance of trade:

$$0 \le q_{jk} \le \bar{Q}_{jk} \tag{11.6b}$$

$$0 \le x_{ij} \le \bar{X}_{ij} \tag{11.6c}$$

$$0 \le m_{ij} \le \bar{M}_{ij} \tag{11.6d}$$

$$\sum_j \sum_k c_{jkl} q_{jk} \le C_1 \tag{11.6e}$$

$$b_i' \le \sum_j (p_{ij}^x x_{ij} - p_{ij}^m m_{ij}) \le b_i'' \tag{11.6f}$$

for all i, j, k, and l, as is relevant.

Equations (11.6a)–(11.6f) are the structural constraints in a mathematical programming problem containing as potential decision variables, unless otherwise fixed, the production, import, and export rates: q_{jk}, m_{ij}, and x_{ij}. The exact solution to this problem will depend on the objective function. In the latter regard, Tardos has suggested three alternative objectives: (1) maximizing some weighted average of total final demand, which by Equation (11.6a) is certain to be satisfied; (2) achieving, at least over the short term, the maximum improvement in the balance-of-payments position; and (3) minimizing the cost of the limited resources to be employed in domestic production. In the first case, letting α_j be the weight assigned to a unit of product j, where α_j might be the domestic price of product j, the objective function would be written

$$Z_1 = \sum_j \alpha_j D_j \tag{11.7a}$$

in the second case, where Π_i is the exchange rate obtaining in country i, the objective function becomes

$$Z_2 = \sum_i \sum_j \Pi_i (p_{ij}^x x_{ij} - p_{ij}^m m_{ij}) \tag{11.7b}$$

and in the third case, where Π_l is the price of resource l, the objective function becomes

$$Z_3 = \sum_j \sum_k \sum_l \Pi_l c_{jkl} q_{jk} \tag{11.7c}$$

Equations (11.6a)–(11.6f), together with any one of the latter three objective functions, define a linear programming problem. Unfortunately, as Tardos correctly points out, in actuality planners rarely have sufficient information to set up the problem, and that which is available is ordinarily incorrect! Thus, in general the relationships that would be built into such a model would tend to be inexact and, moreover, obsolete.

The models that are suggested more often in the socialist countries at the present time conserve the idea of a powerful *planning center,* but also allow for certain forms of *decentralization,* and assign to other types of planning more limited objectives. Thus, for instance, certain models formulated in Eastern Europe (notably in Poland, Hungary, and East Germany) aim at maximizing foreign exchange returns, or minimizing domestic costs, by optimizing the *geographic distribution* of foreign trade, given central planning decisions on the *volume* of imports and exports, without calling into question the commodity structure laid down by the plan. Again, however, optimal plans cannot be obtained since the rates of exchange and the cost structures are distorted to begin with.

Other models posit the problem of minimizing "social labor" outlay so as to satisfy the targeted volume of exportable commodities and foreign trade set out in the plan. In still other models—as in the celebrated two-level planning model developed by Kornai and Liptak [17]—decisions on outputs and inputs are centralized, while price determination is decentralized. The center issues output and input directives, and eventually allocates the supplies within the constraints of the directives; the production sectors plan their investment, productivity, and foreign trade activities so as to maximize their own foreign currency returns. Each sector calculates the dual of its program, which yields the shadow prices associated with each of the constraining factors. These shadow prices then serve the center as the basis for allocating supplies, and for shifting resources among sectors.

In the West, in connection with the so-called gap models discussed in Chapter 7, Chenery and his associates have developed interesting and valuable *procedures* for appraising various qualitative limits to development, and for determining alternative development strategies. In one such study applied to Israel,[18] Chenery and Bruno focus their analysis on six variables. Two of these variables, GNP and the unemployment rate, are policy goals; the remaining four variables, the marginal saving rate, the rate of foreign capital inflow, the rate of exports, and the growth of labor productivity, are *control* variables.

The model is initially formulated in terms of twelve basic equations; these are eventually reduced to three equations corresponding to three basic constraints to growth: the capital limit, the labor limit, and the balance-of-payments limit. In particular, the following relationships are derived: (1) Let Y_1

---

[17] This is just *one* of the applications of the Kornai-Liptak model, which can, assuredly, be used in many other ways. See above, p. 189.

[18] H. B. Chenery, and M. Bruno, "Economic Development in an Open Economy: The Case of Israel," *Economic Journal,* Vol. 72, May 1962.

and Y_0 denote GNP in year 1 and the base year, respectively; let β denote the average product per unit of increase in the capital stock, or the average productivity of investment; let s denote the marginal propensity to save; and let F_1 denote the foreign capital inflow in year 1. Then

$$\frac{Y_1 - Y_0}{Y_1} = \frac{\Delta Y}{Y_1} = \beta s + \frac{F_1}{Y_1} = \beta s + f \tag{11.8a}$$

where $f = F_1/Y_1$, or

$$Y_1 = \frac{Y_0 + F_1}{1 - \beta s} \tag{11.8a'}$$

(2) let N_0 denote the base-year labor supply; let λ_0 denote the base-year average labor input per unit of output; let g denote the annual rate at which the latter decreases, or the annual *increase* in labor productivity; let δ denote the annual rate of growth in the labor force, and let μ denote the ratio of imports to GNP. Then

$$Y_1 = \frac{N_0(1 + \delta)(1 - \mu)}{\lambda_0(1 - g)} \tag{11.8b}$$

(3) Letting X_1 denote exports of goods and services in year 1,

$$Y_1 = \frac{(1 - \mu)}{\mu}(X_1 + F_1) \tag{11.8c}$$

As seen in Equation (11.8c), increases in import requirements can be met either by substituting domestic products for imports (reducing μ), by increasing exports, X_1, or by increasing the foreign capital inflow, F_1. When no limit is placed on the latter, the ultimate limit to growth is placed by the labor constraint, (11.8b), since the other two constraints are removed by increased foreign borrowing. Foreign capital inflow, however, is not an unmixed blessing, since even that part of the inflow that is labeled "aid" is (ordinarily) not an outright grant and entails, in one form or another, future obligations on the part of the receiving country. In particular, at some point the foreign debt incurred through the use of foreign capital inflow will have to be repaid. The ultimate costs of current development might thus be borne through the sacrifices of future generations, via the subsequent outflows of the newly developed domestic natural resources and the industrial products of the newly developed domestic industries. The developing nation, therefore, runs the risk of purchasing development on the foreign capital market in exchange for domestic labor and resources, and in the process getting itself more and more heavily into the debt of its financial benefactors.

Three values are assumed for the control variables: two extremums and an intermediate value, corresponding respectively to a pessimistic and an optimistic assessment, and to a past trend or a specific forecast. These values set the boundaries encompassing the range of feasible combinations of instrument variables that can be considered by the policy makers. The latter must then decide, say by maximizing some objective function, where in the feasible set they wish to be.

To a large extent, four variables characterize the development strategy of any country: the growth rate of GNP; the average savings rate; the foreign capital flow; and the "effective exchange rate"—that is, the rate that serves to adjust imports and exports to the value necessary to bring the balance of payments into balance. Two opposing strategies stand at the extremes—a "low saving–high foreign aid" strategy, and a "maximum savings–low foreign aid" strategy—with a wide range in between. The choice depends on the evaluation of the sectoral implications of the given strategy on the export prospects, and on the policy makers' willingness to rely on, and ability to secure the foreign assistance required to achieve the posited growth of GNP.

11.4 PROJECT SELECTION, EXPORTS, AND THE "MAKE OR IMPORT" ISSUE

We have noted above that increases in import requirements force policy makers to confront the realities of either expanding exports, developing substitute industries, or relying on foreign aid. International trade theory proposes the criterion of *comparative advantage* for determining whether export industries should be set up and, if so, which industries these should be, which commodities should be exported, and whether and to what extent import substitutes should be produced. Planning theorists do not deny the need to take into account the basic aspects of relative efficiency. What they suggest, however, is that it is necessary to develop some *specific techniques* for determining how the ideal could be approximated without losing sight of balance-of-payments effects. We shall examine two interesting approaches in this regard, proposed by Bruno and Frisch,[19] respectively. The first takes as a basic decision criterion minimizing the total resource cost per unit of net foreign exchange earned or saved; the second, optimizing the net creditor position of the country at any point in time, given its investment and expansion policy choices.

Starting from certain policy goals and the usual constraints on the factors a la Chenery (labor, capital, and foreign exchange), Bruno determines the shadow prices to be used in the project planning process. The choice to promote the export of a given commodity is determined by the yield in terms of the foreign exchange *earned,* in comparison to the cost of production in terms of opportunity cost foregone. Similarly, the choice for substitute imports is guided by the minimum resource cost per unit of net foreign exchange *saved.* The method rests on the breakdown of costs into foreign and domestic expenditures—a breakdown worked out with the help of input-output analysis.

Frisch's analysis centers on a country's *net creditor position* at any point during the planning period. He dismisses as a "fad" the interest in industries that can earn or save foreign exchange. Such a policy, he notes, may be

[19] M. Bruno, *op. cit.;* and R. Frisch, *op. cit.*

just as unfounded as one focusing exclusively on the growth of the national product. According to Frisch, even when the foreign exchange power of an industry is properly measured through its total effect, "an extreme emphasis on industries that contribute positively on the balance of payments may lead astray" [20] since the balance-of-payments effect and the national product growth effect are in a very specific sense conflicting, and a politically acceptable compromise must be worked out between the two. A wise compromise could be achieved by the policy makers by considering that for the balance of payments the main criterion to be taken into account is the net creditor position of the country at any time; and, for the national product, the main desideratum is to accelerate the speed of its growth. The pertinent considerations would then be to choose such an investment and expansion policy that: (a) the net creditor position (positive or negative) would at no time fall below a certain lower bound; and (b) to choose an appropriate discounting factor. All this yields a *practical rule* for choosing among projects. To apply this rule properly, Frisch suggests that a comparative gain figure should be computed for *each project* out of a stockpile of projects three or four times larger than one could actually hope to carry out. This computation should be connected with the optimum price for the necessary resources—resources defined in connection with the net creditor position at any point in time, and the primary remuneration of factors (if bounds are also put on these magnitudes). The comparative gain figure should guide the decision on both acceptance or rejection of the project, and on its phasing. Further, the contribution of each project to the GNP should be viewed as depending on two basic data: total investment needed for the project, and the resultant net addition to capacity. Time-shape coefficients of investment input and net additional capacity may be derived as fractions of the total investment. Then, with appropriate yearly interflow tables, the current account inputs needed from all sectors, the decreases in competitive imports it will generate, the increases in exports, and the changes in the country's net creditor position, will be properly ascertained.

Since the effects of investment policies on the future net product can thus be estimated, the optimizing problem may be formalized as that of maximizing the stream of future incomes, discounted to the present (say by some factor reflecting the target rate of speed at which development aims) subject to the constraint that the net creditor position will not fall below the posited bound at any point in time. Frisch's analysis is rich in insights, both with respect to investment analysis and to planning in general.

11.5 CONCLUDING COMMENTS

Planning foreign trade, be it for a country that visualizes its foreign trade sector as *subordinated* to its domestic plan, or a country for which this sector is the pivotal one, is complicated by the facts that (a) a vast number of decision centers exist on the international scene, (b) one cannot predict which particular

---

[20] *Ibid.*, p. 3.

instruments will be used by them and when, and further, (c) one cannot foresee the repercussions that the decisions of *other* policy makers will have on one's own target variables. Even the most extensive planning of imports and exports, and the tightest controls on gold and foreign exchange, may not insure that the foreign trade plan will be successfully carried out. These controls may at best cushion but not cancel the effect of international price fluctuations, and may attenuate but not avoid shifts in the planned composition of imports and exports, or in their planned origin and destination.

The asymmetry between the growth of import requirements and of foreign exchange due to the lack of exportable commodities, often stressed by the policy makers of LDC's, and which has persuaded numerous economists to view the "foreign exchange gap" rather than the domestic "savings gap" as the key constraint to economic growth in these countries, may have some curious consequences as development does get underway. Scarcity in the supply of foreign exchange may encourage what appears to be judicious choices in import substitution—a la Bruno, or a la Frisch—but no matter how judicious these choices are, there are limits to this strategy which are placed by both the size of the domestic market (which is particularly severe for small nations), and the limited demand for the newly produced goods on the foreign markets. Thus it is hardly possible to generalize about the appropriate pattern of import substitution and export promotion, as it were, independently of the particular nation's level of development.

Kalecki suggests an interesting example for analyzing the situation of an already developing country—a socialist economy in his specific case—that neither grants nor receives foreign exchange, so that its foreign trade must be balanced.[21] As that country's foreign demand for imports increases because of its industrialization, its exports *must* rise to cover the imports. The higher the growth rate of GNP, the more rapidly exports must increase, but "the more difficult it is to sell them in view of the limited demand." [22] Efforts to promote exports become associated with price reductions, shifts to less profitable markets, and inclusion of less and less profitable items in the exportable goods list. Concurrent technical and organizational factors arising in the process of development, which hamper the rate of expansion of various sectors, ultimately lead to a situation in which foreign trade difficulties place a definite ceiling on the rate of growth of GNP. At that ceiling rate, "all efforts to equilibrate imports and exports cease to yield positive results." [23] Limited selective demand on the advanced markets, and reduced export prices set in order to gain access to other markets, increase the volume of exports, but not their value. The less favorable markets and less profitable goods thus set a final limit to further growth. Such a problem could disappear in an autarkic economy, but only if that country could escape bottlenecks in its development—hardly a reasonable assumption.

[21] M. Kalecki, *Introduction to the Theory of Growth in a Socialist Economy* (Oxford: Blackwell, 1969).
[22] *Ibid.*, p. 44.
[23] *Ibid.*, p. 47.

The uncertainty inherent in the situation prevailing on the international scene, and its repercussions on the national foreign trade plane, could be removed by coordination or cooperation between policy makers. Various well-known schemes exist, and many more are possible. Tinbergen [24] suggests a world optimal division of labor "in which the total production the world needs is produced as cheaply as possible while using as many of the 'productive forces' as possible;" he also proposes a planning procedure that would lead to the establishment of a "macroeconomic set of target figures for the main variables" to be apportioned among the countries of the world, so that they would adapt their plans and policies to that macro-frame. All this, buttressed with various partial customs unions and ad hoc investment programs. Unfortunately, few policy makers are likely to consider such schemes as practical. Accordingly, they may continue to look upon the international market as an arena of monopolistic competition among nations behaving analogously to corporations with vastly different endowments of technologies, skills, entrepreneurial talents, and selling abilities.

[24] *Op. cit.,* pp. 551–552.

CHAPTER 12

Manpower and Employment Planning

12.1 PROBLEMS OF MANPOWER PLANNING

The synergistic effects achieved by the interdependent components and subsystems of a purposive system—in particular, an economic system—are dramatically illustrated by the outputs realized from the couplings of (1) the human resource component with (2) both the agricultural and industrial-processor subsystems. The former depends on the latter as a source of labor demand and income; the latter depend on the former as a source of labor supply and product demand. In combination they produce economic activity that neither can produce on its own. The system's controller therefore has a vital interest in assuring a smooth flow of labor to the processors that require it, as well as sources of employment for individuals seeking work. This interest once again manifests itself in the planners' concern with both projections and procedures. In the former case, interest centers on labor demand and supply projections; in the latter case, interest centers on the development of policies to effect various labor "qualities," as well as supply quantities, at some future date in order to meet the projected demands of new and changing technologies, shifting economic relationships, and planned increases in economic activity.

Government measures affecting manpower supply and demand encompass a vast field. Indeed, there are few major government policies or programs that are without important human resource *implications*. With respect to labor supply, the government may affect the size, distribution, and skill composition of the total population in general and that of the total labor force in particular, as well as the activity rate—the proportion of the population gainfully employed. With respect to labor demand, decisive roles may be played by policies concerning job creation, and the distribution of employment by groups, by regions, and by industries.

In both MDC's and LDC's, increasing attention is now being paid to the operation of the different elements of population dynamics—fertility, mortality, and migration, and the relations of these elements to changes in age structure—as well as to the formulation of policies concerning population size and distribution. These policies range from family planning and the determination of future urban and rural growth and concentration patterns, to complex regulations affecting the numbers and composition of in-and-out migration. The crucial issues that are raised by rural as opposed to urban populations, and by farm as opposed to nonfarm employment, have long been on the economic managers' agendas in both the developed and the developing nations. In most MDC's, expansion in nonfarm job opportunities, coupled with rapid increases in farm workers' productivity, has led to a systematic decline in the rural population. This decline has not been forestalled by economic growth and a concomitant increase in demand for agricultural products, because of the low income elasticity of farm products. Moreover, although specific measures, such as subsidies and price support schemes, have *tended* to dampen this secular declining trend, their main thrust has been aimed at agricultural *output* rates rather than population distributions, and in the main they have benefitted large land owners rather than encouraged small land owners to remain in agriculture.

In the socialist countries of the Soviet type, the collective organizational set-up in the villages has tended—just as do the traditional sociocultural arrangements in the LDC's—to retain inefficient labor on the farm, and to significantly check the rural-to-urban population drift. This drift still exists nonetheless, and is one of the main contributors to the unemployment problem. Wage controls, slow provision of housing and transportation facilities, and various types of direct controls, such as passports, have, however, also acted in the direction of checking the drift. Finally, a complex of various laws and regulations, notably those concerning child labor, often discriminatory "protection" of female labor, retirement age, obligatory schooling, and support (or lack of support) for certain types of training and education, all act in a determinant way on the size and composition of labor *supply*.

The systematic pursuit of the policy objectives of economic growth and "maximum" employment, and the fiscal and monetary measures used to implement them, along with price and wage policies are the determinant factors for the *demand* for labor in the market-directed economies. In the economies of the Soviet type, direct allocation of capital resources is a major factor in labor demand. A whole gamut of other measures concerning traditional patterns of job access, promotion and seniority, and measures that tend to redistribute jobs between age groups, the sexes, ethnic groups, and regions have, in turn, a heavy bearing on the structure of labor demand. Finally, the government may exercise an important influence on the price of labor relative to the price of capital. It can do so by, for example, directly affecting the supply of capital and the size of investment, and by inducing possible factor "bias" in favor of one factor or another, through its encouragement of technological change, and its financing of R and D programs that result in important technological shifts.

No attempt has been made to place the very complex measures involved within a mutually consistent framework, and to coordinate these measures with the economic activities of the individual enterprises. In most MDC's what has come to be called a "national manpower policy" consists of various broad goals concerning employment, along with some general policies concerning equity and the overcoming of "structural difficulties" in respect to depressed areas, low-income groups, and minorities. Here, programming procedures that *utilize* projections are involved. In other MDC's in which national plans are formulated, "manpower planning" consists of the following kinds of exercises—all of which involve projections *rather than* procedures: (1) projections of total population; (2) projections of labor force activity rates; (3) projections of final and intermediate demands; (4) variations of the demand projections under various assumptions; (5) provision of investments; (6) adjustment of previous hypotheses, and confrontation with the manpower projections; and (7) variations in the demand projections under various assumptions concerning the length of the work week and work year, as well as labor utilization, for a final determination of the overall plan goals.

In the USSR the "balance" of labor resources and their allocation has a more modest role than its name may suggest. The planning sequence does not differ substantially from the one presented above for the planning MDC's: the possible increases in labor resources are prepared via population projections and the utilization of activity rates; the estimates of the so-called "rational allocation" are made with the use of fixed ratios (so-called "basic proportions") among the "productive" (material production) and "nonproductive" (services) complexes, the various industrial branches, and the "social and personal labor" (notably that in agriculture). The differences between this "allocation" and the planned targets may call for "reallocation." This will be mostly of the unskilled, via the system of organized recruitment of workers (Orgnabor), various resettlement schemes of farmers and nonfarmers, and vocational training for the young and their compulsory assignment to production. But the "manpower balance" does not deal with the problems of workers' utilization, working time, or labor productivity, as its name might misleadingly suggest. As we shall see below, the estimates of the enterprises' needs for semiskilled and skilled workers are handled separately, via surveys of enterprises within each administration under centralized controls.

The literature on manpower planning is actually confined to the study of certain *components* of such planning: namely, (a) demographic projections; (b) technical projections of labor availability and of labor requirements given certain policy objectives; and (c) models for educational planning. Most of the studies on "manpower planning" and on "human resources development" are of the latter variety only. Again, J. Tinbergen, in association with H. Correa and H. C. Bos, has been among the most outstanding contributors to this field.[1] Their methodology concerning problems of educational planning, developed by

[1] H. Correa and J. Tinbergen, "Quantitative Adaptation of Education to Accelerated Growth," *Kyklos,* Vol. 15, 1962; J. Tinbergen and H. C. Bos, "A Planning Model of the Education Requirements of Economic Growth," in OECD Study Group in the Economics of Education, *The Residual Factor and Economic Growth* (Paris: OECD, 1964), pp. 147–169.

analogy with planning the requirements for capital goods, has been used, with variations, in a large number of studies. Alternative approaches, developed in relation with the study of the "sources of economic growth," have been suggested notably by the work of E. F. Denison.[2] We shall focus on some of these aspects after a short discussion on demographic relationships and labor availability, on labor requirements, and on the association between these projections for planning purposes.

12.2 DEMOGRAPHIC DYNAMICS AND LABOR AVAILABILITY

a. Demographic dynamics

In economic terms, manpower forecasting implies the identification of all the variables that determine changes in both demand and supply and the analysis of the demand-supply interactions for each type of manpower. With respect to demand, this would require forecasts of changes in final demand, interindustry demands, factor substitution, and wages and prices; with respect to supply, this would require forecasts of changes in population, labor participation (activity) rates, wages and salaries, cost of education, and some other factors.

In *practice,* manpower forecasting of the availability and the requirements of labor—wrongly qualified as forecasts of the "supply" and "demand" for labor—commonly consists of *technical projections* of the interrelations between the growth and changing distribution of the population and labor force on the one hand, and the development of opportunities for employment, or of targeted employment, on the other.

Population projections are made with the help of either the so-called "mathematical" or the "economic" method. The former consists in simple or composite extrapolations of fairly regular growth patterns of the population as a whole, or of population cohorts or segments—by sex, age-intervals, urban-rural division or by some other classification—within a more or less *stable* sociocultural and economic framework. The latter consists in extrapolations within a rapidly *changing* economic framework, when some overriding economic factor—significant changes in in- and out-migration, expansion or contraction of an important industry, or marked changes in transportation and trade patterns—becomes the *primary* determinant of population growth.

Extrapolations of a past datum or of past data follow standard procedures. A certain rate of change is assumed as a function of time for the total population, or for fertility rates, death rates, and in- and out-migration, with reference to the group subclassification chosen. The rates may be constant or

---

[2] E. F. Denison, assisted by J. P. Poullier, *Why Growth Rates Differ,* Postwar Experience in Nine Western Countries (Washington, D.C.: The Brookings Institute, 1967), pp. 78 ff. See also an earlier paper of E. F. Denison, "Measuring the Contribution of Education (and the Residual)," in OECD . . . , *The Residual Factor and Economic Growth, op. cit.,* pp. 13 ff. See also in the same study the comments of A. K. Sen contrasting the approaches of Tinbergen *et al.* and of Denison, pp. 188 ff.

variable, as determined by some specified curvilinear function fitted to historical data—in the past, logistic growth curves that imply increasing annual growth rates up to a maximum level, followed by decreasing annual growth rates were especially in vogue—and presumed to obtain in the future. Cohort-type analysis, wherein the population is divided into particular groups, such as age categories, and the relevant rates determined for each cohort, is also used to determine overall rates. The three decisive rates of fertility, mortality, and migration cannot, however, be treated with equal degrees of confidence for the future. The most statistically reliable rate, that which can be treated with the highest degree of confidence, is the death rate; the least certain is the migration rate—and this rate is particularly important in regional analysis; finally, the most important rate in population change, the fertility rate, usually ranges between these two extremes and is therefore the most likely source of statistical error.

Composite extrapolations that segment the heterogenous population into its component homogenous groups and then aggregate the individual projections into a composite extrapolation, rather than simple aggregate projections for the single heterogeneous population, are evidently preferable since they involve separate analyses of the factors effecting each component. For many purposes it may be important to know not only *what* overall population changes will occur, but the details as to *how* these changes will be brought about, and *where* the effects of these changes will impact; that is, the affected population components, the regions, and the production sectors. But, statistical information is often insufficiently detailed, or inaccurate for the purpose. Lack of demographic data is particularly severe in the LDC's. It is, however, now possible to construct certain models of demographic evolution, and with their help to determine up to a point the demographic characteristics of a population when only *some* of these characteristics are known.

These models concern so-called *stable, semistable,* and *quasistable* populations. The mathematical concept of a stable population, first proposed by the demographer A. J. Lotka,[3] concerns a limit population to which actual populations tend when their mortality and fertility rates remain constant. These populations are particular cases of ''Malthusian'' populations—so-called after Malthus [4] who dealt with populations with a constant rate of natural increase—whose mortality and sex-age structure are constant. The concept of *stable* populations is a purely abstract one; however, most of the populations of the LDC's are semistable, or semi-Malthusian; that is, they also exhibit a constancy of the age structure, but with falling mortality rates, which can in part be interpreted via methods employed in connection with the study of Malthusian populations. Moreover, United Nations demographers have shown that the invariability of

[3] A. J. Lotka and F. R. Sharpe, ''A Problem in Age Distribution,'' *Philosophical Magazine*, 1911, 21, pp. 435–438; and A. J. Lotka and L. I. Doublin, ''On the True Rate of Natural Increase,'' *Journal of the American Statistical Association*, 1925, 20, pp. 305–339; and A. J. Lotka, *Theorie analytique des associations biologiques*, Vols. I, II (Paris: Hermann, 1934, 1939).

[4] T. R. Malthus, *An Essay on the Principle of Population* (London: Reeves and Turner, 1878).

the age distribution of many actual populations can also be studied in an entirely different manner by assimilating such populations into *quasistable* populations—that is, populations whose fertility rates have been constant for a long period, and whose age distribution has remained more or less constant.[5] The concept of quasistable populations is based on experience; it is defined through various statistical procedures. Assuming that we have at our disposal projections for a *network* of quasistable populations, computed by associating a series of model fertility rates with a series of model life tables containing indices reflecting the mortality patterns of a generation, it is possible to study with their help *actual* populations of which only certain demographic characteristics are known. Assuredly, it would be necessary to select from this *network* a population that coincides with the *actual* population—a task that is by no means simple; at best the coincidence between the two can only be approximate. Be that as it may, projections of the total population by sex and by age are the basis on which the estimates for labor availability are made; the quality of the former will evidently be decisive for the quality of the projections of the population of working age.

b. Projections of labor availability

There are three principal methods for projecting activity rates: (1) extrapolations of past trends; (2) simple or multiple correlations of the future rates with specific developmental measures; and (3) utilization of transition probability matrices.

1. Naive extrapolations are the most frequently used means of projecting activity rates. In particular, let a_{ti} denote the *percent* of the population in age group i who are economically active or employed at the beginning of the projection period t—that is, the activity rate. Similarly, $100 - a_{ti} = u_{ti}$ denotes the *percent* of the population in age group i who are economically inactive, or unemployed. It is commonly assumed that the activity and inactivity rates are determinable with a fair degree of accuracy from, say, census data; similar figures a_{0i} and u_{0i} are obtainable for a base year $t = 0$. In general, $0 \leq a_{ti} \leq 100$. This "trivially obvious" condition is worth calling attention to since, in fact, it will *not* necessarily be satisfied in all projection procedures in which the activity (or inactivity) rate is to be estimated over the interval Δt for some time T. For present purposes the time intervals $t = t - 0$ and $\Delta t = T - t$ are assumed to be equal. Where this is not the case, adjustments to allow for the differing interval lengths are readily made, say by computing the *average annual* change in the activity rate.

The simplest extrapolation procedure assumes a fixed rate of change in the activity rate. Thus, suppose the activity rate for age group i has changed by $\Delta = 100(a_{ti}/a_{0i} - 1)$ percent since the base year. It can then be projected to change still further to reach an estimated level of $\hat{a}_{Ti} = a_{ti}(a_{ti}/a_{0i}) = a_{ti}$

---

[5] United Nations, *The Concept of a Stable Population: Application to the Study of Populations of Countries with Incomplete Demographic Statistics* (New York: United Nations, 1968).

$[(100 + \Delta)/100]$ at time T. The fixed *annual* percentage rate of increase over the base period could also be determined, given Δ, by $\Delta_a = 100[(1 + \Delta/100)^{1/t} - 1]$. The latter could then be applied for projecting the activity rate for a time period of differing length from $t = \Delta t$. In particular, for *any* T one could estimate $\hat{a}_{Ti} = a_{ti} [1 + \Delta_a/100]^{T-t}$.

Unfortunately, the initial assumption that the previous two-point trend will be maintained in the future, or that past annual rates of change were constant, is hardly justifiable. Moreover, it can quite plausibly result in implausible projected activity rates in excess of 100. This will occur when the past annual rate of increase in the activity rate was relatively large, and/or when the projection period is relatively long, and past activity rates have been increasing. That is, a_{Ti} can exceed 100, for *any* $\hat{a}_{ti}$, when Δ, Δ_a, and $T - t$ are "big enough." For example, with fixed Δt, an increase in the activity rate from $a_{0i} = 60$ to $a_{ti} = 80$ will result in a projection of $\hat{a}_{Ti} = 80(80/60) = 106.4$, in violation of the previously imposed restriction.

To correct for this, Durand [6] has proposed two alternative weighting schemes for computing $\hat{\Delta}$, the *projected* percentage change from 0 to t:

(a) $\hat{\Delta}_1 = \dfrac{a_{ti}}{a_{0i}} \dfrac{a_{ti}u_{ti}}{a_{0i}u_{0i}} = \dfrac{a_{ti}}{a_{0i}} R$

(b) $\hat{\Delta}_2 = 1 + \hat{\Delta}_1 - R$

Under the first of these, continuing the previous numerical example, $R = .67$ and an estimate of $\hat{a}_{Ti} = 80[1 + (1.33)(.67)/100] = 80.7$ would be obtained; the second yields an estimate of $\hat{a}_{Ti} = 81.1$.

In general, either of these two correction factors retards the rate of growth in the activity rate when the latter is very high, and accelerates the *growth* rate when the activity rate is low. Under admittedly peculiar circumstances, however, neither factor *guarantees* $\hat{a}_{Ti} \le 100$. Thus, for example, if $a_{0i} = 9$ and $a_{ti} = 91$, $\hat{\Delta}_1 = (91/9)(91 \times 9/9 \times 91) = 10.1$ and $\hat{a}_{Ti} = 91(1.1) = 101$. The possibility of this occurring is sufficiently farfetched—even for rapidly developing nations and lengthy time intervals—that it can be confidently ignored. Nonetheless, there does not seem to be any compelling underlying theoretical *basis* for either of the suggested correction schemes.

An alternative procedure that is *alleged* to be superior when activity rates are assumed to be gradually increasing is to project the *inactivity* rates,[7] or $\hat{u}_{Ti} = u_{ti}(u_{ti}/u_{0i})$, and then to compute the activity rates from these projections as $\hat{a}_{Ti} = 100 - \hat{u}_{Ti}$. This method would be clearly superior in the previous illustration, where $u_{ti} = 20$ and $u_{0i} = 40$, and we would obtain $\hat{u}_{Ti} = 20(20/40) = 10$ and $\hat{a}_{Ti} = 90$, as opposed to the impossible result of 106.4. Here too one of the correction factors might be applied to "guarantee" $\hat{a}_{Ti} \le 100$. But, again, there

---

[6] J. D. Durand, *The Labour Force in the United States 1890–1960* (New York: Social Science Research Council, 1948), pp. 238–239.

[7] For a discussion see United Nations, *Methods for Population Projections by Sex and Age* (New York: United Nations, 1956), pp. 10–32.

is no compelling logic to favor either scheme over the other, except insofar as one anticipates that $a_{ti} > 50$ and $u_{ti} < 50$.

A third variant considers the change in the activity rate over the base period for the age group whose activity rate is to be projected, when the members of this group belonged to a *lower* age group. Thus, members of group i at time T may be considered to have belonged to group $i - 1$ during the base period. *At that time,* the percent increase in their activity rate can be computed to be $\Delta^{-1} = a_{t(i-1)}/a_{0(i-1)}$. The simple extrapolation for this group—now belonging to age group i at time T—would be $\hat{a}_{Ti} = a_{Ti}\,(a_{t(i-1)}/a_{0(i-1)})$. Thus, if $a_{ti} = 80$, but $a_{t(i-1)} = 60$ and $a_{0(i-1)} = 60$, we would also project $\hat{a}_{Ti} = 80$, because the activity rates for *these* persons has not previously changed over time, but they presumably will continue to conform to the activity patterns of their *new* age group. Again, one of the correction factors can also be introduced.

Finally, when the activity rate of a particular age group is thought to be quite stable over time, this rate can be used as the basis for the projections for the other age groups. That is, suppose a_{Tk} is judged to be a readily estimated figure, $\hat{a}_{Tk}$. It is then assumed that the ratio $a_{ti}/a_{tk} = r_i$—the ratio of intergroup activity rates—will be constant, at least over the short term. Then, based on this assumption and the estimate $\hat{a}_{Tk}$ we would determine $\hat{a}_{Ti} = \hat{a}_{Tk}r_i$.

2. Each of the former procedures, although naive, can frequently be justified on the basis of data limitations that *impose* upon one the need to extrapolate from only two data points. Where additional data are available, more sophisticated correlation and regression techniques can be employed.

In the event that a time series of activity rates is available, the trend in these rates might be computed under any of several alternative assumptions. Among the more obvious are $a_{ti} = \alpha_{0i} + \alpha_{1i}t$, $a_{ti} = \alpha_{0i}(\alpha_{1i})^t$, and $a_{ti} = \alpha_1^*/(1 + e^{\alpha_{0i} + \alpha_{1i}t})$, where the α_{ji}'s are constants to be estimated by ordinary least squares, and α_1^* might be assessed a priori, say as $\alpha_1^* = 100$ (the random disturbance term being suppressed for convenience). The resultant equations would then be used to project a_{Ti}.

The procedure might be further extended to include *other* variables, such as a technological change factor, some measure of international trade, economic growth, and the like, in a multiple regression. Here, however, the data requirements are considerable and, at least in the LDC's where the activity rates are ordinarily least stable, might be most difficult to satisfy. In fact, despite their conceptual plausibility, these more sophisticated approaches are largely untested and seldom used in practice.

3. A third approach to the projection problem is based on a first-order Markov model in which a person placed in category $i(i = 1, \ldots, n)$ in year t is assumed to move into category j $(j = 1, \ldots, n)$ in year T with fixed *transition probability* p_{ij}. The matrix $P = [p_{ij}]$ is an $n \times n$ transition probability matrix, the elements of which will, in the present context, ordinarily be estimated from survey data. Unfortunately, historically such data have not been gathered

as a regular part of census activities, even in such data-conscious nations as the United States. It is possible, however, to obtain least-squares *estimates* of the transition probabilities from ordinary time series of the number of persons in each category [8]—and such are frequently available. This approach is, therefore, more applicable than might seem to be the case at first blush.

To implement the approach, suppose that four manpower categories are defined: economically active and inactive males and females; categories 1, 2, 3, and 4, respectively. Under this scheme, p_{11} is the probability that an individual that is an employed male (category 1) in the initial period will also be employed one period later; similarly, p_{34} is the probability that an employed female (category 3) will become an unemployed female (category 4) after a single time period.

Suppose, now, that one has an initial row vector $\mathbf{a}_t = (a_{1t}, a_{2t}, a_{3t}, a_{4t})$ whose elements a_{it} are the *number* of employed males ($i = 1$), the number of unemployed males ($i = 2$), the number of employed females ($i = 3$), and the number of unemployed females ($i = 4$) per hundred *persons* in the population at time t. Then, the vector-matrix product

$$a_t P = (a_{1t}, a_{2t}, a_{3t}, a_{4t}) \begin{bmatrix} p_{11} & p_{12} & p_{13} & p_{14} \\ p_{21} & p_{22} & p_{23} & p_{24} \\ p_{31} & p_{32} & p_{33} & p_{34} \\ p_{41} & p_{42} & p_{43} & p_{44} \end{bmatrix} = (a_{1T}, a_{2T}, a_{3T}, a_{4T}) \quad (12.1)$$

yields a vector whose elements are the *expected* number of persons, per hundred, falling into the respective categories. In particular, for a_{2T} one would compute

$$a_{2T} = a_{1t}p_{12} + a_{2t}p_{22} + a_{3t}p_{32} + a_{4t}p_{42} = a_{1t}p_{12} + a_{2t}p_{22}$$

since $p_{32} = p_{42} = 0$. That is, the probability of either an employed or unemployed female becoming an employed male is—some of the more highly publicized counterexamples notwithstanding—zero. The sum, $a_{1t}p_{12} + a_{2t}p_{22}$, adds the *expected* number of initially employed males that will become unemployed ($a_{1t}p_{12}$) to the *expected* number of unemployed males that will remain unemployed ($a_{1t}p_{22}$), and thus gives the *expected* total number of unemployed males, per hundred, at time T. In similar manner, additional categories, such as age and urban-rural distinctions, can be delineated. Even when the probabilities can be estimated from historical data, however, the assumption that these historical estimates provide "good" estimates of the future probabilities is open to considerable question.

Perhaps the most pointed criticism that can be lodged at all of these projection methods is that they are too mechanistic for the purposes at which they are aimed. Employment patterns, particularly beyond the short term, can undergo very considerable shifts as a result of technological change, alterations

[8] H. Theil and G. Rey, "A Quadratic Programming Approach to the Estimation of Transition Probabilities," *Management Science*, Vol. 12, No. 9, May 1966.

in the mortality and fertility rates, and changing economic and social conditions and behavior. The latter are often ignored in the mechanical estimation procedures. Nonetheless, they are especially important in conditioning economic activity rates. Their impact will not disappear through neglect that can cause projections to go awry. It would seem, rather, that our mechanical projections should be tempered by the valuable insights to be gained through observation, and by whatever forecasts of economic, social, and demographic change our other models lead us to expect.

12.3 PROJECTIONS OF LABOR "REQUIREMENTS"

The demand for labor is a derived demand. It depends on both the demand for the various products and services that the labor produces, and the technological conditions—that is, the production function—upon which the production of these goods and services is based. An economy's overall labor *requirements* will therefore depend, on the one hand, on consumer and industrial demands, the policy makers' goals insofar as these effect or inhibit demands for goods and services, and the existing technology, and, on the other hand, on the supply of labor and the other factors of production. That is, decisions reached with respect to "how much labor to employ" will ordinarily depend on technology and prices, as well as on the relative costs of the various factors of production. Projections of labor "requirements" rest on the assumptions that one makes about each of these influential ingredients.

Technical projections of labor demand are usually made by sectors of economic activity, occupations and skills, and the levels and type of training. The first two kinds of projections—and particularly the projections by occupations and skills—which are usually short term, are useful for employment policy; the last type of projections, long term in nature, is most useful for educational policy.

The definitions of "jobs" and "occupations" used in population censuses vary from country to country, and markedly so according to levels of development. As a U.N. study notes,[9] not all jobs are full-time jobs, and some workers holding full-time jobs are in fact "underemployed." In the United States, for instance, the complex concepts of employment and underemployment refer to workers employed during the year *more* or *less* than fifteen weeks, respectively, *and* earning *more* or *less* than $3000, respectively. In most LDC's the concept of underemployment is usually applied to agriculture, where often as much as one-half of the labor force is not employed full time. The concept of underemployment could be extended in both MDC's and LDC's alike to industries where working hours are extremely short.

Lange, whose orientation one must recall is in the Marxist tradition, has suggested the following approach to viewing "underdevelopment:[10] Letting c and w denote the stock of capital goods and the wage bill, the organic composi-

[9] *Methods for Population Projections by Sex and Age, op. cit.*, p. 45.
[10] O. Lange "Some Problems Concerning Economic Planning in Underdeveloped Countries," in his *Papers in Economics and Sociology 1930–1960* (Oxford: Pergamon Press, 1970), pp. 171–179.

tion of capital, or the average degree of capital intensity, is defined as $k = c/w$. With W equal to the average wage rate and N equal to total employment, $w = WN$, so that $N = w/W = c/kW$. Then, if N_0 is the population of working age, the ratio $N/N_0 = c/kWN_0$ is the "measure of underdevelopment," and an underdeveloped economy is one in which total employment falls short of the total population that is of working age; or, one in which $c/kWN_0 < 1$.

In actuality, the labor problem in LDC's cannot be identified just with an unemployment problem; genuine unemployment occurs in LDC's only among those *seeking nonagricultural* jobs. As David Turnham and others have noted, we might expect *unemployment* "to be a more accurate reflection of the state of the labor market in countries and areas where the structure of the labor markets is more developed." [11] Although rates of unemployment are often extraordinarily high in the LDC's, what is probably *more* important, there is "the situation of employed groups who earn and consume very little because their productivity is so low." [12] Since the concepts of employment and underemployment are so difficult to apply to LDC's, constructs such as activity rates and unemployment rates (that is, the ratio of those seeking work to those at work) "are highly sensitive to seemingly trivial and arbitrary differences in measurement procedures." [13]

The projection methods most in use are the various correlation techniques, including simple least-squares trend fitting as well as more advanced econometric models, and particular analytical methods. In the simplest of these procedures, correlations are obtained between expected future population trends, per capita income and employment, aggregated and by sector, and then used via ordinary least-squares estimating procedures. The econometric approach usually involves utilization of models of *employment structures* in countries with comparable or higher per capita income rates, under the assumption that as higher per capita income rates are reached, a *corresponding* employment structure necessarily obtains. Finally, the analytical methods involve mostly fixed labor coefficients per unit of output, and input-output matrices. One of the best known applications of the fixed coefficients methods to manpower requirement projections (MRP) was proposed by H. S. Parnes.[14] This procedure forecasts manpower requirements in *all* occupations, and then translates these forecasts into educational requirements.

In Parnes' approach, the total manpower employed in occupation i, $L_{i\cdot}$, is given by the sum of employment in that occupation for all industries j; or, $L_{i\cdot} = \sum_j L_{ij}$ where L_{ij} is employment in occupation i and industry j. Denoting the rate of output in industry j by Y_j, and employment in industry j by $L_{\cdot j}$, or $L_{\cdot j} = \sum_i L_{ij}$, by definition

[11] D. Turnham and I. Jaeger, *The Employment Problem in Less Developed Countries: A Review of Evidence* (Paris: OECD, 1971), p. 15.

[12] *Ibid.*, p. 15.

[13] *Ibid.*, p. 15.

[14] H. Parnes, *Forecasting Educational Needs for Economic and Social Development* (Paris: OECD, 1962).

$$1 = \frac{L_{.j}}{L_{.j}} \frac{Y_j}{Y_j} = \frac{L_{.j}}{Y_j} \frac{1}{L_{.j}} Y_j$$

Therefore we can write $L_{i.} = (\sum_j L_{ij})[(L_{.j} \backslash Y_j)(1/L_{.j})(Y_j)]$; or,

$$L_{i.} = \sum_j (\frac{L_{ij}}{L_{.j}})(\frac{L_{.j}}{Y_j})Y_j \tag{12.2}$$

The first term in the sum, $L_{ij}/L_{.j}$, describes the "occupational structure" of industry j; the second term, $L_{.j}/Y_j$, describes "labor productivity" in industry j. Forecasts of manpower requirements, $\hat{L}_{i.}$, are then obtained by making projections of the three individual components, including output, Y_j.

As a further extension, let $L_{i \cdot k} = \sum_j L_{ijk}$ denote manpower in a given occupation with an education of level k, and let $L_{\cdot \cdot k} = \sum_i \sum_j L_{ijk}$ denote total manpower with an education at level k. Then we can write

$$L_{\cdot \cdot k} = \sum_i L_{i \cdot k} = \sum_i (\frac{L_{i \cdot k}}{L_{i.}})L_{i.} \tag{12.3}$$

where $L_{i \cdot k}/L_{i.}$ is the proportion of manpower in occupation i with an education at level k. Again, projecting this coefficient, and then combining this projection with the projection for $L_{i.}$ permits a projection of the educational requirements.

In the Soviet Union, a key element in the estimation of the "demand" for skilled labor is a survey by enterprises. The survey is as much concerned with the control of the prospective appointees as it is with the filling of the specific jobs involved. To start with, the central authorities establish a "classified list of jobs" on the basis of the estimated requirements of each enterprise for each of the years of the so-called "perspective" (5 years) plan. The enterprises formulate these requirements on the basis of the projections of output, productivity, and employment for the plan period, and specify their needs in accordance with a detailed "nomenclature" of positions established by the central authorities spelling out the required qualifications for each job. The operational managers tend to overstate their total requirements, while the executive managers tend to understate them. The estimates are finally adjusted at the national level; the actual provision of jobs thus ensures a centralized control on both the job openings and those that fill them.

Projections of labor availability and labor requirements must eventually be compared in order to determine whether the country will have full employment, a labor shortage, or future unemployment problems. Such comparisons raise obvious difficulties since, as stated, the methods involved in these projections vary, the quality of the projections is uneven, and finally, the results are not necessarily consistent. Additionally, difficulties arise because of the possibility of migratory movements, whether desirable or not. Lastly, difficulties arise because significant shifts in labor demand—upward or downward—change the activity rates among various segments of a country's labor force.

Crucial elements in the determination of labor demand, and in the comparison of labor supply and demand projections, are hypotheses about the pace of work during work hours, and the future course of *work hours*—that is, the average weekly hours of full-time and part-time workers—and their probable impact on output and growth rates. As suggested by Edward F. Denison,[15] as the length of the workweek and workyear are shortened, the offset in greater labor efficiency may (in the most advanced countries) progressively decline, and at an increasing rate. Few investigations have been made thus far on the possible impact of different *work patterns* in different industries—that is, of the various possible combinations of daily hours and days, or half-days of work, with varying arrangements for holidays and occasional long weekends. The Centre de Recherches Mathematiques pour la Planification (CERMAP) has, however, constructed a special model for the preparation of the Fifth French Plan, focused on the study of the impact of variations in worktime.

The model divides the economy into twelve major sectors of varying scope, from agriculture, and transportation and communications, to chemistry, textiles, and other services. For each sector there are structural equations describing (1) the necessary twelve sectoral equilibria between output and inputs, (2) the twelve technical restrictions imposed by capacity limitations on production, (3) the forty-eight constraints imposed by the scarcity of each of three factors of production, as well as labor scarcity, and (4) twelve intersectoral labor migration patterns. Additionally, (5) there are two supplementary relations placing (a) an upper limit on total migration, and (b) allowing for the overall growth in the population.

The policy problem attacked by the model is to maximize, for a two-period time horizon, a linear combination of present and future consumption, and present value added, appropriately discounted, with physical production, investment, and consumption as the decision variables. Through simulation, and by altering the assumptions made with respect to what constitutes an average workweek, the model can be used to illustrate the consequences of reductions in worktime on consumption, and in growth rates, on factor substitution, modernization of techniques, workers' migration, and on specified other elements.

In fact, in any sophisticated economy there are several specialized employment markets with only limited "mobility" from one to the other. An interesting approach to forecasting might thus be to combine a sector perspective with the Markov model. Indeed, there is no particular reason why *any* of these approaches need be considered in isolation from the others.

12.4 PLANNING THE "EDUCATIONAL" COMPONENT

A particularly significant kind of national manpower planning is educational planning. A variety of educational planning models exist, the most interesting of which are discussed in some detail by Russell Davis,[16] a discussion that we

---

[15] *Why Growth Rates Differ*, pp. 59 ff. and 109 ff.

[16] R. C. Davis, *Planning Human Resource Development: Educational Models and Schemata* (Chicago: Rand McNally, 1966).

shall only sketch out here. In all of these models, however, the emphasis is on the educational *requirements* imposed by a given structural framework, and a set of production targets and resultant labor demands. The closely related issue of how education affects labor productivity, or more specifically, determination of the precise role in the production function of kth-level educated labor as an *individual* factor of production, and determination of, for example, the elasticities of substitution between these various labor factors, is only now being attacked with any vigor. Yet, to effectively handle *all* educational planning issues, these two sides to the matter should be dealt with simultaneously. Unfortunately, attempts to probe the "other side" of the educational coin have been couched in a foundation of classical economics in which factors are assumed to be paid a wage equal to the value of their marginal products. It is not a foundation that holds up well in a world that is not purely competitive.

To the extent that education is an investment in *human* capital, educational planning is akin to investment planning in general, and can be attacked within either a consistency or an optimizing framework. As is true of investment in general, among the considerations that can enter into a planning model are the resources that are available, the timing of the inputs and the outputs or services received, the anticipated costs incurred and "profits" yielded, and the underlying production relationships. Additionally, however, and uniquely, there may exist—and indeed does exist—a cultural aspect to the educational planning issue which arises because even in the most primitive societies education is considered to be a *right*, with only the minimum *level* at which persons are *entitled* to an education differing among societies.

Within a simple theoretical framework, then, the educational planning problem could be expressed as a mathematical programming problem:

$$\text{Maximize} \qquad Z = \mu(x_1, \ldots, x_n) \qquad \qquad (9.4a)$$

$$\text{subject to } g_i(x_1, \ldots, x_n, b_i) \geq 0 \qquad i = 1, \ldots, m \qquad (9.4b)$$

$$x_j \geq 0 \qquad j = 1, \ldots, n \qquad (9.4c)$$

Here, the objective function is, say, a utility function whose arguments, the x_j, are the number of persons whose terminal education will be at the jth level ($j = 1, \ldots, n$) at some given point in time. If the rate of return from an education at level j is r_j, the objective function might become $Z = \Sigma r_j x_j$; if the cost of educating an individual until the jth level is c_j, the objective might be to minimize $Z = \Sigma c_j x_j$. Such formulations, assuredly, assume that society does not receive any "externality" benefits from education—which is not likely to be the case.

Among the constraints to be recognized is $\Sigma x_j = X$, where X is the total population educated to at least level 1. Similarly, if a_{kj} is the amount of resource k required to provide an individual with an education to level j, where, for example, resource k might represent *existing* educational facilities in terms of classrooms, seats, libraries, and the like, the kth constraint could be written

$\Sigma a_{kj}x_j \leq b_k$, where b_k is the amount available of resource k. Where *at least* $J_l > 0$ individuals educated at the jth level are *required* by the system's technological needs, but no more than J_u individuals with exactly the jth level of training can be employed so as to make full use of their education, one might further demand that $J_l \leq x_j \leq J_u$. In principle, dynamic extensions of such mathematical programming models are also possible, although in practice they may be unsolvable. Similarly, the data inputs required by even the simplest models may be unavailable, and the assumptions necessary to make such models mathematically tractable—such as linearity assumptions—may be so at variance with the empirical facts as to invalidate the models' implications.

A less mathematically complex approach to the problem of educational planning would simply *specify* a priori certain educational goals, and then seek to determine what society must do to accomplish these goals.

Suppose, for example, that the policy makers want to assure the opportunity of a primary education to all persons of primary school age, over the next T years. Suppose, too, that primary school consists of J grades. Data would presumably be available on the number of students, X_{0j}, *currently* enrolled in the jth grade $(j = 1, \ldots, J)$. Similarly, one could project, on the basis of population projections, the number of new entrants to the school system, X_{t0}, at time t.

In addition, assessments might be made of the *probability* that a student in level j will succeed to level $j + 1$, where level $J + 1$ implies leaving the school system, either by dropping out or matriculation. Let us assume these assessments are fixed over time and are summarized in the $(J + 1) \times (J + 1)$ transition probability matrix $P = [p_{jk}]$ where p_{jk} is the probability that a pupil at level j will succeed to level k "next year." If only a one-grade promotion were possible, and all students stayed in school and were promoted, $p_{j,\,j+1} = 1$ and $p_{jk} = 0$ for $k \neq j + 1$ so that

$$
P = \begin{array}{c}
\\ 1 \\ 2 \\ \vdots \\ J \\ J+1
\end{array}
\begin{array}{c}
\begin{array}{ccccccc} 1 & 2 & \cdot & \cdots & \cdot & J & J+1 \end{array} \\
\left[\begin{array}{ccccccc}
0 & 1 & 0 & \cdots & 0 & 0 & 0 \\
0 & 0 & 1 & \cdots & 0 & 0 & 0 \\
\vdots & & & & & & \vdots \\
0 & 0 & 0 & \cdots & 0 & 0 & 1 \\
0 & 0 & 0 & \cdots & 0 & 0 & 1
\end{array} \right]
\end{array}
$$

Hence, given the column vector $X_0 = (X_{01}, \ldots, X_{0J}, X_{0J+1})$ the column vector $PX_0 = X_0^1$ would give the number of persons enrolled at level j (or out of school, in level $J + 1$) at time 1 who were of at least primary school age at time 0.

Now, given X_{10} new entrants to the school system at time 1, $X_0^1 + (X_{10}, 0, \ldots, 0) = X_1$ is the vector of school age or older persons enrolled or matriculated at time 1, and $PX_1 = X_1^2$ gives the number of such persons enrolled at level j (or matriculated) at time 2 who were of at least primary school age at time 1.

This procedure can be repeated so as to obtain an entire time series of enrollments at each level over the next T years. Given various cost factors for educating pupils at each level, factors relating to, say, books, facilities, and teachers, the annual cost of providing an opportunity for education to all persons can be determined—again in *principle*. Unfortunately, however, even in this simplified model these costs are necessarily based on population projections, assumptions about the education-seeking bent of the population, and transition probabilities whose reliability, particularly over time, must be open to serious question.

Perhaps the most interesting approach is that of the Correa-Tinbergen-Bos models.[17] These *assume* both intertemporal shifts in the population between educational levels and the work force, and also *fixed* production relationships between education and output.

In particular, with superscripts indexing education level and subscripts indexing time, two levels of education, secondary $= 2$ and tertiary $= 3$, are considered. The labor force with second and third levels of education at time t is denoted by N_t^2 and N_t^3, respectively. The number of persons *joining* the work force at time t who have second and third levels of education is denoted by M_t^2 and M_t^3, respectively, and the number of *enrollees* at these levels at time $t - 1$ who join the work force at time t is denoted e_t^2 and e_t^3, respectively. Hence given by *assumption* that all persons educated at level 3 join the work force after spending the previous period enrolled at level 3, so that among other things, they are not adversely influenced by the mortality tables,

$$M_t^3 = e_{t-1}^3 \tag{9.5a}$$

and

$$M_t^2 = e_{t-1}^2 - e_t^3 \tag{9.5b}$$

Still further, with λ^2 and λ^3 the proportion of persons with secondary and tertiary-level educations, respectively, who leave the work force, are

$$N_t^2 = (1 - \lambda^2)N_{t-1}^2 + M_t^2 \tag{9.5c}$$

and

$$N_t^3 = (1 - \lambda^3)N_{t-1}^3 + M_t^3 \tag{9.5d}$$

where Equations (9.5a)–(9.5d) hold by definition and assumption. With respect to (9.5d), for example, the work force with tertiary-level education at time t, N_t^3, equals the number of persons with that level of education previously in the work force who remain in the work force, $(1 - \lambda^3)N_{t-1}^3$, plus the number of new entrants to the work force who have a third-level education, M_t^3.

Equations (9.5a)–(9.5d) are basically nonobjectionable, since they are definitional and hinge only upon the specification of the time period, the fairly harmless assumptions, and the measure of education level. The model includes, however, two additional equations that are less easily digested.

[17] *Op. cit.*

First, it is assumed that the number of workers with a secondary education will be proportional to the rate of output, Q_t, or

$$N_t^2 = \alpha^2 Q_t \qquad (9.5e)$$

where α^2 is the factor of proportionality, and with workers with a secondary education employed *only* in production of output, Q_t.

Second, it is assumed that the number of workers with a tertiary-level education who are employed in production is proportional to the rate of output, while the remainder teach at both levels, in proportion to the number of students enrolled at these levels, or

$$N_t^3 = \alpha^3 Q_t + \beta^2 e_t^2 + \beta^3 e_t^3 \qquad (9.5f)$$

where α^3, β^2, and β^3 are factors of proportionality.

Given values for the parameters, the λ's, α's, and β's, and given a set of initial values for the e's, N's, and M's, and Q, the path of output, education and educational structure of the labor force can be traced. The results can then be utilized in two fundamental ways. First, they can provide the planner with output and education *projections* that can be employed in determining future educational resource needs and future economic potential. Second, they indicate how the economic system will behave *if left unaltered,* and to the extent that the parameters can be varied or the structure of the system altered, they provide a means for testing alternative policies in order to assess their effects on the system. Thus, for example, the labor force with a tertiary-level education could be enhanced through migration, and if policies that encourage immigration of educated persons can be effected, the government could in fact increase N_t^3. The effects of such policies could be traced and analyzed through the model. Indeed, each of the equations could be modified to suit the specific structure of the educational system, and the role that the government plays or can play in it. As previously hinted, however, the model ignores the possibility of factor substitutability with respect to education level, and this neglect simply cannot be justified.

12.5 CONCLUDING COMMENTS

Manpower planning entails a series of demographic projections with respect to (a) the size, structure, and distribution of the population, (b) the proportion of the population joining the labor force and becoming part of labor supply, and (c) technical sophistication of the labor force as reflected in the varied educational backgrounds of its members, as well as the demands for labor having varying educational backgrounds and technical skills. The size and disparate skills of the labor force is especially important insofar as these affect the capacity for economic growth and, to the extent that greater skills tend to be reflected in greater earning power, the distribution of economic wealth. Thus, public policy, particularly with respect to growth aspirations and income distribution considerations, must necessarily concern itself with educational planning, manpower training, and cultural attitudes toward work.

On the one hand, technicians can provide planners with projections that enable the determination of, say, the educational facilities that will have to be provided at future points in time if the economy is to maintain its projected growth path. On the other hand, econometric and mathematical programming models can be used to indicate the various manpower-related factors that contribute to, or inhibit economic growth and income equality, and can thereby indicate to the planners directions in which manpower and education policies can and should proceed so as to make developments in the manpower sector compatible with those in the other components of the economic system.

What this seems to suggest is that the human resource sector, as a separate but equal component of the economic system, must be included as an integral part of any national economic planning model. Manpower and education affect, and are in turn affected by, the overall developments in the economy, and it is therefore incumbent upon the economic managers that they fully understand the implications of their acts for these very important elements.

CHAPTER 13

Planning of Industrial Activities

13.1 PROBLEMS OF INDUSTRIAL PLANNING

Any consistent strategy of development involves well integrated policy decisions on (a) the nature and extent of government interference with consumer choice, (b) measures for channeling savings, (c) the scope of international trade, and (d) on the interrelations among major production sectors and major industrial branches. The decisions on industry are crucial because industry commands a web of key economic interrelations, and because industry performs multiple functions in the economy: providing diversified employment opportunities, satisfying demands for a variety of manufactured goods, contributing to national defense, affecting the balance of payments, and raising the level of economic efficiency. But, even when *no unified strategy* is formulated, when no consistent integration of policies is aimed at, and when the market interplays with more or less haphazard policy choices and regulations, decisions concerning industry are bound to have complexly ramified and long-lasting effects because of the centrality of this sector in the modern economy.

The special significance of the industrial sector derives from the fact that it comprises a subsystem of the economic system which is *directly* linked to virtually all other subsystems as well as to the environment. One of these linkages is to the government which even in the West tends to be *directly* involved in industrial activities through its taxation and spending policies as well as via direct controls—rules and regulations—that impinge upon the free market system.

The industrial sector accepts exogenous and endogenous inputs from the components and subsystems to which it is coupled, and sends to them *crucial* endogenous outputs. The individual components of this subsystem are the firms or plants in the economic system, which themselves can be combined into industries as yet further individual subsystems. The transformation functions of

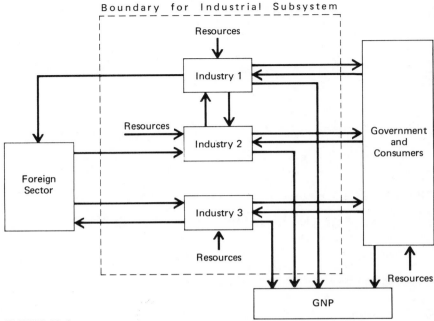

FIGURE 13-1

these components are the plant, firm, or industry production functions, whose operations are guided by managerial decision-making processes. Thus, as seen in Figure 13.1, the decision-making units receive either (a) demand-and-supply *information,* or (b) direct instructions that determine output decisions, and these decisions in turn involve labor, material, and investment decisions. Each industrial component, for example, can be thought of as receiving *input information* in the form of (1) product *demands* from the government, (2) factor *supply data* from labor, raw material sources, other industrial components, and the component's production function, and (3) institutional restrictions that impose constraints on the individual firms and industries, and reduce the feasible set of activities and their rates from which the microeconomic managers can choose. The information is processed, and ultimately the component receives as inputs labor services, raw materials, and industrial products that it subsequently transforms into outputs that may be sent to the government, foreign sectors in the environment, consumers, and other industrial components. Moreover, each industrial component might, in the normal course of events, undertake research and development activity beyond that undertaken by the government or other nonindustrial components, and such activity could result in either (i) an *alteration* in existing transformation functions, or (ii) the *creation* of entirely new transformation functions, or, indeed, new components. And, clearly, the web of interrelationships is so great that such changes could have profound implications for other industrial and nonindustrial components and subsystems.

Because industry is the only sector of a modern economy that can have the capacity to change itself and to change all the other sectors as well, the planning literature contains numerous and often conflicting recommendations as to which industrial strategy a developing country should adopt. Typical in this respect are, for instance, the traditional Soviet emphasis on heavy industry, and certain Western theories emphasizing the special role of (a) "modern industries" (for example, the theory of François Perroux [1]), (b) varying import-substituting industries, or (c) the significance of developing the forward and backward industrial linkages. Suggestions are further made, for example, on the basis of (i) the specific experience of this or that country, (ii) the developmental "spread-effect" of this or that branch, and (iii) empirical observations of the inter-sector relations obtaining at various rates of national product. Although all too often ignored, it is apparent, however, that no clear-cut *uniform* policy can be evolved for countries of different sizes, different factor endowments, different levels of development, and different cultural, social, and political backgrounds.

Moreover, not only do stages of industrialization and backgrounds differ, but so also do the prospects of each given country for further development, as well its policy makers' *appraisal* of these prospects. The concepts of the policy makers as to what is both desirable and possible may mix in a wide variety of ways such objectives as (a) rapid overall industrial growth, (b) broadening the range of certain types of manufacturing outputs, and (c) achieving a variety of "balances," such as those between the public and private industrial sectors, the regional industrial sectors, the "modern" and the "traditional" sectors, and so forth.

In particular, industrialization involves the implementation of specific *projects*. In this respect, decisions are required as to (1) the *source* of the necessary equipment, (2) the *size* of the given project or program, (3) the *type* of *technology* involved, and (4) the eventual *location* site of the project. Trade and foreign-exchange policy play a decisive role in the shaping of the framework in which such programs are to be implemented. Import substitution may to start with require expanding supplies of capital goods and raw materials, and put increasing pressures on the balance of payments. The size and duration of the ensuing balance-of-payments deficits may in turn put severe brakes on further rapid development. Countries at high levels of development may easily interchange and/or adapt to their needs the equipment or machines produced by other highly developed countries, while the assimilation of new techniques may prove complex and difficult when countries at dissimilar levels of development are involved. The technologies suited for MDC's may not be, and often are not suitable for LDC's in terms of plant size, factor proportions, or the methods or techniques governing their operations. All of these problems involve choices, often at the highest policy-making level, and require a wide variety of measures for ensuring that their application is in agreement with the decisions taken.

[1] F. Perroux, "Les industries motrices et la planification de la croissance d'une économie nationale," in *On Political Economy and Econometrics* (London: Pergamon Press, 1965), pp. 463–497.

Industrial development and industrial programs may be, and usually are evaluated by a variety of criteria concerning resources used, contributions made to the growth of GNP, balance-of-payments problems, employment rates, and so on. Less frequently considered, and more difficult to assess, is the *quality* of the goods produced. Yet, product quality may have a crucial and widely dispersed impact, not only on the types and range of the domestic consumption of manufactured goods in general, but also on the conditions for *further expansion*, and for eventual *competition* on foreign markets. Lower quality of equipment produced in certain socialist or LDC countries emphasizing strategies of "autarkic" industrialization may ultimately *handicap* real growth by ensuring further expansion, but only with low-quality equipment that may already be obsolete even when "new," or with equipment that falls below international standards. The question of quality of output thus cannot be divorced either from strategy choice, or from its long-term implications and consequences.

In this chapter we shall first consider the examination of models and recommendations for industrial strategy choice; secondly, the presentation of models and recommendations concerning program integration and project choice; thirdly, the question of quality and its connection to growth and industrial "size"; and, finally, we shall present some concluding comments on the overall problems of industrial growth in the MDC's versus the LDC's. As we shall see, planning in industry, as in the other sectors or subsystems, calls into play a variety of models to which we have already been exposed, including allocation, routing, and dynamic models, but in new and challenging mixes. And, as is also true of the models for the other sectors, here too we run into two distinctly different concerns: (1) optimality; and (2) consistency. In the first instance, planning is concerned with the determination of, for example, an *optimal* portfolio of industrial projects, given a set of desiderata, a systemic objective function, the internal constraints and boundary conditions inherent in the structure of the system, and the external constraints and boundary conditions imposed by the controller, the environment, and past decisions. In the second instance, planning is concerned with the development of *alternative* plans that are *consistent* with both the desiderata, or overall objectives, and the constraints and boundary conditions. Either orientation is compatible with one of the fundamental purposes of planning; that is, the *study* or analysis of the effects of specific *projects* on an overall program, or the effects of controller-initiated *policies* on system-wide objectives.

13.2 LINKAGES, PRIORITIES, AND RATES

a. Linkages

Before trying to assign to the industrial sector a definite role in any overall scheme of development, the policy makers must first visualize the potentials and the constraints under which this subsystem as such, and its individual components could and should operate. Additionally, they must assess a number of development alternatives: (a) the ways in which given changes in industry would affect the subsystem's overall performance; (b) the specific branches or components, which if developed with *priority* would exercise a decisive impact on the growth of other components and subsystems; (c) the "structural weaknesses" that should be corrected; and (d) the overall rates of growth that should be selected as targets. Assessment of these and similar alternatives, and formulation of definite policies requires appropriate studies of interindustry linkages, chains of causal development within and between industries, and comparisons with prevailing international patterns of industrial growth and development at various rates of per capita income.

The study of *interindustry linkages* involves first of all various classifications of industries according to importance of value added, importance of the dependence of a given industry on some critical material (steel, energy, chemicals) or on given imports, importance of interdustry demand in relation to total output, and so forth. Each of these factors can help guide the policy makers' choice under various assumptions. Such studies could then involve, for each component, various manipulations and refinements of the basic input-output approach, so as to assess the impact of, for example, increases in overall economic activity, or the emerging self-sufficiency of other nations that have heretofore been important customers in the export market, on *particular* components of the industrial subsystem.

From the basic input-output framework of Chapter 6, the solution for the vector of production rates by industry, q, can be derived in terms of the vector of final demands, Q, and the technological coefficients matrix A, as

$$q = (I - A)^{-1} Q \tag{13.1}$$

Unlike some of the planning models for the agricultural sector, which we shall introduce in the following chapter, those for the industrial sector *ordinarily* accept as *given* the production processes and choice of factor inputs at the *micro* level of the individual plant. The implication of what is in the main a *macro* orientation of industrial planning models is that the managers in the infimal decision-making units of the individual components of the industrial subsystem are sufficiently sophisticated as to arrive at optimal micro decisions, consistent with industry-wide relationships and the programs initiated for this subsystem as a whole. Conversely, the implication is that the individual farmer can benefit from and, irrespective of the motivation, will be receptive to the suggestions and directives inputed to the agricultural subsystem from the controller. *Neither* implication is necessarily warranted, nor is herein being promoted. Each does, however, represent the *implicit* views of the model-builders.

From the input-output relationships and Equation (13.1), one can then forecast, by industrial branch, the rate of production that will be required as a result of, say, various changes in the *overall* rate of final demand, with the distribution of final demands unaltered; or, that required by changes in the final demands of *individual* sectors. Additionally, one can forecast the impact of such variations on import requirements, as well as labor and raw material requirements. Such forecasts can help to call attention to particular branches that might act as bottlenecks to future economic growth, and thus single out areas to which the economic managers should seek to divert or encourage capital investment, as well as, perhaps, manpower programs. In the latter respect, a prime consideration for both industrial and agricultural planning is the *future* division of the labor force between the two sectors, as well as the overall availability of labor. This consideration demands the projection of future populations, by sector and in total, so as to permit the institution of manpower programs that will effect the necessary labor forces consistent with system and subsystem plans, in the event that these labor requirements would not otherwise be met.

In terms of Figure 13.1, a vector of final demands, Q, is inputed into the industrial subsystem, and the *decision* to generate a vector of outputs q is *automatically* reached for the individual components through the technological qua decision-making process of Equation (13.1). Then, various interindustry exchanges, as well as import, labor, and raw material demands on the part of each industrial component are *automatically* determined commensurate with the decision to produce q. Policy makers can then compare these demands, say, with the projected supplies and capacities, to determine whether the final demands are in fact achievable under existing or projected circumstances, and, if not, why not and what steps might be taken so as to achieve them.

An interesting variant of the above framework, which is applicable when the economy is logically divisible into "clusters" or subsystems of industries, say as in the case of a less developed nation that might consist of both a traditional agricultural sector and a modern industrial sector, is due to Ghosh.[2] This approach seeks to partition the technological coefficients matrix in accordance with these sectoral clusters. In a two-sector economy this partitioning would appear as follows:

$$A = \begin{bmatrix} A_{ij} & A_{ik} \\ A_{kj} & A_{kl} \end{bmatrix} \quad \text{where } i, j = 1, \ldots, r; \quad k, l = r+1, \ldots, s \quad (13.2)$$

Under the least realistic, although perhaps the most useful assumption of complete independence between the two sectors—that consisting of industries 1 through r, and that consisting of industries $r + 1$ through s—we would have $A_{ik} = A_{kj} = O$. This is the situation depicted in Figure 13.1 where industries i, $j = 1, 2 = r$ form a single sector that is not directly linked to industry k, $l = 3 = s$.

In such a two-sector economy, with the first r elements of q and Q contained in the vectors q_r and Q_r, the sector containing industries 1 through r can be analyzed via the system $A_{ij}q_r = Q_r$, with the remaining industries analyzed via the analogously defined system $A_{kl}q_s = Q_s$. In effect, the impact of change can be studied by focusing on the individual sectors, with examination of the sector of particular interest and concern greatly simplified, if only because the computations are simpler. The more detailed study of the interrelationships

[2] A. Ghosh, "Input-Output Analysis with Substantially Independent Groups of Industries," *Econometrica*, Vol. 28, No. 1, January 1960.

within that sector is then undertaken to the possible neglect of the other sector. Thus, an increase in export demand in Figure 13.1 will affect both sectors, but the particular direct effects on industrial component 3 where, say, capacity might be severely limited, can be studied without considering the impact on the other components.

A second important and useful modification can be made when the output rate of one sector can be assumed to be proportional to that of another sector. In the present instance, for example, the historical pattern might reveal that $i'q_r = \alpha i'q_s$, where $i' = (1, 1, \ldots, 1, 1)$ is the sum vector, and α is the constant of proportionality. Then, if the sector consisting of industries $r + 1$ through s is the prime mover in the economy, the impact on these industries of changes in Q_s can be analyzed through the subsystem $A_{kl}q_s = Q_s$; and the rate of production that these changes would imply for the other sector would be immediately determined from the proportionality relationship. In either case, the analysis of industrial components is simplified through clustering and partitioning that permits the *detailed* study of particular sets of components or subsystems of primary interest and concern, without having to perform the more extensive computations and analysis necessitated by the study of the entire economic system and each of the industrial subsystems.

Tinbergen [3] has suggested input-output variants along similar lines. In particular, his so-called semi-input-output method describes a system under which some specified interrelationships simply cannot obtain. A typical example would be the case of a sector or component that is prevented by law or custom from exporting its products. In this case, changes in the rate of international economic activity can be analyzed by first studying the impact on the sectors that do in fact export, and second, considering the effects of the latter impact on the nonexporting industries. In addition, certain sectors might be constrained in their production rate because of capacity limitations, and these too can be incorporated into the analysis. Again, precisely the same sort of thing can be done with respect to individual industries. The advantage of the sector approach is that it focuses attention on aggregate problems and broad areas of concern, as well as simplifies the necessary computations. It thereby permits greater efforts to be devoted to the particular problem areas that are singled out for attention.

Still another dimension can be added to the approach by making the technological coefficients matrix time dependent, and introducing outputs that effect increases in the capital stock. This approach thus allows for both technological change, in the former instance, and capacity changes, in the latter.[4] These variations make the static input-output model more realistic, insofar as they introduce dynamic elements that are indeed present in the real world. At the same time, however, they make the model considerably more complex and

---

[3] J. Tinbergen, *The Appraisal of Investment Projects* (Rotterdam: Netherlands Economic Institute, 1964).

[4] See W. Leontief, "The Dynamic Inverse," in A. P. Carter and A. Brody (eds.) *Contributions to Input-Output Analysis* (Amsterdam: North-Holland, 1970), pp. 17–45.

more demanding in terms of data requirements. From a practical standpoint, the trade-off is not necessarily worth accepting.

b. Priorities and recursiveness

Interindustry linkage studies disclose the likely shifts in interindustry demands, import demands, and final demands which various output changes may entail. Other decisive elements are then necessarily called into play in order to determine policy choice. Such elements are not only the *goals* of the developmental effort, but also *evaluations* and *opinions* concerning the industries that are likely to generate a continuous and self-sustaining process of structural change, the industries that are likely to pull the entire economy along with them—and at a faster pace—and, further, the industries that *must* be developed first in order that other industries *may* be developed later on. Judgmental elements involve, as always, diverging views about the data, and often outright biases in favor of a given industry, or group of industries. The purpose of the analysis is, in a sense, to limit the scope of such biases.

The Soviet approach to industrial development formulated as far back as 1928 by Stalin, directed that the Soviet policy should "proceed from the premise that a fast rate of development of *industry in general* and of the *means of production in particular* is the underlying principle of, and the key to, the transformation of the entire national economy." [5] This fast rate involves—according to what is by now accepted Soviet doctrine—"maximum capital investment in industry," along with the development of a set of specific "leading-link" industries, namely energy, steel, and machine tools. It is the emphasis on "maximum capital investment in industry" and the skewed allocation of these investments within industry itself in favor of "producers' goods industries," and then within the latter in favor of the "leading links," that has become known as the "Soviet method of industrialization"—a method that is *alleged* by the Russians to have "universal validity."

Much has been written about the Soviet emphasis on "producers' goods industries." One of the earliest Soviet growth models, that of G. A. Fel'dman, which we have already mentioned, specifically divides the industrial subsystem into two further subsystems, or sectors: one encompassing all capacity-expanding activities, the second encompassing all the other activities necessary for sustaining the current output rates. The decision variable for Fel'dman is, as in the subsequent germane models of Mahalanobis and Kalecki in particular, the allocation of the output of the capacity-expanding sector between the two sectors. The actual "Soviet model" of industrialization has often been criticized both for its implied need to raise the accumulation rate, and for its underlying "law" of the priority growth of producers' versus consumers' goods industries. The critics have centered their arguments on the possibility of increasing investment either by changing the ways in which some equipment is used, or through

[5] J. Stalin, "Industrialization of the Country and the Right Deviation," in *Foundations of Soviet Strategy for Economic Growth,* Selected Soviet Essays 1924–1930, N. Spulber (ed.) (Bloomington: Indiana University Press, 1964), p. 226.

foreign trade.[6] The "leading-links" options have, in contrast, been character-ized as ad hoc choices of the policy-making establishment bent on developing a heavy-industry base for large-scale domestic armaments, rather than as accept-able "universal" foundations of industrialization.

In 1965, the French economist François Perroux [7] drew attention to the fact that for the MDC's, for any given period, an industrial subsystem can be subdivided into three other subsystems whose components are industries with an *increasing* growth rate, industries with a *medium* growth rate, and industries with a *decreasing* growth rate. Within the first two groups he ranges all the "growth industries" identified with the "modern and entirely modern" indus-tries gaining an increasing share in the total industrial output. Among "mod-ern" industries he includes those that have gained ascendency in the first de-cade before World War I, such as electricity, chemistry, cars, oil, mechanical industries, and the like. In the "entirely new" industries he includes the indus-tries that have developed during the past fifteen or twenty years, such as nu-cleonics, electronics, plastics, aerospace, and the like. These are, in effect, the industries that presuppose the modern industries and that at the same time trans-form them. Within this framework, and with the help of a two-sector model delineating two subsystems, the growth industries and all other industries, Per-roux attempts to clarify the "pull effect" (*effet d'entraînement*) exercised by the growth industries on the entire industrial subsystem.

Perroux's *formal* model is actually quite simplistic. The output growth in the "entirely new" industries is assumed to exceed that in the "modern" in-dustries. The only explicit link between these two subsystems is that the rate of growth of one is assumed to be a constant multiple of the other. This difference in the rates is affected by either of two factors: a higher rate of investment, given equal productivity of capital between the two sectors, or a higher produc-tivity of capital, given equal rates of investment. Clearly, both a greater rate of investment *and* a higher productivity of capital will lead to a greater rate of growth in output.

The overall growth in the economy will be determined by the growth in both sectors, and irrespective of their initial positions, the faster growing indus-tries must ultimately overtake and dominate the lesser growing industries, in terms of their relative positions in the economy. In effect, it is the growth in-dustries that change the character of the economy and that, presumably, and in some unspecified fashion, provide the economic stimulus that carries over to the other industries as well. What this suggests, then, is that when the free market system fails to provide the inventive and innovative activity that un-derlies the "entirely new industries," or when entrepreneurs lack the ability to invest, or fail to perceive profitable investment opportunities, it may be the re-sponsibility of the government to fill this role, or at a minimum to institute policies that encourage such activities. The economy, as Perroux notes, cannot

[6] M. Kalecki, *Introduction to the Theory of Growth in a Socialist Economy* (Oxford: Blackwell, 1969), Chapter 11, "The Structure of Investment."
[7] *Op. cit.*

grow at a faster rate than that at which its most rapidly growing components grow. Thus, it is to these components that he suggests government planners should be directing their attention. The remaining components will then be carried along with the tide.

The question of the choice of *priority* development of given industrial branches can be approached not only by considering any presumed "structural weakness" of the economy, or any beneficial "pulling" effects of this or that industry, but also, more crudely, by considering the need to remove any kind of so-called "limitation to growth," whether it be due to domestic or to foreign trade difficulties. The whole literature on import substitution and "dynamic comparative advantage" could be introduced in this connection, but we shall, regretfully, refrain from the temptation to do so. Rather, an entirely different approach in this respect is suggested by the *recursive* models of industrial development. These draw attention to the facts that (a) all planning decisions depend on decisions already executed, and that, accordingly, (b) a realistic plan is a continuously "rolling" plan—that is, one that *continuously* takes account of decisions already implemented.

In particular, recursive programming models have been developed that incorporate forecast data and exogenous inputs, *together* with the outputs yielded by previous decisions, into a mathematical programming format within which current, and hence future decisions will be reached. In one such model, formulated by Day,[8] optimum output and investment rates in a given industry are determined by solving a linear programming problem. The *direct* inputs into the linear programming model are a set of cost factors, primary inputs supplied, planned production rates, capital stocks, and behavioral bounds on the rates of investment. But, for example, planned production rates depend on sales forecasts, and the latter in turn are made, perhaps through econometric models employing as independent variables actual sales rates in a previous period, exogenous demographic variables and current inventories. Current inventories, however, are the result of previous output decisions reached on the basis of previous linear programming solutions, as well as previous actual sales. Similarly, the capital stock levels that enter the current programming problem as inputs result from alterations in the capital stock that have occurred through previous solutions with respect to optimum rates of investment. Such recursive models are therefore *dynamic* models that call attention to the period-by-period requirements of each industry for, say, labor and other primary factors of production in order to effect the industry's planned rate of output and capacity growth over time. In terms of Figure 13.1, such models incorporate a feedback mechanism that accepts informational and physical outputs from the industrial subsystem, as well as other components, and feeds these back to the subsystem and selected components as either information or physical alterations.

---

[8] R. Day, "Recursive Programming Models of Industrial Development and Technological Change," in Carter and Brody, *op. cit.*, pp. 99–117.

c. Industrialization rates and inter-country comparisons

Strategy choices with respect to the *rate* of industrialization may be enlightened by appropriate inter-country comparisons. Such comparisons could allow the exploration of whether or not the rates chosen are arbitrary, and whether or not other, more realistic alternatives should be formulated.

The United Nations has utilized cross-section regression analysis in making such inter-country comparisons, with respect to both total manufacturing and thirteen individual manufacturing sectors.[9] The purpose of these analyses, which implicitly assume a common structure, was to determine whether, on the basis of a common set of exogenous independent variables, inter-country differences could be found in the projected rates of total manufacturing activity, say as measured by value added, or in the projected rates of manufacturing activity in the individual sectors. The rates, projected on the basis of the estimated regression equations, presumably represent the achievable rates of activity, as determined on the basis of those independent variables that have been found to exercise a *systematic* influence on the *actual* rates on a cross-section, cross-country basis. The extent to which the projected and the actual rates diverge is taken as an *indication* that artificial barriers to industrial activity may exist in those nations that are "under-achieving," which seemingly accounts for the appearance of "over-achievement" in those nations whose projected rates are above the average.

After considering such variables as rate of economic development, government policy, natural resources, trading position, and technological factors, as measured by various surrogate variables, standard statistical analysis revealed that only per capita income and population bore a *systematic* relationship to industrial activity. Subsequent analysis also revealed, however, that the "rate of industrialization," as measured by the extent to which *total* manufacturing activity exceeds or falls short of the projected rate also bore a statistical relationship in determining the rate of economic activity in the individual sectors.

In particular, denote by y_i and P_i per capita income and population, respectively, in the ith nation, and also denote by V_{0i} and V_{ji} value added in total manufacturing and in the jth sector, respectively, in country i. The first hypothesized cross-section relationship is

$$V_{0i} = \alpha_0 y_i^{\alpha_1} P_i^{\alpha_2} \gamma_i \tag{13.3a}$$

where α_k ($k = 0, 1, 2$) is a parameter to be estimated by simple regression, and γ_i is a random disturbance term that accounts for the *nonsystematic* disturbances in country i's value added in total manufacturing from the rates projected on the basis of the systematic relationship $\alpha_0 y_i^{\alpha_1} P_i^{\alpha_2}$. The regression procedure yields estimates a_k of α_k on the basis of which systematic projections of V_{0i} for given values of y_i and P_i can be determined. Then the *deviations* D_i

[9] United Nations, *A Study of Industrial Growth* (New York: United Nations, 1963).

can be determined as the differences between the actual and the projected V_{0i}. These differences are, in effect, deviations from a *conditional* average, conditional upon the values of y_i and P_i. This, under- or over-achievement in the present context is with respect to a statistical yardstick—the conditional average or regression plane.

The second hypothesized relationship is

$$V_{ji} = \beta_{0j} y_i^{\beta_{1j}} P_i^{\beta_{2j}} D_i^{\beta_{3j}} \theta_{ji} \qquad (13.3b)$$

where $\beta_{mj}(m = 0, \ldots, 3)$ is a parameter and θ_{ji} is a second random disturbance term that accounts for the variations of the V_{ji} from the rates projected on the basis of the systematic relationship $\beta_{0j} y_i^{\beta_{1j}} P_i^{\beta_{2j}} D_i^{\beta_{3j}}$. Again, then, one can determine the *deviations* between projected and actual values of V_{ji}. These indicate whether economic activity in a country and industry is below or above the international average—for particular values of per capita income and population, and rates of industrialization.

In addition, the multiplicative form of relationship means that the parameters α_1, α_2, β_{1j}, β_{2j}, and β_{3j} represent elasticities that indicate the relative change in the dependent variable, manufacturing activity, which will occur as a result of a given relative change in the associated independent variable. It is thus possible to project, on an inter-country basis, how exogenous changes in income and population, as well as industrialization, will affect manufacturing activity, in total and by sector.

13.3 PROJECTS AND INTERDEPENDENCIES

The choice of "priority" branches, the study of possible "causal chains" in industrial development, and the selection of some target growth rate, must be accompanied by the choice of *specific projects,* and by the exploration of their eventual interrelations at the firm and industry level with other production and expansion programs, and with the overall direction of development.

Frisch suggested that work should go on constantly in each country, with a view of bringing forth new projects, and that a variety of organizations, government and private, should be called upon to cooperate in this respect: "the extension and diversification of the total national list of projects is only a means of increasing the chance of finding later . . . an optimal solution with highly satisfactory properties." [10]

The planned study of projects and of their complex and ramified interconnections calls into play a number of variants of the traditional mathematical programming and input-output models. These variants are essentially directed at four very broad issues: (1) process choice; (2) project and production interrelationships; (3) locational interrelationships; and (4) branch and overall program interrelationships.

The *choice* among possible projects can also be looked upon as a choice

[10] R. Frisch, *Optimal Investment Under Limited Foreign Resources* (Oslo: Institute of Economics, 1959), p. 99.

among alternative processes.[11] On the one hand, this issue could be resolved by assuming that at any point in time industry will automatically choose the most advanced, and presumably the most technologically efficient production processes. This should be reflected in the input-output tables and coefficients, which should be based exclusively on the most modern technology. Thus, the impact of a particular project or program on the economy or any industrial sector could be studied via an input-output table built on the latter assumption. On the other hand, the various processes that might be employed in the economy, or in any individual branch of industry, could be viewed as activities whose optimal choice could be determined, say, through a mathematical programming approach, such as activity analysis. In particular, in a mathematical programming analysis whose purpose is to determine optimal rates of q_i, the output of industry i, one can further define by q_{ik} the rate of output of industry i produced by industrial process k. Here, $\sum_k q_{ik} = q_i$. Then, with all structural equations, and perhaps the objective function, redefined in terms of the q_{ik}, the optimal solution yields the rate at which q_i is to be produced by process k. In effect, then, the choice of projects can be visualized as a choice among alternative processes, with the selection being made via the optimization of some objective function. In this particular context, however, it is perhaps most appropriate to break down the process choice problem into a *series* of problems, with each branch of industry considered as representing a unique structure within which an activity analysis problem is to be solved. Within this framework, then, the problem is to determine the optimal choice of processes and technology to be employed within each industrial component. A related problem is the determination of the capital requirements, and the time-phasing of investments in each industrial branch, that is, a determination of the feasibility of adopting particular processes and technologies in light of the existing processes, the processes that might become available at various future dates, and the magnitudes of investment necessary to support any and all of the desired undertakings.

A second issue is the *interrelationships* among projects and other production programs.[12] In particular, in considering whether to accept a particular project or program, an important concern is the impact on *other* programs, both those that have been previously implemented, as well as those that are being contemplated. Thus, planners should be concerned with the possibility that, for example, other projects under consideration could, perhaps, provide the inputs for the project in question, or could be an important source of the output of the project. In the latter event, whereas neither of two project alternatives would by themselves appear to be worth undertaking, in tandem, or with a given time lag, both projects might provide a much more advantageous package to a second pair of alternatives that at first seem to be superior. Because of such inter-

[11] H. B. Chenery and P. G. Clark, *Interindustry Economics* (New York: John Wiley, 1959), pp. 126–135.
[12] S. Ishikawa, *Economic Development in Asian Perspective* (Tokyo: Kinokuniya, 1967), and R. Frisch, *op. cit.*

connections it is apparent that not only will the attractiveness of a given project be affected by the price that is assigned to, or determined for, the project's output, but so too will be the attractiveness of projects that might be supplying inputs to, or accepting the outputs of, the project in question. Moreover, from the standpoint of input-output analysis or mathematical programming approaches, it might therefore be advisable to determine appropriate groups of projects to be considered as units to be included in total, or not at all, in any project selection solution. In effect, the problem is to choose an optimal *portfolio* of projects. This observation, and the further recognition that the future returns from any project are only assessable probabilistically, suggests that the project selection problem under uncertainty might best be handled via the previously alluded to Markowitz-type mathematical programming model.[13] Here, however, instead of seeking the minimum-variance portfolio of securities that satisfies a given set of demands, including a prespecified minimum expected rate of return, one might seek, say, the minimum-variance portfolio of *projects* that satisfies certain policy-making desiderata. An important computational complication in this regard, however, is the discrete nature of industrial projects which, for an allocation problem of any magnitude, can inhibit the derivation of an optimal solution.

A third issue is that of *where* the individual projects that are selected should be located. Indeed, in principle the project selection and project location decisions should be inseparable in the sense that the location of a project is one of its very critical aspects. Thus, instead of writing, say, x_j as the level at which the jth project is accepted (where $x_j \geq 0$), and including all x_j in an objective function to be maximized subject to a series of constraints, one might more accurately write x_{jk} as the level at which the jth project is accepted in the kth locale. The coefficients associated with x_{jk} might then be π_{jk}^l, the profit yielded by the jth product produced in the kth locale and sold in the lth locale, where a different coefficient might be associated with each of the k different locales in which the product could be sold.

The fourth important issue is the interrelationship of each project with the other projects in the branch, and with the overall developmental effort. Here, the question is to determine how well the project fits in with the prevailing industrial milieu and that which is projected for the future, as well as how well the project fits in with the overall goals that the policy makers have established for the system. Assuredly, the question would automatically be resolved in any macro-programming analysis in which all interrelationships were defined, and an optimal program determined through a formal mathematical programming analysis. From a practical standpoint, however, such a formal analysis will ordinarily not be undertaken because there are too many projects to consider, the interrelationships are so complex that the model becomes mathematically intractable, and the required data are not available. It is therefore vital, even in less formalistic approaches to the project selection problem, that

---

[13] H. M. Markowitz, *Portfolio Selection* (New York: John Wiley, 1959).

the benefits and costs of each project be assessed in terms of both the overall effects on the system and the policy makers' objectives, and upon the particular industrial branch within which the project is logically classified.

As a final aside, it should be mentioned that this discussion ignores the incentives to investment in industry by the private sector which governments can provide or withhold in the form of social overhead capital. That is, in mixed economies the government can "entice" private investment into certain sectors or regions by helping, in one way or another, to share in the capital costs associated with the preferred sectors or regions.

13.4 SOME SPECIAL ISSUES: QUALITY AND "SIZE"

Quality is hardly a recognized objective of industrialization policies, particularly in "crash programs" in the socialist countries or in the LDC's. Pressures for immediately increasing the national output, developing new industrial branches, and inaugurating new, usually "gigantic" projects is such that only speed seems of the essence. Quality is viewed as a problem devoid of immediacy; it is a thing that in a sense is presumed to take care of itself "once things get under way." This attitude is doubly mistaken, not only because it covers up a number of immediate errors concerning the use of resources, actual costs, and the selections already made, but also because it sets the stage for costly and disappointing results. The new industrial products may indeed prove of lower quality than the imports they purport to replace, be unsalable abroad, and, when capital goods are involved, guarantee further expansion of the domestic industry, but with second-rate equipment only. This kind of "industrialization" becomes the fountainhead of *increasing* technological lags between the "developing" countries and the industrial leaders.

Starting from the idea that the industrial output of a country, irrespective of the quality of that output, depends on its *industrial size,* Ph. Carré [14] has established a valuable development model that assigns an interesting role to industrial imports in relation to the growth of *industrial* output. His key assumption is that the participation of a country in foreign trade is equivalent to an increase in the size of the economic system, since such imports allow the country a higher specialization in domestic activities. Carré then defines the industrial size of an economy by two parameters: the size of its industrial labor force, and the volume of its imports of industrial products. In particular, industrial production, Q, is assumed to be a function of the "total" labor force, L', where the total is the industrial labor force, L_I, corrected by a "fictitious labor force" factor, L_F, attributable to the labor that goes into producing the goods that are imported; or, $Q = f_1(L') = f_1(L_I + L_F)$. Further, the rate of imports, M, is a function of this "fictitious labor force" alone; or, $M = f_2(L_F)$. Hence, by combining the two equations of the model, the "fictitious labor force" can be eliminated as a variable, and either imports or industrial production expressed

[14] Ph. Carré, *Étude empirique sur l'évolution des structures d'économies en état de croissance* (Paris: Editions du C.N.R.S., 1960).

as a function of the other and the industrial labor force; that is, $Q = f_3(L_I, M)$ or $M = f_4(L_I, Q)$. The problem here, clearly, is that the model is oversimplified. In particular, it makes little sense to have imports play a key role in the industrial structure, but to entirely neglect the exports that will have to provide the foreign exchange to purchase the imports.

13.5 CONCLUDING COMMENTS: ON THE "YARDSTICK" OF PERFORMANCE

As is often the case with personal self-evaluations, nations all too frequently seek to evaluate their industrial performance, or to pattern their mode of industrialization, with a view toward the achievements of other industrialized nations with whom they seek to identify. Both individuals and nations, however, have unique characteristics and talents, so that the attempt to imitate the behavior of others without duplicating their virtues and defects is more likely to lead to frustration than to success, or to self-deception than to progress, and attempts to compare performance are often similar to the attempts to compare apples and oranges.

The complexity of the modern economic system is such that it is unreasonable to expect that even the most sophisticated of decision-making models, data analysis techniques, and data processing devices will lead the policy makers to optimal project selection decisions. The input data required by the model are rarely available—at least in terms of accurate data—and the mathematics demanded by models that accurately portray all of the interrelationships between industrial components, and technological relations within individual components, commonly make such models intractable. As a result, the quest for *optimal* solutions to the problem of project choice generally takes a back seat to the quest for *better* solutions than those that would be realized in the absence of formal planning techniques. In light of the unique features that define each economic system—the resource endowments, societal and legal rules, cultural features, and population size, to name a few—this suggests that the system's achievements are perhaps best measured against some hypothetical yardstick or goal that represents knowledgeable judgments of what the system is *capable* of attaining, rather than against the attainments of other systems, even those with similar characteristics. The history of these other systems can provide some guidelines and some "experimental" data; it can provide some evidence of what one can achieve under given technologies, endowments, and economic systems. It cannot, however, provide a forecast of a future that is attainable by all societies and all systems at all times.

CHAPTER *14*

Planning Agricultural Production

14.1 PROBLEMS OF AGRICULTURAL PLANNING

Notwithstanding the populist mystique that enshrouds it, agriculture is *not* the focal point of either development planning in mixed economies or of socialist planning in fully controlled economies. Rather, economic growth in the contemporary world is identified with the *growth of industry,* accompanied by the *decline of the agricultural sector* in terms of labor force, total output, and overall importance in the economic system. Furthermore, the socioinstitutional characteristics, and the specific planning and policy problems of this unique subsystem of the economy apparently differ so strikingly between MDC's and LDC's that at first the economic models devised to deal with the problems of the former seem hardly apt for dealing with the problems of the latter. Finally, for several reasons agriculture seems an almost intractable sector in comparison with industry. First, it involves widely varying multi-period decision phases, along with rigidly determined time-consuming processes. Second, it allows for a wide range of input substitutions and not for fixed coefficients. Third, it is subject to great seasonal fluctuations and to unforeseeable random variations in output. And, lastly, it involves perishable products having long "gestation" periods, so that it is unresponsive to short-run price changes effected by temporary aberrations in supply or demand.

Yet, agriculture is regaining in policy interest and importance. This comeback has been sparked not only by the worldwide population explosion and the resounding agricultural failures of certain socialist countries, but also by a better understanding of the mutually supporting roles of industry and of agriculture in the overall growth process. Further, it is increasingly perceived by planners—if not by policy makers—that, as an outstanding agricultural economist, Earl C. Heady, has rightly pointed out, "differences in size, economic or social organization, market orientation, ownership, goals, and other attributes of farms" do not cause modern planning or decision models to be less appropriate in different countries or in different systems.[1] What must vary are the *types of weights* in the objective function, not the forms, relationships, properties, and functions of the planning or optimization models. The planning *environment* does necessarily vary, but the specification of the optima, and the principles of optimization stay the same. Finally, the unique natural, physical, and social characteristics of farms vary both between and within nations. Despite the recognition of interregional differences in the *specifics,* the universality of the conceptual or practical *tools* of agricultural planning is not in doubt. The vast variety of constraints existing in this sector do raise, however, in isolation or in combination, a number of interesting problems with which we shall deal further below.

"Agricultural planning"—more correctly, formal analysis of the different aspects of food and agriculture—has developed vigorously in the past few decades. Major advances have been made in (a) the study of the interrelations between agriculture proper, the agricultural complex which includes agriculture and all of the industries that depend on it, and the industrial complex (all other industries), (b) the modeling of the food production and marketing systems for agricultural products, and in (c) the construction of various short-term or intermediate-term recursive and/or equilibrium models. In the following sections we shall concentrate particularly on input-output interrelations between the agricultural and industrial complexes, on planning models in different environments, on some feedback recursive sequences, and on some pertinent considerations in projecting demand for agricultural products. Outstanding among the analytical contributors to this field, beside Ragnar Frisch who has devised a scheme for computing all direct and cross demand elasticities in a multi-sector, multi-commodity model, have been Earl O. Heady and Karl A. Fox and his associates at Iowa State University, as well as a number of other economists whose work we shall refer to further below.[2]

14.2 INTERRELATIONS OF THE AGRICULTURAL AND INDUSTRIAL COMPLEXES[3]

As reflected in the previous chapters, input-output techniques have been one of the mainstays of economic planning. This has been the case in the West, and it

[1] E. O. Heady, "Synthesis of Decision and Planning Tools and Environment," in E. O. Heady (ed.) *Economic Models and Quantitative Methods for Decisions and Planning in Agriculture* (Ames: The Iowa State University Press, 1971), p. 9.

[2] For an interesting summary of these efforts, as well as an extensive bibliography, see K. A. Fox, "Spatial Price Equilibrium and Process Analysis in the Food and Agriculture Sector," in A. S. Manne and H. M. Markowitz (eds.) *Studies in Process Analysis* (New Haven, Conn.: The Cowles Foundation, Yale University Press, 1961); E. O. Heady and J. L. Dillon, *Agricultural Production Functions* (Ames: *Iowa University Press,* 1961); R. Frisch, "A Complete Scheme for Computing All Direct and Cross Demand Elasticities in a Model with Many Sectors," *Econometrica,* Vol. XXVII, No. 2, April 1959, pp. 177–196.

[3] For a detailed discussion see K. A. Fox, "The Food and Agricultural Sectors in Advanced Economies," and J. K. Sengupta, "Models of Agriculture and Industry in Less Developed Economies," in T. Barna (ed.) *Structural Interdependence and Economic Development* (Geneva: St. Martin's Press, 1963).

may eventually become the case also in the East, because of the compatibility of the Marxian system and balance methods with the input-output framework. In practice, input-output possesses what is perhaps an unanticipated, additional virtue for agricultural economic planning: the division of the economy into agricultural and industrial subsystems, and the *presumption* of fixed technological coefficients within and between each of these subsystems, yields off-diagonal elements in the coefficients submatrix that are small in relation to the diagonal elements. The import of the latter is that it permits the partitioning of the technological coefficients and transactions matrices into four submatrices, including one that involves agriculture exclusively, and that can be used for analytical and planning purposes in virtual independence of the others.

In particular, suppose that $A = [a_{ij}]$ $(i, j = 1, 2)$ is the matrix of input-output coefficients that describe the interrelationships between and within the agricultural $(= 1)$ and industrial $(= 2)$ sectors of the economy, where $a_{ij} = q_{ij}/Q_j$ is the input of commodity i per unit output of commodity j. Empirical studies reveal that a_{11} and a_{22} will be large relative to a_{12} and a_{21}, and, moreover, a_{21} will be large relative to a_{12}. The latter implies that changes in the final demand for the commodities of the industrial sector will have very little relative effect on the output of the agricultural sector; and, conversely, that changes in the final demand for agricultural commodities will have a somewhat greater, if still relatively inconsequential effect on the output of the industrial sector. Based on 1947 data, for example, Fox estimates that if the agricultural complex "increses by \$1 billion, the gross output of 'all other industries' increases by \$0.36 billion. But if (all other industries) increases by \$1 billion, the gross input required from the Agricultural Complex increases by only \$0.05 billion." [4]

In combination with the former observation, this implies that for all intents and analytical purposes the two sectors can be treated as *independent* of one another. Hence, planning in one sector can, *initially* at least, be carried out independently of planning in the other, which is not to suggest that specific *developments* in one sector cannot have important effects in the other. We have already remarked, for example, on the implications for urban labor supply of increased agricultural productivity, and, assuredly, such manpower shifts can have an important impact on the industrial sector, in terms of prices, processes, and the factor-input mix. Similarly, the development of new industrial products, or technological advances that either improve existing products or reduce their cost, can have important implications for the agricultural sector. In particular, the production of low-cost fertilizers by the industrial sector can have important and favorable effects on the agricultural sector. These effects, however, will not necessarily be enjoyed in the LDC's—if they are enjoyed at all—to the extent that they are enjoyed, or have exploitable potential in the MDC's. Thus, the plans in the two sectors must ultimately be related to one another and reconciled, but to the extent that partial analysis is always simpler than total analysis, the suggestion of virtual independence encourages dealing with each of these sectors as individual entities.

---

[4] K. A. Fox, *ibid.*, p. 63.

What is essential to the use of input-output analysis for planning purposes is the validity of the assumption that, at least over the short term, the empirically determined factor-input to product-output ratios will either approximate (a) fixed technological coefficients that adequately describe the actual production process, or (b) the input-output ratios that will obtain with fixed factor price ratios and a constant-returns-to-scale production process. Although the assumption is tolerable when applied to the industrial sector, insofar as it is neither patently false, nor sufficiently distortive so as to invalidate subsequent analyses, the assumption of fixed technological coefficients is particularly difficult to justify for agriculture where factor substitutability and diminishing returns to the factors tends to be the rule, rather than the exception. Nonetheless, it *can* be argued that treating empirically determined input-output ratios *as if* they represented fixed technological coefficients is not only exceedingly useful, but also readily justified.

Agricultural products can be divided into livestock and crops. Each of the latter can also be divided into its component parts of fowl, beef, and pork; wheat, corn, and barley; and so forth. The level of disaggregation will depend on the problem and the availability of data. Contributing to the complexity of the data problem is the fact that one of the products—crops—is also employed as an input in the production of the other product—livestock.

Every farm product can be "produced" in a variety of ways, or through various *activities* any one of which might be employed on a given farm, at a given point in time. Within the comparatively narrow range of potential outputs which will ordinarily obtain *for a given farm during a particular year,* the assumption of constant returns to scale is not too unreasonable. Hence, for the factor price ratios that obtain during that year, the factor-input to product-output ratios can in fact be assumed to be fixed, for this narrow range of outputs. Thus, the assumption of fixed input-output ratios for each producing unit, the farm, and for each product, is itself defensible. This in turn provides the basis for the assumption of fixed input-output ratios for the agricultural sector as a whole. That is, given the ratios for the individual farms and products, or given a vector of technological coefficients for each activity, the vector for the sector will be determined as a weighted average of the individual activity vectors, weighted in proportion to the relative importance of the output of each activity in the sector's total output. Thus, suppose that the activity vector

$$
_k\boldsymbol{a}_j = \begin{bmatrix} _ka_{1j} \\ _ka_{2j} \\ \vdots \\ _ka_{ij} \\ \vdots \\ _ka_{nj} \end{bmatrix}
$$

contains coefficients $_ka_{ij}$ that represent the optimal input of commodity i per unit output of commodity j on farm k, for that farm's feasible output range.

Suppose, too, that the activity vector $_k a_j$ describes the production process for w_k percent of the output of commodity j. Then the technological coefficients vector for this commodity will be determined by $a_j = \Sigma w_j (_k a_j)/100$.

Assuredly, the individual activity vectors are unlikely to be either known or obtainable. Nonetheless, what is observed is the vector a_j containing the *aggregated* data; or, what is in effect the weighted average of these individual vectors. The question that arises is whether estimates based on aggregated data for one time period are valid for planning purposes in a second time period when either technology may have changed or, as is certainly likely, changes in the factor price ratios will have resulted in factor input substitutions and changes in the input-output ratios. The answer will generally be in the negative.

To skirt this problem, as Fox points out, two similar approaches have been considered,[5] each of which employs a sampling procedure in an attempt to estimate the input-output ratios for either a sample of homogenous agricultural regions, or else a sample of individual farms. Assuming each (a) region or (b) farm to behave as a profit-maximizing decision unit, the data for the individual units are couched in a linear programming framework. The objective function in the model is a linear profits function to be maximized subject to a series of linear constraints. The solutions to these problems yields, for each (a) region or (b) farm, the profit-maximizing activities for each commodity. These individual solutions can then be weighted and combined to obtain estimates of the technological coefficients for the nation as a whole.

Two additional problems occurring in input-output analysis, which while not unique to agriculture seem to be particularly acute in defining and estimating the technological coefficients for this sector, are (1) the extent of intrafirm transactions, and (2) the degree of vertical integration.

As mentioned, livestock and livestock products are major elements in farm output. Yet, some of the factors that go into "producing" these products, such as food products, will often be raised on the same farm that produces livestock. Further, the crops that are fed to the livestock are often not without value, for they may be salable on the open market. The question of how to deal with such factors, both in principle and in practice, is not easily resolved.

Similarly, the production of both crops and livestock to satisfy final demand by households is increasingly becoming the responsibility of the industrial sector, and the food-processing *industry*. Fully vertically integrated firms frequently raise their own livestock, process the meat, and market the final product, whereas nonintegrated meat processors purchase the "factor input" from farms upon which livestock are raised. Again, then, it is unclear as to how to classify the individual operations, or, more precisely, how to define the individual sectors and to obtain estimates of the coefficients in the transactions matrix.

In essence, then, a clear boundary between the agricultural and the industrial sectors in the economy does not exist. Moreover, as the trend toward

[5] *Ibid.*, p. 67.

vertical integration persists, a boundary established at one point in time will not necessarily be appropriate at a later date. This suggests that a very broad definition of the agricultural sector, one that includes foods and fiber processing as well as the traditional agriculture, is likely to be the most practical approach to the problem, although perhaps not the most *theoretically* desirable. A clear distinction between these two sectors has, in addition, the analytical advantage of separating the economy into two sectors that are generally moving in opposite directions: the industrial sector provides the growth stimulus to the economy, while the agricultural sector is declining in importance. In light of our concern with growth, this separation frees the planner to focus specific attention on a smaller subset of industries as the medium for stimulating growth. Simultaneously, it highlights those industries and regions that can be anticipated to provide, say, a future stockpile of unemployed labor.

Indeed, as we have previously seen when discussing the Mahalanobis and Ghosh models, the separation of a sector such as agriculture from the capital-producing industrial sector can provide a useful analytical framework for planning the intertemporal allocation of investment, as well as determining capital capacities within each sector at various future points in time. This determination is crucial, since the potential impact of an additional unit of investment in the industrial sector on the economy and its growth will ordinarily be substantially different from the impact of an additional unit of investment in the agricultural sector. Of perhaps equal significance is the policy makers' objective of self-sufficiency with particular respect to agriculture, to assure that the nation is capable of "feeding itself" if necessary. Isolating the agricultural sector permits planners to determine, for example, the investment requirements and technological changes that will be required *in this sector* in order to achieve and maintain this goal in the future.

The advantages of distinguishing the agricultural sector from the rest of the economy, and the ability to deal with it as an entity apart, has led to the development of a number of models to facilitate agricultural planning, and consideration of several issues peculiar to agriculture. The remainder of this chapter is devoted to a discussion of these.

14.3 PLANNING MODELS IN DIFFERENT ENVIRONMENTS

Conceptually, it seems especially appropriate to deal with planning problems in general by placing them within a mathematical programming format wherein an objective function is to be optimized subject to a series of constraints, and boundary conditions on the decision variables. In practice, however, the complexity of the real world with its abundance of interrelationships among both variables and fixed factors, as well as the sheer magnitude of the number of variables, parameters, and constraints, often makes these models either mathematically or computationally intractable, and forces the technician to impose the simplifying assumptions, such as those of the input-output model, that will ameliorate the difficulties.

There is a uniqueness insofar as agricultural planning is concerned, in that, as previously pointed out, with its boundaries appropriately defined the agricultural sector can for all intents and purposes be isolated from the industrial sector and dealt with *as if* it were independent of the latter; and, moreover, over the long term the possibilities of factor substitution in the production of any one product, and the further possibilities of product substitution on any individual farm or in any region are so considerable that there is great reluctance to assume these out of existence. As a result, mathematical programming methods, in particular *linear* programming, have recently been applied to the long-term planning problems of the agricultural sector in both the West *and* the East, replacing the cruder accounting or balance methods that had been previously utilized for the purpose.

The applicability of the same planning *methods* in the agricultural sectors of Western and Eastern nations alike stems from the similarity in their basic producing units, the individual farms. Although, assuredly, there may be differences in the sophistication of the technology employed on the farms, within *and* between nations, and differences in the specific *problems* faced in, say, MDC's and LDC's, as well as differences in the agricultural potential (productivity) of the land, these are differences in the specific *details* of the programming problem to be solved, rather than differences in its general format. For *any* individual farm, then, one might wish to determine the optimal production *rates* for the various commodities that can be raised on the farm, given a set of commodity prices and production costs, capital and land capacity restrictions, and any other constraints that are implicit in the production process, or explicitly *imposed* by the farmer or the planner. Alternatively, one might wish to determine the optimum production *process* or processes for a given commodity, given a set of factor costs, the technological facts of life, and a set of implicit and explicitly imposed constraints. Technologies may differ between West and East, as well as between farms within an economy; the prices and costs may be determined by the market mechanism in the West, modified, say, by various price support programs, and determined by a Central Planning Agency in the East; but, in either instance decisions are made by treating *some* set of prices and costs as externally determined constants.

Depending on the degree of complexity and sophistication of the programming model, the optimal allocation schemes and production processes can be determined simultaneously for any farm. These procedures can then be extended to include any region—or indeed the entire economy—where a typical planning problem would be to determine the optimal allocation of commodities among farms *within* a region, or the optimal allocation of commodities among regions within an economy. The multi-level aspect of the planning problem is clearly revealed here, for the optimal allocation scheme for any farm in a region will depend on the overall allocation scheme for the region. But by the same token, the optimal regional allocation scheme will depend on the possibilities for the individual farms, and will require that they produce in an optimal manner. Thus, the problem of *coordinating* plans among farms and regions can become an extremely difficult problem to handle. In any event, it is a problem that is best dealt with by first considering the problem confronting the individual farmer.

As discussed in detail by Heady,[6] the basic allocation and production process choice problems of the individual farmer can be defined within a linear programming format without overly disturbing the actual production relationships that obtain on the typical farm. Even in the absence of centrally administered prices, buyers and sellers in agricultural markets are sufficiently great in number such as to prevent any one from having a perceptible influence on price.

In particular, let q_j be the output of the jth commodity on a particular farm. From the farmer's standpoint the commodity price P_j can be taken as a constant to be determined in the market. At the time that production is being planned, this price may be uncertain and the farmer might elect to simply make some best estimate of what P_j will be when that q_j reaches the market. Then the farm's *estimated* total revenue will be given by the linear function $R = \Sigma P_j q_j$. Alternatively, the farmer might assess a probability density over each P_j and then focus on the *expected* revenue of $E[R] = \Sigma E[P_j]q_j = \Sigma \bar{P}_j q_j$. Similarly, within the narrow range of feasible outputs for any one farm, the average cost C_j of producing a unit of the jth commodity could be taken as essentially constant for a given production process, or perhaps assessed probabilistically. In either case, some per unit profit figure, π_j, upon which allocation decisions will be based can be determined. Then some *linear* objective function, $\pi = \Sigma \pi_j q_j$, can be defined. For different farmers, the objective functions may differ in their specific *details* depending on whether the farmer elects to maximize some expected profits function, some additive utility function, or a gross revenue function, or whether the farmer seeks to minimize some total cost function, or an expected loss function. These are, however, details that involve only the *weights* in a *linear* objective function to be maximized or minimized subject to a series of restrictions on the decision variables, the q_j.

The restrictions occur because of the technological and capacity realities that exist on any farm, because of external constraints that might be imposed on the farmers by governmental or social pressures, and because of personal considerations that the farmer might choose to impose upon production decisions. Again, within the comparatively narrow ranges of outputs that are feasible for the outputs of the individual farm, it is quite realistic to formulate these restrictions as linear inequalities and equalities. Hence, the constraints are of the form $\Sigma a_{ij}q_j \leq b_i$ ($i = 1, \ldots, n$), where b_i is the number of units available of the ith resource, or the available capacity of the resource, and a_{ij} is the required utilization rate of the ith resource, per unit output of the jth commodity.

The capacity limitations will derive from the available land, machinery, and buildings. Thus, suppose that b_1 denotes the total acreage of land that the farmer allocates to the production of all crops, and commodity 3 is corn. Then a_{13} indicates the number of acres of land required for the production of a unit of

[6] E. O. Heady, *op. cit.*

corn. Suppose, too, that commodity 4 is wheat. Then a_{13}/a_{14} is the rate of substitution, with respect to land, of wheat for corn. Similarly, the farmer—or the government—might simply *impose,* externally, a restriction on commodity production. Thus, suppose the farmer elects to produce k times as much corn as wheat. Then a constraint, $q_3 - kq_4 = b_k = 0$, will be incorporated into the model; and, if the government limits the farmer to B_4 units of wheat, the constraint $q_4 \le B_4$ will also be introduced.

Since only nonnegative outputs can be produced, a typical commodity allocation problem will be of the linear programming form

$$\text{Maximize} \qquad \pi = \sum_{j=1}^{m} \pi_j q_j \qquad (14.1)$$

$$\text{subject to} \sum_{j=1}^{m} a_{ij} q_j \le b_i \qquad i = 1, \ldots, n \qquad (14.1\text{a})$$

$$q_j \ge 0 \qquad j = 1, \ldots, m \qquad (14.1\text{b})$$

Farms will differ only insofar as concerns the weights π_j in the objective function, the capacity restrictions b_i, the rates of substitution a_{ij}/a_{kj}, and the portfolio of potential commodity outputs q_j.

This linear programming problem can be readily extended to include a variety of different production processes. In particular, let $q_{k_j j}$ denote the rate of output of commodity j produced through process k_j, and let C_{k_j} denote the average cost of producing commodity j via process k_j. Then $\pi_{k_j} = P_j - C_{k_j}$ is the profit per unit for commodity j, when the unit is produced via process k_j; $\pi_{t_j} = \sum_{k_j} \pi_{k_j} q_{k_j j}$, is the total profit derived from producing a total output of $q_j = \sum q_{k_j j}$ of commodity j. Hence, the objective function (14.1) would be replaced by

$$\pi = \sum_j \sum_{k_j} (P_j - C_{k_j}) q_{k_j j}$$

$$= \sum_j P_j q_j - \sum_j \sum_{k_j} C_{k_j} q_{k_j j} \qquad (14.1')$$

Similarly, the a_{ik} would be redefined as $a_{ik_j j}$—the amount of the ith resource required per unit output of commodity j, when the latter is produced via process k_j. Then the constraints (14.1a) would be rewritten as

$$\sum_j \sum_{k_j} a_{ik_j j} q_{k_j j} \le b_i \qquad i = 1, \ldots, n \qquad (14.1\text{a}')$$

and (14.1b) would be rewritten as

$$q_{k_j j} \ge 0 \quad j = 1, \ldots, \text{m}; k_j = 1, \ldots, K_j \qquad (14.1\text{b}')$$

Additional constraints, necessarily including the equalities

$$\sum q_{k_j j} = q_j \qquad j = 1, \ldots, m \qquad (14.1\text{c})$$

might also be introduced. The farm planning problem, then, is to choose values for the decision variables $q_{k_j j}$—the rate of output of the jth commodity produced by the k_jth process—so as to maximize total profits as given by (14.1'), subject to constraints (14.1a') and (14.1c), and boundary conditions (14.1b').

The linear programming format and its specialized variants are also useful in other agricultural planning contexts. One important problem is determining the optimal pattern of shipments of farm commodities to industrial food-processing plants. Simplifying the problem for illustrative purposes, we can define C_{rs} as the per unit transportation cost of a unit of a commodity produced on a farm in region r and shipped to region s for processing. Denoting by q_{rs} the number of units shipped from region r to region s

$$C = \sum_r \sum_s c_{rs} q_{rs} \tag{14.2}$$

gives the total transportation costs in the food-processing process. Then, (1) with

$$\sum_r q_{rs} \le Q_s \qquad s = 1, \ldots, S \tag{14.2a}$$

providing the restriction that total shipments to region s should not exceed the processing capacity Q_s of the region, (2)

$$\sum_s q_{rs} \le Q_r \qquad r = 1, \ldots, R \tag{14.2b}$$

providing the restriction that total shipments from region r should not exceed the region's output, (3) the restriction that total output should not exceed total processing capacity

$$\sum Q_r \le \sum Q_s \tag{14.2c}$$

and finally, (4) the nonnegativity condition

$$q_{rs} \ge 0 \qquad r = 1, \ldots, R; s = 1, \ldots, S \tag{14.2d}$$

an easily solved cost-minimizing transportation problem is defined.

The farm planning problem, with all of its associated uncertainties including the weather, provides a particularly apt setting for the use of stochastic techniques, and chance-constrained programming in particular.[7] Thus, suppose that the availability of resource i is not known with certainty, but that a probability density over b_i has been assessed. Then, in chance-constrained programming, the equation

$$\sum a_{ij} q_j \le b_i$$

would be replaced by its probabilistic counterpart

$$P(\sum a_{ij} q_j \le b_i) = \alpha \qquad 0 < \alpha < 1 \tag{14.1a''}$$

That is, we *impose* the restriction that when selecting an optimal allocation, the *probability* that the constraint $\sum a_{ij} q_j \le b_i$ is ultimately *violated* should not exceed $1 - \alpha$. Similarly, through goal programming we can impose costs for violating certain restrictions, or impose costs for restrictions that *might* be violated due to the vagaries of chance.[8]

[7] See A. Charnes and W. W. Cooper, "Chance-Constrained Programming," *Management Science*, Vol. 6, No. 1, October 1959, pp. 73–79.

[8] See S. M. Lee, *Goal Programming for Decision Analysis* (Philadelphia: Auerbach, 1972).

To extend the linear programming model to the regional level, first define Q_{rj} as the number of units of the jth commodity produced in region r, and π_{rj} as the per unit "contribution" that commodity j makes to welfare (profit, income, product) in region r. The regional linear programming problem [9]

Maximize $\qquad \pi = \Sigma\Sigma\pi_{rj}Q_{rj}$ (14.3)

subject to $\sum_j a_{irj}Q_{rj} \leq b_{ir} \qquad i = 1, \ldots, r_n; r = 1, \ldots, R$ (14.3a)

$\qquad\qquad \sum_r w_{rj}Q_{rj} \leq q_j \qquad j = 1, \ldots, m$ (14.3b)

$\qquad\qquad Q_{rj} \geq 0 \qquad r = 1, \ldots, R; j = 1, \ldots, m$ (14.3c)

can then be defined. Here a_{irj} is the required number of units of the resource i per unit output of commodity j in region r, and b_{ir} is the capacity of resource i in region r. The planners' restriction on the maximum total nationwide production of commodity j is given by Q_j, and w_{rj} is a weight assigned by the planners to a unit of production of commodity j in region r; or w_{rj}/w_{sj} is the trade-off or rate of substitution that planners will accept between commodity j being produced in region s and in region r.

This particular problem is made especially interesting, and is especially conducive to regional agricultural planning, because its computational solution can be simplified by utilizing the *decomposition* principle of linear programming.[10] Specifically, the $r_n \times R$ set of constraints (14.3a) can be partitioned into R distinct "blocks" of constraints, the rth block of which contains r_n constraints

$$\sum_j a_{irj}Q_{rj} \leq b_{ir} \qquad i = 1, \ldots, r_n$$ (14.3a')

or simply

$$\sum_j a_{ij}Q_j \leq b_i \qquad i = 1, \ldots, n$$

with the "r" suppressed. Then, ignoring the national restriction (14.3b), *each of the R regional planning "centers" could be*, in effect, called upon to submit a plan that would solve, for that region, the planning problem

Maximize $\qquad \pi'_r = \sum_j \pi'_j Q_j$ (14.3')

subject to $\sum_j a_{ij}Q_j \leq b_i \qquad i = 1, \ldots, n$ (14.3a')

$\qquad\qquad Q_j \geq 0 \qquad j = 1, \ldots, m$

in which the regional index "r" is suppressed.

[9] See F. K. Bishay, "On the Methodology of Constructing Models for Optimal Spatial Allocation of Agricultural Activities," *The Farm Economist,* Vol. XII, No. 3, 1971, pp. 113–127.
[10] See G. B. Dantzig and P. Wolfe, "A Decomposition Principle for Linear Programs," *Operations Research,* Vol. 8, No. 1, January–February, 1960, pp. 101–111.

The solutions to these regional subproblems will depend on the π'_j—the per unit "contributions," or weights employed in the various objective functions. The decomposition technique involves an iterative procedure for assigning these weights. The procedure utilizes the suggested optima for the regional subproblems, in combination with the national restrictions (14.3b). Without going into the gory details, the central controller, in effect, transmits an initial set of coefficients π'_j to a regional controller whose job is to solve a comparatively small subproblem of the form (14.3'), (14,3a'), and (14.c'). The optimal solutions to R such subproblems are then fed back to the central controller. The latter then uses these optima and the national constraints (14.3b) to generate a revised set of coefficients π''_j to replace π'_j in (14.3'). The constraints (14.3a') and (14.c') are unaltered, but the regional controller must resubmit a solution to the central controller—an optimal solution with respect to π''_j. Once again the optima and the national constraints are used to generate new coefficients π'''_j. The procedure is repeated until an overall optimum, which satisfies an optimum-identifying criterion, is obtained. The advantage of employing this decomposition procedure to reach the optimum occurs when there are a large number of regions, each of which is subjected to a large number of constraints. Then, one very large linear programming problem whose solution may be very difficult to compute, can be replaced by a series of much smaller linear programming problems whose solutions are easily achieved.

It is evident that programming techniques in general provide an appropriate format for agricultural planning. Linear programming is particularly useful in this regard because the linearity assumptions are readily justified, and the computational advantages are indisputable. It should also be evident, however, that for optimal agricultural planning for the economic system as a whole, national plans, regional plans, and plans for the individual farm must *all* be coordinated. This means *both* optimal crop and livestock programs, and optimal process choice at the farm level, in the production of all of these commodities. In principle, an optimal solution can be obtained to the multi-product, multi-process, multi-farm problem. In practice, however, the optimum will have to be sacrificed for mathematical and computational expediency. Thus, undoubtedly the *best* to which planners can aspire in the immediate future is a multi-level planning process in which, at the first level, a national-regional planning model is employed to determine regional optima for the various commodities. Then, these optima are used to provide constraints under which the individual farms are required to operate, with the resulting linear programming problem formulated at the individual farm level dictating the final choice of production processes, and the eventual commodity allocations.

14.4 FEEDBACKS AND PROGRAM SEQUENCES

In agricultural planning, as in planning in general, still more sophisticated models than the above can be built, by explicitly recognizing the *dynamic* nature of the planning process. In particular it should be recognized that decisions reached at time t can influence planning decisions at some later time $t + i (i > 0)$ either because they will impact upon the planning problem to be solved at time $t + i$ in a clear and *deterministic* manner, or because they will have effects on the inputs into the latter planning problem which can only be assessed *probabilistically*. Additionally, perhaps as a result of technological change or other factors external to decisions reached at time t, plans that are optimal at time t will not necessarily be optimal at time $t + i$.

Incorporating the internally known and unknown effects, as well as the external effects into a linear programming model, transforms the problem into one of *recursive* programming.[11] Considering the problem of the individual farm as summarized in Equations (14.1), (14.1a), and (14.1b), we can use the subscript t to index time, and thus initially write the problem as

$$\text{Maximize} \qquad \pi = \sum_{t=1}^{T} \sum_{j=1}^{m} \pi_{jt} q_{jt} \qquad\qquad (14.4)$$

$$\text{subject to } \sum_{j=1}^{m} a_{ijt} q_{jt} \leq b_{it} \qquad i = 1, \ldots, n; \, t = 1, \ldots, T \quad (14.4a)$$

$$q_{jt} \geq 0 \qquad j = 1, \ldots, m; \, t = 1, \ldots, T \quad (14.4b)$$

for a planning horizon of T decision periods.

External factors such as technological change will affect the values of the a_{ijt}—hopefully in a predictable manner—and changes in final demand can be expected to impact on the π_{jt} through the prices that go into their determination. Similarly, a decision with respect to, say, $q_1 = (q_{11}, \ldots, q_{m1})$—the first-period production scheme—may influence the availability of resources in subsequent periods in a determinate manner. This implies the need to include in the problem an additional set of constraints, typified by, for example,

$$b_{12} = f(b_{11}, q_1)$$

and similarly for $b_{it} (t > 2)$. That is, current capacity depends on both past capacity and how it was utilized.

In an analogous fashion, current decisions can impact upon subsequent optimal decisions in a nondeterministic manner. In particular, first-period commodity production and factor input demand might perhaps be thought to influence second-period prices and costs if it is expected that *all* farmers will reach similar commodity and process-choice decisions. But, since this will not *necessarily* be the case, there will be some stochastic factors involved. Thus, for example, the parameter π_{12} might be replaced by $\bar{\pi}_{12} = f(q_{11}, \, \bar{\mu}_{12})$, where $\bar{\mu}_{12}$ is a random disturbance term. Similar substitutions will be effected for the other second-period contributions, and subsequent π_{jt}, and the problem could then be stated as one of maximizing the *expected* total discounted profit $\bar{\pi}$, over the time horizon T. Again, in principle the appropriate, dynamic problem

[11] T. Heidhues, "Recursive Programming Applied to Agriculture," in A. P. Carter and A. Brody (eds.) *Contributions to Input-Output Analysis* (Amsterdam: North-Holland, 1970).

can be stated and solved; in practice, however, neither the definitional problem nor the computational problems are likely to be easily overcome.

14.5 DEMAND AND PRODUCTION POSSIBILITIES

Optimal agricultural planning is a dynamic process that requires short-, intermediate-, and long-term projections of the demand for agricultural products, which in turn permit the projection of optimal short-, intermediate-, and long-term patterns of land use. Econometric models, supported by the selective use of input-output techniques, have become commonplace in the former regard, while linear programming has been basic in the latter. The purpose of demand and production projections commonly tends to be to provide data inputs for consistency-type models, as opposed to optimization models. That is, the results of these projections are analyzed, perhaps quite informally, to determine the extent to which, for example, future production is forecast to be commensurate with future demand, and the extent to which the growth and development of the agricultural sector and the agricultural labor force is consistent with overall policy objectives and aspirations, and with the plans for the industrial and human resources sectors.

a. Demand

From the strict standpoint of planning in the agricultural sector as opposed to planning with respect to human resources, the relevant issue is *total* demand for agricultural products, rather than per capita demand. To obtain the most accurate projections of total demand, it is necessary to disaggregate it in various ways. The disaggregation starts with the distinction between domestic and foreign demand, and proceeds to a further separating out of the various types of agricultural products. The appropriate level of disaggregation depends on what is both useful and feasible. Thus, domestic demand can itself be disaggregated among regions, and foreign demand can be disaggregated among international regions and nations. Similarly, one can consider the demand for wheat, corn, and livestock products, or still further the demand for beef, pork, and fowl. The choice will depend on the requirements of the planners concerned with the determination of optimal land-use patterns, and data availability.

Domestic demand can be disaggregated into final and intermediate products. This distinction can be important because of the different factors that underlie each.

The most important factors determining final demand are the traditional ones of price, income, population, and tastes and preferences. With respect to price, and depending on product definition, it may also be necessary to take into consideration price relatives, or the prices of substitute and complementary products. Certainly these will have to be considered in the absence of ex ante information or knowledge regarding the various price cross-elasticities of demand. Indeed it is in respect to measuring these that the aforementioned contributions of Frisch have been so important. Similarly, and especially in growing economies, it is necessary to incorporate some income measure into a demand analysis. Particularly in intermediate- and long-term analyses the income factor may have to be dealt with in a fairly sophisticated fashion, since the income elasticity of demand cannot be presumed to be independent of the rate of income. Indeed, for certain products, just the reverse will ordinarily be the case. Thus, in any analysis in which a large range of incomes is being considered, allowance must be made for the possibility of a nonconstant income elasticity. The obvious way to deal with this possibility, if the model specification and computational algorithm permit, is to make the income elasticity itself a function of income.

Assuredly, an income variable might at least in part capture and explain changes in tastes and preferences, and the role of a population variable as a determinant of final demand is too obvious to belabor. All of these variables, however, lend themselves to further disaggregation that has great potential importance in arriving at accurate demand projections. Specifically, one can disaggregate along urban and rural lines, as well as along occupational strata. Thus, although ex post analysis may reveal it not to be the case, ex ante it might be expected that consumer tastes and final demand will alter as the population shifts from rural to urban areas, or indeed if technological change effects changes in the number of white collar workers relative to manual laborers. Again, utility and feasibility considerations will dictate the amount of disaggregation and the degree of sophistication with which the problem is treated, but in any event it is important to recognize its potential complexity.

The demand for intermediate products is a derived demand that will depend on the demand for final products, the relative prices of the intermediate products, and technological considerations. Although econometric methods can be employed in this connection, as they are ordinarily employed in estimating final demand, intermediate-demand analysis readily lends itself to the employment of input-output techniques. In particular, *given* projections of final demands, as well as a set of assumptions with respect to price relatives and technological change, the ordinary input-output format is useful for projecting intermediate demand.

Although the same considerations that enter into projecting domestic demand also enter into projecting foreign demand, the latter will generally be (a) less complex in the sense that a higher level of aggregation will generally suffice, so that rural-to-urban population drifts, say, in the foreign sector under consideration would not ordinarily be taken into consideration, and (b) more complex in the sense that additional price, technological, and external factors will also have to be taken into consideration.

In estimating foreign demand for a particular agricultural product, not only can the domestic prices of substitute and complementary products be important considerations, but so too will be the prices of these same products in foreign markets, and in particular the prices of these products in the "domestic" markets of the sector being studied. Further, an important price-related element is transportation cost. This can be an especially difficult factor to assess in an analysis of long-term demand, because transportation costs themselves depend on so many factors, not the least of which is the technological state of the art.

Finally, *effective* foreign demand is always subject to the whims and domestic and international policies of foreign and domestic governments. Thus, on the one hand, a domestic government can interfere in the free market through export embargoes that prevent the sale of domestic products in foreign markets, as well as through international "deals" that effect the sale of domestic produce in the foreign sector. And, on the other hand, foreign governments can institute a system of quotas and tariffs that either limit the amount that can be sold in the foreign sector, or that discourage imports through higher prices. The technological and external factors can ordinarily be assessed with accuracy over the short term, but they make intermediate- and long-term foreign-demand projections extremely hazardous.

b. Production

Because of the fact that food is a prerequisite to survival, the agricultural sector is unique in having an *obligation* to make and fulfill *commitments* to the nation if not to the world at large. Assuredly, there are price, cost, and comparative advantage issues involved in establishing these commitments, but in mixed and controlled economies alike their establishment is a foregone conclusion. The extent of the commitments and the sector's ability to fulfill them depends on both the productivity potential of the agricultural complex, and the intelligence and sophistication of agricultural planning at the national level.

The productivity potential of the agricultural sector is initially determined by the quality and quantity of land suitable for agricultural purposes, as well as the technology that can be effectively implemented in the production process. In addition, however, a sufficient supply of labor to work on the farms, and the development of a food-marketing network, including a food-processing industry and the requisite transportation network, must be achieved. Nonetheless, because "sufficient food supply to meet demand" is a universal dictum, the national agricultural production planning problem is commonly viewed as one of planning aimed at *helping* the agricultural sector to achieve its maximum potential. This can be accomplished via the more obvious, traditional approaches of government-sponsored and encouraged research and development programs, commodity price support systems, national labor policies, and pressures and subsidies for the development of transportation networks. In addition, there exists the possibility of interregional planning for a more effective use of the available land. Here, the issue is to determine the uses to which the land in various regions should be allocated, *given* the demand for various farm products, at *given* or *assumed* factor and commodity price ratios, levels of technology, labor supply patterns, locational factors, and transportation networks and costs.

As previously indicated, this issue can be and has been attacked through various linear programming models.[12] In these models, the regions are usually defined by attempting to group together lands, generally contiguous, that can be considered as being homogeneous in quality for production purposes; that is, lands that are approximately equally effective in a fixed set of agricultural uses, such as the raising of corn, wheat, and barley. The decision variables in such models are the amount of commodity $j(j = 1, \ldots, m)$ to be grown in region $r(r = 1, \ldots, R)$, denoted q_{rj}. Then, given unit profit rates π_{rj} for the average profit per unit of commodity j grown in region r, or average cost figures C_{rj} for growing a unit of commodity j in region r, one can define a linear programming problem having as its objective the maximization of a linear total profit function $\Sigma\Sigma\pi_{rj}q_{rj}$, or the minimization of a linear total cost function $\Sigma\Sigma C_{rj}q_{rj}$, subject to a series of constraints.

The need to satisfy a demand commitment is incorporated into the model through the constraint set $\Sigma q_{rj} = Q_j(j = 1, \ldots, m)$, where Q_j is the estimate of final demand at the assumed price ratios and income rates. Technology is introduced through factors a_{rj}, the per unit input of land in the rth region in the production of the jth commodity. Then, with b_r $(r = 1, \ldots, R)$ the agricultural land capacity in region r, the constraint set $\Sigma a_{rj}q_{rj} \leq b_r(r = 1, \ldots, R)$ is developed. An analogous set of constraints taking into consideration the available labor supply in these regions can also be developed and incorporated into the model.

The model can be extended in various ways, through the inclusion of additional constraints, and dynamic and recursive features. Solving it and implementing its results is not as readily accomplished. The free market does not necessarily respond as rapidly to indicative optimal planning as does a controlled economy to directive plans. As the world becomes increasingly aware of its food scarcity problems, however, it is not unlikely that land-use planning will gain in momentum in mixed as in controlled economies, and that even in the "free" market economies the educational process and government pressures will result in a more effective use of the available labor supply.

14.6 CONCLUDING COMMENTS

Growing human populations are placing an increasingly acute strain on the world's scarce supply of fertile land, and are further aggravating the food shortage problems that have historically plagued the world, and for which there is no apparent satisfactory solution other than the population limitations that many view as ethically and morally reprehensible. Failing to achieve these limitations, or even should they be achieved, the food shortage problem can only be resolved or ameliorated by effective agricultural planning that results in an optimal use of those lands that are employed in the food production process. Although such optimal use ultimately depends on land use of the individual farms, the latter are interrelated components in the agricultural subsystem as a whole, and what is optimal for one farm considered in isolation will not neces-

[12] E. O. Heady and A. C. Egbert, "Spatial Programming Models to Specify Surplus Grain Producing Areas," in A. S. Manne and H. M. Markowitz, *op. cit.*

sarily be optimal when viewed from the perspective of *all* of agriculture. Thus, educating the individual farmer in optimal allocation schemes will not suffice unless supported by national and regional agricultural planning that imposes sufficient constraints on farmers so as to force them into commodity allocation schemes that are compatible with national goals.

Agricultural planning is greatly simplified by the facts that, first, *for many purposes* the agricultural sector can be dealt with *as if* it were independent of the industrial sector, and, second, the basic relationships in the mathematical specification of agricultural planning problems can quite realistically be assumed to be linear. As a result, these problems have generally been formulated as linear programming problems. Even so, the most fundamental of these, planning at the national level, is sufficiently complex and difficult to implement even when mathematically and computationally tractable, that the greatest virtue of the solutions may lie in the *information* that can be extracted by subjecting the models to different assumptions and parameter values.

The solution to a linear programming problem for regional land use, for example, not only indicates land reallocations that would be desirable, but in addition yields a set of shadow prices associated with the various capacity restrictions. Thus, for the model discussed in the previous section, the dual variable associated with the constraint $\Sigma q_{rj} = Q_j$ determines a shadow price to evaluate, at the margin, a unit of the jth commodity. Similarly, the dual variable associated with the constraint $\Sigma a_{rj} q_{rj} = b_r$ determines a shadow price to evaluate, at the margin, a unit of land in the rth region.

Linear programming models are especially conducive to sensitivity analysis in which their solutions are tested for their sensitivity to variations in the individual parameters. Sensitivity analysis could be employed in agricultural planning to determine the effects on optimal land-use allocations of changes in the individual price and cost parameters, anticipated or government-encouraged shifts in regional labor-supply patterns, and technological advances that effect changes in the per unit input of scarce resources such as land, labor, and machinery into the production of any single commodity.

Assuredly, mathematical models cannot by themselves provide the answers to the world's food problems. They can, however, provide planners with information and suggestions as to how the world's scarce resources, in particular those that can be used in the agricultural sector, can be more effectively employed. In conjunction with econometric forecasting models, they can therefore help planners to anticipate the agricultural problems that will evolve in the future, and thereby help the planners to prepare for and deal with these problems in a more intelligent and satisfactory manner than has been the case in the past.

CHAPTER *15*
Locational and Regional Planning

15.1 GROWTH AND CHANGE IN THE SPATIAL CONTEXT

The process of economic growth and change is both uneven and disruptive. The Marxists have long stressed these characteristics, but they have doggedly attributed them *exclusively* to the capitalist mode of production. Lenin, for instance, has asserted that "the uneven and spasmodic character of development of individual enterprises, of individual branches of industries, and individual countries is inevitable under the capitalist system." [1] The reason for this, according to Lenin, is that the capitalists neglect the lagging sectors, particularly agriculture and consumer goods industries, in order to export their capital, in search for super-profits, to the backward countries. "Uneven development and wretched conditions of the masses are the fundamental and inevitable conditions and premises of this mode of production," [2] added Lenin, who, of course, was writing before the emergence of the "communist society."

Be that as it may, interregional and intersectoral unevenness in the growth process is a fact—but a fact with many causes. Beside complex combinations of *historical* factors—economic, social, political, and administrative—that originally favor or hamper the development of a region or sector, there are persistent *contemporary* difficulties that tend to further accent intranational disparities. Principal among these difficulties are relative factor scarcities, the dependence of certain industries on the existence of others, and problems in the transportability of inputs and outputs, and in access to raw materials and markets. Moreover, in developed economies—capitalist, socialist, or mixed—the locus of technological change shifts continuously, its forms vary and embrace successively or simultaneously products, processes, and raw materials, and its

[1] V. I. Lenin, "Imperialism: The Highest Stage of Capitalism," in *Collected Works,* Vol. 22, December 1915–July 1916 (Moscow: Progress Publishers, 1964), p. 241.
[2] *Ibid., loc. cit.*

impact is unavoidably diverse in both range and intensity. As noted by Simon Kuznets, "The emergence of a new industry means ipso facto a change in the industrial distribution of the national output and productive resources." [3] A new industry may involve, moreover, the emergence of a set of other industries and services, alterations in a nation's geography, and unforeseeable modifications in a population's patterns of life and work, particularly when this industry is a "breakthrough" industry such as the automobile or the computer. No society, no matter how extensive its centralized controls, can actually foresee, let alone modify once and for all, such complex consequences of growth and change as (a) the obsolescence of certain enterprises, branches, or industries, (b) the increasing outdating of certain skills, (c) the continuous decay of certain population centers, and (d) the loss in developmental momentum of certain regions, any and all of which can impair the functioning of the economic system.

Indeed, readily observable short-term consequences are subtly interwoven with long-term impacts, combining in a variety of ways with already existing disparities between, say, purely agricultural areas, slowly developing industrial regions and/or rapidly growing and increasingly congested areas. All this requires constant changes in the overall regional balance. The policy makers of capitalist societies are not necessarily moved in this respect by national efficiency considerations alone; and conversely, the policy makers of socialist countries are not moved exclusively by the desire to redress social inequities and to achieve a harmonious and even development on the national scale. In both systems, policy makers are moved by a complex combination of goals and desires effected by the economic, social, and political issues involved, even though their priorities may and do vary. But whatever the case, both need appropriate frameworks for the study of intranational, interregional, and intraregional relationships.

The study of the dynamics of spatial dispersion and of its interactions has given rise to two types of theoretical and applied research. The first has concerned itself primarily with the explanation of this dispersion; the second, primarily with the study of these interactions, and eventually with the management of the regional, interregional, and regional-national activities within the framework of the national economy. In attempting to explain the forces shaping the regional location of activities, pride of place has been given to transportation and distance costs, notably in the pioneering works of J. H. von Thunen, Alfred Weber, and later in the theories of Walter Christaller and August Lösch. [4] Eventually, and conversely, attention has been paid to economies of scale, and to externalities in which transport costs have no part whatsoever, notably in the theories of Gunnar Myrdal, Albert O. Hirschman, and later of

---

[3] S. Kuznets, *Modern Economic Growth, Rate, Structure, and Spread* (New Haven: Yale University Press, 1966), p. 151.

[4] J. H. von Thunen, *Der isolierte Staat in Beziehung auf Landwirtschaft und Nationalökonomie* (Hamburg, 1926); A. Weber (C. Friedrich, transl.), *Theory of the Location of Industry* (Chicago: University of Chicago Press, 1929); W. Christaller, *Die zentrale Orte In Suddeutschland* (Jena, 1933); A. Lösch, *Die raumliche Ordnung der Wirtschaft* (Jena, 1944).

François Perroux.[5] Finally, a useful application of the theory of comparative or absolute (regional) advantage has been proposed in this field by Bertil Ohlin.[6] Some of the concepts of Christaller and Lösch concerning the combination of production and transportation costs have been put to use in conjunction with linear programming techniques by Jan Tinbergen and H. C. Bos,[7] in order to show what the regional distribution of various forms of activities *ought* to be.

In the applied studies of intranational interactions, pride of place has been given to the examination of the problems of how regions constitute a national economy, and conversely how the latter may be disaggregated into various spatial components. Decisive contributions were made in this field most notably by Wassily Leontief, Hollis B. Chenery, Edgar Hoover, Walter Isard, and Richard Stone.[8] Within the framework of two or multi-region, multi-sector models, the analysis of regional policy problems has focused on balanced regional growth and patterns of investment allocation, on regional employment "potentials," and on population transfers and education, on location of developmental projects, and on structure of interregional flows and accounts.

Following a brief discussion of the surprisingly controversial question of regional definition, we shall present some of the frameworks for locational and regional analysis, and then turn to a discussion of (a) the various models proposed for evaluating regional impacts of the dominance of a decision center, nodal centers or "key" industries, (b) the degree of mobility or market range of each commodity or producing sector, and of (c) the substitutability of regional trade flows. We then examine some spatial planning problems at various levels and within different horizons. In conclusion we discuss the goal conflicts involved in national-regional planning, and some of the basic limitations of the techniques prevailing in current planning use.

15.2 CLASSIFICATION OF REGIONS AND ACTIVITIES

Regional planning models proceed by spatially aggregating the interrelated components that comprise the economic system into a set of regional *subsystems*. As with national economies, each of these subsystems has its own unique

[5] On various forms and interpretations of regional *polarization* effects, see G. Myrdal, *Economic Theory and Undeveloped Regions* (London: Duckworths, 1957); A. O. Hirschman, *The Strategy of Economic Development* (New Haven, Conn.: Yale University Press, 1958); and F. Perroux, *L'Economie du XXe Siècle* (Paris: Presses Universitaires de France, 2nd ed., 1964).

[6] B. Ohlin, *Interregional and International Trade* (Cambridge, Mass.: Harvard University Press, 1933).

[7] J. Tinbergen, *Some Principles of Regional Planning* (Rotterdam: Netherlands Economic Institute, 1965); H. C. Bos, *Spatial Dispersion of Economic Activity* (Rotterdam: Rotterdam University Press, 1965).

[8] W. Leontief, "Interregional Theory," in W. Leontief *et al.* (eds.), *Studies in the Structure of the American Economy* (New York: Oxford University Press, 1953); H. B. Chenery, "Interregional and International Input-Output Analysis," in Tibor Barna (ed.) *Structural Interdependence of the Economy* (New York: John Wiley, 1960); E. M. Hoover, *The Location of Economic Activity* (New York: McGraw-Hill, 1963); W. Isard, *Methods of Regional Analysis: An Introduction to Regional Science* (Cambridge, Mass.: M.I.T. Press, 1960); Richard Stone, "Social Accounts at the Regional Level: A Survey," in W. Isard and J. H. Cumberland (eds.) *Regional Economic Planning* (Paris: European Productivity Agency, 1960).

set of characteristics with respect to natural resources, education and training and quantity of labor, and the existing capital stock and its level of technological sophistication. Moreover, each regional subsystem may have its own controller whose primary concern is with planning problems for that specific region, and who views the other regions as part of that subsystem's environment. Generally, the role of these controllers is that of an *infimal* decision maker whose decisions are constrained by the plans adopted by the *supremal* decision maker. The latter is a central planning agency that is concerned with the overall performance of the economic system, rather than simply that of any one of its component subsystems.

The determination of the components that are to be included in a particular regional subsystem, or the choice of the spaces for which the supremal unit will plan in an economy, the classification of the commodities and producing sectors by their degree of mobility, and the examination of possible substitutions among regional trade flows play a significant role in policy formulation and planning problems. Considerable attention has therefore been given in the literature to the question of delineating regional subsystems. Although we have already employed the concept of "a region" with considerable confidence that within the context of the previous discussions the concept would be quite clear, and as if the definition of "a region" clearly delineated some geographical entity—or, in the systems context, as if the components of the economic system could be logically and *uniquely* grouped into a set of regional subsystems—in fact, however, the definitional problem is quite complex, and has occasioned serious and defensible differences of opinion.[9]

Spatial contiguity is generally accepted as a necessary condition for classifying certain areas as being part of a given region. Yet geographical boundaries, whether artificial or national, can establish distinctions between areas that, in very important social and economic respects, are for all intents and purposes homogeneous. From the standpoint of economic planning, it is *homogeneity in the socio-economic plane* that is crucial to establishing both necessary *and* sufficient conditions for a regional definition. What geographical homogeneity commonly accounts for is the political and institutional factors that must also be taken into consideration. The definitional question, then, generally centers around *approaches* for establishing the regional delineations. Three approaches in particular have dominated the literature—that of the homogeneous region, the nodal region, and the program region.

The *homogeneous region* approach requires that spatially small geographic units having the same basic characteristics, say in terms of population composition, economic activities, terrain and institutions, be grouped together. The characteristics required for inclusion in a particular group or region will depend on the problem under attack; and the determination of whether or not a particular unit is included in the group can be based on either subjective evaluations, or quite objective, formula-based criteria. Thus, for purposes of deter-

[9] See J. R. Meyer, "Regional Economics: A Survey," *American Economic Review,* Vol. 53, No. 1, March 1963, pp. 19–54.

mining television-broadcast blackout regions, in the early days of baseball telecasts, blackout regions were defined as geographic areas within a 75-mile radius of second base in any major league park in which a home game was being played. For purposes of studying interregional income differences in the United States, however, a purely institutional-political definition that defines each state as a unique region might not only suffice, but might be quite logical, inasmuch as each state government operates as a unique decision-making unit.

So-called *nodal regions* are distinguished by an interdependence of flows, and are functional in nature. Each region is, in essence, defined around some geographic pole in terms of the sphere of influence exercised by the spatial unit located at that pole. Even such a mundane, if universal problem as the determination of when a telephone call is classified as a local call to be included as part of some regularly assessed fee, as opposed to when it becomes classified as a long-distance call subject to special rates, is ordinarily solved with the sphere-of-influence concept in mind. That is, and although, assuredly, there are other factors that enter in, the extent to which there is a regular and substantial communications flow between population centers is a prime consideration in defining the local-call region. In the nodal approach, then, the problem is to establish that different spatial units have a set of common characteristics, and then to group certain centers together, while separating others, on the basis of these characteristics.[10] This approach is particularly relevant, for example, in the analysis of traffic flows, and in the planning and analysis of transportation networks.

The *program* or *planning region* evolves as the optimal spatial grouping for decision-making or planning purposes, say as the framework for a linear programming model. The level of aggregation will be highly dependent on both the existing administrative hierarchy—that is, the location and influence of the infimal controllers—and the form and availability of the required statistical data. Typical of the problems for which programming regions are employed is that of interregional investment planning. Here, the supremal national controller inputs exogenous investment expenditures into the economic system, and specifically earmarks them for certain regions so as to effect particular patterns of regional development. In a fully coordinated planning system, the infimal regional controllers will then pursue regional policies commensurate with the overall national plan.

Each of these three approaches has its justification and advantages. The homogeneous approach, for example, may be particularly apt and sufficient for the analysis of interregional differences in economic activity, the nodal approach is apt for the study of interregional, inter-industry trade, and the program approach is apt in the solution of economic policy-making problems. There is, unhappily, no clearly appropriate answer to the definitional question. Rather, the answer depends on the problem that is being posed.

[10] An obvious analytical technique for eliciting the "common factors" and determining the appropriate spatial groupings is factor analysis. The applicability of the technique in the regional definition context is discussed in W. Isard, *op. cit.*, pp. 293–305.

15.3 FRAMEWORKS FOR REGIONAL ANALYSIS

Numerous problems of regional development have usually been phrased in terms of a North-South interregional dichotomy, and have been handled within the framework of two-sector models. Either the tools of growth theory or of international trade theory have been applied for the purpose to a closed economy consisting of spatially, rather than of functionally defined subsystems. Much of the literature in economic development is concerned with the causes of the differential rates of growth between and within countries, between advancing and lagging regions—namely, between megalopolises and lagging rural hinterlands, and in the LDC's in particular, between an industrial Western "enclave" and a rural, stagnating, overpopulated "native" economy. (Although not all "enclaves" and native economies are separated spatially; some simply do not interact economically.)

Within this framework, regional and locational planning models have proceeded along two main paths, each of which has itself forked into two separate lanes. The first path, consisting of *dualistic models,* has on the one hand been concerned with exploring the conditions under which the economic system, and each of the regional subsystems, would remain in equilibrium, or more specifically, the conditions for maintaining an *equilibrium rate of growth* for the system and its subsystems. On the other hand, this path has also led to concern with developing *dynamic optimization* models that would establish regional policies for optimizing some systemic objective function, with the emphasis in these models ordinarily being on the system's rate of economic growth.

In contrast to the former theoretical model types, the second path, consisting of interregional, inter-industry models, has on the one hand been concerned with the development of structural models for the empirical analysis of *inter-sectoral movements* of labor, capital, and the like. On the other hand, the specification of regional subsystems has also resulted in the conversion of the more familiar macro accounting models into their regional counterparts, in particular in the development of regional income and product accounts along the classic lines of the national income and product accounts, as well as in the development of regional input-output models that consider both interregional and inter-industry flows.

Typical models of each genre are considered in this section.

a. Dualistic models

The obvious temptation to study regional growth by redefining time-honored macroeconomic models in regional terms has neither been overlooked nor overcome. The two main classes of these models are those that are demand oriented and those that are supply oriented. In each case, however, the regional models will necessarily differ from their macroeconomic counterparts insofar as the latter commonly are built to describe growth in a closed economy, whereas regional subsystems are *open economies* that *necessarily interact* with each other. Thus, one region's opportunities for growth necessarily depend on, and are constrained by, those of the other regions with which it is linked in the economic system. It is in the acknowledgment of these links that the regional models differ from the macroeconomic models, and entail additional complexity.[11]

The Harrod-Domar model is typical of the demand-oriented continuous-time growth models. As previously discussed (Section 6.2c) equilibrium or steady-state growth in a closed economy with a marginal propensity to save of s and a capital:output ratio of k will occur at a rate of $g = s/k$, when planned savings equals planned investment. In order to maintain full employment, this rate must also equal the rate of growth in the population, n. In an open economy, however, equilibrium requires that planned savings S *plus* imports M be equal to planned investment I *plus* exports X; or, in effect, that planned savings plus the *difference* between imports and exports equal planned investment. That is, $S + (M - X) = I$. Hence, if we define net planned savings as the sum of planned savings and net imports, the condition for equilibrium growth in an open economy or region i is that $g_i = s_i'/k_i$. Here, s_i' is the net marginal propensity to save in region i, and k_i is the capital:output ratio in that specific region. Clearly, then, with Y denoting income, and the subscript indexing the region, $S_i' = S_i + M_i - X_i$ and $dS_i'/dY_i = s_i + m_i - x_i = s_i'$.

The equilibrium rate of growth in region i now becomes

$$g_i = \frac{s_i + m_i - x_i}{k_j} = \frac{s_i'}{k_i} \tag{15.1}$$

Moreover, for full employment we require that this rate of growth equal the rate of growth in the regional labor force. The latter rate, in turn, is assumed to be equal to the rate of regional population growth net of the rate of *migration* into the region. Defining both the regional population and migration growth rates with reference to the regional population, and denoting these rates by n_i and n_{mi}, respectively, steady-state growth requires that

$$g_i = \frac{s_i + m_i - x_i}{k_i} = n_i \pm n_{mi} \tag{15.2}$$

Each region cannot, however, be considered in isolation of the others, for it is apparent that growth in one region depends on the maintenance of the requisite imports and exports in the rest of the economy; and, similarly, it is apparent that an inflow, say, of migrants into region i will be achieved only through an outflow of migrants from some region j ($j \neq i$). In particular, it is intuitively apparent that a balanced growth rate of g in the economic system requires that *each* of the R regional subsystems grow at the same rate; or, $g = g_i (i = 1, \ldots, R)$. In a two-region economy, for example, this requires that

[11] For a discussion see H. W. Richardson, *Regional Economics* (New York: Praeger, 1969), pp. 323–336.

$$g_i = \frac{s_1 + m_1 - x_1}{k_1} = \frac{s_2 + m_2 - x_2}{k_2}$$

or that

$$\frac{k_2}{k_1} = \frac{s_2 + m_2 - x_2}{s_1 + m_1 - x_1} = \frac{s_2'}{s_1'} \tag{15.3}$$

That is, balanced growth requires that the ratio of the regional capital:output ratios be equal to the ratio of the regional net marginal propensities to save.

These results can be interpreted in two ways. On the one hand, they provide conditions that *must be respected* for balanced growth to be achieved. Whether these conditions are met then becomes an empirical fact. By the same token, the desire to achieve balanced growth, and the failure to verify the empirical fact, can provide the impetus for actions to redress the failure. Typical of these actions might be the direction of investment into one region rather than into another, in an effort to effect a change in the regional capital:output ratios. Similarly, national policies to encourage migration from one region to another might be suggested by the model, and implemented by the supremal controller.

On the other hand, the model also indicates conditions that *explain* interregional differences in growth rates. As such, it provides the basis for national economic policies designed to exploit these differences, in the sense of taking advantage of the growth potential of the "more promising" regions, rather than permitting the "less promising" regions to hold back the rest.

Supply-oriented models proceed from regional production functions in which regional income or output is generally assumed to be a function of the regional capital stock, regional employment, and the level of technology. Under the classical assumptions of perfect competition and constant returns to scale, each factor will receive as its wage the value of its marginal product; the rate of growth of *regional* output will then equal the weighted average of the regional rates of growth of employed capital and labor, each weighted by the respective factor's share in the total output, adjusted to reflect technological progress. Full employment of the capital stock and balanced growth further requires that the marginal product of capital *in each region* equal the *national* interest rate.

That is, let K_i denote the capital stock in region i, L_i denote employment in region i, and Y_i denote regional output or income. Then,

$$\frac{\partial Y_i}{\partial K_i} \frac{K_i}{Y_i} = a_i = (\text{marginal product of capital}) \left(\frac{\text{capital}}{\text{output}}\right) =$$

$$\text{capital's output share} \tag{15.4a}$$

Similarly, with $Y_i = f_i(K_i, L_i)$ and, as an illustrative simplification, ignoring the possibility of technological change,

$$\frac{\partial Y_i}{\partial L_i} \frac{L_i}{Y_i} = (1 - a_i) \tag{15.4b}$$

and

$$\frac{\partial Y_i}{\partial K_i}\frac{K_i}{Y_i}+\frac{\partial Y_i}{\partial L_i}\frac{L_i}{Y_i}=1$$

whereupon we immediately confirm the classic Euler result of microeconomics,

$$\frac{\partial Y_i}{\partial K_i}K_i+\frac{\partial Y_i}{\partial L_i}L_i=Y_i \qquad (15.4c)$$

Hence, with $\partial Y_i/\partial K_i = r_i =$ the regional interest rate, $r_i K_i/Y_i = a_i$ or

$$a_i\frac{Y_i}{K_i}=r_i \qquad (15.4d)$$

In a two-region economy, under perfect competition, equilibrium requires that $r_1 = r_2$, otherwise capital will shift to the region rewarding it with the higher "wage." Hence,

$$a_1\frac{Y_1}{K_1}=a_2\frac{Y_2}{K_2} \qquad (15.5a)$$

or

$$\frac{a_1}{a_2}=\frac{K_1/Y_1}{K_2/Y_2}=\frac{k_1}{k_2} \qquad (15.5b)$$

That is, equilibrium growth requires that the ratio of capital's share of the total output in each region be equal to the ratio of the regional capital:output ratios.

Similarly, in each region

$$\frac{dY_i}{dt}=\frac{\partial Y_i}{\partial K_i}\frac{\partial K_i}{\partial t}+\frac{\partial Y_i}{\partial L_i}\frac{\partial L_i}{\partial t}$$

Substituting (15.4a) and (15.4b) and then dividing through by Y_i

$$\frac{\left(\dfrac{dY_i}{dt}\right)}{Y_i}=a_i\frac{\left(\dfrac{\partial K_i}{\partial t}\right)}{K_i}+(1-a_i)\frac{\left(\dfrac{\partial L_i}{\partial t}\right)}{L_i}$$

or, where g_i, $_K g_i$, and $_L g_i$ are the rates of growth in output, employed capital, and labor, respectively,

$$g_i = (a_i)\,_K g_i + (1-a_i)_L g_i \qquad (15.5c)$$

That is, the rate of growth of regional output is a weighted average of the rates of growth of regional employment and the regional capital stock. The results of this analysis can then be employed in an analogous fashion to those of the previous model.

Neither of these models is *directly* concerned with optimization. Rather, each is germane to the *study* of growth in dualistic economies, and to the analysis of the structural conditions for national (system) and regional (subsystem) growth. Rahman [12] has presented an optimization model that has been the foundation for several subsequent, more advanced models of the breed.

In Rahman's model, the problem is to maximize national income Y_t at some horizon date T, for a two-region economy. The regional incomes at time t are denoted Y_{1t} and Y_{2t}, where $Y_t = Y_{1t} + Y_{2t}$. The fixed (marginal) rates of saving in the two regions are s_1 and s_2, respectively, and k_1 and k_2 are the marginal capital:output ratios in the two regions. Thus, the rate of investment taking place at the beginning of time period $t + 1$ is $k_1(Y_{1(t+1)} - Y_{1t}) + k_2$ $(Y_{2(t+1)} - Y_{2t})$; and, the savings-equal-to-investment condition requires

$$\sum_{i=1}^{2} k_i(Y_{i(t+1)} - Y_{it}) = \sum_{i=1}^{2} s_i Y_{it} \qquad t = 0, \ldots, T-1 \qquad (15.6)$$

A requirement is imposed that there be no net disinvestment in either region, which is equivalent to the demand that regional income must never decrease. This is written as

$$Y_{i(t+1)} - Y_{it} \geq 0 \qquad i = 1, 2; t = 0, \ldots, T-1 \qquad (15.7)$$

Rahman also introduces a so-called "political" constraint that limits the extent to which income in one region is permitted to exceed income in the other; or

$$\gamma_1 \leq \frac{Y_{1(t+1)}}{Y_{2(t+1)}} \leq \gamma_2 \qquad t = 0, \ldots, T-1 \qquad (15.8)$$

The problem, then, is to choose investment (income) rates so as to

$$\text{Maximize } Y_T = Y_{1T} + Y_{2T} \qquad (15.9)$$

subject to (15.6), (15.7), and (15.8).

This problem is a dynamic programming problem. The solution yields several interesting propositions that Rahman summarizes as follows: [13]

The more productive region (region 1) is favored throughout the entire planning period. This occurs when $s_2/k_2 < s_1/k_1$. In this case the less productive region is unable to offer a rate of saving high enough to offset higher productivity of the other region. Optimality requires that investment be concentrated in the more productive region every year, subject of course to the constraints of the model.

The less productive region is favored in a number of initial years, after which the program switches to the other extreme in favor of the more productive region for the remaining years. This occurs when $s_2/k_2 > s_1/k_1$, and the planning period is large enough so that the initial loss of income resulting from concentrating investment in the less productive region can be recovered, within the planning horizon, with the help of the higher saving rate of this region.

By extreme, we mean that investment takes place so that one region or the other achieves its *maximum possible* rate of income, given the constraints.

[12] M. A. Rahman, "Regional Allocation of Investment," in J. Friedman and W. Alonso (eds.) *Regional Development and Planning* (Cambridge, Mass.: M.I.T. Press, 1964).
[13] *Ibid.*, p. 665.

Subject to this initial maximization, the other region is then provided with the maximum feasible income rate. One of the most interesting implications of the analysis is, then, the observation that the more productive region will not necessarily be the region in which investment is ordinarily concentrated, even when the maximization of total income is the investment criterion. Rather, this will also depend on the propensity to save and, therefore, presumably, on the underlying behavioral patterns.

A related model, due to Datta-Chaudhuri, has as its objective the allocation of "total savings of the nation among the two regions at each instant of time in such a way that the nation as a whole acquires a desired level of capital stock, irrespective of its geographical distribution, in the shortest possible time." [14] In this model, then, the objective is to minimize $T = \int_0^t t_o' dt$ subject to a series of structural constraints. The latter include regional production functions of the form $Y_i(t) = L_i(t) f_i(K_i/L_i)$, employment-growth constraints of the form $L_i(t) = L_i(0) e^{n_i t}$, savings and investment functions, and identities.

The resulting problem can be solved by the calculus of variations for *control variables* $\mu_i (i = 1, 2)$ that determine the optimal rates of transfer of saving from region i to region j ($j \neq i$). The solution to this problem is shown to depend on $\partial S_i/\partial K_i$—the so-called "reinvestment quotient"—as well as on the values of the "multipliers" introduced into the problem in order to solve it. The latter, however, represent the regional demand prices for investment. The solution therefore also depends on the relationship between the demand price for investment in the two regions. In particular, where $(1 - \delta)T_i(t)$ is added to the capital stock of region i ($i \neq j$) at time t, if the region 1-to-region 2 price ratio is less than $1 - \delta$, all investment occurs in region 2, and vice versa for a price ratio that exceeds $1/(1 - \delta)$.

Other, more complex objective functions with more diverse goals can be, and also have been considered. Marglin, for example, has considered spatial planning as a means of *both* increasing aggregate consumption, *and* redistributing wealth to shore up consumption in the low-income region in a two-region economy. [15] The resolution of this problem, that is, the choice of an optimal investment program, depends on the explicit form of the objective function—that is, the extent to which the policy makers are willing to accept trade-offs between growth and redistribution; and the structural possibilities—that is, the extent to which sacrifices in economic growth are required, if indeed they are, in order to effect a redistribution of income.

b. Interregional, inter-industry models

The second major path consists of both empirically based structural models and the input-output and regional accounting models to analyze inter-

[14] M. Datta-Chaudhuri, "Optimal Allocation of Investment and Transportation in a Two-Region Economy," in K. Shell (ed.) *Essays on the Theory of Optimal Economic Growth* (Cambridge, Mass.: M.I.T. Press, 1967), pp. 129–140.

[15] S. A. Marglin, *Public Investment Criteria* (Cambridge, Mass.: M.I.T. Press, 1967).

regional and inter-industry flows. An especially interesting model of the former type is due to Klaassen.[16]

The underlying theoretical model is built with an eye toward empirical testing, and proceeds from the initial specification that a region's working population at time 0, N, is given by the sum of the working population at time -1, N_{-1}, the natural growth of this population gN_{-1}, and net worker's migration, N_M; or

$$N = N_{-1} + gN_{-1} + N_M \qquad (15.10a)$$

Net migration is assumed to be proportional to the difference between the wage rate w in the region and the average wage rate $\bar{w}$ outside the region; or,

$$N_M = \alpha(w - \bar{w}) \qquad (15.10b)$$

where α is a constant of proportionality. Further, the working population and labor supply L_s are taken as equivalent; or,

$$L_s = N \qquad (15.10c)$$

The demand for labor in basic and nonbasic industries, denoted L_{DB} and L_{DN}, respectively, is *specified* as

$$L_{DB} = -\beta(w - \bar{w}) + Z \qquad (15.10d)$$
$$L_{DN} = \gamma N \qquad (15.10e)$$

where β and γ are constants of proportionality, and Z is an autonomous demand factor. Finally, total demand for labor, L_D, is given by the identity

$$L_D = L_{DB} + L_{DN} \qquad (15.10f)$$

and with labor supply and demand equated,

$$L_D = L_S \qquad (15.10g)$$

These seven structural equations can be solved simultaneously to yield two reduced-form equations:

$$N = \theta_1(N_{-1} + gN_{-1}) + \theta_2 Z \qquad (15.11a)$$
$$w - \bar{w} = \phi_1(N_{-1} + gN_{-1}) + \phi_2 Z \qquad (15.11b)$$

where θ_i and $\phi_i(i = 1, 2)$ are functions of α, β, and γ. Fitting Equations (15.11a) and (15.11b) by ordinary cross-section least squares determines α uniquely; but, β and γ are over-identified. Nonetheless, a sensitivity analysis of the basic model itself enables us to explore the implications for regional working populations, and hence industrial growth, of differing values of α, β, and γ, and permits the planner to draw inferences with respect to why, in the past, certain regions have grown, whereas others have declined.

For actual policy problems, a still greater degree of regional disaggrega-

[16] L. H. Klaassen, *Area Economic and Social Redevelopment* (Paris: OECD, 1965), pp. 23–39.

tion may be required. A basic foundation for regional economic analysis and planning is provided by regional *accounts*—namely, income and product accounts, and regional input-output accounts. Richard Stone [17] has been a prime contributor in the former regard, and Walter Isard and Leon Moses [18] have been preeminent in the latter.

The purpose of regional accounting models is to provide a convenient framework for describing interregional and intraregional transactions. The regional accounts disaggregate these transactions in various ways that are convenient for both the supremal (national) and infimal (regional) policy makers who require both informational inputs for the policy-making process, and also a means of analyzing the potential impact, within and among regions, of the various actions that they are contemplating. Unlike the national accounts, the basic focus of which is short term in nature, and the basic policy-related use of which is the regulation of short-term movements in the national economy, the basic focus of the regional accounts is long term in nature, and their basic policy-related use is in studying the long-term interregional and intraregional movements and trends in the location of economic activity.

To accomplish this study, Stone has suggested the division of regional economic activity into three primary categories: production, consumption, and investment. Although the empirical problems in a further disaggregation are considerable, in principle each of these primary categories can itself be broken down into such component parts as production by industrial groups, consumption of durable and nondurable goods, and investment in capital goods and inventory.

Within the broadest disaggregation, production in region r is considered to consist of consumption and investment goods that remain in region r, the value of which is denoted by C_{rr} and V_{rr}, respectively, as well as exports to other regions, denoted X_{rs} ($r \neq s$). These "inflows" into the production account are exactly balanced by payments to the factors of production. The latter "outflows" consist of payments to the consumption sectors in the other regions, denoted Y_{rs}, as well as imports from these sectors, X_{sr}, and depreciation D_{rr}. Similarly, the "inflows" into the consumption account are exactly balanced by a set of "outflows." In addition to the consumption expenditure C_{rr}, these consist of interregional "gifts and grants," denoted G_{rs}, and regional savings, denoted S_{rr}. Since all interregional trade is assumed to take place through the production sector, there is no *direct* interregional consumption, and $C_{rs} = 0$. Finally, the "outflows" from the investment account consists of the regional investment purchases, V_{rr}, and interregional borrowing, denoted B_{rs} ($r \neq s$).

Figures 15.1 and 15.2, which are due to Stone,[19] illustrate the regional accounting system for three regions. In the first case, the accounts are ordered by region, and then by type of account within each region; in the second case, the

[17] R. Stone, *op. cit.*

[18] L. N. Moses, "The Stability of Interregional Trading Patterns and Input-Output Analysis," *American Economic Review,* Vol. 45, No. 5, December 1955.

[19] R. Stone, *op. cit.,* p. 268.

		Region 1			Region 2			Region 3		
		P	C	K	P	C	K	P	C	K
Region 1	P	0	C_{11}	V_{11}	X_{12}	0	0	X_{13}	0	0
	C	Y_{11}	0	0	Y_{12}	G_{12}	0	Y_{13}	G_{13}	0
	K	D_{11}	S_{11}	0	0	0	B_{12}	0	0	B_{13}
Region 2	P	X_{21}	0	0	0	C_{22}	V_{22}	X_{23}	0	0
	C	Y_{21}	G_{21}	0	Y_{22}	0	0	Y_{23}	G_{23}	0
	K	0	0	B_{21}	D_{22}	S_{22}	0	0	0	B_{23}
Region 3	P	X_{31}	0	0	X_{32}	0	0	0	C_{33}	V_{33}
	C	Y_{31}	G_{31}	0	Y_{32}	G_{32}	0	Y_{33}	0	0
	K	0	0	B_{31}	0	0	B_{32}	D_{33}	S_{33}	0

FIGURE 15-1

		P			C			K		
		1	2	3	1	2	3	1	2	3
P	1	0	X_{12}	X_{13}	C_{11}	0	0	V_{11}	0	0
	2	X_{21}	0	X_{23}	0	C_{22}	0	0	V_{22}	0
	3	X_{31}	X_{32}	0	0	0	C_{33}	0	0	V_{33}
C	1	Y_{11}	Y_{12}	Y_{13}	0	G_{12}	G_{13}	0	0	0
	2	Y_{21}	Y_{22}	Y_{23}	G_{21}	0	G_{23}	0	0	0
	3	Y_{31}	Y_{32}	Y_{33}	G_{31}	G_{32}	0	0	0	0
K	1	D_{11}	0	0	S_{11}	0	0	0	B_{12}	B_{13}
	2	0	D_{22}	0	0	S_{22}	0	B_{21}	0	B_{23}
	3	0	0	D_{33}	0	0	S_{33}	B_{31}	B_{32}	0

FIGURE 15-2

accounts are ordered by type of account, and then by region within each account type.

The accounts can be aggregated in various ways to derive various figures of interest to policy makers and planners. In particular, $Y_{11} + Y_{21} + Y_{31} = Y_{d1}$ is "domestic" income, or the net domestic product at factor cost of region 1; and, in general, $\sum_s Y_{rs} = Y_{dr}$ is the net domestic product of region r. National income will then be given by $\sum_r Y_{dr} = Y$. Gross income in region r will then be given by $Y_{dr} + \sum_s G_{rs}$. This income will be spent on consumption goods, savings and grants, and gifts to other regions. That is, the outlays of the consumption sector of region 1 will equal $C_{11} + S_{11} + G_{21} + G_{31}$; and, in general, the outlays of the consumption sector of region r will equal $C_{rr} + S_{rr} + \sum_s G_{sr}$. Net exports of region 1 will be given by $X_{12} + X_{13} - X_{21} - X_{31} = X_1$; and, in general, net exports of region r will be given by $\sum_r (X_{rs} - X_{rs}) = X_r$. Clearly, $\sum X_r = 0$.

The specific aggregations obtained in any particular instance, and the most useful format for the presentation of these accounts, will depend on the particular policy-making problem under consideration. Given a set of such accounts over even a moderately long period such as, say, five or ten years, it might further be possible to distinguish certain trends in, say, the interregional balance of payments and investment flows, as well as to derive suggestions as to possible explanations for regional disparities in economic wealth. This approach also encourages the taking of the additional steps and assumptions required by input-output analysis, a technique that, as we have already seen, has proven to be so very valuable for planning at the national level.

The crucial input-output assumption is that $a_{ik} = q_{ik}/Q_k$ is a constant, where q_{ik} is the input of the ith commodity into the production of the kth commodity, and Q_k is the total output of the kth commodity. For purposes of interregional analysis, this assumption is extended to *each region's share* in the production of commodity k. That is, it is assumed that $_rb_k = {_rQ_k}/Q_k$ is a constant, where $_rQ_k$ is the output in region r of commodity k. As we shall see below, it is feasible to modify these assumptions slightly. In particular, we could define fixed *regional* technological coefficients that specify a fixed proportion of one region's inputs to another region's outputs where that proportion might vary among regions. That is, we could define fixed technological coefficients, $_{rs}a_{ik} = {_{rs}q_{ik}}/{_rQ_k}$, that represent the proportion of the kth commodity in region r that is comprised of an input of commodity i from region s. Additionally, some of the $_rb_k$ can equal unity. This is the case of the so-called regional commodities that are produced and sold exclusively in a single region, the rth.

Given a set of demands for all the commodities, in particular national demands for the commodities sold nationally and regional demands for the commodities sold regionally, the familiar balance equations can be defined and solved for the regional outputs and interregional, inter-industry flows.[20]

Denote by Y_i the known final demand for commodity i ($i = 1, \ldots, m$). The output of this commodity used as a factor input is $\Sigma q_{ik} = \Sigma a_{ik}Q_k$. Thus

$$Q_i - \sum_k a_{ik}Q_k = Y_i \qquad i = 1, \ldots, m \qquad (15.12)$$

is a system of m linear balance equations in m unknowns which is readily solved for the m values of the Q_i.

For those commodities that are balanced nationally, say commodities $i = h + 1, \ldots, m$, the regional outputs are now immediately determined from

$$_rQ_k = {_rb_k}\,(Q_k) \qquad r = 1, \ldots, R;\, k = h + 1, \ldots, m \qquad (15.13)$$

Commodities $i = 1, \ldots, h$, however, are also balanced *regionally*. That is, there is a set of known regional final demands, $_rY_i(r = 1, \ldots, R;\, i = 1, \ldots, h)$, that must also be satisfied. By analogy to (15.12) we obtain

$$_rQ_i - \sum_k a_{ik}Q_k = {_rY_i} \qquad r = 1, \ldots, R;\, i = 1, \ldots, h \qquad (15.12a)$$

[20] See W. Leontief, *op. cit.*, pp. 95–97.

which is actually R systems of linear equations, each system containing h linear equations in h unknowns—the commodities $_rQ_k$ $(k = 1, \ldots, h)$.

Assuredly, at the regional level the data problems of input-output analysis multiply, and the fixed coefficients assumptions exercise still a greater strain on credulity than in the case of national input-output models. Potentially, however, the approach is pregnant with possibilities. In particular, it has been used to study the impact at the national level of changes in regional industrial structure, the impact on the regional balance of payments of changes in interregional trade, and the effects on interregional flows of exogenous changes in national demand.[21] In principle, at least over the short term, the results of such studies will be valid, and with respect to the long term the model can be made dynamic, say by permitting the coefficients to vary over time. In practice, however, the problems and limitations would seem to outweigh the usefulness of the results. Indeed, in the United States where a tremendous amount of work has been done on input-output models, their effect on policy formulation has been nil. Their major virtue may well be the pedagogical one of illustrating the interdependence of the sectors in the economy; or, in LDC's, they might prove useful provided that the coefficients are based on engineering data in which the authorities know what production techniques will be used or are being used.

15.4 NODAL CENTERS AND THE SPATIAL MOVEMENT OF GOODS

a. Nodal models

Nodal models are concerned with the delineation of regions having a functional unity. The purpose of these models is to assist in an understanding of how the regions so delineated tend to develop and grow, in order to improve efforts to plan and control this development, as well as to provide a definitional structure amenable to the analysis of interregional flows. Central place theory, gravity models, and the growth-point concept have been the major models of nodality.[22]

Central place theory begins with the observation that urban populations tend to be distributed among urban centers of different sizes. These centers comprise an urban hierarchy in which the larger centers dominate in the flows of economic activity, acting as the centers for market areas that are served with a set of products and services, including governmental services. There is, however, a multi-level system of centers that emerge when, for example, the population in a given urban area is sufficiently large from the standpoint of economic efficiency to serve as a center for its own market area, or when the distance between the largest center in the hierarchy and the "infimal" centers is sufficiently great as to justify the establishment of a second center, albeit one

---

[21] See W. Isard, *op. cit.*, pp. 349–363, and H. W. Richardson, *Input-Output and Regional Economics* (London: World University, 1972).

[22] For a discussion see H. W. Richardson, *Elements of Regional Economics* (Baltimore: Penguin Modern Economics, 1969), pp. 89–107.

that services a smaller market area than that served by the primary, "supremal" center. There is a relationship between size-class and the distance between centers, with the larger urban centers in the lower order of the hierarchy.

Viewing the development of urban centers from the hierarchical standpoint is convenient to the extent that it provides a useful framework for planning decisions, in particular decisions concerning the allocation of resources. The central place concept suggests the impact of decisions involving urban centers on the network of infimal centers lying within their aegis. In addition, the concept provides a basis for helping us to understand urban systems and how they grow. This is, however, a very narrow basis because in the models emanating from central place theory, growth depends solely on an increase of population in the hinterland of the cities. In fact, much if not most of the growth in industrially advanced or in industrializing countries comes from technological change and from capital accumulation (human or physical) rather than from a mere increase in people.

The simplest of the formal models along these lines, the rank-size rule, states that the population of any center in a hierarchy will be proportional to the population of the largest center in the hierarchy; or,

$$M^{\alpha}P_M = P_A \tag{15.14}$$

where P_A is the population of the largest urban center, P_M is the population of the center of rank M, and α is a constant to be determined empirically. This model has been extended by Beckmann [23] to one that results in the pair of equations:

$$P_M = \frac{R_1 n^{M-1}}{(1-K)^M} \tag{15.15a}$$

where P_M is the population *served* by place of order M, R_1 is the rural population served by place of lowest rank, K is the proportion of the total population in the hierarchy located in the central place, and n is the number of places in order $M - 1$ served by places in order M; and,

$$C_M = \frac{KR_1 n^{M-1}}{(1-K)^M} \tag{15.15b}$$

where C_M is the population of place of rank M. These equations follow from the definitions $C_M = KP_M$ and $P_M = C_M + nP_{M-1}$ after a bit of algebraic manipulation. For planning purposes, Equations (15.15a) and (15.15b) can help to explain and anticipate the growth of urban centers, in light of their place in the urban hierarchy.

The gravity concept provides a useful operational device for delineating regions, a device that recognizes the importance of distance between centers, as well as some measure of their attraction. In this context, the concept of attrac-

[23] M. Beckmann, "City Hierarchies and the Distribution of City Size," *Economic Development and Cultural Change*, Vol. 6, 1958, pp. 243–248.

tion is neither easily nor unambiguously defined. It relates, for example, to the ability of a center to attract retail trade in particular, or economic activity in general. Thus, the size of the center, the rate of economic activity in the center, and the size of the "downtown" area, are some measures that have been suggested as appropriate surrogates for attraction.

Specifically, with A_r a measure of the attraction of center r, say its population, d_{rs} a measure of the distance between centers r and s, and α, β, γ, and θ positive constants, the degree of interaction between centers r and s is defined to be

$$I_{rs} = \frac{\alpha A_r^\beta A_s^\gamma}{d_{rs}^\theta} \qquad (15.16)$$

That is, interaction is directly related to attraction, and inversely related to distance. Similarly, the "potential" of center r is defined by

$$P_r = \alpha \Sigma \, \frac{A_s^\gamma}{d_{rs}^\theta} \qquad (15.16a)$$

That is, the interaction of a center with *all* other centers will be directly related to their attraction, and inversely related to their distances from the center in question.

The appropriate measure of attraction will depend on the purpose for which the gravity model is being employed. The interaction measure itself can serve two purposes. First, it provides a descriptive measure that can serve as the criterion for delineating nodal regions by requiring certain levels of the measure to include different centers in the same region. Second, it can provide an empirical basis for testing theories and hypotheses with respect to urban growth and inter-center flows, and it can assist in the location of industry, in the planning of towns, and so forth.

In particular, it can be suggestive insofar as it signals centers, or "bedroom" and business communities, whose connecting transportation and communication links might warrant reconsideration and subsequent restructuring. An especially attractive planning procedure in the development of an interregional transportation or communications network is to follow a minimax criterion in which, for example, one would seek to determine the road network that *minimizes* the *maximum* expected number of automobiles in any road lane during peak-use hours, or the number of telephone trunk lines that *minimizes* the *maximum* expected delay in making a telephone connection, subject in either case to a set of constraints. The attraction of this approach is twofold: first, it effects the optimization of a straightforward, readily understood, and not unappealing objective function under conditions of risk, and thereby finesses the issue of specifying the less-easily developed von Neumann-Morgenstern preference function; and, second, it commonly results in a programming problem that is much more mathematically tractable than that which would result from the likely alternatives of equal sophistication.

Finally, the growth point concept, which is primarily due to Perroux,[24] distinguishes between the key "propulsive" industries that expand and induce development, and the stagnant and declining industries. It is these propulsive industries that provide the nucleus for regional growth around which other industries will agglomerate. Planning at the regional level requires the control of these so-called growth points, inasmuch as decisions concerning, say, the location of the growth points will, simultaneously, if indirectly, result in decisions regarding other industries that tend to agglomerate with the propulsive industries. For planning purposes, then, such growth point decisions are critical in effecting interregional disparities in economic growth, or in ameliorating or aggravating the existing disparities.

b. Commodities and sectors market ranges

The Netherlands School has formulated an interesting linear programming model for planning the location of (commodity and service) sectors $h(h = 1, \ldots, H)$ in prespecified regions $r(r = 1, \ldots, R)$.[25] The movement of a sector into or out of a region is indicated by the value of the decision variable Y_{hr}, which denotes the increase in income or value added of sector h in region r. For illustrative purposes, we shall assume that $Y_{hr} \geq 0(r = 1, \ldots, R;$ $h = 1, \ldots, H)$—that is, regional production never decreases for any sector—although the variables can be redefined for the purposes of using the simplex algorithm, so as to make this assumption unnecessary.

The model assumes that the sectors can be classified in various ways. In particular, it distinguishes between sectors that can exist in all regions, those that can exist in one region only, and those that can exist in some, but not all, regions. These are called *shiftable, nonshiftable,* and *partly shiftable,* respectively. These same distinctions can be maintained on national-international lines.

The basic model assumes that (1) transport costs are negligible, (2) the production function is defined by linear input-output relationships, (3) the ratio of income to output in each sector is the same in all regions, (4) the increase in demand for each nonshiftable national or regional sector is proportional to the increase in national or regional income, respectively, and (5) prices are fixed and interregional price differences can be ignored.

Defining C_{hr} as the cost of scarce resources required to effect a unit increase in income of sector h in region r, the objective of the model is to

$$Minimize\ C = \Sigma\Sigma C_{rh}\,Y_{rh} \qquad (15.17a)$$

subject to a series of constraints. Typical of the latter would be constraints derived from fixed target rates for income in each region, and income in each sector. For example, a constraint of the form

[24] F. Perroux, "Les poles de dévelopment," *Économic Appliquée,* Vol. 5, 1952.
[25] For discussion of these efforts see: J. G. Waardenburg, "Economic Planning for Regions Within Countries: Purposes, Methods, Difficulties, and Results," in *Policies, Planning and Management for Agricultural Development* (Rotterdam: Oxford Institute for Agrarian Affairs, February 1972).

$$\sum_r Y_{rh} = Y_h \qquad h = 1, \ldots, h_n \qquad\qquad (15.17b)$$

would specify that the total increase in income for each of the regional sectors $h = 1, \ldots, h_n$ should equal some fixed target rate. Similarly, the constraint

$$\sum_h Y_{rh} = Y_r \qquad r = 1, \ldots, R \qquad\qquad (15.17c)$$

would demand that the income increase in all sectors in each region equal some fixed target rate.

In addition, a targeted rate of increase for *national* income Y can be introduced. Then, given constants n_h describing the increase in demand for product h, measured in value added, per unit increase in national income, constraints such as, say,

$$\sum Y_{rh} = n_h Y \qquad r = 1, \ldots, R \qquad\qquad (15.17d)$$

can be introduced. Similarly, given constants n_{rh} describing the increase in total demand for product h in region r per unit increase of region r's income, constraints

$$Y_{rh} = n_{rh} Y_r \qquad r = 1, \ldots, R; h = 1, \ldots, h_n \qquad\qquad (15.17e)$$

would also be introduced.

The resulting problem is an easily solved linear programming problem the solution to which specifies regional increases in production. Further modifications, including upper bounds on, say, regional increases in income and changes in the balance of trade, the introduction of transportation costs, explicit input-output relations and employment targets have also been suggested and are feasible. There are, however, ample and obvious data problems, as mathematical problems that result when nonlinearities and indivisibilities occur are recognized. The basic approach, however, even at its present stage yields solutions that are at worst suggestive, and holds considerable potential as the data availability increases, and computer technology permits the solution of larger, and mathematically more complex programming problems.

c. Substitutability in trade flows

The previous programming and input-output models assumed that the interregional input flows were in fixed proportion to regional outputs, or that, in effect, an input of commodity i from region t could *not* be substituted for an input of commodity i from region r in the production of commodity k in region s. That is, it has been assumed—in what has thus far been the most relaxed assumption—that $_{rs}a_{ik} = {}_{rs}q_{ik}/Q_k$ is a regional *fixed* technological coefficient of production. Ghosh [26] has suggested that a relaxation of this assumption would be particularly appropriate for rapidly changing (growing) economies in which the emergence of new demand and supply patterns and sources, and the operation of some regional sectors at full capacity, force alterations in existing pat-

[26] A. Ghosh, *Planning, Programming and Input-Output Models* (Cambridge, Mass.: Cambridge University Press, 1968), pp. 90–97.

terns of interregional flows, for reasons of economy and expediency. That is, the substitution of one region's commodity for *a like commodity* of another region is effected by yet a third region.

There are many factors, for instance base price and transportation costs (including time, money, and accessibility) that influence the choice of a source of supply. Ghosh summarizes these in a Paasche-type price index $_rP_i$, the price relative of commodity i in region r in base period 0 to its price in current period 1.

The fixed technological coefficient for commodity i in region r in the production of commodity k is

$$_ra_{ik} = \frac{\sum_s {}_{rs}q_{ik}}{_rQ_k} \tag{15.18}$$

where $\sum_{rs}q_{ik}$ is the total of *all* inputs included in the Frischian *ring* (see Section 8.3) for commodity i. The proportion of the total input of commodity i in region r, contributed by region s in the base period, is

$$_{rs}K_{ik} = \frac{_{rs}q_{ik}}{\sum_s {}_{rs}q_{ik}} \tag{15.19}$$

so that the input-*weighted* price index for the ring will be

$$P_i = \sum_r {}_{rs}K_{ik}\,(_rP_i) \tag{15.20}$$

Letting the superscript index the period, from (15.18) and (15.19),

$$\frac{_{rs}q_{ik}^0}{_rQ_k^0} = {}_ra_{ik}\,(_{rs}K_{ik}) \tag{15.21}$$

Ghosh suggests that this *ratio* of the input of commodity i from region s to the output of commodity k in region r will change during period 1 when the *price* of this input in period 1 changes relative to the average price. In particular, he hypothesizes that

$$\frac{_{rs}q_{ik}^1}{_rQ_k^1} = {}_ra_{ik}\,(_{rs}K_{ik})\frac{_rP_i}{P_i} \tag{15.22}$$

Thus, when $_rP_i = P_i$ for all r, the interregional flow will be the same in the current and the base years, relative to the total output of commodity k in region s. When, however, $_rP_i > P_i$ this indicates that the price of commodity i in region r has *decreased* relative to the average price in all regions, and this decrease effects an *increase* in the use of this commodity as an input in the production of commodity k in region s. The reverse is true when $_rP_i < P_i$. In this model, then, both the regional flows *and* the sectoral flows can change; that is, substitutions can occur because of price changes.

Ghosh also suggests an optimization model that recognizes transport costs $_{rs}C_{ik}$, in which the objective is to minimize

$$C = \sum_r\sum_s\sum_i\sum_j {}_{rs}C_{ik}(_{rs}q_{ik}) \tag{15.23}$$

subject to the production function (15.16) and a set of regional balance equations. In this model, however, the price effects are not introduced, and thus the model is only apt for planning under fixed price ratios.

d. Development of spatial programs

The interregional, inter-industry programming models that we have discussed serve two basic purposes. On the one hand, they provide a convenient medium for the analysis of interregional commodity flows, and the potential impact of regional and sectoral prices, transportation costs, and the development of transportation networks. On the other hand, from the standpoint of the controller concerned with regional and locational planning, they provide a decision-making framework for the allocation of investment expenditures.

Within this decision-making framework two distinct issues arise. The first is concerned with planning at two separate levels: the sectoral level and the regional level. The second is concerned with planning over a given time horizon. Assuredly, both these issues ordinarily arise in a given planning problem, but it is important that they be singled out lest they be overlooked.

The Rotterdam model in particular focuses on the first of these issues. In this model, no fewer than three distinct regional levels are defined for planning purposes: the international level, the national level, and the regional subsystems that comprise the national system. Additionally, one might also define, for example, urban and rural components of the regional sub-subsystems. It is only the data availability problem and, perhaps, the computational difficulties that argue against this further disaggregation. With respect to sectors, the model distinguishes between shiftable, nonshiftable, and partially shiftable sectors. Fortunately, the computational problems are eased by the various linearity and proportionality assumptions, but for actual planning purposes in multi-region, multi-sector economies they will, nonetheless, be considerable.

Planning for a particular time horizon, or with respect to a particular target date, requires the specification of an objective function with specific respect to that date. Thus, it requires that the policy makers' preferences concerning, say, the rates of income and industrial development in the various regions at some *future* date, be elicited and quantified; and, that judgments be reached with respect to the available transportation networks and technological processes to be employed at that time.

Assuredly, problems such as these are not unique to regional planning. An awareness of them, however, forces recognition of the fact that while regional and locational planning problems can be framed within the general analytical and decision-making contexts employed in the solution of sectoral planning problems and macro-planning problems, their resolution, and the application of their solutions, makes data demands and imposes additional conditions and assumptions that are often insoluble, infeasible, and untenable.

15.5 Concluding Comments

Regional and locational planning is a complex subject, the complexity of which is at least in part due to the difficulty of determining appropriate groupings of spatial units into uniquely defined regions. It seems reasonable to demand, however, that any such grouping define a unique *administrative* unit that is responsive to the decisions of its own policy-making body.

Although regional planning models and techniques can benefit from our experience with national planning models and techniques, at best this can be only a partial benefit. There are two *major* reasons why this is so. First, regional economies are always *open* economies that *must* trade with one another, that can benefit from or suffer the consequences of population flows that result in regional changes in commodity demands and labor supply, and that are directly influenced by the establishment and deterioration of transportation networks. Second, the *instruments* available to the national planner differ from those available to the regional planner, so that national models developed to determine the optimal rates of a specific set of instruments will be inappropriate for spatial planning purposes when these instruments cannot be employed at the regional level.

In addition, the delineation of regional subsystems points up the fact that the national economic system is a multi-level, multi-goal hierarchy and, as is commonly the case in such hierarchies, there can be goal conflicts at the regional and national levels. Thus, for example, the optimal solution for achieving the maximum rate of national economic growth may have, as one of its implications, the reduction of the rates of consumption in any number of individual regions, and an increase in investment, employment, and consumption in others. Such conflicts require trade-offs and can be resolved—but not to the satisfaction of every region.

Finally, the regional goals themselves must be recognized and determined, and here too there is a uniqueness in the situation. Maximum economic growth, industrialization, population growth and control, and increased interregional trade—objectives that are common at the national level—may be of relatively minor concern, or of no concern at all, at the regional level. For all of these reasons, efforts at regional planning in, for example, France, Britain, India, and Italy have proved to be interesting experiments of dubious success. In the United States, one particularly promising area of research activity is in regional econometric forecasting. Here, using regional (state) models that are linked to a national forecasting model, along the lines of Project LINK, econometric forecasts are obtained—both short term and long term—that are particularly useful to (state) government officials, as well as to private industry, planning budgets in the first instance, and planning future corporate activity in the second.

What this suggests, then, is that notwithstanding the considerable attention that has been given to spatial planning, and the vast knowledge that has been amassed and devoted to the subject, the complexities in the problem have left us with a long way to go.

PART THREE
Economic Control: Scope and Issues

It is by now clear that *any* economic system, *as well as* each of its component subsystems, is amenable to economic management. In particular, as discussed in Part I, the basic *conceptual* issues in economic management are the specification of the *structure* of the system, the determination of the *instrument* variables available to the managers, and an explicit statement of systemic *objectives*, together with the associated issues of *information, implementation,* and *control*. As discussed in Part II, a variety of tools and techniques are available for the *practical* issues of problem and model formulation, and solution; and, moreover, the *same* battery of tools and techniques are universally applicable to system *or* subsystem problems. Part III considers the extent to which the economic systems of the East and West, as exemplified by the communist state of the Soviet Union in the former case, and by the capitalist state of the United States in the latter, have tended to differ insofar as the conceptual issues are concerned. That is, with respect to their basic structures, choice of instruments, and specification of objectives, as well as with respect to how they deal with issues of information, implementation, and control, whether any differences that do exist are tending to narrow over time, as well as whether in the process of evolutionary change, which is common to all systems in a world of technological change and developmental opportunities, each system is tending to approach an ideal form, the unique *optimal economic system* or economic order through which all societies can best achieve what is evolving as a common set of societal goals.

Chapters 16 and 17 are concerned with the state's "agenda" under capitalism and socialism, respectively. In these chapters we discuss the *theoretical* foundations upon which each of these systems has been built, and the *philosophical* developments that have occurred over the past century, which have resulted in the current views of economic planning that obtain in these differing societies. In particular, in Chapter 16 we see that, notwithstanding the immense growth of the public sector and the state's "agenda," and the increasing encroachment of the state on the activities of the individual—both human and corporate—the economic systems of the West remain oriented toward the *individual* as opposed to the collectivity. The supremal controllers—that is, the economic managers—retain their basic faith in the free market as a means of best solving the fundamental problems of what to produce, how and for whom, in a world of scarcity. In Chapter 17 we trace the development of Eastern thought, beginning with Marx and Engels. We see that, notwithstanding an occasional bow in the direction of individual freedom, the economic systems of the East remain oriented toward the *collectivity qua state* as opposed to the individual. The supremal controllers retain their basic distrust of the free market as a means of solving economic problems, eschew the possibility of private ownership of the means of production, and remain adamant in their view that intervention and control is necessary to guard against the latter possibility and to replace the former means.

In light of these observations, Chapter 18 considers the current views "in vogue" with respect to "convergence"—that is, the alleged tendency of the two disparate systems to converge to the same unique economic system, an optimal economic order consistent with what such important and influential observers of the economic scene as Galbraith and Tinbergen variously see as merging goals and the evolvement of comparable technological and organizational structures. Our conclusion is that despite the aesthetic, if not utopian appeal of the convergence hypothesis, a look at the facts, at a distance as it were, suggests that an acceptance of this hypothesis is clearly premature. In its well-meaning intention to stress the *similarities* between the systems, the hypothesis neglects, understates, or undervalues the sharp and important *differences* that persist between them: notably, differences in their views of the ownership of the means of production, and therefore of the *locus of decision-making* power; differences in their views of what constitute appropriate *instruments of economic management;* differences in their views of the appropriate *structure of the economic process,* and of the extent to which *efficiency versus control* should guide productive activity in the state; and, dominating all, differences in their views of *the individual versus the state,* and in particular, whether the individual serves the state, or the state serves the individual. These differences, which are at the core of each system, are not easily eroded. *Plus ça change, plus c'est la même chose.*

CHAPTER 16

State's "Agenda" under Capitalism

16.1 ECONOMIC THEORY AND THE STATE

When the economy is described as a purposive system of interrelated components, (a) the government plays *singly* or *jointly* with other elements (for example, the markets, and various large-scale organizations assuming in some form quasi-governmental functions) the role of one of the systems' controllers, (b) government intervention, or the conscious injection by the policy makers of inputs into the system, becomes an unexceptional consequence of this role, and still further (c) the clear implication is that the government should seek the optimal choice of instruments coincident with systemic goals; in effect, that *some* economic planning is both necessary and natural in *any* economic system, with only the extent of the planning and the government interventions being subject to dispute. Our focus has therefore been on the *techniques* of economic planning, rather than on its rationale. Although in the modern era in which growth, inflation, and unemployment have become pedestrian concerns there is nothing terribly startling in this view, it has not always been thus. Rather, government intervention in the economy, and the presentation of a state "agenda," have only become commonplace after a lengthy period of scholarly debate, and the reconciliation from various perspectives of a diverse potpourri of economic, social, and political theories and thought. In this chapter and the next we sketch the philosophical developments that have led to the current views of economic planning, and where it should be focused, in the economic systems of the West and the East.

a. Liberal order and indirect *demand* management

Two basic socio-political philosophies have traditionally divided policy makers and economists alike in the perception of the role of the government and in the formulation of a theory of the state. The first has emphasized the primacy of the *individual* and of his liberty under the law; the second, the primacy of the *collectivity* (national, state, or class) to which the individual is deemed to be subordinated. The first has attempted to disengage in its analysis the forms and conditions under which the government's activity could be "beneficial to those governed in the sense that it assists them to attain their own ends." [1] The second has focused on the ways in which an economy should be "administered in the public interest"—an interest defined by the government at its discretion in the name of the collectivity (national, state, or class) it proclaims to represent. More recently, it has been pointed out that governments—*qua* politicians, bureaucrats, or system controllers—have clearly perceptible interests of their own, such as power expansion or reelection, whose pursuit need not coincide with either assistance to individuals "to attain their own ends," or with any of the alleged interests of the "collectivity" as such.

Notwithstanding substantial conceptual changes with respect to the *scope* of governmental activities and of the criteria for assessing them, the two basic socio-political philosophies have remained typical of the leading countries of Western capitalism (above all, the United States and England) on the one hand, and more recently of the leading countries of socialism (the USSR and China) on the other. The primacy of the individual and of his liberty under the law involves, as Hayek correctly puts it, "the enforcement of universal rules of conduct, protecting a recognizable domain of individuals." [2] This can be achieved only in a state based on the rule of law—that is, within what the Germans have aptly called a *Rechtsstaat*. Conversely, supremacy of the "collectivity" implies absence of a well-defined domain of individuals—that is, a compulsory order and a widely discriminating and utterly formalistic legal framework, as well as various forms of compulsory economics (of the Nazi or Soviet type). Each philosophy, however, is firm in its belief that it, and it alone, is the basis for optimizing individual welfare—that of *all* the individuals in the first case, that of the "elected" in the second case, although a true collectivist would argue that only in maxmizing collective welfare can every individual optimize his or her own welfare.

Within the Western liberal tradition, basic conceptual changes toward restraining, regulating, or improving the *modus operandi* of capitalism by the agency of government—changes, or government interventions, that continue to be considered as aberrations by the extreme partisans of classic liberalism—can be easily dated. For over a century and a half—from the beginning of the last quarter of the eighteenth century to the end of the first quarter of the twentieth century—the influence of the classical economists moved the Western governments away from specific and detailed interventions in the economy and toward general constraints in the economy. In the vision of the classics (Smith, Ricardo, Mill, and Senior, in particular) the economy had a great capacity to tend

---

[1] W. J. Baumol, *Welfare Economics and the Theory of the State* (Cambridge, Mass.: Harvard University Press, 1965), p. 180.

[2] F. A. Hayek, "The Principles of a Liberal Social Order," *Il Politico*, Vol. XXXI, No. 4, December 1966, p. 603.

toward a stable, self-regulating, self-optimizing mechanism; government interferences with the functioning of this mechanism as such had to be demonstrated case by case. Certain interferences were, however, considered indispensable not only in respect to the provision of such things as education, defense, public works, and so on. More generally, such interferences were viewed as necessary, notably, as responses to changing circumstances, evolving public sensibilities, and changing development levels. This was particularly true with respect to redefinitions of the rights of the market's participants, specifications of legitimate forms of organization, and acceptance of state obligations with regard to welfare and related issues. Increased development—increased "opulence" as Bentham put it—would simultaneously condition decreases in the scope of the agenda and better integration of all existing elements that blend together in the market's functioning. The decrease in the scope of the agenda would result, according to Bentham, from the expansion of the *sponte acta* of the individuals—that is, from an increase in the scope of their initiatives—while better coordination in the state's action and in its interaction with the activity of the individuals would be obtained from the systematic erection of an institutional structure creating the "good society." The economic system was thus visualized as embedded in a perfecting legal-ethical-social framework fashioned by both accepted patterns of individual behavior, and by responsive legal changes favoring the development of individual initiative. This, it should be noted, never did imply the absence of responsiveness of government action to continuously changing problems, from balance-of-payment issues, to welfare, or to education.

Neither the classical vision of a system tending to optimizing, nor the fully elaborated theory of general, perfectly competitive, full-employment, equilibrium—crowned by the end of the nineteenth century by the works of John Bates Clark—proved fully suitable for the world that emerged only a few decades later in the wake of the First World War. The "Economics of Tranquility" and of "Confident Foresight" patiently built by the greatest economists, from Walras onward, became obviously inadequate and partially inappropriate.[3] At a time when chronic unemployment seemed to become the hallmark of advanced capitalism, and when "risk, uncertainty, and ignorance" seemed to transform "business into a lottery," Keynes suggested in a remarkable essay published in 1926, "The End of Laissez-Faire," that the time was ripe for distinguishing anew between the "agenda" and the "nonagenda." Keynes proposed then, *inter alia,* that the state's agenda be henceforth so defined as to *include* "decisions which are made by *no one* if the state does not make them," namely, "things which at present are not done at all"[4] with respect to uncertainty and the dissemination of information, and with respect to the management of demand—that is, the coordination of overall savings and the pattern of investment.

[3] See G. L. S. Shackle, *The Years of High Theory, Invention and Tradition in Economic Thought 1926–1939* (Cambridge, Mass.: Cambridge University Press, 1967), pp. 290 ff.
[4] J. M. Keynes, *Essays in Persuasion* (New York: Harcourt, Brace, 1932), p. 317.

Keynes, and others along with him and after him, thus helped move economics as a discipline into new planes: from the consideration of scarcity alone, to the consideration of scarcity *cum* uncertainty, and of their interrelations and ramifications; and from the contemplation of a seemingly orderly world, to development in certain forms of state control, in a restless and unstable world whose natural condition of efficiency is not a static optimum. The scope of the agenda started to both expand and shift its focus, although not without strenuous opposition from many quarters, most particularly of the modern philosophical liberals, who have always considered the establishment of the "mixed economy" as a permanent system of capitalist economic management to be an aberration, insofar as it abridges individual freedom. A decade after his essay on laissez-faire, in his *General Theory,* positing unemployment as the key problem of modern capitalism, Keynes (who himself believed his theories to be more applicable to a totalitarian state than to the liberal type of state envisioned by the Cambridge classics) focused his analysis directly on the specific interplays of the instruments of state control; that is, on the interplay of income-expenditure and expenditure-income, or on the role and place of what came to be eventually called "functional finance" in the government's agenda. With the receding of stagnation and unemployment from the center of the stage, and with the successive emergence of other key issues, such as rapid growth, inflation, and eventually stagflation and slumpflation, both expansion of the agenda and stimulation for the opening and reopening of certain avenues of economic thought (growth, development and change, forms of economics of control) gathered momentum. Increased "opulence" did not necessarily lead to the decrease in government's action anticipated by Bentham. As inflation and all its noxious variations come into day-to-day focus, and as anti-Keynesian trends of various persuasions gained attention, continuous and methodic efforts have been pursued, if not for establishing an all-encompassing economic theory of the state, at least for theorizing about various aspects of logical government behavior. In this regard, theories have been proposed concerning criteria for government action, concerning the interrelations between given goals, instruments, and the economic structure, and concerning procedures for assessing the impact of any specific policy. We shall turn to these criteria, interrelations and procedures, further below in Section 16.3

b. Compulsory order and direct *supply* management

A number of disparate trends merge, at times unexpectedly, in the evolution of the conception of a compulsory economic order stressing the primacy of the state over the individual. Some of the basic strains that have had a lasting impact on this conception are the German (or, more precisely, Prussian) nationalist tradition, and curiously enough the pre- and Marxian socialist traditions, which are often dismissed by professional economists as influences of noneconomists on economics.[5] The German nationalist tendency proceeded

[5] L. Von Mises, *Socialism, An Economic and Sociological Analysis* (J. Kahane, transl.) (London: Jonathan Cape, 1969), p. 531.

originally from the pre-nineteenth century German version of mercantilism (called "Kameralism" from "Cameral Wissenschaft") aiming at the efficient administration of the domains and regalian rights of the sovereign, the "statolatry" of well-known philosophers such as Fichte and Hegel, and the anticlassical protectionist economics of a number of writers, among them Friedrick List, so well fitting an underdeveloped, badly splintered, and ambitious Germany ardently desirous of "catch up" with an advanced, industrial Great Britain. The socialist tendency—"utopian" first and so-called "scientific" afterwards, according to Marx's preferred terms—continued for its part in a number of ways, and with varying dosages, the complex traditions and currents of the French Revolutions from Robespierre to Babeuf, and on to the Paris Commune of 1871 (see below, Chapter 17).

The ideas that nations must be fully independent of one another and autarkically organized, that the state must ensure a suitable livelihood for each of its citizens, that the state must, accordingly, control production, engage in compulsory buying and selling at fixed prices, and conduct what foreign trade it may require through a total state monopoly, were first methodically stressed by John Gottlieb Fichte in his *Closed Commercial State,* by the turn of the eighteenth century.[6] A whole series of subsequent contributors to the theory of the national corporatist state—that is, a state based on the tight organization of the entire population into professional fields ("Korporationen")—as well as to the theory of a state-administered national economy, appropriately paid homage to Fichte's conception of the closed commercial state. Fostered by evidently vast and seemingly unbridgeable inequalities among nations, and thriving within less developed countries seeking to rapidly build up their military and economic power, nationalist, neo-mercantilist, anticosmopolitan, antiindividualist, and protectionist theories that emerged early in nineteenth century Germany, dominated the thought of policy makers and economists throughout Europe, far into the twentieth century. Eventually, a number of tenets of these theories influenced the socialist schools, and eventually found great favor in renewed forms in the less developed countries, particularly after the Second World War.

Among the most notable contributors to the early nineteenth century attacks against the "atomistic, individualist, and cosmopolitan" tenets of the classics were the German nationalists—ranging from the philosophic romanticist Adam Heinrick Müller to the pragmatic protectionist Friedrick List—all of whom stressed in various ways the importance of the nation as an entity between the "individual and humanity," the fundamental significance of national power, and the need of extensively protectionist developmental policies in order to foster rapid national industrial growth. The nationalists and "romanticists" of the early 1800s were eventually followed by the "historicists"—partisans of the "historical method of Political Economy"—who continued the attacks against the cosmopolitanism and universalism of the classical economic theory, albeit from a different angle. These "antitheoretical empiricists," as

[6] R. H. Bowen, *German Theories of the Corporative State* (New York: McGraw-Hill, 1947), p. 27.

Hayek later called them,[7] saw in any observed economic phenomenon not reflections of economic problems, but "historical categories" produced by changing social or legal institutions. Accordingly, they directed their main efforts against the method of classical economic analysis, particularly against its "abstract deductions" from ideal postulates. Instead they stressed, in theory, the validity of "inductive" reasoning based on the "realities" of the various stages of industrial evolution of the national economy, and eventually, in practice, the importance of massive government interventions in the economy.[8]

The triumph of the idea of the state as the main organizer of the national economy for achieving an overriding national goal finally took place in Germany in World War I. An industrialist, Walther Rathenau, and an army-career man, Wichard von Moellendorff, contributed seminal ideas to the organization of this type of compulsory economy. Their conception of the *Kriegswirtschaft* (war economy) eventually became a model of centralized state administration, not only for the fascist or Nazi corporatist states, but also for the Soviet Union (as we shall see in Chapter 17). The ideas of Rathenau and Moellendorf were predicated on the vision of an integrated national community in which individual values would be entirely subordinated to the needs of an overriding national goal—the goal of victory in the war. To achieve this cohesion, and in order to place the entire economy in the service of the war, Rathenau conceived a machinery that placed in the hands of the state virtually the full control of the supply and distribution of *raw materials*. Rathenau's assumption was that the country was a "beleaguered fortress" whose survival depended on the organization and administration of raw materials. Without resorting to nationalization—that is, while maintaining private ownership and market exchange—the German War Office, at the suggestion of Rathenau, took into its hands the power of regulating, through the control of raw materials, and eventually through the control of labor assignments, the entire economic and industrial life of the country. To start with, all raw materials were "sequestered" and placed at the disposition of the state. The latter indicated to its owners those to whom the raw materials should be allocated, according to the needs of the war. Eventually, new agencies were created for gathering, storing, and distributing these raw materials in quantities corresponding to the government's orders, and at the prices fixed by the government.[9] This compulsory order, or "Zwangswirtschaft," collapsed with the German defeat. But many of its underlying assumptions, ideological tenets, and methods of control, found a new and fruitful terrain during the ascension of Nazi Germany, and during World War II. The nationalist, antiuniversalist, anticosmopolitan, antiindividualist, anticlassical economic current, à la Heinrich Müller, was maintained alive from the early 1900s on by the writings of Othmar Spann, Friedrich Lenz, and of many other economists.[10] After Hitler's accession to power, the Nazis also maintained

---

[7] F. A. Hayek, *op. cit.*

[8] See L. H. Haney, *Economic Thought* (London: Macmillan, 1936), pp. 539 ff.

[9] See R. H. Lutz (ed.), *Fall of the German Empire* (Stanford: Stanford University Press, 1932), p. 82.

[10] Haney, *op. cit.*, p. 671.

private ownership of the means of production, entrepreneurship, and market exchanges. But the Nazi government tried even before the outbreak of the war to decide whenever it deemed necessary what and how their entrepreneurs, now called "enterprise leaders" or *Betriebsführers,* should produce, for whom and at what prices, at what terms they should borrow, and at what wages workers should work for them. During the war, the state supplied these Betriebsführers with slave labor, at no wages at all. This interventionism on an increasingly broad scale, under the form of injections of commands and prohibitions into the workings of an exchange economy, neither elicited the full compliance of the industrialists, nor accomplished the expected output results. Much of the official commands and prohibitions went unheeded. Finally, as in both Britain and the United States, the Nazis did ultimately attempt to inflexibly subordinate the competing objectives of the economy to the central purpose of winning the war. But ruthlessness is not equivalent to efficiency; contrary to the impression carefully exposited by the German propagandists during the War, the German economic administration remained riddled by continuous conflicts among numerous and competing administrative organizations, displayed patent inefficiency in the planning of its various programs, and finally failed to meet many of its key output or distribution objectives.[11]

16.2 FROM HAPHAZARD MEASURES TO COORDINATED MANAGEMENT

a. In MDC's

In the history of doctrines, economic management by the state agency has signified a break with liberal economic thinking. As Gunnar Myrdal has pointed out, in countries such as England and the Scandinavian nations, state intervention in the economy "have originally been introduced *ad hoc* to serve limited and temporary purposes, often to meet an emergency of one sort or another. . . . The demand for order and rationality has been an afterthought, when it was becoming apparent that it had been an illusion to believe the need for intervention to be temporary, and when the interventions proved to be cumbersome to administer and irrational and damaging in their secondary effects." [12]

As we already indicated, then, in England and the Scandinavian nations the economy was considered as fundamentally self-regulating. Within the government, up to World War I, economic policy in the modern sense of "policy toward the economy as a whole" was nonexistent. The term *management* came in broad use most prominently with the ideas of Keynes, and, initially, essentially referred to *currency* management. When the term expanded to include budgetary measures, it emphasized as its objective the regulation of demand in

---

[11] See B. H. Klein, *Germany's Economic Preparations for War* (Cambridge, Mass.: Harvard University Press, 1959) and A. S. Milward, *The German Economy at War* (London: Athlone Press, 1965).

[12] G. Myrdal, "The Trend Towards Economic Planning," *Manchester School of Economic Studies,* Vol. XIX, January 1951, p. 6.

order to eliminate cyclical fluctuations. Assuredly, management of demand never did imply equal degrees of control over *all* decisions. While the rate of aggregate demand started to be viewed as dependent upon governmental decisions of various kinds, decisions on the rate of demand for individual products were definitely to be left—if not exceptionally and temporarily for some key products—outside of governmental control. Similarly, the government's interest in the division of the national income between consumption and investment was never intended to mean *detailed* controls of the constituents of either of the two. Keynes ultimately recognized that a durable disequilibrium could exist with respect to demand and employment which could not be cured by the market mechanism. This recognition, while somewhat out of vogue, nonetheless had been shared earlier by the Physiocrats and the Marxists, as well as by Keynes' contemporaries of the Chicago School who submitted that there were infinite equilibria only one of which was at full employment. Where the latter differed with Keynes was on theoretical issues. For his part, Keynes never showed concern with the "long pull" but with the short term only. In the long run, equilibrium was to prevail again, and the classical theory of the self-regulating system was to come back into force.

It is important to mention in this context that a crucial distinction exists between *demand* management and *supply* management. The first concerns regulations within a prevailing framework of supply responses, while the second involves structural changes within this framework itself. The transition from demand to supply management has accordingly proceeded cautiously and hesitantly in the West; moreover, outright coordinations between the two have usually not been attempted—except, perhaps, for a few Western countries. As Cairncross has noted,[13] the distinction between the two forms of management corresponds roughly to the classical preoccupations with *stability* (of demand) and *growth* (of productive capacity). In this respect it reflects the conflict between short-term and long-term objectives. It is only toward the end of the 1940s that the interest in the growth of productive capacity itself—and not only in the growth of market demand in relation to the growth in the productive capacity—came increasingly into government focus in the West; and this, in no mean measure under the competitive pressure of Soviet growth!

Approaching Keynes in the critical spirit in which the latter had approached the classics, Roy F. Harrod pointed in his *Economic Dynamics* to the crucial concept of *positive savings*—imbedded by Keynes "in a treatment which in broad lines follows the method of static equilibrium analysis"—and stressed then the significance of the so-called "paradox of thrift" which, according to him was "likely to play a prominent part in the dynamics of a steadily advancing economy." [14] Harrod finally underlined a key reason for savings: to provide for continuous output growth. At the same time, Domar stressed the significance of the impact of investment on the accumulation of physical capital

---

[13] A. Cairncross, *Essays in Economic Management* (Albany: State University of New York Press, 1971), p. 168.

[14] R. F. Harrod, *Economic Dynamics* (New York: St. Martin's Press, 1973).

goods. Soon after, the path opened by Harrod-Domar was producing a plethora of growth models emphasizing either capital accumulation or optimal consumption streams—all actually assuming a controllability of the economy which no economic planner has ever been able to experience.

Along with the development of interest in growth in production expansion, in priorities to particular industries or regions, and so on—that is, along with the interest in long-term objectives for the economy as a whole—and concomitantly with the formulation of national economic plans (notably in France, England, and Scandinavia) the study of policy and planning gathered momentum. A whole new branch of economics started to focus its attention precisely on the *process* of economic policy, on the formulation of economic policy *goals,* and on the *interrelations* between the goals, instruments, and the economic structure. The theory of quantitative policy and planning with which we have been dealing in this book is thus essentially a product of the last fifteen to twenty years, reflecting a new and hitherto unrecognized aspect of the government activity in an economy primarily market-directed; namely, the deliberate, systematic, integrated intervention of the government on both the demand and the supply sides, in order to further certain national economic objectives. The state's "agenda" is thus visualized henceforth as opened to a wide variety of short-term and long-term objectives whose achievement, given the acceptable trade-offs between them, is to be effected by the optimal selection of measures.

b. In LDC's

For the neoclassical theory, the existence of differences in economic development levels—among countries and among groups and regions within a country—avowedly raises a serious challenge. Factor differences cannot explain these vast gaps. The differentials may reflect, according to Arrow,[15] differences in production-possibility sets among countries. But this, continues Arrow, would imply that contemporary firms occupying similar economic positions would face different constraints on their optimization due to differences in productive knowledge. Then the constraints, instead of being constant, would have to be interpreted as variables. While not raising questions about the underlying optimization assumptions of the firm, this would, however, raise serious questions concerning the nature of this optimization.

Neoclassical economists do not in fact attempt to formulate an overall theory of economic development. Such an attempt, they know, escapes them, since it involves knowledge about the entire macro system—social and cultural—an endeavor toward which they are not inclined. What economic theory has offered until now are partial explanations and frameworks of analysis of some of the economic conditions prevailing in the LDC's. Such an approach, however, is often viewed as insufficient either by some of the policy makers of these countries, or by various kinds of "pragmatists." Falling back on many of the theories and contentions of the European "antiuniversalists" and "anticos-

---

[15] K. J. Arrow, "Limited Knowledge and Economic Analysis," *American Economic Review,* Vol. 64, No. 1, March 1974, p. 1.

mopolitans'' of the last century, these pragmatists stress again the importance of the "nation" above the individual, the necessity of "protectionism" if not of "autarky," and the relevance of the neomercantilist or of the "historicist" kind of thought.

Attacks against the applicability to LDC's of conventional economic theory and against the uses of the market mechanism in these countries actually encompass a wide variety of forms. Starting from the unique characteristics of MDC's as opposed to those of the LDC's, some economists (Dudley Seers,[16] for instance) contend that this *differentia specifica* makes the theoretical framework devised for the former inapplicable to the latter. Others, starting precisely from the reverse side, that is, from the unique characteristics of the LDC's as opposed to the MDC's, contend that the market mechanism is "qualitatively" different there—that is, more imperfect in its workings; that a "fundamental" disequilibrium prevails there between capital and labor (the former scarce, the latter in surplus), a disequilibrium that cannot be corrected by improving allocative efficiency; that most LDC's are trapped into a stable low-income equilibrium trap out of which they cannot escape without large "structural" changes; that the free play of the market tends to "fossilize" prevailing imperfections, thus further accenting the differences between MDC's and LDC's, and so on. Hla Myint [17] has pointed out in response to these latter contentions that much of this critique is addressed to the laissez-faire approach with which some critics persistently identify "orthodox" theory; that often the role of the market is viewed narrowly, in relation to resource allocation only, and not also in respect to its long-run effects on factor supply, especially capital; that the problems raised by any kind of structural change involve complex interrelations the analysis of which actually requires many of the theoretical frameworks produced by modern economists; and that some of the cumulative disequilibrating and disequalizing effects allegedly resulting from the play of the market are rather suggestive hypotheses, and not proven facts.

In any case, the historic example of early nineteenth-century Europe and the United States seeking to emulate Great Britain, stressing at times, at least, growth as a national objective, encouraging protectionism and, in continental Europe, exhibiting a large and methodic governmental participation in industrial and technological development, tends to influence the thought and behavior of policy makers in the LDC's of today. Many of the leaders of these countries ultimately tend to establish a curious symbiosis between ideas and practices borrowed from nineteenth-century Europe, with concepts and tools of mid-twentieth century economics—particularly Keynesian income determination, growth models a la Harrod-Domar, and planning—all recast into contemporary socialist propaganda language. The tragedy of a large number of LDC's—notably of those that are devoid of critical raw materials such as

[16] D. Seers, "The Limitations of the Special Case," *Oxford Bulletin of Economics and Statistics,* Vol. 25, No. 2, May 1963, p. 77.
[17] Hla Myint, *Economic Theory and the Underdeveloped Countries* (London: Oxford University Press, 1971), p. 3.

oil—is, however, that the technological gaps between them and the MDC's is increasingly difficult and costlier to bridge. Neither a better understanding of the problems raised by this widening gap, nor a much more sophisticated manipulation of the parameters involved seem, therefore, sufficient for the attainment of the elusive purpose of sustained growth and development. The "agenda" of the governments of the LDC's may indeed involve responsibilities and obligations that transcend national frontiers.

After World War II, making development plans became the more popular activity of the governments of the newly independent LDC's; and according to W. Arthur Lewis, "also nearly their biggest failure." [18] Almost every government has issued at least one plan, and most governments have issued several. Yet, plans are afterwards usually put on the shelf; they do not guide, in any significant way, government action. The reasons for failure, that is, of the absence of correlation between goals and performance, are complex. They stem in many cases not only from poor planning, overambitious evaluation of actual resources and of their potential development, deficient utilization of the narrow range of instruments available, and continuous expansion of already high administrative costs, but also and often primarily from the inability of effectively interfering, on the one hand, with large nonmonetized sectors of the economy, and, on the other hand, with the prevailing influences and policies of foreign corporations and foreign powers.

16.3 EFFICIENCY CRITERIA FOR THE "AGENDA"

The classics were interested in efficiency with respect to the self-regulating, self-stabilizing market mechanism; in their vision, the "agenda" consisted, therefore, as we have stated, only in defining the rules of the game, and in providing for certain narrowly defined collective needs, although there was additional interest on the part of such as Marshall in the possibility of taxing increasing-cost industries in the name of efficiency. The latter policy was efficient to Marshall, because it provided more goods that are becoming cheaper at the expense of less goods that are becoming more expensive to produce, which would contribute to the well-being of mankind. Keynes, who may well have gotten some of his ideas from Paul Douglas and Jacob Viner, led his followers' interest toward efficiency with respect to the full utilization of resources: from this vantage point they introduced in the agenda the imperative of coping with below full-employment equilibria. The welfare economists, like the classics, again have focused on market efficiency (that is, Pareto optimality) adding notions of distributive justice, notions that, however, they do not know how to implement. Nevertheless, they have systematized and rationalized the possible contents of the agenda, by specifying that state interventions are inherently warranted under several diverse circumstances, generally involving market failures, for example, (a) in the case of monopolization, stock manipulation, or even unemployment involving patent misuse of resources; (b) in the

---

[18] W. A. Lewis, *Some Aspects of Economic Planning, op. cit.,* p. 37.

case of increasing-returns industries (where a government subsidy would be required to cope with the fact that marginal cost would be below a declining average cost, leading otherwise to output reductions and price increases), and of decreasing-cost industries where, conversely, a tax would be appropriate, (c) in the vast and complex case of externalities—always to be envisaged in conjunction with explicit cost-benefit considerations, and so on. On the basis of the externality argument and its extensions, Baumol, for instance, feels that a vast number of programs involving the welfare of all clearly belong on the "agenda," programs designed, for example, to reduce unemployment, eliminate inflation, provide for education, fight urban decay, and the like, since "in each of these cases, private initiative alone cannot be depended upon to eliminate the difficulties because self-interest must lead many persons to behave in a manner which is not optimal from the point of view of the community as a whole. Nor can any individual or any small group of individuals, even with the best of intentions, do much about any of these matters." [19]

Ideally, we have also arrived at a "maximum total welfare" vision with respect to governmental budget policy: on the side of revenue, the tax bill should be so distributed as to equate, between citizens, marginal sacrifice; and, synchronously and complementarily, on the side of spending, expenditures should be so allocated as to equate the marginal benefits, yielded by each program. Unfortunately, the debate is not yet closed with respect to the nature and the determination of the wants to be provided for by the budget, nor of the evaluation of the benefits. With respect to public *and* private wants, the individualist tendency remains predicated on the idea that *both* originate with the community's individuals, and that the budget plan must accordingly be derived from individual preferences; the collectivist tendency assumes for its part that social wants are of an entirely different nature—deriving not from the needs of the individual, but from the needs of the collectivity *qua* collectivity. With respect to benefits, often what is actually measurable is but a part of the whole, and not always the most significant part.

Statistical progress has, however, been made in evaluating the welfare costs of various tax measures and in the exploration of pricing criteria for public enterprises. In practice, many projects have been evaluated in a manner that accords at least broadly with the prescription of welfare analysis; and an increasingly systematic effort has been made for assessing—with various degrees of success—the benefit-cost interrelations of the governmental programs and of governmental agencies.

The possible contours of the agenda have thus tended to become clearer under the impact of welfare economists. An effort has thus been made, notably to dispel the apparent arbitrariness of the classical method of selection of the "agenda" items, and to suggest instead the circumstances in which an extension of government authority would be perceived by the community's individuals as "requisite for the most efficient pursuit of their aims." [20] The approach

---

[19] W. Baumol, *op. cit.*, pp. 29–30.
[20] *Ibid.*, p. 51.

is politely criticized by those who, like Mishan, for instance, note that by accepting GNP as a measure of real goods and the Pareto improvement as implying a continuous pushing outward of the production frontier, we may neglect to remember that social *profits* also have social *costs* associated with them, and that GNP is an unreliable measure of welfare, insofar as it adds up "goods" along with "bads." The approach, assuredly, is violently criticized by those that attack its underlying premise: namely, the acceptance by the theorists of the interests of the individuals as worth defending and realizing more "efficiency," by broadening because of them the role of the state.[21]

16.4 GROWTH OF THE PUBLIC SECTOR AND PERSPECTIVE PLANNING

A key characteristic of our century has been the spectacular growth of the public sector in all the countries of the world, and more particularly in the MDC's themselves since the 1930s. A complex number of factors—economic, social, political, and military—have brought about significant changes in the conception of public administration and public management, and along with them, a continuous and multi-faceted expansion of the public sector. The reliance on the government as a *balancer* or adjuster between the organized conflicting interests—of giant corporations, labor, farmers, trade associations; the reliance upon government as a *promoter or protector* of business enterprise, of agriculture, or of the consumer; the reliance upon government as a *regulator* of certain type of services—transportation, communication, and utilities—as well as of certain trade practices; the reliance upon the government as an *investor and public trustee*—in the conservation of natural resources, in the development of public enterprises of various kinds, and in the development of complex welfare programs—have all brought about vast changes in the nature and extent of the public sector in the modern capitalist economies.

The growth of the public sector, and in the scope of its activities, has not necessarily been accompanied by expansion in state ownership—although this has up to a point been the case in France, Germany, and England—but by a complex interweaving of regulatory controls, social welfare activities, and public enterprise. Ultimately, as public investment has started to exceed by far private investment, its total impact on the economy has become so evident and compelling that, on the one hand, it cannot be neglected in the calculations of the private industries, and, on the other hand, it must itself be subject to coherent and comprehensive management. Even in the United States, Great Britain, or Scandinavia, "we have moved from a world in which the government played a very subordinate part in economic life, to one in which the pronouncements and actions of government are of overwhelming importance to a large sector of industry. The government is expected to take responsibility for almost everything—particularly if things go wrong—and to be correspondingly ready

[21] J. O'Connor, "Scientific and Ideological Elements in the Economic Theory of Government Policy," *Science and Society,* Vol. 33, 1969, p. 392.

with statements of policy and well conceived measures on every imaginable occasion.'' [22]

In this new setting, the traditional liberal idea that we have a choice between controls or no controls by the government, and that we must reject all controls, has actually been superseded by a more specific question: what *forms* of controls do we actually want? In this respect, the choice is, as we have pointed out, essentially between controls on the *demand* side, letting the market operate freely within the resulting ceiling, and multiplicity of controls on the *supply* side. In most MDC's, controls have been exercised primarily on the demand side, along with selective and temporary uses of administrative controls on consumers or producers. The question that arises now is, once again, whether these controls can by themselves cope with the combined phenomena of unemployment and inflation; that is, with all kinds of noxious variations between stagnation in some sectors, and inflation in other sectors of the economy. It has long been the contention of various anti-Keynesians that reliance on Keynesian or neo-Keynesian fiscal policy to support full employment may eventually become impossible "as an inflationary bias arising out of monopolistic trade union activity and large industrial concentrations may permit both unemployment and inflation to occur simultaneously'' [23]—as Paul J. Strayer had already noted a quarter of a century before apparent fulfillment; and, in fact, the problem may be somewhere else.

As Wassily Leontief has pointed out, the modern industrial economy is a gigantic and intricate machine: "a serious malfunction of any one of its component parts, affects, *sometimes with a long delay,* the workings of all the other parts." Decisions affecting the future, by both the state and by the great corporations, could be better founded if the state would monitor "all the branches of the economy in their mutual interrelationships"—with a view to the impact of different lags—thus providing a basis for a better analysis of the available options "not from the point of view of an individual company or sector but of the system as a whole." [24] The concept of a methodic *firming up of business expectations* via the provision of a consistent, integrated, *indicative* rolling-plan framework—rather than a directive plan of any kind—may eventually become standard practice even in the United States, the last country in which the idea of a National Economic Planning Board seemed, up to now, confined only to exceptional periods of stagnation or of war preparation.

---

[22] A. Cairncross, *op. cit.,* p. 30.

[23] P. J. Strayer, "Public Expenditure Policy," *American Economic Review,* Vol. 39, No. 2, March 1949, p. 384.

[24] W. Leontief, "For a National Economic Planning Board," *New York Times,* March 14, 1974, p. 37.

CHAPTER 17

State's "Agenda" under Socialism

17.1 THE MARXIAN THEORY OF THE STATE

The Marxian theory of the state is a complex agglomeration of a number of ingredients, the most important of which are: (1) Marx's own conception of the sociohistorical process as an unfolding class struggle; (2) Marx's ideas on the form of the workers' state, as they evolved through the analysis of the short-lived activity of the Paris Commune of 1871, following the Franco-Prussian war; (3) Marx and Engel's absorption of the ideas of the French "utopians" of the early nineteenth century, particularly those of Saint-Simon concerning the interactions between industrialization, politics, and economics.

The fundamental aim of Marxian socialists (or communists) is the transfer of the means of production from private ownership to the ownership of organized society. The aim is not arbitrarily chosen; it is viewed both as a social *necessity* and as an ineluctable *result* of the historical development itself. "Utopians" such as Charles Fourier and Robert Owen had suggested a similar goal before Marx and Engels, the founders of "scientific socialism." But the former could not have perceived what allegedly became subsequently clear to the latter: namely, the *need* of "harmonizing . . . the modes of production, appropriation and exchange with the socialized character of the means of production," a harmonization that "can only come about by society openly and directly taking possession of the productive forces which have outgrown all control except that of society as a whole." [1] This alone, says Engels, can transform the means of production "from master demons into willing servants," eliminate the prevailing "social anarchy of production," and give place "to a social regulation of production upon a definite plan." [2]

---

[1] F. Engels, *Anti-Dühring, Her Eugen Dühring's Revolution in Science,* trans. from the 1894 ed. (Moscow: Foreign Publishing House, 1959), p. 384.
[2] *Ibid.,* p. 385.

How is this to be accomplished? Are the "producers working together" going to take over the existing state administrations? Are they going to "regulate" production, and, if so, how? These and related questions have been an unending subject of contention among socialists. We shall consider here only the main lines of the *theoretical* arguments developed by Marx and Engels, their interpretation and adaptation for *practical* application by Lenin and Stalin, and their eventual *modifications* in the Soviet-type economies after Stalin's death.

In Marx's conception, the state is the creation and the instrument of the *dominant class*. Under the system of private ownership of the means of production, the capitalists—or the "bourgeois" as they were known in Europe before the end of the feudal regime—form the dominant class. Under their "dictatorship," or under the "dictatorship of capital," the state—whatever its passing "governmental" form: monarchy, republic, or democracy—is but a parasitic, continuously expanding bureaucratic-military organization "for managing the common affairs of the dominant class." It is a *determined*, not a *determining* force. The state may *become* a determining force, "independent and superior to all social classes," in special circumstances only; for instance, under an authoritarian personal rule (called "Bonapartism" from the two reigning Napoleons) that expropriates politically the other classes, but does not change the fundamental purpose of the state: namely, the defense of the given property relations.[3] The state may also become independent of all classes, in what Marx calls the "asiatic form" of society, a peculiar traditionalist Asian society in which, allegedly, "there is no private property or land, but only individual possession, because the community is, properly speaking, the real proprietor." [4]

The workers' revolution aims at raising the proletariat to the position of the ruling class. In Lenin's exegesis, such a revolution puts an end to the "dictatorship of the bourgeoisie" and establishes the "dictatorship of the proletariat." In the process of assumption of power, the workers "wrest by degrees all capital from the bourgeoisie," abolish all land property, centralize in the hands of the state all instruments of production, the credit system, and the means of communication and transport, and increase the totality of productive forces "as rapidly as possible." [5] The specific *form* assumed by the workers' state is perceived by Marx (in "the rough sketch which the (Paris) Commune had no time to develop") as a pyramidal structure of highly autonomous rural communes, town-based district assemblies formed by these communes' revocable delegates, and a National Delegation of these assemblies themselves [6]—a structure broadly comparable to that set up eventually in Russia during the revolution of 1917.

---

[3] K. Marx, *The 18th Brumaire of Louis Bonaparte,* as quoted in R. Milbrand, "Marx and the State," *Socialist Reporter* (1965), pp. 283 ff.

[4] *Ibid.,* pp. 286 ff.

[5] K. Marx and F. Engels, *The Communist Manifesto* (New York: Modern Reader, 1968 ed.; orig. 1848), pp. 39–40.

[6] K. Marx, "Civil War in France," quoted in S. H. M. Chang, *The Marxian Theory of the State* (New York: Russell and Russell, 1935), pp. 112–113.

Revolutionary socialism, Marx further affirms, is "the declaration of the permanence of the revolution." [7] The workers in power incessantly revolutionize production, abolish the distinction between town and country, surmount the old division of labor and generate a new "race of producers with an all-around training." [8] As the former enemies are disposed of, production relations changed, and class antagonisms disappearing, state interferences in *social* relations become superfluous. The state withers away, and eventually "the government of persons is replaced by the administration of things, and by the conduct of processes of production." [9]

The latter, rather elusive idea is borrowed by Engels from Saint-Simon, whom Engels quotes approvingly as having indeed foretold the "complete absorption of politics by economics" and the "future conversion of political rule over men into an administration of things and direction of processes of production—that is to say, the abolition of the state." [10] In Saint-Simon's view, society is in complete harmony with itself only when it is fully industrialized. As industry becomes the unique substance of social life, and society a vast producer company, its direction is naturally placed in the hands of a Supreme Council of Industry, assisted by a subordinated organ, the Supreme Council of the Learned. As nothing is more socially central than economic activity, no place is left within the society for *another* central organ; all power—political, legislative—is concentrated in the hands of the Supreme Council of Industry. As Emile Durkheim, the great French sociologist points out in his study on Saint-Simon, in the latter's views:

"in exercising its functions, it (the Supreme Council of Industry) will proceed according to an entirely different method than that which governments of all times have employed. As its authority stems not from the fact that it is strongest but because it knows what others are ignorant of, its action will have nothing arbitrary or coercive about it. It will not do merely what it wishes, but what fits the nature of things, and as no one wishes to act other than in conformity with the nature of things, one will do as it says without having to compel it." [11]

Thus society passes, in the vision of Saint-Simon, "from governmental or military rule to administrative or industrial rule." [12] The Supreme Council of Industry is the *administrative council* of the vast company formed by the whole society, while its members are society's *trustees*.

For Saint-Simon, these eventual trustees were to be "working bourgeois, manufacturers, merchants, bankers" who, as Engels notes, "were still to hold vis-à-vis the workers, a commanding and economically privileged position." [13] This Engels necessarily rejects, however, since it is only *after* the

---

[7] K. Marx, *Class Struggles in France*, quoted *Ibid.*, p. 90.

[8] F. Engels, *Anti-Dühring, Her Eugen Dühring's Revolution in Science, op. cit.*, p. 409.

[9] *Ibid.*, p. 387.

[10] *Ibid.*, p. 356.

[11] Emile Durkheim, *Socialism and Saint-Simon* (Le Socialisme), R. W. Gouldner (ed.), C. Sattler (transl.) (Antioch: The Antioch Press, 1958), pp. 154–155.

[12] *Ibid.*, p. 155.

[13] F. Engels, *Anti-Dühring, Her Eugen Dühring's Revolution in Science, op. cit.*, p. 355.

workers' revolution and their accession to power that the whole sequence—transformation of the society into a production company, dying out of state's interferences in social relations, and passage to "administrative rule"—may take place. But Engels does not try to expressly work out in detail, or to combine into an integrated whole, the apparent contradictions between the vision of a decentralized state of communes—Marx's own vision—and the centralized tasks devolved upon it; the liquidation of "commanding and privileged positions," and the civil service or managerial tasks within the vast company to be formed by the whole industrial society; the immediate and violent destruction of the civil-military apparatus—part and parcel of the old state machine—and the slow dying out of the state. It is Lenin, the principal founder of the Soviet state, that in 1917 works out various answers to these questions, with an eye to the texts of the masters, and with another eye to the progress of the revolution itself.

Lenin posits first—with some quotations from Engels—that broad local self-government can easily combine "with the voluntary defense of the units of the state by the 'communes' and districts"; specifically, he states that centralism and local autonomy are possible, and that along with "the complete elimination of all bureaucratic practices and all 'ordering' from above." [14] How is this "complete elimination" to be carried out? To start with, by "converting the functions of the civil service into the simple operations of *control and accounting* that are within the scope and ability of the vast majority of the population, and, subsequently, of every single individual." [15] For Lenin, the "vast majority" of the population cannot only discharge all civil service jobs—since capitalism has rendered literacy universal—but also replace all the capitalists "overnight" in "the control over production and distribution." As for the "scientifically trained staff of engineers, agronoms, and so on, "they can be put to work for the workers just as they did for the capitalists." [16] Finally, the military apparatus can be destroyed and replaced "by the simple *organization of the armed* people." [17] In short:

"Accounting and control—that is *mainly* what is needed for the proper functioning of the *first phase* of communist society. *All* citizens are transformed into hired employees of the state, which consists of the armed workers. *All* citizens become employees and workers of a *single* countrywide state 'syndicate'." [18]

In the conception of Marx, Engels, and Lenin, the state's agenda under socialism—"the first phase of communist society"—is then necessarily shaped by the workers' state's "dying out," that is, its eventual *transformation* from *politic* to purely *economic* (or purely administrative). While eliminating its enemies, this state of "communes" (or of Soviets "voluntarily united") wrests

[14] V. I. Lenin, "The State and Revolution" in *Collected Works,* Vol. 25, June–September 1917 (Moscow: Progress Publishers, 1964), p. 447.
[15] *Ibid.,* p. 452 (Emphasis supplied).
[16] *Ibid.,* p. 473.
[17] *Ibid.,* p. 463.
[18] *Ibid.,* p. 473.

the means of production from private ownership, centralizes the conduct of economic affairs, organizes the economy "as a single office and a single factory," [19] and replaces the former "anarchy of production" with a "plan performing conscious organization."

In the actual construction of the Soviet state, the theoretical scenario was changed in many respects. The old state machine was indeed shattered, but in its stead arose a new, even more formidable civil-military bureaucracy. Far from dying out, the new state developed means and methods of coercion on a grand scale. The "self-governing" structure of Soviets overnight lost all real power; the ruling *communist party* became the lord and overseer of the interlocking top administration of the state and economy, staffed in all key decision positions by its men. Yet, no matter how distorted the theoretical scenario may seem in the practice's mirror, its underlying Saint-Simonian conception of the society as a vast producer company—a single office and a single factory as Lenin puts it—has not been basically changed in Soviet-type economies. The party's leadership visualizes itself as the Board of Directors of the economy and society, its Supreme Council of Industry. This, of course, does not mean that this Supreme Council can eliminate or overcome by injunctions the extremely complex production, technical, and organizational problems that push toward division rather than cooperation within this theoretically unique "office and factory." But the built-in tendencies of the system are toward centralization rather than decentralization, and toward the blurring of the frontiers between the top management of the economy as such and the top civil and military state administration as such.

In the capitalist economies, the state's agenda is ultimately shaped by the social, economic, and political needs of coping with market imperfections and market failures, in order to exist. Tendencies toward centralization are constrained not only by production, technical, and organizational factors typical to any industrialized society, but also by the existence of private ownership. The ensuing decentralization may or may not be optimal in specific cases, but it exists and at times may be insurmountable. Ownership as a barrier does not exist in Soviet-type economies; in fact, the basic vision of the economy as a single office and factory constrains the attempts at decentralization, even though, in principle at least, it may allow the search for *optimal* decentralization.

17.2 CENTRALIZATION, DECENTRALIZATION, OPTIMIZATION MODELS

Since its inception, the Soviet economic system has been built on the principle "the state governs the economy, the party directs the state." [20] The idea of "governing of the economy" taken to mean *direct administration via instructions* (or commands) has been changed in the case of a single economy which has evolved from a Soviet-type framework: Yugoslavia, particularly between

---

[19] *Ibid.*, p. 473.

[20] See Bela Csikos-Nagy, *Socialist Economic Policy* (London: Longman, 1973), p. 76.

1951 and 1970. There too, however, the party's control over the state has not been weakened, and eventually the state's control over the economy has been progressively reinforced (since the early 1970s).

On the indicated foundations, three basic types of economic organizational models—or "economic mechanisms" as they are called in the socialist camp—have been developed in the USSR: (1) the economic system of war communism (1918–1920): (2) the economic system of the "New Economic Policy" (NEP, 1920–1928); and (3) the centralized "planned" administration system of Stalin (from 1929 on). The essential feature of the first system is the tendency toward complete liquidation of monetary market relations in the economy as a whole; of the second system, the reliance on market relations on a vast scale; of the third, the tendency toward all-encompassing day-to-day administration of all basic economic activities from a single center of command. Each of these three mechanisms can be modified in a wide variety of ways: the first one was rapidly abandoned; the second one remains in many respects even now the ideal of certain East European system directors, and is analogous to the system prevailing in Yugoslavia; the third one is typical of what is usually called a "Soviet-type" economy, and is indeed the one that is characteristic—with various modifications and adaptations—of all contemporary socialist economies, exclusive of Yugoslavia.

War communism is usually described in the Soviet textbooks as the "proletarian form of war economy." Actually, the system had its own well-developed ideological foundations, which had little or nothing in common with the specific conditions in which the system was finally implemented. Characteristically, the economic system of war communism displayed the following features: (1) continuous extension of state ownership with a view toward liquidating all private ownership; (2) extension of state control of all aspects of production and distribution, eventually through a network of communes; (3) forced mobilization and allocation of labor; and (4) "naturalization" of the economy, that is, direct exchange of goods and liquidation of monetary exchange relations. The utter collapse of this barter economy by the beginning of 1920, complete disorganization and widespread famine, compelled the party to institute a number of key changes—some of which became irreversible.

The extension of nationalization in agriculture was halted; collectivization finally took place more than a decade later, and even then, in face of peasant resistance, the directors of the system had to concede some form of private possession of land (the so-called "private plots" of the collectivized peasants). State control over production was reduced to the "commanding heights" of the economy: large-scale industry, banking, transport and communications, and wholesale trade. While the "commanding heights" remained essentially centrally administered as a multi-branch corporation, market relations were introduced between the state complex and the rest of the economy freed from centralized control—private agriculture, small-scale industry, handicrafts, and retail trade. The forced mobilization and allocation of labor were discontinued and never reinstituted as such, except in partial forms including the eventual institution on a large scale of concentration camps for a significant part of the labor force. Finally, the attempts at "naturalization" of economic relations within the state complex were abandoned, although these relations have long been viewed as being of a different nature from "simple commodity production and exchange."

The NEP—that is, the coexistence and interaction of a state-run industrial-banking-transportation complex, with a largely peasant-dominated agriculture—remains, as we said above, the "ideal" of many would-be reformers of the Soviet system. Actually, it was never viewed within the ideological framework of bolshevism as being valid for a relatively prolonged period of "transition to communism." Rather, the institution under Stalin of the so-called system of "planned organization," and the application within it of the so-called "planning principle," are viewed by orthodox Marxists as the pure embodiment of the Marxian prediction of "planning" under socialism.[21] Actually the Soviet "planned organization" is in fact an attempt at centralized day-to-day administration of the main economic activities of the entire country, and the "planning principle" a misnomer for both policy decisions *and* arbitrary manipulations of cost-price considerations and of incentives; both the forms of administration and the application of the "principle" have been subjected to various changes, and are susceptible to further changes, as we shall see below.

In the contemporary Soviet system, the directives and instructions concerning outputs and inputs issued by the system's managers—the top party-state leaders—are coordinated and operationalized by the Central Planning Board and by industrial ministries and banks—the actuators or controllers of the system. The Planning Board issues instructions in the form of global physical production targets to the industrial sector and their divisions (departments or industrial associations of various types of enterprises). The latter apportion the tasks among their units (the enterprises), while a special organization of supply—the "Material Technical Supply" reminiscent of Walter Rathenau's supply organization of the German *Kriegswirtschaft*—channels the resources earmarked for fulfillment of the specific production targets.

Output information goes to a variety of identifying mechanisms, such as planning committees, statistical services, supervisory agencies, and sometimes the market, as when quantities of labor and goods are to be determined in accordance with the plan. The data are subsequently processed and sent back to the Central Planning Board via various feedback networks. The actual results of the original plan are then compared with the desired results, and further instructions designed to correct any deviations are issued to the actuators.

Reforms of the system have traditionally involved restructuring of the components and of their couplings, changes in overall informational flows—particularly instruction forms and content—changes in performance indicators, and variations in the nature of the identifiers of performance. Various changes during the Stalin "plan" era (1929–1953) sought to vertically consolidate on a

[21] P. M. Sweezy, *The Theory of Capitalist Development, Principles of Marxian Political Economy* (New York: Oxford University Press, 1942), pp. 52–54.

national level actuator jurisdiction of the Moscow-based national (so-called All-Union) ministries. In the late 1950s, during Khrushchev's tenure, regional or territorial supervisory agencies were substituted for the nationally unified ministerial organizations. After Khrushchev's fall, the ministerial organizations were reestablished. Subsequently, in the early 1970s, emphasis was placed in this latter frame on *associations of enterprises* in order to promote better industrial cooperation and higher specialization.

Each of these systems—arrangements and rearrangements—have incorporated some basic elements of the other. In the *ministerial* system, the principle of organizing each branch of industry as a consolidated organization has included territorial subdivisions and, eventually, enterprise associations. In the system of *territorial councils* of the national economy (or sovnarkhozy), the planning committees expanded their branch-of-industry divisions and assumed many of the functions of the previous ministries. Both systems—"pure" or "modified"—have shown a marked inability to deal simultaneously and equally effectively with departmental and regional problems. Under the ministerial system, departmental barriers have traditionally led to duplication of activities in various ministries; under the territorial system, regional barriers have led to localized distortions of the national interest and have thwarted the goals of the top policy makers and central planners. In the more complex relationship of the actuators with the central coordinating level, responsibility for allocating investable funds has been shifted in various ways from the state budget office to the banks. In either situation, however, decisions on the actual physical allocation of resources have remained of primary significance.

Various reforms are aimed at reducing the volume, complexity, specificity, and ranking of instructions, with a view toward eliminating the multiplicity of commands that often leads to duplication and confusion. Nevertheless, an enormous amount of redundant information still circulates within the vast reaches of the Soviet state bureaucracy. According to V. A. Trapeznikov, an examination of information reporting within a ministry in the late 1960s showed that for a number of divisions in that ministry, information, for which nobody, from the lower production level up to the ministry itself, could ascribe a purpose, amounted to 90 percent of the total information transferred to the superior levels. Each month the redundant information submitted from the lower to the upper level amounted to thousands of statistic-filled pages, reprinted several times along the chain of command.[22]

The selection of a performance criterion for assessing output has led to innumerable difficulties. The policy makers have traditionally used *gross value of output* as a performance criterion, but since the 1960s its increasingly obvious shortcomings have forced a shift toward another objective: the *"profits"* made by the enterprises. Profit orientation is one reason that prices have had to be made more meaningful than in the past. Nonetheless, in the view of the Soviet-system managers, prices essentially remain priority signals rather than

[22] V. A. Trapeznikov, "Problems of Control of Economic Systems," transl. from *Automatika i Telemekhanika,* in Joint Publications Research Service, No. 47, April 1969, p. 802.

scarcity indicators. Finally, as far as choice of identifiers is concerned, strong reliance has always been placed on direct rather than on roundabout controls, and on nonmarket mechanisms rather than on market or other spontaneous mechanisms.

The main contemporary thrusts of improvement of this centralized system concern, on the one hand, what may be called *optimal planning* (officially called "optimal functioning of the economy"); and, on the other hand, *optimal system design*. To clarify these general directions, consider the hierarchical structure of the system and its three basic layers: (1) supreme *coordinating* tier, represented by the Planning Board, and including the supremal policy-making level; (2) the *controlling* tier, represented by the heads of ministries and banks (possibly including also the heads of large enterprises' associations); and (3) the *operational management* tier, directly in charge of production processes. Assuredly, without changing this basic type of hierarchical arrangement, a great number of changes could be envisaged in the scope and nature of the respective assignments, responsibilities, and of the couplings within each layer.

The members of the prestigious Central Mathematical Institute (TsEMI) of the Soviet Academy of Sciences, for instance, have suggested that in plan formulation the supremal coordinating unit could base itself on the national optimality criterion for the development of the economy (defined by the directors of the system), the inter-industrial constraints (specified by the controllers), and the technological coefficients (furnished by the operations managers, reviewed and aggregated at the level of each industry). With these data, a first variant of the plan could be calculated, determining as a result of the solution of an extremal problem, the aggregated physical indices (the resources consumed and the outputs produced) and the corresponding prices for each industry. With these prices, the industries and the operational managers would then solve these specific optimization problems "without superfluous tutelage by higher organs." [23] Perspective plans would be continuously revised ("rolling plans") and plan fulfillment would not have an obligatory character, as it presently has.

Some interesting variations have been envisaged along the lines of the so-called Kornai-Liptak planning model (see Chapter 8). In this model, the coordinating unit proposes a given distribution of resources and the enterprises compute their shadow prices and report them to the coordinating unit. The latter then computes a new distribution and the enterprises compute new shadow prices—and so on until a distribution is found that equalizes the shadow prices among all the enterprises (there can be, however, more distributions showing equal shadow prices—only one of which is optimal). [24]

In the perspective of the technological changes for the balance of the century, or beyond, one could envisage still other possible linkages among

[23] See N. P. Fedorenko, "Optimal Planning and Functioning," transl. in M. Ellman, *Planning Problems in the USSR* (Cambridge, Mass.: Cambridge University Press, 1973), p. 67.
[24] See A. ten Kate, *Decentralized Decision Making in the Point of View of a Mathematician who is not Allowed to Use any Formulas* (Rotterdam: Netherlands School of Economics Centre for Development Planning, Discussion Paper No. 9, January 1971), pp. 4–5.

plans and activities within a hierarchical structure of the Soviet-type. Eventually, the infimal units may consist of fully automated plants . . . without workers *or* managers. The processes occurring there could then be conveniently described by deterministic mathematical models and be readily monitored in all their phases. At the controllers' level, humans and machines would then have to cooperate to develop activities that could be described by deterministic and stochastic models, while machines would perform data-processing functions. Finally, at the top coordinating level, where the system's directors would determine the direction of growth and production development, some decisions could be made with the help of programming techniques. But all this, assuredly, is as yet far into the future.

Improvements concerning the system's design could also run a whole gamut from modifications required by the computerization of the entire network of planning and statistical linkages, to new assignments of responsibilities within the planning structure, to redeterminations of the sequence of principal plan functions, to standardization of instructions, and formalization of all operations connected with the national plan.

Easily conceivable, and understandable within this frame, are certain suggestions also made, for instance, by Kornai with reference to the characteristic "tautness" of Soviet-type plans, and by Lange with reference to the need for "reliability" in regulation systems. Kornai [25] has suggested that one of the principal and perennial difficulties of Soviet-type economies is the planned tightness of inventories, and the ensuing inability of the system to cope with fluctuations in demand. Lange [26] has stressed that for any system forced to operate with a large, or a very large number of elements coupled in series, the provision of alternative couplings would increase the reliability of operations: the alternate elements would become active if a given element fails to perform. What Kornai would thus introduce in the system are *capacitors* to cope with surges in demand; what Lange would introduce in the system are *reserve channels*. Combining the two, we could envisage that Kornai's capacitor would not only level off given fluctuations, but also open up alternative channels when a particular channel becomes overloaded.

These and similar suggestions pale, however, in comparison with the intent of cyberneticists—commonly associated with the Scientific Council for Optimal Planning and Management of the USSR Academy of Sciences—who have made various proposals concerning optimal controls for the economy as a whole, along with self-regulating controls for branches and regions,[27] and optimal control for the entire macrosystem, including all of its subsystems and their interactions.[28] The macrosystem's subsystems are viewed as being (1) na-

[25] J. Kornai, *Anti-Equilibrium* (Amsterdam: North-Holland, 1971), pp. 256 ff.

[26] O. Lange, *Introduction to Economic Cybernetics* (Oxford: Pergamon Press, 1970), pp. 154 ff.

[27] A. Berg, "Economic Cybernetics," transl. in *Problems of Economics*, Vol. XI, No. 2, June 1968.

[28] See E. Z. Maiminas, "Economic Cybernetics," transl. in *Mathematical Studies in Economics and Statistics in the USSR and Eastern Europe*, Vol. II, No. 3, Spring 1966.

ture, in the form of resources and environment, (2) the economy as the processor of resources, and (3) the society or web of social relations, which according to Marxian theory, is engendered by the "mode of production," where production techniques change with various systems at various levels of development (see Figure 1.8). The purpose of the research is to uncover the optimal linkages of the subsystems and of their optimal performance, via mathematical model-building, and studies of information theory, management science, and systems theory in general. The Soviet contributions to the theory of optimal systems in mathematics and engineering are impressive [29]; they are far less interesting in the social sciences. The supporters of "optimal planning" expressly reject as not yet "fully worked out" the theories of the system redesignings for an "optimal functioning economy," which thus far have not received any encouragement from the Soviet leadership.

"Improvement" of the traditional Soviet system of centralized administration—erroneously referred to as Soviet "planning organization"—could thus involve almost countless reshufflings and reorderings of linkages, information flows, performance indicators, and so on, each of them open to some immediately obvious, and some less immediately obvious drawbacks. The suggested decentralizations, optimizations a la Fedorenko (of TsEMI), Kornai-Liptak (or for that matter the famous Lange-Lerner scheme) are no exceptions. Aggregation problems and rigid sequences of decisions involving time are present in all of them. It is impossible now to report to the center all the characteristics of the elements involved in the decision-making process; and accordingly, information selections have to be made, and decisions are to be based on these selections and ensuing aggregations. Much depends, accordingly, on whether, on these bases, plan fulfillment is rigidly defined and rendered obligatory or not. Further, other important information may be needed and possibly forthcoming when the participants are already locked-in in their particular decision-making sequence. Finally, difficulties arising in actual implementation may require reformulation of the problem; but that would be excluded, since the formulation step has already been completed. [30]

In practice, in the case of the Soviet Union, the full computerization ideal remains elusive, and even the formulation of an articulated economy-wide network of computer centers encompassing all levels of management is only at its beginnings. Soviet planners and engineers are still uncertain as to whether the development of the network should start with the individual enterprises and firms and proceed upward, or whether it should start with the center and proceed downward to the development of branch and finally enterprise systems— or in both directions. While the ideal of "computopia" is far and elusive, the controlled return of NEP schemes—in some East European countries at least— is jealously watched from Moscow. Various decentralization schemes with a NEP flavor have, however, been implemented in the socialist camp.

[29] See A. A. Fel'dbaum, "Optimal Systems" in J. Peschon (ed.) *Disciplines and Techniques of Systems Control* (New York: Blaisdell, 1965), pp. 317–373.
[30] See A. ten Kate, *op. cit.,* pp. 2–3.

Instead of directives on *all* quantities and *all* prices—determined necessarily, independently and simultaneously, at the same level, or at different levels—various changes can be envisaged also with respect to *some* quantities and *some* prices. Decentralization with respect to the determination of a large number of prices in Hungary, for instance, allowed the subsequent elimination of most output targets, increasing freedom for enterprises with respect to their financial and investment decisions, and increasing openings for direct contacts between producers, suppliers, and customers—first domestic, then foreign.

An important break with respect to the ownership barrier allowed the Yugoslavs some interesting, although ultimately ineffectual experimentations. The Yugoslavs replaced the principle of social ownership of the means of production with that of collective trusteeship of each enterprise by its personnel. To this they associated the idea of *self-management* by each collective, freeing the latter of central tutelage on either quantity or price determination, and substituting market relations to centralized directives. Within this collectively based, and apparently self-managed enterprises' framework, the economic controls from the center took only various *indirect* forms, as in any market-directed economy. Yet, even when these controls were at their weakest point, the governmental organs, and behind them, the communist leadership, exercised pervasive manipulations with respect to the *staffing* of all key economic and managerial positions. Actual "self-management" by the collectives, and especially by the lower personnel, varied, for this and other motives that have been examined elsewhere,[31] inversely with the significance of the enterprise. After two decades of experimentation (1951–1970) the Yugoslavs have proceeded under the same leadership that led them to decentralization, back to centralization—a retreat that is not yet fully stabilized.

17.3 EFFICIENCY AND INTERACTION-COORDINATION MODES [32]

Within the Soviet-type system, the question of *efficiency* has been limited to the evaluation of the specific results achieved by the enterprises, the industrial associations, and their controllers, with relation to the specific assignments set. While it is perfectly clear that the question of efficiency is complexly connected with the modes of interaction-coordination chosen for determining and assessing performance, the nature of prevailing incentives, and the scope and significance of price determination and manipulation, the matter has been tackled, so to speak, independently of its decisive connections. Emphasis has been placed on various suggestions concerning, for instance, payments for the use of capital assets, rent payments for the use of land, use of pay-back standard periods for choices among investment projects, use of profits as sources of investment financing and as incentive bonuses, and so on. Various changes have also been

---

[31] See N. Spulber, *Socialist Management and Planning* (Bloomington: Indiana University Press, 1971), pp. 61 ff.
[32] This section draws heavily on a paper by N. Spulber and E. M. Kloc, Jr., "On Conflict and Conflict Resolution in Policy and Planning," presented at the Annual Meeting of the Public Choice Society in New Haven, Conn., March 21, 1974.

made with respect to the disbursement of investment, by expanding the role of the banks and by curtailing the scope of activity in this respect of the budget office. But hardly any official consideration has been given to the deeper problems of, first, the overall *mode* of interaction between the supremal coordinating unit, the controller, and the infimal units, and, second, of the possible impact of the choices involved and of the ways in which they are carried out, on the nature of the plans themselves, and on the scope of the state agenda in its entirety.

For simplification purposes, consider a two-level hierarchical system composed of both a single central coordinating unit that also sets the constraints on the actions of the firms' managers, and the lower-level controlling managers themselves. Through its coordination of the interaction between lower-level units it becomes the responsibility of the center to ensure that the actions of the enterprises' managers motivated by their own self-interest, attain in concert the system's overall objective. Processing informational feedback from the decision makers of the lower level, the center attempts, then, to influence these combined decisions so that the optimal system performance is achieved.

In this two-level system three types of decision problems may be distinguished: the *overall* problem, the *central* problem, and the *lower-level* problem. Each problem in turn involves different goals and "images" (or "Gestalt" and "patterns"). For the system as a whole, the goal or goals—for example, stabilization, full employment, growth, and a set of output targets—may be defined, explicitly or implicitly. The attainment of this goal or goals is governed exclusively by the performance of the economy's *process*, with all variables exogenous to the system treated as being in the environment. The problem at the central or at the lower levels has other characteristics and variables. The objectives of the central decision-making unit *need not* be congruent with the goals of the overall system; this unit's "image" of the process in its entirety is made up of *all* lower-level decision problems. Put otherwise, the transformation of these actions into results is regulated by the process itself and constrained by the actions (and the objectives) of each lower-level unit. Finally, the lower-level decision makers view choice in terms of their own objectives as constrained by that *portion* of the process whose operation they can envisage— that is, the formal structure of the process in which they are engaged. Peripheral to their vision are the *remainder* of the process and the actions of the other decision makers, both viewed as exogenous and treated, in the form of interface inputs, as part of the environment.

If we assume that the central decision-making unit has as its concern the attainment of the overall system's objective, the distinction between the overall objective and the central objective would seem unnecessary. Actually, such a distinction is essential. Faced with a set of goal-seeking lower decision units, the central unit has, in principle, the option of either assuming the overall objective as its own goal, or of formulating *new aims* as the central objective by which to govern its own choices. But the eventual assumption of the overall goal places severe burdens upon the central unit. Suppose for a moment that it were capable of assuming total control of the process by removing decision-making authority at the lower level. (Such a supposition is indeed cardinal to optimal control theory. The latter allows the decision makers to reformulate the overall objective function in terms of a set of control variables initially endogenous to the process, but whose values are directly determined by the decision makers.) The existence of lower-level managers, however, implies precisely that the central unit *cannot* control directly the variables defined in the process. Such control ultimately rests with the lower-level decision makers. Rather, the center must view itself as a *coordinator* whose power to influence the outcome of the process is limited by the ability to affect the lower-level decision-making process through a set of *coordination variables*. Certainly the overall objective could be reformulated in terms of the lower-level managers' decisions, decisions that directly affect the outcome of the process. But such an approach would essentially involve: defining the overall objective function in terms of the process variables, determining the optimal solutions, and transforming this solution into its corresponding values in terms of the coordination variables. An alternative approach would be to reformulate the overall objective function into a form designed to reduce the complexity of the problem and the time required to find and implement a solution.

If we assume that the central authority wishes to avoid the assumption of *all* decision-making powers, it must: (a) select a mode of coordination defining clearly the *center to lower-level relationship;* (b) modify lower-level *goals and subprocesses,* thus altering the structure of the lower units' decision problems; and (c) establish a method for determining and implementing an *optimal* solution. With the selection of a mode of coordination, the central unit must establish the type, quantity, and quality of information that each lower-level unit will receive concerning its interaction with the rest of the system. Several modes of interaction-coordination are available: *estimation, prediction,* or *decoupling.* When the central unit chooses an estimation mode, it must specify the *range* of values that inputs to and/or outputs from any subprocess must take. With the choice of a prediction mode, the central unit must specify the *particular values* (for example, quotas) that these inputs and/or outputs must take. Finally, when it chooses a so-called decoupling mode it places *no constraints* on the quantities of either inputs or outputs. Achieving optimal values of the overall system objective depends on the center's ability to: (a) recognize an optimal solution when it occurs; (b) realize compatibility between the overall objective and the lower-level decision problems; and (c) enjoy the capacity to influence the action of the lower-level units in the desired way.

With each coordination mode one can associate a particular coordination principle; that is a rule telling the center that the optimal strategy has been chosen. When applying the estimation mode, the center seeks assurance that when the actual values of all interface inputs (resulting from lower-level action) fall within the interval estimates made, the overall solution has been attained. When choosing the prediction mode, the center seeks assurance that equality of actual and ordered interface values will yield the solution to the overall problem. Finally, when resorting to the decoupling mode, the center seeks assurance that when actual interaction values coincide with the interface values desired by each unit at the lower level, the overall decision problem has been solved.

In order to "speed up" performance the center may be inclined to treat any autonomous action as an impediment on the achievement of the overall objectives. The center may then choose to directly intervene in the production process, bypassing or ignoring the lower managers. Put otherwise, the center will seek to *circumvent goal conflict* by treating the entire system as if it were *single-level, single goal*. Actually, even under the most rigid specification of the eventual actions of the operational managers, the center can hardly hope to reduce the entire economic system to a manipulable, fully integrated, single-level, single-goal servomechanism, as it were, combining "all production establishments in the country into *one enterprise*". But, as the author of this remark, Oskar Lange, has pointed out, this "would be a purely fictitious operation": within that single enterprise the already mentioned differences in *technical* stages of production would not disappear, problems of *cooperation* between divisions would not be avoided, and *organizational* issues of all kinds would not be removed.[33] No matter how narrowly defined and how detailed the central specification of the process or subprocess, each variable will still represent various kinds of *aggregations* of a more detailed, unspecified structure capable of manipulation by the lower-level unit. Specification of a particular value will serve, then, only to constrain the lower-level unit's ability to maneuver in a *given* way, but not in all possible ways.

In arriving at the overall national economic targets, the Soviet planner views himself as an absolute controller of an integrated servomechanism whose objective is defined by the Politburo, and whose image consists of the nation's existing productive structure. Solving this overall problem, using sectoral and regional resource allocation as instrument variables, the coordinator (and his controllers) derive preliminary national output rates, as well as the values of each input (control) variable. In so approaching the problem of choice, the coordinator is forced to a large extent to ignore the oft-times conflicting goal-seeking activity of the operational managers of the individual productive units. With delegation of output and input specifications down the hierarchy through the controllers (actuators), the individual decision agent is presumably fully integrated into the plan. Actually, an ambivalent situation is created. Although explicitly formulated for an apparently single-level, single-goal structure with the input of each productive unit treated as a control variable, the plan must be made operational *within a multi-level, multi-goal framework*. The specification of the firms' input and output rates via the actuators constitutes, in fact, the implicit choice by the center of a *prediction* mode of coordination. While thus ensuring satisfaction of the system's physical (material input-output) interface linkages, the approach requires that the number of degrees of freedom available

---

[33] O. Lange, *op. cit.*, p. 171.

to each lower-level unit be sufficient to ensure reproduction of the desired values for the constellation of the firm's input-output linkages. Now, when faced with an insufficient number of traditional instruments by which to meet the production constraints imposed from above through the initial specification of physical balances, the Soviet manager is bound intuitively to seek *new* instruments of control.

To remove the overdetermination within his subsystem, the operational manager chooses, as instruments, parameters whose value had been *implicitly understood* rather than explicitly specified by the central unit. The lower-level units perform their own image modifications upon the system in order to ensure the feasibility of a solution given the balance specifications of the supreme coordinator and of the controllers. Thus, for example, a textile manufacturer given an output requirement of so many yards of material and a set of input specifications initially making such a quota impossible, may introduce a new instrument, *width,* into his model as a control variable. Choosing to modify the system by the reduction of the width of his output, he can ensure the achievement of the output goals. Realizing what has occurred, higher level decision units may then decide to specify fabric width. But the higher level's difficulties are not resolved by such action. Faced again with a set of excessively restrictive constraints the manager searches for another instrument, such as fabric *thickness,* assuring compliance with input and output specifications through the production of sheerer fabrics. As a result the lower levels, although having goals possibly quite compatible with overall national objectives, find themselves forced to suboptimize in terms of the stated objectives. Although *quantitatively* national balance may be attained, the failure of the central planner to recognize and fulfill the role of coordinator results in severe, multiple, and unpredictable *quality* imbalances. Having provided the lower-level units with a subprocess for which the number of coupling (interface) variables exceeds the number of control variables, the planner finds that the lower-level manager is forced to assume the role of *system modifier* in order to find a locally feasible solution. It is also possible that the infimal units have objectives different from those of the supremal unit, which they try to disguise by "feeding back" misleading information.

It is precisely for these reasons that some partisans of the "optimally functioning planning system" suggest that the *prediction* mode be abandoned, and that the *estimation* mode be substituted for it. Other economists suggest the decoupling of the decision makers of the infimal units, while others still, on the Yugoslav example, suggest complete disconnection between a broadly formulated national plan and the specific plans and operational decisions of the industries and of their enterprises. Thus, the introduction of the estimation or decoupling modes involve both the abandonment of *directive* planning, and in this sense, also a change in the socialist state's agenda.

As the directive plan is part and parcel of the traditional Soviet method of "governing the economy," and as its results are increasingly unsatisfactory, the Soviet and East European system controllers pursue simultaneously conflicting and elusive targets; they stick to the system of injunctions, but try at the same time to rely on economic instruments (actually faulty and distorted) in order to change managerial behavioral patterns (conditioned by the very structure of centralized administration); they continue to interfere in the day-to-day operations of industries—and the actuators, in the day-to-day operations of the enterprises—while at the same time they try to extend the enterprises' investment horizon and its own financial decisions, and so on. The rationale of this apparently illogical or inconsistent behavior is not too difficult to fathom: what is involved in the switching from one mode of interaction-coordination to another is ultimately the scope and nature of the state's role in the economy as a whole.

17.4 THE STATE AS A PERPETUAL PRIME MOVER

The Marx-Engels vision of the economic regime of the "dictatorship of the proletariat"—a vision that the communist parties in power have tried to implement in practice in its essentials—can be easily grasped from their writings. The founders of "scientific socialism" recommend the centralization of "all instruments of production in the hands of the state," abolition of property in land, "conscious and prearranged control of society on a common plan," and eventually "concentration of all production in the hands of a vast association of the whole nation." [34] All the countries directed by communist parties have carried out these recommendations, with the exception of some East European countries in regard to the nationalization of land. All these regimes, without exception, have abandoned some other crucial recommendations such as "centralized distribution of labor power and means of production to the different lines of occupation," and the elimination of money [35] which only the economic system of war communism implemented, and then with disastrous results.

The establishment of such a type of organization and management of the economy is meant to emphasize the passage to a *collective way* of achieving the wants of the population, as opposed to the primarily individualist way typical of capitalism. Indeed, on the basis of the centralization of the means of production, the proletariat, the new class in power, is supposed to continuously transform production and production relations. In the process, the proletariat imposes on the society as a whole its class-determined conception of what the wants of society *should* be. No self-interested private parties can act as quasi-governments to block the preferred reorganization of the economy as envisioned by the "proletariat"—actually by the communist party in power which claims to represent it.

In its extreme form, the imposition of government's will on society involves every possible form of activity, and in the economic field, not only the overall perspective of development, the specific division of income into investment and consumption and their structure, but also all the conditions of produc-

[34] See K. Marx and F. Engels, *The Communist Manifesto, op. cit.,* pp. 39–41; also R. Freedman (ed.), *Marx on Economics* (New York: Harcourt, Brace, 1961), pp. 263 ff.
[35] *Marx on Economics, op. cit.,* p. 266.

tion, of sanctions and rewards, of work and leisure. The government, and its inspiration and guide, the party, use as a criterion their "class-conscious" view of the ways in which society should develop and industrialize "until the completion of communism." This is what the Chinese Marxists call putting "Politics in Command of Everything." The slogan implies not only disregard for economic constraints, or for all kinds of constraints, and disregard of material incentives, consumer choice, or individual values, but also a "heroic" reconstruction of society and of the economy on a new, allegedly "higher plane" than that of capitalism.[36]

This extreme imposition of the "proletarian" view and will on the society is sure to bring about, according to Marx and Engels, "unbroken, constantly accelerated development of the productive forces and . . . a practically unlimited increase of production itself" as well as, eventually, the dying off of the state, and its transformation—or reduction—to a simple administrator of the "processes of production." [37] Actually, the various difficulties in achieving "accelerated development," except from very low levels and in relatively short and exceptional conditions, eventually transformed most of the communist-led economies into "mixed" socialist economies: (1) mixed in terms of ownership—particularly with respect to land (in countries like Poland and Yugoslavia, for instance, but also even in the Soviet Union where the persistence of private plots of the collectivized peasants and the importance of their output are also an expression of the significance of mixed ownership at the margins of the state complex); (2) mixed in terms of welfare rationale—up to a point, at least, consumer preferences could no longer be disregarded and consumer choice could not be considered as "insignificant" and "neglible" at will; and (3) mixed in terms of the utilization of centralized administration and the uses of market mechanisms—the existence of markets for labor and for consumer goods (and Yugoslavia alone also has true markets for producers' goods) have opened the way to various market influences, not only at the margins of the state-run complex, but within the complex itself with respect to prices, incentives, and economic calculus in general.

In the Soviet interpretation of the "political economy of socialism," a *transition period* takes place, after the overthrow of capitalism, from capitalism to socialism, during which the nascent and the defeated systems continue to be locked in overt and covert combat. As socialization expands, planned production is installed, economic "anarchy and competition" are abolished, and the state overcomes the inherited economic backwardness through industrialization; socialism triumphs! After the establishment of socialism, the role of the state in no way diminishes: it is now its task to prepare "the material and technical basis of communism." Since communism is supposed to ensure abundance for all, and distribution according to needs, *another* period of transition is said to exist between socialism and communism, in which production is further revolutionized, continuous progress in science and technology is carried out, higher

---

[36] Wan Jen-Chung, *Red Flag,* April 6, 1966, Peking Radio Report.
[37] F. Engels, *Anti-Dühring, Her Eugen Dühring's Revolution in Science, op. cit.,* p. 389.

levels of technical and general knowledge are created, and productivity is enormously increased.[38] While the Soviet and East Europeans have asserted that some 20 years after the accession of the respective communist parties in power the first transition period—to socialism—has been completed, they have been less keen to specify the time-table for the second transition—to communism. In any case, the Russians have stated that during this transition they could not " 'wait' for the lagging countries and give them everything which the advanced countries had created in comparison with the lagging." The Chinese have retorted, not only by accusing the Russians of nationalism, chauvinism, and disregard of the need of the poorer socialist countries, but also by specifying that as far as they knew, communism was nowhere in sight, and that the "transition" to it would last for centuries.[39]

Be that as it may, the role of the party-state as guide, perpetual prime mover, and agent of history, extends thus, far into the future. Instead of dying off, the state prepares "from above" a series of "leaps in different spheres of social life." In short, the new state, by destroying the old economic base, "becomes a constantly improved tool for building communist society." [40] The state must therefore "be protected like the apple of one's eye, constantly strengthened and allowed greater freedom of expression" than ever.[41] While the socialist state is thus glorified, its role exalted, and its motivating force at times deified—*vide* Stalin and Mao not to speak of the lesser deities—obvious difficulties rent the socialist economies. Difficulties in maintaining a sustained rate of growth, incapacity in achieving technological progress comparable to that of the capitalist MDC's, glaring and persistent discrepancies between the levels of development of various economic sectors and branches, slow rises in the standards of living, and irritating and persistent conflicts among the socialist countries concerning their own national development and their interrelations, have all led to a number of disclaimers as to what this apparently all-powerful and beloved socialist state could do.

Mao, for instance, has stressed that many "contradictions" subsist in a socialist country like China "between the government and the people." These contradictions include "contradictions among the interests of the state, the interests of the collective, and the interests of the individual," as well as contradictions among and within the various strata of the society as a whole.[42] In the same vein, all kinds of other contradictions—that is, of persistent and insoluble problems—have been noted by others with respect to the socialist economy and its efficiency, technology, quality of output, growth, and interrelations between

---

[38] See G. N. Khudokormov (ed.), *Political Economy of Socialism* (Moscow: Progress Publishers, 1967), pp. 9 ff and pp. 263 ff.

[39] See N. Spulber, *Socialist Management* . . . , *op. cit.,* p. 165.

[40] B. Kedrov, "On Forms of Leaps in the Development of Nature and Society," *Bolshevik,* August 1951, quoted by V. A. Aspaturian, "The Contemporary Doctrine of the Soviet State and its Philosophical Foundations," *The American Political Science Review,* No. 48, December 1954, p. 1050.

[41] V. A. Aspaturian, *ibid.,* p. 1051.

[42] See "The Correct Handling of Contradictions Among the People," in *Quotations From Chairman Mao Tse-Tung* (Peking: Foreign Language Press, 1966), pp. 46–47.

centralized directives and market mechanisms.[43] Stalin pointed out shortly before his death that the socialist state could not actually do everything since it had to recognize the existence of certain objective constraints—so-called "basic laws"—that it must respect in order to assure "an unbroken process of perfecting production on the basis of higher techniques." [44] Finally, the "reformers" pointed out after the death of Stalin that behind the discussion on "contradictions" and "laws" loom specific policy issues concerning growth strategy, investment choices, financial and monetary policies, and the articulation of the budget office and the banks to the enterprises, prices, and income policies, policies toward agriculture and distribution, internal economic policies—and the overall interrelations between centralized planning and the market mechanism. The study of these issues had been previously disregarded: "it was assumed that the knowledge of general economic policy can be practically integrated with the theory of national economic planning; it was feared that the independent study of economic policy might eclipse the theory of planning." [45] These policy issues have now started to be debated, sometimes timidly, sometimes more vigorously in at least *some* socialist countries, thus opening the way toward an evaluation of what precisely the agenda of a socialist country should be, and what criteria should be used for the purpose.

Notwithstanding the enormous changes undertaken in the structure of these economies, notwithstanding the enormous expansion of the state power and of its bureaucracy, notwithstanding the attempt at running the entire national economy as a "single office and single factory" which at a moment seemed almost under grasp—the questions typical for capitalism, which seemed already solved under socialism, namely *where* and exactly *how* should the state intervene, reappear again in all their vigor. The socialists have not arrived at specific answers that are any more satisfactory than those of the welfare economists, as to the exact *scope* of the agenda—even though, in principle, nothing limits it under socialism. As for *how* these interventions are to be carried out and how their impact is to be measured, the socialist system can and does borrow: *rational policy choice,* as we have already seen in this book, has made enormous progress in the West, in both the study of setting objectives and in the study of the decisions for optimally implementing them, and it is from the West that covert and overt borrowing and adaptations are now carried out in both planning and policy analysis.

[43] See N. N. Constantinescu, *Problema Contradicţei in economia socialistă* (Bucharest: Editura Politică, 1973).
[44] J. Stalin, *Economic Problems of Socialism in the USSR* (New York: International Publishers, 1952), pp. 19 ff.
[45] Bela Csikós-Nagy, *op. cit.,* p. 9.

CHAPTER 18

Convergence Theories and Optimal Systems

18.1 THE PROBLEM POSED

a. A preview

The intra-socialist debates on reforms of the socialist economic mechanism and the discussions "in vogue" in the West concerning convergence between the socialist and the capitalist systems, raise one and the same question, albeit from different angles: namely, that of *optimal economic systems*. Optimal systems can, however, assume many and varied forms, an observation that we interject in classic literary tradition to hint at the denouement of our plot: to wit, that the reports of imminent convergence have been greatly exaggerated! We shall arrive at this conclusion after first setting forth a framework within which optimal systems can be conveniently viewed. We shall then discuss convergence tendencies between East and West, and the classical paradigms used to explore any such propensities, turning subsequently to the major distinguishing features between economic systems—the controllers, the process, and information. Recognizing, as we do, that the concept of optimality in the present context is relative to the social preference function and the society's endowments, we shall go on to consider the extent to which "the" optimal systems toward which the Eastern and Western nations are heading are themselves tending to converge toward a single optimum.

b. An analytical framework

There are two basic reasons for the absence of a unique and invariant optimal system. First, the *concept* of optimality necessarily pertains to a situation for which both an objective function for the system, and the deterministic or stochastic nature of the system have been specified. Thus, under certainty one can delineate *uniformly optimal systems* that are governed by a decision-making process that *always* selects the optimal inputs into the system, given the processors' transformation functions and the decision makers' objective function. Alternatively, under uncertainty, one can distinguish between *statistically optimal systems* and *minimax optimal systems*. In the former instance, inputs are chosen so as to optimize some objective function under uncertainty, but an optimal solution is not *guaranteed ex post* because of stochastic elements that also impact upon the controllers and the processors; in the latter instance, perhaps under competitive pressures, the decision makers take an extreme risk-averse position and select inputs that maximize some objective function, given that the *worst* of the possible stochastic or competitive effects actually obtains. In either event, different objective functions can imply different optimal systems.

Second, there will not *necessarily* be a *unique* arrangement of the system components for optimizing any *given* objective function under either of the three conditions. Thus, without some classification scheme of manageable size, no unified approach to the fundamental problem of optimal systems is conceivable. Nonetheless, a simple classification suggested by A. A. Fel'dbaum [1] in connection with automatic control systems can be usefully expanded here for our purpose.

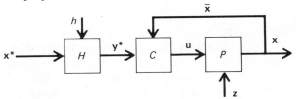

FIGURE 18-1

Consider the block diagram of an automatic control system presented in Figure 18.1. Here, C is the *controller* and P is the *processor*. The process generates a vector of outputs, x, in response to a vector of inputs u, received from the controller, and inputs z received from the environment, where z, u, and x are compatible with the respective transformation operations. Thus z is a vector of exogenous, *perhaps* random disturbances that impact upon the system. The vector of outputs that is optimal for the system, say in the sense that they represent, *if correctly perceived,* the outputs that are compatible with the optimization of the society's social welfare function, is x^*. Unfortunately, however, the controller's *perception* of the social welfare function, or the controller's interpretation of the ''message'' sent to it from the environment may, and indeed generally will be imperfect. Therefore, when x^* is the *desired* output vector, some other vector, y^*, may be ''inputed'' to the controller through the *communication channel H*, where y^*, say as a function of x^*, may itself be stochastic because of random noise, h, that interferes with communications. Finally,

[1] A. A. Fel'dbaum, ''Optimal Systems,'' in J. Peschon (ed.) *Disciplines and Techniques of Systems Control* (New York: Blaisdell, 1965), pp. 315–373.

the vector of outputs that is *actually* generated by the processor in response to the inputs that it receives from the controller and the environment is denoted $\bar{x}$.

In this system there are four basic transformation operations, one at the *initial* communications level, two at the supremal decision-making level of the controller, and one at the infimal decision-making, or production level for which the processor is responsible. In the first case, the communications channel, consisting, say, of a set of technicians, transmits society's desires to the controller; in the third case, the processor, consisting, say, of a set of plants, converts the controller's outputs—physical inputs and instructions that may additionally have been filtered through an actuator—into outputs for society; and, in the second case, the controller either translates the messages that it receives from the communications channel into outputs, u, that are destined to be sent to the processor as inputs, *or,* alternatively, it receives *feedback* information as to the actual output resulting from the initial set of inputs, and subsequently transmits to the processor another vector of inputs.

In this system, the decision-making unit, including the communications channel, or *C and H,* as well as the processor, *P,* are subjected to various *requirements* and *restrictions*. It is precisely according to these that we may draw important distinctions between optimal systems. In particular, we can distinguish five primary modes of classification:

1. The characteristics of the controller, C (and H);
2. The requirements made upon C (and H);
3. The characteristics of the processor, P;
4. The requirements made upon P;
5. The nature of the information about P (and the environment) which is supplied to C.

Characteristics, in the sense in which the term is used here, refer to the *transformation operations* that govern the particular component, be it controller or processor. Thus, the controller is a *supremal* decision-making unit that selects as *its output* a vector u, which becomes an input to the processor, in accordance with a *decision rule* or transformation operation such as

$$u = F(y^*, \bar{x})$$

Similarly, the processor is a production unit, or *infimal* decision-making unit, whose output vector x is determined in accordance with a *production function,* decision rule, or transformation operation such as

$$x = G(u, z)$$

The functions, F and G, thus represent the restrictions on the decision-making and production processes, respectively.

Requirements, in the present sense, refer to the external demands that are *imposed* upon the component, or upon its transformation operation. Thus, for example, the controller might be required to operate in accordance with a linear decision rule such as

$$u = \alpha(y^* - \bar{x})$$

or one might simply require that the decision rule not be "too complex," or that the controller's actual *physical* plant, say in terms of the magnitude of its administrative operations, not be too grandiose. Similarly, the processor might be required to minimize the *expected* sum of squared deviations, say, between actual outputs in $\bar{x}$ and the desired outputs in y^*, given the presence of a stochastic disturbance term z. In effect, then, the requirements of a component are analogous to the *objective function* or controller-initiated constraints that govern the choice among alternative processes or programs, whereas the characteristics of a component are analogous to the structural *constraints* that determine the feasible set of processes or programs that *might* be chosen. The design of the controller, for example, could be undertaken with the objective of selecting the decision *process,* say the *quadratic* decision rule for determining u, that minimizes the difference between the *perceived* desired output y^* and the actual output $\bar{x}$; the processor operations might be carried out with the objective of selecting the production *program* that, say, minimizes some quadratic objective function, subject to the given transformation operations.

The nature of the *information* that is supplied to the controller about the processor has two distinct aspects. On the one hand, in order to determine the inputs to transmit to the processor, the controller must understand the processor's transformation operations; on the other hand, in order to ensure that it truly controls the process, that is, that outputs in y^* are actually effected, the controller must obtain feedback with respect to the outputs that have resulted from its initial inputs to the processor. In either or both respects, the information available to the controller may be complete or incomplete. *Complete* information, it must be recognized, does *not* mean *perfect* information in the decision-theoretic sense. Rather, it refers to the fact that the controller has full knowledge as to the *transformation operation* and all of the *inputs* of the processor, as well as the *desired* outputs, where *either* the inputs x^* (and therefore u) and z are known with certainty a priori, or else their statistical properties are known a priori. *Incomplete* information refers to the fact that the inputs, whether in fact deterministic or stochastic, are treated by the controller *as if* either they and/or their generating functions are stochastic; but, as in the best decision-theoretic tradition, the controller can *learn* more about these inputs and the densities governing their behavior by subsequent observation that leads to the revision of prior judgments. In particular, feedback information $\bar{x}$ as to the output generated by the input u will, together with knowledge of the processor's transformation operation, enable the controller to *infer, ex post,* the exogenous input z that actually obtained, and therefore to revise prior judgments about z and its statistical process. Alternatively, the controller itself will not necessarily receive perfect information with respect to x^*. Instead, when x^* is the output that is really optimal for the system, errors in the communications channel—perhaps random errors—might lead the controller to the erroneous observation that $y^* \neq x^*$ is the optimal output. Then the information-processing problem confronting the controller is to determine either x^* or its governing process, given that the information y^* has been transmitted.

In approaching the question of *the* optimal system, the Eastern socialist "reformers" as well as the Western debaters on convergence deal, if with different emphases and completeness, with the same *type* of issues: namely, the *structure* (characteristics) of the individual components of the system, whether processors or controllers; the *demands* (requirements) imposed upon each of these individual components, including *objectives;* and, the nature and scope of the information possessed by the controllers with respect to both the inputs from the environment into the system, and the components' operations. As we shall see below, on the one hand convergence theorists ignore certain issues that the socialists tend to emphasize, and vice versa. On the other hand, the convergence discussion expands the horizons of the quest for an optimal system from production and its control, to distribution and to the questions of equity and inequality both within and between nations. In any case, the convergence theorists raise important issues with respect to optimal socio-economic systems, even if their efforts have not as yet led to the integrated theory that would produce these optima.

18.2 CONVERGENCE TENDENCIES AND PARADIGMS

Numerous writers representing many disciplines have propounded convergence theories. We shall limit ourselves here to the economic theories, wherein the main forces that are alleged to make for convergence among capitalism and socialism *qua* systems are the complex and widely ramified impact of the technical-scientific-managerial-revolution of large-scale production and large-scale organization, and of continuous high rates of economic growth. Separately, or in conjunction with these main forces, other factors are also alleged to make for convergence in the mature industrial states: notably, tendencies of systems' adaptability; the influences of experience and of each system upon the other; and a "changeover from ideology to rationality" in tune with the technico-scientific changes themselves. These tendencies are *alleged* to have effected a number of systemic changes. In particular, the significance and role of large-scale industry in the economy; the importance and the functions of the state; the nature and the inner working of the abstract institutions that carry out the society's goals—property rights, markets, and the degree of centralization and decentralization in production decisions and prices; the ways in which the production process is run, coordinated, and expanded; and the nature, uses, scope, and the concept of information, in ways affecting the system in its entirety.

Some current views of convergence originate with the early socialist concepts and theories—utopian or "scientific"—on the impact of the industrial revolution and the advent of the industrial society. Other ideas originate in the theories of evolutionary capitalism (of the German historical schools, of the American institutionalists, or the theoreticians of various aspects of the "managerial revolution"). Others proceed from unqualified abstractions, a la Frank Knight for instance, according to which socio-political changes do not "logically or necessarily imply any change whatever in the empirical course of economic life."[2] Still others transpose concepts from sociology or biology into economics. All of these theories then branch out into the future, with or without "optimistic" or "pessimistic" connotations. Assuredly, these underlying concepts and ideas are blended, completed, and expanded in *different* ways: the vision—or the paradigm—of the "mature industrial state" (capitalist or socialist) differs substantially from one writer to another. Among the most representative modern contributors to the economic theory of convergence are John K. Galbraith,[3] Jan Tinbergen,[4] and, to a lesser extent, W. W. Rostow.[5] Indeed, only the former two address themselves to most of the basic issues that their theses raise. One may recognize in their respective paradigms and underlying arguments some of the contentions of the "New Left," of the older "revisionist" (social-democratic) Left, and of the still older German historicist school—including here and there various echoes from Marx, Veblen, Berle, and Means.

In the Galbraithian vision,[6] the economic nucleus of the mature industrial state is formed by the complex of large corporations—which he specifically designates as the industrial system, or the modern economy. This complex is in fact the locus of key decisions for the economy in its entirety, and for the society at large. The "brain" of the corporation is not, as is usually assumed, its management, but the specialized knowledge, talent, and experience of the firm's *technicians*—engineers, product planners, market researchers, sales executives, and the like—which management mobilizes through continuously

[2] Frank Knight quoted by G. N. Halm, "Will Market Economies and Planned Economies Converge?" in E. Streissler *et al.* (eds.) *Roads to Freedom: Essays in Honor of Friedrich A. von Hayek* (New York: A. M. Kelly, 1970), pp. 75–88.

[3] J. K. Galbraith, *The Affluent Society* (Boston: Houghton Mifflin, 2nd ed. rev., 1969); *The New Industrial State* (Boston: Houghton Mifflin, 2nd ed. rev., 1971); *Economic Development in Perspective* (Cambridge, Mass.: Harvard University Press, 1962).

[4] J. Tinbergen, "The Theory of the Optimum Regime," in H. Klaassen, L. M. Koick, and H. J. Wittereen (eds.) *Jan Tinbergen, Selected Papers* (Amsterdam: North-Holland, 1959); "Do Communist and Free Economies Show a Converging Pattern," *Soviet Studies,* Vol. XII, No. 4, April 1961, pp. 333–341; *Lessons From the Past* (Amsterdam: Elsevier, 1963); *Central Planning* (New Haven, Conn.: Yale University Press, 1964); "The Significance of Welfare Economics for Socialism," in *On Political Economy and Econometrics: Essays in Honor of Oskar Lange* (Oxford: Pergamon Press, 1965), pp. 591–599; (with H. Linnemann and J. P. Pronk) "Convergence of Economic Systems in East and West," in *Disarmament and World Economic Interdependence* (Oslo and New York: Universitetsforlaget and Columbia University, 1967), pp. 246–260; *Development Planning* (New York: McGraw-Hill, 1967); "Some Aspects of Long-Term Planning" (Rotterdam: Erasmus University, mimeo); "Some Suggestions on a Modern Theory of the Optimum Regime," in *Socialism, Capitalism and Economic Growth: Essays Presented to Maurice Dobb* (Cambridge, Mass.: Cambridge University Press, 1967), pp. 125–132; "Development Strategy and Welfare Economics," *Co-existence,* Vol. 6, 1969, pp. 119–126; "Some Thoughts on Mature Socialism" (Rotterdam: Erasmus University, mimeo 1970); "Once Again: the Use of Welfare Economics" (Rotterdam: Erasmus University, mimeo 1971); "Some Features of the Optimum Regime," in *Optimum Social Welfare, A Comparative View* (New York: New York University Press, 1972), pp. 21–51.

[5] W. W. Rostow, *The Stages of Economic Growth: A Non-Communist Manifesto* (Cambridge, Mass.: Cambridge University Press, 2nd ed., 1971).

[6] See notably Galbraith, *The New Industrial State, op. cit.,* Chapter I, pp. 392 ff. and *passim.*

constituted and reconstituted committees according to tactical needs. This "technostructure" is the corporation's guiding intelligence. To implement its decisions, the corporation binds the consumer to its needs, brings the supply of capital and labor, the unions, and also the universities under its control, and extends its influence deeply into the state. It is to its planning—that is, to its control of demand, control of supply, provision of capital, and minimization of risk—that the state's own policies and instrument use, from taxing to spending, civil or military, are closely attuned (*mutatis mutandis*—this view encompasses the "mature" socialist states, as we shall see further). Juxtaposed to the "industrial system" with its large-scale processes is the world of small firms. It is within this world only, and up to a point in some of its interactions with the "industrial system," that market relations and "consumer sovereignty" function. To implement its day-to-day decisions, long-term planning and expansion, the "technostructure" requires a high measure of *autonomy,* which it eventually secures whatever the socio-political system. Convergence between the two systems begins indeed "with modern large-scale production, with heavy requirements of capital, sophisticated technology, and, as a prime consequence, elaborate organization."

In the Tinbergian vision,[7] the imperatives of technological development, of experience, and of adaptability inexorably push the capitalist and socialist systems alike toward a similar mix of goals, controlling devices, processes, and information use. The "West" moves from the traditional factory optimization and management to the complex organization and coordination of "hundreds of thousands of simultaneous actions" for entire industries, sectors, and finally for the economy as a whole. The "East" moves through growth and experience from the narrow military concepts of the German *Kriegswirtschaft* and from extreme scarcity to different patterns of organization and to accelerated growth. In the natural search for optimality it revises, or *should* do so— Tinbergen often changes from the positive to the *normative,* and back again— its commitments to total nationalization of the means of production, comprehensive planning, tight centralization, and direct instrumentalities. While West and East converge toward an optimum that can be rationally determined and sought after, the underdeveloped "South" is in its turn drawn through the spreading and modernization of technology toward new, more appropriate institutional blends.

Finally, in the Rostovian vision,[8] as in all stage theories, *all* societies lie "in their economic dimensions" within one of a number of categories. For Rostow, these "stages of growth" are the traditional society, the preconditions for take-off, the take-off, the drive to maturity, and the age of high mass-consumption; beyond, "it is impossible to predict," although one can foresee some of the issues. The indicated stages are defined not only in terms of real per capita income growth and patterns of income distribution between consumption, savings, and investment, but also in terms of leading sectoral com-

---

[7] Tinbergen, *Lessons from the Past, op. cit.,* Chapter I and *passim.*

[8] Rostow, *The Stages of Economic Growth, op. cit.,* Chapters I, II, pp. 159 ff. and *passim.*

plexes of production. All countries move normally along the indicated sequence. Communism is a kind of harsh "last resort," a *possible* form of organization, capable of launching and sustaining the growth process. Put otherwise, "it is a kind of disease which can befall a transitional society if it fails . . . to get on with the job of modernization." Then, as income per capita reaches a certain level, the communist society also enters into the phase of high mass-consumption. Provided the consumers' income elasticity of demand is not frustrated by public policy, the communist society will also eventually develop the "sectoral complexes," such as the "automobile sectoral complex" and the related industries and services associated with it, going into this particular stage.[9]

Let us then consider how these convergence theorists deal with the *specific issues* raised by convergence, in the context of optimal systems. The purpose is to determine what is actually *relevant* in this respect, and to call attention to what is in fact emphasized, as well as what is neglected. We shall deal, then, successively with: (1) the characteristics of, and the requirements on, first the controllers and second the processes; (2) the nature and scope of information; and (3) the optimal system at which we are aiming.

18.3 THE ISSUES

a. Controllers

Economic systems can *first* be distinguished from one another by focusing on the controllers, and on the *abstract institutions* (or mechanisms)—(i) property rights; (ii) markets; and (iii) patterns of centralization or decentralization in production decisions and prices—as opposed to *technological processes,* that help the society to carry out its goals, and that give each system its unique character. What is meant by "convergence," then, is that *evolutionary changes* are taking place within *each* of two economic systems of fundamentally different character, with respect to these distinguishing institutions, changes that are bringing the two systems into ever-sharpening coincidence. Convergence theorists, those that uphold the view that such evolutionary changes are in fact occurring, have given a stimulating diversity of interpretations to the ways in which this is being accomplished. Let us consider these interpretations in relation to each of these institutions, which jointly and in varying combinations determine the control functions that serve to regulate the economic process; that is, let us consider *characteristics* and *requirements* of *both* the supremal and infimal *controllers,* the decision-making units of the economic system. In particular, we shall focus on the disparate interpretations of Galbraith and Tinbergen, which taken in concert place the problem in true perspective.

(i) Galbraith sees decision-making power in the mature industrial states as passing from the owners—public or private—to the corporate *technostruc-*

[9] *Ibid.,* pp. 11, 104, 164.

ture. This is alleged to occur because modern technology *requires group decision;* that is, it requires pooling, processing, and use of specialized knowledge and data within an appropriate organizational framework. In fact, there are few corporations in which the owners—the shareholders—exercise any important *direct* influence in the decision-making process (although it should be acknowledged that to varying degrees corporate decision makers *do* maintain an *awareness* of shareholder interests and concerns). Further, for effective performance the corporation *must* defend its own decisions—that is, its power and autonomy for implementing decisions—against the challenge of any authority (public or private, or both as the case may be) in either a capitalist *or* in a socialist economy. In the Soviet Union there are two major sources of interference with this autonomy: that of the state planning apparatus, and that of the Communist Party. Even in the Soviet Union, however, the managers stress the need for autonomy, and the result is an uneasy compromise between the manager and the Party Secretary within the firm, so that ultimately "the resolution of the problem of authority in the industrial enterprise is not unlike that in the West— although no one can be precisely sure." [10]

Tinbergen sees convergence in property rights and decision-making authority on a different plane. Starting from the "most striking difference" between East and West, namely, the respective sizes of the public sector, Tinbergen stresses the *expansion* of this sector in the West (a process also noted by Galbraith) via what he calls "stepwise nationalization" *and* continuous limitations of various attributes of property rights. Following the Swedish Professor Unden, Tinbergen notes that ownership can be visualized as a "bunch of decision rights each of them showing a range of alternatives." These rights have been progressively narrowed as capitalism has evolved, via public legislation. Converging tendencies might manifest themselves by different approaches to the question of the scope of public ownership in various socialist states as well as via the shifting of decision powers from the state to the state-owned production units. [11]

(ii) Tinbergen and Galbraith also bring to bear different concepts on their views of planning—which is actually a decision-making *strategy*—and on converging plan-market combinations. For Galbraith, planning "in all cases means setting aside the market mechanism in favor of the control of prices and individual economic behavior." Planning refers here to planning by *autonomous firms* under their own authority. Since these are large and very large firms interpenetrating various state administrations, it is *their* plans and strategic decisions that largely overshadow the market and the decisions of *its* agents; and, it is these plans that are supported by the state's regulation of aggregate demand, stabilization of prices and wages, manpower training, and so on. Eventually, according to Galbraith, the Western interpenetration of the industrial system with the state will be such that "in time the line between the

[10] Galbraith, *The New Industrial State, op. cit.,* p. 107.
[11] Tinbergen, "Some Thoughts on Mature Socialism," op. cit., pp. 4 and 7.

two will disappear.'' [12] This would apparently yield an industrial-state decision-making complex not unlike that of the USSR, even though their *theoretical* ownerships and decision centers would be different.

For Tinbergen, planning means *planned economic policy;* that is, coordinated economic measures (that is, decisions *taken*) by *governments.* This planning—indicative macro-planning in the West and directive micro-planning in the East—combines in entirely different ways with the markets and market mechanisms. Convergence is viewed as resulting from ''tendencies of expanding the scope of planning in the West for developmental aims and that, sectorwise, still using indirect instruments for the private sector but affecting the public sector directly; and, conversely, tendencies'' of decentralizing planning decisions in the East, that is, ''less items to be planned at the center, more at lower levels, down even to the single factory.'' [13]

(iii) Galbraith advances two ideas with respect to centralization and decentralization of decisions. First, that there is a discrepancy between the *appearance* of power and the *reality* of power within the corporation; and, second, that the leadership of the corporation has one paramount objective in relation to the formal owners and the public authorities, notably its *autonomy.*

East and West differ sharply in corporate centralization. The power of decision is defined in the West in ways allowing the infimal units to decide on various matters outside the control of the higher levels. In contrast, Soviet centralization of decisions with the supremal unit remains very high with respect to investment, inputs, outputs and prices; little is left to the discretion of the managers of the infimal units. These differences may be differences without much substance. Indeed, according to Galbraith, in the Western-type corporation, on which his analysis focuses, the Board of Directors only *imagines* that it has decision powers in the selection of the corporate decision makers, in the determination of changes in capital structure, or in decisions on lines of credit, and so on. Actually, Galbraith adds, one should not confuse *ratification* of decisions with the real *process* of decision making. What the appointed Director *qua* manager ratifies has already been, in effect, decided ''by the group which has provided the information.'' When the Board ''acts'' it actually ratifies the technostructure's decisions; the technostructure manipulates its sources of savings and capital supply. In short, leadership is defined not by organizational charts—and this *mutatis mutandis* should hold for the USSR also—but by the ways of coping with the task, via *group* decision making. [14] The technostructure is everywhere, and in every case intent on preserving its autonomy, free of outside interference, in order to carry out its goals. Thus, Galbraith notes that ''to gain autonomy is what, in substantial measure, the Communist theoretician calls reforms.'' [15]

[12] Galbraith, *The New Industrial State, op. cit.,* p. 396.
[13] Tinbergen *et al.,* ''Convergence of Economic Systems in East and West,'' *op. cit.,* pp. 249–250.
[14] Galbraith, *The New Industrial State, op. cit.,* pp. 83–84.
[15] *Ibid.,* p. 393.

Tinbergen has a much more complex view of the implications of centralization, and of the possible patterns of decentralization in the East and West. He first notes that significant differences exist between East and West in respect to industrial democracy in general, freedom of decision of the infimal units in particular, and methods of control. He then notes the following converging tendencies: increased centralization, whether public or private, and increased central regulation in the West; and, conversely, reforms in planning concepts, in pricing, and in incentives, in the East. Tinbergen, accordingly, pays close attention indeed to all the changes in the Soviet-type economies concerning the scope of central planning, planning procedures, uses of capital, choice of projects, shifts in managers' success indicators, changes in pricing policies, and so forth.[16] For Tinbergen, the devolution of decision-making power requires a close and detailed study; the patterns of devolution do indeed play a decisive role in his subsequent definition of the "optimal regime."

We thus see different emphases among the convergence theories, as epitomized by the Galbraithian and Tinbergenian views, with respect to the evolution and significance of property rights, the ways in which markets are alleged to be superseded or controlled, the perception of the patterns of centralization and decentralization with the hierarchical structures that act on the economic process, and, eventually, the conception of the "optimal regime" itself.

b. The process

As in the case of the controllers, the possibility, if not the fact of convergence between East and West with respect to the *process* can also be analyzed in terms of requirements and characteristics. Here, however, the impact of the modern scientific-technical revolution is visualized on two different, but interrelated planes: first, in respect to requirements, on the plane of *specialization* and *organizational forms* required by the technological sophistication of modern production processes; second, on the plane of changes in the basic structure—that is, in the characteristics—of the industrial complex as such.

According to Galbraith, six consequences flow from the extensive application of technology to modern production, and from the attendant needs of vastly subdividing the production tasks into fractional and microfractional jobs: (1) an increasing time span must necessarily elapse from the beginning to the completion of any such task; (2) the capital committed to production must be very large; (3) investment must be inflexibly committed to the task; (4) specialized manpower on a large scale becomes necessary; (5) a complex and large organization becomes imperative; and (6) planning is required for fitting into a given perspective the various jobs that finally complete the task.

The more sophisticated the technology, the greater in general will be all the foregoing requirements. For the intricate technology of modern weaponry, which has given rise to an industrial complex of its own, "a quantum change in these requirements will be necessary." Specialization, organization, and plan-

---

[16] Tinbergen *et al.*, "Convergence of Economic Systems in East and West," *op. cit.*, pp. 249–250 and Tinbergen, "Some Thoughts on Mature Socialism," *op. cit.*, p. 4.

ning are thus a consequence of technology and, effect in their turn, technological development on an increasing scale: "the imperative of technology and organization, not the images of ideology, are what determine the shape of economic activity." [17] Convergence, as previously noted, starts for Galbraith with the appearance and the need of elaborate organization. Above all, the intricate requirements of modern weaponry being the same for the most advanced countries, resources permitting, the underlying tasks will also be the same.

Galbraith emphasizes specialization, organization, and planning in general, but to a large extent the fulcrum of the modern large corporate activity is for him the armament industry and its requirements. Other convergence theorists visualize, in different ways, changing industrial complexes according to various stages of growth or innovational processes. Following the European model of the third quarter of the nineteenth century, the Russians emphasized, according to Rostow, coal, iron, and heavy engineering in their "drive to maturity" started in 1929. As they enter into the stage of high mass-consumption, they naturally emphasize another leading sector, such as the automobile industry, plus those parts of other industries linked to it (such as strip steel, rubber tires, petroleum refining, and so on). [18] Perroux, as we noted earlier (see Chapter 13), sees as characteristic for the present-day MDC's, various specific clusters of industries with an increasing, decreasing, or medium growth rate, with the former "pulling along" the economy and those industries that agglomerate around it.

Be it on the *organizational* or on the *structural* plane, the choices in respect to the processors are thus *technologically* motivated; policy choices may interfere "to a degree," but apparently do not change, and cannot change in any significant way technologies' imperatives. [19]

c. Information

Any control system or subsystem—firm, industry, sector, or the economy as a whole, together with its various parts—requires *information* on the *demands* of the "operator(s)," the *purpose* of the control, the *state* of the output, and the impact of *disturbances.* This information is conveyed by such mechanisms, or *communications channels,* as markets or plans. Of decisive importance in hierarchical systems are, in addition, the role of information both *between* and *within* the decision-making levels, the *forms* of information (for example, nonprice or price-type information), and the *cost* and *effectiveness* with which it is handled.

Convergence theorists have concentrated their attention mostly on the nature and origin of the *demands* on the system (in our notation, x^*) and only in passing, and in relation to certain related aspects—for example, the question of the optimal degree of decentralization—on the very decisive problem of the relationship between such demands and the controls *within* the decision-making

[17] *Ibid.,* pp. 7 and 11 ff.
[18] Rostow, *op. cit.,* pp. 59, 187.
[19] *Ibid.,* p. 59.

structures (namely, between x^* and the controller inputs u, and between u and the processor outputs x, as well as between the *actual* demands x^* and the demands y^* that are transmitted to the controller via the communications network).

With respect to demands, Galbraith has noted that the standard economic questions of what to produce, how to produce, and for whom are decided in the main, in the capitalist as in the socialist system, by the infimal decision units of the producing organizations that form the industrial system—a system increasingly merging in the West with the state, and already merged with the state in the East. The consumer has lost considerable "sovereignty" in the West—a "sovereignty" that no one claims he ever held under the communist "thorough going" planning of the East.

The consumer has little to say: the corporation "reaches forward to control the markets that it is presumed to serve, and beyond, to bend the consumer to its needs." The industrial complex decides, in the main, on savings, and provides the major wherewithal for the expansion of the economy. In comparison to these decisions, the decision of a much larger number of individuals, on dwelling and consumer goods, are of secondary import. The state finally gives certitude, stability, and support to the industrial system's planning, through the control of aggregate demand, the underwriting of the costs of research and development, the maintenance of a high rate of public expenditures (particularly military), and so forth. The goal of output expansion seems to be a *social* goal, but it is in fact derived from the goals of the technostructure. The latter both imposes and responds to changes in social attitudes. In short, whatever the "planning instrument"—the corporation under capitalism, the state in the socialist system—the key decisions are removed from the consumer, who is bent to needs essentially defined by others.[20] In effect, the information that would be conveyed in a free market is to varying degrees ignored.

Tinbergen has been mostly concerned with how to *maximize* a social welfare function, rather than with the problem of how exactly one arrives at this function. He has, however, noted that the *normative* goals were similar in East and West; namely, a high average consumption and equity in the distribution of social justice. He has concluded that the *derived* goals were accordingly congruent; namely, high and stable employment, high investment, stable prices, and so on.[21] Elsewhere he has posited that what emerges "from new technologies as well as from a better understanding of the operation of economies" was a long list of governmental tasks rather than of private activities, and he has included in the latter, beside the usual tasks of regulation of unstable markets, aggregate demand, and the investment rate, the less usual tasks of macro-planning, and of various activities in the field of information and communication.[22]

The questions of the nature and function of the controls *within* the

[20] Galbraith, *The New Industrial State, op. cit.*, pp. 37 ff; 159 ff; 312.

[21] Tinbergen *et al.*, "Convergence of Economic Systems in East and West," *op. cit.*, p. 247.

[22] Tinbergen, "Some Thoughts on Mature Socialism," *op. cit.*, p. 11.

system—of crucial import for a capitalist-socialist systemic comparison—of the form of information, and of the effectiveness of its handling, have thus not been *directly* examined by the partisans of convergence. They bear heavily on the issue, however, and we shall turn to them later on.

d. The "optimal regime"

Logically, convergence supposes change and movement toward a *unique system*. For Galbraith, convergence tendencies, resulting from "industrialism's" extensive needs of superseding both the market and consumer sovereignty, (a) push the West toward the "fusion" of the industrial system with the state under the dominance of the former, and (b) push the East, where this fusion has already occurred, toward a shift in power from the state to the industrial system (namely, managerial autonomy). For Rostow, convergence consists in the natural gravitation of the Soviet Union, at a given per capita income, toward the United States' sectoral complex of high mass-consumption. We are not told whether these systems are optimal in some given sense; this is only implicit in the case of Rostow, who assumes that in the West the consumers exercise their sovereignty, whereas in the East they "hunger" for these complexes, and may eventually overcome with their pressure the hesitations of their leaders. Tinbergen alone sees the process of convergence essentially as a *rational* process in both East and West, and tries accordingly to define the "optimal regime" toward which he feels the two systems are "groping." Capitalism, which has grown spontaneously out of a certain historical framework, evolves through growth and technological transformation in such complicated ways that the need for rational correctives of various market consequences becomes imperative. And socialism, which has grown from extreme scarcity, the ideological assumptions of revolution, and the arbitrary rules of the *Kriegswirtschaft,* into a mature and complexly developed society, is also compelled by experience to change in rational ways. What *is,* or *should be,* the optimal system toward which they are really tending?

Tinbergen has tackled this issue a number of times,[23] continuously refining his argument, while starting from the same premises. For him, behind the usual questions of what, how, and for whom to produce, lies the deeper problem "by what 'arrangements,' that is, by what social order these production figures, etc. can be attained." Taking as given the social welfare function, he tries to find the set of institutions making for maximum welfare, given the usual constraints on production and on the costs of institutions and of the information flows they require. From his earliest paper on the subject, the direction of his research is clear.[24] In the spirit of convergence, he notes that in the West the following issues are debated: (a) Is the size of the public sector (which he

---

[23] See notably the following studies, cited in footnote 4: "Do Communist and Free Economies Show a Converging Pattern"; "Convergence of Economic Systems in East and West"; "Some Suggestions on a Modern Theory of the Optimum Regime"; and "Some Features of the Optimum Regime."

[24] See "Do Communist and Free Economies Show a Converging Pattern," *op. cit.,* pp. 120 ff.

stresses is not too *small*) adequate? (b) What "degree of plan detail" is most appropriate? (c) What should be the scope of "industrial democracy" and, given the inflationary pressures, is "some new form of price setting necessary?" Conversely, he perceives that eventually the following questions must be raised in the East: (a) Would a gain in efficiency—that is, achieving the same effect with a lesser expenditure of resources—not result "from making a large number of small enterprises in essence 'private' enterprises?" (b) Should not the scope of central planning be limited? (c) Would decentralization with respect to production and prices not yield quicker and better output results more in keeping with the consumers' rising requirements? [25] Continuing his exploration as to which specific institutions should do what, Tinbergen and his associates note finally that in the "optimum order" we would have: (a) a public sector with "at least small and medium production units;" (b) public regulation of total demand, total investment, of unstable markets and of income redistribution; and (c) distribution of policy tasks over authorities of "different levels." [26]

In brief, with various refinements and expansions, Tinbergen centers his search for and definition of the optimum on the various modifications of the controllers' parameters, under the assumption that the directors of the two systems approach rationality and efficiency in the same way. This, however, is far from being the case. Indeed, it is not clear that efficiency is in fact a desideratum of Eastern economies, or at any rate one that weighs heavily in the social preference function.

18.4 OTHER PARADIGMS

Hardly any one could deny the ramified impact of the scientific-technical-managerial revolutions, including the development of large and very large-scale production and organization, the multiple effects of sustained economic growth, and the efforts of the "directors" of capitalism and socialism of "learning from experience." But recognition of these facts does not mean acceptance of the theses that these revolutions are the beginning of convergence, that economic growth leads to the development of the same structural complexes in all MDC's, and that everybody learns the same lessons from the same experience, thereby leading to the same mix of goals and instruments whatever the sociopolitical system may be. Both Marxists and anti-Marxists take a variety of positions on these matters.

Consider first the "Marxist-Leninist" thesis, or the Communist vision of the changes occurring in the two systems. In the Marxian frame of reference, capitalism is in continuous decay, while socialism is continuously "perfecting" itself on the way to communism. Large-scale capitalist production and organization, corporate planning, and the "fusion" of corporations with the state—which Berle, Galbraith, and others are "forced to admit"—are "a law gov-

[25] *Loc. cit.*

[26] "Convergence of Economic Systems in East and West," *op. cit.*, p. 256; and "Some Suggestions on a Modern Theory of the Optimum Regime," *op. cit.*, pp. 129 ff.

erned process engendered by capitalism." As a Soviet writer puts it: "Concentration of production and concentration of capital engender monopoly which inevitably coalesces and interlaces with the state becoming state-monopoly capitalism." [27] As concentration increases, the small shareholder becomes a formal owner, while the large shareholder and the higher bureaucracy of the corporation form "the higher stratum of the capitalist class which exercises 'control ownership'." [28] Capitalist monopolization and capitalist planning have nothing to do with socialist reality; capitalist planning suppresses competition and thus, as Marx foresaw "disintegrates the production method on which it is based" while increasing the system's instability. [29] All of these phenomena are "the fullest material preparation for socialism" and for "mounting class battles." [30] Convergence theories on a "mixed society," an "industrial society" and so on, are "directed against the revolutionary ideology of the working-class." In short, no scientific or technical revolution can obviate the need for a *proletarian* revolution. [31]

The non-Marxian economic visions of the various processes taking place in the two systems range variously between two widely separated extremes. At one extreme it is posited that given the socio-political differences between the two, a workable symbiosis between market and planning is not achievable; and, that those mixes that have already been achieved, are revealed to have produced undesirable results. At the other extreme, Tinbergen's convergence theory assumes, as we have already seen, the possibility of the two systems converging toward the *same* optimal system.

In contrast to these positions, our view is that a *large variety of combinations between the two extremes* with respect to the characteristics of, and the requirements on the economy's controlling mechanisms and processes is actually possible in *both systems*. Additionally, however, we also contend that the respective choices, East and West, among the *available* sets *could not and would not coincide!* In particular, even should the *characteristics* of controllers and processors in both types of system tend to assume similar forms as a result of their taking advantage of, and adopting similar *technologies* which we are convinced they will *not do*—the *requirements* imposed upon them give every evidence of remaining divergent. Convergence theorists a la Tinbergen actually take a narrow view of the requirements issue, focusing on the *economic* objectives of the system as they are incorporated into a social welfare function; specifically, they focus on income distribution and economic growth as the arguments in such a function. They then posit that *all* systems are tending to

---

[27] S. Dalin, "John K. Galbraith's Theory of State Intervention," in S. Dalin, A. Anikin, and Y. Olsevich, *Economic Theories and Reality* (Moscow: Progress Publishers, 1967), p. 124.

[28] A. Anikin, "Monopolistic Corporation and Development of Capitalism, Adolf Berle's Conception," in *Ibid.*, p. 172.

[29] Walter Ulbricht: Speech on 'Das Kapital' Anniversary, *Neues Deutschland*, September 13, 1967 (Transl. in Foreign Broadcast Information Service, September 20, 1967 FB 183/67245), p. 19.

[30] See *Pravda*, October 16, 1967.

[31] *Pravda*, April 25, 1968.

adopt similar views with respect to these arguments and the shape of the welfare function, whereupon, given similar characteristics, convergence is the logical outcome for systems striving toward an optimum. If, however, one also recognizes that objectives *qua* requirements can also be *imposed* upon the components—both controllers and processors—as additional *constraints,* and that the socio-political-economic *philosophies* of the two systems are *not* necessarily converging, and that the constraints imposed upon the components do not coincide—and show no tendency to do so—convergence toward the same optimum seems less likely than otherwise.

Certainly, the form of ownership is one of several system parameters, and for many purposes, not the most important one: it tells little about consumer-government welfare rationales, and about the incentive structure on which the output of any system depends. Yet, one should remember that the *fundamental aim* of the Marxians is *abolition* of private ownership of the means of production, and hence a change in the social locus of decision making. Ultimately, then, under a Marxian socialist system, the subsistence of this type of private ownership would *necessarily* be viewed as transient (small or medium plants meant to respond quickly to consumers' changing tastes and needs could, of course, be organized on the basis of other forms of ownership—but that is another matter). Both capitalist and socialist economies could be reconciled with various mixes of consumer-government sovereignty, although the former would more typically be inclined toward the mix with higher consumer sovereignty, and the latter more typically toward a mix with higher government sovereignty. Finally, both economies could experiment with various patterns of centralization and decentralization with respect to production and pricing decisions. One should remember, however that a crucial tenet of Leninist ideology is that whatever the "decentralization" scheme may be, the Communist Party *directs* the state, which *governs* the economy; as Pravda puts it: "he who speaks against the leading role of the Communist Party in socialist society encroaches on the very foundations of this society." [32]

Since various mixes are possible, could not a socialist system select from all of the available sets the ideal mix suggested by Tinbergen? Our contention is that this would be impossible even if the posited constraints (with respect to the *extent* of public ownership and to the specific *ways* in which the party would guide the economy) were to be flexibly interpreted. The additional reasons why the directors of Soviet-type socialist economies could not choose the most efficient combinations of public-private ownership, market-plan mixtures, and centralization-decentralization patterns—assuming that the optima are those suggested by Tinbergen—are a number of further, hidden, subtler constraints. The *fear* of the directors of the Soviet-type economies that small ownership could and would generate capitalism—as Lenin contends with respect to small agricultural ownership—indeed precludes the possibility of the normal development in these economies of "small and medium enterprises"

[32] *Loc. cit.*

quickly responding to the changing tastes and needs of consumers, that is, to the *market*. The Party's *fear* of losing its control over the division of the national product into consumption and investment, and over the detailed patterns of both (and particularly the latter) precludes the resort to efficient plan-market combinations, either with respect to the domestic market or with respect to foreign trade. The Party's *fear* of allowing the development of important decision centers in production outside the Party's control precludes the search for efficient decentralization. Choices of the optimum mix with respect to controllers is thus confined in the logic and mentality of the manipulators of the Soviet-type system to the search for *accuracy* rather than to the search for efficiency: in particular, accuracy in the ways in which the central instructions are translated into the process' control imputs; and further, accuracy with respect to the ways in which the process' outputs and inputs match the control inputs; and, further back, accuracy in the central instructions to be received by the supremal controller. It is also incorrect to assume that the character of the plant (the Processor P in our notation) would or could be the same in both systems. The fear that managers, scientists, and technicians could or would "overrule" Party decisions *precludes* efficient choices also in this respect: choices of techniques, size, and location would remain, therefore, biased and distorted in various ways. Finally, the information required by a system that emphasizes efficiency, and the flows required by a system that emphasizes accuracy in execution, are bound to diverge both in nature and content, and evidently also in costs.

Detailed examination of a number of specific aspects of the convergence theories with respect to the controlling mechanisms in the two systems, the imperatives of technology, and the role of information, tend to further reinforce our doubts as to the merits of this hypothesis—as we shall discuss further below.

18.5 THE ISSUES RECONSIDERED

a. Controllers

(i) The convergence theorists' views on the questions of ownership and control in the two divergent systems of the East and West, and on the internal organization of large-scale industries tend to oversimplify the situation and to overlook a number of important elements. It is certainly true that in the West—as a critic of Galbraith concedes—"the modern corporation *is* largely free of stockholder control; it *does* supply internally a large part of its capital requirements; it *is* run by its managers; and the managerial bureaucracy *is* a coherent social-psychological system with motives and preferences of its own." [33] But, the Galbraithian concept of technostructure tends to both overstress the monolithic nature of the corporation and to obscure the nature of

[33] S. Gordon, "The Close of the Galbraithian System," *Journal of Political Economy,* Vol. 76, No. 4, July–August 1968.

its workings as an economic institution. It notably overlooks the facts that: (a) corporations are not single-level, multi-goal organizations, but rather *hierarchical* systems with complex goals, controls, and coordination problems; (b) corporations can and do take a *variety* of growth-oriented *organizational forms and functions* (for example, the multi-nationals, the conglomerates, and so on); and (c) the *characteristics* of a Western corporation differ sharply from the industrial associations and "conglomerates" of a Soviet-type setting where the Party-state appoints the managers, supplies the capital, and determines each organization's patterns and prospects of development.

Tinbergen's idea that ownership can be visualized as a "bunch of decision rights each of them showing a range of alternatives" may be in principle helpful, but in practice of little use as far as "convergence" is concerned. Certainly, the "bunch's" range has been increasingly restricted in the West; but the Communists refuse to consider these restrictions as important, and focus instead on the institution itself. Whereas in the West, nationalization is the *least desirable* means to achieve society's ends, the Communists' *main objective* remains the *complete* nationalization of the means of production, not only because of the inner logic of their doctrine, but also because they *believe* that through *total* nationalization they can root out the danger of the "revival" of capitalism, and simultaneously secure total control over the economy. Tinbergen may plead that "we should not stick to doctrinaire views based on antiquated theories, sometimes on scientific views of a hundred years ago," [34] but his appeal is bound to remain unheeded. The disparate views may bend, but neither shows an inclination to break, or to lean far enough to conjoin with the other.

(ii) The convergence concepts on planning and plan-market combinations are often based on hasty and shallow generalizations. It has been pointed out by various writers that Galbraith's views on planning lack understanding of the nature of the limitations of any type of planning, and of the relationship between firms' planning and a national plan. A Shell corporate executive has pointedly noted that the Galbraith-posited goal of the corporate planner, "the elimination of uncertainty," is extremely elusive: uncertainties abound, in the political, technological, and "environmental" fields—from aleatory contracts and explorations to aleatory weather—which no planner can eliminate. [35] That national planning is merely "corporate planning writ large" is baseless. As another critic correctly notes, Galbraith glosses over a whole range of issues: "How is the economy organized in a coherent system? By means of what mechanism or procedure are the activities of the 'five or six hundred firms' that constitute 'the heartland of the modern (U.S.) economy' . . . made to mesh? Galbraith rejects the market mechanism of traditional economics, but he offers no answer of his own to these fundamental questions . . . Galbraith slips from the proposition that the firm plans to the proposition that the economy is

[34] Tinbergen, "Some Thoughts on Mature Socialism," *op. cit.,* p. 11.
[35] F. S. McFadzean, "The Economic Planners Viewed From Inside a Large Corporation," in A. Cairncross (ed.) *The Managed Economy* (New York: Barnes and Noble, 1970), pp. 30 ff.

planned, without realizing that such statements possess only a verbal similarity." [36]

As we saw, Tinbergen's schema stresses converging in the planning *concepts* and *procedures*—East and West. While significant changes have undoubtedly taken place in this respect, as we have indicated throughout this book, vast differences in the methods and scope of planning continue to exist between East and West. It is interesting to note that in countries like the United States, no matter how sophisticated planning and programming can be in some administrations or in the case of vast military and space projects, that competence has not infiltrated the policy-making process. In contrast, as far as the USSR is concerned, no matter how much the Soviet econometricians stress the significance of the "introduction of mathematics in planning and decision making," after decades of experimentation Soviet planning remains centralized, directive to the last detail, bureaucratic, and quite primitive. A former Polish planner, Professor Zielinski, provides the key to this paradox: "The broader the scope of central planning (and hence the more difficult its tasks) the more primitive the planning techniques it must employ. This sounds paradoxical, to say the least, but it is nevertheless true. The reason is obvious: sophisticated planning techniques are unable at present to cope with a quantitative task of the dimensions of the yearly plan." [37] Only an administrative iterative process can cope with such a task.

(iii) Galbraith affirms that in general decisions are really made by those who *provide* the information—the "technicians"—rather than by those who *ratify* it—the "directors." This may be true, at least up to a point, in some corporations, although it singularly simplifies the question of power relations within a hierarchical structure. In any case, in the Soviet system the lines of decision making are much more sharply drawn. The assumption that a flexible technostructure rather than the rigidly controlled Party itself could fix the main decisions—not in the plant, at the infimal level, but at the higher and highest levels—is not acceptable. The Party's innate distrust of the "spets" (specialists) and managers of all types, hamstrings the operational managers and places in executive positions only Party members. There are certainly inputs from specialists at all levels; but the Soviet planning history is replete with decisions overruling the "pessimism" of the specialists. In fact, it is a sort of ritual, meant to stress the farsightedness of the Party.

Tinbergen's examination of the processes of centralization in the West, and of decentralization in the East, stresses the increasing similarities rather than the differences between the two, as significant and valid in many respects. There has been, indeed, a powerful expansion in the role of the public sector in the West, leading to increased uses of fiscal and monetary instruments, expanded scope of transfer payments of all kinds, and an enhanced role of the

[36] Gordon, *op. cit.*
[37] J. G. Zielinski, *Poland: Economic Reforms in East European Industry* (London: Oxford University Press, 1973), p. 80.

state as investor. But these changes have, of course, taken place without significant changes in ownership—even in countries like Great Britain or France—and without changes in the control of production. Similarly, decentralization in the Soviet-type economies—excepting Yugoslavia—have not led to effective devolution of power to the operational managers, as we have already noted (see Chapter 17).

Convergences in respect to ownership, market-plan combinations, and patterns of decentralization are incidental, widely different in import, and all in all as significant as the divergences between the main representatives of the two systems, the United States and the Soviet Union.

b. The process

Both Galbraith and Rostow envisage the "imperatives" of technological development as necessarily leading to the same consequences in the U.S. and Soviet systems; both of them point, however, to different *consequences* as concerns the processors. Galbraith stresses the needs of extensive *specialization,* vast *organization,* and *planning;* Rostow stresses the tendency toward the creation of the same *industrial complexes,* or processor subsystems, at given levels of development.

There is truth—but only partial truth—in each of these contentions. Indeed, vast organizations for the mobilization and manipulation of manpower can be created even on the basis of the most backward techniques—as ancient Egypt or ancient and modern China could testify. Large-scale organization is not the hallmark of advanced technology alone. Further, technological adaptation can take highly diverse forms, including the neglect of certain branches, the "priority" development of other branches, and the use of heterogeneous technological blocks even in the "priority" branches—as was indeed done in the USSR. No matter what technology is transferred from one country to another—and *a fortiori* from one systemic arrangement to another—adaptations and changes are inevitable. The emphasis with respect to control in the two systems being so sharply different—namely, primarily (although not exclusively), the pursuit of *efficiency* in one, and of *accuracy* in carrying out instructions in the other—one should naturally expect significant differences in branch, project, and plant choices, between the two. At the beginning of its industrialization drive, the USSR's leadership did indeed attempt to copy *in the main* the industrial framework existing in the United States (see Chapter 9, p. 198); it ultimately ended up with substantially different interdependencies, except in some select industries. In certain respects, given doctrinaire constraints in agriculture, for instance, in trying to develop modern skills, create large land compounds for advanced methods, and raise outputs by the "modern methods," the USSR actually moved *further away* from the West. Professor Gerschenkron once pointed out that in order to develop skills and increase outputs, Peter the Great made serfdom effective—that is, he further increased the distance with the West; the magnitude of the challenge (to "catch up") may thus change the "quality of the response." [38] (The *modern* kolkhoz is in many respects but *modern* serfdom.) In fact, there is no reason whatever to assume that even on the basis of the same technology entirely differently structured societies could not arise; even Marxists do not fully subscribe to such narrow determinism. Further, as far as strategies of development are concerned, that is, as far as the future is concerned, there is no reason whatever why ideological biases should not assert themselves and shape different "industrial complexes" in different countries—quite apart from the usual constraints and differences.

c. Information

Who defines the society's preferences and how—East and West? As we saw, for Galbraith an implicit convergence takes place in this respect because of large-scale organizations of production, of group decisions within them, and of their planning. For Tinbergen, the same goals are posited East and West for the manipulation of the systems and for their states by both failure of markets to exist (for example, externalities) and by a common drift toward "rationality." Thus, let us note in passing, Galbraith seems to see convergence in the relegation of the state to an increasingly subordinate and peripheral role, while Tinbergen sees precisely in the enhancement of the role of the state the very outcome of converging tendencies.

Be that as it may, we cannot at all agree with Galbraith's assumption that the competing decisions of the large corporations form a decisive interlocking pattern of preferences for the economy as a whole, but rather that the government and the consumers along with the corporations shape the demands on the economy through both market and nonmarket mechanisms. As for the USSR, the Party-state's preferences clearly govern those of the economy—not as the managers at large demand, but as the Party envisages them. Neither in the West nor in the East can the complex of state administrations—no matter what the competing influences exercised upon them—be viewed as deprived of their own decision-making powers.

As to the nature of the information on which decisions are taken, substantial differences exist between the East and the West. In the USSR both prices and quantities are determined centrally; in the West, with its "free," if oligopolistic markets, neither prices *nor* quantities are so determined. Convergence would imply—as ten Kate [39] has suggested—say, (a) renunciation of quantity determination in the USSR and (b) enforcement of price controls for plan purposes in the West—or some other similar combination; no convergence theorist has, however, examined these issues.

---

[38] See A. Gerschenkron, *Economic Backwardness in Historical Perspective* (Cambridge, Mass.: The Belknap Press of Harvard University Press, 1962), p. 18.

[39] A. ten Kate, *Decentralized Decision Making in the Point of View of a Mathematician who is not Allowed to Use any Formulas, op. cit.*

d. The convergence hypothesis and optimal systems

Convergence theory assumes, then, that the two systems tend toward a similar system, and as we saw, Tinbergen assumes that the system will necessarily also be the most efficient. This, however, seems to us a highly questionable proposition.

1. Returning to the model presented at the beginning of this chapter, let us note that Tinbergen posits that both systems will tend to choose the most efficient characteristics of the controllers—including communication systems *and* actuators—whose parameters or requirements—property rights, markets, and centralization patterns—are simultaneously tending in both systems toward the optimal mix. Both in the West and in the USSR, however, the range of the parameters is restricted in different ways, thus leading to different requirements and different characteristics. Further, the final selection between the latter is made in the West on the basis of the highest *efficiency,* in the USSR on the basis of the highest *accuracy* and/or *reliability,* that is, of the highest correspondence (or conformity) between the output x and the control input $u,$ and between the latter and the instruction y^*. The Western decision maker tacitly assumes that the most efficient choice is also the most accurate, that is, it best reflects the demands on the system's input and output correspondences.

2. With respect to the economic process, the convergence hypothesis assumes a tendency toward the same type of industries, branches, processes, and plants with the same mix of components—with various possible characteristics determined by, say, the following parameters: efficiency, returns to scale, elasticity of substitution, and input mix. Further, the hypotheses assume the same choice, East and West, among the resulting characteristics. Actually, projects, plants, and so on, will be selected with different requirements, or optimization criteria, such as maximization of output over time in the USSR rather than maximization of profits, and moreover, among the characteristics generated, the Soviets would tend to choose those reflecting the highest correspondence between x and $u,$ while the Western decision maker would tacitly assume that the most efficient characteristic is the most accurate (although actually a trade-off may be involved in both cases).

3. The type of information chosen in these systems may be considered optimal with respect to entirely different criteria: the criterion in the West is most information possible and "necessary" at least cost; in the East, most information on *all* the elements involved in *control,* whatever the *cost.*

The optimal models usually discussed in the West, with or without reference to convergence, focus on the most efficient characteristics of the controllers and processors, and the most information at least cost; the optimal models usually discussed in Eastern theory do likewise, but with emphasis on the requirements—especially control—and with an outright different choice in respect to the nature of information. Essentially, then, the two systems *tend toward divergent optimal choices.*

18.6 CONCLUDING COMMENTS

Convergence theorists usually focus their analyses on the United States and the Soviet Union—the so-called "mature" industrial representatives of the two systems. But quite often some of them convey the impression that what is happening in a less representative sample made up of this or that Western country (usually France) and this or that Eastern country (usually Yugoslavia) evidences, necessarily, what will happen in the most representative sample (the United States and the Soviet Union).

Assuredly, there are similarities between the two systems; but there are differences as well, and the latter can be substantial. *Even in principle,* there will *not necessarily* be a *unique* optimal regime, or an optimal economic order defined with specific reference to a given social welfare function, a given structural framework, and a given set of decision variables. Moreover, in practice the social welfare functions of the two systems do *not* coincide—that is, their goals are not the same; the structural frameworks—that is, the political, social, and legal requirements and restrictions—do not coincide; and the decision variables that are *in and of themselves* most palatable to the controllers—that is, the *preferred* instruments—also differ between the two systems.

Assuredly, both the modern capitalist and communist systems *are* susceptible to change and to the extent that they are at opposite extremes the changes that they do adopt tend to bring them closer together. Nevertheless, *several* important philosophical differences persist between them which are so deeply imbedded in the respective societies as to make any middle ground impractical, and any complete reversal of beliefs inconceivable. In particular, the adoption of social programs in the West, and the increased freedoms for the individual in the East, do *not* reflect a shift in emphasis from the individual to the collectivity in the former instances, and from the collectivity to the individual in the latter. Instead, they represent policy *adjustments* that are seen as benefiting the overwhelming *majority of individuals* in the former instance, and the *collectivity* in the latter, consistent with societal goals with respect to equity, economic growth, and ownership of the means of production. Similarly, public policy in the West specifically *aims* at the *preservation* of free markets and the *maintenance* of decentralized price and production decisions, whereas state policy in the East specifically *aims* at the *elimination* of the market and the centralization of price and production decisions. Again, neither system is completely successful in these aims. Thus, centrally administered controls are in fact imposed upon some markets in the West, and the emergence of large-scale oligopolies has had the effect of eroding other markets. These, however, are *aberrations* that as a matter of *conscious* public policy are either reluctantly instituted, or in the absence of adequate legal remedies, reluctantly tolerated; and, in either event, in some long-range view those aberrations are seen as being temporary. In contrast, the *small* free markets that actually exist in the East are seen as minor *concessions* on the part of the state which, in the total scheme of things, are basically unimportant. In effect, then, Western policy seeks to *protect* free markets, whereas Eastern policy seeks to *prevent* them. The result of these contrasting views of the individual and decentralization of decision-making authority, versus the collectivity and centralization of decision-making authority, is that on the one hand *profit* maintains its imposing position as a prime mover in the West, and *efficiency* of markets and production processes remains the vehicle for effecting profits. On the other hand, state *control* maintains its imposing position as the prime mover in the East, and the *accuracy* of keeping track of economic quantities remains the vehicle for effecting control. Thus, managerial decisions in the West are taken with some form of *profit maximization* objective in mind, whereas managerial decisions in the East are taken with some form of *error minimization* objective in mind. And, clearly, these conflicting objectives will not ordinarily imply the same decisions, nor give rise to the same optimal regime for effecting these decisions.

As A. G. Meyer once noted, convergence theories "as variants of development or modernization theory share with it one methodological weakness: theories of modernization have a tendency to be explicitly or implicitly teleological about the end product of development." [40] And it is precisely this end product at every point in time which escapes us.

[40] A. G. Meyer, "Theories of Convergence," in C. Johnson (ed.) *Change in Communist Systems* (Stanford: Stanford University Press, 1970), p. 337.

Accounting, 57, 160, 234, 295, 350; computer, as device for, 15, 41; identity $(x_i = m_i)$, 245, 246; models, 312, 317, 319–321; relationships, 133–146; social, 151, 157

Activity: analysis, vi, 155, 158, 181, 285

Actuator, 23, 24, 30, 36, 37, 38, 41, 43, 44, 47, 49, 51, 58, 64, 107, 178, 205, 212, 354, 361, 363, 369, 389

Advanced countries. *See* MDC's

Agriculture/agricultural sector, 154, 155, 307, 308, 345; communism and, 352, 383; demand, 302–304; as instrument, 107, 112; labor force, 185; manpower planning and, 256, 257, 278; planning, 289–290, 305–306; planning models, 277; processor, 255; production/productivity, 164, 180, 304–305; related to industrial subsystem, 290–294; two-sector models, 169; underemployment, 264

Allocation: of capital, 235, 256, 342; decisions, 178; of demand, 184; of economic variables, 61; farm commodity, 295–297, 300, 306; of goods, 185; of investment, 74, 169, 187, 188, 215, 230, 231, 232, 234, 235, 280, 294, 309, 328; of labor, 188, 257, 342; of land-use, 304, 306; of market shares, 9; models, 276; of output, 235; problems, 286; processes continuum, 56; of raw materials, 335; regional, 214; of resources, 27, 92, 109–111, 129, 153, 161, 185, 199, 323, 342; of savings, 317; of supplies, 249

Arrow, Kenneth, J., 1, 26, 88–89, 90, 214, 234, 341

Automaticity, v, 80; in control systems, 13, 25, 30–31, 356, 368; of formalized planning procedure, 177; in production planning, 185; in resolving project interrelationships, 286; in simulation, 181; in technological coefficients matrix, 138; in technological forecasting, 206

Automation, 356

Ayres, Robert U., 209

Babeuf, F. E., 337

Backwardness: economic, 199, 364; technological, 387. *See also* LDC's

Balance: equations, 321; of equilibrium growth, 313; government as balancer, 345; between industrial sectors, 275; of labor resources, 257; regional, 308; of regional growth, 295; in Soviet/Eastern economic planning models, 139, 141, 164, 165, 166, 184, 186, 188, 257, 291, 295, 362

Banking: international, 129; under socialism, 349, 352–353, 355, 359, 366; system, as economic structure, 62. *See also* Central Bank

Bargaining, 88, 163

Basic Policy Chart, 93, 99–102, 178

Baumol, W. J., 214, 228, 344

Bayes' Rule, 49, 54, 81, 179, 203

Beckermann, W., 239

Beckmann, M., 323

Bellman, Richard, 157

Benefits, 188, 287; direct and indirect, 188, 225; from education, 268; foregone, 228, 229; function, 55; future, 227–228, 229–230; intangible, 225; longer-term, 165; marginal, 344; social, 125, 231–232; state, 176. *See also* Cost-benefit analysis

Bentham, Jeremy, 335, 336

Bergson, A., 87, 88–89, 105

Berle, A., 372, 381

"Black box," 30, 42, 54

Bor, M., 176–177

Borrowing: consumer, 116; foreign, 236, 250; government, 110, 111; technological change and, 194; terms, 339

Bos, H. C., 158, 257, 270, 309

Brainard, W., 126

Brookings Institution, 78

Brookings model, 78, 79, 243–244

Bruno, M., 240, 249, 251, 253

Budget: under capitalism, 339, 344; constraint, 64; expenditures, 186, 223; national, 109; planning, 329; problems of investment planning and, 211, 222, 230, 231, 232; short-term plan and, 186; under socialism, 359, 366

Bureaucracy: corporate, 382; decision making and, 13, 230; managerial, 384; under socialism, 178, 348, 350, 351, 354, 366, 386

Cairncross, A., 340

Capacitators, 356

Capacity: of central authority, 57; channel, 48, 51; effect, 171, 232, 233; locational and regional planning and, 326; in planning agricultural production, 294, 295, 296, 297, 298, 299, 301, 305, 306; in planning foreign trade, 242, 244, 245; in planning of industrial activities, 278, 279, 280, 282; in planning models, 164, 165, 166, 171; in planning for technological change, 196; in problems of investment planning, 216, 230, 232, 233; productive, 72–73, 187, 232, 340; self-regulating mechanism of, 334–335; in Soviet planning techniques, 184, 185; of a system, 52–53

Capital: accumulation, 139–140, 199, 280, 323, 341; available, 187; concentration, 382; dictatorship of, 349; disequilibrium of, 342; equipment, 212; expropriation, 348; flow, 237; fixed, 139, 165; formation, 221, 222; growth rate, 141, 142; human, 268; inflow, foreign, 242, 249, 250, 251; intensity, 265; investment, 141, 142, 168; level of, 141; market, 236; needs, 373; new, 168, 208, 221; organic composition of, 140, 142, 162, 174; -output ratios, 162, 164, 165, 166, 167, 168, 170, 243; overall, 164, 187;

owners of, 110, 142; for production, 377; productivity, 220, 281, 294; replacement, 139; requirements, 172, 285; restrictions, 295; scarcity, 342; sectoral, 167; shifts, 315; social overhead of, 287; stock, 62, 104, 155, 165, 188, 219, 220, 221, 222, 250, 282, 310, 314, 315, 317; structure, 376; supply, 132, 150, 155, 185, 256, 373, 376, 384; utilization, 165, 235, 256, 377, 385; variable, 139

Capitalism/capitalists: controller under, 211; in convergence theories and optimal systems, 367, 371, 379, 380, 381–383, 385, 390; economic control in, 331; locational and regional planning and, 307–308; planning foreign trade and, 237, 238; as owners, 139, 140; programming, 176–177; in relation to state's "agenda" under socialism, 350, 351, 363, 364, 365, 366; state's "agenda" under, 333–346

Carré, Ph., 287

Carry-on effect, 171

Cartel, 112, 293–294, 346

Causality, 64, 79, 146–149, 206

Central Bank, 110–111, 211

Centralization: of administration, vi, 106; of allocative processes, 56–57; in convergence theories and optimal systems, 371, 373, 374–377, 383, 386, 389, 390; of decision-making authority, 26; of economic control, 3, 35, 159; in economic systems, 42, 58; of investment planning, 212, 214, 215, 230, 232, 234–235; in locational and regional planning, 308; in manpower and employment planning, 257, 266; of planning, vi, 158, 178, 185–186; in planning agricultural production, 296, 300, 305; in planning foreign trade, 249; of planning for technological change, 208; in state's "agenda" under socialism, 351–358, 359–361, 363, 364, 366

Central place theory, 322–324

Central planning agency, 185–186, 295, 310, 346, 353, 355, 359–360

Centre de Recherches Mathematiques pour la Planification (CERMAP), 367

Certainty: convergence theories and optimal systems and, 367–368, 370; in deterministic models, 10, 67, 68; -equivalent, 5; of information, 39; instruments and measures and, 123, 127;

investment alternatives and, 226; theory of consumer behavior under, 94, 95, 96

Chakravarty, S., 213, 215, 216

Chance, 120; in policy models, 13, 60, 80; "random shocks," 68, 206; -constrained programming, 298

Change: adaptability to, 80; administrative, 56; analyzing, 184, 202; anticipating, 161, 199, 200; in controllers, 178; in debt, 234–235; in demand, 291; demographic, 165, 255–272; directed, 132, 177; in economy, 258, 279, 281, 331, 363, 366, 390; effects of, 10; in employment, 263; endogenous/exogenous, 194–195; equivalents, 221; in income source, 171; industrial, 258, 275, 277, 322, 377–378; in input-output relationship, 135, 138, 277; in instruments, 108, 112, 113, 116, 124, 127; internal, 163; intertemporal, 171; inventory, 137, 233; and investment, 145; in labor needs, 255–272; in land use, 306; long-term, 97, 208; magnitude of, 200, 201; model, 177; output, 75–76, 280; population, 256; in preferences, 97; in productive capacity, 73; in public sector, 345; rate of, 160; rates of national income, 77, 164; in ratios, 314, 327; regional, 322; seasonal, 289; simulated, 79; structural, 340, 342; in system, 348–358, 371, 383; in target rates, 66, 79; technological, 101, 165, 179, 180, 194–210, 256, 262, 307, 355; in thought, 336, 339; in trade balance, 326; in variables, 95, 139, 141; in the West, 386–387; in world needs, 168

Channels, 59; communications, 41, 48–49, 368–369, 370; in investment, 171, 211, 233; noisy, 50–51; reserve, 356; for savings, 273; transmitting, 38, 40, 41, 50–51

Chaudhuri-Datta model, 317

Chenery, Hollis B., 132, 150, 154, 157, 158, 164, 172, 225–226, 230, 240, 249, 309

Chicago school, 340

China, 334, 364, 365, 387

Christaller, Walter, 308–309

Clark, John Bates, 335

Clark, P. G., 158

Coding: equivocation and, 51; of instructions, 44, 49; of messages, 38–39, 41, 46; optimal, 52; of signals, 38, 41

Communication(s): channels, 40, 41, 368, 369, 370, 378; device, 37; efficiency, 43, 49, 52; engineering, 31; format, 51; network, v, 3, 36, 48, 57, 324, 379; between nodal regions, 311; rate, 48, 49; signals, 41; speed, 52; state control of, 352; subsystems, 38, 291; systemic, 18, 34–35, 37–43, 55, 379; theory, 36, 45, 49; types of, 38; uses, 56

Competition/competitive, 211; and capitalist planning, 382; decentralization and, 28; economy, 30, 135, 136; education and, 268; and entropy, 55; in foreign trade, 110, 237, 240, 243, 244, 245, 247, 252, 254; market, 161; and optimal systems, 368; perfect, 314, 315, 335; pressure of Soviet growth, 340; producers, 32–33; quality of industrial goods and, 276; systems, 209

Complementarity, 171, 194, 211

Computer, v, 34; activity analysis and, 182; capacities, 40–41; center, 26; in economic system, 65; electronic, 67, 180, 181; experimenting via, 18, 27, 52, 55, 66, 180–181; in feedback model, 148; instruments and, 107, 110; large-scale, 14, 15, 37, 40, 52, 181; managing, 24; planning models and, 189; preference functions and, 84, 90, 92; simulation, 18, 180–181; technological forecasting and, 207; technology, 77, 308

Constraints: in convergence theories and optimal systems, 370, 380, 383, 388; on government intervention, in economy, vi; instruments and measures and, 117, 118, 121, 123, 124, 128; in locational and regional planning, 310, 313, 317, 324, 325–326; in manpower and employment planning, 267, 268; noninstitutional, 40, 43; in planning agricultural production, 290, 293, 294, 295, 296–300, 301, 305, 306; in planning foreign trade, 238, 239–240, 247–248, 249, 250, 252, 253; in planning of industrial activities, 274, 276, 279, 286; planning models and, 161, 162, 164, 165, 172; in planning techniques and procedures, 177, 181, 182, 185, 187; in planning for technological change, 196–198, 199, 201, 203–204; in policy models, 9, 11, 12, 13; preference functions and, 84, 85, 90, 93, 98, 105; in problems of investment planning, 215, 219, 231, 232; on processor, 3; in ration-

Constraints (*continued*)
al policy choice, 3, 42, 59, 60, 61, 63, 64, 65, 66, 67, 70, 71, 73; sectoral, 154; of sequences, 48; in state's "agenda" under capitalism, 335, 341; in state's "agenda" under socialism, 351, 355, 359, 361, 362, 364, 366; in structural framework, 131, 134, 135, 150, 151; in systems, 17, 34, 57; in technological forecasting, 155

Consumer, 18, 20, 135, 167, 200, 205, 213, 214, 265, 274, 345, 346, 364, 373, 379, 380, 381, 383, 384, 388, 390; behavior, 12, 64, 92, 94, 113, 166, 303; borrowing, 116; choice, 272, 364; demand, 134, 135, 264; goods, 143, 174, 184, 280; income, 64; preference, 106; productivity, 61; purchasing power, 24, 27; and rational choice theory, 1; spending, 53, 62, 78, 110, 211; theory of the, vi

Consumption, 2, 16, 21, 56, 62, 164, 198, 219, 220, 221, 233, 235, 276, 317, 363, 383; autonomous, 75; capacity, 169; control, 104; function, 146; goods, 73, 141, 169, 222, 320; growth, 216, 373–374, 378, 380; patterns, 218; personal, 144, 150; private, 100, 101, 137; public, 187; rate, 167, 168, 214, 215, 216, 217–218, 227, 234, 329; regional, 319; sector, 26, 27, 72, 134, 140, 142, 143, 147, 165; subsectors, 169–170

Control: of change, 198, 322; corporate, 373, 385; cybernetic, 3, 31, 35; of demand, 112; direct, 111, 113, 224, 308, 332; economic, 331–332, 341, 350, 358, 373, 384, 385; engineering, 31; government, 108, 110–112, 144, 224, 338, 340, 345–346; import-export, 236; inadequacy, 32; information, 2, 38, 54, 163, 389; input, 389; instruments, 107–116, 235; job, 266; measure, 81; mechanism, 7, 13, 20, 23, 42, 382, 384; ownership, 382; political, 161; population, 256, 329; price, 62, 112–113, 118, 129; problems, 25, 41, 54, 67, 154; process, 52, 57, 60, 360, 374–377, 384–391; programmed, v; quantity, 111; rent, 111; state, 336, 337; systems, 15, 20, 30, 33, 34–35, 37, 47, 51, 52, 59, 162, 199, 368, 378; theory, vi, 1, 2, 31, 158, 182, 219; of variables, 62, 67–69, 79, 107, 215; wage, 62, 111, 112

Controllers, 2, 3, 12, 15, 17, 24, 25, 27, 30, 36, 37, 38, 40, 41, 43, 44, 45, 46, 47, 48, 49, 51, 55, 58, 62, 63, 64, 65, 97, 99, 103, 106, 132, 137, 147, 148, 153, 177, 178, 179, 182, 211, 212, 234, 238, 239, 247, 248, 276, 277, 328, 358, 359, 361, 367, 368, 369, 370, 371, 381, 382, 384–387; central, 300, 355, 356; conditioning, 100; function, 162, 238; infimal, 3, 28, 38–39, 106, 311; input, 138, 163, 379; markets as, 32, 33, 42; network, 178; regional, 300, 310; single, 59; supremal, 2, 3, 28, 38–39, 311, 314, 332, 384; systems, 107, 160, 255, 333, 334, 374–377, 384–388

Convergence theory, 332, 367–391

Coordination, viii, 3, 17, 20, 26, 30, 33, 34, 35, 36, 37, 43, 59, 84, 85, 90, 91, 154, 162, 183, 230, 254, 257, 295, 311, 335, 339–341, 355, 356, 358–363, 376, 385

Corporate state, 337

Corporation, 1, 6, 7, 8, 26, 62, 129, 254, 332, 343, 346, 381–382, 384–385, 388; borrowing, 146; cartelization, 112; control, 379, 390; giant, 345, 371–372, 374–378, 381; needs, 373; planning, 208, 329, 386; profit, 78, 106, 111; tax, 110, 211, 212, 213, 228

Correa, H., 257, 270

Cost(s), 117, 183, 188, 231, 232, 249, 250, 287, 353, 384; adjustment, 127; agricultural, 291, 296, 298, 301, 303–304, 305, 306; assigned, 66; average, 344; balancing, 52–55, 134; capital, 287, 358; constraint, 64; curve, 20; direct and indirect, 188, 225; of education, 258, 268, 270; experimentation, 180; factors, 183, 282, 327; function, 34, 305; holding, 29; of information, 37, 41, 58, 378, 380; instrument, 117, 119, 129, 130; intangible, 224–225; of investment, 211, 223–224, 228–229; marginal, 20, 344; minimizing, 33–34; opportunity, 66, 229, 232; overrun, 223; political, 117; production, 135, 254, 295; research and development, 204; resources, 251, 252; shipping, 298, 303, 308–309, 325, 326; social, 117, 225, 345; of technology, 198, 210; total, 136, 143; welfare, 344

Cost-benefit analysis, 54, 234, 344

Couplings, 15–16, 17, 21–22, 34, 35, 42, 57, 60, 63, 108, 112, 131, 132, 153,

154, 162, 163, 176, 177, 195, 199, 212, 255, 273, 353, 355, 356, 362
Currency: foreign, 63, 111, 236, 247; hard, 237; management, 339
Customs union, 254
Cybernetics, 2, 3, 18, 19, 30, 34–35, 36, 356–357
Cycles, 180, 340

Dadaian, V. S., 159
Davis, Russell C., 267
Day, R., 282
Decentralization: of allocative processes, 56–57; in convergence theories and optimal systems, 371, 374–377, 378, 381, 383, 386, 387, 390, 391; of decision-making authority, 26; of economic control, 3, 35; in economic systems, 42, 58; of planning, viii; in planning foreign trade, 249; of policy-making process, 13; in state's "agenda" under socialism, 351–358; in systems control context, 26–28; techniques, 155
Decision-making: agricultural, 295, 300–301; in behavioral and causal relationships, 146–149; centralization and, 26–28, 57, 376; in communication system, 37–43, 55; by controller, 24, 27, 29, 103, 239, 310, 369; convergence theories and, 332, 368, 372, 374–377, 378–380, 386, 389, 390–391; costs in, 129; feasibility and, 2, 131; in firms, 5–8; in foreign trade, 239, 241–242, 247, 248, 249, 251, 252–253; government, vi, vii, 7, 8, 9, 38–39, 110–111, 150–151, 214, 277, 376; industrial, 273–288; infimal vs. supremal, 33–34, 310, 369; information in, 6–7, 13, 24, 37–43, 53–57, 130, 378–380, 386, 388; in institutional relationships, 150; interdependency in, 13; investment, 214, 215, 222–230, 231, 233, 274, 366; on labor "requirements," 264–267; in locational and regional planning, 309, 310, 311, 323, 325, 328, 329; Marxism and, 383, 384; in multi-level systems, 28–30; in optimal systems, 368, 389, 390; by people vs. machines, 31; in planning models and procedures, 157, 161, 178, 180–181, 186, 203–204, 207, 209; in policy models, 10, 11, 12, 13–14, 17, 20, 59–83, 117, 123; preference functions and, 12–13, 43, 84–106; risk and, 6, 54, 57, 67, 95, 97, 209, 368; single-goal, 2, 29; in state's

"agenda" under capitalism, 335, 340, 346; in state's "agenda" under socialism, 356, 357, 359–360, 362
Decision theory, vi, 49, 54
Decoding: of messages, 38, 41; of signals, 41
Decomposition, 46–47, 51, 55, 155, 182, 300
Decoupling, 360, 361, 362
Deficit: balance, 147, 148, 150, 236, 238, 275; spending, 91, 110–111
Delphi technique, 207
Demand, 5, 6, 11, 20, 21, 27, 40, 42, 57, 90, 112, 145, 150–151, 155, 158, 171, 185, 187, 200, 205, 206, 244, 247–248, 253, 256, 257, 273, 325, 341, 346, 374, 375, 379, 381; agricultural, 290, 302–304, 305; curve, 33; educational, 269; final, 134, 136–137, 143, 176, 196–197, 215, 216, 233, 242, 248, 277, 278, 280, 291, 293; 303, 305, 321; import-export, 279; for investment, 214; labor, 255, 264, 271, 273, 318; management, 335, 339–340; market, national, 322; -oriented, 312–313; price, 26, 32–33, 72, 289, 302, 303, 317; regional, 329; resource, 230; social, 60, 227; and supply, 75, 135, 140, 172, 189, 199, 258, 274, 289, 326; total, 74, 184, 326; values, 137
Demographics, 165, 200, 206, 257–260, 264, 271, 282
Denison, Edward F., 256, 267
Depreciation, 72, 134, 164, 165, 185, 216, 217
Depressed area, 257, 307, 308
Depression, 157
Developing countries. See LDC's
Development: agricultural, 302; under capitalism, 335, 336, 337, 341–343; foreign trade and, 253; industrial, 273–288, 337, 342; information and, 57; in LDC's, 341–343; planning and, 189–190, 376; and projections of labor availability, 260, 262; regional, 307–329; under socialism, 357, 363; "Soviet strategy of," 199; technological, 342, 373, 387–388; uneven, 307, 308, 338, 365; variables in strategies of, 249–251
Dictatorship, 86, 89, 91; Bonapartist, 348
Directive planning, 153, 160, 177, 184, 185, 186, 189, 190, 198–199, 212, 249, 277, 305, 346, 362, 376

Discounting, 218, 220, 223, 252, 301; rate, 63, 213, 214, 223, 227, 229; social rate of, 226, 228–229
Distribution, 61, 64, 87, 109, 110, 111, 113, 129, 132, 150–151, 197, 210, 225, 249, 317, 338, 366, 371; industrial, 308; investment, 211–213, 215; labor, 255; population, 194, 256–260, 271, 308; regional, 309; resource, 355; tax, 344; of technology, 195; wealth, 317
Dividends, 134, 138, 171
Domar, E. D., 340. *See also* Harrod-Domar model
Douglas, Paul, 343
Durand, J. D., 261
Dorfman, R., 87–88
Durkheim, Emile, 349

East. *See* Europe, Eastern; Socialist economies
Economic: order, 9, 60, 331, 336–339, 390; planning, vi, vii, 51, 61, 155–175, 178, 237, 290, 310, 333, 341, 346; policy, v, vii, viii, 7, 8, 17, 19, 24, 61, 108, 116–119, 179, 246, 314, 341; stabilization, 2, 67; stimuli, 57, 281; structure, 12, 20, 40, 60, 62, 64, 67, 70, 80, 84–85, 93, 98, 99, 101, 105, 116–117, 119, 133, 246, 336, 341, 381
Economics: classical, 334–335, 337–338, 340; of control, 336; empirical, 337–338; Marxian, 347; modern, 57, 289, 371, 391; welfare, 343, 366
Education, 155, 194, 208, 257, 265, 267–272, 305, 306, 309, 310, 335, 349; right to, 268
Efficiency: in capitalist West, 308, 391; in communications systems, 48, 49, 52–53, 57; vs. control, 332; in criteria for state's "agenda," 339, 343–345; industry and, 273, 285; of instruments, 116–117, 130; labor, 267; in optimal system, 381; in planning, 154, 161, 183, 251; policy makers and, 130, 131, 308; policy-planners and, 106; in public investment, 228; under Soviet-type socialism, 256, 358–363, 365, 383, 384; state's ruthlessness and, 339
Egypt, 100, 101, 387
Elasticities, 241, 243, 247, 256, 268, 284, 290, 302, 303, 374, 389
Employment, 12, 62, 90, 91, 92, 93, 96, 97, 99, 106, 118, 125, 162, 170, 185, 186, 242, 256, 273; full, 71–72, 79, 105, 112, 147, 148, 234, 236, 313, 335, 340, 343, 346, 359; nonfarm, 256; planning, 255–272, 309, 326; rate, 276; regional, 314, 317, 329
Energy, 19, 33–34, 62, 104, 138, 184, 199, 202, 238, 277, 280, 342; flow, 36; human, 211
Engels, Friedrich, 332, 347–350, 363, 364
Engineering, vi, 30–31, 42, 54, 208, 350, 357, 372; data, 322; heavy, 378
England, 329, 334, 337, 339, 341, 342, 345, 387
Entrepreneurs, 5, 6, 7, 10, 29, 135, 138, 144, 145, 176, 187, 254, 281, 339, 345
Entropy, 47, 48, 49, 50, 55
Environment: adaptive systems and, 25; constraints imposed by, 163; exogenous variables in, 17, 62, 106, 148, 180, 359; industrial link to, 273, 276; inputs from, 36, 37–38, 40, 41, 101, 106, 147–148, 238, 359, 368, 369, 371; international, 148, 238, 239, 274; as macrosystem's subsystem, 356–357; planning models and, 290, 294–300; regional subsystems as, 310; technological change and, 195, 205
Equilibrium, 75, 76, 135, 136, 174, 189, 195, 221, 253, 267, 290, 312, 313, 315, 320, 335, 340, 342, 343; condition, 139–143
Equipment, 185, 186, 234, 237, 242, 275, 276, 280
Equity, 9, 257, 272, 379
Ethics, 106, 220, 227, 335
Europe, 243, 244, 337, 341, 342, 348, 378; Eastern, 190, 249, 352, 357, 362, 365
Exploitation, rate of, 139, 140, 174
Exports, 103, 134, 137, 147–148, 150, 154, 165, 168, 169, 172, 184, 187, 236–254, 277, 279, 287, 304, 313; regional, 320
Expropriation, 347–348, 350–351, 363
Externalities, 225, 268

Farm, 290, 292, 293, 295, 297, 298, 300, 301, 305; buildings, 296; collectivization, 352, 364; labor, 256, 257, 289, 302, 304. *See also* Agriculture
Farmers, 169, 277, 296–297, 301, 306, 345
Fascist states, 338

Feasibility, 2, 3, 116, 131, 137, 157, 158, 161, 162, 177, 178, 182, 185, 187, 195, 235, 250–251, 274, 285, 292, 296, 302, 303, 317, 321, 328, 362, 370

Feedback: in agricultural planning models, 300–302; control and, 23, 36, 37, 59, 84, 92; in cybernetic approach, 2–3, 36; decision process and, 13–14, 28, 36, 70, 161; in determining preference, 93, 103; identifier function of, 23–24, 36; information, 36, 37–38, 42, 65, 103, 107, 147–148, 282, 353, 359, 362, 370; OECD model and, 245; in planning models and procedures, 161, 162–163, 182; in policy models, 13, 23–24, 25, 32, 59, 65, 67, 68, 70; in recursive sequences, 147–148, 290; in technological forecasting, 200, 205–206

Fedorenko, N. P., 357

Fel'dman, G. A., 221, 280

Fichte, J. G., 337

Finance, 358; foreign, 250; functional, 336; public, 109, 110–112, 113, 116, 129, 188

Firms: analyzing competition of, 55; in convergence theories, 378, 384–385; direct controls on, 111–112; fixed factor commitments of, 64; models of, 5–8, 20, 29; optimization of, 341; planning procedures and, 160, 184, 186–187; profit-maximizing, 5–6, 20, 29, 135, 293; small, 373; social responsibility of, 106; in Soviet-type system, 359, 362, 375; in systems control context, 18, 27; in technical and accounting relationships, 133–135, 136; theory of, vi; vertically integrated, in agriculture, 293

Fiscal, 2, 78, 108, 172, 199, 256, 346, 366, 386

Flows, 16, 79; capital, 237; cash, 211; diagram, 17, 21, 32, 70; economic, 19; energy, 36; of funds, 158, 188–189; information, 19–20, 28, 36, 37, 40, 42, 54, 55, 56, 57–58, 59, 79, 138, 208, 353, 357, 380, 384; intercenter, 324; interindustry, 136, 137, 233, 318; interregional, 309, 311, 318, 322, 326–328; inventory, 134; investment, 211, 321; labor, 255; payments, 246; population, 329; of returns, 223; sectoral, 327; trade, 60–61, 243, 244, 246, 309, 326–328; traffic, 311

Fluctuation, 77, 127, 340

Food, 238, 290; processing, 293–294, 298, 304; production, 304–306; scarcity, 305. *See also* Agriculture

Forecasting: in agricultural planning, 290, 296, 302–304, 306; errors in, 42, 70; in foreign trade, 238, 239, 240–247, 250, 252; industrial, 282, 283–284; information and, 42, 55, 57; instruments and, 128; as interaction-coordination model, 360, 361–362; in investment planning, 223–224; in manpower planning, 255–272; models and, 61, 63, 67, 68, 70, 80, 160, 163, 165, 172, 282, 329; in planning techniques, 179–180, 185, 186, 187, 188, 189; in policy analysis, 6, 7; sales, 282; technological, 155, 199–210, 304; uncertainty and, 6, 126, 204, 209

Foreign: aid, 62, 150, 162, 172, 183, 236, 250, 251; capital, 236, 242, 249, 250, 251; corporations, 343; countries, 242–243; currency, 63, 111, 236, 247, 249; debt, 100, 101, 250; demand, 302, 303; exchange, 111, 129, 150, 154, 158, 169, 172, 184, 185, 215, 226, 236–254, 275, 288; goods, 110; governments, 111; influence, 238; investment, 101, 237, 242; labor movement, 236; powers, 343; relations, 132; sector, 134, 135, 155, 238, 252, 274, 276, 304; technology, 194, 205, 210; trade, 2, 59, 60, 62, 111, 112, 113, 148, 150, 154, 164, 165, 172, 233, 236–254, 262, 273, 281, 282, 287, 304, 312, 337, 358, 384

Fourier, Charles, 347

Fox, Karl A., 290, 291, 293

France, 157, 208, 267, 329, 337, 341, 345, 387, 390

Frisch, Ragnar, 85, 98, 100, 101, 150–151, 154, 157, 158, 164, 171, 172, 213, 230, 232, 233, 237, 240, 251–252, 253, 284, 290, 302, 327

Function, 24, 40, 126; adjustment, 25; benefit, 54–55, 109; borrowing, 146; complex, 149; concave, 69, 102–103; consumption, 146; control, 36, 162, 374; convex, 68; cost, 34, 305; import-export, 244–247; individual, 86, 87; of industry, 273; investment, 146, 233; loss, 68–69, 70; market, 153; objective, 19, 25, 64, 66, 69, 92, 97, 120, 123, 126, 177, 182, 217, 238, 245, 249, 251, 268, 276, 285, 290, 293, 294, 296, 297, 300, 312, 317, 324, 328,

Function (*continued*)
360, 367, 368, 370; optimum, 219,
357; plan, 356; preference, 2, 3, 11,
12–13, 42–43, 60–61, 62, 63–64, 65,
68, 69, 70, 84–106, 110, 117, 118,
120, 121, 128, 162, 324, *see also* Preference; production, 64, 65, 133, 134,
135, 264, 274, 312, 325, 328, 369;
quadratic objective, 71, 230; sum of,
67; transportation, 32, 42, 146, 177,
181, 273, 274; unique, 145; utility, 54,
87, 89, 94–95, 96, 218, 221, 296. *See
also* Welfare function

Galbraith, John Kenneth, 332, 372,
374–380, 381, 384, 385, 386, 387, 388
Game theory, 2, 30, 88
Gaps, 94, 158, 172–174, 190, 237, 249,
253, 341–343
General Planning Commission (GPC), 186
Germany, 177, 334, 336, 337, 338, 371,
372; East, 249; West, 345
Gerschenkron, A., 387
Ghosh, A., 278, 294, 326, 327
Goals: ambiguous, 106; broad, 98, 257;
divergent, 60, 106, 212, 289, 389–391;
coordinating, 153; educational, 269;
formulating, viii, 1, 99, 101–105,
116–119, 131, 160, 162, 305, 308,
366, 383; fulfilling, 179; growth,
185, 275; limited, 249; multiple, 2,
29–30, 128, 157; national, 236–238,
336, 338, 342–343, 362, 385; normative, 9, 10, 172, 199, 208, 379; policy,
vi, 11, 12, 59, 63, 130, 160, 188,
214, 249, 251, 286–288, 294, 302,
341; regional, 318, 329; single, 29,
199, 217; social, 162, 203, 371; system's, 25–26, 33, 41, 57, 186–187,
234, 256, 276, 331, 333, 354,
359–361, 371–373, 374, 381, 388;
technological, 198; war, 339
Goods and services, 27, 42, 56, 64, 87,
92, 206, 211, 237, 243, 249, 276, 343;
agricultural, 307; allocation of, 185;
basic, 184, 199; capital, 73, 168, 169,
170, 221, 222, 258, 264, 275, 319,
340–341; consumer, 72, 139, 141, 166,
168, 174, 221, 222, 307; in different
economies, 72, 100, 101, 112–113,
139–144; diffusion of, 194, 199; domestic, 238, 240; durable, 21, 218,
319; export, 147–148, 168, 250, 253;
foreign, 110; imported, 287; industrial,

27, 143, 250, 273; intermediate, 187;
investment, 166; military, 103, 109,
184; movement, 322; physical capital,
340–341; priority, 184; producers',
139, 174, 199, 280; properties of, 57;
real, 345; sector, 169, 185; taxed, 211
Government: action, 108, 117, 149–150,
158–159, 160, 255, 343; agencies, 344;
bonds, 111; central, 162; choice, 273;
controls, 59, 107–112, 113, 144, 224,
345–346, 390; debt, 63, 110, 234–235;
decision-making, vi, vii, 7, 8, 9,
38–39, 110–111, 150–151, 214, 227,
376; fiat, 154, 160; information center,
21, 22; input, 205, 331; intervention, v,
vi, viii, 1, 9, 10, 27, 33, 132, 157,
172, 213, 235, 256, 332, 334–335,
338, 363, 366, 379; investment, 77,
212, 228, 233, 234, 345, 386–387;
laboratories, 205; participation, 342;
planning, 157, 177, 189–190, 281–282,
329, 343; policy, 283, 306; pressure,
111, 287, 296, 305; purchasing, 134,
137; revenue, 110; role, 1, 2, 208, 271,
274, 281, 284, 304, 333, 336, 363,
364, 383, 388; services, 322; spending,
12, 21, 22, 24, 25, 31–32, 62, 64, 77,
108–110, 116, 137, 147, 148, 194,
211–212, 273; structure, 60, 108, 297,
304; taxing, 25, 109, 273
Grain, 292, 296–297, 302, 305
Grants, 237, 250, 253, 319, 320
Gravity concept, 322–324
Gross national product (GNP), 8, 14, 24,
31, 94–95, 96, 97, 137, 144, 145, 150,
162, 164, 172, 184, 205, 240, 241,
242, 243, 244, 249–252, 253, 276, 345
Growth, vii, 61, 106, 141, 153, 155, 252,
273–288, 289, 294, 333, 356, 359; agricultural, 302; balanced, 104,
314–315; and change, spatial, 307–329;
consumption, 215, 216; export-import,
150, 236–254; industrial, 275–279,
318, 380; knowledge, 194; long-term,
79, 164; maximum, 169, 250; model,
62, 74, 144–146, 154, 159, 160, 280,
341, 342; national income, rate of,
164–165; national industrial, 337, 342;
optimal, 214; -oriented, 71, 164,
342–343, 385; output, 198; points, 322,
325; policy, 237; population, 162, 169,
185, 194, 258–260, 267, 318, 329; in
public sector, 331, 345–346; rapid,
336; rate, 71, 90, 141–142, 145, 166,

167, 168, 169, 172, 174, 201, 202, 217, 222, 234, 235, 251, 253, 267, 281, 312, 365, 378; regional, 173, 309, 312–329; stimulus, 294; strategy, 366; theory, 157, 159, 213, 312; unlimited, 281–282; urban, 323–324
Growth point concept, 322, 325

Hansen, B., 105
Harrod, Roy F., 340
Harrod-Domar model, 144–146, 164, 165, 167, 172, 187, 313, 341, 342
Hayek, F. A., 334, 338
Heady, Earl C., 289–290, 296
Hegel, G. W. F., 337
Hierarchies, 3, 6, 12, 13, 28–29, 38–39, 49, 55, 56, 57, 79, 84, 106, 132, 149, 154, 178, 186, 230, 311, 322–323, 329, 355, 356, 359, 361, 377, 378, 385, 386
Hirschleifer, J., 213, 226
Hirschman, Albert D., 308
Historical: empiricism, 338, 342; factor, 307, 347, 380
Hitler, Adolf, 338. *See also* Nazi
Holland, 157
Holmes, Sherlock, 40
Homogeneous region approach, 310
Hoover, Edgar, 309
Housing, 256, 379
Hungary, 159, 189, 247, 249, 358
Hurwicz, Leonid, 26, 56

Ichimura, Shinichi, 166, 243
Identifier, 23, 36, 38, 43, 50, 300, 353, 355
Imports, 113, 134, 137, 147, 148, 162, 165, 167, 168, 172, 184, 185, 213, 236–254, 275, 277, 278, 280; categories, 242; substitution, 275, 282
Impossibility theorem, 88–89, 90
Incentives, 358, 364, 377, 383
Income: balance, 188–189; classes, 150–151, 171; constraint, 135; consumer, 64, 302; corporate tax, 211; current, 146; determination, 342; differences, 311; disposable, 2; distribution, 2, 55, 110, 111, 112, 113, 129, 132, 225, 303, 382; division, 363; domestic, 245, 320; entrepreneurial, 135, 138; entropy, 55; equality, 272; forecasts, 158; future, 252; import, 241, 242; increase, 325–326; increment, 226; individual, 55; -investment ratio, 235; low, 257,

317, 342; national, 71–72, 73, 74, 75, 77, 100, 101, 138, 147, 164, 165, 166, 167, 184, 185, 216, 225, 316, 325–326, 340; per capita, 12, 14, 265, 277, 283, 284, 373, 374, 380; personal, 16; policy, 366; rate, 76, 148, 164, 168, 247, 303, 305, 328; ratio, 150, 214, 336; real national, 14, 148; regional, 312, 314, 316, 317, 325; rural, 256; tax, 62, 109, 149–150; theory, 157; transformation, 171; total, 137, 148–150, 298
India, 72, 169, 329
Industrial, 18, 25, 27, 135; cartel, 112; change, 258, 275, 277, 322, 377–378; complex, 290, 387; concentration, 346; context, 286; countries, 237, 243, 246; demand, 264; development, 328; framework, 387; goods, 27, 143, 250, 273; information center, 22; interaction, 136, 137, 158, 187; investment, 280; jobs, 255; laboratories, 205; -military, 377; obsolescence, 308; origin, 184; planning, 273–288, 379; plant, 133, 184, 223, 273–274, 277, 298; research and development, 198; rule, 349; sector, 143, 144, 153, 166, 169, 174, 185, 195–196, 214, 278–279, 280, 283, 284, 285, 287, 289–306, 345–372; strategy, 273–276, 283; structure, 377; subsystem, 277, 280–281, 282, 391; West, 312
Industrial Revolution, 371
Industrialization, 57, 194, 198, 199, 237, 253, 275–288, 323, 329, 347, 349–350, 364
Industry, 133–134, 135, 136, 155, 168, 171, 172, 177, 187, 189, 190, 197–198, 211, 245, 264, 266, 274, 279, 282, 284, 285, 294, 362; auto, 374; basic, 280–281, 318, 378; categories of, 277; decreasing-cost, 344; dependence, 307; domestic goods, 168; giant, 381; heavy, 162, 199, 275, 280–281, 378; increasing-cost, 343; key, 309; large-scale, 384; locating, 324; major, 273; modern, 275, 281; new, 308; output, 171; private, 275, 329; small, 162; substitute, 251; Supreme Council of, 351; work patterns in, 267
Inequities, 9–10, 56, 113, 117, 308, 337
Infimal unit, 3, 28, 30, 33–34, 38, 39, 79, 149, 277, 310, 311, 319, 322, 323,

Infimal unit (*continued*)
356, 359, 362, 369, 374, 376, 377, 379, 386

Inflation, 62, 129, 333, 336, 344, 346, 381; rate, 90, 91, 93, 96, 105, 110

Information: analysis, 41, 42, 54–55, 138, 360; bids, 56; center, 21, 22, 52; classes of, 42; comprehensive, 181; content, 43–48, 55, 370, 374, 378–380, 388; and control, 2, 17, 25, 37–43, 386–387; conversion, 15–16, 30; cost, 37, 53–57, 58; defining, 87; dispersal, 56, 335, 379; evaluating, 43; exchange, 37; flows, 19–20, 28, 36, 37, 40, 42, 54, 55, 57–58, 59, 138, 208, 331, 353, 357, 380, 384; gain, 50, 55; -generating technique, 181; historical, 9, 14; imperfect, 6, 7, 40, 249, 259; inputs, v, 3, 65, 81, 97–98, 99, 107, 110, 147–148, 160, 171, 274, 302, 319, 367; measure, 43–48; minimal, 92; necessary, 56, 154, 155; networks, v, 3, 36, 37–43, 48, 52, 57; new, 49, 97, 103, 187, 203, 306; output, 79; perfect, 53, 54; precise, 6; primary, 40; prior, 53–55, 62; properties, 45, 46–48, 55; recycled, 38, 42; redundant, 354; reliable, 56, 57, 77; reverse, 37; role of, 37, 56; source, 37–38, 39, 40, 43, 45, 48, 50, 52, 54, 57; statistical, 49, 54; storage, 14, 38, 41; technical, sources of, 208; technological, 201, 202; theories, vi, 37; transformation, 148; transmission rate, 50–51; value, 54–55, 92; volume, 56–57, 58, 98; yield, 66

Innovation, 194, 195, 198, 199, 208, 281, 378

Input-output, vi, 1, 18, 21, 22, 37, 41, 42, 64–65, 81, 107–108, 162, 163, 180, 181, 273, 277, 279, 286, 361, 362, 368; accounts, 319; agricultural, 290; analysis, 158, 181, 196, 225, 251, 291–292, 293, 321, 322, 360; control, 23, 384, 389; conversion, 15–17, 20, 30, 32, 110, 131; data, 3, 7, 10, 14, 23–24, 25, 36, 41, 53, 54, 60, 66, 92, 130; decisions, 42, 177; economic model, 72, 73, 84, 133, 134, 135–138, 144; economics, vi, 154, 238; equilibria, 267; investment, 212; labor, 139–141, 185, 250; matrix, 151, 265; model, 135–138, 170, 171–174, 179, 187, 189, 195, 198, 216, 232, 233, 268, 294, 317, 326; period, 195; physi-

cal, 208, 307, 369; price ratios, 135; ratios, 293; regional, 312, 325, 326; research and development, 204; sets, 13–14, 78–79; table, 151, 224, 242, 285; techniques, 290–291, 302, 303

Instructions: actuator's, 49, 369; in communications system, 36, 38, 39, 41–42, 47–48, 49, 51; controller's, 24, 38, 41, 44, 47–48, 51, 58; by Eastern planners, 179, 351–352, 353, 384

Instruments: and changes in institutional framework, 112, 115, 116; controller's selection of, 24; cost of, 117, 119, 129, 130; criteria for selection of, 116–119; of direct control, 111–112, 114, 116; diversification of, 127–128; efficiency of, 116–117, 130; foreign trade and, 111, 114, 236, 238; instability, 127; as measures, 24, 108; of money and credit, 110–111, 115, 116; nature of, 107–108; and objectives in West and East, 112–116, 128, 373, 379; planning and, 190, 333, 379; policy, 12, 212, 238; primary classifications of, 108–112; of public finance, 108–111, 115, 116; qualitative, 107–108, 118, 125, 130, 190; quantitative, 107, 108, 118, 130; selection of measures from, 119–130; in state's "agenda," 333, 336, 343; Tinbergen model and, 119–123

International, 60, 93, 111, 112, 117, 252, 283, 284; banking, 129; bodies, 246; borrowing, 236; conditions, 168, 279; environment, 132, 148, 238, 239; growth pattern, 277; labor, 112; market, 184; models, 239; obligations, 222; planning, 172; sector, 236, 238–239, 243, 302, 325, 328; standards, 276; relationships, 308; techniques, 194; trade, 236–254, 262, 273, 312

Invention, 194, 199, 205, 208, 281

Inventories, 6, 29, 57, 134, 137, 139, 158, 184, 233, 319

Investment, 2, 9, 10, 134, 137, 159, 164, 169, 170, 189, 234, 235, 257, 313, 340–341, 359, 363, 373, 376, 389; alternatives, 165, 194, 230, 239; analysis, 252; autonomous, 75; capacity, 72–73; capital, 36, 141, 278, 280; concentration, 199; decision-making, 214, 215, 222–230, 231, 233, 274, 366; demands on, 183; domestic, 8, 9, 137, 172; educational, 268; financing, 209;

flow, 211; foreign, 101, 237, 242; function, 146, 233; goods, 166, 167; government, 77, 212, 228, 233, 234, 345, 386–387; human, 41; induced, 75–77, 145, 256; industrial, 280; intersectoral, 221; overall, 204; periods, 186, 194, 196; phasing, 230, 232, 233, 285, 294; physical, 208, 234–235; planning, 24, 77, 100, 104, 158, 171, 174–175, 211–235, 309, 311, 335; policy, 222, 252, 254; portfolio, 127, 204, 230, 231; private, 22, 25, 74, 144–145, 155, 211–212, 213, 214, 228–229, 231, 234, 235, 287, 345; productive, 165, 168, 250; profit ratio, 226; public, 155, 223–230, 233; rate of, 62, 76, 143, 164, 165, 187, 198, 199, 212, 281, 282, 379; regional, 314–317, 319–321, 328, 329; sectors, 61, 74, 141–143, 170, 174, 176, 187, 211, 212, 249; securities, 230; shiftable, 221; specifics, 188; total, 101, 196, 215
Isard, Walter, 309, 319
Israel, 249
Italy, 205, 329

Jantsch, Erich, 200

Kalecki, M., 159, 164, 184, 253, 280
Kantorovich, L. V., 159
Keynes, John Maynard, 31–32, 132, 335, 336, 339–340, 342, 343, 345
Khrushchev, N., 354
Kirschen, E. S., 108, 110, 112
Klein-Goldberger model, 78
Knight, Frank, 371
Knowledge: new, 43, 44, 194, 205, 206, 237; productive, 341; specialized, 375; technical, 365. See also Information
Koopmans, T. C., 103
Kornai, J., 159, 356
Kornai-Liptak model, 189, 249, 355, 357
Kuhn, H. W., 213
Kuhn-Tucker conditions, 124
Kurz, M., 213, 214, 234
Kuznets, S., 308

Labor, 1, 26, 36, 62, 63, 106, 110, 111, 118, 125, 134, 135, 141, 143, 150, 162, 185, 198, 212, 234, 236, 242, 274, 277, 278, 282, 302, 315, 345, 352, 353, 363, 364; assignment, 338; conditions, 112; distribution, 140, 141, 153, 155, 174; division, 254, 349; educated, 268; industrial, 287–288; international, 112, 236; policy, 304; productivity, 140, 162, 165, 207, 249, 256–257, 266, 268; sectoral, 170, 289; skills of, 158, 194, 208, 254, 255, 257, 264, 266, 271, 308, 387; slave, 339; social, 249; supply, 135, 136, 138, 140, 150, 162, 164, 184, 187, 188, 215, 222, 250, 255–272, 278, 291, 294, 304, 305, 306, 310, 313, 329, 340, 373; surplus, 342; training, 194, 257; value, 139–140. See also Employment; Manpower; Unemployment; Work, force
Laissez-faire, 335, 342
Land, 295, 296–297, 302, 304, 305, 306, 348, 352, 358, 363, 364; owner, 250, 256
Lange, Oskar, v, 1, 159, 213, 234, 235, 264, 356, 361
Lange-Lerner model, 357
LDC's (less developed countries), 8, 278, 307; closed commercial state and, 337; demographic activity rates, 261, 262; demographic data, 259; development planning and growth in, 189–190; economic development in, 341–343; foreign trade planning in, 236–237, 239–240, 242, 253; imports from, 172; locational and regional planning in, 312, 322, 323; manpower and employment planning in, 256; planning of agricultural production in, 289, 291, 295; planning of industrial activities in, 275–276, 287; problems of investment planning in, 211–213, 235; technological change in, 207–210; unemployment in, 265; underemployment, 264
Lenin, V. I., 307, 348, 350, 351
Lenz, Friedrich, 338
Leontief, Wassily, vi, 3, 19, 135–138, 143, 144, 154, 174, 216, 232, 309, 346
Less developed countries. See LDC's
Lewis, W. Arthur, 189–190, 343
Liberals, philosophical, 334, 336, 346
LINK, Project, 246–247, 329
Linneman, H., 239
List, Friedrick, 337
Lösch, August, 308–309
Lotka, A. J., 259

Machine tools, 199, 280
Machinery, 31, 234, 237, 242, 275, 296, 306, 356

Macro: -economic, 7, 15, 60, 63, 134, 188, 246, 254, 312–313; -models, 163, 201, 202, 277; -planning, vi, 158, 187, 188, 286, 328, 376, 379; -system, 356–357
Mahalanobis model, 62, 71–74, 139, 164, 166, 169, 170, 221, 280, 294
Malthus, Thomas R., 259
Management: in convergence theories, 384–387; corporate, 1, 6–7, 8, 26, 106, 384; decision-making, *see* decision-making; as entrepeneurs, *see* Entrepeneurs; in firm and policy models, 5–8; government role in, *see* Government; information and, 6–7, 42, 43, 49, 52, 92; investment planning and, 212, 222–223, 224, 228, 229–230; operational, 212, 266, 361; planning and, 159–161, 183, 189, 277–278; preference functions of, 84–106; public, 15, 43, 52, 345; Soviet, 190, 332, 351, 356, 358, 359, 360, 361, 375, 377, 388; in systems approach, 15, 17, 26; technology and, 198, 199, 207, 208; theory of, vi, vii; under Western capitalism, 106, 332, 335, 336–343, 391
"Managerial revolution," 371, 381
Manpower, 2, 255–272, 278, 291, 375, 387; requirement projections, 264–267; specialized, 377. *See also* Labor
Mao Tse-Tung, 365
Margolin, S. A., 213, 317
Market, 92, 106, 113, 178, 333, 358, 371, 374, 377, 378–380, 382, 383, 384, 387, 389; allocation, 9; competitive, 161; control of, 379; as controller, 32, 33, 42; domestic, 111, 167, 253; economy, 34, 57, 58, 62, 157, 175, 256, 281, 305, 341, 351; exchange, 339; export, 277; factor, 20, 177, 273; failure, 343; foreign, 253–254, 276, 287; free, 332, 390–391; industrial, 26, 27; labor, 265, 267; manipulation, 113; mechanism, 9, 33, 87, 153, 154, 176, 295, 342, 343, 346, 364, 366, 375, 376, 388; operation, 111; participants, 335; period, 186; price, 33; private, 235; range, 309, 325–326; regional, 322–323; research, 372; share, 244–245, 246, 247; structure, 113; world, 243–244, 247–248
Marketing, 29, 184, 289, 290, 304
Markowitz, H. M., 204, 213, 230, 286

Marshallian framework, 64, 68, 87, 89, 94–95, 96, 97, 186–187, 343
Marx, Karl, 19, 138, 139, 140, 307, 332, 337, 347–350, 363, 364, 372, 382
Marxian, 3, 159, 162, 184, 264, 291, 340, 353, 357, 381, 383, 388; models, 138–144, 174–175
"Mature industrial state," 371–376, 380, 390–391
MDC's (more developed countries), 199, 267, 281, 365, 371, 378, 381; economic management in, 339–340; exports, 242–243; foreign trade planning in, 236–237, 239; growth of public sector in, 345–346; investment planning in, 211–213; and LDC's, economic development compared, 342–343; manpower planning in, 256–257; planning agricultural programs, 289, 291, 295; planning of industrial activities in, 275, 276; technological change in, 194, 198–201, 207–210, 307, 323; underemployment in, 264
Mercantilist, 337, 342, 349
Mesarović, M. D., 29, 33
Message: ambiguity, 51, 52–53; coding, 38, 39, 41; decoding, 38; interpretation, 37–38, 368, 369; reproduction, 37, 38, 40; selection, 43–44; storage, 38; three-symbol, 49; transmission, 37, 38, 39, 49; two-symbol, 46; value, 54–55
Meyer, A. G., 391
Micro: -economic, 7, 60, 61, 134, 234, 274, 315; -model, 7, 60, 163, 201, 202, 277; -planning, vi, 376
Migration, labor, 256, 258, 259, 266, 267, 271, 303, 308, 313, 314, 318
Mill, John Stuart, 334
Mishan, E. J., 213, 345
Mishustin, D. D., 237
Model(s): activity analysis, 181; agricultural, 294; analysis, 66; approach, 2, 8, 163–164; building, 8, 10, 13–14, 17, 18, 121, 154–155, 163–175, 177–178; closed, 31, 60; complex, vi, 7, 10, 14–15, 16, 77–81, 134, 157, 204, 240; consistency, 214–215; core, 177, 184; decision, 41, 53, 92, 130, 178, 288, 290; demographic, 259; deterministic, 10, 60; dualistic, 312–317; dynamic, 10, 60, 61, 67, 74–77, 155, 171, 216, 312, 322; econometric, 67, 79, 80, 132, 246, 302; educational, 257, 258, 267; electric power, 33–34; firm, 5–8,

20, 29; forecasting, 245–246; formal, 81, 128; formulation, 331; gap, 172–178, 249; general policy, 123–128; gravity, 322–324; growth, 144–146, 154, 159, 160, 280, 341, 342; input-output, 135–138, 170, 171–174, 179, 187, 189, 195, 198, 216, 232, 233, 268, 294, 317, 326; interregional and interindustry, 317–329; intuitive, 206–207; investment planning, 212–223; large-scale, 7, 13, 14–15, 77–81; linear, vi, 3, 31, 66, 67, 70, 189, 215, 304, 305, 311, 325; locational, 312; macroeconomic, 246; mathematical, 158, 161, 214, 215, 247; microeconomic, 61, 163; multi-period, 77–81; multi-sector, 169–172, 216, 221; neoclassical, 7, 60; nodal, 322; nonlinear, 123–128; normative, 9, 200, 203–204, 205, 208; one-sector, 216–221; open, 60; open loop, 50; optimization, 215, 316; overall central, 164; perspective planning, 160; planning, viii, 8, 18, 61, 67, 68–81, 155–175, 177, 187, 189, 221, 238, 239, 276–280; policy, vii, viii, 2, 8, 10, 12, 25, 36, 59–81, 84, 117, 121, 123, 124, 133, 134, 154, 160, 181; quadratic, 3; realistic, 18, 80; recursive, 148–149, 290; regional, 155, 309–319, 329; selection, type, 172; sensitivity, 180; simultaneous equation, 206; single-decision, 13; solving, 14–15, 61, 126; specifications, 162, 164, 195; static, 10, 60, 62; structural, 149, 150, 163, 317; structure, 60, 61, 80; systematic, 200; trade, 243–244; as tool, 81, 175; traditional, 98–99; two-sector, 138–144, 166–169, 174–175, 216, 221–223, 312; TF, 200–207
Moellendorff, Wichard von, 338
Monetary: flows, in Soviet system, 188–189; instruments, 2, 62, 78, 108–116, 129, 386
Monopoly, 161, 254, 343, 382
More developed countries. See MDC's
Mortality, 258, 259, 264, 270
Moses, Leon, 319
Müller, Adam Heinrick, 337, 338
Multi-level system, vi, 2, 28, 29, 30, 38–39, 42, 49, 59, 61, 79, 149, 153, 157, 295, 322, 329, 361, 385. See also Hierarchies
Multi-national corporation, 8, 112, 385

Musgrave, R. A., 109
Myint, Hla, 342
Myrdal, Gunnar, 308, 339

National: cost, 224; debt, 110; development, 308; economic policy, 7, 162, 238, 246; economy, 309, 329, 338, 361; export, 245; goals, 306, 341; growth, 315; income, 14, 55, 71–72, 73, 74, 75, 77, 100, 101, 138, 147, 148, 164, 165, 166, 167, 184, 185, 216, 225, 320, 325–326, 340; independence, 236; interest rate, 314; manpower, 257; models, 322; planning, 153, 157, 161–162, 176, 181, 208, 272, 293, 304, 306, 311, 329, 341, 385–386; plans, 341; policy, 314, 319; product, 8, 14, 137, 144, 145, 345, 361, 384; projects, cost, 224–225; regional activity, 308, 309; restrictions, 299–300; savings, 317; sector, 328; space, 155; subsystems, 239; system, 154; trade, 242–244
Nationalism, 336
Nationalization, 363, 373, 383, 385
Nazi, 177, 334, 338–339
Nemchinov, V. S., 159
Networks: in agricultural production, 304; decision-making, 13; information, 37–53, 324; of precedence relations, 147; of quasi-stable populations, 260; in systems, 19, 20, 24–25, 132, 357; theory of, 183; transportation, 304, 311, 324, 328
Nodal region, 310–311, 322–326
Noise, 38, 39, 40, 41, 50, 51, 52, 63, 368
North, 312
Novozhilov, V. V., 159

Ohlin, Bertil, 309
Oil, 343, 385
Oligopoly, 388, 390
Optimal, 367, 378; consumption, 341; controls, 356–357, 360; economic system, 331–332, 367–384, 389–391; growth, 214; investment, 215, 216, 222; linkage, 357; output, 370; planning, 355, 362; production, 185, 295; savings, 217; science, 182; sequence, 182; solution, 284; time, 183
Optimization: in agricultural planning, 290, 294, 295, 298, 300, 301, 302, 305–306; in communication system, 52; convergence theories and, 367, 373,

Optimization (*continued*)
378–379, 380–381, 389; in educational planning, 268; in foreign trade, 249, 251, 252, 254; in industrial planning, 276, 277, 282, 285, 286, 288; in investment planning, 214, 215, 216, 217, 219, 230, 231, 235, 282; mathematical techniques of, vi, 117; in models of firm, 6; in planning models and procedures, 154, 159, 170, 178–179, 181, 182; in policy analysis, 11, 12, 13, 16–17, 24–25, 59, 61, 62, 66, 67, 68, 70; preference function and, 2, 3, 61, 62, 84, 90, 91–92, 96, 97, 98, 99, 104, 105; in regional planning, 155, 312, 315–317, 324, 327–328, 329; in selection of instruments and measures, 117, 124, 125, 127, 130, 151, 333; in state's "agenda," 333, 334, 335, 341, 351–358, 360; in structural frameworks, 131–132, 133, 151; in systems design, 18–19; in technological planning, 203, 204
Oslo model, 150–151, 171, 172, 179, 232
Output: agricultural, 292–293, 296, 297, 298, 299; allocation, 235; and capital ratio, 73, 164, 168, 169, 170, 187, 214, 216, 217, 221, 222, 243, 313, 314–315, 316; changes, 75–76, 280, 327; data, 161, 163, 238; economic, 61, 111, 134, 178, 180, 379; flow, 136; gross, 137, 291; growth, 198, 207, 340, 389; improved, 381; independent, 200; industrial, 171, 237, 242, 274, 275, 281, 285, 287; information, 3, 36, 42, 79, 378; labor, 140, 165, 255, 265; lag, 186; limits, 113, 344; mix, 177; national, 287; net, 137, 166; pattern, 162, 271; perishable, 32; physical, 282; plan, 157, 190, 355; price of, 135; production, 6, 29, 62, 136, 204, 266; productive capacity, 73; quality, 276; rate, 23, 61–62, 65, 103, 167, 234, 256, 267, 271, 297, 361; regional, 314, 321; response, 146; sectoral, 72, 197, 233, 325; standards, 185; and supply, 74–75; targets, 189, 358, 359; technological, 154; total, 2, 74, 134, 145, 219, 277, 289; values, 137, 354
Owen, Robert, 347
Ownership: agricultural subsidies and, 256; convergence theories and, 374–375, 376, 382, 383, 384, 385, 387; investments and, 141, 142; Marx-

ian view of, 347–348, 350–351, 363, 382, 383; by private entrepreneurs, 5, 6, 135, 338–339; profits and, 5, 139, 140, 141, 174; in Soviet-type economy, 352, 358, 364, 383

Pareto, V., 86, 89, 343, 345
Paris Commune, 337, 347, 348
Parnes, H. S., 265
Payments, balance of, 335; effect of technological change on, 194; locational and regional planning and, 321, 322; in models of rational policy choice, 62, 79, 80; planning industrial activities and, 273, 275, 276; planning for trade and, 236–239, 244, 246, 248, 249, 251, 252; problems of investment planning, 225, 226, 234; problems in planning models, 162; in a recursive model, 147, 148; as short-term objective, 112
Perroux, François, 275, 281, 309, 325, 378
Phillips model, 62, 74–77
Physiocrats, 340
Planning, v, vi, vii, viii, 17, 19, 20, 24, 38, 104, 153–175, 318, 382, 384; agricultural, 289–306; alternative, 239; analysis, 366; budget, 329; capital projects, 214; center, 249, 252, 299, 309, 310, 346, 349, 351–353; for change, 195; communications in, 51; concepts, 377; 386; context, 163; corporate, 208, 385; current approach to, 163–164, 182–183, 208, 331; decentralized, viii, 57; development, 189–190, 273–288, 289, 322, 323, 342–343; economic policy, 376; educational, 257–258, 267–271; foreign trade, 236–254; implementation of, 12, 13, 65, 66, 117, 123, 134, 136, 153, 154, 155, 159, 160, 161, 162,170, 172, 178, 179, 184, 186, 190, 194–195, 208, 212, 214, 275, 282, 285, 304, 305, 306, 314, 331, 343, 348, 357, 360, 373, 375, 384, 387; indicative, 153, 160, 177, 190, 305; industrial, 273–288, 379; inputs, 171, 184–185; international, 172; investment, 24, 77, 100, 104, 158, 171, 174–175, 211–235, 309, 311, 335; literature, 275; locational, 307–329; long-term, 164, 186–187, 209–210, 220, 223, 266, 273, 276, 295; manpower,

255–272, 294; mathematical, 158; medium-term, 186–187; models, viii, 8, 18, 61, 67, 68–81, 155–175, 177, 187, 189, 221, 238, 239, 276–280; national, vi, 208, 257, 300, 366, 383–384; overall, viii, 153–155, 164; pattern, 35, 162; periods, 158, 167, 169, 171, 174, 179, 186, 203, 233; perspective, 186, 194, 266, 267, 345, 355; price, 185; quantitative, 341; rate, 214; regional, v, 2, 8, 10, 155, 182, 187, 299, 305–306, 307–329; schedule, 185; sectoral, 164, 166, 186, 187, 195, 234; short-term, 186–187; specifications, 160–161, 289, 306; stages, 155, 178, 187–189; techniques, viii, 154, 155, 176–193, 288, 309, 321; theories, vi, viii, 157, 375; types, 176–178; unified, 188–189

Poland, 159, 164, 249, 364

Policy makers: of capitalist vs. socialist countries, 308; cybernetics and, 31; foreign trade and, 236–237, 240, 241–242, 251, 252, 253, 254; industrial planning and, 273, 275, 277, 280, 281, 286, 287, 288; instrument choice of, 116–119; investment planning and, 211–212, 214, 216, 217, 220, 225, 228, 230, 231; of LDC's, 341, 342; locational and regional planning and, 311, 317, 319, 320, 328, 329; in manpower and employment planning, 255, 264, 269; in models of firm, 5–8; policy models and, 10, 11–13, 19, 24, 59–83, 123–128, 136, 137; policy problem of, summarized, 3; preferences of, 12–13, 43, 84–106, 117, 118, 120, 123, 128, 131, 139, 151, 162, 177, 181, 231, 328; and role responsibility of, 12; Soviet, 139, 176–177, 184–185, 198, 199, 354; structural frameworks and, 131–151; technological change and, 194, 198, 199, 203, 208–210

Political: change, 165, 345, 348; context, 13, 132, 154, 175, 275, 347, 390; cost, 17; decision-making, 117, 252; definition, 311; economy, 337, 364; factor, 307, 308, 316, 351, 385; feasibility, 116; forecasting, 200; forces, 161; institutions, 106, 310; mathematics, vi; power, 348–351, 364; problem, 163; science, vii; standpoint, 106, 113, 117, 367–391; structure, 9, 10, 12, 13; students, vii; theory, 333

Pontryagin, L. V., 219

Population: centers of, 311, 322–324; composition of, 256, 259, 310; education planning and, 269, 270, 309; growth of, 162, 185, 267, 289, 305, 313, 318, 329; manpower and, 255, 256, 259, 260, 278, 308, 313, 318, 350; of scientists, 201–202; size of, 256, 288; urban vs. rural, 194, 256, 303

Pöyhönen, P., 239

Preferences (preference function): Basic Policy Chart approach to, 93, 99–102; future, 178, 220, 303; individual vs. social, 87–90; opportunities, commitments and, 103–104; as ordinal vs. cardinal, 11–12, 91; of policy makers, 12–13, 43, 84–106, 117, 118, 120, 123, 128, 131, 139, 151, 162, 177, 181, 231, 328; in policy models, 2, 61, 62, 63–64, 65, 66–67, 68, 69, 70, 120, 121; priorities approach to, 102–103; risk and, 54, 95, 97, 230, 231, 324; "Santa Claus" approach to, 93, 94–99; social, 12, 20, 60, 84–87, 91, 103, 106, 110, 123, 129, 162, 165, 217, 218, 227, 364, 367, 381, 388, 390

Present value (PV) criterion, 223

Prices: in agricultural planning, 289, 293, 295, 296, 301, 302, 303–304, 305; control of, 62, 111, 112–113, 129, 154, 375, 388; demand conditions and, 26, 32–33, 72, 289, 302, 303, 317; fluctuations in, 187, 253, 289, 344; in foreign trade, 240, 241, 242, 243–245, 246–247, 248, 303, 304; industry and, 286, 291, 292; as information, 42, 56, 57–58, 378; labor and, 256, 258, 291; preference and, 92, 105, 118; in regional planning, 317, 325, 327; setting of, 5, 6, 9, 26, 27, 32–33, 158, 344, 381, 383; shadow, 26, 66, 159, 249, 306; in Soviet-type economies, 33, 178, 184, 185, 190, 249, 353, 354–355, 364, 376, 377, 383, 390; supply and, 26, 33, 72, 289; support of, 256, 295, 304; as system elements, 20, 135, 136, 137, 149, 164, 168

Priorities: as established by policy makers, 11, 90, 94, 102–103; in industrial planning, 277, 280–282; in Soviet-type economies, 164, 179, 184, 208, 234, 280, 354, 387

Probability: in agricultural planning, 296, 298, 301; analysis of, 55; forecasts and,

Probability (*continued*)
62–63, 126, 128, 179, 180, 199, 203, 209; information and, 39, 40, 44, 45, 46, 47, 48, 49, 50, 51, 53, 54, 97; in investment planning, 223–224, 225, 229, 230, 231; in manpower planning, 260, 262–263, 270; preference and, 95–96, 97; in simulation, 181

Processor, 29, 30, 36, 38, 43, 49, 52, 58, 131–151, 255, 293, 382, 383

Production, 57, 64, 188, 215, 220, 221, 247, 268, 285, 295, 296, 363–364, 381; activity, 132, 271; agricultural, 297, 304, 305, 306; assignments, 177, 190; categories, 170, 171; centers, 181; concentration, 382; control, 350, 371, 387; cost, 309; cycle, 57, 170; decisions, 371, 383, 384, 390; domestic, 184, 248, 379; expansion, 284, 341, 356, 364, 371; expenditure, 164; export, 168, 237; flow, 36; forecast, 180; frontier, 345; function, 64, 65, 133, 134, 135, 264, 274, 312, 325, 328, 369; industrial, 287; large-scale, modern, 371–373, 381, 388; material, 257; means of, 139, 141, 174, 280, 332, 338, 347, 350–351, 363, 373, 383, 385; of messages, 37; mode, 307; modern, 377; nationalizing, 383; output, 42; period, 6, 39; planning, 347, 369; possibilities, 98–100, 302–305, 341; problems, 20, 29, 205, 351; process, 37, 139, 170, 194, 195–197, 215, 277, 285, 291, 292, 293, 295, 296, 300, 304, 307, 328, 391; purpose, 379, 380; quota, 184; rate, 168, 169, 185, 187, 215, 277, 279, 282; regional, 319–321, 325–328; relations, 170, 195, 233, 268, 270, 296; revolutionizing, 349; sector, 137, 151, 171, 176, 180, 259, 273, 310, 372–373; standards, 112, 170, 215; state control of, 337; structure, 112, 230; systems, 112; techniques, 198, 322, 351; technology, 195, 233; transformation process, 181; unit, 299, 375, 381; workers, 134, 170; world, 254

Productivity, 61, 72–73, 98, 103, 187, 232; agricultural, 164, 256, 292, 304; equal, 281; increased, 207, 208, 365; labor, 140, 162, 165, 185, 249, 250, 256, 265; of land, 295; regional, 316; scientific, 202

Profit: in agricultural production planning,
293, 296–300, 301, 305; in educational planning, 268; industrial location and, 286; in investment planning, 211, 226, 228; in Leontief and Marxian models, 138, 139, 143–144; maximization of, by firms, 5–6, 20, 29, 135, 293, 389; vs. output maximization (Soviet), 389; in policy model, 78; social, 345, 354; vs. social responsibility, 106; in Western economy, 307, 389, 391

Programming: dual, 70; dynamic, 158, 182; linear, 64, 65, 66, 67, 69, 70, 121–123, 126, 181–182, 189, 215, 249, 295, 296, 298, 299, 300, 301, 302, 305, 306, 309; mathematical, 181–183, 185, 189, 213, 215, 232, 247, 248; model, 8, 12, 61, 269, 272, 282, 285, 296, 325, 326; problem, 3, 63, 66, 67, 131, 162–163, 205, 316, 324, 326; procedure, 257; quadratic, 3, 69, 70, 230–231; research and development, 203–204; solution, 12, 41; technique, 126, 170, 204, 300, 356

Projection Evaluation and Review Technique (PERT), 183

Protectionism, 110, 337, 342, 345

Public: consumption, 187; debt, 149, 234–235; enterprise, 345; ownership, 375; finance, 108, 111, 112, 113, 116, 129; health, 110; informed, 92; interest, 105–106, 162, 334; investment, 211, 212, 214, 223–234; policy, 171, 374; preference, 85, 87, 88, 90, 91, 92, 95, 99, 104, 105; projects, 103, 109, 224–225, 231, 244; sector, 275, 331, 345–346, 375, 376, 380–381, 386; spending, 147, 155; welfare, 344; works, 335

Quantitative: analysis, vii, 85, 153, 241; complexity, 386; economic control, vii, 12; instruments, 107–118, 126, 128; policy, 8, 341; precision, 131; prediction, 190; techniques, 179, 182–183, 206; variables, 123, 125

Quesnay, François, 19

Rahman, M. A., 316
Ramsey, F., 213
Rathenau, Walter, 177, 338, 353
Receptor, 38, 39, 40, 41, 43, 50
Recursive, 78–79, 148–149, 198, 280–284, 290, 301, 305
Recycling, 38, 42, 206

Redundancy, 48, 52–53, 58, 342
Reforms, 125, 130; agricultural, 107; economic, 56, 108, 116, 118
Regions: in agricultural planning, 293, 294, 295, 298, 299, 300, 302, 304–305, 306; analysis of, 312–322; centers and trade flow of, 322–328; classification of, 309–311; growth and change in, 307–309; interregional planning for, 304–314, 318, 322–328; in planning process, 187, 188, 328–329
Reproduction: expanded, 141, 142, 174; of messages, 37, 38, 40; simple, 139, 141, 142
Research and development, 195, 198–200, 201, 203–206, 208, 222, 256, 274, 304
Rhomberg, R. R., 245
Ricardo, David, 334
Ring equations, 171, 233
Risk: decision-making and, 6, 54, 57, 67, 95, 97, 209, 368; investments and, 10, 211, 223, 229–230, 231; reduction of, 128, 373; in stochastic vs. deterministic models, 10, 60, 67, 71
Robespierre, Maximilien, 337
"Rolling" plan, 282, 346
Rostow, W. W., 372, 373, 378, 380, 387
Rotterdam model, 328
Rules: decision, 28, 85–86, 89, 180–181, 182, 241, 242, 369–370; as direct controls, 273; institutional relationships and, 132; instrument-per-target, 126; investment decision, 214, 222–230; practical, 252; as qualitative instruments, 107–108, 125; rank-size, 323
Rural, 169, 194, 256, 258, 263, 303, 312, 323, 328, 348
Russian Revolution, 348–350

Saint-Simon, Comte de, 347, 349, 351
Sampling, 49–50, 53, 54, 55, 293
Samuelson, Paul A., v
Sanctions, 177
Santa Claus approach, 93–99
Savings, 172, 226, 320, 340, 376, 379; investment and, 212, 214, 215, 216–217, 335, 373; as marginal propensity, 74, 75, 145, 146, 162, 165, 166, 167, 168, 249–250, 313–314, 316, 317; ratio, 150
Scandinavia, 339, 341–345

Seers, Dudley, 342
Self-sufficiency, 242, 276, 277, 294, 338, 342
Senior, Nassau, 334
Services. *See* Goods and services
Servomechanism, 30, 33, 42, 54, 56, 361
Signals, 24, 36, 37, 38, 41, 49, 91, 324
Simulation, 18, 57, 65, 66, 79, 179, 180–181, 246
Size: in agricultural planning, 289–290; in convergence theories, 375, 377, 380–381, 387; in industrial planning, 275, 276, 285, 287–288, 377; investment planning and, 211, 213, 215, 234; in regional planning, 322–325; in technological forecasting, 200, 201
Smith, Adam, 334
Social: change, 264, 345; class, 19, 150–151, 348, 363; cost, 117, 125, 129, 224–225, 380; factor, 307, 308; forces, 25; homogeneity, 310; inequity, 9, 10, 308; institutions, 2, 9, 10, 163, 172, 275, 289, 338, 341, 371, 374; order, 380; overhead capital, 287; philosophy, 105, 106, 264, 331–332, 383; preference, 367, 381; pressure, 296; production, 347; relations, 357, 390–391; responsibility, 106; security, 109; status, 350, 351; system, 335; theory, 333; welfare, 9, 25, 27, 28, 63, 68, 69, 84–106, 130, 172, 203–204, 206, 217, 218, 219, 220, 222, 225, 227, 269, 345, 364, 368, 379, 380, 382, 390
Social marginal product (SMP), 225–226
Socialist economies: agricultural planning in, 289, 291, 295; changes in, 56, 348, 364–365, 373; in convergence theories, 367–391; cybernetic approach to, 34; direct government control in, 33, 113, 159, 166, 186, 214, 351–358; efficiency in, 256, 358–363, 365, 383, 384; firms in, 359, 362, 375; foreign trade in, 237, 247, 249, 253; industrial growth in, 276, 287, 307–308; investments in, 233–234, 235; labor control in, 256; Marxian model used in, 3, 138–144; planning in, vi–viii, 158, 159, 176–179, 186, 189, 376; state's "agenda" in, 331–332, 347–366; technology in, 214, 234, 295, 355–356, 357, 364–365; Western economies and, viii, 7, 57–58, 86–87, 105–106, 108, 128, 130, 132, 133, 155, 186,

Socialist economies (*continued*)
233–234, 290–291, 295, 367–391. *See also* Marxian; Soviet Union
Sociopolitical: change, 271; issues, vii; order, 60, 373; philosophy, 333–334, 383, 388; system, 381, 382
South, 312, 373
Soviet Union, 340; centralized economy in, vi, 26, 29–30, 56, 113, 338, 351–357, 362–363, 386, 388; industrialization in, 275, 280–281, 375, 376, 378, 380; labor allocation in, 257, 266; Marxian model as used in, 138–144; planning in, vi, 153, 158–159, 164, 176–177, 184–185, 188–189, 190, 237–238, 361, 386, 389; technological development in, 208, 209, 387; transition periods in, 364–365; U.S. and, 198, 199, 331, 334, 380, 387–388, 390. *See also* Socialist economies
Space industry, 386
Spann, Othmar, 338
Spending: actual, 77; autonomous, 144, 145; capital, 185; consumer, 74, 78, 110, 144–145, 146, 211, 227; deficit, 91, 110–111; domestic, 168, 251; government, 12, 21, 22, 24, 25, 31–32, 62, 64, 77, 108–109, 110, 116, 137, 147, 148, 172, 194, 211–212, 223, 232, 273, 344, 373, 381; income-generating, 148; inputs, 154; investment, 223–224, 230, 311; nondiscretionary, 186; pattern, 183; productive, 164; ratio, 336; regional, 328; research and development, 203–204, 205, 206; total, 147, 148
Spillover effect, 129
Stability, 25, 62, 67, 74–77, 79, 105, 109, 111, 113, 234, 258, 259, 260, 262, 340, 343, 358, 359, 375, 379, 382
Stages, 157–175, 180, 182, 183, 187–189, 275, 300, 373, 378
Stagflation, 336
Stagnation, 346
Stalin, J. V., 158–159, 177, 280, 353, 364, 366
Standard of living, 161, 164, 165, 184, 187, 212, 264, 365
State: capitalist, 331–332, 333–346, 351, 371–373, 381, 382; fascist, 338–339; goals of, 9; monopoly, 337; ownership, 375; socialist, 347–358, 363–366, 379, 390; statism and, 9, 42, 211; theory of

the, 333–334, 336. *See also* Government
Steiner, P. O., 230, 231
Stochastic, 5, 9, 10, 20, 29, 40, 53, 60, 61, 62, 67, 68, 71, 183, 204, 298, 301, 356, 367, 368, 370
Stock: capital, 104; -holders, 375, 382, 384; market, 38; manipulation, 343
Stone, Richard, 309, 319
Storage: of information, 14, 36, 37, 38, 40, 41; product, 29; raw materials, 338
Strayer, Paul, 346
Structure/structural: approach, 247; change, 199, 340, 342, 366, 378; constraints, 68, 85, 117, 124, 181, 187, 204–205, 215, 248, 317; continuity, 132; difficulties, 257; equation, 118, 125, 126, 133, 205, 285, 318; framework, 131–151, 390; imbalance, 162; model, 149, 150, 317; organization, 108; regional, 155; regression, 53; relationships, 63, 118, 136, 138, 139, 181, 187; specifications, 67, 132; weakness, 277, 282
Subsidies, 112, 226, 236, 256, 304, 344
Substitutions: of agricultural factors, 292, 295, 301; import, 253, 275, 282; of labor factors, 258, 267, 268, 271; in planning, 158; product, 302, 303; rates of, 66, 95, 97, 102, 118, 226, 227, 297, 299; of regional trade flows, 209, 310, 326–328
Subsystems, viii, 2, 3, 12, 18, 28, 33, 38, 41, 42, 54, 64–65, 71, 72, 79, 133, 146, 153–155, 161, 162, 163, 166, 169, 182, 188, 189–190, 194–210, 238, 255, 273, 274, 276–277, 278, 279, 280–281, 282, 291, 305, 312–313, 331, 356–357, 378; regional, 309–315, 328, 329, 387
Supply: capital, 155, 256, 275, 373; curves, 33, 243; exports, 165; food, 304; government and, 341, 346; information, 57, 274; labor, *see* Labor; oriented, 312, 314; of parts, 210; price and, 26, 33, 72, 289; raw materials, 275, 278; response, 340; of savings, 214; time factor in, 186; in trade flows, 326–327. *See also* Demand
Supremal unit, 2, 3, 28, 30, 33–34, 38, 79, 90, 106, 149, 162, 310, 311, 314, 319, 332, 349, 355, 359, 362, 369, 374, 384

Surplus, 174–175; labor, 342; for trade, 238; value, 139–140, 141, 162

Synergism, 17, 18, 255

System(s), 15–35, 105–108, 153–155, 174, 287, 341; adaptive, 25; analysis, 18, 30, 34–35, 42, 52; approach, 15, 138; autoregulated, v, 13, 30–31; change in, 108, 113; characteristics, 20, 150; closed, 135; closed loop, 24; communications, 37–43, 48, 52–55, 389; competitive, 209; complexity, 18–19, 25, 48, 57–58; components, 133, 134, 146, 163; concepts, 15, 19, 20; context, 310; control, 2, 3, 5, 15, 17, 26, 37, 42, 47, 51, 54, 162, 199, 333, 386–387; design, 19, 30, 42, 48, 52; different, 17, 382; directors, 162; and environment, 17, 101, 147–148, 180; evaluating, 27; feedback, 23–25, 92, 147–148; free market, 157, 281; functions, 16, 308; future, 199; goals, 286; growth, 315; hierarchical, 2, 28, 55, 132; industrial, 371–373, 379; inputs, 137, 181, 206, 211–212, 333, 368; learning, 154; managers, 36, 198; model, 8, 180, 195; modification, 70, 362; multi-goal, 29, 30; multi-level, vi, 2, 28, 29, 149, 153, 157; national, 154, 328; off line, 28; on line, 28; open, 135–138; open-loop, 20–23; orientation, 19, 55; organization, 56; output, 37; performance, 103; and plans, viii; price support, 304; principles of various, 20, 59; production, 135; purposive, 255; redesign, 17; regulated, 2; rule, 182; self-regulating, 340; single-goal, 29; size, 16; socioeconomic, 371; stimuli, 42; structure, 21, 63, 131, 136, 195, 271, 276, 331; theory, 28; types of, 35; uncertainties of, 45; urban, 323; value, 59. *See also* Economic

Tableau Economique, 19

Tardos, M., 247–249

Tariffs, 110, 213, 226, 304

Tax, 25, 92, 110, 134, 138, 226, 234, 273, 343, 344; corporate, 212, 213, 228; income, 62, 109, 149–150; liquor, 110; loss, 224–225; policy, 211, 373; rate, 12, 107, 110, 118, 129, 133, 149, 212, 214; sales, 211; system, 113, 116; tobacco, 110; variables, 78, 79

Team theory, 2, 30, 85–88

Technology: in agricultural planning, 291, 292–293, 294, 295, 301, 303, 304, 306; change and progress in, 37, 77, 90, 98, 101, 143, 165, 179, 180, 194–210, 222, 232, 255, 256, 262, 263, 279, 291, 294, 301, 303, 306, 314, 323, 331, 342, 355–356, 364–365; coefficients of, 135–136, 138, 170, 171, 181, 233, 242, 277, 291, 292–293, 321, 326, 327; constraints of, 11, 60, 73–74, 135–144, 151; in convergence theories, 332, 374–375, 377–378, 381, 382; economic growth and, 207–210, 275, 287, 342–343; forecasting, 158, 199–210, 304; foreign trade and, 242; in industrial planning, 275, 277, 278, 279, 283, 285, 287, 288; information and, 36, 37, 40, 43, 56, 77; investment planning and, 216, 232, 233, 234, 235; labor productivity and, 140; in Leontief model, 135–136, 138; "linear," 216; in locational and regional planning, 310, 314, 321, 323, 326, 327; in manpower planning, 255, 256, 262, 263, 264; in Marxian model, 138, 140, 143–144; in Marxian vs. Leontief models, 143–144; in planning models and procedures, 153, 154, 161, 163, 165, 169, 170, 171, 179, 181, 187; in policy analysis, 10, 11, 27; public policy on, in MDC's and LDC's, 207–210, 342–343; in Soviet-type economy, 214, 234, 295, 355–356, 364–365

"Technostructure," 372–373, 374–376, 384, 386

ten Kate, A., 388

Theil, H., 3, 59, 62, 68–71, 74, 96, 126

Theory, 3, 80, 151, 385; capitalist economic, 333–346; central place, 322–323; communications, 36–37, 45, 49; comparative, 35; control, vi, 25, 31, 158, 182, 189, 360; convergence, 367–391; decision, vi, 37, 370; economic, 341–342; evolution, 337–338; game, 2; growth, 154, 157, 213, 312; import-substituting, 275; income, 157; information, vi, 37; international trade, 312; management, viii, 5–7; microeconomic, 7; network, 183; optimal systems, 357; policy, viii, 1, 2, 3; regional, 309; signal structure, 37, 39; socialist economic, 347–366; stage, 373; of the state, 333, 363; statistical decision, 49,

Theory (*continued*)
54; systems, 357; team, 2, 30, 85–88; trade, international, 251; utility, 11

Tinbergen, Jan, 1, 2, 3, 59, 61, 62–68, 69, 71, 77, 79, 80, 96, 117, 119–123, 126, 146, 157, 158, 187, 230, 239, 254, 257, 270, 279, 309, 332, 372, 373, 374–376, 379, 380–381, 382, 383, 385–386, 388, 389

Trade: balance of, 97, 237, 238, 242, 248, 253, 326; controls, 236; deficit, 148, 150; flow, 60–61, 243, 244, 246, 309, 326–328; foreign, 2, 59, 60, 62, 111, 112, 113, 148, 150, 154, 164, 165, 172, 233, 236–254, 262, 273, 281, 282, 287, 304, 312, 337, 358, 384; internal, 60–61, 111, 168, 324, 352, 384; interregional, 326–329; organizations, 345, 358; partners, 243, 246; patterns, 258, 283; policy, 275, 304; regional, 275, 304; relations, 246

Trade unions, 346, 373

Transport, 111, 112, 118, 202, 211, 256, 258, 267, 298, 303–304, 307, 308, 309, 311, 325, 352–353; interregional, 322–328, 329

Trapeznikov, V. A., 354

Trusts, 62, 112

Tucker, A. W., 213

Two-level planning, 189, 249, 359

Two-sector: economy, 278; model, 138–144, 159, 163, 166–169, 174, 214, 221, 281, 312

Uncertainty, 57; in communication theory, 45–48, 50–51; convergence theories and optimal systems and, 368–385; in decision-making, 5, 6, 67; deterministic models and, 60; in environment, 13; farm planning problem and, 298; flexibility and, 103; and forecasting, 179; of information, 36–37, 40; instruments and measures and, 118, 126, 127; Keynes and, 335–336; planning foreign trade and, 238, 254; problems of investment planning and, 214, 229, 235; project selection and, 286; simulation and programming and, 181; statistical decision theory and, 54, 55; in stochastic policy models, 10, 59, 60; technological forecasting and, 204, 209; theory of consumer behavior under, 95, 96

Underdevelopment, 264–265, German,

337; the ''South'' and, 373. *See also* LDC's

Unemployment, 12, 90, 91, 93, 105, 118, 125, 150, 162, 225, 226, 249, 256, 260, 263, 264–265, 266, 294, 333, 336, 343, 344, 346; chronic, 335; disguised, 162

United Nations, 259, 264, 283

United States: convergence theories and, 371, 380, 385, 387; foreign trade model of, 243–244; institutional relationships in, 149; instruments in, 129; manpower and employment in, 263, 264; model of economy, 78; preference functions in, 87; regional planning in, 311, 322, 329; state's ''agenda'' in, 334, 339, 342, 345, 346; technological change in, 207–208; technology in, 198, 199. *See also* Western economies

Urban, 169, 194, 256, 258, 263, 291, 303, 322–323, 328, 344, 348

Utility: of consumption, 135, 220, 221, 222, 303; individual (Marshall), 87, 89, 94–95; as risk-preference function (von Neumann-Morgenstern), 54, 55, 96, 97, 229–230; social, 124, 128, 218; as target-preference function (Tinbergen), 63–64; theorists, 11, 54, 63

Viner, J., 20, 343

von Neumann, J., 213

von Neumann-Morgenstern concept, 54–55, 68, 96, 97, 229, 325

von Thunen, J. H., 308

Wage, 92, 134, 137, 138, 139, 140, 141, 142, 143, 151, 171, 264, 314–315; control, 62, 111, 112; minimum, 111; policy, 79, 256, 258, 375; rate, 135, 136, 318; ratio, 140, 174; worker, 255, 268, 339

Walras, Leon, 19, 135, 335

War, 57, 80, 108, 132, 157, 179; communism, 352–353, 363; economy, 338; Franco-Prussian, 347

Wealth, 112, 171, 317, 321

Weber, Alfred, 308

Welfare function, 12, 14, 28, 61, 66, 103, 105, 108, 128, 172, 203–204, 206, 298, 334, 335, 343, 344, 345, 383

Western economies: agricultural planning in, 290–291, 295; capitalists in, 139; convergence theories and, 367–391; economic control in, 366; foreign trade in, 243, 249; industrial planning in, 273, 275; instruments used in, 3, 112, 113; investments in, 233–234; and LDC's, 312; planning in, vi–viii, 153, 155, 157, 159, 166, 179–183, 186; planning for technological change in, 199, 208; socialist economies and, viii, 7, 57–58, 86–87, 105–106, 108, 128, 130, 132, 133, 138, 155, 351, 367–391; state's "agenda" in, 331–332, 334, 340, 345; systems in, 28, 30. *See also* United States

Wharton model, 78, 79
Wiener, Norbert, v
Women, 256, 263
Work: age, 260, 265; conditions, 112; force, 134, 135, 138, 185, 255, 270, 271, 277–278, 287–288, 289, 291, 302, 304, 305, 310, 313, 318, 339, 340, 356, 363; input, 135; pattern, 308; time, 61, 185, 257, 264, 267
World: change, 345; economic model, 246; food, 304, 305, 306; trade, 236–254
World War I, 177, 281, 335, 338
World War II, 108, 177, 180, 189, 237, 337, 338–339, 343

Yugoslavia, 113, 351–352, 358, 362, 364, 387, 390

Zielinski, J. G., 386